COMRADES

DATE DUE

'A timely and ambitious book . . . vast in its scope. He writes best when he offers an unabashed personal and moral perspective on the human cost of the totalitarian society' **Tim Gardam**, *Observer*

'A splendid achievement . . . Service writes with fluency and verve with a nice sense of historical irony and barrowloads of sarcasm. He mercilessly dissects the ideas and personalities of the communist greats' *History Today*

'An outstanding book, written with grace and style . . . Service's conclusion is powerful and disturbing. Soviet-style communism inspired by Marx, created by Lenin and fine-tuned by Stalin will never return, but it will have an afterlife. Totalitarianism can mutate. The system of unrestrained state power penetrating all areas of life can rise again, adopting the USSR circa 1950 as a grim model, and seek to oppress us under a new kind of quasi-religious dictatorship. This is a warning, as well as a masterful book' **Victor Sebestyen**, *Daily Telegraph*

'The decency of communism's ideals and the horror of its effects form the basis of Robert Service's masterly handling of the beginning, progress and (all but) end of communism . . . It is also a finely tuned description of what life was like under communism' **John Lloyd**, *Financial Times Magazine*

'Service has read widely – using the extensive archives and poster collection of Stanford University's Hoover Institution to good effect – and he has organised his material in an analytical narrative that sweeps the reader along' **Michael Burleigh**, *Sunday Telegraph*

'A deceptively ambitious book. Neither unreasonably long nor overwhelmingly theoretical, it swiftly chronicles the movement from its philosophical origins to the collapse of the Soviet Union and the economic transformation of China . . . an ideal introductory history' **Anne Applebaum**, *Spectator*

Robert Service is the author of the highly acclaimed *Lenin: A Biography*, *A History of Twentieth-Century Russia*, *Russia: Experiment with a People* and *Stalin: A Biography*, as well as many other books on Russia's past and present. He is a Fellow of the British Academy and works at St Antony's College, Oxford. He is married with four children.

Also by Robert Service

LENIN
A Biography

RUSSIA
Experiment with a People

STALIN
A Biography

ROBERT SERVICE

COMRADES

COMMUNISM: A WORLD HISTORY

OAKTON COMMUNITY COLLEGE
DES PLAINES CAMPUS
1600 EAST GOLF ROAD
DES PLAINES, IL 60016

PAN BOOKS

First published 2007 by Macmillan

First published in paperback 2008 by Pan Books
an imprint of Pan Macmillan Ltd
Pan Macmillan, 20 New Wharf Road, London N1 9RR
Basingstoke and Oxford
Associated companies throughout the world
www.panmacmillan.com

ISBN 978-0-330-43968-8

Copyright © Robert Service 2007

The right of Robert Service to be identified as the
author of this work has been asserted by him in accordance
with the Copyright, Designs and Patents Act 1988.

The publishers would like to thank the Hoover Institution Archives
for supplying all the pictures.

Every effort has been made to contact copyright holders of material reproduced
in this book. If any have been inadvertently overlooked, the publishers
will be pleased to make restitution at the earliest opportunity.

All rights reserved. No part of this publication may be
reproduced, stored in or introduced into a retrieval system, or
transmitted, in any form, or by any means (electronic, mechanical,
photocopying, recording or otherwise) without the prior written
permission of the publisher. Any person who does any unauthorized
act in relation to this publication may be liable to criminal
prosecution and civil claims for damages.

1 3 5 7 9 8 6 4 2

A CIP catalogue record for this book is available from
the British Library.

Typeset by SetSystems Ltd, Saffron Walden, Essex
Printed and bound in the UK by
CPI Mackays, Chatham ME5 8TD

This book is sold subject to the condition that it shall not,
by way of trade or otherwise, be lent, re-sold, hired out,
or otherwise circulated without the publisher's prior consent
in any form of binding or cover other than that in which
it is published and without a similar condition including this
condition being imposed on the subsequent purchaser.

Visit www.panmacmillan.com to read more about all our books
and to buy them. You will also find features, author interviews and
news of any author events, and you can sign up for e-newsletters
so that you're always first to hear about our new releases.

CONTENTS

CONTENTS

CONTENTS

FIVE: MUTATION: 1957–1979

SIX: ENDINGS: FROM 1980

Preface

This book began with an idea and a plan. The idea was to put together a general account of communism around the world; the plan was to do this mainly by assembling the secondary literature on country after country with experience of communism. Surprisingly few attempts have been made at such a project, and nearly all of them were written before the collapse of communist states in eastern Europe and the USSR in 1989–91.

The initial idea was knocked about like a punch-bag. As I learned about the five-sixths of the world's land mass that was not the Soviet Union, the structure and contents of the book underwent much remodelling. This is what happens with most books that have ever been written. Yet the plan was scrapped – and for a very positive reason. In 2004–5 I spent a sabbatical year at the Hoover Institution at Stanford University. Archives are the water of refreshment for the historian. When I discovered the vastness of resources available to scholars in the shadow of the Hoover Tower, I went through box after box of documents like a thirsty traveller. The endnotes give some idea of the exceptional holdings on countries such as Hungary, Cuba and India. Just as instructive for me were the boxes on the Soviet Union, especially on its relationship with the 'world communist movement'. And although I did not have it in mind to do much on American and British communism, any reluctance was dissolved when I examined the boxes themselves. There were also many moments when odd little files suggested themselves from the catalogue: Ivy Litvinov on Rose Cohen; Soviet officials on Arthur and Yevgenia Ransome; Herbert Hoover's food-relief officials on the regime of Béla Kun; defecting Cuban ministers on Castro and his entourage; Eugenio Reale on Togliatti's difficulties over eastern Europe; and the Russian diary of Malcolm Muggeridge.

The book investigates communism in its many aspects. This obviously requires an examination of communist states, their leaderships and their societies. Of equal importance are communist ideology and its appeal to people outside such states. Likewise I have given a good deal of space to twentieth-century geopolitics. Moreover, a truly global account of communism must also cover countries where communists failed to get anywhere near to national power.

The archival research nudged me towards modifying the interpretations I started with. It also brought events and situations to life – and I hope that this conveys itself to those who read the chapters. The staff at the Hoover Institution Archives were extraordinarily knowledgeable and helpful. I owe a debt to Elena Danielson, Linda Bernard, Carol Leadenham, Ron Bulatov, Lora Soroka, David Jacobs, Lyalya Kharitonova and their colleagues, who pointed me in the direction of several boxes I would have missed. My gratitude goes too to Robert Conquest for originally encouraging my stay at the Hoover Institution and to Director John Raisian and Board of Overseers member Tad Taube for making it a practical possibility. Deborah Ventura and Celeste Szeto, who supervise arrangements for visiting scholars, were models of helpfulness.

My wife Adele was a tremendous help throughout the process, carrying out research in the National Archives at Kew as well as reading up and discussing Asian communist history while we were in California; she also scrutinised and improved the entire text. I also want to express thanks to those who advised on one or more of the following chapters: Alan Angell, Arnold Beichman, William Beinart, Leslie Bethell, Archie Brown, Richard Clogg, Robert Conquest, Valpy Fitzgerald, Robert Evans, Paul Flewers, John Fox, Timothy Garton Ash, Roy Giles, Paul Gregory, Jonathan Haslam, Ronald Hingley, Michael Kaser, Alan Knight, Simon Sebag Montefiore, Norman Naimark, Brian Pearce, Silvio Pons, Alex Pravda, Paul Preston, Martyn Rady, Harold Shukman, Steve Smith, Geoffrey Swain, Steve Tsang, Amir Weiner and Jerry White. My literary editor David Godwin was encouraging from the earliest stage of the project. Georgina Morley at Macmillan and Kathleen MacDermott at Harvard have been characteristically constructive editors. Peter James has copyedited the printout with exemplary care.

A few words are in order here about the book's organisation. Certain chapters on particular countries or periods repeat information given in other chapters. This, I know, is authorial sin; but I ask indulgence on the ground that the basic details need to be kept in the foreground of so lengthy an account. I must also mention that the following usages are adopted: the Democratic People's Republic of Korea appears as North Korea; the Democratic Republic of Vietnam as North Vietnam; the German Democratic Republic as East Germany. A further alert: I have employed simplified modes of transliteration in the book. Occasionally they are inconsistent, especially as regards Chinese. Thus the modern Guomindang appears more traditionally as Kuomintang. Nor did I seek to render Zinoviev as Zinovev but instead stuck to the conventional English rendering. Dates are given exclusively according to the Gregorian calendar, place names in the bibliography in concordance with the contemporaneous habit of the local authorities. I have minimised reference to the full names and acronyms of those many communist parties which frequently changed them.

My own acquaintance with communism happened intermittently. At the conscious level it began in 1956. At my primary school, with the newspapers filled with pictures of the USSR's forces crushing the Hungarian Revolt, we schoolchildren – or at least the boys in the class – welcomed the chance to complete our diary assignments sketching tanks, soldiers and explosions. The Chinese communist invasion of Tibet was another event which left its mark on our minds. The annual prize books at Sunday school included accounts of Christian endurance under assault from Marxist-Leninist totalitarianism. The achievements of Soviet technology, though, turned the mind of our geography master at grammar school. He had read in the newspapers that the USSR had developed a technique to grow wheat north of the Arctic Circle. He concluded that the USSR might well win the struggle with the West for economic mastery. In the early 1960s I learned Esperanto and acquired foreign penfriends. One was Chinese, another from Czechoslovakia. We corresponded about our daily lives for a year or two before the exchanges with China petered out. Looking back, I have to assume that my Chinese partner was victimised in the Cultural Revolution.

Inexperience of communism was not unusual in the United Kingdom in those years. A personal incentive to make sense of communism came when I studied Russian literature at university. It became obvious how vital it is to understand the historical background to the Soviet order. That was a period, moreover, when students debated Marxism. There was endless discussion about whether communism was inherently despotic or potentially liberating.

This book is an attempt to answer that basic question, among several others. The chapters examine whether the Soviet historical experience was unique; they also enquire into the Kremlin's involvement with communist parties around the world. Above all, though, this is a world history of communism. Countries covering a third of the world's earth surface underwent communisation to a greater or lesser extent in the twentieth century. Communist parties have existed in almost every area of the globe except the polar ice-caps. The engine of my argument is that, despite all the diversity of the states committed to communism, there was an underlying similarity in purpose and practice. Communism was not simply a veneer coating diverse pre-existing national traditions. It adapted itself to those traditions while suffusing them with its own imperatives; and it transformed those countries where it held power for more than a few years. The book provides a narrative and analysis but is not an encyclopaedia. I have not investigated absolutely every communist idea, leader, party or state. I have made choices in order to hold the account together. The book is dedicated to the memory of Matthew Service, Ulsterman, gardening-enthusiast and wonderful father and grandfather.

Robert Service
October 2006

Maps

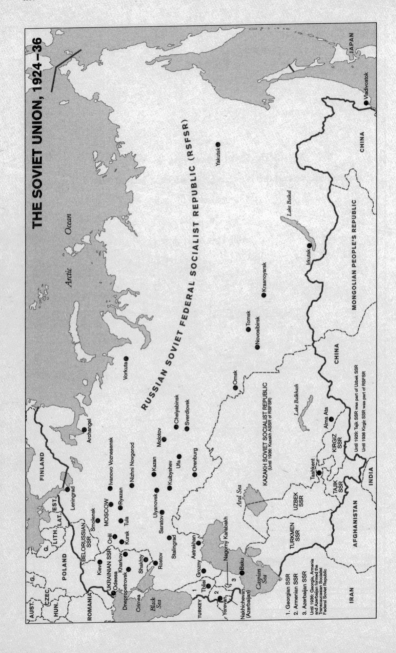

THE SOVIET UNION, 1924–36

RUSSIAN SOVIET FEDERAL SOCIALIST REPUBLIC (RSFSR)

Arctic Ocean

JAPAN

CHINA

Vladivostok

Yakutsk

Lake Baikal

Irkutsk

Krasnoyarsk

Tomsk

Novosibirsk

Omsk

MONGOLIAN PEOPLE'S REPUBLIC

CHINA

KAZAKH SOVIET SOCIALIST REPUBLIC
(Until 1936: Kazakh ASSR of RSFSR)

Lake Balkhash

Alma Ata

KIRGIZ SSR

Until 1929: Tajik SSR was part of Uzbek SSR
Until 1936 Kirgiz SSR was part of RSFSR

INDIA

AFGHANISTAN

TAJIK SSR

Tashkent

UZBEK SSR

TURKMEN SSR

Aral Sea

IRAN

Caspian Sea

Vorkuta

Archangel

FINLAND

LITH. LAT. EST.
G.
Leningrad
ESTI.

BELORUSSIAN SSR
Smolensk

Ivanovo Voznesensk

MOSCOW
Ryazan
Nizhni Novgorod

Molotov

Kazan

Ufa

Kuybyshev

Orenburg

Chelyabinsk

Sverdlovsk

Orel

Tula

Kursk

Ulyanovsk

Saratov

POLAND

UKRAINIAN SSR
Kiev

Odessa

Kharkov

Dnepropetrovsk

Shakhty

Rostov

Stalingrad

Astrakhan

Crimea

Black Sea

ROMANIA

AUST.
CZEC.
HUN.
G.

Grozny

Nagorny Karabakh

Baku

TURKEY
Tbilisi
Yerevan

Nakhichevan
(Azerbaijan)

1. Georgian SSR
2. Armenian SSR
3. Azerbaijan SSR
Until 1936 Georgia, Armenia
and Azerbaijan formed the
Transcaucasian Soviet Socialist
Federal Soviet Republic

EASTERN EUROPE AND THE WESTERN USSR AFTER THE SECOND WORLD WAR

SWEDEN

DENMARK

Copenhagen

Leningrad

Tallinn

ESTONIA

RUSSIAN SOVIET FEDERAL SOCIALIST REPUBLIC (RSFSR)

Riga

LATVIA

KALININGRAD PROVINCE (RSFSR)

LITHUANIA

Kaliningrad

Vilnius

Minsk

BELORUSSIA

Berlin

GERMAN DEMOCRATIC REPUBLIC

Warsaw

POLAND

Prague

Kiev

UKRAINE

CZECHOSLOVAKIA

Vienna

AUSTRIA

Budapest

HUNGARY

MOLDAVIA

Kishinëv

ROMANIA

Belgrade

YUGOSLAVIA

Bucharest

ITALY

Rome

Sofia

BULGARIA

Istanbul

Tirana

ALBANIA

GREECE

TURKEY

Athens

The USSR

Countries which acquired communist governments | ALBANIA

300 miles

400 kilometres

N

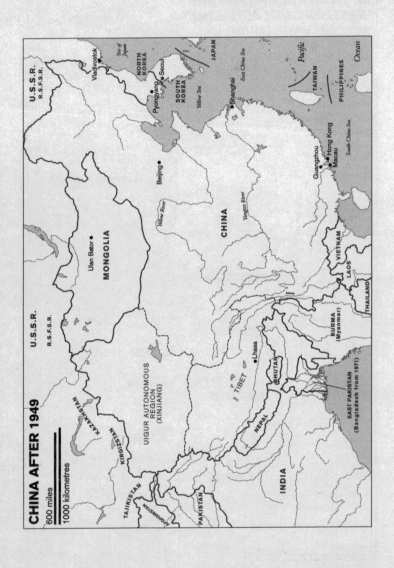

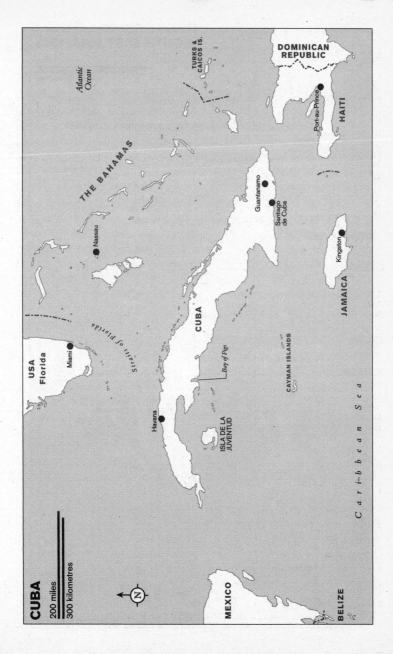

CUBA

200 miles

300 kilometres

N

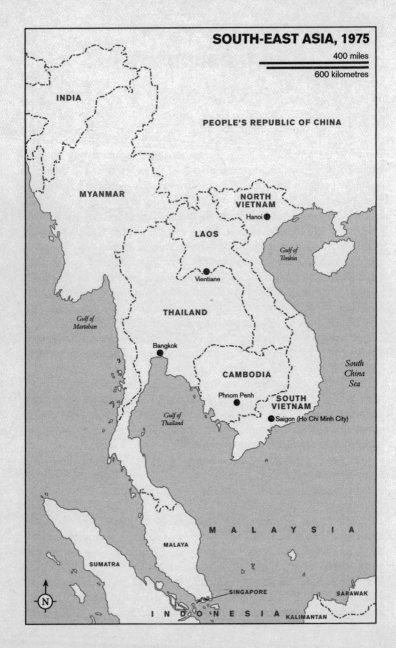

SOUTH-EAST ASIA, 1975

400 miles

600 kilometres

INDIA

PEOPLE'S REPUBLIC OF CHINA

MYANMAR

NORTH VIETNAM

Hanoi ●

LAOS

Gulf of Tonkin

Vientiane ●

THAILAND

Gulf of Martaban

Bangkok ●

CAMBODIA

South China Sea

Phnom Penh ●

SOUTH VIETNAM

● Saigon (Ho Chi Minh City)

Gulf of Thailand

M A L A Y S I A

MALAYA

SUMATRA

SINGAPORE

SARAWAK

N

I N D O N E S I A

KALIMANTAN

INTRODUCTION

People in 1989–91 had to pinch themselves to make sure they were not hallucinating. Something extraordinary had happened in world politics. Suddenly communism had collapsed. Until then it had been one of the most powerful and widespread types of modern state. Coming to power in the October 1917 Revolution in Russia, Lenin and his comrades established an order which was reproduced in eastern Europe, China, east Asia, Cuba and elsewhere after the Second World War. In 1989 this communist order was removed from the face of Europe. In 1991 the same thing happened in the Soviet Union. Although China still claimed to be communist, its fundamental economic reforms meant that this was no longer accurate as a comprehensive description. Communist parties clung on to office in a few countries such as North Korea, Vietnam and Cuba; their geopolitical importance was a long way short of the power and prestige of the 'world communist movement' in its years of pomp. Communism was fast becoming a historical relic.

Such a transformation brought an end to the struggle known as the Cold War. This was predominantly a conflict between coalitions led by the USSR and the USA, and the Soviet disintegration in December 1991 signalled a definitive victory for the Americans. For years the Cold War had involved the nightmarish possibility of a nuclear strike by one side against the other. Unable to match American advances in the development and dissemination of technology, the Soviet Union had lost the military parity it had possessed. This was not the sole index of defeat. Throughout the contest between the superpowers the Americans had claimed to stand for the market economy, liberal democracy and civil society. Although the USA had often honoured these principles only in the breach, they were the principles widely thought to have triumphed when communism expired in eastern Europe and in the USSR. The West's political leaders and commentators were proud and excited. Communism had been exposed as an overwhelmingly inferior kind of state order. Many believed that history had come to a close. Liberalism in its political, economic and social manifestations had consigned the ideology and practice of Leninism to the dustbin of the ages. The suggestion was that communism had been a puffball which too many people had walked around as if it was a great oak tree.

Word got about that, if only the Western powers had adopted a more militant political and security policy in the 1920s or even the 1940s, the USSR would have imploded. Presumably historical development could have been terminated seven decades earlier if Churchill's advice had been heeded and the communist infant – the early Soviet state – had been strangled in its cradle.

Yet communism endured. By 1941, when the USSR was attacked by the Third Reich, the child had grown to a powerful maturity and threw back Hitler's forces. Soviet forces overran the eastern half of Europe. From Poland to East Germany and from the Baltic shores to the Black Sea the map was repainted. Communist states covered the entire region. In 1949 the communist armies under Mao Zedong seized power in Beijing and proclaimed the People's Republic of China. North Korea and North Vietnam soon acquired communist states. In 1959 there was a revolution in Cuba and Fidel Castro announced his adhesion to the world communist movement. At last communism had spread from Eurasia across the Atlantic. A communist-led government was also installed in Chile in the early 1970s. There were further successes for communists as several governments in Asia and Africa announced their commitment to communisation. By the mid-1980s, just before the first mortal blows were delivered to world communism, such states had a record of astonishing expansion. From being just a dream before the First World War it turned itself into a potent reality threatening the capitalist order around the globe.

Debates on communism are as old as communist theory. The communists themselves always loved an argument. They disputed mainly among themselves and with others throughout the nineteenth century. The October Revolution introduced a practical urgency. Communist apologists asserted that a new world was being built in Russia. The party's monopoly of rule was condoned. Dictatorship and terror were purportedly instruments for the direction of a comprehensive system of welfare for working people. The revolutionaries of Russian would put an end to political, economic, cultural and national oppression. Capitalism, according to its enemies, was about to be eradicated. This image of the Soviet state was reproduced down the decades. This happened not only in the USSR but also in the many countries which acquired communist governments after the Second World War. In eastern Europe and China the message went out that a superior order of state and society was being constructed. Privilege was about to be ended, economic waste about to be abolished. Communism was proclaimed as scientific, humanitarian and unstoppable: it was said to be the inevitable, desirable future of humankind. Thus the ultimate vision of Marx and Engels seemed ready to be realised.

What had not been anticipated were the internal divisions in the international communism. Trotski, deported from the Soviet Union in 1928, argued that the October Revolution had been betrayed. After 1945 the schisms increased in number. The USSR and Yugoslavia condemned each other's variant of communism. The Chinese communists turned against the Soviet Union and denounced the Kremlin leadership as 'revisionist' – there was no sin greater for Marxist-Leninists than attempting to revise the unalterable precepts of the founders of Marxism. Only Albania was unconditionally on China's side. Troubles recurred in eastern Europe as governments sought to loosen the Soviet grip on their countries. As this was occurring, many communists tried to rethink the nature of a desirable communism. In western Europe, especially Italy and Spain, the communist parties start to chip away at the model offered by the USSR. 'Eurocommunism' was born. The ideology and politics of communism were far from being monolithic. There were almost as many variants of communism as there were communist states.

People who were not communists joined in the debates about the essential nature of communism. Some of the twentieth century's finest minds were engaged in this. They included philosophers from Bertrand Russell to Jean-Paul Sartre, novelists from André Gide and George Orwell to Alexander Solzhenitsyn and religious leaders from Patriarch Tikhon to the Dalai Lama and Pope John Paul II. The diverse answers they gave enriched the wider discussion about human society in past, present and future. Nothing comprehensive could be said or written about the world after October 1917 without account being taken of the communist project.

The world had an urgent need to find out about communism. There was also a moral imperative. With the exception of Salvador Allende's communist-led coalition government in Chile from 1970 to 1973, the record of communist rule was universally associated with dictatorship, police terror and gross infringements of human rights. It was vital to explain and publicise what was happening in communist states. This was easier planned than done. Communist rulers were like submarine commanders who shut down their engines and enforced radio silence. Stalin managed efficiently to cover up the scale of the famine he had caused in Ukraine, Kazakhstan and southern Russia in 1932–3. Mao outdid even Stalin in 1958–60 by preventing news of the largest instance of policy-induced starvation in history from seeping out beyond his borders. The resort to news black-outs was copied by most communist rulers, even if they did not go to the lengths of Kim Il-sung and his son. Marxist-Leninist rulership was systematically mendacious about its internal affairs and external purposes. Wherever possible, the ambition was to eliminate unofficial sources of information. Politicians, journalists and scholars in the rest of the world had a hard time establishing even quite basic facts about the real circumstances.

This blockage of information enabled communists to go on claiming to possess a superior way of organising society. The boasts were the same from Lenin to Pol Pot and Fidel Castro. Communism supposedly out-matched capitalism's capacity to provide political freedom, cultural opportunity and social and material welfare. Between the two world wars there was only one communist state: the USSR. Only a tiny minority of hostile states by the late 1930s were liberal democracies even in Europe. It was an authoritarian age. There had never been many democracies on the other continents. Africa remained the property of European empires, and most countries in Asia and South America were dominated by one great power or another. Those were also years of economic malaise as market economies sought to surmount the Great Depression of 1929. It was natural for foreigners to wonder whether the Soviet Union with its industrial growth, educational advance and full employment might afford lessons worth learning. What is more, Moscow claimed unprecedented success in resolving national tensions and providing healthcare, shelter and social insurance. Was there perhaps something positive to be borrowed from the Soviet experiment?

The USSR emerged in 1945 as a superpower contesting with the USA for global dominance. The number of communist states increased in the post-war period. Yet another image of communism was disseminated. Stalin's USSR was said to conform to a totalitarian model. Like Hitler's Third Reich, the Soviet order suppressed fair elections and the rule of law and prescribed terror. It was dedicated to propagating its ideology at the expense of all others. It treated its people as a resource to be mobilised. Politics were severely centralised. Labour camps were built for real and potential dissenters. Religious believers, monarchists, cultural free-thinkers, political liberals and socialists, nationalists and other dis-senters were arrested.

Earlier autocracies had come nowhere near to such intensity of control over their societies. Important things changed in the twentieth century. One was the development of technology allowing rapid communication, especially telephones, the telegraph, railways and aircraft. With the expansion of literacy and numeracy, the opportunity for administrative and ideological penetration had never been greater. A second factor was of equal importance. Even the most ambitious dictatorships of the past had shied away from trampling down many traditions and eradicating groups and organisations. Political movements were formed after the nineteenth century to turn their societies upside down and reconstruct them in their own image; and these movements – the communists on the left and the fascists on the right – destroyed, wherever possible, every vestige of autonomous association. They had a totalising perspective. Nothing was to be regarded as unpolitical. The totalitarian rulers had no respect for private life. They derided customary culture and religion. They pulled the media, sport and recreation into their grasp. They eliminated all opposition. They filled the jails and conducted a campaign of permanent terror. They poured the bottles of their ideology into the minds of those whom they ruled.

Whereas fascist totalitarianism in Italy and Germany was crushed in 1945, communist totalitarianism was reinforced in the USSR and other Marxist-Leninist states. Fascism lived on in Spain and Portugal; it re-emerged fitfully and partially in Latin America and elsewhere over ensuing decades. Communism was much more successful. It characteristically lasted a long time wherever it was installed.

No single analysis has the monopoly of historical insight. But few have denied that the Soviet order was truly innovative: there had been nothing like it in world history. Fascism was in many ways a structural copy of it, albeit with a different set of ideological purposes. The totalitarian interpretation incurred criticism because it seemingly implied the end of history wherever communism was established. If a ruling elite achieved a position of such power, it was hard to imagine how change could be engineered. Dictatorship, terror and ideological monopoly were surely sufficient to keep totalitarianism in permanent dominion. Yet the totalitarian theory was only proposing an 'ideal type' of rule. No communist state was without its deviations from the perfect model. Opponents of the theory pointed out that even the USSR under Stalin fell short of a totally secure system of vertically imposed commands. Nor was the Soviet Union ever emptied of social, cultural and economic dissent from the policies of communist rulers. But enough was achieved in the pursuit of comprehensive political monopoly for the USSR – as well as most other communist states – to be rightly described as totalitarian.

Totalitarian theory needs to undergo further revision. Communism in power had problems everywhere. It never overcame social resentment or apathy about its purposes. Nowhere did it fully eradicate the pre-revolutionary culture. It persecuted religion without successfully eliminating it. Its labour discipline was usually woeful. The communist order beneath the apex of supreme leadership had to accommodate itself to a degree of disobedience and obfuscation unmatched in liberal democracies. It had clientelist groups and unreliable mechanisms of information. The point is that these phenomena were not the grit in the machinery of totalitarianism but the oil. Without them the entire order would have ground its way to a standstill. A 'perfect' totalitarianism cannot give an attractive enough incentive for people – from middle-ranking officials down to state-employed factory workers – to co-operate. People had to be allowed to contravene strict requirements. What is more, the rulers needed their entourages of personal patronage in order to get things done in the localities. Communist systems, being based on formal principles of vertical command, could not survive without resuscitating some traditions of the nation. This was not an accident. It was the common pattern of all Marxist-Leninist states. It was the key to their effectiveness.

These phenomena would have surprised Marx and Engels, the fathers of contemporary Marxism. They would have baffled Lenin, who saw them in their incipient form with his very own eyes. They went on disconcerting communist rulers in Asia, eastern Europe, Cuba and Africa after the Second World War. Nobody had a realistic answer to the problems of enhancing economic performance and political consent. There was also difficulty in achieving even a modest degree of social integration. A chasm existed between officialdom and the people under communism. Marx and Engels had predicted a 'withering away of the state'. Communist history moved in the opposite direction. State power increased exponentially. Labour camps proliferated. Repression of individuals and groups hostile to communism continued to be necessary for the maintenance of the status quo. Civil society was crushed. Many communist rulers pointed to their achievements in free education and healthcare, as well as the easy access to shelter, employment and food. But the regimes never enjoyed genuine consent. Dictatorship had to remain dictatorship.

Why the bright hopes of Marxism were disappointed has been a constant topic of controversy. Some blamed the original doctrines of Marx and Engels. There is much in this. The founding fathers saw force as the midwife of historical progress and never blenched at the prospect of dictatorship, terror and civil war. But there was another side to them, and it was the side which appealed to most Marxists in central Europe before the First World War. The truth was that Marx and Engels left behind an unfinished, incoherent legacy. Their heirs were legitimately free to hold opposite opinions. Ideological dispute informed the genes of Marxism. Among the Marxists who refused to adopt a peaceful road to the perfect society of the future were Lenin and the Bolsheviks. They inherited the authoritarian strands of Marxism's DNA. And it was they rather than the more moderate Marxists who established the first revolutionary regime. They formed the Communist International and offered a model to socialists on the extreme political left in other countries.

Even the Bolsheviks had peace, prosperity and harmony as their ultimate objective. The 'revolution from above' was meant to be harnessed to a 'revolution from below'. The fact that the actual outcome was different had multiple roots. Leninist doctrine had an anti-libertarian core. At the slightest obstacle the reaction of the Bolsheviks was to use force – and the obstacles were huge after the October Revolution. Most of those who made the subsequent revolutions in Marxism's name applied immense coercion. Communists were foolish in not anticipating the difficulties that beset them. The other Russian socialists had warned the Bolsheviks before the October Revolution. Leaders of succeeding communist revolutions had even less excuse: they had the Soviet experience to look back on and learn from. Communism in its Leninist variants stemmed from a simplistic analysis. That was partly the fault of Marx and Engels and partly attributable to a failure of reconsideration by Lenin, Stalin, Mao and Castro. They held to ideas in the teeth of the evidence. Social and economic affairs, moreover, changed drastically in all sectors after the late nineteenth century. All communists were shown to underestimate capitalism's capacity for self-regeneration and to exaggerate the working class's potential to act as the saviour of the planet. They were the prisoners of their delusions.

Communist affairs, moreover, were conditioned by geopolitics. Not even the mighty USSR could exist in the world without maintaining relations with the other great powers. The treaty of Brest-Litovsk, signed by Soviet Russia with Germany and Austria-Hungary in March 1918, was the first in a series of compromises with capitalist states made by communist rulers. Smaller communist countries such as Cuba, North Korea and North Vietnam had always to adjust their policies to the likely attitude of the superpowers. Internal policy had also to be adapted to unpredicted conditions. The search for popular support induced communist rulers everywhere, including the internationalist fanatics of the Hungarian Soviet Republic of 1919, to play the national card. Mao would have made little progress after seizing power in 1949 if he had not stressed his credentials as a Chinese patriot. In many cases communist rulers were genuinely surprised that the degree of obstructiveness in society did not quickly subside. There were exceptions: Béla Kun in Hungary and Pol Pot in Cambodia in 1975 were extremists who spilled the blood of others in advance of serious resistance to the Marxist experiment. Communist states also fell behind the capitalist West in technological progress. Ways had to be found to compensate for this chronic lack of competitiveness by increasing imports and intensifying espionage.

When the old utopianism of Lenin and Stalin reared its head, as it did with Mao in the Cultural Revolution of 1966–8, the results were disastrous. Communists frequently displayed historical amnesia. Pol Pot as Mao's pupil drew only catastrophic conclusions from the career of his master. Yet communist history around the globe also had much variety. Expectations were altered. Practices evolved. Communist regimes, if they lasted several decades, modified their policies so as to avoid the bloodbaths of the past.

But how many communisms were there? Communists themselves have never ceased to argue about this. Some suggested that the communisms of Lenin and Stalin were like chalk and cheese: others – and I am one of them – have argued that the foundations of the Soviet order were laid down under Lenin and lasted unreformed under his successors through to the late 1980s. Curiously, few have made similar attempts at periodisation for the People's Republic of China. Mao's regime is acknowledged to have had roughly the same political and economic structure from the 1950s until the introduction of capitalism from the late 1970s. Cuba, East Germany, Cambodia, Romania and North Vietnam switched many policies in the course of their existence but nobody seriously maintains that the early years of those states were radically different from the later ones. The exceptions prove the rule. Hungary in 1956, Czechoslovakia in 1968 and the USSR in the late 1980s introduced reforms of so radical a nature that they teetered on the brink of decommunisation. Invasion stopped this happening in Hungary and Czechoslovakia at that time. (They, like other countries in eastern Europe, had to wait until 1989 to free themselves of communism.) The USSR leaped into the unknown under Gorbachëv: at the end of 1991 it ceased to exist.

Nobody maintains that Cuba with its colourful, noisy bars and restaurants is administered exactly the same as North Korea. Mao's China was not a replica of Gomułka's Poland or Hoxha's Albania. Life in Stalin's USSR was not the same as in Allende's Chile. The national aspects of each communist order have always been of importance.

Yet communism's characteristics have been basically similar wherever it has lasted any length of time. Allende did not institute a one-party, one-ideology state. But he held on to power for only three years and was overthrown by a military coup. Durable communist regimes had much in common. They eliminated or emasculated rival political parties. They attacked religion, culture and civil society. They trampled on every version of nationhood except the one approved by communist rulership. They abolished the autonomy of the courts and the press. They centralised power. They turned over dissenters to forced-labour camps. They set up networks of security police and informers. They claimed infallibility in doctrine and paraded themselves as faultless scientists of human affairs. They insulated societies against alien influences in politics and culture. They fiercely barricaded their frontiers. They treated every aspect of social life as in need of penetration by the authorities. They handled people as a resource to be mobilised. They showed little respect for ecology, charity or custom. These commonalities make it sensible to speak of a communist order. It is to the history of that order that we now shall turn.

PART ONE

ORIGINS

TO 1917

1. COMMUNISM BEFORE MARXISM

The seeds of modern communism germinated long before the twentieth century. The word itself – communism – was invented late, gaining widespread currency in French, German and English only in the 1840s. It has consistently denoted a desire to dig up the foundations of society and rebuild. Communists have never been half hearted about their purposes. They have focused a constant hatred of the existing order on state and economy. They have suggested that only they – and not their many rivals on the political left – have the doctrinal and practical potential to transform human affairs. Some kind of egalitarianism lasted in their objectives. Determination and impatience to achieve change have been permanent features. The commitment to militant organisation has endured. But communism itself has not ceased to defy attempts at definition. No final meeting of minds is likely. One communist's communism is another communist's anti-communism, and this is a situation unlikely to change.

What became known as communism in the twentieth century was the outcome of many influences. Its principal expression was the official ideology of the USSR and other communist states. Marx and Engels themselves – the originators of the doctrines which became known as Marxism – acknowledged three main sources of inspiration. Politically they were deeply affected by what they learned about Maximilien Robespierre and other radical politicians in the French Revolution at the end of the eighteenth century. In economics they admitted to having drawn strongly on the ideas of David Ricardo and other theorists who examined the extraordinary propulsive energies in production and commerce unleashed by capitalism in the United Kingdom. Philosophically they were fascinated by the writings of Hegel. Their fellow German had insisted that history proceeds through stages which condition the way that humankind thinks and acts and that the great changes in social life are not merely of a superficial or cyclical character: Hegel regarded the historical record as a sequence of progress towards an ever better condition of people and things.[1]

Marxism's co-founders were never uncritical admirers of Robespierre, Ricardo and Hegel. Indeed Marx claimed to have turned Hegel
upside down;[2] and, of course, he neither accepted Robespierre's specific
political analysis nor condoned Ricardo's advocacy of private enterprise.
Marx and Engels thought of themselves as working to synthesise the
crucial discoveries of those who had influenced them; and they went on
developing this synthesis through their middle and late careers.

Both wished to be taken seriously as propagators of 'modern',
'scientific' and 'contemporary' communism.[3] Their ideas were not to be
sullied by association with most previous and contemporary thinkers.
They were men in a hurry; they thought they were living at the end of
the capitalist era and that the communist era was nigh. Neither had an
introspective personality – and, apart from Marx's brief comment on
Robespierre, Ricardo and Hegel, they seldom enquired about the influences which had shaped their world-view. (If indeed they examined
themselves in this way, they did not breathe a word about it to others.)
Crucial to Marxism was the dream of apocalypse followed by paradise.[4]
This kind of thinking existed in Judaism, Christianity and Islam. Marx
had been brought up in a Jewish family which converted to Christianity;
the Engels family were Protestants. Marx and Engels as atheists later in
their lives denied that true believers would be rewarded by eternity in
heaven; instead they contended that they and their supporters would
create the perfect society down here on earth. Christian doctrine predicted that unbelievers would meet a miserable end at the return of the
Messiah. Likewise, according to the founders of Marxism, those who
obstructed the advance of communism to supremacy would be trampled
underfoot. The ruling classes of the day would come to rue their lordship
over humankind.

The New Testament also laid an emphasis on the universal sharing
of material goods. Christ's Sermon on the Mount eulogised the poor
and the oppressed. When he learned that the crowd had only five loaves
and two fish among them, Christ divided them equally, and a miracle
was witnessed as everyone present had enough to eat.[5] This was one of
the great influences on subsequent endeavours for all people to have an
adequate means of subsistence. No other statement more potently disseminated egalitarian principles. Organised Christianity did not adhere
to them for long after the crucifixion of Jesus Christ. Even before Roman
Emperor Constantine turned it into the state religion in AD 313, most of
its spiritual leaders justified the traditional hierarchy of political and
social power. Slavery was sanctioned, wars of conquest approved. The

poor were instructed to put up with poverty and wait until after death for relief from their suffering. The New Testament stated otherwise – and religious reformers such as St Francis of Assisi and John Wycliffe, being able to understand the Latin Vulgate, spoke out against the rich and powerful. The sharing of goods was always treated by some Christians, even if only a minority of them, as a virtue. And under communism the means of sustenance were to be equally distributed and there would be no one left to want for more.

Christians were not the only Jewish sect in the time of Jesus Christ which practised forms of social and material egalitarianism. The Essenes, whose scrolls were found in caves near the Dead Sea nearly two millennia later, were committed to such principles. Like the Christians, Essenes looked forward to an apocalypse and to the divine instatement of a perfect society in heaven.[6]

Christ's message was spiritual in nature and omitted to indicate the institutional means to achieve its ultimate aim. Certain thinkers in later centuries suggested that state power should be used to bring about equal access to food, shelter and reward. Two influential works were Thomas More's *Utopia* in 1516 and Tommaso Campanella's *City of the Sun* in 1601. More could not imagine that the common man, still less the common woman, might independently attain the perfection of society without orders from above. Campanella's tract depicted a society which instituted universal fairness by means of gross intrusion into private life.[7] More and Campanella advocated thorough indoctrination of their people. This was a reversion to the attitude of the Greek philosopher Plato who, in the fourth century BC, called for philosopher–kings to introduce a reign of universal virtue. Neither More nor Campanella prospered in temporal affairs. Having faithfully served his master Henry VIII, More refused to accept the termination of the Pope's supremacy over the English Church. He died on the executioner's block in 1535. Campanella was the victim of the Catholic Church. Incarcerated in Naples, he spent years in a confinement relieved only by the many curious and fervent Christian believers who came to his cell. The Church accused him of communing with a demon who inhabited the space underneath his fingernails. He died in 1639.

It was in the sixteenth century AD that movements arose to seek to realise some egalitarian objectives, and Marx and Engels certainly took note of this in their historical writings. The Anabaptist Christian sect in sixteenth-century Germany and Switzerland put such ideas into practice by abolishing private property. To this end they adopted an authoritarian regime in Münster. Having expelled the town elders and the Catholic clergy, they set about transforming a whole way of life and undertook a rigorous application of their interpretation of God's word. They were fanatically intolerant. They were certain that the Second Coming of the Messiah was nigh. Exploratory curiosity among them was discouraged by savage punishments. Indeed the Protestant sects throughout northern Europe reacted to their experience of persecution by the Catholic Church by persecuting those inside – as well as outside – their sects who refused to adhere to their doctrines.[8] Neither Marx nor Engels saw anything wrong in such behaviour. They regarded the religious rebels as enthusiastic precursors of nineteenth-century political radicalism. Their main point was that the Anabaptists and others had come into existence too early to be able to benefit from economic as well as intellectual modernity.

Their argument was similar about the course of the English civil war of 1642–9. They were especially interested in the Levellers and the Diggers. These were radical groups which fought in the parliamentary forces and advocated plans to redistribute property on an egalitarian basis. Their personal decency was beyond cavil, and unlike the Anabaptists they were without fanatical zeal. Oliver Cromwell valued their military proficiency while distrusting their ultimate intentions. Proof came for him in the Putney Debates which happened outside London and alongside the Thames. Members of the New Model Army, confident that victory would be theirs in the civil war, discussed what kind of state and society should be constructed. Levellers and Diggers hated the England of property and privilege. They despised materialism.[9] They were principled republicans and supported Cromwell when he resolved to execute Charles I. But their hostility to political and social hierarchy was anathema to Cromwell, who never failed to protect the interests of landowners and merchants. He sent in the rest of the Model Army to suppress trouble in 1649. For Marx and Engels, they were revolutionary martyrs.

Equality in material possessions was not the aim of most militants in the French Revolution from 1789. But some espoused it. Jean-Paul Marat hated the aristocracy and its inherited wealth and authority. He was killed in his bath by Charlotte Corday, who hated his Jacobin extremism. Gracchus Babeuf maintained the fanatical tradition. Babeuf's Conspiracy of the Equals strove after the revolutionary elimination of differences based on a person's origins, upbringing or current condition. They made allowances solely for age and sex. The Conspiracy set up groups and canvassed for support in Paris. Babeuf enjoyed his politics until in 1796 the government ordered his arrest. By then his radicalism was thought dangerous to public order. His trial was perfunctory, the verdict known in advance. Babeuf, complacent advocate of the guillotine in previous years, was driven in a cart to the place of his execution.[10]

Yet ideas about forcible equalisation of status and property were catching the imagination of others. Although Napoleon Bonaparte imposed a personal dictatorship in 1799, France remained a forcing bed for revolutionary ideas well into the nineteenth century. Among the influential figures was Henri de St Simon. He and his followers called for the gathering of the 'instruments of labour, land and capital in a social fund'. Hereditary wealth was to be expropriated. St Simon aimed at creating a vast 'association of toilers' who would be organised from above. They would be assigned tasks according to their talent and rewarded according to their work. St Simon's doctrine envisaged an end to war and the start of an endless era of plenty for humankind. This was meant to come about through dutiful propaganda. Such a prediction convinced Louis Blanc, a Frenchman born towards the end of the Napoleonic wars. Blanc rejected calls for a violent seizure of power. He wanted the revolutionary regime to proceed by democratic means while acting as the banker of the poor and biasing economic policy in favour of associations of working people. Private enterprise would steadily be squeezed from industry, agriculture and trade. Blanc was more radical than St Simon about the future: he planned for people to be paid not according to work done but according to whatever need they experienced.[11]

Then Charles Fourier attracted public attention in the first quarter of the nineteenth century. Working as a clerk in Lyon, he had no patience with existing society; he proposed that people should withdraw to 'phalansteries' where they might form self-ruling communities. This was not unlike the summons of the medieval Catholic Church to young men to become monks. Fourier's fantasies had an appeal to some intellectuals for their passionate denunciation of private profit: 'Truth and commerce are as incompatible as Jesus and Satan.' Another French author who wanted to remove the state from the centre of revolutionary strategy was Pierre-Joseph Proudhon. His famous slogan was 'Property is theft.' Proudhon hated all authority and rebuked anyone planning a dictatorial form of socialism. He abhorred government altogether and made the call for a free federation of independent communes. He rejected all laws as instruments of oppression; he wanted communes to conclude agreements with each other about how their members should live.[12]

If Fourier and Proudhon were annoyed by Louis Blanc, they raged about Louis-Auguste Blanqui, who preserved the French Jacobin tradition of terror and dictatorship. Blanqui was a master conspirator, having started out as a member of a secret insurrectionary society. He advocated violent revolution to overthrow the ruling classes and establish a dictatorial regime that would promote socialism. The task would be to enable the proletariat to liberate itself from political and economic thrall. Blanqui aimed to change France – and later the world – root and branch. The aristocracy and the middle classes would lose their civil rights. The standing army would be disbanded. The administration would be dismantled and replaced by an apparatus of power committed to 'continuous revolution'. The ultimate objective was to bring about communism. This would be the last stage in the development of humanity's organisation. Blanqui practised what he preached. He led several uprisings. All of them failed. He was repeatedly imprisoned, but he always returned from confinement with yet another desperate scheme.[13] His writings were not his strongest point and his *Social Critique* was published only posthumously; but the gist of his message contributed strongly to discussions among revolutionary groups in later years.

Communist groups were no longer confined to France. The ideas had spread around Europe, and artisans and craftsmen as well as students and writers picked them up. In Germany, Belgium and Switzerland the police were perplexed by the surge of interest in ultra-radical versions of socialism. Secret societies sprang up wherever political persecution occurred. (It was already notable that the freest countries in the world, the United Kingdom and the USA, had only weak stirrings of communist agitation.) One such organised gathering was the League of the Just in Germany. Its leader Wilhelm Weitling, a journeyman tailor, could scarcely believe how his thoughts – expressed in his *Gospel of Poor Sinners* – quickly found fertile ground abroad. Even London acquired a group of his supporters.

Politics and economics were not the only matter exercising the minds of the radicals. By the early nineteenth century a strong trend had emerged among many thinkers. Physics, biology and chemistry made strides forwards greater than any achieved in the previous two millennia. For most thinking people – at least those who were not hewing coal, working weaving machines or digging canals – a positive excitement was in the air. They gulped it down. Then along came Darwin. *Origin of the*

Species oxygenated intellectual life around the planet. Darwin's achievement was to link the natural and human sciences. His theory of evolution postulated that the various animal species derived over millions of years from crude, simple life-forms which adapted themselves to their physical environment in a struggle which ended in the 'survival of the fittest'. Higher forms of life supplanted lower ones. The struggle had been constant since the beginning of time and had not yet finished. Nothing was eternal except change itself, and competition among life-forms was inevitable. This way of thinking had enormous appeal for radical militants who eulogised the need for political battle and asserted that one specific group – the working class – would win it.

Darwin wrote about aeons of successive microscopic changes which had led to the natural world of his day. When he went to the Galapagos Islands in 1835, he found turtles and birds which because of their insular isolation and specificity of climate had developed differently from their nearest relatives in the rest of the known world. Marx and Engels thought in terms of stages of transformation which involved ruptures of a macroscopic nature. Despite their admiration for Darwin, they were drawn to notions of sharp breaks between one kind of political and social 'order' and another. A preoccupation with historical stages from the beginning of recorded time to the present was not new. The Greeks since the poet Hesiod, if not before, had believed that the golden age had yielded to the silver and then to the bronze. Hesiod was a pessimist: each age was worse than the one before. Later thinkers contended that big changes were inevitable but that deterioration was not inevitable. Down to Giambattista Vico in the eighteenth century, they argued that transformations were of a cyclical kind. Things underwent alteration but after time reverted to their original condition – and then, needless to say, they moved further round the old circle.

Not everyone accepted such ways of thinking. Auguste Comte in France and Herbert Spencer in Britain proposed that historical transformation had always taken a progressive path. Ever higher, ever better. They predicted that humankind would advance towards ever greater social complexity and general happiness in the course of future years. Comte and Spencer were exponents of evolutionary and peaceful change.[14] Marx and Engels disagreed. Like Thucydides and Machiavelli, they contended that people could divert the course of development by sheer force of will and intelligence. History lay in the hands of those who chose to make it. Thucydides thought this was what had happened in the Athens of Pericles. Machiavelli longed for a 'prince' who would grab the reins of Florentine politics and build Italy into a single nation feared and admired throughout Europe. Marx and Engels disliked the notion that an individual could do more than take advantage of the circumstances of their time. They also ridiculed the importance of accident in human affairs. For them, a Luther or a Napoleon merely embodied the rise of broad social forces in their countries and had no particular talent of their own. But they shared the confidence of Comte and Spencer that history was constituted by stages of development and that the best stage was yet to come.

The founders of Marxism put class struggle at the forefront of their analysis; they said the working class (or the proletariat) would remake the politics, economics and culture of the entire world. Messianism had crept in again here. Judaism and Christianity projected the arrival on earth of a Saviour who would strike down the enemies of God and raise up a community of perfection. Believers were asked to work to ready themselves for that day. The Judaeo-Christian tradition postulated that the preceding human era was a history of man's lapsed condition. Wars, oppression, thievery, deceit and debauchery were the reflection of original sin; there was no reforming this state of affairs: it had to be swept away in a single ruthless movement. Christians and Jews trusted that the Messiah would know and tell how this was to be achieved. Salvation according to Marx and Engels would come not through an individual but through a whole class. The proletariat's experience of degradation under capitalism would give it the motive to change the nature of society; and its industrial training and organisation would enable it to carry its task through to completion. The collective endeavour of socialist workers would transform the life of well-meaning people – and those who offered resistance would be suppressed.[15]

Politics, they suggested, would cease to exist. This was no new idea. Jean-Jacques Rousseau in the late eighteenth century had suggested that public affairs ought to be guided by what he called the General Will. Rousseau had little interest in institutions. He spurned notions of representative democracy and any theory of checks and balances. He disliked the idea of a plurality of political parties; in fact he wanted no such party to exist. Somehow, he assumed that enlightened doctrines and popular participation by themselves would lead to the creation of a truly just, egalitarian and free society. If anyone fails to conform to the General Will, however it might be expressed, he or she would automatically have abandoned the path of goodness. In a striking phrase, Rousseau wrote of the need to train people to 'bear with docility the yoke of public happiness'. Personal, partial interests had to be given up. Loyalties other than to the whole society had to be foresworn. Privacy was unimportant to Rousseau in theory and he deemed every aspect of life to merit public interference. Unanimity of purpose was natural and desirable. Rousseau conceded that, left to themselves, the people do not always know where the good lies in any great matter of state. But he argued that the General Will is always right and should be unquestioningly obeyed.[16]

Although neither Marx nor Engels wrote much on Rousseau, the imprint of his way of thinking is unmistakable. Rousseau's politics were fundamentally anti-political and authoritarian even while he looked forward to an ultimate era of universal harmony. Not without reason he is seen as an intellectual progenitor of twentieth-century totalitarianism.[17]

Other thinkers and practical leaders were more direct than Rousseau in stressing the desirability of a lengthy period of authoritarian rule, and they too had a formative influence on Marxism. The fact that Marx and Engels were men of the political left does not mean that they failed to soak up ideas from the political right. In the nineteenth century there were plenty of reactionary thinkers who pointed to the corruption possible and likely in the growing institutions of representative democracy. Yet the most remarkable case for authoritarianism was contained in the works of Niccolò Machiavelli. The fifteenth-century Florentine writer and diplomat objected to the philosophical axiom that moral goodness was the prerequisite of sound rulership. Machiavelli would have none of this. The true 'prince', he insisted, had to be severe on his people. They needed to fear him: this would engender respect and obedience. Gentleness would result in endless political ineffectiveness. Machiavelli claimed that a period of exemplary brutality would be salutary in wiping thoughts of rebellion from everyone's mind. It would clear the road for the ruler to attain glory and unity for his city or nation. Machiavelli looked back fondly to those ancient commanders in the histories of Livy who were tough on themselves and their people in the cause of the Roman republic.[18]

Marx and Engels followed Machiavelli in rejecting morality as a principle for action. They wanted to focus a glacial eye on their situation. They embraced scientific principles of analysis and recommendation. This was a legacy of the European Enlightenment. Scottish, French and English thinkers exercised a huge impact on them. David Hume and Voltaire had taken a scalpel to the fat of superstition and prejudice. There was open season on the intellectual inadequacies in the defence of

anciens régimes in the late eighteenth century.[19] 'Science' became a substitute religion. The notion that ideas should be scrutinised with a sceptical
eye using procedures unconditioned by the need to arrive at predeter-
mined conclusions predated the Enlightenment. Towering figures
such as Galileo and Copernicus had challenged the conventional wisdom
of their day. Galileo had been disciplined by the Catholic Inquisition
for his audacity; Copernicus had escaped persecution only by lying low
in distant Poland. In still earlier centuries most individuals whom
we nowadays call scientists confined their researches to the natural
sciences. But in ancient Greece this had not been the case. Aristotle
himself had written as easily about human affairs as about the movement
of stars in the heavens or about the peculiar properties of snail, toad
and horse. Marxism's co-founders saw themselves as upholders of this
tradition.

They denied being sentimental in their politics and rejected the
notion that the poor in society were inherently decent and altruistic.
They scoffed at many socialists of their day for succumbing to sentimentality about the poor in their societies. Idealisation of the poor and
oppressed did not come new with socialism. As with many influences
upon them, Marx and Engels refused to accept that they shared such
assumptions. But this was self-deception. Whenever they spoke of the
'masses', they explained away all faults and deficiencies as the responsibility of the ruling classes. They eulogised the 'proletariat' as a class and
argued that capitalism diverted its members from the path of truth and
rationality.

And so it came about that vast intellectual and political detritus
existed where the seeds of Marxist communism could breed. The
aspiration for a perfect society was an old religious thought in Judaism,
Christianity and Islam. Although definitions differed, many writers had
also called for a redistribution of goods and power on egalitarian
principles. Millenarian moods and beliefs were not uncommon in
previous centuries; there had frequently been movements to build the
kingdom of heaven on earth and to effect its instant completion. Global
objectives had frequently been pursued. Militants had enjoined the need
for cosmopolitanism and an end to national, class-based or parochial
concerns. Divisions had inevitably existed in the camp of radical change.
Dictatorship and terror, while not appealing to everybody, had their
adherents. And several influential thinkers had proposed that history was
not a random or a cyclical process but moved stage by stage to its
ultimate condition. What is more, the belief that society in past, present

and future could be subjected to scientific analysis was a widespread one. How this might be brought to its political realisation caused unending dispute. Not a few religious, social or political movements had rested their confidence in the poor and oppressed as the perpetrators of transformation. They were often intended too as the main beneficiaries.

These yearnings were like conch shells swept on to the beach after a storm at sea. They were picked up by radical anti-capitalist groups in the early nineteenth century and carried to workers, artisans and intellectuals. These groups were a diverse bunch, stretching out across several European countries. They itched to put their ideas into effect after gaining the necessary support to come to power. They called themselves communists, socialists or even anarchists. They were vociferous and increasingly bold and organised. Communism was placing its feet firmly in Europe's political arena.

2. MARX AND ENGELS

Karl Marx and Friedrich Engels provided the inspiration for twentieth-century communism. No one else so effectively captivated minds on the political far left or drew other minds to that standpoint. The gusto of their writings and their politicking was tremendous. Few other variants of communist ideology any longer came under consideration outside the rarefied atmosphere of scholarly or sectarian groups. Marxism and communism for most people were co-extensive. The kind of Marxism which they knew about was to a greater or lesser extent linked to the interpretation offered by Lenin and the makers of the October 1917 Revolution in Russia.

They died in exile in the United Kingdom. Marx expired on 14 March 1883 in his family house in north London. Engels lived a dozen years more; he passed away on 5 August 1895. Both were Germans. Marx had been born on 5 May 1818 in Trier, Engels on 28 November 1820 in Barmen (now part of Wuppertal). The Marxes had been observant Jews until Karl's father, a competent and ambitious lawyer, converted to Christianity. The Engels family were Protestant industrialists. Marx and Engels were bright students. They were well schooled; they read voraciously in European literature and contemporary public debates – Marx was especially expert in ancient Greek philosophy. They quickly rejected the staid bourgeois life projected for them. As young men they had joined free-thinking intellectual circles and advocated the communist cause. They avidly followed current affairs. They detested the restrictions on intellectual freedom of expression in their homeland; they equally hated the oppressive conditions of working people there. In 1843 they left Germany seeking greater opportunity to publish their opinions. They moved restlessly between Brussels and Paris and made frequent trips to London. In 1846 Marx set up a Communist Corresponding Committee. Together they wrote one of their most influential pamphlets, *The Communist Manifesto*, a year later.[1]

Their predictions of revolutionary upheaval seemed likely to be fulfilled in 1848, when uprisings occurred in many countries of central and western Europe. Engels took part in military action against the Prussian armed forces. Marx, Engels and others edited *Die Neue Rhein-ische Zeitung*. (Marx was editor-in-chief.) All were hoping for a total recasting of politics across the continent. Co-ordinated action by the Holy Alliance of Austria, Russia and Prussia, however, crushed the revolutions. The rebels everywhere were executed, imprisoned or scattered into foreign exile. Marx and Engels hung on for as long as was safe and then fled to London in 1849. The United Kingdom was the sole country in Europe where they could go on researching, writing and publishing with the necessary facilities and without fear of state persecution. The British government and police, unthreatened by any revolutionary movement at home, saw no reason to prevent the flotsam and jetsam of continental extremism fetching up on their shores. The application by the Prussian authorities for the extradition of Marx and Engels was therefore refused.

Disgust with 'bourgeois society' did not stop Marx and Engels from benefiting from capitalist industry and bourgeois society. Engels's father had acquired a Manchester textile factory. The son worked there until 1870, securing an income and learning about capitalism from the inside. Marx lacked personal finance but was expert at avoiding the bills of tradesmen. He was also a cheerful scrounger. Engels many times rescued his friend and his growing family from destitution. Neither of them denied themselves the pleasures of everyday life. Few other contemporary philosophers would have got drunk as they did and run up the Tottenham Court Road pursued by policemen who wanted to nab them for breaking the lights on lampposts.[2]

They had declared in *The Communist Manifesto*: 'A spectre is haunting Europe – the spectre of communism. All the powers of old Europe have entered into a holy alliance to exorcise this spectre: Pope and Tsar, Metternich and Guizot, French Radicals and German police-spies.' They declared, with more than a little exaggeration: 'Communism is already acknowledged by all European powers to be itself a power.' Then came the call to action:

The history of all hitherto existing society is the history of class struggles.

Freeman and slave, patrician and plebeian, lord and serf, guild-master and journeyman – in a word, oppressor and oppressed – stood in constant opposition to each other, carried on an uninterrupted –

now hidden, now open – fight, a fight that each time ended either in
a revolutionary re-constitution of society at large or in the common
ruin of the contending classes.

The future was specified. Marx and Engels predicted a final struggle
between the 'bourgeoisie' and the 'proletariat' under capitalism. The
outcome, they said, was inevitable: the supremacy of the proletariat.

The proletariat was the name used increasingly by socialist intellectuals for the working class. Marx and Engels saw employed workers as
the future saviour of mankind. They gave little mind to the unemployed.
They, like most bourgeois of the period, had no time for those people
at the very base of society who had no regular occupation; they despised
the so-called lumpenproletariat as a bunch of thieves and indolent ne'er-
do-wells. The great revolution, they believed, required an active force of
organised, skilled and literate industrial labourers.

The expected transformation would not be restricted to 'property
relations'. In response to their critics, Marx and Engels admitted that
communism 'abolishes eternal truths, it abolishes all religion and all
morality, instead of constituting them on a new basis; it therefore acts in
contradiction to all past historical [sic] experience'.[3] This was the long-
term perspective. For the moment, however, they restricted themselves
to calling for certain reforms. They aimed only to abolish landed
property and inheritance rights. They also demanded a graduated income
tax. They planned for 'the extension of factories and instruments of
production owned by the state'. They aspired to universal, free education.
They demanded universal liability for labour and proposed the creation
of 'industrial armies, especially for agriculture'. They aspired to the
abolition of the family. They summed up their vision in striking words:
'The working men have no country. We cannot take from them what
they have not got. Since the proletariat must first of all acquire political
supremacy, must rise to be the leading class of the nation . . .'[4] Exactly
how this could be achieved was not spelled out. Somehow the 'united
action' of what Marx and Engels called 'the leading civilised countries'
would supply 'one of the first preconditions for the emancipation of the
proletariat'.

Marx wrote up his analysis of recent French history in The Class
Struggles in France and The Eighteenth Brumaire of Louis Napoleon. His
essential argument was that the course of change had been conditioned
not by the brilliance of 'great men' or by dynamic governments but by
the clashes of social classes – and Marx insisted that classes pursued their

objective economic interests. The French 'proletariat' had lost its recurrent conflict with the bourgeoisie since the end of the eighteenth century. But Marx was undeterred. He had asserted in his *Theses on Feuerbach*, penned in 1845: 'Philosophers have hitherto only interpreted the world in various ways; the point is to change it.'[5]

The ultimate objective for Marx and Engels was the creation of a worldwide communist society. They believed that communism had existed in the distant centuries before 'class society' came into being. The human species had supposedly known no hierarchy, alienation, exploitation or oppression. Marx and Engels predicted that such perfection could and inevitably would be reproduced after the overthrow of capitalism. 'Modern communism', however, would have the benefits of the latest technology rather than flint-stones. It would be generated by global proletarian solidarity rather than by disparate groups of illiterate, innumerate cavemen. And it would put an end to all forms of hierarchy. Politics would come to an end. The state would cease to exist. There would be no distinctions of personal rank and power. All would engage in self-administration on an equal basis. Marx and Engels chastised communists and socialists who would settle for anything less. They were maximalists. No compromise with capitalism or parliamentarism was acceptable to them. They did not think of themselves as offering the watchword of 'all or nothing' in their politics. They saw communism as the inevitable last stage in human history; they rejected their predecessors and rival contemporaries as 'utopian' thinkers who lacked a scientific understanding.[6]

They spent the rest of their lives working out how to underpin this vision with an intellectual justification. They were among the nineteenth century's most innovative thinkers. Marx aimed to produce a multi-volume analysis bridging politics, economics, philosophy and society. Having made a rough plan, he started with the volume on capitalist economic development. Everything had to be grounded in scientific examination. The result was *Capital*. The job took him years longer than he had expected; and, although his friend Engels begged him to deliver the manuscript to the publishers, he kept rewriting large sections. The first volume appeared in 1867.[7]

By then Marx and Engels had helped to establish the International Workingmen's Association. This was to become known as the First International. It was an organisation whose founding meeting took place in St Martin's Hall in central London in 1864 and brought together revolutionaries of diverse sorts. The unifying aim was to bring down capitalism across Europe and North America. Marx was elected to the General Council. His pre-eminence in the International had been attained by his success in the furious disputes he had had with the Russian anarchist Mikhail Bakunin. Marx and Engels sought to bring all the parties and organisations over to their specific doctrines. Members of the International, however, showed fissiparous tendencies. They disagreed about practically everything – and Marx's involvement in the disputes gave him an excuse for being slow to deliver any of *Capital* to the publishers. The General Council was a little more tranquil. Even so, there was continual disagreement about political strategy, national specificity and revolutionary methods. Marx waded into every controversy. Being more learned and domineering than his comrades in the Council, he got his way more often than not. Congresses were held in Geneva, Lausanne and Brussels between 1866 and 1868. All participants were fired by an enthusiasm for worldwide revolution.[8]

Most of them were also committed to the cause of international peace and were horrified by the outbreak of the war between Prussia and France in 1870. But Prussian military success led to the fall of Napoleon III, and a revolutionary situation erupted in the French capital. Workers and socialist agitators set up the Paris Commune in March 1871. This was an attempt to establish an administration of popular self-rule. Each representative was elected and remained subject to instant recall if ever the electors objected. Wages and salaries were equalised; welfare provision was disseminated. The Commune heavily regulated the metropolitan economy. Marx and Engels were ecstatic. To them it seemed that the model of their kind of revolution was being created by the 'proletariat'. Then disaster happened. The forces of counter-revolution were assembled outside Paris by Adolphe Thiers. In May they marched against the insurgents, scattered the weak resistance and carried out a brutal suppression. Marx and Engels continued to uphold the memory of the Paris Commune, criticising its leaders only for their failure to arm and train the workers in due time.[9]

The International was moved to New York in the following year. This was a sensible way of making its activities more secure at a time when European police forces were hunting for the General Council. Marx and Engels were safe in London; but they were distant from the Council's new base and lost much of their influence over it. Both men tended to focus their work on their writings. Marx himself was constantly short of funds; he was profligate with the money he received for the many articles he had written for the *New York Daily Tribune* since the

1850s. Although they did not abandon interest in the International, Marx and Engels spent more time on developments in particular parties. Chief among these were the socialist groupings in Germany. The German Social-Democratic Party was created in 1875. Marx and Engels judged that it could be brought close to their viewpoint and worked hard to this end. They criticised the Gotha Programme adopted at the party's inception, and they campaigned for a more radical analysis and strategy. The German Social-Democratic Party picked up followers in their thousands and Chancellor Otto von Bismarck outlawed it in 1879. Under such conditions the call by Marx and Engels for greater audacity was echoed by many socialists in Germany. The opportunities for Marxism to impose itself on the German social-democrats were growing.

Yet what was Marxism? This is a question that has caused endless political and scholarly debate. Unfortunately Marx was more fertile in ideas than prolific in print. He was an inveterate jotter and an incorrigible master of second thoughts, a publisher's nightmare. Even his short pieces of journalism, such as those for *New York Daily Tribune*, had to be torn from him like a gazelle from the teeth of a lion. Engels, loyal, enduring Engels, pitched in with psychological encouragement and editorial advice; sometimes he even wrote the commissioned pieces for his friend.[10] But Marx's was the superior intellect, and Engels understood that the difficulties of research and analysis were immense. Marx and he were exploring the fundaments of social existence from the distant past into the distant future. This required them to examine and process theories of philosophy, economics, sociology, politics and culture, as well as to keep abreast of everything new that was happening in contemporary public affairs around the world. The task proved too much for Marx. He had lost the capacity for popularisation of this kind. In his last years he struggled to understand why so many certainties of the first volume of *Capital* were being disproved by actual economic developments. The complexities he was observing obstructed a synthesising vision. Life had taken a heavy toll on him. His financial debts and the illnesses of his wife and children, as well as the relentless reading and writing, finally wore him out at the age of sixty-four.

At his death in 1883 he left behind a pile of manuscripts which he had failed to complete in a fashion satisfactory to himself. These included work of importance for later generations of Marxists – or at least for some members of those generations. Among them were his *Economic–Philosophic Manuscripts*, his *Theses on Feuerbach*, *The German Ideology*, the *Grundrisse*, the two final volumes of *Capital* and the *Critique of the*

Gotha Programme. It was not that he thought them unimportant to his oeuvre. The opposite was the case: most of them meant so much to him that he wanted to get them just right before exposing them to others' scrutiny.

Marx was forever changing his practical recommendations in the light of experience. A Russian socialist, Vera Zasulich, wrote to Marx in February 1881. She belonged at the time to the clandestine movement associated with the project to build a socialist society on the foundations of the peasantry and the village land commune. Her question for Marx was whether Marxism treated industrialisation as the prerequisite for the introduction of socialism. To the delight of herself and her comrades, he replied that his ideas did not exclude the possibility of a revolution being made by Russia's agrarian socialists (or *narodniki*). Marx had for some years admired the works of one of their founding figures, Nikolai Chernyshevski, and had begun to study Russian with a view to learning more about intellectual thought in Russia. The narodniks were pleased with the correspondence. Admittedly they overlooked certain reservations Marx had expressed, especially his comment that such a revolution would need to take place at the same time as revolutions in some countries in Europe which had already undergone industrialisation. Nevertheless this episode, at the end of Marx's life, indicated that he did not prescribe a uniform sequence of stages of political and economic development for all societies; and his Marxism remained an inchoate system of thought.[11]

If Marx fell short in putting his ideas into print, what chance did Engels have? His personality was no more dour than Marx's. By the standards of Victorian morality he was a bit of a rogue, and for years he lived with his lover Lizzie Burns while outwardly conforming to the requirements of the successful northern mill-owner. But he had a dose of common sense lacking in his intellectual companion. Above all, he saw the need for readable summaries of the gist of Marxism. In his own last years he was preoccupied with projects of this genre. Polemicising with fellow socialist Eugen Dühring, he published his *Anti-Dühring* in 1878 in an effort to prove the scientific basis for Marxist theories about society and revolution. Intrigued by the growing literature on the natural sciences, anthropology and palaeontology, he put together *The Dialectics of Nature* in 1883 and *The Origins of the Family, Private Property and the State* in 1884. The first was intended to show that the Marxist way of thought was in line with discoveries in physics and chemistry; the second sought to do for human pre-history what Darwin had done for evolutionary biology. These books were wide in scope and important in content; but they were a long way from offering a summation of the full range of Marxist thought as Marx and Engels had been developing it in their many writings.[12]

Later generations of Marxist intellectuals, especially in the West, tended to play down Engels's attainment as a summariser; some even thought that the process of summarisation led inevitably to a distortion of the essential ideas. As happens in every great school of thought, the exponents of Marxism strove to establish where the original misinterpretation had taken place.

Yet the greatest obstacle to codifying Marxism was the fact that the ideas of Marx and Engels changed as their thought matured and their researches continued. They were affected by the alterations in the world they observed. As intelligent people, they did not expect to go through life without second thoughts. And sometimes they trimmed their opinions in public for immediate political purposes. At the same time, however, they propagated an image of themselves as the only scientific analysts of modernity. This was tantamount to claiming intellectual infallibility. They acted as if their followers had no right to gainsay or criticise them. They actively encouraged devotion. The consequence was that they were treated as prophets whose every word had to be treasured. Marxists turned to the works of Marx and Engels in the manner of Christians examining the Bible. Where contradictions existed in *Capital* or in the *Anti-Dühring*, they had to be denied or else somehow brought to appear as insignificant or resoluble. Marxism from its inception fostered the growth of 'theorists' in its midst. Attempts proliferated to prove that Marx and Engels had laid down stones for an edifice which brooked no possible revision as later conditions might have demanded. Marxism from the start offered a shelter to the kind of intellectuals who in the Middle Ages had argued about how many angels could stand on the point of a needle.

This in turn meant that no single line of inheritance descended from Marxism's co-founders. At various times both Marx and Engels had subscribed to revolutionary dictatorship and terror. They scoffed at moral arguments. They ridiculed what they called the sentimentality of other brands of socialism (or communism). They asserted the scientific basis of their doctrines and maintained that they alone discerned the direction of historical development. The terminal point of change, they declared, was inevitable. Communism would come sooner or later, but come it definitely would. Capitalism was doomed by its inherent contradictions. The working class needed to have such ideas explained to it since only that class could head the revolution against capitalism. A party had to be formed which could undertake the task.

Although their predictions lacked close definition, Marx and Engels indisputably desired a workers' movement committed to unified action. They believed in the benefits of large-scale organisation – and they intended to implement this in politics and economics if ever they came to power. Central revolutionary discipline was a key to success for them. In the longer term, of course, they expected that communist society would give opportunities for individuals to pursue their wishes without being constrained by a state of any kind whatever. Until such an epoch began they emphasised the need for firm, uncompromising struggle. They were harsh polemicists. It came easily to both of them to mock and denigrate their socialist adversaries. They were interested in ends and untroubled about means, and nowhere in their writings did they acknowledge the merits of legal and constitutional procedures. They despised liberal theory about the division of powers. For them, parliamentary democracies were really bourgeois dictatorships which allowed legislators, administrators, police, judges and army to collude in the suppression of the 'proletariat'. They eulogised revolutionaries who took a gamble and who refused to be bound by doctrinal commitment.

The precautionary principle was weak, to say the least, in their doctrines. They themselves benefited from political tolerance in the United Kingdom. Despite being overt subversives, they were left alone. In their daily lives they enjoyed the protection of the rule of law. Engels's industrial profits and Marx's free access to the British Museum Library were theirs by legal right – and without them their revolutionary propaganda and activity would have been hobbled. Yet they eulogised the kind of society where no constraints on 'proletarian' power would be installed. Individuals would have to submit to authority or suffer punitive consequences. They blithely stood forth as the destroyers of democracy, legality and institutional checks and balances. Everything had to be pulled down before rebuilding could commence. The ideas of Marx and Engels indeed contained seeds of oppression and exploitation under a Marxist revolutionary regime.

This is not to say that their legacy lacked ideas and aperçus of enduring value. They were right about the irresistible march of economic globalisation. They foresaw the ever greater scale of industrial and commercial activity. Their analysis of capitalism's inherent tendency to reward those entrepreneurs who could maximise technological improve-

ment and minimise labour costs has proved accurate. Fundamental to
their writings, moreover, was an insistence that human consciousness
was not unchanging. Advanced industrial society produced an unprecedented set of attitudes and practices. People were shaped by their
environment; they were profoundly affected by the type of economy,
political regime and culture which surrounded them. Marx and Engels
were convincing in predicting that changes in consciousness would
continue to occur as conditions underwent transformation. They were
brilliant in showing how the rulers in any society disguise the nature of
their dominance. Some of their best writing was about the rituals
invented to get the lower social orders to accept inequality as an eternal
and natural phenomenon. As atheists they delivered coruscating denunciations of the connivance of organised religion in the prolongation of
material and social hardship.

Yet, if Marx left a confusing legacy in his general theory, he also
bequeathed little guidance for decisions on crucial practical policies. An
especially tortuous question was about how socialists should organise
themselves while operating under various types of regime ranging from
parliamentary republics to absolute monarchies. Marxists also had to
decide what dealings to have with other sorts of socialists. Should they
ally with them or treat them as misguided enemies? Marxists at the turn
of the century tended to believe that revolutions had to follow a sequence.
First there had to be a 'bourgeois–democratic' revolution against feudalism. Only then could socialists prepare for a revolution against capitalism
and 'the transition to socialism'. But was this sequence fixed in stone?
Could there not be a telescoping of two stages into one? And what about
that brief but significant exchange of letters between Marx and Zasulich
about treating the peasantry rather than the industrial working class as
the pivotal group in the advance towards socialism in Russia?

Marx and Engels, moreover, had said nothing definitive about the
kind of socialist regime they aimed at. Sometimes they espoused a violent
seizure of power and a provisional dictatorship. At others they called for
a peaceful assumption of power. About the institutions and policies of
either type of revolutionary authority they remained silent. They were
complacent about the tasks of consolidating a Marxist regime in power.
They assumed that the revolution would have the fervent support of the
overwhelming majority of society's members. Sometimes they wrote
enthusiastically about the uses of state terror. They praised the Jacobins
in the French Revolution. But they also understood that, if terror needed
to be used, the Jacobin leadership must have had very weak support.[13]

Having raised the problem, though, they dropped it. They tended to believe that any difficulties of analysis and prediction would be surmounted by 'practice' in the forthcoming revolutionary situation. So much for their claims to be scientists of human development! At bottom they were just as speculatively minded as the 'utopian socialists' whom they ridiculed. The basic truth was that they expended more intellectual energy on the economics of capitalism than on the politics of socialism. This was a catastrophic cavity in the corpus of Marxism.

Nor did Marx or Engels have much to say about the 'national question'. Some of their utterances, moreover, were uncongenial to their followers in the smaller national and ethnic groups. They were scathing about some of the Slavs.[14] Supposedly the best outcome would be their absorption in German culture and an end to the ambitions of their nationalist intellectuals. Marxism's co-founders put their faith in the civilising mission of the great industrial powers. They railed against the economic exploitation of indigenous peoples carried out by the European empires; but imperialism was not in their eyes a bad thing in itself. The world was changing as the factory system was extended. It was, for them, a harsh but inevitable process.

They assumed that large nations with advanced economies and culture would assimilate them; and they no more regretted this prospect than they worried about the elimination of the peasantry by the capitalist economy. But generally they made few statements on such problems, leaving the discussion to their successors. They hardly talked much more about the 'agrarian question' despite the fact that the predominant part of the global population consisted of peasants. They were convinced that capitalism was about to transform all traditional modes of cultivation and husbandry. The gigantic industrial factories of the cities were seemingly about to be joined by huge farms – the new latifundia – which would be organised on capitalist principles.[15] Similarly they seldom spoke about the 'colonial question'. They were living through a time of rapid expansion of European empires across Asia and Africa. By the end of the nineteenth century there was hardly a country which had escaped direct or indirect dominion by one or other of the great capitalist powers. The perspective of Marx and Engels had intellectual limitations. Their ambitions were boundless but the extraordinary tumult of change in the world of the late nineteenth century eluded their desire for comprehensive understanding and prescription. Deified by their followers in later generations, they themselves were thwarted in their endeavour to achieve a total science of humankind.

Yet this never stopped them from striving after the unattainable. Their whole careers were devoted to assimilating fresh evidence and adjusting their analysis and recommendations to take account of it. They enjoyed themselves. Research for both was a pleasure, and they delighted in the tasks of politicking and propaganda. Their partnership brought out the intellectual best in both of them. They lived in an age when it was easy to denounce the political and economic status quo. Yet Marx and Engels as Victorian intellectuals had little presentiment of the uses which would be made of their extraordinary doctrines. Marxism encoded their dangerous brilliance.

3. COMMUNISM IN EUROPE

Engels continued to supply the German Social-Democratic Party with advice and encouragement till his death. When Bismarck's anti-socialist law was revoked in 1890, the authorities were recognising that persecution was counter-productive: it only increased the resentment of working people and turned them against the political and economic structures of the status quo. The removal of the ban on the German Social-Democratic Party, however, came too late to stop the party leadership from endorsing Marxism. To the delight of the ageing Engels, its party programme and basic ideology were already pervaded by a Marxist commitment – and there was no serious effort by any party leaders to change this. Meanwhile Engels and the party leadership avoided saying anything that might provoke renewed prohibition. They were confident that events would move in their favour as an ever greater proportion of the working class sided with them electorally. Other parties, including socialist ones, competed with them for the votes of factory workers and miners. But the German Social-Democrats as Marxists believed that their analysis alone made sense of the country's future. They felt sure that they would eventually monopolise the loyalties of the 'proletariat'. With their newly obtained freedom to proselytise for their cause they set about their tasks with eagerness.[1]

Organising itself for the Reichstag elections, the party immediately obtained a fifth of the vote. It celebrated as if it had won an absolute majority; and even though it exaggerated its achievement, the influence of 'labour' in Imperial Germany was unmistakably on the rise. A full network of local committees and newspapers was established. The party also took care of the recreational needs of its members. It supplied educational facilities. Promising militants were given additional training. Leaders such as August Bebel and Wilhelm Liebknecht became prominent public figures.

The German Social-Democrats were the most influential member-party of the Socialist International. This was the body created in 1889 to replace the defunct International Workingmen's Association; it quickly became known as the Second International. Many parties elsewhere had to contend with serious difficulties. Some were outlawed or banned by their governments; others were hit by internal dispute. Others again were not sure about whether to ally themselves with the liberal parties. The German Social-Democratic Party from the start stood proud and independent. Its electoral successes mounted. By 1912 it was the largest party in the Reichstag with over a third of the available seats. Although this was still not an absolute majority, the party's spokesmen – their leaders as well as 'theorists' such as Karl Kautsky – saw this as the start of an unstoppable wave of success. They did not forswear the need for armed insurgency in principle; but they no longer behaved like revolutionaries. They talked a good revolution. But it was a revolution postponed to an ever more distant future. Their true preoccupation was with making the best of the present and gradually improving the living and working conditions of the 'proletariat'.[2]

It is a fallacy that Marxism's flaws were exposed only after it was tried out in power. Marx and Engels had been controversial figures in the First International which they helped to found. They handed out and received criticism by the plateful, and wounding blows had been delivered to their claim to intellectual solidity. The only wonder is that so many Marxists ignored the damage. Marxism had become an infallible set of doctrines and political substitute for religion for its followers.

Marx and Engels themselves had not been able to overlook the criticisms. In their time they had faced a formidable opponent in a Russian aristocrat and anti-tsarist militant. This was the anarchist Mikhail Bakunin. Where Marxism's co-founders sought scientific validation of their doctrines, Bakunin picked up ideas as they happened to appeal to him, and he developed them after his own fashion. Bakunin had a chaotic life. Marx and Engels despised him as a mischief-maker and hated his insights. Bakunin dissected Marxism's claim to produce a 'withering away of the state'. His point was that the doctrines were inherently incapable of attaining that end. Bakunin saw the fatal flaws before anyone else. Marx and Engels were know-alls; they always thought they had discovered the absolute truth even when they said they were offering up ideas that needed testing by revolutionary experience. They were centralisers. While talking about 'free associations of producers', they advocated discipline and hierarchy. Their ideology condescended to working people; their political orientation was premised on the need for such people to be herded into regiments of revolt under their exclusive control. Bakunin delivered this judgement to the rest of the European labour movement.[3]

There was no letting up in the challenge to Marxist doctrines. Marx's most scrupulous work had been on economics and he had offered his 'labour theory of value' as a fundamental contribution to the understanding of all past and present societies. Although it was a flimsy basis for his politics, it became an article of faith for Marxists from his day to ours. Marx had convinced himself that additional value was added in the process of production exclusively through the efforts of manual labourers. He finessed this somewhat in the second and third volumes of *Capital* but never expressly abandoned his hypothesis. Among the first to assail him was Max von Böhm-Bawerk, who pointed out that technological inventiveness and entrepreneurial initiative had wrongly been omitted from Marx's economic analysis. His name was reviled by generations of Marxist economists who included Rudolf Hilferding and Rosa Luxemburg. Yet they failed to refute Böhm-Bawerk's fundamental proposition.[4]

This was only the opening campaign in the twentieth-century intellectual attack on Marxism. The German sociologist Max Weber, despite being hugely impressed by Marx and Engels, took them to task for picking out economic factors as the primary motor of great historical movements. Weber insisted that cultural and religious factors were also influential. He indicated the role played by Protestantism in the inception of European capitalist economies. Weber introduced multidimensional complexity to the explanation of the emergence and expansion of capitalism, and he challenged Marxist analyses of advanced industrial societies at the end of the nineteenth century. He exposed the implausibility of the sociological predictions made by Marx and Engels. Germany, far from developing into a society consisting simply of a few 'big bourgeois' owners and a mass of 'proletarians', was experiencing a demographic explosion of professional and administrative specialists. Weber predicted that it would be the bureaucrats who would dominate and not the bankers and industrialists. He had picked apart Marxist politics by highlighting cultural, religious and sociological factors which Marx had only just begun to broach in his notes for the third volume of *Capital*. And, of course, it would have been impossible for Marx and Engels to accept Weber's standpoint without abandoning the cause they had dedicated their lives to.[5]

Robert Michels and Gaetano Mosca piled into the mêlée. They denied altogether that any future society was feasible without hierarchical authority. Elites, they contended, were an operational necessity as well as an inevitable consequence of political disputes. The stateless human paradise predicted by Marx and Engels was consequently a futile dream. Michels impishly subjected the German Social-Democratic Party to scrutiny and found that its officials fell a long way short of eradicating authoritarian procedures. They cut themselves off from control by the ordinary party members and decided policy outside a democratic framework. They paid themselves better than the average industrial worker. Furthermore, they quietly moved the party away from any activity which might invite trouble from the Imperial government; they talked revolution while in practice co-operating with the political status quo. Their Marxism was a mask for setting up a self-serving bureaucracy. Michels argued that, if they behaved like that before they came to power, there was little chance that they would ever establish an egalitarian social order. Marxism, far from being based on scientific observation, was just as utopian as the nineteenth-century rival variants of socialism which had drawn the ridicule of Marx and Engels.[6]

Practically every sector of intellectual thought involved discomfort for Marxists. Historians questioned whether societies had followed the simple sequence of stages described in most works by Marx and Engels: primitive communism, slave-owning society, feudalism and capitalism. Eduard Bernstein, the amanuensis of Engels, was the first leading Marxist to feel the need for entirely new wheels to be fixed to the doctrinal carriage. Few people were better acquainted with the writings of Marx and Engels, and in most ways Bernstein was a devoted follower. But he had a mind of his own. Like his masters, he avidly watched current developments. Without disregarding the terrible living and working conditions of most German workers, he recognised that an improvement was happening. The organised labour movement was exacting concessions from employers. Strikes were having an impact. Big business increasingly accepted collective wage bargaining as a normal necessity. The government encouraged this. Otto von Bismarck, German Chancellor until 1890, introduced a rudimentary system of pensions and social security. The purpose was no secret. Germany's political and economic elites aimed to empty the well of working-class support for revolutionary action. They hoped to make German workers feel integrated in society and identify themselves as 'true' Germans.

Challenging his comrades, Bernstein argued that workers should exploit this opportunity. The German Social-Democratic Party should engage in peaceful, legal contestation with the government and big business. It was Bernstein's belief that the working class would emerge victorious. He had no illusions about Kaiser Wilhelm II's Germany and knew that the current freedoms could at any moment be suspended. But for the time being he advocated staying within the constitutional framework. Bernstein had a horror of violence. Marx and Engels had talked casually about past civil wars and dictatorships. Bernstein was a man of more sober attitudes. He was shocked by all the jovial talk about the French Revolution; he urged that German social-democrats should abandon their preoccupation with violent struggle and dictatorship. Teasing out his conclusions from the posthumously published third volume of Marx's *Capital*, he urged that the future did not lie in a neat division between bourgeoisie and proletariat. Bernstein highlighted the growth of intermediate social groupings. He urged that Marxism had to be adjusted to take account of the changes being brought about under contemporary capitalism.[7]

Among those who sided with Bernstein was Eduard David, who proposed a revision of the basic economic predictions of Marx and Engels. David conducted a survey of contemporary agriculture and found that small-scale farms, far from disappearing under pressure from large landowners, were flourishing. He drew the conclusion that Marxists should not automatically assume that every sector of the economy would increase its average scale of production.[8]

There were plenty of efforts to defend revolutionary Marxism against the 'revisionism' of Bernstein and his friends. These included Karl Kautsky, Otto Bauer, Rudolf Hilferding and Rosa Luxemburg in central Europe as well as Georgi Plekhanov, Vladimir Lenin, Yuli Martov and Lev Trotski in the Russian Empire.[9] They were important political and intellectual figures in the Second International. Kautsky had the greatest influence. In moderate language – he wanted to be legally published – he affirmed the need for the party to hold fast to its revolutionary objectives. He refrained from advocating immediate direct action but suggested that the time would eventually come when the Imperial regime of Wilhelm II would be terminated. Kautsky knew as well as Bernstein that advanced industrial societies were changing in ways unpredicted by Marx and Engels. But he set himself up as the Pope of Marxism in opposition to Bernstein as Anti-Pope. He protected 'orthodoxy' against attacks on its fundamental doctrines. He honoured the memory of Marxism's co-founders. He wrote a lengthy disquisition on the agrarian question querying the evidence and analysis adduced by Eduard David.

Nor did he fail to stress that developments around the world in industrial organisation were following the path predicted by Marx and Engels.[10]

Yet none properly confronted the damage done to Marxist doctrines by its critics. They wanted to hold on to their faith in Marxism. They required a bedrock of political and economic axioms and invested a vast deposit of cleverness in their attempt to vindicate Marx and Engels. They were not the fundamental rethinkers of the contemporary world. Albert Einstein, Sigmund Freud, Ernst Mach and Max Weber existed on an entirely higher level. Admittedly some Marxists tried to take ideas from some of them. Kautsky, for example, had no principled objection to Mach's denial of the possibility of absolute truth. Others were fascinated by Freud. But by and large the process was going in the opposite direction as Marxist thinkers sought to isolate Marxism from infection by alien bacilli.

Marxism went on expanding its appeal in Europe. Although it had its largest following in Germany, there were also lively Marxist organisations in Holland and a growing interest was noticeable in Italy and France. But these were the exceptions. Generally there was little responsiveness to the doctrines of Marx and Engels in western Europe. So little impact had they in the United Kingdom that the police continued to place no obstacle in the way of foreign Marxists holding gatherings in London. Marxism still appeared an exotic trend unlikely to plant deep roots among the British. Harassment of Marxists as subversives, it was thought, would only give them the publicity of a persecuted sect. To the east and south-east of Germany it was a somewhat different story. Marxist organisations were growing in Bulgaria and in the Czech and Polish lands of the Habsburg Monarchy, as well as in the Russian Empire. The membership was not as numerous as in Germany; the reason for this was mainly that industrialisation was at an earlier stage in those countries and the incentive to join a movement directed at gaining support among factory workers was weaker.[11]

This growing prestige induced critics to continue to mount assaults on conventional Marxism. The history of the labour movement became controversial. Marx and Engels had suggested that the key to the advance of the working class was the establishment of large political parties. The assumption was that 'proletarian' interests would be served by such parties. Not everyone concurred. The Polish writer Jan Machajski produced a work claiming that socialist parties typically enabled intellectuals rather than workers to run their committees. He saw this as a logical development. Machajski pointed out that the intelligentsia had the technical skills to set up a proper administrative apparatus. From this it was a short step towards the suppression of working-class interests. He suggested that if ever a socialist revolution were to occur it would ensconce an elite of middle-class origin in power.[12]

There was a growing literature on this. Robert Michels, a socialist by inclination, had gone off to Turin University and exposed the compromises which lay at the core of the party's practice in Germany. (As a leftist sympathiser he could not get a professorial chair in Germany.) He gave a devastating sociological analysis. Michels indicated that party officials had an interest in the maintenance of the German political status quo. They would lose their comfortable incomes if the party were to be suppressed. As negotiators with employers and government they had a crucial role to play. They could point to the steady accumulation of positive results. They had deputies in the Reichstag; they were recognised as spokesmen for an entire class. Michels suggested that the German Social-Democratic Party was run by its 'apparatus' and for the interests of that 'apparatus'. Its officials had metamorphosed into a conservative stratum without an incentive to upset the Imperial political establishment.[13]

Critics of the German social-democratic leadership also existed in the Second International. The sharpest arrows were shot by foreigners. Among them were the Poles Rosa Luxemburg and Karl Radek and the Dutchman Anton Pannekoek. Luxemburg and Radek, fluent German speakers and refugees from 'Russian' Poland, had multiple party allegiances. They simultaneously belonged to the Social-Democracy of the Kingdom of Poland and Lithuania and the Russian Social-Democratic Workers' Party, as well as to the German Social-Democratic Party itself.[14] Luxemburg, Radek and Pannekoek sensed the lack of a lively commitment to revolution in their German comrades. They did not need to earn the Berlin leadership's approval. They had confidence and passion, and continually urged more radical policies at party congresses. All of them contended that contemporary German Marxism was strong on rhetoric and weak on preparations for action. They asked what the German social-democratic leadership was doing to plan for the ultimate conflict with Kaiser Wilhelm and his government. They derided any steady dedication to wage-bargaining. What was the point of this if the party's leaders genuinely believed that the era of unconditional socialism was nigh? Was there not a danger of political degeneration if the party went on working for goals achievable under the Wilhelminian regime?[15]

Luxemburg set up an informal 'leftist' opposition to put the case for confrontation on the streets. Her favoured method to destabilise and overturn state power was the 'mass strike'. Drawing on her observation of Russia in the revolutionary situation of 1905–6, she argued that Germany could equally be engulfed by a sudden emergency. The party should encourage workers to engage in industrial conflict. Strikes would breed further strikes. They could be used to politicise the entire working class. Workers should be encouraged to think for themselves and develop their initiatives. The final struggle between bourgeoisie and proletariat would occur and the revolutionary vision of Marx and Engels would be realised.[16]

Another aspect of German Marxism which caused unease was its silence on the 'national question'. Karl Kautsky and others argued that Polish immigrant workers in Germany ought to receive equal treatment; and the social-democrats welcomed recruits among people who were not German citizens. But fundamental ideas about how to organise a multinational state were few. This was noted by Marxists living in the lands of the Habsburg Monarchy. The Austrian followers of Marx and Engels were keenly aware of the many tensions among the various national groups in the empire. Hostilities between one nation and another were likely to occur when the Habsburgs were removed. Marxists in Vienna thought hard about possible solutions. It helped little to ransack the writings of the founders of Marxism.[17] Neither Marx nor Engels had said much about the 'national question'; and what they had said or written was often pretty disrespectful to the smaller nationalities. The Austro-Marxists, as they became known, were annoyed by this. They thought that national consciousness, far from fading at the beginning of the twentieth century, would continue to grow. They attributed this to the combined expansion of capitalist economic production, mass education and the public press. The tendency was for people to exchange a local – especially a rural – identity for a national one. Writers such as Otto Bauer and Karl Renner argued that Marxism could not afford to bury its head in the sand about the phenomenon.[18]

They denied that breaking up the empire into separate nation-states would resolve the problems among the nations. The Habsburg Monarchy was a patchwork quilt with several national minorities living in many regions. There could be no neat division of administrative districts. Instead the Austro-Marxists devised a scheme whereby each nationality would elect its central political authority in parallel to the government ruling the entire multinational state. The idea was to enable nations to

acquire 'national-cultural autonomy'. An end would be put to the
national and ethnic oppression and the government would be able to get
on with the achievement of a socialist society.[19] Such ideas would
probably have produced a bureaucratic entanglement. But the eagerness
of Bauer and his comrades to make allowances for nations had a deep
appeal for Marxists elsewhere. The Mensheviks in the Russian Empire
picked up the project of national-cultural autonomy with enthusiasm.

At the Second International's Stuttgart Congress in August 1907 there
was an attempt by Marxists as well as other by socialists to prescribe
policy for the member parties on war and peace. This was a crucial
enterprise. The world was entering a new phase of change and uncertainty. The European powers competed with each other to acquire
overseas colonies. British, French and German interests frequently col-
lided. Europe itself was undergoing a fresh territorial demarcation as
the countries of the Balkans sought and obtained independence from
the Ottoman Empire. Wars broke out in the Balkans in 1912–13. The
Habsburg Monarchy also had severe internal tensions. Its nationalities,
especially the Hungarians and the Czechs, resented what they regarded
as Austrian oppressiveness. An arms race began between the United
Kingdom and Germany. Other powers too, including France and Russia,
laid plans for their defence. The danger of a continental war – and even
a world war – was evident. Congress resolutions opposed militarism
and imperialism. But what was to be done if such a war broke out? The
gist of the Congress's decision was that, if the great powers were to go
to war, the duty of socialists was to oppose their own governments.
Parliamentary representatives were enjoined to refuse to vote war credits.
A political campaign was to be organised to bring about peace. The
parties of the Second International agreed to act in fraternity with each
other and to extract the sting of chauvinism from European public life.[20]

Quite how this would be achieved was left unclear. Some parties
suggested that a revolutionary insurrection would be necessary; others
wanted to stay within the law and avoid violent methods. But it was a
universal article of faith that total opposition to any war was a socialist
duty. Bankers and arms manufacturers were said to be the only beneficiaries of military conflict. Monarchs too were brought under suspicion.
The Second International took a stand against each and every move by
governments to exacerbate the situation in Europe.

This also left open what kind of society it was that Europe's Marxists
were aspiring to create. Hardly any of them regularly mentioned communism – and, of course, non-Marxists in the Socialist International

avoided it altogether. No country had an organisation naming itself as communist. Germany had set the precedent for using designations which were thought less obviously subversive. The result was that socialism, social-democracy, communism and even anarchism continued to be employed interchangeably by the enemies of the political left; and the political left itself remained vague or confused about its ultimate vision. (The fog of terminology was to be lifted a little by Lenin's *State and Revolution* in 1917, but it was never entirely removed.)[21] The German Social-Democrats kept up a formal commitment to the establishment of communism worldwide. They attracted members who were genuinely inspired by a communist vision. They included Germans such as Karl Liebknecht and foreigners like Luxemburg. But the ultimate goal – communism – was not frequently discussed or even contemplated. Marxists in most countries were getting on with leading strikes, fighting for welfare reforms and denouncing and undermining conservative and liberal governments. Thus it came about that the case for communism was elaborated most pungently in a country to the east of Germany. That country was Russia.

Yet the Marxists of the Russian Empire were not alone in seeking to keep the Marxist faith. This was a pan-European phenomenon before the First World War. Marxists and other radical leftists were a minority on the European far left, but they constituted a restless corpus of enemies of capitalism. Plenty of militants believed that the larger socialist parties in western and central Europe were neglecting their political obligations. They seldom abandoned their own parties. They made an effort to bring their more moderate comrades over to their side. It was a fluid situation. Marxism remained the official ideology of only the German Social-Democratic Party and a few other large parties in Europe. A battle for hearts and minds in European and North American socialism was under way. Practically every country in the two continents acquired some kind of Marxist organisation. The weakest instance was the USA, where Marxists tended overwhelmingly to be recent immigrants and the Social-ist Party was hostile to them. But each party on the political left had many militants who were frustrated by the compromises made by their leaders with the political status quo. These were circumstances which were bound to be exploited by any extremist and internationalist party if ever it came to power.

4. RUSSIAN VARIATIONS

It had been the expectation of Marx and Engels that Marxism would first strike roots in a country like Germany. They pinned their hopes on industrialisation, on the expanding cities and on factory workers and miners; they naturally looked to the more advanced economies to supply the political following for their ambition. Yet other countries produced plenty of Marxist revolutionaries. These included Poland, Bulgaria and Italy. The disappointment for Marx and Engels was the weak impression their ideas made on radical socialists in their country of exile, the United Kingdom, where a strong Marxist party failed to emerge in the early twentieth century even though the authorities did not much interfere with the labour movement. Civil freedom and material comfort, despite their limitations even in Britain, acted as an antidote to political extremism – and Marx and Engels were aware of the connection and wrote about it.

It was turning out that poverty and oppression constituted the best soil for Marxism to grow in. Accordingly the Russian Empire eventually dwarfed every country except Germany in the eagerness of its reception of Marxist ideas. Russia in the 1870s, when Marxism began to have a wide impact there, was an autocracy. There were no legal parties or trade unions. No parliament existed. There was strict censorship of political debate. The government was slow to spread a network of popular schooling. Most of the peasants, who constituted the huge majority of the people, found it impossible to escape from dire poverty. Several nations of the empire, especially the Poles, aspired to independence; and others such as the Georgians and Finns were deeply annoyed at the restrictions on the expression of their nationhood. Corruption was endemic in the bureaucracy. The Russian Orthodox Church was fiercely reactionary. Although novelists and poets found ways to make criticisms of the social order, organised groupings of dissent were subject to efficient persecution. Usually the punishment involved banishment to the wilds of Siberia – and in the worst cases the convicts were put to forced labour.

The Romanov dynasty after the Crimean War of 1854–6 understood that their future security depended on their success in promoting industrial expansion and modern methods of transport, communication and administration. It was also essential to encourage a rising number of professional cadres. Such changes, however, brought their own dangers. Unemployed or disenchanted former students were easily drawn into revolutionary circles. Ill-paid factory workers felt little impulse of loyalty to the Imperial throne. Peasants, even if they were ardent monarchists, were embittered by the 'agrarian question': there was only one fair solution in their eyes – the transfer of all the landed property into their hands.

The political police (Okhrana) coped well despite its small budget. It infiltrated the organised rebels of each generation, arrested and deported them to Siberia. Yet this never cleared the grounds of discontent, and the government came to recognise that revolutionary activity would continue for the foreseeable future. The Okhrana refined its techniques, playing off one militant faction against another. It was frequently handy to let a group go on operating, on a weaker basis, so that the authorities might stay informed about its activities. The Okhrana also recruited agents from among the revolutionaries. Blackmail, financial blandishment and ideological persuasion were employed. Informers penetrated every subversive organisation. Revolutionary groups had to improve their conspiratorial security. Caution was exercised about who should be allowed to join and there were investigations of suspect members. Central control was reinforced. Organisations typically established a base abroad so that their newspapers, correspondence and discussions could function. Geneva, London and – later – Paris were favoured sites. The police reacted by extending the geographical scope of their operations. Although they could not obliterate the organisations, they succeeded in disrupting, demoralising and restricting revolutionary activity. In the nineteenth century they went about their business with impressive efficiency.

The game of cat and mouse between the Okhrana and the rebels had lasting consequences. The Russian revolutionary movement, having no opportunity for positive participation in legal public life, became fixated by 'theory'. Its adherents started up exhausting internal disputes about the country's social order and harangued each other about politics, economics and philosophy. Their mental abstractions became hard-baked because they could not be tested in practice. A highly theoretical orientation was integrated into the life of revolt against the authorities.

There was also an internal trend towards eulogising the leader of any revolutionary organisation. Some leaders relished the praise and ruthlessly suppressed any opposition. The most notorious example was Sergei Nechaev, who in 1869 ordered followers in his little group to murder an internal critic. In order to induce total submission to his will he pretended to be the representative of an imaginary international agency known as People's Retribution.

Until the early 1880s the revolutionaries of the Russian Empire upheld the axiom that their socialism should take account of the predominantly agrarian and backward nature of the economy. Britain, France and Germany had accomplished a vast industrial and cultural advance. Russia and its borderlands had lagged behind. The revolutionary thinkers made the best of this by proposing to put peasants at the core of their ideas. Inspiration for the future socialist society was drawn from the Russian village land commune. The peasantry's tradition of periodic redistribution of the land could serve as the basis of an egalitarian transformation. Such thinking, however, started to lose its grip. Peasants themselves were persistently indifferent to calls for revolution. Furthermore, a surging growth in factories, mines and railways was taking place. Many socialists in the Russian Empire began to deny that it was any longer realistic to repose hope in a peasantry which seemed destined for the scrap heap of history. A certain Georgi Plekhanov decided that enough was enough. Russia, he declared, was already taking the economic path of the advanced capitalist powers. A 'proletariat' was in the making. Instead of peasants it would be the workers who should lead the revolution.[1]

According to Plekhanov, the solution was for revolutionaries to adopt the Marxism that was spreading in Germany. He and his comrades in the Emancipation of Labour group had fled Russia to Geneva. As they proselytised among Russian intellectual dissenters from a distance, they quickly gained followers. Vera Zasulich was a member of the tiny group in Switzerland. She it was to whom Marx had written in 1881 to explain that he did not exclude the possibility that a peasant-orientated revolutionary movement might succeed in the Russian Empire.[2] The Emancipation of Labour group put all this correspondence out of sight. For them, the important thing was that Russian economic and social development pointed in the opposite direction to the peasantry, the villages and the communes.

The fact that Marx did not appreciate their efforts as Marxists did not discourage them. They had caught the contagion of faith and would spread the gospel of Marxism. Pamphlets were smuggled back to the Russian Empire. Circles of supporters sprang up in Vilnius, St Petersburg, Tbilisi and elsewhere. The Marxists started to contact workers and draw them into classes of indoctrination. They tried to lead strikes as industrialisation proceeded. By the 1890s they were the most vibrant trend in the Russian revolutionary movement. They aimed to consolidate this position by forming a proper party, and the founding congress was held in Minsk in March 1898. Although its delegates were quickly taken into custody, the struggle to set up a Russian Social-Democratic Workers' Party continued. One of Plekhanov's followers, Vladimir Ulyanov, left Russia after his period of Siberian exile and established a newspaper – *Iskra* ('The Spark') – so as to co-ordinate and dominate these efforts. A Second Party Congress took place in summer 1903 and broadly endorsed the ideas of Plekhanov. But Ulyanov, who had adopted the pseudonym Lenin, was emerging as the prime organiser. He had got fed up with being bossed around by Plekhanov. He thought he alone had a clear conception of what needed to be done in the party. He did not mind how many Russian Marxists he offended.[3]

Who was this Lenin? At the time he burst on to the scene he was respected as one of the party's leading intellectuals as well as a trouble-making factionalist. Now he was mocked by his own protégé Lev Trotski. Lenin's vituperations and manipulations at the Second Congress had disconcerted him. Trotski predicted that Leninist ideas end in a 'dictator' taking over the party. He wrote this in a sarcastic tone. He did not seriously argue that Lenin would become the despotic leader. Instead he was suggesting that, if Lenin were to rise to the top, the result would be a political farce.[4]

Vladimir Lenin, born on 21 April 1870, came from a family of what might be called new Russians. His father was possibly of Kalmyk background; his mother was definitely of Jewish and Scandinavian descent. Both yearned for a better Russia, a Russia more educated and modern. Their children were given a grammar-school training to fit them for a prominent role in this desired future. All of them, however, rejected liberalism and became far-left revolutionaries. Vladimir's elder brother Alexander was hanged in 1886 for involvement in an assassination attempt on Emperor Alexander III. Vladimir joined the clandestine rebel groups. Caught by the Okhrana, he was exiled to Siberia in 1897. There he wrote a treatise on Russian economic development, claiming that capitalism was already the dominant mode of production in the country. He made his name, though, with *What is to be Done?* This booklet urged the need for severe rules in the party to guarantee centralism, discipline and the vetting of recruits. The result was a brouhaha at the Second Party Congress of the Russian Social-Democratic Workers' Party when the *Iskra* group, which had dominated the proceedings, fell apart. Scarcely had the organisation been formed than it succumbed to factionalism.

The strict rules proposed by Lenin as well as his argumentative zeal and underhand methods annoyed even many of his allies. He won a majority at the congress by a whisker, and this enabled him to refer to his group as the Majoritarians (or *bol'sheviki* in Russian and Bolsheviks in English) and his opponents as the Minoritarians (or *men'sheviki* and Mensheviks). His dominance of the central party bodies was in fact short lived. Plekhanov, the grand old man of Russian Marxism, defected to the Mensheviks and tipped the balance in their favour. The schism was at its most bitter among the émigrés. Lenin accused the Mensheviks, led by his former friend Yuli Martov, of being usurpers. The Mensheviks charged Lenin and the Bolsheviks with obsessive authoritarianism. The two factions started to produce their own newspapers and to run their own agents in the Russian Empire.

Both Bolsheviks and Mensheviks were taken aback by the sudden revolutionary outbreak in Russia. The trigger was Bloody Sunday on 9 January 1905, when a peaceful procession of protesters was dispersed by violence and hundreds of people were killed or wounded. Months of disturbance followed. Strikes were organised. Workers' councils (or 'soviets') were elected. The most famous of these was the Petersburg Soviet, whose leading figure was the brilliant young Marxist orator Lev Trotski. Soviets demanded basic reforms of the state order and strove to supplant the local agencies of government. Mutinies occurred in the armed forces. Peasants began to expropriate the possessions of their landlords. By October the Emperor felt compelled to issue a manifesto promising to introduce a parliamentary system. This took a lot of the steam out of the agitation by liberal groupings such as the Constitutional-Democratic Party (or Kadets). Liberals had been shaken by the direct action taken by socialist parties in recent weeks. Most socialists – Bolsheviks, Mensheviks and Socialist-Revolutionaries – suspected that Nicholas II would restore his autocratic powers at the first opportunity. The Bolsheviks pressed on with efforts to mount an uprising. When this happened in Moscow in December 1905, the armed forces suppressed it with efficiency. After less than two years the Marxist leadership streamed back into the 'emigration'.

Lenin had started his revolutionary activity as a supporter of narod-
nik terrorism but, like others of his generation, moved across to what he
considered orthodox Marxism. He continued to admire the narodniks
and advised the Russian Social-Democratic Workers' Party to adopt
some of their ideas. His insistence on a tightly organised clandestine
party organisation had come from them. From 1905 he was declaring
that any successful revolution in Russia would require an alliance of
parties representing the workers and the peasantry. This broke with the
conventional assumption of Russian Marxists that they should seek out
the middle classes as allies in the struggle against the Imperial monarchy.

Lenin had lost control of the central party leadership in factional
strife in 1904. As Russia became enveloped in revolutionary turmoil, he
ceased to dominate his own Bolsheviks. Many of them refused to enter
the soviets, thinking them too much the products of spontaneous
working-class activity: Bolsheviks expected to guide and not to follow
events; and the majority of them rejected the idea of competing in the
parliamentary elections to the new State Duma. A leading exponent of
such opinions was Alexander Bogdanov. He and others contended that
no compromise should be made with the aim of revolutionary insurrection. Bogdanov in particular argued that workers should eschew any
connection with official Russia and should set about developing their
own separate 'proletarian culture'. Lenin was annoyed by all this. For
him, it was obvious that Bolsheviks should exploit every available
opportunity to increase their prominence and influence. Not to enter
the soviet or join the Duma electoral campaign seemed folly to him. He
railed against the intellectual inflexibility of his factional comrades.[5]

What is more, he began to appreciate the benefits of co-operation
with the Mensheviks, if only to counteract the extreme position taken by
the Bolsheviks; and the Bolsheviks and Mensheviks reunited at the
Fourth Party Congress in London in 1906. At the same time, though,
he announced a general strategy that was deeply uncongenial to Menshevism. He declared that the Russian middle classes were finding common
cause with the monarchy. His proposal was for Marxists to treat the
peasantry rather than the urban and rural bourgeoisie as allies of the
proletariat. He also contended that any successful revolution against
Nicholas II would require insurrection. A peaceful transfer of power in
his view was inconceivable. Lenin declared that a provisional revolutionary dictatorship of the proletariat and the peasantry would be needed to
install civic freedom as well as to facilitate capitalist economic development.

Not surprisingly, then, Russian Marxism inevitably remained a house divided against itself. Mensheviks and others may have agreed even to the inclusion of 'the dictatorship of the proletariat' in the party programme decided at the Second Party Congress in 1903; but they understood it differently. They had no intention of setting up a class dictatorship such as Lenin intended. They construed the phrase more as Marx and Engels had probably meant it.[6] The Mensheviks saw advanced capitalist society as a bourgeois dictatorship only in the sense that the fundamental direction of economics, laws and politics was tilted in favour of the interests of the bourgeoisie. But they wanted to work with the liberals to get rid of the Imperial monarchy. They also accepted the desirability of universal electoral suffrage. They wanted universal civil rights for citizens and rejected any suggestion that a socialist government might introduce class-based restriction of such rights. They strove to involve themselves in the legal workers' movement in the Russian Empire. But they remained radical revolutionaries. They expected that the monarchy would have to be brought down by street demonstrations and violence; they intended to fight for the interests of the working class. While talking Marxist language in common with Bolsheviks, however, they projected a very different political future for Russia.

The so-called Party Mensheviks and the Leninist Bolsheviks were the best co-ordinated of the factions of the Russian Social-Democratic Workers' Party in the Russian-inhabited territories of the empire. The first had an Organisational Committee combining the activities of émigrés and local militants, the second did the same through their Central Committee. Other factions also existed: the Plekhanovites, the Liquidators and various Bolsheviks who rejected Leninism. What is more, several national organisations existed. Some operated within definite territorial limits in Lithuania, Russian-ruled Poland, Armenia and Georgia; and there was also the Jewish Bund, as well as the Hümmet for Marxist adherents of Azeri background.

Lenin aimed his criticisms at all rival factions at one time or another, claiming that they had betrayed Marxism in crucial respects. He presented himself as the paladin of Marxist orthodoxy. In his own idiosyncratic way, indeed, he could not have been more loyal to the doctrines and doings of Marx and Engels. The co-founders of Marxism had approved of violent revolution, dictatorship and terror; they had predicted and hoped for the 'dictatorship of the proletariat'. They had ridiculed socialists who preferred caution to action. They had never claimed that each country would come to its great revolution through a uniform series of stages. Many assumptions of Leninism sprang directly from the Marxism of the mid-nineteenth century. Lenin and Bolsheviks of all sorts were dedicated to industrialisation and urbanisation; they yearned to promote education. They believed that large-scale organisation was the key to modernisation. They aimed to eradicate religion, rural traditions and old Russia. They were committed to economic planning and social engineering. They were uninterested in constitutional procedures and political niceties. They aimed to form a monolithic 'vanguard' for revolutionary transformation.[7]

But both the Bolsheviks and Mensheviks had only an intermittent impact on the Russian labour movement. The émigré leaders, regardless of factional allegiance, lived in the same European cities. Their places of choice were Geneva, Zürich, Paris and London. (Lenin was unusual in detesting Paris; his feelings were not enhanced when someone stole his treasured bicycle from outside the Bibliothèque Nationale and the woman he had paid to look after it displayed no particular concern.)[8] On their holidays they sometimes went hill walking in Switzerland. Sometimes a large group of them would find houses to rent in towns on the Breton coast. Otherwise they might try the island of Capri off the south Italian coast where the novelist Maxim Gorki kept open house. Whether they were living in cities or taking a summer break, they nearly always stuck together in Russian groups. Bloomsbury in London attracted leading revolutionaries from the Russian Empire. The Rue Carouge in Geneva was a microcosm of radical Russia with its Russian libraries, kefir shops, presses and cafés. The emigrants spoke Russian most of the day. They read the St Petersburg newspapers. Although they followed political developments in their countries of exile, Russia remained their focus of attention.[9]

The Okhrana disrupted their activities by infiltrating its agents into the Russian Social-Democratic Workers' Party at home and abroad. Organisations based in Russia's largest cities were regularly broken up. Leaders were sent into Siberian exile. The party suffered years of dejection after the revolutionary emergency of 1905–7. Its membership tumbled from a peak of 150,000 to a handful of thousands.[10]

Marxists reacted to the disappointments by becoming intransigent when talk of compromise was in the air. No leading revolutionary worth his salt would agree to work for the Imperial bureaucracy or in the higher reaches of the economy. The exception, Lev Krasin, proves the rule. Krasin was a wonderfully employable engineer who earned his salary in Russia and Germany for the Siemens electricity company – and at the same time he supplied expertise on finance and weaponry for the Bolsheviks to carry out bank raids before the Great War.[11] The revolutionaries were not simply alienated from the regime. They would have nothing to do with it in case they compromised their political integrity. Inadvertently they rendered themselves impervious to any need to question their fundamental assumptions about the world. They argued nastily with each other, and this gave the impression to the world that they were led by free-thinking intellectuals. But the reality was that the leaders had imbibed a set of ideas which they protected from the slightest sceptical enquiry. The Bolsheviks were intellectually the most inflexible of all. They thought and acted constantly from certain premises; they had inoculated themselves against contrary notions about 'revolution'.

European socialists who had been meeting the Russian revolutionaries since the middle of the nineteenth century had always found them a strange lot. Novels such as Fëdor Dostoevski's *The Devils* and Joseph Conrad's *Under Western Eyes* stressed the rupture with ordinary standards of morality which typified many anti-tsarist organisations. The Socialist International, however, came to a less jaundiced conclusion. Not all revolutionaries from Russia were fanatics. In particular, the Socialist-Revolutionaries and the Mensheviks appeared reasonable and accommodating in their politics. Even the Bolsheviks were forgiven their frequent excesses. They could be exasperatingly uncompromising, but the assumption of the German Social-Democratic Party was that Russia, an exotic and underdeveloped country, was bound for the time being to produce wild revolutionaries as well as oppressive emperors and uncouth peasants. European socialists accordingly turned a blind eye to the peculiarities of their Russian comrades. When the Russian Social-Democratic Workers' Party met for its Fifth Congress in London in 1907, the Christian socialist Revd Bruce Wallace put the Brotherhood Church in Hackney at its disposal.[12] Evidently he had no inkling of the militant atheism and readiness for dictatorship, terror and civil war espoused by the Bolshevik participants.

Not everyone shared this indulgent approach. Rosa Luxemburg certainly discerned the menace in Bolshevism. Holding simultaneous membership of the Russian Social-Democratic Workers' Party and the German Social-Democratic Party, she had an exceptional vantage point for saying: 'The ultra-centralism advocated by Lenin is not something born of the positive creative spirit but of the negative sterile spirit of the watchman.'[13] She also disliked Lenin's policies on the agrarian and national questions and saw them as an opportunistic diversion from the authentic spirit of Marxism. Not even she, however, subjected his penchant for dictatorship to criticism. The Second International through to the Great War treated the Bolsheviks as a legitimate section of the European socialist movement.

This anyway had little immediate importance in the Russian Empire until the labour movement picked up strength again in 1912. An industrial boom followed the years of recession. Workers became less worried about unemployment. They returned to militant postures. The authorities exacerbated the situation as usual by their over-aggressive response. A massacre of striking miners in the Lena goldfields in Siberia in April 1912 provoked protest demonstrations across the country. There were 2,404 strikes in 1913. The monarchy and the big employers across the Russian Empire were rocked back on their heels. A second revolutionary emergency seemed in the offing. Both the Bolshevik and Menshevik factions aimed to take advantage of the turbulence. Mensheviks tried to reunify the Russian Social-Democratic Workers' Party. Their effort was in vain. The Bolsheviks – or rather the Leninist sub-group of Bolshevism – held their own separate conference in Prague in January 1912, electing a Central Committee which laid claim to be the party's sole legitimate leadership. This called forth anger and ridicule in equal measure; but Lenin had ceased to care what other Russian Marxists thought of him: he intended to break permanently with all other factions and harness the labour movement in Russia to the political purposes of Bolshevism.

The elections to the Fourth State Duma in 1912 had produced seven seats for the Mensheviks and six for the Bolsheviks. The new 'Central Committee', which based itself in and around Kraków in Austrian Poland, goaded the Bolshevik deputies in the Duma to organise themselves separately from the Menshevik group. A separate Bolshevik legal daily newspaper, *Pravda*, was established in St Petersburg. In the trade unions the Bolshevik militants were enjoined to operate without collaborating with the Mensheviks. Lenin was even willing to incur the obloquy of the Second International for holding tight to funds which in fairness should have been shared with the Menshevik faction, and it looked probable that he would fall out with Karl Kautsky over the matter.[14]

But the ultimate clash in the Second International between Lenin and Kautsky never occurred. Bigger events overtook their squabbles. War erupted in Europe in July 1914. On one side were the Central Powers: Germany and Austria-Hungary. Confronting them were the Allies: Russia, France and the United Kingdom. It was a titanic struggle. The

Russian armed forces made a rapid advance into East Prussia only to be caught in a pincer movement at the battle of Tannenberg. German military success was not confined to the conflict with the Russians. Despite the precautions taken by the French, the armies of Imperial Germany raced across Belgium into northern France. The fronts then stabilised. Warsaw and Brussels fell to the Germans but the Allies mobilised immense human and material reserves to prevent disaster. The Allies and the Central Powers faced each other across the trenches in 1915–16 with little sign of either coalition being able to develop a strategy to break the stalemate. Far from being over within weeks, as most people had expected, the Great War continued to drain the resources of every belligerent state. The struggle quickly involved whole societies. Conscription of recruits was universal. Industrial enterprises were co-opted into the economics of the war effort. Official propaganda whipped up extreme forms of patriotism.

The Second International before 1914 had committed its member parties to opposing their governments' participation in any continental war. Russian revolutionaries were divided in their reaction to the actual outbreak. Even some Bolsheviks rallied to Russia's patriotic cause. But many Bolsheviks, Mensheviks and Socialist-Revolutionaries stuck to their principles. The war for them was an inter-imperialist conflict which would benefit the bourgeoisie of one or other military coalition but could only bring poverty and death to the ordinary working people of the world. Socialists in other countries tended to vote in favour of war credits for their governments. But some leftists held to their pre-war commitment. These included groups of French, German, Dutch and Swiss socialists, and it was the Swiss leader Robert Grimm who convoked a conference of the anti-war political left in the little Alpine village of Zimmerwald in 1915. There were only three dozen participants. Trotski quipped that far-left socialism could be fitted into a couple of charabancs to travel up the mountain.[15]

Unity was not easy to achieve, and the fault lay with Lenin, who demanded that each socialist party should actively seek the military defeat of its army; he called for 'European civil war' between the continent's bourgeoisie and proletariat. These were fanatical eccentricities. Many of his own factional comrades thought he had finally gone off his head. Why, they asked, should Bolsheviks seek victory for the jack-booted armies of Kaiser Wilhelm?[16] What persuaded Lenin that workers of any European nation would want to follow the current ghastly war with a further civil war? The Zimmerwald movement, closely scrutinised by the intelligence agencies, had next to no influence on events. They produced pamphlets. They conducted propaganda in POW camps. They kept in touch with each other and argued in a less than comradely spirit about political strategy. Yet they were sure that the day of socialist revolution was about to dawn. The war and its hardships would accelerate history. They wanted to be ready for a revolutionary situation whenever and wherever it presented itself. The death knell of conservative and liberal politics in Europe was already ringing; and those socialists who had abandoned the Second International's opposition to participation in war would soon rue their pusillanimity.

It was the situation in Russia which offered the best revolutionary opportunities. As the war continued beyond the expected few weeks, the strains intensified. The government succeeded in mobilising twelve million men to the garrisons and the front. Its contracts with the metallurgical and textile factories generated the output to equip the armies. The high command steadied the defence against the Central Powers. But this came at a price. Inflation rocketed as the Ministry of Finances printed money to supplement foreign loans. Peasants had less and less incentive to trade their grain since industry no longer produced very much that they wanted. Urban amenities deteriorated. Although wages increased in the armaments factories, they failed to keep pace with the rising cost of living. The civilian administration, barely able to cope in peacetime, was falling apart. The court came into ever deeper disrepute. Nicholas II unwisely moved to military headquarters in Mogilëv, leaving his wife Alexandra and their confidant Grigori Rasputin in the capital. Rumours grew of financial corruption and an illicit sexual liaison. Rasputin was murdered in December 1916. Duma politicians discussed in private whether the end of the monarchy was nigh, but they did nothing. Generals pondered in the same way; they held back from action. Workers, however, felt pushed beyond endurance. Strikes broke out in Petrograd (as St Petersburg had been renamed to give it a less Teutonic ring) in late 1915 and again in late 1916.

5. THE OCTOBER REVOLUTION

By 1917 the Russian Imperial monarchy was discredited beyond redemption. Moderate conservatives and the more right-wing liberals hoped that a constitutional monarchy might be formed on the British model. Other liberals wanted to get rid of the dynasty altogether; and the Mensheviks and Socialist-Revolutionaries, planning for a 'bourgeois–democratic' revolution, aimed to form an opposition protecting the interests of workers, peasants and serving conscripts: their chief demands were to limit the Russian war effort to defensive aims and to install an order of comprehensive civic freedom.

Nicholas II failed to appreciate the seriousness of his situation. The moment of truth came in the last week of February 1917 when women textile workers went on strike in the capital. Workforces in the armaments factories joined in. Garrison soldiers took the side of the strikers. The Emperor came to his senses too late. Unable to restore control, he abdicated and after a few days of confusion a Provisional Government was formed. Its leader was the liberal Georgi Lvov and Kadets and other liberals filled most places in the cabinet. New policies were announced. The Provisional Government would stay in power until a Constituent Assembly could be elected. Until that time the cabinet would engage in a defensive war against the Central Powers. The expansionist war aims of Nicholas II were renounced. Ministers proclaimed a full range of civic freedoms. People could talk, write, pray, assemble and organise as they chose. The hope was that these reforms would be repaid with popular gratitude. The cabinet also banked on assistance from the Western Allies and sent out the message that, now that Russia was a free country, its forces would fight more effectively. Optimism was the dominant mood in the early weeks after this February Revolution.

Yet the Provisional Government was already severely constricted in authority. A Petrograd Soviet had been elected by workers and soldiers and its leadership was provided by Mensheviks and Socialist-Revolutionaries. Neither the Mensheviks nor the Socialist-Revolutionaries wished to form a cabinet, thinking Russia unready for socialism. But they wanted to influence the Provisional Government and their sanction was needed for the liberal ministry to survive. A condition of dual power existed. Lvov understood this; his Foreign Minister Pavel Milyukov did not. Milyukov in April sent a telegram to Paris and London reaffirming Russia's expectation that it would gain territory at the Ottoman Empire's expense if and when the Allies won the war. Workers and soldiers came out on to Petrograd's streets to protest at the abandonment of a purely defensive strategy, and Milyukov had to resign. Menshevik and Socialist-Revolutionary leaders were persuaded to enter the coalition, agreeing to share governmental responsibility with them. This co-operation was always fractious. Liberals objected to autonomy being granted to Finland and Ukraine; they also disapproved of their socialist fellow ministers introducing industrial arbitration tribunals and allowing 'land committees' to hand over uncultivated fields to peasant village communes. In late June they had had enough and resigned from the cabinet.[1]

By then the Provisional Government faced menace from the Bolshevik party. Initially there had been disarray among Bolsheviks. Their original plan had been to establish a provisional revolutionary dictatorship with other socialist parties, but this had not happened. The Bolshevik Central Committee under Lev Kamenev and Joseph Stalin decided to avoid open confrontation with the Provisional Government and barged aside those militants who wanted a more radical agenda. This annoyed Lenin, who sent angry telegrams to Petrograd from Switzerland. Many Bolsheviks in Russia were longing for a leader like him to take command. Lenin and other anti-war émigrés gained permission from the Berlin government to cross Germany in a sealed train. The Germans wanted to exploit their dedication to Russia's withdrawal from the war. Lenin's group arrived at the Finland Station in Petrograd in the early hours of 4 April.

Lenin had returned to political conditions he knew he could exploit. His 'April Theses' called for the cabinet to be replaced by a socialist administration. This was essentially a summons to revolution. Lenin argued that the Provisional Government would never solve the country's problems. Land, he insisted, should go to the peasants. The workers ought to exercise 'control' over industrial production. There should be national self-determination for all peoples. The war on the eastern front should be ended. The soviets as elective bodies of workers, peasants and soldiers should be turned into the organs of government. These arguments were treated as the raving of a madman. Many Bolsheviks rejected them and left the faction. But others were attracted by the man and his project even though the Mensheviks and Socialist-Revolutionaries at the time enjoyed the support of factories and garrisons. Kamenev and Stalin came over to his side and the Bolshevik Central Committee ratified his strategy. The fracas over the Milyukov telegram in late April convinced further doubters that Lenin was right that the Provisional Government was unworthy of trust. At their Conference in late April the Bolsheviks broke definitively with the rest of the Russian Social-Democratic Workers' Party and established themselves separately as the main party of opposition.

Industry was dislocated by shortage of finance and material supplies; things were made worse by the strikes. Workers, fearing unemployment, turned to the militants who urged a curtailing of the freedom of employers and managers. Food deliveries to the cities were dipping. The peasantry was getting less for its goods in real terms than earlier and scarcely any factory products were on sale. There was not much incentive to sell the harvest. Peasants also felt cheated by the government's refusal to turn over all the agricultural land to them. They hearkened to socialist leaders – mainly the left wing of the Party of Socialist-Revolutionaries – who told them to grab whatever they wanted. There was no popular sympathy for the patriotic calls of ministers. The Russian offensive on the eastern front in June resulted in military defeat and the further loss of territory in Ukraine. Soldiers no longer had the slightest confidence in the competence and sincerity of their officers. First the garrisons and then the men in the trenches demanded an end to the war. The government was powerless to improve the situation. The liberal-led coalition gave way in July to a ministry headed by the Socialist-Revolutionary Alexander Kerenski. He was a brilliant orator, but circumstances were beyond his capacity to rectify. Russia was plunging into chaos.

The Bolshevik political advance had momentarily stalled in early July when the Provisional Government charged the party with subversive activity. The party had helped to organise an armed demonstration in Petrograd; there was also some evidence that Bolsheviks had received money from Berlin. When the Ministry of Internal Affairs accused Lenin of being a German agent, he fled the capital and hid away in Helsinki. Yet the party managed without him. Bolsheviks made gains in the elections to the soviets, factory-workshop committees and trade unions. They operated dynamically. Unlike the Mensheviks and Socialist-Revolutionaries, they had no responsibility for governmental policies.

Their committees in the provinces picked up local grievances as well as the party's more general agenda.[2]

Their growing success was fed by Kerenski's gross incompetence. In August he decided to bring the soviets to heel and ordered his chief commander Lavr Kornilov to redeploy a force from the front to Petrograd. Kornilov, based at military headquarters in Mogilëv, was the darling of the political right. Anti-socialist groups in Russia had been the dog that did not bark after the February Revolution, but the call for a 'strong man' to assume office was gaining acceptance among the propertied elites. Whenever he visited from military headquarters Kornilov was fêted by salon society. At the last moment Kerenski panicked after becoming convinced that Kornilov was plotting a *coup d'état* against him. Kerenski countermanded his own order for the redeployment of troops to the capital. Kornilov at that point considered that Kerenski had lost the will to restore order to the factories and garrisons – and he resolved to undertake the very coup which he had earlier not intended. The February Revolution was put at risk. Kerenski turned to the Mensheviks, Socialist-Revolutionaries and even Bolsheviks for help. Socialist agitators sped out to the trains that were carrying Kornilov's troops. Words, not rifles, were their weapons as they brought the contingent to obey the Provisional Government. Kornilov was taken into custody and the coup was over before it had properly begun.

The Bolsheviks gained support for their case that Russia faced a choice between themselves on the left and a military dictatorship on the right. As the result of its recurrent elections, the soviets in Petrograd and Moscow provided them with majorities. In September, isolated in Helsinki, Lenin called on the party to seize power in the name of the soviets. The Bolshevik Central Committee rejected his demand as premature. But its members, enlivened by the adhesion of Lev Trotski to the party in midsummer, agreed that the time was approaching for the Provisional Government's overthrow.

Their thoughts were not confined to Russia. They contended that world capitalism's final crisis was imminent and that the period of European socialist revolution was about to begin. Lenin encapsulated this idea in *The State and Revolution*, which he wrote while reclining on a sofa in the friendly Helsinki police chief's home. The parties of the Second International, he declared, had betrayed Marxism by concentrating on peaceful, legal political methods and by assuming that the 'bourgeois state' would be retained when socialists eventually came to power. The parliament, army and bureaucracy would be preserved.

Lenin predicted that this was a step on the road to further compromises with capitalism; and he suggested that in the age of imperialism it was already clear that 'finance capital' in the imperial countries had learned the tricks of buying off the opposition. The skilled segments of the working class in the advanced economies were paid ever higher wages, and they became less committed to radical social change. Socialist parties sometimes kept up the rhetoric of revolution. The reality, though, was growing collusion between their leaders and the ruling classes.[3]

Lenin had searched for evidence that Marx and Engels believed in violent revolution and the dictatorship of the proletariat. He accepted that they had allowed for the possibility of a peaceful 'transition' to socialism in the United Kingdom and Holland; but his argument was that twentieth-century developments in both countries had given rise to a militarism which made a socialist seizure of power the only practical revolutionary strategy.

Marx and Engels had not really had a fixed standpoint on violent revolution and proletarian dictatorship. But they had written frequently about violence, and it would seem that Marx used phrases like 'the dictatorship of the proletariat' about a dozen times. Lenin scoured their writings for references like an intellectual detective. His analysis, while having a degree of justification, therefore rested on the props of a highly selective treatment of the inconsistent writings by his intellectual heroes. He professed to be merely expounding their purposes and represented himself as their modest pupil. The most he claimed for himself was that he was applying their analytical principles to the changed conditions in the twentieth century – and he believed that his interpretation fitted Europe as a whole, not just Russia.[4] Lenin maintained that the 'bourgeois state' had to be smashed to smithereens by armed uprising and proletarian dictatorship. In its place a wholly new state order had to be created. He expected this to be built on the foundations he witnessed in Russia in 1905 and in 1917: the soviets. Since these were bodies elected and organised by workers and soldiers by themselves, according to Lenin, they were to be turned into the nucleus of a Marxist proletarian dictatorship.

Lenin insisted that it would absolutely have to be a dictatorship. Nothing else, he declared, could secure the 'transition to socialism'. The middle and upper classes would inevitably support counter-revolution. They would have to be suppressed whenever they raised their heads. Their civil rights needed to be withheld. Lenin let it slip out that dictatorial rule would involve the use of state terror. But he coupled this with the prediction that, once the soviets held power, the power of the 'people' would weigh decisively against the counter-revolutionary forces. The revolution would be a fairly easy affair. If a civil war were to break out, it would soon be over.

The State and Revolution permanently changed the discourse of left-wing politics. After 1917 no socialist group could formulate its ideas without taking Leninism into account, even if only to repudiate it. With endless recourse to the sacred texts of Marx and Engels, Lenin postulated that two historical stages had to be traversed after the overthrow of capitalist rule. Marxism supposedly taught that the first stage would be socialist, the second would be communist. The first stage itself was to be initiated by the dictatorship of the proletariat which would start by introducing radical social and economic reform while suppressing the rights of the middle classes and implementing the principle: from each according to his capacity, to each according to his work. People would be rewarded for what they contributed to the good of society. As the coercive requirements of the authorities diminished and the proletarian dictatorship became a distant memory, the second stage would start. This would be communism itself. Kitchen maids would do their share of administration. History would be coming to an end. Then the operational principle would at last be: from each according to his abilities, to each according to his needs. The prophetic vision of Marx and Engels would be fulfilled.

This was a heady and idiosyncratic interpretation of Marxism. Lenin was vulnerable because of his absolute insistence that a peaceful socialist strategy had become absolutely impractical and that a violent uprising followed by a dictatorship of the proletariat was the sole available path of development. Just as controversial was his claim to exclusive correctness in his understanding of the 'teachings' of Marx and Engels. He stood forward unashamedly as their 'pupil'. Other interpreters such as Kautsky, he affirmed, had prostituted the pure doctrine. Lenin and the Bolsheviks sought to convince far-left socialists in Europe and North America to adopt the Bolshevik strategy. They intended a mighty Third International – a Communist International – to rally them to their red banner.

Lenin's summons was not lacking in ambiguity and incoherence. While calling for communist policies, he demanded socialist reforms and a 'European socialist revolution'. On the far left it was only the more sophisticated activists who grasped the meaning of his theory. There had always been diversity among socialists in ideas and methods.

There had never been a time when terms such as communism, social-ism, social-democracy and even anarchism had not overlapped to some extent. Lenin was appropriating communism as a term to demarcate his party and its ideas from the rest of the political left.[5] He particularly aimed to monopolise Marxist debates. Kautsky, as Marxism's most influential interpreter at the time, came in for intensive criticism. Most socialists outside Germany – and many German social-democrats, prob-ably – had never heard of Kautsky. *The State and Revolution* dealt obsessively with him. This was not just a psychological quirk of Lenin's mentality. It sprang too from his ambition to assemble all far-left revolutionaries under his international banner and to thrust aside those groups which refused to respond to his summons. The book itself was not published until 1918. But the basic ideas underpinned everything said and written by Lenin after his return from Switzerland. This was a leader with a mission.

If it had only been Lenin who thought this way, he would have remained a columnist for extremist but ineffectual newspapers. Indeed he had given this impression to his followers a few weeks before the February Revolution. In fact he had made himself leader of a large, dynamic party and it was this party which was about to seize power in Petrograd. His ideas were not yet shared by everyone in his party and he as yet lacked the disciplinary sanctions to impose them. Even in the Central Committee a majority were to oppose his refusal to share posts in government with Mensheviks and Socialist-Revolutionaries after the Provisional Government's overthrow. Lower down the party there was the same disquiet about ideas of a one-party dictatorship. Bolsheviks, whether they were local officials or ordinary new recruits to the party, expected to form an 'all-socialist government' and to hold to democratic procedures. Lenin and his close supporters kept nicely quiet about their intentions. They needed the maximum of internal party unity before seizing power. Not for nothing did Lenin say that making revolution was an art rather than a science. He might have added that this art involved dissimulation as well as intuition and audacity.

He had a coterie of leading comrades who, despite occasional reservations, were his willing adjutants. These included Joseph Stalin and Yakov Sverdlov, who together had run the Central Committee in his absence from July. But the person who bulked larger than Stalin and Sverdlov was the former anti-Bolshevik Lev Trotski. There was no finer orator in the entire party. No one wrote prose of such coruscat-ing brilliance for *Pravda*. Trotski, with his pince-nez and his shock of auburn, curly hair, became one of the most readily recognised Bolsheviks. His strengths lay as much in organisation as in propaganda. When the Petrograd Soviet formed a Military–Revolutionary Committee to co-ordinate its work in the capital's garrisons Trotski was a natural choice for the party to deploy to it as a member. He had always wanted to telescope the two stages of the Russian revolutionary process – as envisaged by conventional Russian Marxists – into one. Lenin in his *April Theses* implicitly endorsed this desire. The two of them had no problem in working together after years of mutual antipathy.

Yet Lenin's theory of revolution was at the same time thought too moderate by Nikolai Bukharin and several other Bolshevik leaders who called for the state to own the entire economy. The Bolsheviks lived and breathed the desire to transform the world – and this was also true of those from the less radical side of the party who regarded Lenin as proposing a course of action which would dangerously isolate the party. All were millenarian in spirit. The remaking of Russia, Europe and North America was going to happen within weeks, perhaps within days. Bolsheviks simply could not imagine that capitalism might survive the current war. 'The epoch of socialism' was nigh. In their more sober moments they may have pondered whether this was guaranteed by what they knew about strikes and mutinies to the west. But these moments faded. As soon as they were with Bolshevik comrades they resumed their apocalyptic perspective. Their optimism was increased by the ease of their intermittent political advance after the February Revolution. Soviets, trade unions and factory-workshop committees tumbled under their thrall. If this could happen in Russia, it surely made sense to predict revolutionary successes in Germany, Austria, Britain and France. Bolsheviks assumed that Russian workers, despite their merits, were 'backward' and 'uncultured' in comparison with the industrial labour forces in central and western Europe.

Central Committee members Kamenev and Zinoviev at the last moment doused these notions with scepticism. But then they quickly recoiled. Solidarity with comrades took precedence over calm consideration. Their lives had meaning for them through membership of the party. They needed to feel part of the group. Individuals who were too sensible to go along with Lenin's project simply left the party. There had been millenarian movements in the distant and not so distant past and the Bolsheviks admired some of them. They admired the sixteenth-century Anabaptists of Münster in Germany. They eulogised the Jacobin terrorists in the French Revolution. Tommaso Campanella and Thomas

More figured prominently in their reading. Bolsheviks were inspired by these old dreams about the perfect society almost as much as by Marx and Engels; and they were sure they could bring them to completion. They refused to be depressed by the difficulties in state and society. It was as if they had eyes in the backs of their heads but no peripheral vision: they looked fondly at the reveries of their forerunners. Most of them scoffed at contemporary ideas outside the Marxist canon. They refused to glance sideways and consider whether they had something important to learn from the great innovative thinkers of their day.

Like all Marxists, they nonetheless credited themselves with having a scientific understanding. They thought they knew everything they needed for a successful revolution. They would not be sparing in repressive measures. The Paris Commune of 1871 had fallen, they contended, because its leaders had failed to get properly tough with its enemies. They would not make the same mistake. Alexander Herzen, one of Russia's greatest essayists in the mid-nineteenth century, expressed fear of bloody revolution in his country. He thought that, if ever the peasantry rose against their masters, they might be led by some 'Genghis Khan with the telegraph'. His prophetic idea was that modern technology would enable terror to be applied with unprecedented ferocity. His aperçu was wrong in one main respect. The Bolshevik leaders were not bringing an alien power to Russia; they were born and bred in the empire of the Romanovs. Nor were they interested only in power and glory: they aimed also to alter minds. Theirs was a secular gospel which they intended to take to the willing and impose on the unwilling. They studied the French Revolution relentlessly; they were Jacobins with the telephone and the machine-gun. There had not been their like in previous centuries.

If ever they experienced doubt, they instantly repressed it. What sustained them was their certitude about the condition of the world. War in Europe had discredited the entire international system. Millions of people had been killed or were suffering in the trenches. Profiteering by financiers and arms manufacturers was notorious. Nationalism had been exploited by all governments. Churches had become megaphones for the military cause of their countries. The rhetoric about 'the war to end war' failed to convince many far-left socialists in Europe and North America. To them it was unlikely that the current war would be the last world war. The likelier outcome was a victors' peace which would be challenged in the next generation by the resurgent losers. The era of

empires was not over. Whoever won the Great War would seize control
of the colonies as well as subjugate the defeated imperial powers.

The conclusion seemed self-evident on the extreme political left.
Capitalism was the disease and had to be cured by the surgery of
revolution. The Bolsheviks claimed there was no alternative. The Mensheviks and Socialist-Revolutionaries had brought about no discernible
benefit for the people by joining the Provisional Government. Military
and economic collapse was in prospect. Bolsheviks had consequently
been correct in spurning fraternal socialist parties in Russia. They were
proud of being independent and thought history to be on their side.
From a small Marxist faction before the February Revolution they had
become a mass party. Workers who had not heard the name of Lenin
were crowding to Bolshevik mass meetings and voting Bolshevik in
elections to soviets. The Bolsheviks had always been sceptical about the
autonomous revolutionary potential of the 'proletariat'; but their concerns were allayed by the political advance made by Bolshevism with
working-class support in summer and early autumn 1917. They assumed
that their success would become permanent in Russia and that the rest
of Europe would follow their example. They could not care less about
the warnings given them by Mensheviks and Socialist-Revolutionaries on
the perils of a revolution based on dictatorship and civil war.

They had made their choice. They were going to create revolution in
their own way and damn the consequences. But how and when? Lenin
returned secretly and in disguise to Petrograd, for fear of arrest, around
the beginning of October. He stayed in the city's outskirts where an
adoring Central Committee secretary, Margarita Fofanova, gave him a
room and a bed. From there he bombarded the Central Committee with
intemperate demands for an insurrection. What agency should organise
it and what kind of government should be installed, he did not say. The
main thing for him was to get assent to an armed uprising.

On 10 October, still wearing his wig as a disguise, he attended the
Bolshevik Central Committee and thrust his arguments on his comrades
at a meeting that went on for hours. His intellect and temperament won
the debate. By a vote of ten to two it was resolved to seize power. The
details were left undetermined. There was also a feeling that so important
a decision required a further Central Committee meeting on 16 October
with representatives from the party committees of Petrograd, Moscow
and other large cities. Lenin again attended: he wanted no shilly-shallying
at the last moment. The revolutionary opportunity would not necessarily

be repeated. It was now or never. He need not have fretted. For the second time the vote went strongly in his favour and the Bolshevik Central Committee set about preparations for a seizure of power. This was going to be done cleverly. The Second Congress of Workers' and Soldiers' Deputies was about to meet. The Bolshevik leadership needed to avoid giving the impression that a single party was using violence to monopolise revolutionary authority. Consequently they operated through the Military–Revolutionary Committee of the Petrograd Soviet. It was this organ, with its influence over the capital's garrison troops, which was to oust the Provisional Government and present power to the Second Congress.

People in Petrograd on 25 October 1917 were to remember how normal everything had been that day. The shops opened as usual in the Russian capital. Schools functioned. The trams were running – luckily for Lenin, who used the network to travel from the outskirts to the Smolny Institute where the Second Congress was taking place. It had been obvious that a clash between the Provisional Government and the armed units controlled by the Military–Revolutionary Committee of the Petrograd Soviet was getting nearer by the day. The Bolshevik Central Committee had agreed to an insurrectionary strategy on 10 October. Lenin had returned from Finland to make the case. Then he went back into hiding, in the apartment of Margarita Fofanova, to await the Central Committee's recall to action. The insurrection began on the night of 24–25 October, but Lenin suspected that insufficient resolve would be displayed. There was no other option: he bandaged his head as a new disguise and took the tram line to the centre of the city. In the Smolny Institute he found his Central Committee plotting the details of the overthrow of Kerenski's Provisional Government. This was still not enough for Lenin, who demanded fanatical urgency and dedication – and by his presence he was able to ensure the completion of the task.

The Provisional Government was running on an empty fuel tank. Kerenski had a genuine commitment to democracy, patriotism and fighting for victory in the war. But he lacked support of genuine substance. The liberals did not oppose him, but then again they had hardly tried to stop the Kornilov coup in its tracks along the railway from Mogilëv to Petrograd. The economy was in free fall. Industry was ruined by financiers who refused to finance and by suppliers of raw materials who ceased to trade. Army generals never trusted Kerenski again after the Kornilov affair. His writ hardly ran beyond the walls of the Winter Palace. The Mensheviks and Socialist-Revolutionaries were beginning to consider supplanting him and introducing more radical reforms. But they had internal divisions and lacked the will to act. The Bolsheviks meanwhile showed unity of purpose. They detested Kerenski and openly called for his overthrow. They promised immediate solutions: land to the peasantry, workers' control in the factories, national self-determination. They promised, above all, to bring about peace. They had made their preparations in the Military–Revolutionary Committee of the Petrograd Soviet. Whereas others had talked about socialist revolution, they would make one.

Kerenski had tried to pre-empt a rising by closing down Bolshevik newspapers. This action was altogether too little, too late. Troops loyal to the Petrograd Soviet began to seize key buildings. The telegraph offices and the railway station were occupied even before the Winter Palace was surrounded. By 10 a.m. on 25 October it was possible for Lenin to issue the proclamation that the Provisional Government had been overthrown. Angered by the coup, the Mensheviks and Socialist-Revolutionaries walked out of the Second Congress of Soviets. This allowed Lenin to go ahead and form a new government. On Trotski's suggestion, it would be called the Council of People's Commissars (or Sovnarkom in its Russian acronym). The era of socialist revolution was announced. Bolsheviks believed they were sounding the death knell of world capitalism.[6]

6. THE FIRST COMMUNIST STATE

The Bolsheviks came to power without a detailed template for the new state order. They did their inventing almost as an afterthought. In the first weeks of the October Revolution they concentrated on establishing their authority and announcing their fundamental policies. Lenin quickly issued his Decree on the Land. This expropriated crown, Church and gentry estates without compensation and put them at the disposal of the peasantry. Also from Lenin's pen came the Decree on Peace. This called for an immediate end to the war and urged all belligerent states to cease fighting. Russia sought an armistice on the eastern front. Bolsheviks continued to believe that this would spark off revolutions in Germany and Austria. The Decree on Workers' Control empowered labour forces to exert supervisory authority over managers of their enterprises. This was meant to increase order in the factories as well as to enhance conditions for waged employees. The Decree on the Eight-Hour Working Day further improved the rights of the labour force. Lenin and Stalin signed the Declaration of the Rights of the Peoples of Russia abolishing all privileges based on nationality and guaranteeing self-determination for every national and ethnic group. The Decree 'on the Separation of Church and State' was also introduced.

Banks were taken into state ownership without reimbursement. Loans contracted by the governments of Nicholas II and Kerenski were unilaterally cancelled. The private import-and-export trade was banned. The largest factories and mines were seized by the government and their owners dispossessed. Lenin at the same time affirmed the need to protect capitalism. The paradox was explained by Marxist economics. Bolsheviks recognised that many sectors of the Imperial economy were 'backward' and needed to undergo capitalist development so as to attain a concentration of production. Once this had taken place, it would supposedly be easy for the party to expropriate and switch them to producing goods for the benefit of the entire society.

Lenin accorded paramount importance to consolidating Bolshevik political power. The Decree on the Press was one of the first measures of Sovnarkom, empowering him to close down any newspaper hostile to the new revolutionary administration. He had trouble in his own Central Committee over his refusal to invite Mensheviks and Socialist-Revolutionaries into a government coalition. By supporting the Provisional Government, they had ceased for ever to be acceptable political partners in any capacity. Several leading Bolsheviks resigned their posts of authority in protest at his intransigence. The Railwaymen's Union went on strike with the purpose of forcing Lenin and Trotski to negotiate. But Lenin's group held its ground and the strike petered out. It suited Lenin and Trotski to introduce the Left Socialist-Revolutionaries as junior partners in Sovnarkom because the Bolsheviks, unlike them, had little following in the countryside. This was the limit of political compromise. The Bolshevik Central Committee pressed forward with enforcing the authority of the revolutionary administration. A security police force – the Extraordinary Commission for Combating Sabotage and Counter-Revolution (or Cheka) – was set up under Felix Dzierżyński; the task was to root out and crush the resistance to the October Revolution. Enemies were to be eliminated. Lenin for years had preached the virtues of the 'dictatorship of the proletariat'. No one had known whether his bite would be as fierce as his bark. It turned out to be fiercer.

Few people would have bet on the survival of the Soviet regime. The assumption everywhere was that it stood no better chance than the ineffectual Kerenski. The Bolsheviks themselves kept their suitcases packed; they knew that at any moment they might have to flee Petrograd. The Constituent Assembly elections in November 1917 gave early cause for concern. Less than a quarter of the electorate voted for the Bolsheviks. The Socialist-Revolutionaries, a designation that admittedly included left-wing candidates who had abandoned their party allegiance, gained nearly two-fifths of the seats. The combined vote of the two parties in the Sovnarkom coalition did not add up to an electoral majority. The decision was taken simply to suppress the Constituent Assembly. This was a tragedy for the people of the former Russian Empire, its democracy and its socialism. If the votes for socialist parties are put together, four-fifths of the electorate supported some kind of socialism. The largest party were the Socialist-Revolutionaries led by Viktor Chernov, but they lacked the armed power to protect themselves. The Assembly itself met in an atmosphere of fear on 5 January 1918 and, at the behest of Lenin, Sovnarkom ordered the building to be cleared and closed the next day. Zhelezhnyakov, the chief of the guard, announced brusquely that his men were tired. Russian democracy was terminated on the pretext of the sleepiness of a few armed janitors.

International affairs had changed decisively in the meantime. The Bolsheviks parleyed with the Central Powers at Brest-Litovsk, the nearest town to the eastern front. Trotski as People's Commissar for External Affairs dragged out the discussions. He made 'neither war nor peace' into his slogan since he understood that the Reds could not beat the armies of Germany and Austria-Hungary. But the ultimatums became ever more threatening and by January 1918 Lenin had resolved that a separate peace had to be signed to prevent a German occupation of Russia. A furious dispute broke out. Trotski and Bukharin, leaders of the so-called Left Communists in the Bolshevik Central Committee, admitted that the military prospect for Russia was dire. Yet they refused to condone a separate peace. Better to go down fighting than to collude in the preservation of 'German imperialism'. They called for a 'revolutionary war'. Neither workers nor soldiers in Russia were in a mood to go on fighting against Germany and Austria-Hungary.[1] The administration and the economy were in chaos. Steadily Lenin clawed his way to a majority in the Central Committee. By 23 February a definitive vote was taken and permission was given for peace to be signed at Brest-Litovsk.

This 'obscene peace' on 3 March 1918 removed Ukraine, Belorussia, Lithuania, Latvia and Estonia from Russian control. Soviet diplomats relinquished any claim to rule nearly half of the population of the former empire, and with this disappeared a vast chunk of the coal and iron industry and the bulk of the most fertile agricultural land. The humiliation was endured so that a 'breathing space' might be obtained for the regime to deepen its social and economic reforms. Class enemies would be rooted out and Bolshevism would expand its authority.

The Left Socialist-Revolutionaries shared the disgust of all Russian political parties with the treaty of Brest-Litovsk, and walked out of the Sovnarkom coalition. So too did many Left Communists, leaving behind the rump of the Bolshevik party. Almost without being noticed, the Soviet republic became a one-party state. Meanwhile the Socialist-Revolutionaries had removed themselves to Samara in the Russian south-east and set up a rival government known as the Committee of Members of the Constituent Assembly (or Komuch). Chernov readied himself for conflict. The onset of civil war was only a matter of time as both sides built up their armed forces. It broke out in the oddest way at the end of May. A legion of Czech former POWs was travelling to Europe along the Trans-Siberian Railway when its members suspected the Bolsheviks of arresting and maltreating some of their comrades. They turned back from the middle of Siberia and suppressed the soviets en route. Arriving in Samara, they threw in their lot with the Socialist-Revolutionaries. Within weeks they had pushed north towards Kazan. Constituent Assembly and Sovnarkom were at war, and the Czechoslovak legionaries led an offensive against Bolshevism in the Volga cities. The Bolsheviks assembled a Red Army and, inspired by Trotski as People's Commissar for Military Affairs, halted the advance of Komuch forces on Moscow.

This success was nullified at the end of the year when so-called White Armies began to emerge from the edges of the Russian heartland. The first of these was led by Admiral Kolchak in Omsk. Kolchak overthrew Komuch and directed his forces towards central Russia. Another military contingent under General Denikin was assembling in the south. A third, headed by General Yudenich, gathered recruits and equipment in Estonia. All aimed to bring down the Soviet republic and restore the old social order. Their officers were typically monarchists. The Imperial family itself had been executed in Yekaterinburg in July 1918. The Whites, almost as furious with liberals as with the Bolsheviks, aimed at a military dictatorship to bring back order and territorial integrity to the country. The Red Army picked them off one after the other in 1919: Kolchak from April, Denikin in summer and Yudenich in November. They had geography on their side. By holding on to northern and central Russia, they retained the advantage in quantity of military equipment and conscripts. The main railway and telegraph lines radiated from Moscow and Petrograd. The Reds fought politically as well as with armed might. They did not let workers, peasants and soldiers forget that the Whites would reverse the reforms made since the fall of the Romanovs in February 1917.

The Bolsheviks were never very popular. They reacted to dissent with a concentration of state violence. Strikes against them were put down in the first year of 'Soviet power'. When workers voted for Mensheviks in city soviets, the Bolsheviks declared the elections invalid and sent in their armed units. Peasants, far from feeling gratitude for the Decree on the Land, withheld their produce in protest at the continuing low payments received. Sovnarkom dispatched armed squads to seize grain. Rural revolts proliferated. There were mutinies even in the Red Army. But the Bolsheviks survived and triumphed. They used officers from the Imperial Army to lead the Reds. They drew willing elements from the old administration into the new people's commissariats. They instigated a Red Terror to 'cleanse' the cities of 'enemies of the people':

restrictions on the Cheka were removed. Even so, the intensity of popular resistance increased in 1920–1. Whole provinces rose in rural rebellion. The strike movement caused disruption even in Petrograd. In February 1921 the Politburo decided to make economic concessions. The New Economic Policy (NEP) was passed by the Tenth Party Congress in March and implemented the next month. Its essence involved replacing forcible grain requisitioning with a graduated tax-in-kind set at a low enough level to allow peasants to conduct private trade. Meanwhile the Red Army suppressed the revolts, including a mutiny by the Kronstadt naval garrison in March. The carrot was accompanied by a very thorny cudgel.[2]

The other reason for the Bolsheviks' survival was the state order they developed. Power was monopolised by a single party and increasingly by a single ideology. Terror was openly advocated as a necessary weapon in the party's arsenal. By the end of the civil war they had seized huge sectors of the economy. All industry was owned by the state. The grain trade was a state monopoly. Schools and the press were brought under communist supervision. The party became the supreme agency of statehood. Government and other public institutions emitted a constant stream of instructions about policy; they were staffed at the highest levels by loyal Bolsheviks. Centralisation of command was prioritised. Elective procedures became a ceremonial formality. The people in whose name the October Revolution had been made – the workers, the poor peasants and the conscripts in the armed forces – were treated as a resource to be mobilised for whatever tasks the central party leadership specified.

The Bolsheviks had always believed in strict centralism and discipline and had faith in themselves as the omniscient 'vanguard' of revolutionary militancy. Such had been their credo since the birth of Bolshevism. But they had never properly practised what they preached. It was the conditions of power which pushed them into actual compliance. They faced great political and military resistance. They confronted chaos in administration, communications and transport. Hardly an institution existed at the 'centre' which could secure obedience from the 'localities'. The normal lines of hierarchy had disintegrated. The communists had to restore the situation fast. The economy, especially the food supply, had to be restored and the orders of central authority fulfilled. The armed forces had to be recruited, trained, equipped and shipped to the fronts. Revolutionary rhetoric alone would not achieve this; nor would endless meetings in smoke-filled rooms. Lenin and the Central Committee could clearly see that organisational reform was a matter of life and death as much as the debate on the treaty of Brest-Litovsk, and they did not have to impose this on an unwilling party. Local Bolshevik leaders appreciated the practical necessity of a unified system of command.[3]

At every territorial level from the Kremlin to the smallest district it was the communist party which dominated. Having moved to Moscow in March 1918, the Central Committee had gathered its functionaries and their families within the walls of the Kremlin. Twelve months of revolution had turned the place into a mess. The horses of the Imperial cavalry had left their ordure everywhere. Repairs had been neglected. Few Central Committee members stayed there for long. Trotski and most other members sped away to bolster regional government or to ensure political control of the Red Army. By the beginning of 1919 the decision was taken to set up two inner bodies of the Central Committee. These were the Political Bureau (Politburo) and the Organisational Bureau (Orgburo). The first was charged with overseeing virtually all public affairs including economic management, military strategy and foreign policy as well as political command; the second was to oversee the internal organisational dispositions of the party and to direct business in the Secretariat. The result was to devolve immense daily responsibility to a small number of leaders. Even the five-person Politburo met infrequently. Lenin and Yakov Sverdlov operated a virtual diarchy until Sverdlov's death in March 1919.[4]

The same trend existed at lower levels. As leading activists volunteered or were mobilised for army service, party business fell to committee chairmen acting alone or with a handful of subordinates. Although in 1920 the chairmen were redesignated as 'secretaries', the more modest title disguised an increase in their power.[5] While fighting the civil war, the party was becoming militarised in organisation and outlook. It instructed the bodies of government at the centre and in the provinces.

The People's Commissariats were the successor bodies of the Imperial ministries; their inherited staff were a perennial object of the party's suspicion. Bolsheviks constantly sought to invent ways of investigating and controlling governmental machinery. One of the institutional innovations was entrusted to Stalin. This was the Workers' and Peasants' Inspectorate, which sent its personnel into administrative offices to examine the financial accounts and to assess the loyalty of officialdom to party policy. Occasional attempts were made to establish bodies which were outside regular party control. The 'political departments' in the Red Army were an example of this. These were heavily sponsored by Trotski,

who had been an anti-Bolshevik before 1917; and his enthusiasm for
them led to a fear that they might become vehicles for an army-inspired
movement against the party. There was a precedent for this in the French
Revolution, when the radicals of 1789 had eventually been superseded by
Consul and then Emperor Napoleon Bonaparte. Perhaps the same thing
could occur in Soviet Russia. The worries sharpened in 1920, at the end
of the civil war, when Trotski sought to extend the political-department
model to the tasks of restoring order on railways and rivers. Trotski also
tried to set up 'labour armies' of Red Army conscripts to carry out repair
jobs for the government.

But the order inaugurated in 1917–19 was otherwise reinforced as the
party asserted its rule. Central party bodies decided all important
postings. The Politburo, acting on behalf of the Central Committee,
reserved the key decisions for itself, and the rest were left – in descending
order of significance – to the Orgburo and the Secretariat. Party leaders
were eager to allocate such postings exclusively to fellow communists.
Sverdlov relied on his capacious memory to pick old comrades. But as
the Soviet state underwent consolidated expansion both in territory and
in administrative reach the need arose to create a reliable filing system
in the Secretariat. A Files and Assignment Department (Uchraspred) was
created in 1919 by Sverdlov's successor Yelena Stasova.[6] In 1923 the policy
was confidentially introduced of listing all the posts crucial to the party's
interests. This was called the 'nomenklatura'. At first it was applied to
the 'centre'. Jobs from the Sovnarkom chairmanship to the Kremlin
precinct guard commander as well as each provincial party committee
chairmanship were included. These procedures were then reproduced in
the 'localities'. In this way the party could insert its reliable cadres into
public institutions and ensure compliance with central policies.

The pay and conditions associated with each post were laid out with
exactitude. There was a graduated hierarchy of material rewards. This
told only a part of the story. Appointment to particular posts gave access
to shops, clinics and sanatoria denied to other citizens. The higher the
position on the nomenklaturas, the greater the privileges available. The
comforts of official life had not yet reached their climax. In August 1918,
when an assassination attempt was made on Lenin, his sister Maria
refused to send out for medicine from the nearby pharmacies. Knowing that most medical professionals were anti-communist, she feared
that one of them might poison the stricken leader.[7] What is more, the
penetration of public institutions by the communists was weaker than
it seemed. In mid-1919 Lenin paid a visit to the outskirts of Moscow. It

was a snowy day and visibility was poor as his limousine entered the Sokolniki district. Three robbers leaped out on to the road, held up the vehicle and robbed Lenin of his revolver. It made no difference when he exclaimed: 'My name is Lenin!' On being captured by the Cheka, they said they had misheard their victim as claiming to be a certain Levin. They evidently believed that robbing people with a Jewish name was an extenuating factor in their crime.[8]

The country was in chaos at the time and the Soviet order retained many informal features. To get a job in the Kremlin it was an advantage to be a relative of one of the leaders. This was how Stalin's young wife Nadya, who had left grammar school without finishing the course, began work as one of Lenin's secretaries; and when Nadya's family was short of food, she turned to Kremlin quartermaster Abel Enukidze, her godfather, for additional supplies.[9] There was much intermarriage among communists. Trotski's sister Olga was the wife of fellow Politburo member Kamenev. Nepotism – or better, perhaps, 'familism' – was rife and had its roots in the isolation of the party. Communists could rely only on communists. The same kind of environment encouraged the development of cliental arrangements in politics. Leaders at each level acted as patrons to selected personal followers. Although networks of this kind had characterised Russian public life for centuries, they had been losing influence as the professionalisation of the bureaucracy and other sectors increased. Under communism the wheel was turned in the opposite direction. It mattered more how long you had been a communist and which leader you knew personally than how competent you were at the functions of your post. Loyalty counted for more than ability.

The party imposed control over the Red Army, the Cheka and the People's Commissariats. The trade unions too were brought under strict control. Trotski urged that such unions should be turned into agencies of a 'workers' state' dedicated to the interests of the proletariat. Trotski's extremism was rejected. But when Mikhail Tomski surreptitiously tried to increase trade union autonomy, Lenin threatened to expel him from the Party Central Committee.[10] An ideological monopoly too was enforced. Religious organisations had had their landed property expropriated. Priests, imams and rabbis were routinely murdered throughout the civil war, and show trials and executions were held of Russian Orthodox Church leaders in 1922. Novelists, philosophers and scholars were spared such brutality (although the poet Nikolai Gumilëv was shot in 1921). In June 1922 a censorship office – Glavlit – was established. The Soviet order required hegemony not only over institutions but also over ideas. Nicholas II had abolished pre-publication censorship in the 1905–6 revolutionary crisis. It returned with a vengeance under the NEP. Every artistic and scholarly publication had to pass through the sieve of the regime's appointed vetters. Dozens of intellectuals, including the Christian philosopher Nikolai Berdyaev, were summarily deported on the *Oberbürgermeister Haken* steamship in September 1922.[11] The Soviet order was to be put into quarantine while the authorities set about indoctrinating people with the ideas of the Leninist variant of Marxism.

Electoral competition had long since disappeared. In Russia only the Mensheviks survived the civil war. They maintained a few newspapers and they could offer occasional criticisms of the communists in the soviets. But many of them were arrested; and after the show trial of the Socialist-Revolutionaries in June 1922 Lenin wanted to apply the same treatment to the Menshevik leadership. In fact the Politburo decided against instituting judicial proceedings against Menshevism,[12] but the remnants of opposition in the Soviet state were eliminated. A few socialist organisations agreed to be incorporated in the communist party. These included the Borotbists, who were the Ukrainian equivalent of the Left Socialist-Revolutionaries in Russia.[13] Many members of the Jewish Bund were also induced to come over to communism. This happened because Lenin thought it the only quick way to acquire Ukrainian and Jewish activists for the Bolshevik party in Ukraine and the former Jewish Pale of Settlement. The newcomers had to accept strict political control from Moscow in return for their local power. Not every Bolshevik leader thought this a safe manoeuvre – and the gamble fell to pieces in the party's hands by the end of the 1920s. But such was Lenin's personal influence that the experiment was tried out.

The one-party political system was tautened in 1921. Factions inside the communist party were proscribed. Disputes had divided the party throughout the civil war. First there had been the controversy between Lenin and the Left Communists over the treaty of Brest-Litovsk. Then in 1918–19 the Military Opposition, inspired behind the scenes by Stalin, had objected to the policy of employing officers from the Imperial Army. No sooner had the dust settled than the Democratic Centralists campaigned against internal party authoritarianism. By 1920 the Workers' Opposition was complaining about the clampdown on direct working-class influence on economic policy. The Politburo ordered the 'purging' of such troublemakers from the party.

The Soviet leadership aimed to construct a neat slope from top to bottom of the pyramid of power. The exception to this was the establishment of Soviet republics alongside the original Russian Soviet Federative Socialist Republic (RSFSR). Lenin and Stalin fell out over this. Stalin had been willing to accept 'national liberalism' as an expedient to win the civil war; but his ultimate objective was for the RSFSR to incorporate the other republics at the end of the fighting. Lenin, though, believed that the intense feelings of the diverse peoples of the former Russian Empire had to be accommodated by introducing a federal constitution. Thus the Ukrainian Soviet Republic would exist as the formal equal of the RSFSR. Lenin was not really as gentle as he wanted to appear. The communist party would remain centralised and non-federal, and the Politburo in Moscow would continue to give commands to the Ukrainian communist leadership which staffed the government of the Ukrainian Soviet Republic. Lenin, despite his illness in 1922, won the political tussle, and it was largely his scheme which lay at the basis of the Union of Soviet Socialist Republics (USSR) that was sanctioned at the end of the year. This combination of a rigidly realised centralism with a formal appearance of federal powers was to last through to all but the last couple of years of the communist state.

The party had granted freedom to the non-Russians to publish and teach in their own languages. They also introduced a policy of positive discrimination in favour of young recruits from each nationality whom they could train to become fervent party and government officials. A close watch was kept for the menace of Russian nationalism, and Russia's Church and intelligentsia were more heavily supervised than their counterparts in the other republics. The aim remained to create a community of peoples who would meld together in a socialist society without political, economic or national oppression. The global perspective was also maintained. Lenin aimed to form a Communist International (or Comintern) consisting of all Marxist parties which rejected the compromises accepted by parties belonging to the Second International; and he expected that when the 'European revolution' eventually happened, a Comintern congress would be held in Berlin and the working language would be German rather than Russian.[14] Much that happened was different from what was officially intended. Moslem inhabitants of central Asia felt that Russian communists in the civil war behaved little differently from Imperial armed forces in the past. Ukrainian peasants thought the same about the depredations and oppression undertaken by the Reds. But as the heat of military conflict cooled, communism gained a chance to appeal to the national and ethnic groups.

Not all Bolshevik leaders approved of these concessions; some of them thought that nationalism would be the result. But Lenin and Stalin persisted. They made the case that, by allowing a degree of freedom for cultural self-expression for the nations of the USSR, they would allay suspicions of 'Great Russian chauvinism'. Communists were people of the book and treated Marx's *Capital* as their sacred text. People would not study and learn the doctrines effectively unless they could be taught in the language they spoke. Belorussian peasants did not even understand Russian, but once they learned to read in their mother tongue they could be indoctrinated with Leninist precepts. Tolerance of national sensitivities would constitute a bridgehead into socialism.[15]

The communist party encouraged citizens to participate in what was meant to be their own revolution. Unfortunately, people who were hungry and out of work were in no position to build such a state. The ambition of a 'proletarian dictatorship' was turned into the reality of a dictatorship of the party. Voluntary extra days of work – *subbotniki* – were introduced in the civil war. Lenin led the way by putting in a few minutes shovelling snow in the Kremlin precinct. In fact these special days were not free from compulsion. At a time when urban inhabitants depended on state food rations it was difficult to refuse to comply with the calls to work for nothing. Members of the former middle classes had still less choice. The communists evicted aristocrats and landlords from their homes and ordered them to clean the streets. Such practices were relaxed but not eliminated after the civil war. Not every instruction involved heavy work. The central party leadership tried to engage the minds of people by organising great ceremonies and putting on state festivals. May Day and the October Revolution anniversary became holidays when the heroes of revolutionary communism could be celebrated. Parades took place across Red Square.

Yet a vast amount of economic ownership and regulation survived the civil war. Although trade in agricultural produce was liberalised and small industrial enterprises were transferred back into private ownership in 1921–2, the 'commanding heights of the economy' – large-scale industry, banking and foreign trade – remained in the state's possession. The communists hated having to denationalise enterprises. But, compared with every other country at the time or in the past, the USSR had an economy heavily controlled by its central political leadership.

The main features of the Soviet order were in place by the early 1920s. The USSR was a one-party, one-ideology centralised state deploying terror to thwart resistance and to indoctrinate and mobilise its people. This order mutated in subsequent years and the most complete model of the order had yet to be constructed. The party remained more fractious in reality than official policy demanded. The Cheka's resources were restricted and its repressive functions were somewhat moderated with the inception of the NEP. Religion was openly practised. Age-old peasant customs were left undisturbed. Whole sectors of economic activity were released from state ownership. The country's general condition served to limit what the communists could do. Administrative linkages still bore the damage of the civil war. Communications were shaky, and Russia and its borderlands remained underprovided in roads, telephones, radios and literate officials. Whenever the Politburo looked at reports from the 'localities', its members regularly learned that its grip on society left much to be desired. The communist party was a cork bobbing on a sea of indifference, resentment and opposition.

Yet the Reds had invented a state order which provided the basis of Soviet rule for another seventy years. They had done this without a grand plan. Even so, their early doctrines pushed them in the direction they had taken. There had been many influences at work. Marx and Engels had been important, as had the specificities of the Leninist interpretation of Marxism. Russian traditions fed parts of this interpretation. So did the experience of Bolsheviks in their struggle against the Imperial monarchy. Several Bolshevik leaders had been positively impressed by Germany's centralised war economy from 1914. Coming to power with this bundle of ideas, they encountered a situation they had not expected, and the ensuing difficulties at home and abroad compelled them to think up practical solutions. Their instinct was to force the pace of developments down a line which led towards the Soviet one-party, one-ideology state. Despite not having intended this specific result, they very much liked what they had done. Their invention would be clamped down like a steel hood over other countries undergoing communisation in the decades ahead.

PART TWO

EXPERIMENT

1917–1929

7. EUROPEAN REVOLUTIONS

The Bolsheviks had never aimed to restrict themselves to action in Russia and its borderlands. Their seizure of power, they proclaimed, had inaugurated 'the epoch of European revolution' and what they were doing in Russia would soon be repeated elsewhere. At least, this was their belief. If they had thought differently, they would not have made their revolution. Russian socialists who disagreed with their assessment of revolutionary prospects in Europe belonged to parties such as the Mensheviks and Socialist-Revolutionaries. When Kamenev and Zinoviev poked holes in Lenin's international predictions before the October Revolution, Lenin denounced them as 'strike-breakers' who had betrayed their comrades and the world proletariat.

The Bolshevik party had sanctioned the treaty of Brest-Litovsk with reluctance in March 1918. But its leaders intended to assist fellow revolutionaries on the far political left as soon as they had the chance. It was their firm belief that the great states of the continent were ripe for fundamental change. The Bolshevik party waited and hoped for Germany to be defeated because this would increase the chances of revolution in central Europe – and if the Germans won the Great War, they would have torn up the Brest-Litovsk treaty and overthrown the Bolsheviks in Russia. But when the Allies forced the German surrender in November 1918, the Bolsheviks were preoccupied by the civil war with the Whites. Agents, literature and money were hurried to Germany; but the assistance was nothing in comparison with what Lenin had wanted to supply. Since summer he had been building up the Red Army and Soviet grain stocks with a view to aiding revolution in central Europe if and when German military power collapsed.[1] When the German armed forces surrendered, he was helpless to put his plan into effect. In fact a government of social-democrats led by Friedrich Ebert and Gustav Noske assumed power in Berlin. Its ministers had a record of support for the German cause in the Great War. Moscow assumed that they would be no more able to survive than Kerenski's cabinet in Russia in 1917.

The German collapse on the western front caught most people by surprise. But the political far left was prepared. Karl Liebknecht cabled Moscow with the news about the fall of the monarchy in Berlin: 'The revolution of the German proletariat has begun. This revolution will save the Russian revolution from all attack and will sweep away all the foundations of the imperialist world.'[2] Liebknecht was a leading comrade of Rosa Luxemburg and Leo Iogiches in the Spartacus League, which they had formed out of disgust with the German Social-Democratic Party's support for the national war effort. The Spartacists were looking for revolutionary action. Their manifesto announced: 'The question today is not democracy or dictatorship. The question that history has put on the agenda reads: bourgeois democracy or socialist democracy.' On 29 December they brought together their followers in the Spartacus League for the founding congress of the German Communist Party. On 1 January 1919 they 'organised' a rising in Berlin. They may have had a readiness of the intellect; they utterly lacked the aptitude for practical planning. Luxemburg did nothing to halt the enterprise, despite her well-founded doubts. The government turned to the unofficial Freikorps units eager to take vengeance on enemies of the patriotic spirit. The insurrection was a débâcle. Its leaders were hunted down and Luxemburg's corpse was dumped outside the Zoological Gardens.[3]

The communists in Hungary were more fortunate. The November 1918 armistice delivered a terminal blow to the Habsburg monarchy, and the great multinational state fell apart. Hungary claimed its independence in advance of the peace settlement about to be imposed by the victor powers. A provisional government was established in Budapest under Count Mihály Károlyi. Hungarians were ruling Hungary without interference from foreigners. The cabinet faced huge problems in keeping public order and maintaining food supplies; it stood no chance of success once the Allies' intention to effect a severe reduction of Hungarian territory became public knowledge[4] – and the communists, few though they were, gained prominence for opposing what was being planned. National opinion was deeply offended by the plan to reduce Hungary to a third of its previous size by transfers of land to Romania, Czechoslovakia and Yugoslavia. The economic devastation made things worse. Károlyi stepped down with his cabinet on 20 March 1919. This was the day when the French authorities delivered their note demanding the further withdrawal of Hungarian troops and made his position untenable. Károlyi had intended a government of social-democrats to take over. Next day, however, he learned that the social-democrats had done a deal with the communists to form a coalition: both parties were determined to resist the humiliating peace terms being prepared by the Allies.[5]

Although the social-democrats had taken the initiative, Béla Kun and the communists provided the continuing impetus. Hungary was about to be enveloped in a storm of revolution. Under the umbrella of a leftist political coalition, the Hungarian Communist Party was resolute in its ambition to make an impact. If any communist revolutionary lost his senses in government it was Béla Kun. Lenin took months to open wide the gates of his Red Terror; Kun unlocked them on his first day of power. Son of a Jewish notary, he had drifted into journalism and political militancy before being conscripted into the Austro-Hungarian army in the First World War. The Russians took him prisoner in 1916. He was released when the Bolsheviks seized power, and quickly offered his services to them as a Hungarian-language propagandist. The Bolshevik party had sent him back into Hungary after the military collapse of the Central Powers in November 1918. His hatred of the old regime was ferocious. The burning fires were stoked by his experience on returning to Budapest. He was arrested and beaten up by his jailers. On release he still bore the scars on his head.[6] His optimism was undiminished. Kun's admiration for the Soviet order as it had been developing in the civil war was boundless. Short and stocky, he wanted to be Hungary's Lenin.

'Communism', he said to visitors from the American Relief Administration in July 1919, 'seems to me practically obtainable in the course of time and we shall ultimately have it. The system is going better in Hungary all the time.'[7] He made this claim when famine, administrative chaos and corruption had never been greater and popular resistance to his government was intense. Kun's solution was for the Allies to lift their economic blockade and send across raw materials for the country's regeneration. In the same breath he indicated a wish to form a communist league with Austria, Bohemia, Germany, Italy and Russia. He surely knew capitalist powers would not find this attractive. Then came another feint: 'I am myself a socialist rather than a communist from the standpoint of present policy.' He suggested that he had only allowed his party to call itself communist so as to distinguish it from German right-wing social-democrats like Philipp Scheidemann.[8] If he thought this smoke-and-mirrors act would confuse the American officials, he was fooling himself. With other visitors he got away with it. For example, he told an inquisitive Englishwoman, Alice Riggs Hunt, that the government had released its many hostages without harm – and Hunt repeated this falsehood on her return to London.[9]

Hungarian communists had an eye for image and style. The red flag was run up over the Imperial palace. The Grand Hotel Hungaria, where the families of the People's Commissars were housed, was renamed the Soviet House.[10] Appeals were made to workers and poor peasants in speeches, posters and leaflets. Béla Kun and the young Mátyás Rákosi were remarkable orators. They announced the termination of the capitalist period in Budapest. Everyone was called 'comrade'. Porters and concierges were instructed to refuse tips and to tell foreign travellers that they were already adequately paid. Housewives were officially recognised as an integral section of the working class. The cinemas and theatres were taken out of private hands. Ninety per cent of the tickets were given to the trade unions for distribution among their members; performances were brought forward to five o'clock in the afternoon so that workers could enjoy them at the end of their shifts.[11]

Communist propaganda was a fantasy: the real conditions in Hungary were dreadful. Although Kun was right that most people wanted social and economic change, they did not endorse the extremism of the Budapest Soviet. The last thing they wanted was a civil war, and few could understand why dictatorship should be imposed once the Habsburg regime had been dismantled. The proclamation of a Soviet republic had put Hungary into quarantine. The Allies enforced an economic blockade. Kun's troops increased the isolation by firing on ships passing up and down the Danube.[12] The Americans would have been happy to see Allied forces topple Kun but thought this should be done by European armies without their help. French commander Marshal Foch considered he would need 350,000 troops, and this was not politically feasible at the time. An American food-relief official opined that 'a battalion and a bugle under the Stars and Stripes' would be enough.[13] Hungary was left to itself. The British and French appeared to have hoped that an internal counter-revolution would quickly arise and bring Bolshevism in Budapest to an end.

Hungarian communists wished to induce revolutionary ferment across the Hungarian border. Vienna already effervesced with political conflict. The Austrian security agencies claimed to have discovered Kun's secret plan for the occupation of Vienna.[14] There was in fact no such plan, but Austria's government had reason for general concern. Moreover, far-left socialist organisations operated in Italy and Czechoslovakia.

The Western Allies were worried that the revolutionary contagion might spread its spores to them. Kun himself sent some of his forces into Slovakia, where a large Hungarian minority lived. He was looking out for any chance to expand the zone of trouble for the Allies. Close wireless contact was kept with Lenin in Moscow and Trotski on campaign, and Kun begged them to send him forces from the Red Army in Ukraine.[15] (Little did Kun know that the Americans based in Vienna were picking up his messages.)[16] If the Red Army had not still been embroiled in the USSR's own civil war, the Bolsheviks would undoubtedly have deployed it to Kun's assistance.[17] But Lenin would also have brought Kun to heel: he saw no point in policies which caused avoidable resistance. This was the pot calling the kettle black. Lenin could evidently more easily identify foreign communist 'adventurism' than he could his own, and this continued to be the case in respect of Soviet advice to other countries after his death.[18]

Food shortages in Hungary grew worse. Industrial activity plummeted as owners of coal mines and textile factories were dispossessed and finance for post-war reconstruction disappeared. Land reform pleased the peasants who took possession of their landlords' property. But they hated being compelled to hand over whatever stocks of produce they had left after the long winter of 1918–19; they also resented Kun's decision to turn the big landed estates into collective farms. Rebellions proliferated. The revolutionary government reacted by intensifying mass terror. Tibor Szamuely formed a squad called the Lenin Boys and marched out to subdue the rural rebellions; his repressive extravagance appalled even Kun.[19]

The underlying difficulty for Kun was the international situation. In April the Hungarian forces, commanded by Habsburg officers under the scrutiny of political commissars, threw back the invading Romanians and Czechs.[20] Kun marched Czech prisoners through the streets of the capital to show off the regime's military effectiveness.[21] He resumed the campaign against the Romanians in July. Kun was impressed by the orderliness of the general staff, which he compared favourably with the Red Army in Russia. But when he complained about nationalist talk, he was firmly told that conscripts would fight only under the national flag and not under the red flag of communism.[22] By then he was so desperate that he backed down. But this made no difference. Romanian troops seized the northern territories of the already reduced Hungarian state. Peasant revolts distracted the Red forces. Urban discontent with communist abuses and inefficiency mounted. The Romanians continued their advance, occupying Budapest on 4 August. They stripped the country of flour, sugar, medicine and railway equipment, and the result was famine.[23] Only political intervention by the Western Allies saved Hungary from perdition. The Hungarian Soviet Republic collapsed in blood and ignominy.

Kun scuttled off to Austria and eventual sanctuary in Soviet Russia. Szamuely was less lucky, being shot in flight at the Austrian border. Known communists were rounded up and executed in a White terror started by the Romanians and completed by the Hungarian government headed by Admiral Miklós Horthy. Kun had lasted only 133 days in power.

This was longer than the leaders of the Bavarian Soviet Republic managed. Munich, Bavaria's capital, shared in the national humiliation, mass unemployment and food shortages experienced by Germany immediately after the war. The situation was aggravated by uncertainty about the peace treaty about to be imposed. There was talk about Germany being broken up and Bavaria being made either an independent state or somehow amalgamated with Austria. Strikes, demonstrations and workers' elected councils (*Räte*) spread to Munich with its large industrial base. From November 1918 the Prime Minister was Kurt Eisner, Jewish theatre critic and leader of the Independent German Social-Democratic Party in Bavaria. Eisner danced between the factions in his party; and although he gave private assurances that he would hold out against communist-style measures, he was widely detested in other political circles as a Red extremist.[24] On 21 February 1919 a young aristocrat of the far right assassinated him. The result was tumult on the streets of Munich. The Workers' Council, established weeks earlier, resolved to assume power. Eisner's death removed the last obstacle to the surge of the local communists on power. A Bavarian Soviet Republic was proclaimed on 7 April.

The communist leader was a certain Max Levien, who became even more widely detested than Eisner. Levien, like several in the leadership of the Bavarian Soviet Republic, came from a Jewish family. Unusually, though, he had not lived in Germany most of his life. He had been brought up in Russia, leaving for central Europe in 1906 when things got hot for revolutionary militants. While studying zoology in Zürich, he stayed in touch with far-left politics.[25] He greeted the October Revolution in Russia with enthusiasm. He and his political partner Eugen Leviné had opposed German participation in the Great War and despised the German Social-Democratic Party. They dreamed of setting up a Soviet republic in Bavaria. The opportunity to make a socialist revolution came to them suddenly, and they aimed to emulate Lenin in seizing their chances. Like the Bolsheviks, they were adept at issuing proclamations. The bearing of arms by anyone but the men of the Workers' Council was prohibited. Large factories were taken into state ownership. Levien cabled Moscow with the good news that revolution in the German lands had broken out, and Lenin sent his congratulations in reply. The 'European socialist revolution' had apparently started in the country predicted for the event.

Yet although Munich had some heavy industry and a large working class, it also possessed plenty of people who hated communism. Antisemitism was strong among the Catholic clergy, the urban middle class and the peasantry. Papal nuncio Eugenio Pacelli, later to become Pope Pius XII, recorded seeing 'a gang of young women of dubious appearance, Jews like all the rest of them ... with provocative demeanour and suggestive smiles'; he noted that Levien was 'a young man, about thirty or thirty-five, also Russian and a Jew. Pale, dirty, with vacant eyes, hoarse voice, vulgar, repulsive, with a face that is both intelligent and sly.'[26] Pacelli was expressing the conventional anti-communist attitude of his time. Communists for him were filthy Jewish fanatics. Munich had to be cleansed of them.

Levien and his comrades seemed no less likely to consolidate their power than the improbable Bolsheviks of 1917 in Russia. They were drawn from the usual professions, journalism being a favourite trade. They contained several outstanding orators and, in the case of Ernst Toller, a prominent writer. They were fired up by confidence that history was on their side. They declared that the military, economic and religious authorities of the Imperial regime were co-responsible for the deaths of millions of their fellow countrymen. They saw the 'proletariat' of the Bavarian capital as more than adequate to rise to the challenge posed by the counter-revolutionary forces. But in other respects they, like Béla Kun, fell a long way short of Lenin's Bolsheviks. Their revolutionary steel had not been tempered by decades of state persecution and 'underground' political activity. They had not been tested for psychological and physical hardness when the going got rough. Their organisational networks were new and frail; their objectives for Bavaria's future were cloudy. They had slight links with socialists elsewhere in Germany and Austria. They readily assumed that if a speech were well received at a workers' meeting the tasks of making revolution would be rather simple and easy.

Unemployment spread. The crime rate soared after the release of common criminals from prison. The Council leadership grabbed supreme economic authority. It shut all Munich's shops – this meant that when Leviné went to buy flowers for his wife he found the florist's closed.[27] The mixture of ruthlessness, incompetence and dottiness continued after Levien and Leviné had shunted the impractical Toller out of the way. Toller did not mind; he donned a soldier's uniform and announced his willingness to die in the ranks under their leadership: he loved the grand gesture.[28] Foreign Minister Dr Lipp tried to borrow sixty rail locomotives from Switzerland. When the Swiss authorities turned him down, Lipp declared war on Switzerland. Meanwhile Levien and Leviné ordered the formation of a Red Army and tried to strengthen ties with Soviet Hungary and Soviet Russia.[29]

They stood little chance of success. Freikorps units had gathered in Bamberg in northern Bavaria. The German government in Berlin sought an end to the Soviet Republic and Gustav Noske, its Defence Minister, had already turned a blind eye to military excesses against the Spartacists.[30] When regular troops reached Munich in May there was news of a massacre of ten hostages at the hands of Council supporters. Retaliation was brutal. Officially six hundred communists and their sympathisers were killed, but this was probably about half the real number. Levien succeeded in escaping. Leviné, however, stood at his post despite knowing that further resistance was hopeless. At his trial he declared: 'We communists are all dead men on leave.'[31] Toller, who passed the time by issuing an open letter 'to the young people of all lands',[32] got off with a lengthy term of imprisonment. Noske's use of both his regular forces and the armed units of the political far right had proved highly effective. The Bavarian Soviet Republic had been a botched adventure from start to finish. When Russian communists discovered how Levien and Leviné had behaved there was no eagerness in Moscow to commemorate them as revolutionary heroes.

Sputterings of revolt started to occur at the same time in northern Italy. Factories in Turin and Milan were hotbeds of far-left agitation. Strikes and political demonstrations brought production to a halt. The Italian Socialist Party was being torn apart by factional disputes and the radicals were drawn towards splitting off to form their own communist party. This duly occurred in 1921. Among the advocates of revolutionary action was the young Sardinian militant Antonio Gramsci. Like his comrades, he was attracted by what he heard about the October Revolution. Gramsci edited *L'Ordine Nuovo* ('The New Order') in Turin. He welcomed the factory councils elected by workers in the city from summer 1919 through to 1920. It looked as if northern Italy would follow the path just taken by Hungary and Bavaria – and perhaps with greater success for communism.

By then the civil war in Russia was over and Lenin wanted to exploit every opportunity to induce the 'European socialist revolution'. Military conflict between Polish and Soviet forces had occurred sporadically throughout 1919. Borders and states had yet to be stabilised east of Warsaw. The Peace Conference in Paris confined itself to decisions which could readily be imposed. The treaties of Versailles, St Germain, Trianon and Sèvres between June 1919 and August 1920 decided the fate of the lands of the German Empire, the Habsburg Monarchy and the Ottoman Empire. Russo-Polish relations were in any case outside the terms of reference of the Paris Conference. Polish army commander Józef Piłsudski, who already dominated his country's politics, itched to make Poland more secure by forming a federation with Ukraine. This naturally required preliminary conquest. After one of the recurrent clashes in the borderlands in spring 1920 he announced this ambition and committed his troops to action. Success was immediate. On 7 May his troops entered Kiev. The movement of Polish forces was so rapid that Red Army soldiers were surprised at bus stops as they waited to go into work. The Reds, however, recovered and picked up recruits from many Russians and Ukrainians – including former Imperial officers – who were stirred by the call to repel the traditional national enemy. Piłsudski beat a retreat, his dream of expansion in tatters.[33]

Lenin was cockahoop. At last, he believed, he could begin a 'revolutionary war'. Ever since the treaty of Brest-Litovsk he had promised that if ever the Red Army was strong enough he would hurl it westwards. The purpose would be political revolution, not territorial conquest. He had Germany and not just Poland in his sights. Lenin faced down those of his comrades who doubted that Red forces were strong enough. They included leaders who, unlike him, had military experience. Inside the Politburo both Trotski and Stalin demurred. But they were on military campaign and distant from Moscow, whereas Lenin held the levers of power in the Kremlin. He cajoled everyone into acceptance of his vision. Red commanders and political commissars on active service, however, were soon brutally disillusioned. The Polish workers and peasants failed to rise up against their factory owners, priests and landlords and rallied instead to Piłsudski. The Reds meanwhile pursued a confused strategy, which was made worse by Stalin's obstreperousness. They were pulled up short of Warsaw and went down to defeat at the battle of the Vistula. This was not the only reason for communist dispiritedness. The Italian government suppressed the Turin rebels before they could seize the city. Gramsci and his comrades remained at liberty, but their revolution was over before it began. Communism had been crushed at both ends of Europe.

The frame of Lenin's geopolitical perspective had been shattered. He was seldom one to confess to mistakes, but on this occasion he forced out a semi-apology. (At the same time he let Stalin take the brunt of the blame!)[34] It was all very different from a few weeks earlier when the two of them had confidently considered how best to organise the European states after their 'sovietisation'. Lenin had planned to expand the Soviet federation westwards so as to cover Poland, Germany and the other 'liberated' lands of the continent. Stalin, despite having travelled little abroad, thought this implausible. He could not imagine Germans or Poles feeling comfortable inside a state founded and run by Russians. His solution was to create two vast, fraternal federations, led by Soviet Russia and Soviet Germany. The usual duel by telegrams ensued. Lenin shot at Stalin's scheme for abandoning genuine internationalism; Stalin fired backed that Lenin underestimated German national sensitivities.[35]

The foreign policy of Soviet Russia changed abruptly in autumn 1920. Peace was sought with Poland and a treaty was signed in Riga in March 1921. Lenin told his party that the Red Army for the foreseeable future would not try to export revolution at the point of a bayonet. Russia's communists were lucky. France and the United Kingdom had ruled out military action against Soviet Russia from the end of 1919. Paris and London faced daunting tasks of economic recovery and would have stirred up the opposition of their own socialist parties and trade unions if they had instigated an anti-Soviet crusade. There was dissent beyond that point. France resented Soviet action in unilaterally annulling the debts contracted by the governments of Nicholas II and Alexander Kerenski. Prime Minister Georges Clemenceau stated that the French would block any rapprochement with Moscow until its financial responsibilities were honoured. The British government, however, was being pushed by industrial and commercial circles to resume trade with Russia.[36] This suited Prime Minister David Lloyd George, who believed that Soviet fanaticism would be sedated by a dose of capitalism ingested through foreign trade. An Anglo-Soviet trade treaty was signed in London in March 1921 and Lenin had to promise to desist from spreading subversive propaganda in the British Empire.[37] In return the

USSR would be able to breach the walls of its isolation and regenerate its shattered economy. Until such time as 'capitalist stabilisation' was over and a 'revolutionary situation' recurred in Europe, this was the best that Lenin and Trotski felt they could hope for.

The British government, yielding to French pressure, rejected deeper reconciliation with Russia at the Genoa Conference in April 1922. Lenin told Georgi Chicherin as External Affairs People's Commissar to seek out a deal with Germany. This was done in the utmost secrecy a few miles down the coast at Rapallo. (Actually the hotel where they met was up the coast in well-heeled Santa Margherita.) There the two black sheep of the European flock – the USSR and the Weimar Republic – signed a treaty. Its terms publicly promoted large-scale trade and confidentially provided Germany with the opportunity to conduct secret military training on Soviet soil. This was not the geostrategic outcome previously expected by the Bolsheviks. But it was better than some alternatives. The Soviet Republic could get on with political consolidation and economic recovery. Yet communists in Russia and Europe still trusted that 'European socialist revolution' would happen in their lifetimes.

Béla Kun was up to his tricks in Berlin in early 1921, just weeks before the treaties were signed with Poland and Britain. He had been sent there, apparently without Lenin's knowledge, with instructions from Zinoviev and Radek that remain obscure. What is clear is that on arrival he agitated for an uprising by German communists against the government. Fresh from conducting a massacre of amnestied White officers in Crimea, Kun overrode sensible objections by German comrades Clara Zetkin and Paul Levi to his insurrectionary summons. His hallmarks were on display: rhetorical bravado, haphazard planning and complete self-delusion. The uprising in the last days of March was unsupported by Berlin's 'proletariat' and was swiftly suppressed by police and army: 145 insurrectionaries were killed. Kun fled back to Moscow and to Lenin's stern judgement.[38] Across Europe the embers of the revolutionary conflagration faded. Yet Lenin and his comrades did not give up. They believed that the 'Versailles system', which meant for them the entire settlement of international affairs by the Paris Peace Conference, had transmitted germs of disruption to European affairs – and they assumed that Germany would sooner or later rise up against its 'enslavement'. Comintern was blamed for practical ineptitude and not for fundamental misjudgement.

A further attempt at a communist uprising was made in Germany on Zinoviev's orders in October 1923. Yet again the political assessment and revolutionary planning were woeful. Zinoviev entertained the pseudo-romantic idea of undertaking the action on the anniversary of the Bolshevik seizure, and it resulted in predictable failure. Probably he wanted to prove his insurrectionary credentials as the contest for the Lenin succession intensified. Stalin was the only Soviet leader to express scepticism about the scheme, but the reports of German working-class unrest won him over. The Politburo, including Trotski, supported the attempt.[39] The result, though, was again a disaster: police and army were more than a match for the insurgents. Lenin, if his health had allowed, would surely have emptied the lexicon of sarcasm on them for outdoing Kun in crass mismanagement. The communist fiascos of 1921 and 1923 in Germany had a single salutary consequence in Comintern: they demonstrated that revolutionary initiatives outside Russia had to be handled with extreme care for some time to come. This was a lesson bought with the blood of the working class in Hungary, Italy and Germany.

8. COMMUNISM AND ITS DISCONTENTS

The revolts against the Bolsheviks in 1920–1 had put a knife to the throat of Soviet communism. Workers, peasants, soldiers and sailors were furious with them. People were fed up with communist mobilisations and annoyed by forcible grain requisitioning; they were convinced that a fundamental change in the political system was necessary. The freedoms of the February Revolution were fondly remembered. Introduced in spring 1921, the NEP was the minimum concession necessary for the party's survival in power; any other government in Moscow would have granted a lot more.

Yet Lenin and the Politburo got away with it. The regime had superior force and co-ordination. It had reunited the country territorially or, as the Russians put it, had 'gathered the lands'. It also played on the fatalism of millions of people who had been oppressed for centuries. Brief explosions of popular rebellion had been separated by long intervals of sullen acquiescence in central political power. The authorities exploited this situation. Lenin was turned into an official hero. His health was frail after a heart attack in 1922. Preparing himself for an early death, he grew worried about who might succeed him. In his confidential testament he suggested that not one of his comrades was fit for the task. Picking out Trotski and Stalin as the likeliest winners, he criticised them for overdoing the administrative side of rulership. This was rank hypocrisy, coming from a leader who had plunged his country into a vat of dictatorship and terror. He feared that if Trotski and Stalin were to compete for the succession, the outcome could be a schism in the party. Confident in progress only when he was in personal control, Lenin did not think he was leaving structures and practices robust enough to endure without him.

He wrangled with Stalin from his sickbed, castigating him for wanting to weaken the state monopoly in foreign trade. He also charged that Stalin, despite being a Georgian, was acting like a 'Great Russian chauvinist' towards Georgia. It was his contention that Stalin as Party

General Secretary had used bureaucratic and authoritarian methods. The two men did not in fact disagree about fundamental questions. But Lenin had been angered by Stalin's offensive demeanour. Furthermore, he was mentally overwrought by his illness and by his annoyance that Stalin refused to show automatic obedience. He suggested that Stalin should be removed from the post of General Secretary.[1]

Dying on 21 January 1924, Lenin was cheated of his desire. His corpse became an object of veneration in a mausoleum constructed on Red Square in Moscow, and Stalin set himself up as chief celebrant in the new cult. Factional dispute erupted. There had already been trouble in the previous year when Trotski and the Left Opposition objected to the slowness of industrial investment growth under the NEP, as well as to the continuing 'bureaucratisation' of the party. The ascendant leadership of Zinoviev, Kamenev, Stalin and Bukharin rejected Trotski's case and deprived him of his important posts in government. But these same leaders quickly fell out among themselves. Zinoviev and Kamenev were unnerved by Stalin's rising power; they also believed that, as Trotski had been asserting, the Politburo was turning away from communist radicalism in Russia and abroad. Their Leningrad Opposition was crushed by Stalin and Bukharin. Zinoviev and Kamenev in panic reached out to Trotski and formed a United Opposition with him. But Stalin and Bukharin did not flinch. They packed party meetings with loyalists willing to heckle oppositionists. Fresh appointments of personnel were made on the basis of allegiance to the party line. The media were held tight in the grasp of the Politburo majority.

Lenin was proved right about the danger of a party split. He had been wrong, though, about how it would occur. His idea was that Trotski and Stalin would found competing movements of the working class and the peasantry. The reality was that neither Trotski nor Stalin roused a large number of supporters outside the party. Trotski tried his best, but the working class declined to respond to his appeal; Stalin used state violence to ensure that neither workers nor peasants would influence the course of events.

The factional conflict in the Russian Communist Party in the 1920s reached a climax never to be matched elsewhere. Foreign communist leaders, observing the history of the USSR, took precautions against things getting out of their control. But they could not avoid the Soviet experience in certain other ways. The Bolsheviks in Russia were the first communists to run into specific obstacles. One difficulty was the party's inadequate readiness for its revolutionary tasks. This should not have been a surprise.

Active Bolsheviks at the time of the February Revolution numbered a few thousand members at the most. The party grew immensely in subsequent months. Many of those new recruits, however, walked away from the communists after the October Revolution. Others died in the civil war. There was constant change in the party's composition, and the circumstances did not make it easy to spread the doctrines of Marxism. Practical tasks had a higher priority. Those who joined the party did not always distinguish themselves by their dedication to revolutionary ideals or even by their standards of literacy and numeracy. The regular surveys indicated that the 'cultural level' of the party gave grounds for concern.[2]

There were also unwelcome phenomena higher in the party. Many communist officials were new to Bolshevism, and the veterans in central and local leadership distrusted them and usually made crucial appointments from the small pool of 'old Bolsheviks'. This was done with thoroughness for postings to party committees. But there was a severe shortage of cadres; communists of recent vintage as well as non-communists (and, indeed, secret anti-communists) had to be given jobs in government and other public institutions. The central party leadership knew this and suppressed information about the depth of the problem for fear of stirring up criticism at party congresses. The spine of the Russian Communist Party was constituted by the men and women who had fought against the Romanov monarchy. They were a tiny section of a mass party which had yet to be turned into the kind of organisation they wanted. The party itself was a ship floating on an ocean of popular hostility; and almost as bad for the prospects of communism was the fact that most workers were apathetic about it at best. Communism, if it was to function successfully, needed an environment of enthusiasm. It never converted more than a minority to zeal for the revolutionary cause.

This is not to say that communists in the USSR entirely lacked support outside the party. Many people had come to see the Bolsheviks as modernisers and even as patriots. At last, seemingly, there was a ruling elite with an unconditional commitment to economic and cultural competitiveness at the global level. The Change of Waymarks group emerged among Nikolai Ustryalov and fellow Russian émigrés across the Siberian border in China's northern city of Harbin; they took the line that the Bolsheviks were evolving away from their original fanaticism.[3] Ustryalov praised Lenin and his comrades for 'gathering the lands' of the old empire and imposing order where, from 1917, there had been chaos.

The group's members also believed that the communist party was removing the old obstacles to talented individuals rising up the ladder of state and society. The Bolsheviks were widely regarded as meritocrats. Unlike their rivals, they had the ruthlessness and competence to realise their purposes. Their predilection for economic planning commended itself to many observers as a sign that the Soviet Union – or Russia in its latest manifestation – would successfully harness its energies and direct its resources towards turning the country again into a great European and Asian power. Even people who had never heard of the Change of Waymarks group hoped that such an analysis was correct.

Communist leaders themselves worried about the trends in their party and gathered information about them. According to a 1923 survey of the Petrograd city organisation, 60 per cent of its party members were 'politically illiterate' and only 8 per cent were conversant with Marxism.[4] Such exactitude demonstrated an earnestness about assembling pointless data – everyone in the country knew this without the need for laborious surveys. The party lost and gained members for the wrong reasons. Recruits walked out when they discovered that communism was not fulfilling the genuine idealism of earlier years. The opposite phenomenon was equally strong: recruits were joining the party because they hoped to improve conditions for themselves and their families; careerism was an ineradicable difficulty.

Most workers had never wanted anything to do with the communist party. Much hostility or apathy had been noted before the October Revolution but the Bolsheviks had assumed that their policies would change this.[5] They were wrong. Physical exhaustion and political annoyance with Bolshevism became acute. Dissenting communist groupings such as Workers' Truth strove to galvanise the discontent into a solid anti-regime force. The Cheka quickly broke up each successive attempt. But the working class remained sullen and hostile in factories and mines. Stoppages of production continued through the 1920s. Party and police recognised that blatant repression might make things worse, and they took to bargaining with strike leaders. The plan was to keep a lid on the trouble and localise it. Strikers were promised improved conditions and higher wages; their leaders were guaranteed immunity from punitive sanctions. This usually did the trick. Once the workers had given up and returned to their jobs, the Cheka snatched those who had fomented the challenge to the authorities. The idea was that regular decapitation of militancy would produce a compliant workforce.[6]

Political demonstrations against the communist order did not take place in the capital or other cities; the authorities had kept a grip on things since 1921. Yet trouble never truly disappeared. It was only exacerbated by the utopian promises made by the communist party. A workers' paradise had been predicted. No one living in the degraded urban landscape or labouring in the shattered factories after the civil war could believe that this was likely to be created in the near future. The party went on professing a commitment to 'proletarian self-activity'. This concept was never properly defined but everyone knew it implied some kind of governance by and for the proletariat. The reality was starkly different: the party and the Cheka dominated politics. Official exhortations to drop restrictive practices at work and to 'rationalise' production were a cause of exasperation to most people. Communist functionaries strutted around. The penchant of many of them for black leather jackets and boots – not to mention their habitual homilies on the omniscience of Marxism-Leninism – grated on the 'toiling masses'. Bolsheviks were more intrusive than had ever been the case with officialdom before 1917. Decrees came down from on high. Moscow ruled.

Yet the working class was not battered into total submission. The ill-discipline on the job that had characterised workplaces since after the February Revolution was never eradicated. The sanctions of unconditional capitalism were absent and the regime could hardly threaten the workforce with sacking if it wanted to be a beacon of socialist achievement in the eyes of the world. Anyway, skilled workers and technicians were in short supply. Enterprise directors needed to keep them on the books.

The intelligentsia was another crucible of hostility to the communist rulers. Bolsheviks came to power with next to no party members who were active in the arts, taught in universities or conducted scientific research. Few intellectuals went over to communism in the civil war. The poet Vladimir Mayakovski was an exception – and even he committed suicide in April 1930. Not having had time to raise up a young generation of writers, painters, thinkers, technologists and scientists of its own, the party settled for reaching out to 'fellow travellers' (as the sympathisers of the Soviet regime were known). Trotski and Zinoviev promoted the policy. In return for limited freedom of expression and a comfortable lifestyle, individuals had to avoid criticising Bolshevik policies. The inducement was hard to resist. Private facilities for publication and research were exiguous in the 1920s and opportunities to flee abroad dried up as the security police sealed the frontiers. Failure to co-operate with the authorities meant self-administered hardship.[7] Many intellectuals in fact developed a degree of sympathy with communism, especially because it advocated education, science and industry. Perhaps, they also thought, the communist state would moderate its repressive proclivities. They shared the Change of Waymarks group's hope that Politburo leaders would turn out to be civilised modernisers. Certain Bolsheviks such as Kamenev and Bukharin were thought to represent the more malleable side of Marxism-Leninism.

The Bolshevik party meanwhile allowed some cultural experimentalism. A classical orchestra was formed which denied the need for a conductor. This was approved as an attempt to align musical performance with an orientation towards 'collectivism' and 'mass activity'. Mayakovski produced his 'futurist' poetry with the party's approval (even though Trotski had to have its principles explained to him and Lenin simply hated it). Marc Chagall set up a painting school in Vitebsk – and his willingness to reach out to the workers as his pupils helped to gain the resources he needed to go on creating his mystical pictures of fiddlers, cows and comely young women in the Jewish towns of the former Pale of Settlement. Yet generally the intellectuals resented being humbled. Persecuted in Imperial Russia, they had been regarded as an 'alternative government' by emperor and people alike. They had surmounted censorship by using indirect ways of criticising the state order. In 1917 they had had a brief few months when they could say, write or paint whatever they liked. The wish to function as the conscience of society remained. They objected to the communist eagerness to rule on what types of art and science should and could exist. It was not only the artistic and scholarly intelligentsia which jibbed at these conditions. Engineers, teachers, librarians and doctors hated the intrusion of the state into their professional business. The bossy commissar was a figure of contempt among them.

Disgruntlement rose at the sight of the kind of people who flourished during the NEP. The security agencies had repressed the old middle classes in the civil war. Bankers, big industrialists and mine-owners had been eliminated; they now appeared only as bugaboos in Soviet cartoons. The quintessential entrepreneur in the 1920s was the 'nepman' showing off his luxurious fur-coat, brandishing his expensive cigars and groping his latest floozy. Such individuals were usually petty traders who made their money by getting hold of products in scarce supply. Many had links to the criminal underworld and had to duck and dive so as to avoid the trammels of official investigators. The Cheka made frequent raids on their shops and stalls. Yet really it was they who made the commercial cogwheels whirr after the civil war. If the nepmen were to be systematically suppressed, the NEP would fall apart. Workers, however, asked how this was reconcilable with Marxism-Leninism. The USSR was meant to be a 'proletarian state' and not a breeding bowel for 'parasites'. The kind of capitalism prevalent in the 1920s was represented by spivs, crooks and fly-by-nights. Party officials shared the popular unease about them.

Communists were equally suspicious of the better-off peasants. These were stigmatised as kulaks ('fists') who held the rest of the peasantry tight in their grasp. They exploited the other households of their village by buying or renting their land and by hiring them as labourers. The Bolsheviks saw them as capitalists in the making. The landed gentry had long since departed; traditional peasant-style cultivation was universal except for the few state-owned collective farms. But communal land ownership did not prevent some peasants getting richer through the return of the commercial economy.[8]

Bolsheviks hated the market economy both in principle and in practice. They failed to appreciate its growing success in introducing new techniques of cultivation. At the same time they were correct in sensing that the longer the NEP lasted, the further the villages slid away from the objectives of Marxism-Leninism. Soviet communism was never going to be implanted in the minds of the peasantry without fresh measures. The wealth of peasants in the USSR by the yardstick of the rich capitalist countries was no wealth at all. In some parts of the country, indeed, there was no chance of profit from agriculture. The Russian north was poor in soil and harsh in climate. The Bolsheviks felt they had an answer to this. They had always believed that the future lay with the 'industrialisation' of Soviet agriculture. Tractors were almost unknown to inhabitants of the rural areas, including to those designated as kulaks. (This, of course, was still true in regions of Europe and North America.) Small fields, wooden ploughs and horses had been used for centuries. The technology of the advanced West had to be incorporated in new collective farms. The land had to be taken away from the peasantry. The enemies of communism in the countryside had to be defeated. Their consolidation since 1921 had to be undone.

Tied to the party's concerns about economic and social developments in the 1920s was an acute worry about the 'national question'. The policy of concessions to the non-Russians in schooling, publishing and recruitment backfired spectacularly. Nationalists, to the Politburo's annoyance, were taking advantage. The conservative historian Mykhaylo Hrushevsky gave lectures in Kiev explaining the chronic mistreatment of the Ukrainians at the hands of the Russian Imperial state. Georgian and Armenian bishops as well as Azeri imams told their congregations how badly their forebears had suffered in the recent past. Such individuals barely concealed their anti-Soviet feelings. The OGPU, as the Cheka was known from 1924, regularly reported to the Politburo on the unsettling effects of religious fervour on the country's communisation. The problems of dissent did not end at the Soviet frontiers. Traffic of people and goods continued despite official prohibitions. It was not insuperably difficult for individuals to travel abroad without being stopped at customs posts. This was a two-way problem. Poles, Turks and Chinese gained entry to the USSR. The Poles were a bugbear for the central party leadership. The fear was that Poland's ruler Józef Piłsudski was sending agents into Ukraine to foment trouble. Supposedly they could slip unnoticed into the sizeable Polish communities of Soviet citizens in the republic.[9]

A more insidious cause for worry was to be found in the communist party itself. Bolshevik officials, especially at the lower levels, quietly gave preferment to their co-nationals. The communists after the October Revolution recruited frantically in the borderlands of the former Russian Empire. In some cases the recruitment was collective in nature. Because the party was weak in Ukraine and its leaders and militants who originated from there tended to be Jews, Poles or Russians, Lenin in 1919 had recourse to inducting the Borotbist Party as a whole into the ranks. The Borotbists were a radical Socialist-Revolutionary organisation dedicated to the peasant cause. Ukraine was overwhelmingly an agrarian country and most Borotbists were Ukrainians. Lenin argued that there was nothing for it but to bring them into the Russian Communist Party and use them as an instrument for the spreading of socialism.[10] In the south Caucasus there was a similar difficulty. In Azerbaijan the central party leadership in desperation was willing to recruit left-leaning imams to the revolutionary cause. The newcomers to Bolshevism were given high posts in their public life of their region.[11] This was the reality of the policy to 'root' the party in the localities (*korenizatsiya*). Bolshevism was becoming a secular church of the willing; it was seeking to evangelise by means of compromises which would have seemed unimaginable before October 1917.

Social traditions, especially in the frontier areas, were reinforced. The political system was riddled with the practices of patronage. Each patron, once in post, promoted his clients. Crony communism was on the rise. This sometimes had a basis in family networks as ways were found to give jobs to relatives and friends regardless of their professional qualifications. What is more, party bosses distant from supervisory control by the Kremlin packed their administration with loyal followers. Loyalty was demanded first to the republic, region or city and only then to the Kremlin. The neat vertical line of command and obedience set out in the Bolshevik textbooks was constantly interrupted. The phenomenon was not peculiar to the 'borderlands'. It was observable throughout the USSR, being as strong in Moscow as in the smallest township or village.

This situation was to prove common to societies subsequently undergoing communisation. In country after country in the years ahead a similar pattern of disgruntlement and non-compliance with the objectives and practices of the revolutionary government was to the fore; and knowledge was accumulated in advance of revolutions about the intensity of hostility to communism likely to occur. Communists came to power in eastern Europe, China, Cuba and other parts of the world aware of the difficulties awaiting them. The difficulties in the USSR – the setbacks, the frustrations, the tricky calculations and the dangers – were openly discussed in the 1920s: they were not kept secret from Comintern. What happened in Russia after October 1917, however, had caught Lenin and his Bolsheviks by surprise. They recoiled at first and then reconsidered how best to deal with the situation. Soviet leaders tried to tell themselves that they were merely dealing with 'remnants from the past'. They appreciated as good Marxists that 'consciousness' lags behind objective change in political and social conditions. They could not expect to win over many priests, landlords or bankers to the cause of the revolutions. Those 'former people' (*byvshye lyudi*), as they were chillingly called, were bound to be a thorn in the party's flesh.

For a while the communists expected the difficulties to fade away as the generations of people who had lived under the Russian Empire died off. They also tried to hurry forward a solution by campaigns of incarceration as well as indoctrination. Their experience, though, was already a clear indication that any communist party coming to power in the years ahead would have to prepare for revolution in a more sober spirit than Lenin and Trotski in 1917, Béla Kun in 1919 or Antonio Gramsci in 1920. Kun was in power too briefly to learn the lesson for himself. Gramsci never formed a revolutionary administration and in 1926 was thrown into one of Mussolini's prisons. The Soviet communist experience after the civil war, however, was applicable to communism in every country and at every time. Communists might seize power elsewhere and withstand attempts at political and military counter-revolution; yet they would still have to deal with the long haul of sullen hostility, quiet disobedience and obstruction that assailed the communist party in the USSR in the 1920s. The establishment of a one-party, one-ideology state would not by itself solve the problems. Such a state, indeed, would generate its own internal pressures. The history of the USSR in the 1930s was about to show that Stalin's alternative to the compromises of the NEP was riddled with problems of an equal weight.

9. THE COMMUNIST INTERNATIONAL

Among the few practical plans in Lenin's head when he seized power in Petrograd was one to establish a successor organisation to the Second International. He had talked about the need for a Third International throughout the Great War and this remained on his mind even after the treaty of Brest-Litovsk in March 1918. Yakov Sverdlov formed a small organising group working on a practical scheme in September 1918.[1] Invitations to Moscow had therefore been prepared even before the German military surrender two months later. Lenin and Trotski were in exalted mood. The founding Congress of the Third International realised Lenin's dream in March 1919. It was also known as the Communist International (or Comintern) to give a sharp signal that its purposes were more radical than those of the parties of the Second International. Fifty-two delegates arrived representing twenty-five countries. The 'European socialist revolution', they thought, was drawing near.

Communists aimed to split the worldwide socialist movement into two and bring the far left under their leadership. They themselves claimed that the objectives of socialism were unattainable without violent revolution and revolutionary dictatorship; they did not flinch at the possibility of civil war, foreign military intervention and terror. They scoffed at calls for multi-party elections and universal civil rights. They were determined to use coercion to eradicate religious, cultural and social traditions inimical to Marxism. They believed that they alone had the correct policies and regarded their enemies on the left as traitors to the cause. Their ambition was to foster the creation of communist parties in their own image around the globe. They shared many policies with the socialist, social-democratic and labour parties they despised. Common to them was a commitment to state economic ownership, a comprehensive welfare system, universal employment and an end to social privilege. All of them had once belonged to the same Socialist International. Some had been Marxists, others not. They had been held together by the belief that the future lay with political action of benefit to the working class – and they fervently believed that this would ultimately create a perfect earthly society.

But high walls now separated them. Communists wanted the kind of state which the enemies on the left thought the very antithesis of the socialist tradition. By renaming themselves the Russian Communist Party, the Bolsheviks had stressed the differences between themselves and the other socialists. Lenin's theoretical disquisitions had deepened the rift. 'Socialism' for him and the other Bolsheviks was an inferior stage to 'communism' in the future development of humankind. Yet Bolsheviks still called themselves socialists as well as communists. The result was that liberals and conservatives were able to tar the socialist parties of their countries as being indistinguishable from the communist parties. It was a confusion that lasted for decades.

Lenin was a masterful manipulator. Many delegates arrived in Moscow without any formal mandate from their party. Some spoke on behalf of parties which did not yet exist. A few already lived in the Soviet republic and were members of the same party as Lenin and subject to its discipline. Those socialists who hated communism were neither invited nor tempted to participate. The assumption was that all the world's potential member-parties would need to be represented before any gathering could be called a full congress. Lenin let the delegates think this until the opening session. He then announced that the gathering should designate itself as the founding congress. Rosa Luxemburg and Karl Liebknecht had suspected Lenin of plotting to build a Moscow-directed world organisation; they had seen what he had got up to in the Russian Social-Democratic Workers' Party before 1917 and knew about his methods.[2] If Luxemburg had attended, she would have made difficulties since she was a match for Lenin in debate. Her death in the Spartacist uprising removed this possibility. The German delegate who turned up in Moscow, Hugo Eberlein, argued stoutly that the 'congress' had been called on a false premise; but he got nowhere as Lenin impressed himself on the proceedings.

He and the Soviet leaders saturated delegates to the First Congress of Comintern in experiences designed to induce a collaborative spirit. They were taken on a trip to Petrograd to visit the famous sites of the October Revolution: the Finland Station, the Smolny Institute and the Winter Palace. They were awed by the sense of history recently made. On the streets there were the banners and posters of the October Revolution. Principal speakers included the finest orators of the Russian Communist Party: Trotski, Zinoviev, Bukharin and – like an impassioned schoolmaster

– Lenin himself. Workers and soldiers in Petrograd had a confidence not witnessed in other countries; their refusal of deference to their 'betters' contrasted with the behaviour of the lower social orders at home. From being the object of suspicion and condescension in the international socialist movement the 'Russians' had risen to pre-eminence. They had made a socialist revolution and acted while others – most others – had theorised or dithered. They had survived against every prediction. Now they were fighting their civil war, and it was by no means certain that the Reds would win. The sympathetic visitors, who were put up in comfort at the Hotel Lux, were minded to stand by their hosts.

An Executive Committee was then formed under Grigori Zinoviev with representatives from various countries. The Bolshevik central leaders handpicked the new body. They evidently intended to minimise any objections to Moscow's ideas and practices. Soviet control was going to stay tight for the foreseeable future.

Diplomatic representatives and clandestine agents were dispatched to Europe and North America. They carried with them the bacillus of revolution. Communists as well as their enemies used this medical imagery; everyone at the time regarded the societies of advanced capitalism as organisms vulnerable to communist infection. Karl Radek was arrested in Germany in February 1919 but the authorities allowed him plenty of visitors and he turned his cell into a political salon for far-left socialists disaffected from the German Social-Democratic Party. Radek relished his role. A chain-smoking Polish Jew with a line in acerbic jokes, he grabbed the opportunity to ridicule his old political enemies while enjoying legal immunity from imprisonment. When Germany was defeated in the First World War the Soviet republic in Russia became internationally isolated again. It sought to rectify this situation by sending further representatives to Sweden, Switzerland and the United Kingdom. Politburo member Lev Kamenev and Foreign Trade People's Commissar Lev Krasin went to London seeking a trade deal and diplomatic recognition (and, in Kamenev's case, to wine and dine himself at the Café Royal).[3]

The general aim of Comintern in its first few years was to enable leftist socialists to break away from their existing parties and set up their own communist parties. The Party Politburo and the People's Commissariat of External Affairs released funds to the Communist International. Among the dispensers of money was Willi Münzenberg, known to Lenin in his years of Swiss exile. Münzenberg's task was to travel around Europe searching out places and people for the making of revolution. He was a colourful figure. Like Kamenev, he had a penchant for the high life; and indeed he succeeded in combining politics with entrepreneurship. His business interests made him a very rich man before he was killed in 1940 by Soviet security agents.[4]

The Moscow leadership was falling back on techniques used before 1917, sending couriers with the finance for sympathisers abroad. A secret list was kept in the spidery handwriting of a People's Commissariat of External Affairs official in 1919–20. Couriers could be searched at customs posts so that it was impractical to carry paper currency. Instead they travelled with diamonds and pearl necklaces. Although Soviet manufacturing was at a low ebb, Cheka-led expropriations were a thriving industry. The Imperial propertied elites had left behind whole cellars of valuables which were put to use in the cause of the Revolution. Jewellery was more easily hidden than cash; indeed it could be openly worn by female agents. On arriving at their destination, communist groups could sell the jewels and recoup their value in the local currency. Europe was the main recipient of this largesse. Krasin, according to the records, received goods worth more than seven million rubles for political use abroad.[5] Not every emissary was very discreet; in the early days some of them broke their cover by giving fiery speeches en route.[6] Such was the revolutionary spirit of the period. Nor were all of them honest, so that Comintern sent out agents to track down the swindlers. (The story went about that the bookish communist György Lukács was sent with a pistol to Vienna to get funds back from one of them.)

As Comintern adjusted and oiled its administrative machinery in Moscow, it assembled an international network of communists to counsel – really to instruct – the member-parties abroad. Individuals with multilingual skills, political reliability and experience of clandestine party work were favourite choices. They did not have to have been Bolsheviks before 1917. Above all, they were tested as instruments of the Executive Committee's will. Thus a certain 'Williams', also known as Mikhailov among dozens of other aliases, was sent as Comintern representative in Berlin in 1922. He was present when the abortive 1923 rising took place in Hamburg. This did not blight his career. By 1924 he was performing the same functions for Comintern in Paris since his French was as good as his German. In 1926 he was moved to the United Kingdom, then back to Germany. From there he was dispatched to India to stir up anti-imperial sentiment. Arrested by the British secret services, he lay low after his release, and in 1930 was sent to Argentina and Chile. After a lifetime of false passports and 'underground' activity he ended up as press officer at the Soviet embassy in Paris.[7]

It was understood in Moscow that communism in other countries had to acquire a distinct political profile and organisational formation. Demarcation from mere 'socialist', 'social-democratic' and 'labour' parties was essential for this. Attracted by the Bolshevik example, many far-left activists readily agreed. The problem for Lenin was that their eagerness was a mite too casually developed. They could not be trusted. By July 1920, when the Second Congress of the Comintern took place in Moscow, the Politburo was confident of imposing its frame of desired behaviour on member-parties. The Reds had essentially won the civil war with the defeat of Anton Denikin at the end of 1919. The Whites were fleeing in disarray. The reputation of the leaders of the October Revolution was at an unprecedented height and the Red Army's success in repelling Piłsudski's invasion of Ukraine elevated it still further. The subsequent failure of central and western far-left socialists to reproduce this revolutionary success added to the status of Lenin, Trotski and their comrades. It was in this situation that the Comintern Second Congress agreed to the twenty-one conditions for membership which Lenin had drafted.

These conditions were modelled on the rules of the Russian Communist Party. Principles of centralism, obedience and selectivity were imposed. The Executive Committee of Comintern was empowered to guide and discipline member-parties. In theory, at least, the Russian Communist Party was equally subject to its command. Co-ordinated action was demanded on the ground that actions by communists in one country could affect the well-being of communist parties elsewhere. Every communist was to be a militant in the army of the world communist movement.

The claim of Comintern and its member-parties was that the Soviet order constituted the only authentic embodiment of socialism. Competition in the labour movement was intense after the world war. In its wake, several social-democratic, socialist and labour parties entered governmental office. The German Social-Democratic Party formed a national administration in November 1918 and remained formally committed to a Marxist party programme. The British Labour Party came to power in October 1924. The Second International, despite being badly disrupted in wartime, began to restore its old linkages between countries. Its member-parties aimed to eradicate inequalities in social opportunity and to provide education, healthcare, pensions and shelter free of charge. They planned an end to unemployment as well as to all corruption and injustice. They were committed to terminating discrimination based on race, nationality, gender or religion. The fact that communists and their left-wing rivals were dipping into the same baggage of objectives served to exacerbate hostility between them. Communists asserted that they alone were thoroughly implementing what they preached. Their enemies retorted that ideas of dictatorship and terror precluded communism from making fundamental improvement in the societies they wanted to rule.

Yet enough of a common purpose survived in the 1920s to dissuade anti-communist socialists in Europe from supporting military crusades against the Soviet republic. Socialists had discreet allies among businessmen who wanted to resume trading links with Russia. Western governments regardless of type – conservative, liberal or socialist – fitted in with the trend. Foreign companies turned a blind eye to Soviet dictatorial oppression. Entrepreneurs responded readily to the invitation to sign 'concessions' in industry. There was even a tender put out for companies abroad to set up farming enterprises,[8] and the German firm Krupp negotiated just such a deal. The managers and experts sent by Krupp found it a dispiriting experience. It would have been surprising if the indigenous peasantry had welcomed the Germans any more warmly than they did the Bolshevik party officials who had made the first attempt at agricultural collectivisation during the civil war. But other sectors of the economy benefited from the infusion of foreign capital. Technological advances made in manufacturing and mining under the NEP were usually associated with the concessionaires.[9] The difficulty was that businesses remained worried about the reliability of Soviet official promises, and this inevitably made for only a moderate infusion of European and American capital into the USSR.

What is more, the Politburo had acute concerns about the geostrategic pretensions of the great powers. There were recurrent war scares in Moscow. As there was no obvious sign of an imminent crusade by any of them against the USSR, Soviet leaders nervously expected that a 'proxy' state on their borders would move against the first socialist state – if not Poland, then probably Romania or Finland. The expectation was that Britain or France would arm such a state to the teeth and prod it into a military offensive.

Things were still creaky in practice. Comintern agent Ramison arrived in Rio de Janeiro to speed the foundation of a communist party in Brazil. Soon he encountered the prominent journalist and anarchist Edgard Leuenroth: 'Why won't the gentleman found the Communist Party of Brazil?' Leuenroth replied: 'Because I'm not a Bolshevist!'

Ramison would not be put off: 'In that case give me the name of someone capable of this task.' Leuenroth after a short pause relented: 'I'll give you a name. Make a call to Astrojildo Pereira. He's living in Rio de Janeiro.'[10] Ready-made communists existed nowhere outside Russia, where the Bolshevik ideology had been invented. The richest source of foreign left-wing ore from which to smelt communist iron lay in the existing socialist and labour parties. These were typically riven by disputes. Comintern's device was to engineer a formal split and lead off the extreme leftists into forming national communist parties. The Great War and the October Revolution had shifted the contours of political discussion.[11] This was how the Italian Communist Party came into existence. Antonio Gramsci had long chafed against the compromises of the leadership of the Italian Socialist Party. Comintern's foundation gave him the practical incentive he needed to make the organisational rupture.[12]

By the mid-1920s, when dozens of countries had established more or less normal relations of diplomacy and commerce with the USSR, Soviet agencies could abandon jewellery for paper currency. Young Henri Barbé, rising leader of the French Federation of Communist Youth, was surprised to be asked to take suitcases filled with three million dollars to Paris in denominations of between ten and a hundred dollars.[13] World communism was becoming ever more self-assured and couriers now had to have the strength of weightlifters.

The Fifth Congress of Comintern in 1924 passed an explicit resolution on Bolshevisation. The few remaining peculiarities of organisational structures and practices were eliminated and Russia became the model of virtue and the judge of its imitators. Party schools were set up in Moscow for foreign communists from over the world. The curriculum involved physical exercise and training with guns as well as Marxism-Leninism; sometimes the students were sent out to work in factories in the provinces to get a close glimpse of the fabled Russian proletariat.[14] This did not always turn out as Comintern wanted when inquisitive foreign youngsters witnessed the sloppy work and poor conditions of the labour force. Young Waldeck Rochet, later to head the French Communist Party, said to a friend while attending his courses in Moscow: 'If we were to tell French workers what we are seeing here they would throw rotten apples at us.'[15] Party schools were also established in those other countries where sufficient freedom existed. The French set one up north-east of Paris at Bobigny. This way of overcoming the shortage of qualified personnel was known in France as Bobignisation:[16] the curriculum was subject to approval by Comintern officials who strove to produce a set of obedient parties at Moscow's disposal.

Alongside Comintern there were other bodies designed to spread communist policies and organisation. These included the Red International of Trade Unions (Profintern), the International Organisation of Assistance to Fighters of the Revolution (MOPR), the International Peasants Council (Krestintern) and even the Red Sports International (Sportintern). It was hoped that, even if Comintern met political obstacles, influence could continue to be leached into the labour movement in all countries. Despite generous funding from Moscow, the new agencies made little impact. But their creation demonstrated that faith in worldwide communist revolution was by no means abandoned.

Comintern had to act with some circumspection after Lenin, in approving the Anglo-Soviet treaty in March 1921, agreed to suspend Soviet interference in the politics of the British Empire. Ambassadors from the USSR outwardly observed the diplomatic proprieties in the rest of the decade. The People's Commissariat in Moscow insisted that it had no control over Comintern. This was indeed true. It was the Politburo of the Russian Communist Party which took the decisions, and throughout these years it searched for any sign that the 'relative stabilisation of capitalism' was coming to an end. Money, agents and instructions continued to issue from Moscow. The problem – the only problem for the Politburo and Comintern – was that the West's great powers were successfully alleviating the social distress which motivated people to turn to communism. Marxism-Leninism contended that rivalries among these powers were ultimately uncontainable; it also laid down that capitalism could not avoid recurrent economic crises and that the working classes would inevitably turn to the political far left. But conditions in the middle of the decade were disturbingly placid. Harbingers of the final crisis of capitalism stubbornly refused to arrive.

Comintern was getting nowhere, and the Politburo gave the order for Comintern to instruct communist parties abroad to change policy and to establish a 'united labour front'. The idea was that communists would get together with rank-and-file members of socialist, social-democratic and labour parties and campaign against the capitalist order. They would not stop denouncing such parties; indeed they would continue to declare that communists and communists alone had the necessary determination to effect a drastic improvement in working people's conditions. They would also infiltrate those rival left-wing parties (and although the British Labour Party prohibited them from joining it as individuals from 1925, the ban was ineffectual).[17] Communists were encouraged to achieve dual party membership and struggle for the communist party's objectives. This later became known as 'entryism'. Frustrated about making an independent impact, communist militants became parasites on socialist parties which had achieved a greater electoral impact than they had. The 'united labour front' was a total misnomer. Communist policy in the 1920s was to intensify the bitter polemics on the political left and the 'class struggle' against capitalism.

But in 1926 the politics of Europe suddenly entered a turbulent phase. The British Labour Party had been ousted from office two years earlier and the Conservatives formed a government. The new government was firmly anti-Soviet. It was also determined to rein in the pretensions of the labour movement in the United Kingdom. The Trades Union Council struck back in the same year by organising a general strike. The strikers' demands were more material than political. This was a situation which could not be neglected by the Communist Party of Great Britain. With Comintern's endorsement, it tried to politicise the discontent. But the British labour movement was averse to breaking the law. Communist agitators were welcomed when they urged the need for higher wages and were ignored when they espoused a total change of regime. Government and police handled the opposition intelligently and the strike petered out. This was the pattern across Europe. Germany disappointed the hopes that Comintern placed in it. Although France was repeatedly disrupted by industrial conflict, it never looked seriously likely to succumb to communism. Italy was firmly under the thumb of the fascist dictatorship installed by Benito Mussolini in 1922. Communists watched and waited.

They also continued to set up parties wherever they did not already exist. They made progress even outside the advanced capitalist countries. In 1920, balked by their failures in Europe, the Soviet leaders had called a Congress of Peoples of the East in Baku. They aimed to act as midwives at the birth of communism in Asia. If the great imperial powers would not succumb to red revolution, perhaps countries such as China, Turkey and India would. And surely such an outcome would disrupt political stability around the world. If revolution could not enter through the front porch, why not by the back door? Just one success occurred in those early years. As the civil war drew to a close in Siberia, the Red Army crossed over into Mongolia and occupied the capital Urga in July 1921. Soviet military power ensured the proclamation of the Mongolian

People's Republic in 1924. Essentially it became a puppet regime and conformed its internal policies to the changing shape of the Kremlin's policies for the USSR. Repression of social and religious custom was severe even before Mongolia followed Russia into the bloodbath of the 1930s. The manhandling of the Mongolian People's Republic gave an early sign of how the USSR would treat the so-called people's democracies of eastern Europe after the Second World War.[18]

But Mongolia remained an isolated exception as a 'fraternal' regime for the USSR; and Comintern's Executive Committee busied itself with setting up a permanent commission for each large region of the world. The appointment of commission chairmen was done cunningly. Citizens of countries in the region were not eligible; this was a provision designed to restrict the capacity of 'nationals' to interfere with the Executive Committee's wishes and to prevent 'national' vendettas being played out in the Communist International. Russian Bolsheviks had behaved badly towards the Second International and its International Socialist Bureau before 1914, and they were not going to let others mess them around in the same way. The regions included 'America', the 'East' and Latin America. Comintern functionaries kept their political antennae attuned both to the demands of the Russian communist leadership and to shenanigans in the Communist International's parties. Neither Comintern's chairman Zinoviev nor, after his removal in 1926, his successor Bukharin had time to keep an eye on everything as their higher need was to attend to politics in the Russian Communist Party. They relied on the Secretary, Osip Pyatnitski, to keep them in touch. 'Le père Piat', as he was known to the French,[19] did his level best. But he too was paddling against a fast current of work and the commission chairmen became the linchpins of the world communist movement.

These same chairmen knew that their power hung by a thread spun down to them from the Politburo. A few maintained their youthful exuberance and stood up for themselves. These included occasional visitors to Comintern offices in the Kremlin who refused to toe the official line automatically. The Italians were frequent troublemakers. (German, French and British militants were always tame in comparison through to the 1980s.) From Amadeo Bordiga in 1922 to Angelo Tasca at the end of the decade they spoke their mind to Muscovite authority.[20] But independent spirits became ever rarer. Comintern had a whole apparatus for isolating them and, if they persisted in being troublesome, sacking them from the leadership of their party.

The model of a communist party member was a person who was

studious, punctilious and devoted to the cause. Zhen Bilan, a young woman who joined the Chinese Communist Party, rescinded her engagement to be married to a family friend and renounced any interest in 'love'. She was taking a frightful risk: families in China sometimes murdered disobedient fiancées.[21] Zhen, though, was determined to deepen her Marxist education. Members of study circles had to explain their conclusions and open themselves to criticism. Once the official line was set, all had to accept it. Faith in the distant communist future – but perhaps it was really going to be sooner rather than later – was compulsory. Communists were thrust into trade unions, schools and many kinds of bodies hostile to the ruling classes. It was a criterion of party membership that they should be highly active. They also had to give automatic allegiance to the policies of Comintern. Zhen Bilan was a thoughtful, independent individual. She objected to the Chinese Communist Party incorporating itself in the nationalist Kuomintang led by Chiang Kai-shek. In 1929 she was expelled from membership.[22]

But generally the mentality of obedience was quickly assimilated. The Northern Regional Committee of the Chinese Communist Party sent out a circular to subordinate bodies describing the party cell as follows:

1) It is the basic organ and organisational unit of the party.
2) It is the school of the party for education and propaganda.
3) It is the kernel of the party among the masses.
4) It is the instrument for development of the party.
5) It is the centre of life of the party.
6) It is the party's weapon of struggle.[23]

This mantra was designed to raise spirits and improve co-ordination and unity, as well as to point the entire party in the direction demanded by the central leaders – and the leaders themselves were to behave like the Kremlin's political annexe.

Comintern – and the Politburo as its overseer – seized whatever opportunities came its way. Under constant criticism from the Bolshevik left, it also itched to prove its internationalist credentials. If an opportunity failed to arise, it would make one by artifice. In 1925 the Bulgarian Communist Party, which had already organised a rising two years earlier, was encouraged to undertake armed action again. Commissions of the Politburo and Comintern had spent two years discussing the question so as to avoid the casual planning of the German revolutionary putsches in Germany in 1921 and 1923.[24] The authorities in Bulgaria, however, pre-empted such a scheme and the party was vigorously suppressed. The Bulgarian disaster did nothing to staunch the flow of revolutionary orders from Moscow. The focus next time was on China. Stalin and Bukharin through to the mid-1920s had insisted that the communists should ally themselves with nationalists such as Chiang Kai-shek and his Kuomintang. Abruptly they changed their stance, having convinced themselves that the Chinese Communist Party was strong enough to stand alone. A revolution was heralded and a rising duly took place in Shanghai in April 1927 on Comintern's orders. But instead of defeating the Kuomintang, the Chinese communists suffered a savage beating.

The ascendant group in the Politburo had got everything badly wrong. Defeated in the factional struggles in Moscow, Trotski crowed over the misjudgements by Stalin and Bukharin. Comintern's reputation lay in shreds. The only positive aspect was the proof given, not for the first or last time, that the Kremlin was by no means reconciled to the containment of communism within the borders of the Soviet Union. It still thought that, if the October Revolution was to survive, eventually it had to spread abroad. Lenin's original vision had not yet faded.

Trouble arose two months later for communism in the United Kingdom. The Anglo-Soviet treaty stipulated that the USSR would not use Comintern to subvert governments and private enterprises. Communists winked at each other while signing such documents. Comintern, working to the Kremlin's orders, turned London into a clandestine hub of communications and organisation for worldwide political subversion. British security officers knew that the All-Russia Co-operative Society (Arcos) in Hampstead was a front for Soviet intelligence. They raided the premises in May 1927 and carted off compromising documents. The Conservative cabinet immediately broke off diplomatic relations with the USSR. The Politburo's worries increased that a crusade might be started against the Soviet Union. The Arcos affair appeared to indicate that 'international imperialism' was about to go on the march yet again. The volatile condition of world politics was exposed. Trotski suggested that the episode constituted a case for a more aggressive foreign policy. He wanted to put global socialist revolution back on the immediate agenda. Comintern policy towards the great capitalist powers, he complained, had been neither chalk nor cheese. He had no inkling that his enemy Stalin was about to order communist parties around the world to become more militant.

10. PROBING AMERICA

American communism was spawned in pools of political sectarianism imported from the Russian Empire. The October Revolution excited all left-wing militants in the USA. Some were enraptured, others were sceptical or downright hostile. Among the enthusiasts for Lenin and his comrades were socialist veterans who had never had much time for each other. Their disputes were conducted with vicious intensity at both the ideological and personal levels. The result was chaos. In fact not one but two parties formed themselves in 1919. These were the Communist Party of America and the Communist Labor Party. Each claimed to stand for Leninism better than its rival. Charles Ruthenberg stated bluntly on behalf of the Communist Party of America: 'We reaffirm our opposition to unity with the Communist Labor Party.'[1] The Communist Labor Party reacted in kind. Each party banked on winning the political beauty contest in Moscow. They were disappointed. The Comintern Executive Committee insisted on amalgamation. Otherwise neither party would be allowed to affiliate itself to Comintern.[2]

This conclusion was unavoidable once the details of the dispute reached Moscow from across the Atlantic. Comintern leaders, arch-splitters to a man and woman before 1917, could not afford to allow a couple of competing communist parties to represent it in challenging the world's most advanced capitalist economy. Personal jealousies and factional disagreements were to be set aside and priority was to be given to the tasks of making revolution. In December 1921 a founding convention took place in New York. The united organisation was baptised as the Workers' Party of America, which pulled together all parties willing to accept Comintern as the supreme authority. This designation, it was hoped, would ward off the attention of the government and police at a time when known communists were routinely being arrested as subversives.

There had never been a realistic chance of communist revolution in the USA. And this continued to hold true. Informed Marxists before the

First World War had always been pessimistic about the American labour movement.[3] But Russia's communists did not speak like this in public in their euphoria after the October Revolution. Forgetting earlier doubts, they treated all capitalist societies as 'ripe' for 'the transition to socialism'. Two leading members of the Moscow leadership, Bukharin and Trotski, had been resident in the USA before 1917. They knew the country well enough. Party duty, however, required them to parrot that American conditions were propitious for communist revolution. They knew in their marrow that it was going to be an uphill struggle for the comrades across the Atlantic. Comintern's line was that the USA was one of the prime targets for revolution and Sovietisation. The newly formed communists of America agreed. They had joined their party because they shared a belief in revolutionary possibilities – and they accused the country's socialist parties of lacking the stomach and strategy to bring about fundamental changes in the American order.

The USA bore similarities to the old Russian Empire. Factory working conditions and wage rates were abysmal and the influx of European immigrants made it difficult for trade unions to secure betterment. The labour movement was persecuted. Police and courts supported employers. Violent gangs were paid to break strikes. The Italian immigrant anarchists Nicola Sacco and Bartolomeo Vanzetti were arrested in 1920 in Boston and charged with murdering a factory paymaster. The accusation was baseless; but the pair were found guilty after a trial tainted by bias. They were executed in the electric chair in 1927. Judicial murder served to warn radicals about the dangers of joining subversive groups. Such conditions had existed in Russia where the outcome of the struggle between the government and the revolutionaries had been the overthrow of the Romanovs and, months later, the October Revolution. Oppression had made heroes of the Bolsheviks in the eyes of radical opinion before 1917, and the tsarist authorities had not succeeded in extirpating Bolshevism. Communists in the USA hoped for a similar denouement.

American industrial growth after the First World War was impressive, turning the country into the first economic power around the globe. Technological advances in the automotive, electrical and chemical sectors were enormous. The universities were turning out graduates of quality. This success was achieved despite elections which, after Woodrow Wilson left office in 1921, produced a string of presidents undistinguished by abundant initiative. America stood out as a society that was thrusting forward despite its political leadership.

Mass immigration assisted the economic upsurge; for without cheap foreign labour it would have been impossible to sustain the remarkable rates of growth. Newcomers swarmed across the Atlantic, especially from Russia and eastern Europe. Few measures were taken by the authorities to welcome and assimilate them. They lived huddled in the factory and mining districts. They were poorly paid and badly treated. Their presence in the workforce introduced resentment and division, as had been the case in Petrograd in the First World War. Many refugees from Russia also brought radical political ideas with them. Communists hoped to exploit this situation. They were not going to have to start from scratch. A Socialist Party already existed, led by Eugene Debs, which took 6 per cent of the votes in the 1912 presidential election.[4] The socialists were divided by strategic dispute and factional conflict, and local groups in that vast country frequently acted in defiance of national policy. If strong communist parties could emerge from the womb of socialist parties in old Europe, there was no reason why the New World could not follow suit.

Comintern increased its contacts with the Workers' Party of America. Telegrams were regularly dispatched between New York and Moscow and agents criss-crossed the Atlantic by steamer. Soviet leaders were annoyed by the endless internal American wrangling, and sprinkled their correspondence with detailed instructions: they were determined to keep a tight hold on the emergent communist organisation.

When police raided the party's offices in New York in August 1922 they found a ten-page document signed by Nikolai Bukharin, Karl Radek and Otto Kuusinen 'concerning the next tasks of the Communist Party of America [sic]'. Communists were told that their primary task was to support Soviet Russia in every way. They were also to form a legal party without dropping illegal forms of activity – it would be foolish to 'liquidate' work in the 'underground'.[5] Their practical task was to be the building of a mass party. Yet the 'real party' would remain the core of leaders and militants who flouted the law in their operations. Theirs would continue to be the supreme power and responsibility. They had to train the new recruits. And the mass party was to infiltrate and manipulate left-wing organisations. The Politburo and Comintern leadership could hardly disguise its low expectations of the American comrades. Moscow patiently explained that they should enter trade unions and 'Negro' bodies but on no account should they function inside the Ku Klux Klan. They should campaign against anti-strike legislation such as the Kansas Industrial Court Law. They should link up with small-holding farmers and agitate against bank foreclosures. They were also to set up a communist press: 'As long as the party does not possess at least one or two legal dailies in the English language, it is still crawling around on all fours.'[6]

Jules Humbert-Droz, a boisterous, multilingual Swiss, headed Comintern's American Commission and liaised with the Americans from Moscow. He did not always get the results demanded by Zinoviev and the Executive Committee. The problems for communist strategy in the USA were complex. Furthermore, Moscow could not operate without detailed information and advice from the American comrades themselves. This made an opening for the same comrades to skew decisions in the direction they desired. Sometimes the Americans appeared to have the upper hand. Their emissary to Moscow in May 1924 exulted that the Communist International had 'accepted our basic analysis which stated that there is a social-political crisis in the United States'.[7] Yet his satisfaction was also a sign that the key to success was a capacity to plead a national case at the 'centre'. American communist leaders had to be effective supplicants.

Their authority was sapped by internal party conflicts. Policies were endlessly disputed. Clashes among personalities bedevilled party life. It often seemed that leaders were more exercised in doing each other down than in proselytising for communism. The party's multinational composition did not help the situation. The industrial workforce had a heavy component of recent immigrants who spoke little English, and this was also true of recruits to communism: half of them in the mid-1920s were born outside the USA.[8] Sections were established for Czechs, Estonians, South Slavs, Lithuanians, Italians, Jews, Bulgarians, Germans, Finns, Hungarians and several others. There was even an English section.[9] All the Slavs caused endless trouble and American communist Max Eastman wrote to Trotski and Lenin in 1923 urging that the party should cut its ties with them. Eastman thought them just too much trouble.[10] The Jews were the most disputatious, always saying the worst of each other and arguing with the party leaders (nearly half of whom were themselves Jewish).[11] A report despaired of sorting them out: 'This is chaos.'[12] Only the 'hundred odd farmers', who had their own small section, failed to cause trouble – and probably this was only because it was not a very active section.[13] Comintern instructed the party to scrap all its national sections in June 1925.[14]

The American leadership put on a brave face and took pride in holding together a party combining people from all backgrounds. Comintern was unconvinced. The largest national or racial minority in the USA were the Negroes (as Blacks or African-Americans were known). The party was formally committed to integrating them in its ranks but did next to nothing. When in 1925 the American delegation to Moscow was quizzed about this by Stalin, its members admitted that 'prejudice and discrimination' existed.[15] Moscow put its foot down. In 1927 Comintern ordered the party leadership to send ten suitable Negroes for training at the Communist University for the Toilers of the East in Moscow.[16] This caused panic in the American party. The Political Committee thought it possible to round up two or three suitable candidates at the most.[17] Comintern had its own concealed racism; for why should American Negroes, descendants of slaves from Africa and wholly assimilated to America's culture and economy, be associated with Asia? On arrival in Moscow the Negro students objected to being segregated and made to suffer from 'white' chauvinism.[18] Problems also remained in the party in the USA. To its shame, the Negro members were still being refused admission to its miners' relief ball in 1929.[19]

Comintern eventually got its way. American communists did not confine themselves to reaching out to Negroes but disseminated a project to carve an independent republic for them in the southern states. The chief promoter of such ideas was Harry Haywood, himself a Negro. Haywood had gone to party school in Moscow and worked there for Comintern till 1930.[20] His project became Comintern policy. The same ideas were relayed to communists in South Africa, where the party was told to campaign for 'an independent native South African republic'.[21] In neither party was this popular, but Comintern insisted on it. No one seems to have queried how a Second Civil War would be avoided in the USA. Perhaps it was only as a device to win Negro recruits for the communist party.

Some communists had always disliked Comintern's interference. A letter to party leader Charles Ruthenberg complained: 'Essentially the [communist party] was a hip-hip-hurrah society for the celebration of good news from Russia.'[22] But this sort of complaint became rare as the grumblers and sceptics left the ranks. American comrades bowed regularly to the east like Moslems praying to Mecca – and 'Mecca', as it happens, was the codeword for the Moscow leadership in their telegrams.[23] A demeaning psychology developed among them. The ascendant leadership in a message to the party in March 1926 stated: 'If we are trying to be Bolsheviks we must practise the method of ruthless self-criticism.' This attitude was displayed whenever criticism was relayed from Moscow. And joy was unrestrained when Moscow gave its nods of approval: 'We are the party. The Communist International has said so.'[24] Young James Cannon, later to walk out and join the Trotskyists, was not one to toe any line automatically; but even he was bowled over by the opportunity to meet Politburo members in the 1920s. Late in his life he still remembered his experience in Soviet Russia as 'an incomparable school'.[25]

The factions in the Workers' Party of America saw Moscow as the court of arbitration in disputes. The Comintern Executive Committee was not always pleased. In April 1927 it told the party to end its internal disputes and to agitate against the invasion of Nicaragua by the American Marine Corps.[26] Jay Lovestone and the ascendant group in the leadership obeyed the injunction. But they did not stop conspiring; they informed Comintern that they had achieved only an artificial unity and that the opposition continued to agitate for Lovestone to be sacked as General Secretary in favour of William Weinstone. Nevertheless, they claimed, they themselves were resolutely avoiding provocative activity.[27]

Eventually Lovestone was sacked even though he apparently had the support of nine-tenths of the membership.[28] This happened in 1929 on Moscow's orders, and what did for him was his political closeness to Bukharin. In September 1928 Lovestone had warned Bukharin in writing that foreign leaders, notably Heinz Neumann from Germany, were speaking ill of him.[29] This was like shouting to a drowning man that the water was coming over his head. It was not as if Bukharin was unaware that Stalin's group was moving among the delegations spreading dirt on his reputation. This was always how Stalin operated before organising an open assault. Lovestone was called to the Comintern offices and given a dressing-down by Otto Kuusinen in April 1929 for being sympathetic to the Right Deviation.[30] A few weeks later a delegation of American communists came to supplicate before the victorious Stalin. He judged them insufficiently compliant: 'Who do you think you are? Trotski defied me. Where is he? Zinoviev defied me. Where is he? Bukharin defied me. Where is he? And you? When you get back to America, nobody will stay with you except your wives.'[31]

Comintern's disappointment in the USA was constant. William Z. Foster stood as the party's candidate in the American presidential elections in 1924. He scored a pathetic 0.1 per cent of the votes cast. The communists alleged that they had been the victims of electoral fraud. Secretary Ruthenberg and candidate Foster cabled to Russia: 'Capitalist

Memento of the Fourth Congress of Comintern, 1922. Lenin declares:
'Let the ruling classes tremble before the communist revolution.'
He stands on a globe pointing confidently to a radiant future.
Note the characteristically shiny shoes.

Biro's poster of an improbably musculated worker, painted for Budapest's May Day in 1919. The mallet is as supple as the torso. It is almost an integral part of the worker himself.

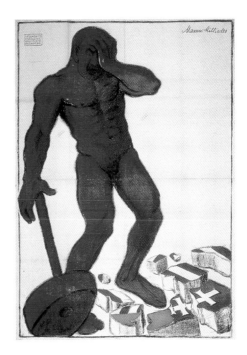

Counter-revolutionary response to Biro's poster: the distressed Red worker in 1919 finds he has destroyed the country, symbolised by a block in the colours of the national flag, with his hammer blows.

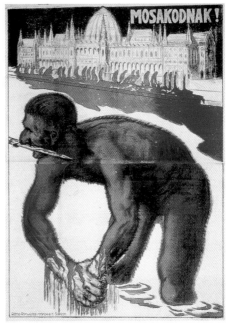

Hungarian anti-communist poster: 'They wash themselves!' A beast-like comrade cleanses himself of the blood that pours from the country's great buildings of state.

JAK BOLSZEWICY RZĄDZĄ

U SIEBIE ZNISZCZYLI
ZIEMIĘ I FABRYKI, SPROWADZI-
LI GŁÓD I NĘDZĘ. ZIEMIĘ POL-
SKĄ PRZEZNACZAJĄ DLA
ROSYJSKIEJ BIEDOTY I CHCĄC
ZROBIĆ MIEJSCE DLA SWOICH
PĘDZĄ NASZYCH W REKRUTY
A TYCH CO ZOSTALI RABU-
JĄ I MORDUJĄ.

JAK TEMU ZARADZIĆ?
PRAĆ TO PLUGASTWO ZA-
CIEKLE A UWOLNIMY ZIE-
MIĘ POLSKĄ OD KRWA-
WYCH TYRANÓW.

JEŚLI
DZIŚ
NIE PÓJDZIESZ
W POLE
Z ŻOŁNIERZEM
TWYM
BRATEM

JUTRO
ODDASZ
WSZYSTKO
POD
BOLSZEWICKIM
BATEM

Na co wy czekacie?

Above. Polish patriotic message in 1920: the Soviet Reds will arrest and pillage if their invasion succeeds. A triumphant Russian soldier torments the lifeless body of his victim. Cattle and pigs are driven off while the farmstead burns.

Left. Warning to Poles about the consequences of Sovietisation: 1920. A Polish soldier tells a fellow Pole that unless he leaves his farm to fight for his brother Poles, he too will suffer under Bolshevik rule. Jackbooted Red Army men wield a whip and a rifle. In the distance a Pole dangles by the neck from a rope.

RSFSR poster condemns Polish aggression in 1920. Poland is portrayed as 'the latest dog of the Entente'; its old-style whiskers and blood-red eyes signify the most reactionary intent.

Ukrainian communist paean to Stalin and agricultural collectivisation. Stalin looks calm and reflective. There is no indication of the famine afflicting Ukraine in the early 1930s.

Soviet workers in the 1930s happily promise to deliver greater output than demanded by the five-year plan for grain, fuel and metal. As usual, one of them points skywards.

Appeal to Spanish youth by the anti-Stalinist communist POUM in the Civil War.
A brawny-shouldered youth waves the hammer and sickle – the POUM refused to let
Stalin monopolise possession of the symbol of the USSR.

Spanish Republican summons to comrades to work and fight for the revolution.
The two figures are bare to the waist, one wielding a sickle and the other a rifle.

dictatorship will not count communist votes.'[32] The capitalist order would always connive at doing them down.

The subsequent history of American communism confirmed the frail potential revealed in the party's first decade. The Wall Street Crash in April 1929, according to Comintern's global prognosis, should have led to a massive increase in the party's popularity. Yet membership grew from 7,500 in 1929 to only 90,000 in 1939.[33] By the mid-1930s Stalin had concluded that Comintern should moderate its struggle against F. D. Roosevelt, whose New Deal included a commitment to state intervention in the workings of the economy.[34] The Kremlin sanctioned the formation of an Abraham Lincoln battalion to fight in the Spanish civil war. Not a Lenin battalion but one commemorating an American president not known for his socialist sympathies. Earl Browder became the communist leader in 1934, and it was he who stood as the party's candidate in the US presidential elections of 1936. He fought a languid campaign and garnered a little over eighty thousand votes. In effect Roosevelt was allowed to run less as a Democrat than as the unofficial leader of a coalition for 'progressive' politics. The Kremlin, at least temporarily, identified its interests with helping to secure his victory and gave appropriate instructions to the American communist leadership. If it had been a horse race, there would have been a stewards' inquiry.

Nevertheless the Communist Party of the USA, as it was known from 1930, enjoyed its growing prominence. Browder appeared in published photos smoking a pipe like his overseer in the Kremlin. The difference was that, with an eye towards gaining conventional respectability, he wore a striped tie. Priority was given to making an impact on public opinion. Approaches were made to fellow travellers who submitted pro-communist articles to weekly journals. The party dressed itself up as the only organisation in American politics with an unconditional devotion to social justice, economic fairness, racial equality and the struggle against fascism and imperialism. It put a new slogan into circulation: 'Communism is Twentieth Century Americanism'. Although the communists were a spectacular failure at every election, they undoubtedly increased their influence, especially among intellectuals. What is more, companies with contracts for business in the USSR had no incentive to criticise Stalin or Browder.[35]

The party's general policies were controlled from Moscow, and Browder was an obedient enthusiast for them. When the Second World War erupted in September 1939 after the signature of the Nazi–Soviet pact and the German invasion of Poland, he urged that the USA should stay out of the conflict as Stalin required. Communist militants, whatever their private opinions, were told to show as much reluctance as any conservative isolationists to pull European chestnuts out of the fire. Until December 1940 Browder toured the country making the case at factory and dockyard gates. Arrested and tried, he was thrown into Atlanta prison 'as the first political prisoner in the second imperialist war'.[36] He and his party continued to declare that the United Kingdom was tricking the USA into an unnecessary and undesirable alliance. Browder vigorously supported Irish neutrality and did not object to the Dublin government's soft policy towards the Third Reich. At the same time he opposed the 'forces in Jewish life' which he alleged were inveigling the USA into the military carnage in Europe.[37] The gains in the party's influence were tossed away by this subservience to the instructions of the Communist International.

Policy was turned on its head when Hitler invaded the USSR in June 1941 and the party was instructed to be the cheerleader for America to open a 'second front' in western Europe. This made no difference until the Japanese attack on Pearl Harbor in December 1941. War broke out between the USA and Japan, and Hitler declared war on the USA. American communists could suddenly parade theirs as a patriotic party and Browder was released from prison in May 1942.[38] Hammering nails into the coffin lid of past policy, he – dutiful as ever but this time with a more natural fervour – eulogised the potential of a Grand Alliance of the USSR, USA and UK. According to Browder, the objective of military victory overrode the traditions of 'class struggle'. He opposed strikes and protests for the duration of the war. Stalin wanted to assure Roosevelt of his commitment to the wartime partnership. (Not that this stopped Stalin from getting American communist agents, with Browder's connivance, to go on spying for political and technological secrets.)[39] In May 1944 Browder shut down the party and formed a Communist Political Association – this was really a way of retaining a party organisation without appearing to have one: the aim was somehow to reassure the American government.[40] Communist community clubs were set up to promote the Grand Alliance, study Marxism-Leninism and lobby national and local politicians.[41] Browder and his comrades canvassed for harmony between the USA and USSR. They urged workers to intensify production. They encouraged voluntary enlistment in the army and navy in the war against Germany and Japan.

Browder's perspective on the post-war future was distinctively his own. He sprayed his ideas out on the world. In 1943, for example, he called on Roosevelt not to demand that the USSR should enter the Pacific theatre of the world war once Germany had been defeated.[42] More importantly, he asserted that 'capitalism and socialism have begun to find a way to peaceful co-existence and collaboration' on a durable basis.[43] This was an idea that a later communist generation known as the Eurocommunists redeveloped. He also proposed continued collaboration between employers and workers. Moscow became perplexed about Browder and knew that he had aroused opposition from his rival William Z. Foster.[44] Moscow sought each side's explanation. Foster criticised Browder for recommending an avoidance of industrial strikes and other forms of 'class struggle' in the post-war future – and the International Department of the Soviet Party Secretariat agreed with Foster.[45] Stalin did not immediately become involved. But Browder's ideas grated with him and leading French communist Jacques Duclos, encouraged by Moscow, denounced him in April 1945.[46] This started the ball rolling for Browder to be expelled from the ranks of American communism as a revisionist. Although Moscow did not supervise all details of policies in the communist parties around the world, it demanded obedience to its strategic standpoint. Browder had gone out on a limb and paid the price.

Yet the newly reconstituted Communist Party of the USA was a weak force in American politics. The communists therefore supported Roosevelt's former Vice-President Henry Wallace, who stood against both Democrats and Republicans as presidential candidate of the Progressive Party in the electoral campaign of 1948. Wallace had shown eager favour to the USSR in earlier years.[47] But the Democrats under Harry Truman after the Second World War treated Stalin as the greatest threat to world peace. The Cold War had begun.[48] American communists continued to fetch and carry on the orders of the Kremlin. This stretched far beyond campaigning against US foreign policy. Soviet intelligence agencies continued to recruit party members and sympathisers as spies. Confidential diplomatic files were passed to Moscow. The secrets of the US atomic bomb projects were made available to scientists in the USSR.[49] Yet the party's puppy-like devotion to the USSR had thoroughly discredited it. Senator Joe McCarthy in the early 1950s campaigned noisily against communist infiltration of government and media.[50] Communist party members fell in number. By 1957 there were only three thousand of them.[51] By then their internal disputes and public campaigns hardly merited attention in the national media.

General Secretary Gus Hall, the dullard devotee of the USSR, welcomed the suppression of the Hungarian Uprising in 1956 and the Prague Spring in 1968.[52] If the USSR had invaded Alaska he would probably have interpreted it as a happy incursion of garlanded peace-lovers. This was no more and no less than Moscow expected of a CPUSA leader. Just a few embers of indigenous Marxist fire were still glistening in America. The young black woman Angela Davis emerged from the anti-government movement of students and Blacks in the late 1960s. She joined the party. But her fame flickered briefly on TV screens and then faded. The communist party never pushed its way to the front of the public protests against American military intervention in the war in Vietnam.

Hall and his comrades as Soviet stooges through all the years of détente between the USA and the USSR urged the maintenance of diplomatic, commercial and cultural exchanges. They eulogised Leonid Brezhnev as the world's greatest promoter of peace and progress. The Soviet Union was represented as a beacon of democracy. Gorbachëv's reforms in the late 1980s came as an unwelcome surprise to Hall.[53] The worm turned in the American communist party only when the USSR embarked on fundamental reform. Hall signed a receipt for two million dollars from the Soviet party in 1988.[54] But his scarcely veiled criticisms annoyed Gorbachëv, who withdrew Moscow's subsidy in the following year. Hall scoffed that Gorbachëv's 'new thinking' had nothing new about it but was essentially the same as what the disgraced Earl Browder had been saying in the Second World War.[55] (This was not wholly inaccurate about Gorbachëv in respect of USA–USSR relations.)[56] He was therefore delighted by the coup attempt against Gorbachëv in August 1991. But when Gorbachëv was freed from confinement and returned to Moscow, it was Hall who was in trouble. An initiative group, including Angela Davis, emerged in the American party to challenge Hall at its national convention in November 1991.

By then in his eighties, Hall complained angrily about Gorbachëv's 'misleadership'.[57] Facing down the 'Dump Gus' campaign, he came out the winner. He had been party leader since 1959 and the party's vanquished candidate in four presidential elections. He died in 2000, unlamented except by the dwindling band of comrades who kept the faith even after the fall of communism in eastern Europe and the Soviet Union. They no longer had many foreign countries to admire. China and Vietnam were taking the capitalist road in economic policy. Although Cuba was still thought worth supporting as a plucky survivor of the American blockade, its reliance on tourism and its rapprochement with the Catholic Church were hardly propitious for communist advancement. Only North Korea was left for the armadillo minds of the USA's communist veterans to approve.

The communist party in the USA had never had a healthy, independent life since its birth in 1921; and the American 'failure' to go communist exemplifies the inherent flaw in the vision of Marx and Engels. The USA was the world's largest industrial power from the First World War onwards. Its technological dynamism over the generations had no equal. The assumption had been that miserable living conditions would turn the American working people into followers of communism. Tens of millions of Americans indeed lived and live in poverty. But most people experienced material betterment. Marx and Engels had begun to take this into account even at the end of the nineteenth century. Kautsky, Lenin and Trotski recognised that capitalist America was going to be a difficult political nut for communists to crack. They rightly indicated that American workers shared in the benefits brought to their country by its leading position in the global economy and politics. They were correct in stating that the more skilled members of the working class were drawn away from radicalism by high wages and that they became – in the Marxist jargon – a 'labour aristocracy'.

But they stuck to the tenet that capitalism in the USA was on the brink of irretrievable collapse. Successive generations of the American communist party, following the Soviet leadership from Lenin onwards, upheld those basic assumptions in the teeth of their lived experience. In the end, in 1991, it was to be the USSR and not the USA which tumbled into oblivion.

11. MAKING SENSE OF COMMUNISM

Bolsheviks declared that a 'proletarian revolution' had taken place in Russia and that a workers' state was being created. Occasionally they admitted to having failed to prevent 'bureaucratic distortions', but generally they claimed to be realising the dream of Marx and Engels. Nikolai Bukharin and his friend Yevgeni Preobrazhenskii explained the rationale for this state order in *The ABC of Communism* in 1920. They intended it as a primer for the party.[1] Their chapters, however, scarcely mentioned the party itself. Only in 1924 did a party functionary, Lazar Kaganovich, produce a pamphlet on the party's workings.[2] Kaganovich, already one of Stalin's close associates, spelled out the system of vertical command needed in the party-state if the communists were to enhance their power.[3] Most Bolshevik 'theoreticians' said little about the discrepancy between pre-revolutionary promises and post-revolutionary realities. The party had been meant to seize power and then let the proletariat rule. This was the fundamental theme of Bolshevik policies in 1917.[4] Occasionally Lenin and other party leaders blurted out the truth that politics were characterised by a dictatorship of the party; but usually they preferred to draw a veil over reality.[5] Yet they had to concede, however faintly, that the working class was not really running the Soviet state. They blamed this mainly on Russia's cultural backwardness. It would not be long, they asserted, before the situation was rectified.

Most commentators abroad rejected this rosy view of Bolshevism. But accurate information was difficult to obtain. After the treaty of Brest-Litovsk, when the Western Allies withdrew their embassies, only the Central Powers maintained their representation. German ambassador Count Wilhelm von Mirbach paid the ultimate price in July 1918 when he was assassinated by a Left Socialist-Revolutionary hit squad. The German embassy disappeared at the end of the Great War. Meanwhile London and Paris sent counsellors not to Moscow but to the high commands of the White armies. The West relied ever more heavily on its clandestine spy networks to keep itself acquainted with communism in Russia.

The British did not succeed in providing their agent Sir Paul Dukes in Petrograd with a regular stream of funds. Dukes enlisted in the Eighth Army of the Reds in order to receive food rations and even joined the Russian Communist Party: 'My party ticket was everywhere an Open Sesame.'[6] He was free from rancour about how the Secret Intelligence Service had handled him. His last instructions in London, before his mere three weeks of training, had been: 'Don't go and get killed!' He spoke Russian with a bit of an accent and decided to pass himself off as a Ukrainian. To throw off surveillance he took out (or put back in) his front tooth.[7] His memoir on escapades in Petrograd and on the fronts of the civil war is among the harum-scarum classics. Another raconteur was Robert Bruce Lockhart, both in the reports he made to the Secret Intelligence Service and in his subsequent memoirs. Lockhart, like Dukes, was a confirmed conservative in politics. He had been ordered to get on friendly terms with the Bolsheviks and to try and keep them in the Great War. He met Lenin and Trotski and had hopes of bringing Trotski over to some kind of alliance against the Germans. Then came the treaty of Brest-Litovsk. Lockhart maintained a precarious presence in Moscow and, after the attempt on Lenin's life in August 1918, Dzierżyński ordered the Cheka to seize him. He was later released in an exchange with a Russian communist suspect held by the British.[8] Such misfortunes disrupted the flow of information and analysis available to the cabinet in London. Policy was made on guesswork.

American officials hoped to do a better job in the early Soviet years. President Woodrow Wilson, ever the optimist, sought to bring the civil war in Russia to an early end. For this purpose in 1919 he sent his personal emissary William C. Bullitt to negotiate with Lenin in Moscow. Bullitt was a bright young man who wanted Washington to accord official recognition to the Soviet regime. He took the Bolsheviks at their word when they claimed to be willing to compromise with the Whites. He also believed that Bolshevism would moderate its dictatorial ferocity. Bullitt did not stay long enough to test out his judgements – and the Reds went on fighting the Whites into the ground until they achieved unconditional victory.

Intelligence agencies sought help from newspaper correspondents. Several brilliant reporters, exploiting the chance to interview Bolsheviks, gained privileged access to the party leadership. The *Manchester Guardian* correspondent Arthur Ransome was one of them. Ransome publicly endorsed the Bolsheviks so warmly that leading Soviet propagandist Karl Radek wrote an introduction to Ransome's *Letter to America* which was translated for distribution in New York.[9] Ransome in the course of his work had fallen in love with Trotski's attractive secretary Yevgenia Shelepina. Later they married and moved to Cumbria in the north of England.[10] All the time he was in Russia, however, Ransome was an informer for the Secret Intelligence Service.[11] Undoubtedly he played down the oppressive nature of the Soviet state. But he was also a British patriot, thinking that friendly relations with the Bolsheviks would serve the interests of the United Kingdom. This is not the end of the tangled thread of intrigue because the new Mrs Ransome was not the innocent secretary she seemed. In October 1922 she was the recipient of a gift from the People's Commissariat of External Affairs beyond the wildest dreams of Soviet citizens: diamonds to the value of 1,039,000 rubles.[12] She and her husband were leaving the country for good and the Soviet state was not in the habit of handing out wedding presents. Obviously she was a Soviet agent in some capacity. In all probability she was smuggling financial assistance to the British communists.

Whether she did sustained work for the Leninist cause in the Cumbrian fells, three hundred miles from the English capital, is doubtful. She and Arthur gave up their previous lives for the rural idyll they had promised themselves, and Arthur achieved fame not for his politics but for *Swallows and Amazons* and the other books he wrote for children. It is an intriguing episode: a British secret informer married a Soviet secret agent. There was really no basic contradiction here. Ransome had been an enthusiast for the Bolsheviks and his purpose in reporting to the Secret Intelligence Service was to bring the United Kingdom's policy over to acceptance of Sovnarkom; Yevgeniya had volunteered to work for the Bolshevik leadership. The likelihood is anyhow that she passed her valuable package to a designated contact as she had passed through London and then had nothing more to do with Bolshevism; but the truth at present remains as unfathomable as the deepest waters of the Lake District.

Other journalists kept a greater distance between themselves and their intelligence agencies. Among them was the American reporter Albert Rhys Williams, a Congregational minister and socialist of Welsh descent. Williams worked in Russia for the *New York Evening Post*. His sympathy for Sovnarkom was such that Bolshevik newspapers reproduced some of his dispatches on their pages.[13] John Reed was another supporter of revolutionary politics in Russia. He too was a socialist journalist. Reed was drawn to the world's trouble spots like a moth to a lighted candle and was present at the Second Congress of Soviets when power was seized from the Provisional Government. His book *Ten Days that Shook the World* earned the approval of Lenin, who read it 'with never-slackening attention' and wrote a preface for editions worldwide.[14] Reed and his wife Louise Bryant went back from Moscow to the USA on a speaking tour to expound the merits of communism – they were given items valued at over one million rubles to assist revolutionary propaganda and organisation.[15] They founded the Communist Labor Party. On returning to Russia, however, Reed contracted typhus and died in 1920. He received a state funeral and was buried beneath the Kremlin Wall with the fallen heroes of the Revolution. American communists established John Reed Clubs in his honour.

In fact Reed had broken with Zinoviev over American trade union strategy and resigned from the Comintern Executive Committee. A hail of criticism was directed at Reed until he retracted.[16] Whether he would have maintained an allegiance to Comintern is an open question. What is clear is that many on the political left in the West came to abhor Soviet communism. Anarchists were to the fore in this. Emma Goldman and Alexander Berkman, arriving from the USA in 1919, were willing to give the benefit of the doubt to the Leninists. They were horrified by the persecution they witnessed everywhere in Soviet Russia, including the brutal treatment meted out to their anarchist comrades. Communists had needed the assistance of anarchists in their civil war. As soon as the military balance tilted decisively in favour of the Reds, the political conflict was resumed and the Cheka arrested and killed prominent anarchists.[17] Goldman and Berkman learned from their anarchist friends how cunningly the communists sanitised the political scene before visitors came to Soviet cities. The troublesome leaders of non-communist groups were invariably removed. Everything was done to create the illusion of a regime beloved of its people. The lie was put about that those who struggled against the Bolsheviks – including the Kronstadt mutineers of March 1921 – were the willing tools of foreign capitalist powers.

Goldman's experiences turned her forever against the October Revolution. She was furious with Lenin and Trotski. Reviewing her general principles, she abjured her lifelong advocacy of violence as a means of changing society. 'Never before in all history', she wrote, 'has authority, government, the state, proved so inherently static, reactionary, and even counter-revolutionary.'[18]

Rosa Luxemburg, Lenin's long-standing antagonist, had criticised the Soviet regime. She detested his contempt for democracy and universal civil rights as prerequisites for socialism. No pacifist, she was convinced that force of some kind would be needed to consolidate any socialist government in power; but she railed against Russian communism's contempt for democracy. She also despised Lenin's readiness to compromise with the aspirations of Russian peasants and non-Russian national minorities. In her eyes he was turning his back on the urban and internationalist traditions of Marxism. Luxemburg's critique was published posthumously as *The Russian Revolution*.[19] Another opponent of Leninism, Karl Kautsky, shared several of her ideas on democracy. Kautsky responded with alacrity to the writings of the Bolsheviks in 1917 with his own *Dictatorship of the Proletariat* in the following year. He denied that Marx and Engels had intended a constriction of civil rights as their revolutionary strategy; he also pointed out that Lenin's assumption that society would irresistibly become divided between two great classes, the proletariat and the bourgeoisie, was not borne out by demographic trends. A strategic gamble on proletarian leadership of the transition to socialism was therefore neither scientific nor likely to be effective.[20]

Kautsky's arguments dovetailed with the thought of the Menshevik leader Yuli Martov. After his death in 1922 a collection of Martov's writings on the Soviet communist regime was published in Berlin.[21] His work had not appeared in his own country since the civil war. The Mensheviks in Russia had no legal facilities to spread their ideas. Their party organisations had been closed down, their leaders banned from standing in elections to public office. Many of them were imprisoned on the old monastery island of Solovki in the White Sea or sent into administrative exile, and the rest lived under the menace of persecution. Martov, however, had already sketched out the reasons why he thought the October Revolution was a ghastly mistake. The Bolsheviks in his estimation had introduced ideological contraband into Russian Marxism, especially with their absolute adherence to dictatorship and terror. Mensheviks traced the onset of an oppressive bureaucracy with an interest in aggrandising its economic and social power. They hoped – and they persuaded themselves – that the Revolution could be 'straightened out' when the Bolsheviks were forced to recognise that they had driven the country into a cul-de-sac. The October Revolution was deeply flawed, but it was the only revolution that was available and it had to be reformed.

While censorship prevented Soviet readers from learning what the anti-Bolsheviks had written, the USSR poured funds into translating works by Lenin, Trotski and other communists. Left-wing bookshops in central and western Europe sold tens of thousands of cheap copies. Bukharin's *ABC of Communism* was popular as a statement of communist intent. The best face was put on developments in the USSR. The Red barbarities in the civil war with the Whites went unmentioned and the official line on the malign involvement of capitalist powers in the Kronstadt mutiny of 1921 was maintained.

Yet not even Soviet propaganda could drown out everybody on the left of Western politics. Socialists went out to Moscow in delegations to discover the situation for themselves.[22] Two British authors of the first rank were so intrigued by the Soviet experiment that they too travelled out to Russia to interview Soviet leaders. These were the novelist H. G. Wells and the philosopher Bertrand Russell. The authors had read up on Lenin and Trotski as well as Marx and Engels. They were impressed by Lenin's intelligence when they met him; but they disliked having to endure his diatribes against capitalist iniquities before they had their chance to put their own points. Wells drew attention to the chaos and inefficiencies of administration in Russia; he also remarked on the oppressive methods of communism.[23] Russell levelled criticisms at Lenin for Red behaviour at the front and in the rear in the civil war. Wells, a member of the Fabian Society in the United Kingdom, had a soft spot for radical social engineering, but he understood the dangers of Lenin's utopianism and impatience and said so. Russell too was a Fabian Society member; but he was also a liberal in politics and was even more appalled than Wells about the treatment of the individual in Soviet official policy and practice.[24] The books by Wells and Russell were bestsellers. They gave the communists a fair hearing before delivering their damning verdict: neither of them wanted the replication of the Soviet regime in England's green and pleasant land or anywhere else.

Yet they had a lingering affinity with certain socialist objectives proclaimed by the Bolsheviks. They could not but admire them for striving after a welfare state system, free education, central economic planning and the abolition of social privilege. (Russell was himself an aristocrat who decried the British class system.) Austrian Marxists such as Otto Bauer shared the willingness to show some approval. Unlike Kautsky, Bauer did not come out unequivocally against the Soviet regime even though Lenin continued to harangue him over his writings on the 'national question'. Bauer was a democrat and an enemy of dictatorship. His opinion was that the Soviet order, barbaric as it was, was suited to the conditions of the former Russian Empire. Austria and Germany, he thought, could do better for themselves. But Marxists in Russia had to contend with a society lacking in traditions of political and social forbearance. The Great War had aggravated the difficulty. It was altogether unrealistic to expect backward Russia to develop the sophisticated socialism propagated by Marx and Engels. The Bolsheviks were themselves barbarians; they were the kind of modernisers appropriate for the country they ruled.

Wells, Russell and Bauer wrote in a measured tone and were widely influential. Generally, however, such self-restraint was not in vogue, and most people looked for simple descriptions and a simple prognosis. Supporters of the Soviet political experiment were drawn to John Reed; the opponents welcomed memoirs in the style of Sir Paul Dukes. On both sides there was a strongly exotic flavour. Pro-Soviet writers insisted that citizens of the USSR had been elevated in spirit and been granted opportunities to improve their conditions to a level unparalleled in other countries. Supposedly communists were developing a model of society surpassing every great achievement of humankind. Such writings had a vivid touch of otherworldliness. Russians were made to appear unlike the rest of the nations of the world. This experiment in exotic portraiture had a hostile twin in the work of anti-Soviet writers. For them, the entire period since October 1917 had been a human abattoir. Communists, far from being inspiring idealists, were depicted as fanatics who had steeped their hands in the blood of their victims. The Soviet republic was no utopia but a nightmare for its people. The Bolshevik party had presided over some of the greatest horrors in history: police terror, dictatorship, fiendish tortures, military carnage, malnutrition and disease.

Communist parties used fair means or foul to refute their critics and concentrated their effort on workers and intellectuals. They also appealed to national groups which suffered from discriminatory treatment. They went on fostering communist ideas in the colonies of the European empires as well as in South America. Angry, alienated and idealistic men and women existed in the working classes of the world. Communist parties worked to bring them into their ranks. The recruits were offered a vision of a perfect future as well as a sense of dignity and purpose through party membership. Rivalry among the parties on the political left remained ferocious; but although the communists had no monopoly of success in their recruitment campaigns, they did increasingly well in the course of the 1920s.

They also had greater success with some national, ethnic or religious groups than with others. Jews had supplied leaders and activists to revolutionary parties in the Russian Empire wildly out of proportion to their size in the population. Not only the Bolsheviks but also the Mensheviks and Socialist-Revolutionaries attracted many talented Jewish recruits. The anti-socialist political parties, both in Russia and abroad, exploited this. The most extreme position was taken by the European far right, which called the October Revolution a Jewish conspiracy against civilised values. Hitler, the Austrian corporal who fought in the German armed forces in the First World War, was already putting this accusation into his rabble-rousing speeches in the Weimar Republic. Antisemitism, stretching back nearly two millennia, was abruptly intensified by the reports that Jews filled crucial posts in Sovnarkom. The fact that Sovnarkom also aimed unequivocally at world governance fed resentment towards Jewish people living in many societies which faced basic problems of recovery from the Great War. Trotski, Zinoviev and Kamenev became whipping boys for fascist agitators, cartoonists and sensationalist authors.

But, if the unwholesome propaganda is laid aside, Jews were certainly attracted to communism in the 1920s to an extraordinary extent. Not all Jews joined communist parties. Far from it: most of them stayed outside politics altogether. In New York the authorities were amazed by the higgledy-piggledy complexion of Jewish religious sectarianism which had flooded into the city since the turn of the century. But an important and noticeable minority of young Jews, including women as well as men, took up Marxism as they rejected the faith of their ancestors.[25] The leadership of the Communist Party of the USA was overwhelmingly Jewish by background. Why did they and their followers flock to Marxism? Among the factors was a quest for a set of ideas resting on internationalist premises. Communists were meant to be nationally blind. Another specific attraction of communism was its replication of Judaic traditions of book-learning, exegesis and prediction. And since Jews in many countries, including the USA, came from communities still mired in poverty and exhausting labour it was no surprise that they turned in large numbers towards an ideology of the far left. They could immerse their religious identity in a secular credo which promised heaven on earth to those who were willing to struggle for their beliefs.

Marxism was immensely inspiring to those national minorities in many societies which placed a premium on educational achievement and social advancement. This characteristic was not confined to Jews. Wherever minorities felt that the existing order of things was tilted against them there was an opportunity for communist organisers to make their presence felt. The Chinese in south-eastern Asia were to be notable examples after the Second World War. What impressed many recruits to communism around the world was the determination of Marxists to eliminate racist prejudices. The Indian communist M. N. Roy recalled attending congresses where people had their first experience of 'brown and yellow men [meeting] white men who were not overbearing imperialists but friends and comrades, eager to make amends for the evils of colonialism'.[26]

Soviet communist leaders exploited their opportunity with muscular panache. Their Agitation-and-Propaganda department in the central party apparatus, abetted by Comintern's publishing arm, turned out newspapers and pamphlets extolling the policies of the day. Pluralism existed only to the extent that factional disputes arose in Moscow. These usually took place in a circumscribed fashion. Although Trotski called for an increased amount of state economic planning, he still supported the NEP. Kamenev and Zinoviev too asked that the policy should be adjusted rather than jettisoned. The Democratic Centralists urged the adherence to democratic procedures in the one-party state while seeing no contradiction between their calls for 'soviet democracy' and the dictatorship of a single party. The nearest that any Bolshevik faction came to overturning basic principles of Bolshevism occurred with the Workers' Opposition. Shlyapnikov and Kollontai in 1921 had campaigned for the 'producers' – the workers and the peasants – to have some control over decisions about how the production of goods was organised and how their subsequent distribution was undertaken. Lenin called the Workers' Opposition an anarcho-syndicalist deviation. This was polemical hyperbole. The Workers' Opposition had put together a mishmash of ideas. Their wish was to reform the system of power sufficiently to allow ordinary working people to have influence; but they did not advocate the dismantlement of a centralised party dictatorship.

Outside the ranks of organised Marxism, Alexander Bogdanov continued to agitate for 'proletarian culture' (which had been among the reasons for his rift with Lenin in 1908).[27] The communist authorities indulged him to the extent of subsidising the Proletkult movement which ran classes for workers in sculpture, painting and natural sciences as well as reading, writing and arithmetic. Bogdanov was firmly convinced that a socialist seizure of power was worthless unless the working class developed confidence in its autonomous capacities. He hated the bossiness of the intelligentsia and thought Lenin and Trotski were prime examples of the type. Authoritarian thought, according to Bogdanov, pervaded official Bolshevism. Salvation lay in getting workers to apply their collectivist mentality to the tasks of building a new and better society without interference by the radical bourgeoisie. He did not welcome the October Revolution but accepted it as a fact of life and tried, within the limits imposed by the Soviet regime, to strengthen Proletkult. He was the movement's inspiration. Yet he was soon a disappointed man: his dream of helping the working class to attain the collective confidence, ambition and independence to elaborate their own version of socialism was unfulfilled. Bogdanov killed himself in a mysterious blood-transfusion accident – or was it suicide? – in 1928.

Another Marxist who thought about such questions was Antonio Gramsci, who founded a Proletarian Culture Institute.[28] Gramsci was a communist with a touch of the libertarian about him. Friendly, even boyish in appearance, he was the Italian Communist Party's much loved leader. Unlike Bogdanov, he revered Lenin. But he told a friend: 'I'm Italian, I study Marx, I study the Russian revolution, I dwell on Lenin and see that he did not apply Marxist theory by simply parroting it. So why shouldn't I adapt Marxism and the Russian revolution to the Italian situation?'[29] Gramsci never forgot his experience of revolutionary ferment in Turin in 1919–20. He remembered his Italian cultural heritage and cherished the works of the great Italian social thinkers, especially Niccolò Machiavelli and Benedetto Croce. Apparently he had never heard of Bogdanov but he would surely have queried whether the autonomous development of a 'proletarian culture' was truly practicable. Yet he shared with Bogdanov a distaste for the narrowing confines of Soviet communism. Gramsci understood the need to change the fundamental culture if ever politics were to be basically changed.

What did he mean by this? As leader of the Italian Communist Party, he wanted his own ideas to be taken seriously. He never advertised his objections to Comintern's instructions. Imprisoned by Mussolini in 1926, he cloaked his written thoughts in Aesopian language as the authorities were ever on the alert. Gramsci also lost close contact with what was happening in the world communist movement. He had a lot to say none the less. He was deeply affected by what he had learned about ancient Roman and then Renaissance Italian history. As a Marxist he accepted that economic and political coercion was important for feudal or capitalist society, but he did not stop at that: he asserted that the ruling classes under both feudalism and capitalism had depended on asserting their cultural 'hegemony'. The monks gave indispensable help to the feudal knights; the clergy, academics and scientists assisted the bankers and industrialists. In order for socialism to succeed, its advocates had to impress their ideas on the working class. Workers needed to have the self-confidence in their culture which would impress most other groups in socialist society: they had to develop their own hegemonic position.

Gramsci disliked the militaristic side of Bolshevism. In his *Prison Notebooks* he pointed to the undesirability of Trotski's labour armies, and he was to reach a similar verdict on Stalin's reliance on 'the virtue of arms'. He also had his reservations about Bukharin, who seemed to him to hold to a crude belief in the objective reality of the external world. Gramsci wanted communists to test out all their ideas in practice rather than start from axiomatic propositions.[30] He detected problems in the 'rigidification' of the communist party. Among the books from his library he sent for was the classic study of political parties by Robert Michels, who exposed the tendency of leaders to cut themselves off from their followers.[31]

Sick and neglected, Gramsci was to perish in prison in April 1937. Even if he had escaped his confinement, it is doubtful that he would have been gently treated by a Comintern that stuck to the current Bolshevik precepts. (He had been beaten up by his comrades in confinement for objecting to Stalin's execution of Zinoviev in 1936.) Gramsci was not the only foreign Marxist to pursue the quest for a less rigid and narrow Marxism. György Lukács, People's Commissar for Public Education in the Hungarian Soviet Republic in 1919, had found refuge in the USSR and wrote *History and Class Consciousness*. Like Gramsci, he retained belief in the need for a 'proletarian revolution' characterised by the working class emancipating itself. In 1917 such a notion would have been acceptable among most Bolsheviks. At least, it could have been accepted if it could have been understood; for Lukács expressed himself in Hegelian terminology impenetrable to anyone lacking postgraduate competence in philosophy. Be that as it may, times had changed. In a period when the primacy of the party's role in revolutionary action was axiomatic, Lukács's book was thought heretical. When Zinoviev denounced the ideas, Lukács immediately recanted: he could not bear to live outside the embrace of official communism.

The global wrangling among Marxists went entirely over the heads of most people who took an interest in communism. But by the end of the 1920s the reportage on Soviet Russia had greatly improved. The structures, practices and policies of communism were becoming better known through the work of diplomats, newspaper correspondents and intelligence agents. Emigré revolutionaries added their informed perspective to the picture. Their statements were contested by the communist parties and their fellow travellers. Throughout the decade there was a wrestling over ideas as each side laid claim to an exclusive capacity to make sense of communism.

12. THE USSR IN TORMENT

In January 1928 Joseph Stalin set off on a tour of inspection in the Urals and Siberia. With him he took a picked team of officials. The stimulus was the deficit of food supplies to the cities. Famine seemed possible by the winter's end if nothing was done. The terms of Stalin's assignment had not been defined; he relished the vagueness. He travelled along the Trans-Siberian Railway in a carriage that was far from being luxurious – it was not until the Second World War that he had one built for his exclusive personal use. His destination was Novosibirsk in mid-Siberia. En route he barked at administrators at the meetings he held at his stopovers. No longer watched over by Politburo members, he behaved as he pleased.

Party officials in the region heard from Stalin's lips that something far beyond the restoration of commercial equilibrium was required. On his own initiative he ordered the seizure of grain and, ultimately, the formation of collective farms. Functionaries would be assessed severely. Only practical results counted for him. Some of the recommended procedures were akin to those used in the civil war – Stalin did not have to invent them. The kulaks – the better-off peasants – were to be isolated from the other rural inhabitants. The party was to work with poor peasants to uncover grain hoards, and those who helped would be rewarded with a share of what was found. The General Secretary was changing policy out of sight of the Politburo. His intimidating presence had an immediate impact and he returned to Moscow in February with wagonloads of grain. But he had shredded any lingering trust in the government among the peasantry. Having withheld grain from the market because of the low agricultural prices as well as the shortage of industrial products on sale, rural households reacted angrily to what became known as Stalin's 'Urals–Siberian method'. He had not just undermined the NEP: he had destroyed it.

Brusque and volatile, Stalin declared that the time had come to thrust the party on to the road of fundamental economic transformation.

He aimed to resolve the other basic questions that had been tormenting the minds of party leaders. He would settle accounts once and for all with his internal party enemies as well as with the social groups hostile to the October Revolution; and he would answer all criticism that the objectives of Bolshevism had been forgotten. He bristled at Trotski's jibe that he was the 'gravedigger' of the Revolution. One advantage that he had over his enemies was that they underestimated him. They frequently expressed fears about his conduct.[1] But they did nothing serious in consequence; and Stalin, like Napoleon, thought it bad form to interrupt his enemies while they were making mistakes. They relapsed into complacency until such time as he went after them. They never got the true measure of him. His rivals for the succession to Lenin gauged him by the wrong criteria. He did not speak German, French or English. He was a poor public speaker. He had never been an émigré. He lacked poise in any genteel milieu. He was downright ill-mannered.[2]

But he was more intelligent and dynamic than his enemies appreciated, and no one was more concupiscent of power. Born in 1878 to the family of a poor cobbler in Georgia, he had been picked out to train for the priesthood. Bright and unruly, he hated the seminary discipline. First he turned to poetry and then he found Marxism. Despite often being imprisoned, he stuck to the life of the revolutionary. Stalin was a competent organiser and editor; and although he cultivated a working-class image, he was a well-schooled man with a voracious eagerness for books. By 1912 he had been co-opted to the Central Committee. Four years in Siberia followed before he returned to active politics. In 1917 he undertook important political, editorial and administrative work for the party. After the October Revolution he was the People's Commissar for Nationalities' Affairs. He entered the first permanent Politburo and Orgburo in 1919. He knew his Marxism and was a dedicated Leninist. He was bursting to prove his worth; he raged to avenge the many slights that, in his own mind, he had unfairly endured. He would be the leader to take the October Revolution forward. He did not intend to go down in history as a bureaucratic footnote.

Stalin was the most violent of the leading Bolsheviks. His terror campaigns in the civil war were gruesome. He adopted a military-style tunic and knee-length black boots, and his soup-strainer moustache indicated a pugnacious man. At tactics and conspiracy he was masterful. He had reached dominance in the party before Trotski, Zinoviev, Kamenev and Bukharin knew what had happened. There was no keeping a bad man down in the politics of the USSR. He was moving with the current of attitudes of many officials in the party, its youth organisation – the Komsomol – and the Cheka. The USSR was falling behind the advanced capitalist countries in industrial technology and military might. The NEP was never going to close the gap. Existing policies, moreover, generated social, national, religious and cultural problems for the Soviet state. Militant Bolshevism was becoming humbled. Veteran Bolsheviks had not made the October Revolution and fought the civil war in order to preside over such a deviation from their revolutionary dreams. Stalin knew that he could count on the support of central and local elites if he threw aside the NEP. All he needed was tactical finesse and political willpower, and he had both these qualities in superabundance.[3]

Returning from the Urals and Siberia in February 1928, he broke up his partnership with Bukharin. As Bukharin predicted, rural intransigence intensified. The Politburo zigzagged in policy over subsequent months but in the end decided that Stalin's emergency measures had to be prolonged if grain supplies were to be secured. Stalin began to argue that the moment had arrived to replace household-based peasant agriculture with collective farms. Traders in towns and villages were put under arrest.[4] Stalin's hostility to the kulaks was equally fierce. No kulak or his relatives could enter the new farming system. Severe repression was ordered for them. Some were shot, others deported to inhospitable regions of the USSR like Siberia and Kazakhstan; the luckier ones were simply banished from the district of their current residence and forced to start their lives again with meagre resources. Officially the rest of the peasantry was to be induced to accept collectivisation by methods of persuasion. In reality the authorities used whatever force was required to herd peasants into the system devised for them in Moscow. The centre fixed the tempos for collectivisation. Stalin sent emissaries to enforce compliance and they dared not return without being able to report success. A blitzkrieg was waged on the countryside.

The assaults in 1929 took the peasantry unawares. As the intentions of the authorities became plain, there was active resistance. It was strongest in regions like the north Caucasus and central Asia where national and religious sentiment was strong. Southern Russia too was on fire with revolts against communism. The regime smashed down these peasant uprisings. The Politburo deployed the Red Army despite having worried that the conscripts might side with the peasantry. The regime also assembled 25,000 volunteers in armed squads empowered to enforce agricultural collectivisation. Party and soviet officials too were mobilised. All these agencies had been indoctrinated to look on starvation as the outcome of kulak sabotage and resistance. As peasants got wind of the fate intended for them they banded together to repel the collectivisers. The insurgents were no match for the invaders. The authorities possessed vastly superior firepower and were better placed to co-ordinate their operations over large areas.

A millennium of peasant customs was violently cast aside. By March 1930 the proportion of collectivised households in the countryside had reached 55 per cent. Complaints about 'excesses' disconcerted Stalin at this point, and he called for moderation. But he had let loose the collectivisers again within months. He chastised any party committee which failed to ensure an uninterrupted realisation of policy. He achieved what he wanted. Almost 99 per cent of all cultivated land had been pulled into collective farms by the end of 1937. The ghastly price paid by the peasantry has yet to be established with precision, but probably up to five million people died of persecution or starvation in these years.[5] Ukrainians and Kazakhs suffered worse than most nations. Ukraine, rich in agricultural soil and independent farmers, was afflicted by famine in 1932–3. Stalin's instruction to stop people leaving Ukraine in search of work and food made things worse. The situation was no better for the Kazakhs. These people belonged to tribal groups of nomads who knew nothing of settled agriculture. About half their population perished while undergoing sedentarisation. Ukrainians and Kazakhs trapped mice, chewed bark and boiled leaves as their normal supplies vanished. The rest of them perished.

Stalin had originally intended that the revenues from grain exports – or the 'tribute', as he privately called it – would pay for higher real wages as well as for investment in rapid industrial growth. The working class was promised a drastic betterment in conditions. The State Planning Committee (Gosplan) was ordered to compose a five-year plan for industrialisation. Whenever Gosplan submitted a draft, the Politburo raised the targets of output still higher. Iron, coal, steel and machine tools were given greatest emphasis. Advice from most economists was ignored. Sergei Strumilin, a proponent of 'teleological' planning, was a rare one who spontaneously supported Stalin. The Politburo and Gosplan thought up quotas for the economy regardless of predicted difficulties. The goal of the first five-year plan, scheduled for completion by the end of 1933, was to secure the USSR's progress along the road to becoming a modern, industrial and socialist society.

Industrial managers and local party bosses were commanded to achieve the dream. Rough methods were condoned; results alone counted. This was hardly planning as anyone had ever envisaged it. The communist leadership was like a blind man painting a picture. The idea had been to export grain in return for technological imports. Yet world cereal prices had unexpectedly collapsed. Stalin did not flinch. Rather than do without up-to-date machinery, he budgeted for a lowering of living standards. Wages tumbled. Shop shelves were poorly stocked. Factory labourers, even those with skilled jobs and above-average wages, could rarely feed themselves well. Most of them became involuntary vegetarians. Cities were founded in places where valuable natural resources had been discovered. Magnitogorsk, the new steel-making centre, was the great example. Conditions were grim for most urban inhabitants there and elsewhere. Budgetary precedence was given to industrial output over the housing and feeding of employees and their families. The barracks where they sheltered at night were little better than byres.

Yet this was also a period of revolutionary élan and a cultural revolution was proclaimed. The authorities were bent on transforming an entire society as they reinforced the drive for industrialisation. The network of schools was expanded. Evening classes were organised for the illiterate and innumerate. No sooner had teachers been trained than they were sent out to staff the new schools. Workers who gave any sign of talent were guaranteed the chance of academic or professional training. Promotees bustled around enterprises and offices spouting the official rationale for state policy. There were hundreds of thousands of them.[6] They joined the party, urging workers and peasants to work hard to build the foundations of a perfect society. The task of the current generation was to devote itself to the ideals of Marxism-Leninism. Communism was thought constructible within a single lifetime. Youngsters lined up to carry out the ruthless measures demanded by Stalin and the Politburo. Industry was expanding rapidly and jobs were abundant in the cities. Demoralised peasants were spilling in from the countryside in search of employment. Anything was better than what they left behind. The migrants, arriving fearful and penniless, put up with conditions which in the 1920s would have sparked strikes and demonstrations.

Industrialisation was undertaken with coercion. At Shakhty in the Donets Basin, on Stalin's orders, dozens of directors and engineers were arrested and charged with industrial sabotage. Among them were foreign advisers. Stalin was going for broke as he terrorised the entire managerial stratum into compliance. The defendants were brought out on 'show trial'. After being beaten up by the OGPU, they were in no condition to resist the demand that they confess to criminal activity. Trials followed in the big cities elsewhere and Stalin supervised the process. He organised the fabrication of cases against anti-Soviet conspiracies by former Mensheviks and Socialist-Revolutionaries working in the state planning agencies. These included brilliant economists such as Nikolai Kondratev, Vladimir Groman and Alexander Chayanov. Stalin arranged for the 'conspirators' to be accused of having links to the Rightists in the communist party itself. Bukharin was made to look like a traitor to the party's cause. The Shakhty trial ended in sentences ranging from long prison terms to execution. Judges in the other cases, which were directed by the Moscow political authorities, usually consigned the defendants to years of hard labour.

These travesties of judicial process achieved their intended outcome as Soviet planners, directors and managers strove to prove their enthusiasm for the economic transformation. The linkage between industry and agriculture was stressed. According to the Politburo and Gosplan, the rural economy would be boosted by 'tractorisation'. One hundred thousand tractors were to be manufactured as the modernisation of the economy picked up pace. Up-to-date weaponry was to be made available to the Soviet armed forces. The USSR was set to become a great power again in Europe and Asia. The first five-year plan was completed a year ahead of schedule in December 1932. Although the authorities fiddled the books and pretended that practically every sector of the economy had hit its official targets, there was no denying that the country had gone a long way towards achieving industrialisation.

Economic policy began to be moderated in 1933. The second five-year plan specified that priority should be shifted to bringing the newly built factories into production and eliminating the disorder in industry and trade. Output quotas were lowered. Managers and workers were called upon to toil as hard as ever but were promised a higher level of reward. The budget for consumer goods, welfare and shelter was increased; schools, theatres and parks were to be constructed. Military requirements were not to be forgotten. The worsening international situation, especially after Hitler came to power, accentuated the need for the technological modernisation of the armed forces. Yet the emphasis remained on making the best use of what had already been put in place rather than continuing with reckless industrial expansion. This did not happen without heated discussion in the Politburo, but Stalin came down on the side of those advocating moderation. Yet the little internal grouplets in the party which levelled criticisms at him kept reproducing themselves. For the moment he found it prudent to go easy on lower-level politicians, enterprise directors and society at large. But he remained edgy about the political situation.

The Politburo had also changed policy on the 'national question' at the end of the 1920s. Previously the non-Russian peoples had been allowed considerable scope for self-expression in their press, schools and administration. The party leadership became determined to tame their assertiveness. Public figures who had promoted their respective nations' causes during the NEP were denounced and sacked. Mykola Skrypnik, an outstanding Ukrainian communist veteran, committed suicide in despair at the new political line. Trials were held of professors, clerics and old activists who were accused of 'bourgeois nationalism'. The charges were trumped up that they had formed counter-revolutionary organisations and were plotting the overthrow of the communist party. At first the anti-nationalist repression was applied as much to the Russians as to the other peoples. Proceedings were instituted in 1930 against the fictitious All-People's Union of Struggle for Russia's Regen-eration.[7] But Stalin decided that it was mistaken to treat the Russian nation in this fashion. In 1932 he stopped arresting Russians for 'bour-geois nationalism'. Russia and its virtues started to be celebrated. At the same time he drastically restricted the already limited freedom of the other peoples.

The idea was to assimilate the Russians to a Soviet identity which everyone else would copy. This would exclude all association with religion. Stalin let loose the League of the Militant Godless to persecute clerics. Priests, imams, rabbis and shamans were liable to arrest. Thousands were shot. Churches, mosques and synagogues were razed to the ground. Religious treasures were ransacked. 'Little god' was mocked in official publications.

The Seventeenth Party Congress in the USSR, opening in January 1934, was called the Congress of Victors. Stalin had defeated the internal party opposition, secured his industrialisation and collectivisation pro-gramme and defended the rationale of 'Socialism in One Country'. Delegates hailed him as the 'Lenin of Today'. He towered over his own Politburo in power and prestige. Yet there was disquiet in the party as the delegates massed in Moscow. A rumour spread that a sizeable proportion of the Congress delegates were minded to replace him with his Politburo colleague Sergei Kirov. Yet Stalin survived and enjoyed his public triumph. But he remained wary – and on a personal level he was extremely lonely and anxious after his wife's suicide in 1932. Then in December 1934 an assassin killed Kirov in Leningrad. Whether Stalin had ordered the murder remains unproven. What is certain is that he exploited the situation as an opportunity to introduce emergency powers enabling three-person tribunals (*troiki*) to hold trials of suspects without the usual judicial procedures. Stalin aimed to eliminate any real or potential resistance among the upper echelons of the communist party.

He also moved to get rid of 'anti-Soviet elements' in the wider society. His measures since 1928 had caused immense resentment. He had persecuted kulaks, clerics, 'bourgeois nationalists', members of already suppressed parties, ex-oppositionists and 'former people'. Tens of millions of people fell into these categories. Many of them were returning from the camps and resettlement areas after serving out their time. Others had escaped the clutches of the OGPU during the first five-year plan. They hated Stalin and his associates. The cult of Stalin left no doubt about who was responsible for the traumas they had been suffering. Stalin did not have to invent his enemies. His activity had created a vast number of them in town and countryside in the USSR.

Repressive activity was intensified after the Kirov assassination. Hundreds of thousands of 'former people' – the surviving old nobles, bankers, landlords and their families – were deported at a moment's notice from the largest cities. This programme of social 'cleansing' was designed to increase political security. Passports had been introduced for urban residents in December 1932, which made it easier for the police to 'cleanse' the cities. On the slightest pretext the returnees from the camps were resentenced and sent back to confinement. Penal servitude was run by the Main Administration of Camps (or Gulag) – and the term Gulag quickly became a synonym for the entire camp network. Political prisoners, especially ex-Trotskyists, were never released from it. Stalin was ensuring that the resentful strata of Soviet society could never find a leadership to guide them. Blame for the death of Kirov was attributed to Kamenev and Zinoviev. The actual killer was Leonid Nikolaev, who had adhered to a Zinovievite group in the late 1920s. This was enough for Stalin to load moral and ideological responsibility on to the heads of Kamenev and Zinoviev and to put them on trial. The proceedings were filmed for the newsreels. Threatened with capital punishment, the defendants agreed to admit guilt in return for a term of imprisonment. They agreed to be suitably abject. At the same time a hunt was started to discover anyone harbouring sympathy for the ideas of the crushed internal oppositions of left and right.

By the winter of 1936–7 Stalin had made up his mind to conduct a systematic campaign of arrests and executions nowadays known as the Great Terror. His Politburo was accustomed to bending to his demands. Even so, he had to cajole them. One Politburo member, Sergo Ordzhonikidze, committed suicide when he saw where things were heading. The Central Committee too had to be brought to heel. Stalin arranged plenary sessions where Nikolai Yezhov, recently appointed head of the NKVD, explained that treacherous activity had been detected throughout the party. The NKVD was the People's Commissariat of Internal Affairs; in 1934 it had taken over the functions of the OGPU. Yezhov said that reports indicated that Bukharin and others were up to no good. When Bukharin denied the charge, Stalin brought him face to face with his denouncer. Not only Bukharin but also the entire Central Committee were being terrified and demoralised.

Stalin wished to impose his unconditional despotism. The party was the sole remaining institution with the capacity to change the direction of events. Many communist leaders in the republics and the provinces, even while praising him in public, were horrified by his political and economic fanaticism. Stalin cut into the flesh of the party to assure himself that only the 'healthy' elements survived. He had the same intentions towards the Red Army high command. Mikhail Tukhachevski and other military leaders were arrested in May 1937; they were shot in June after being forced to admit to state treason – the bloodstains remained on Tukhachevski's signed confession. The Central Committee met in plenary session and was asked to sanction what had been going on. Osip Pyatnitski, high-ranking functionary in Comintern, objected to the massacres. He expressed doubt that the charges against party comrades were valid. This was tantamount to calling Stalin a tyrant and fraudster, but Pyatnitski refused to back down. His Central Committee membership was withdrawn and then he was snatched by the NKVD and executed. No one in the supreme party organs repeated his suicidal act of courage.

Yezhov and Stalin together formulated a plan for a mass 'operation', scheduled to start in late summer. Decree 00447 stipulated that 259,450 'anti-Soviet elements' should be taken into custody. Twenty-eight per cent of them were to be executed, the rest to be sent to labour camps for lengthy periods. Categories of people were specified who were to be hunted down; they included anyone who had been a kulak, priest, Menshevik, Socialist-Revolutionary, 'bourgeois nationalist', aristocrat or banker.[8] Other such operations followed. Particular national groups, especially those living in the borderlands of the USSR with compatriots in nearby foreign states, were targeted: Poles, Greeks, Germans and Koreans.

The Great Terror was not brought to an end until November 1938; Stalin started to behave with greater prudence only after exhausting the alternatives. It had been carried out according to the system of numerical quotas established in economic planning. Stalin could not trust the NKVD and party to go about their tasks effectively without this. The result was the chaos characteristic of the Soviet industrial campaign. When the purgers could not find people in the social and political categories set for them by Stalin and Yezhov, they simply set out to meet the numerical quotas – and frequently they set out to over-fulfil them. Local police chiefs who failed to achieve their quotas immediately became victims themselves. The incentive was to seize just about anyone off the streets. Stalin himself chose his victims in the most arbitrary fashion. Three hundred and eighty-three 'albums' were presented to him. Against some names he scrawled a '1' (for shooting), against others a '2' (for ten years in the Gulag). Where he placed a '3', he left the decision to Yezhov's discretion.[9] Evidently he was intent on replacing most of the USSR's public leadership. His working assumption was that holders of high posts should be treated as traitors unless there was pressing reason to spare their lives. Although he had reason to suspect that many wanted him removed from power, the real plots against him were few and weak. Essentially Stalin was overseeing a preventive operation to get rid of people who had the slightest potential to oppose him.

Stalin had a gross personality disorder: he did not care that he was murdering wholly innocent comrades, including several who were shot while proclaiming their affection for the Leader. He could not have got away with this unless he had the co-operation of Politburo members. He also relied on the party, the police and the government; he had built up their institutional strength in previous years and could deploy state power without fear of popular resistance. He could draw on the ruthless ideology of Leninism.[10]

The process was facilitated by the opportunity it offered for promotion. Plenty of ambitious young officials in every institution were ready to denounce their superiors. They took their jobs and apartments and bought up their personal possessions; they themselves hoped against hope to stay out of range of the terror machinery. Workers and peasants were not always averse to collaborating with the NKVD. There had been awful hardship for most members of society. The authorities suggested that responsibility lay with treacherous officials who had acted as saboteurs and spies for foreign powers and sought the restoration of capitalism. Working people, after years of resentment, eagerly denounced their tormentors: party militants, farm directors, enterprise managers, teachers and engineers. It was dangerous to be thought to have protected an 'enemy of the people'. The best way to stay on the right side of the NKVD was to be eager to denounce. There had been huge disruption of the settled patterns of social life. Millions had moved from the country-side to the cities. Neighbours were strangers to each other. Families had been broken up. It was tempting for individuals to look after themselves by showing unkindness to others.

From the mid-1930s there were always around two million convicts in the labour camps. There were further millions of forced settlers torn from their homes and livelihoods and hurled into the grimmest parts of the country. They were used as labour for important projects of the second and third five-year plans. They dug canals, sawed timber, mined for gold and built new cities. Labour camps were set up in Siberia and north Russia wherever an economic purpose was served.

13. THE SOVIET MODEL

Stalin and his cronies had stirred up the revolutionary storm and must have worried that it would end up by blowing them away. But, if they felt such concerns, they kept quiet about them. Stalin stamped on any vacillation inside the leading group. He would finish the job he had started. They would obey or suffer his punishment.

The last components of the Soviet model of communism had been bolted into place. Other variants of the model would have been tried out if Trotsky, Zinoviev or Bukharin had secured the political succession; but quite what each alternative leader would have developed is difficult to say. Like Stalin, they had frequently changed their policies since 1917 and could easily have done so again. The important point, however, is that they approved of many features of the USSR under Stalin. They agreed that communism should include the one-party dictatorship, the ideological monopoly, revocable legality, societal mobilisation and militant urbanism. Even Bukharin went along with this. Nor is it clear that they would have stuck with their alternatives if there were to have been resistance in the country (as would surely have been the case). Trotski in particular had a record of talking sweet reason in opposition and behaving ferociously in power. He had been beaten to supreme power in the party by a man who had consistently talked and acted ferociously in the early years after the October Revolution. Yet no one had expected even Stalin to build the ziggurat of the Soviet terror-state so high. They repeatedly claimed that Lenin's legacy had been abused.

Stalin's personal supremacy was not yet entirely secure in the early 1930s. Trotski and Bukharin still hoped to return as leaders of the USSR, and both of them retained their admirers. Bukharin was rehabilitated in 1934 and made chief editor of the government newspaper *Izvestiya*; he was no longer in the Politburo, but if Stalin had stumbled he would have been in a useful position to tread him underfoot. Trotski, after having been deported from the USSR in 1929, kept up limited clandestine contact with supporters in Moscow and published his *Bulletin of the*

Opposition. He said that collectivisation should have been undertaken on a voluntary basis. He also claimed that he would have managed state affairs much more competently across the range of policies. Since 1923 he had criticised the decline in democratic procedures in the party. He had even come to call for greater authority for the soviets. Bukharin, while agreeing with Trotski in condemning the violence of collectivisation, was eager to reinstate the NEP in full order (whereas Trotski had been demanding a rapid increase in industrial investment throughout its duration); he also gave much emphasis to a scheme for workers and peasants to write and publish complaints about corruption and inefficiency in politics.

These differences, however, were mainly about tactics and strategy and not about ultimate objectives. Bukharin in the mid-1920s had urged the removal of the regime's harshness: 'I consider that we must as soon as possible move towards a more "liberal" form of Soviet power: fewer repressions, more legality.'[1] Yet this was hardly a proposal for fundamental reform, and anyway it was contained in a confidential letter to the security police and he never campaigned openly for his proposal.

Bukharin, like all Bolsheviks, aimed to sustain communist political power and prevent the Mensheviks, Socialist-Revolutionaries or Kadets from returning to public life. The USSR was to remain a communist monopoly. Both Trotski and Bukharin wanted an economy entirely owned and planned by the state. The market sector in industry, agriculture and trade was supposed to disappear as soon as was feasible. Although this might take longer than Stalin had allowed, no leading Bolshevik intended to allow capitalism to exist for ever. It is true that Trotski and Bukharin called for increased freedom of discussion for Bolsheviks, but they did not abandon their commitment to a strictly centralised party. They idealised the party's organisational arrangements in the civil war which had been criticised by oppositionists at the time as intolerably authoritarian. They had no objection to severe censorship or to the state monopoly of the press. Like Stalin, they aimed to expunge religion, national assertiveness and other anti-communist ideologies from the media. While disapproving of the mayhem of the early 1930s, they endorsed the persecution of communism's enemies in general terms. In fact they no longer thought of it as persecution: they shared the assumption that revolutions had to be defended by merciless measures.

They went on believing, with minor reservations, that the central party leadership had the right and duty to decide everything. Popular opinion could always be rejected. Bolshevism after 1917 picked up its old theme that the 'masses' needed to be told what was good for them. Constitutional and legal discrimination against the former ruling classes and their supporters was to be maintained. Aristocrats, priests and ex-policemen could be discarded as 'former persons'. Meanwhile party organisers and communist propagandists should work on the rest of society – the 'people' itself. Demands by workers for higher wages should be resisted. Peasants who called for a lowering of taxes should be ignored. Everyone should struggle for the greater communist good.

Communists had preached and commanded since the October Revolution, and the habit was reinforced in the 1930s. Party officials became punitive know-alls. As the NEP was eliminated, the state penetrated more and more areas of life. Space for a civil society was virtually abolished; all organisations with the slightest autonomy from communist control came under attack. The Russian Orthodox Church was subjected to the harshest treatment. Tens of thousands of priests were killed. Ecclesiastical buildings were demolished – most notoriously, the Cathedral of Christ the Saviour in central Moscow was blown up at night in 1932 to make room for a Palace of Soviets which was so grandiose in conception that it could never be built. The League of the Militant Godless was let loose with its propaganda. Publication of sacred texts, including the Bible, was forbidden. No religious edifices were built in the new cities that were constructed across the country. Church bells were removed to foundries to be melted down for industrial use. The auditory landscape was transformed. No longer did the peals of bell-ringers summon the faithful to services. Not that there were many bell-ringers, vergers or priests at liberty after their intensive violent suppression.

The Academy of Sciences was intimidated. This was one of the bodies which even the Romanov emperors had been reluctant to bully. Stalin refrained from actually appointing academicians but he arrested those whom he suspected of disloyalty, and he was pleased to accept honorary membership of the Academy. The radio and press, moreover, were state monopolies. Nothing could be broadcast or printed without prior clearance by the authorities. Even musical scores were checked in this way.

Several great artists were summarily arrested by the NKVD and thrown into the Gulag or executed. The poet Osip Mandelshtam was sent into exile in Voronezh. Temporarily reprieved, he perished of malnutrition and exhaustion on his way to a labour camp in 1938. In all the arts – literary prose, poetry, painting, film and drama – the repression continued. Stalin set up a structure of institutional control. In 1932 he induced the novelist Maxim Gorki to convoke a congress to establish the USSR Union of Writers. Individuals wanting to make a living as authors had to join it and operate inside its regulatory framework. Its secretary, Alexander Fadeev, was literature's policeman. With membership of the Union of Writers there came attractive benefits: access to dachas and sanatoria, large royalties and official prestige. On every branch of the arts and scholarship there sat a pot of gold available to intellectuals of the slightest talent if only they would bow down before Stalin. Trade unions and professional organisations were run by stooges subject to control by party and government. Whatever the occupation, there was an agency for it: lawyers, metalworkers, physicists and even militant atheists. This had been Trotski's idea in 1920 in calling for the 'statification' (*ogosudarstvlenie*) of the unions.

The state's reach was meant to be ubiquitous. Football, gymnastics and other sports were under exclusive state-sponsorship. The NKVD ran the Moscow Dinamo soccer club, the Komsomol was in control at Spartak. Stalin was present in Red Square to watch a demonstration football match on Physical Culture Day in 1936.[2] Even tiny recreational groups were pulled into the maw of the state. Harmless pursuits such as Esperanto or philately were judged subversive. By 1937 Esperantists were routinely arrested as agents of the great powers; enthusiasts who collected foreign stamps fared no better. The rule of thumb was that people who gathered together under one roof for any leisure pursuit had to be regulated.

The nomenklatura system of graduated privileges was reproduced in all spheres of public life. The only men and women who were not state employees in some fashion or other were the criminals, the mentally ill, the priests and the very elderly. Most people of pensionable age needed a job of some kind to have any income. Even the worst-paid workers, however, could use the cafeterias, kindergartens and residence-barracks of their enterprises. Incentives fostered active co-operation at least among a minority of the labour force. In 1935 the Donets Basin miner Alexei Stakhanov broke the records for hewing coal on a single shift. His example was advertised in *Pravda*, and the call went out for Soviet workers to emulate him. They received prizes in the form of extra rations and wages. The luxuries available at the apex of power were unimaginable to ordinary citizens. Kremlin politicians had dachas, nannies, governesses, special food deliveries and smart clothes. The system of

privileges was extended in a calibrated form down through the administrative levels. If an office clerk received only a packet of sugar or butter
over and above his salary, this was more than the average person could
get from the shops.

People had to fight to look after themselves and their families.
Manners were rough and ready. Life was never 'a stroll across a ploughed
field' and was unendurable without the dodges developed in the 1920s.
People idled knowing they would not be sacked. They showed no
conscientiousness on the job; they stole from their enterprises and sold
products illegally on the side. Groups of friends showed solidarity with
each other, thumbing their noses at state policies. The system of patrons
and clients existed throughout the regime.

The central authorities in the 1930s regretted the abandonment of
the old social proprieties. The cohesion of communities was breaking
down. The Kremlin therefore changed direction and demanded that
youngsters should automatically defer to their elders and betters. Women
were encouraged to have as many children as they could – and kindergartens and cafeterias were made available to enable them to remain in
the workforce. Divorce and abortions were made more difficult. In 1932
the media praised a boy, Pavlik Morozov, who had been murdered after
denouncing his father for undermining the management of their kolkhoz
(which was the name for the most widespread type of collective farm).
Patriarchal authority was subsequently reasserted. Stalin demanded
orderly relationships at home and at work. School uniforms were
reintroduced and the girls had to wear their hair in pigtails. Military
training was expanded. Even the personnel in the People's Commissariat
of External Affairs dressed like soldiers. The turbulence of industrialisation and collectivisation had to be moderated. Order, hierarchy, compliance and vigilance were the watchwords. The social effervescence of the
first decade after the downfall of the Romanov monarchy became an
object of disapproval. In return the regime widened the avenues for
promotion. Opportunities for education, industrial training and cultural
access were guaranteed. Citizens were told to expect ever better provision
of material goods and recreational facilities.

The architecture of the Soviet order as redesigned by Stalin was not
like one of those rambling country houses where wings, turrets and
pigeon lofts were added at the whim of the generation of the family in
possession. The USSR has frequently been compared to an Egyptian
pyramid with the stones at the top supported by a widening platform of
layers from top to bottom. Yet the resemblance is not a close one. The

simple outward appearance of a typical pyramid hid a maze of secret tunnels; and many pyramids over the ages lost their highest stones without collapsing under the winds of the desert. Without its supreme leadership the USSR would not have survived a single day. The communist order had an architectonic tautness unknown in physical buildings. Politics was highly centralised and, at local levels, reduced as much as possible to a process of administrative instruction and compliance. Central politicians intruded directly and deliberately into all sectors of social existence. Ideology, economics, leisure, family life and personal habits were subject to state penetration and held together by unbreakable cross-ties.

The elimination of autonomous civil associations strengthened the Soviet order. The Kremlin could set policies without consultation across the entire range of politics, economics, society, ideology and culture. Drastic switches of line were possible whenever the ascendant leadership required. Equally impressive was the capacity to concentrate resources. Factories could be nationalised, farms collectivised and social groups arrested. The organisational hierarchies were trained to relay decisions from the centre to the furthest tiny corners of the periphery with implicit obedience. The supreme leadership had endless punitive sanctions at its disposal. Communist ideology gave validation and confidence to the administrators who carried out the instructions. The country's insulation from the rest of the world facilitated operational efficiency; and the authorities were in a better position to inoculate citizens against the contagion of alien ideas.

Questions arose about the nature of the USSR. A fresh answer began to be offered in the last years before the Second World War. This was that the Soviet Union constituted a new kind of state. The word for it was 'totalitarian'. It had been coined by Benito Mussolini, who produced it to define his purposes for fascist Italy. It acquired currency in descriptions of Stalin's USSR and Hitler's Germany. Precise definitions were few on the ground until after 1945, but the general idea was widely agreed. What struck the minds of observers was the common imperatives of these three dictators to suppress political pluralism, quell criticism in the media and minimise the propagation of alternative ideologies. Due legal process was overthrown. The cult of the Leader was installed. A single party operated. A millenarian creed was poured into the minds of all citizens. Commands came down from on high without recourse to consultation with the lower levels of the political system or with the people. Associations of civil society were eliminated or emasculated. It was recognised that none of these three dictatorships fully achieved its objectives. Mussolini left the monarchy in place and signed a concordat with the Catholic Church. Hitler co-opted big business to his purposes without wholly eradicating its freedom. Stalin never liquidated the Orthodox Church or eradicated private profit from the economy. Totalitarianism failed to be comprehensively realised anywhere.

The order entrenched by Joseph Stalin involved centralism, hierarchy, discipline, mobilisation and terror; state power on a scale unprecedented in world history – until Hitler's Third Reich – had been amassed. Political intrusion into social life was like a dagger plunged into butter. Privacy was devalorised. The state counted for everything, the individual for nothing. People were treated like coal or wheat: they became a resource exploitable for the public cause. To outsiders it appeared that communism had already acquired a comprehensive – perhaps even a total – control over an entire society.

Yet fraud, corruption and misinformation inevitably proliferated even more strongly than in most liberal-democratic states. Measures were formulated on the basis of false data. Although the supreme leaders wanted to know about difficulties, lower-level officials had reason to keep the truth to themselves and deliberately misled the leadership.[3] Governments in the West operated alongside bodies which on occasion might oppose them: churches, the press, the judiciary and the various social associations of citizens. Communists regarded such bodies as a 'bourgeois' scam. The Marxist-Leninist argument was that capitalist society gave the impression of looseness and diversity while ruthlessly pursuing the fundamental interest of the ruling class. Communists grossly overstated the monolithic nature of capitalist societies; this had been a principal defect in Lenin's *The State and Revolution* and was not peculiar to Stalin and his clique. The Soviet order consequently lacked the components which enable the self-correction and self-renewal of looser systems of rule. In the USSR there was no press to object to politicians who acted dishonestly or incompetently. There was no religious institution which could point up the moral inadequacies of rulers. There were no universities whose scholars could publish criticism of official policy with impunity.

As administrative arbitrariness mounted, the amount of compulsion needed to get anything done had an effect on popular attitudes. Although sections of society were enthusiastic about Stalin's policies, millions of individuals complied only out of dread of punishment. Genuine approval was always difficult to obtain from society. Such a situation created a cycle of passive disobedience by ordinary people – and, in many cases, administrators – followed by massive state pressure to mobilise them to carry out their designated tasks. It is true that this had been an old Russian tradition. The communists were stultifying the developments which had been moving in the opposite direction before 1917. They did this unconsciously; after seizing power with the intention to destroy old Russia, they restored many of its worst customs; and when further communist states were installed after the Second World War, the same phenomenon of popular resentment and alienation occurred because of the same imposition of unelected and unconsultative authority.

The way round this was to establish bureaucracies to supervise and regulate bureaucracies. So-called control organs proliferated. Neither party nor government bodies could be trusted to get on with their tasks. The organs of control intervened regularly in institutional affairs to carry out checks on personnel, finance and due procedure. This had been happening in the first decade of communist power. The difference in the 1930s was the regular prominence of the NKVD in the investigations. From having been subordinate to the party it rose to being a counter-weight to its authority. Stalin used it to keep party officials and committees in a condition of constant willingness to carry out his orders. The NKVD was also the agency for surveying and analysing popular opinion. Confidential reports were forwarded to Stalin on a monthly basis; they were directed at gauging the extent and nature of any discontent. The authorities were always especially concerned about attitudes among workers, peasants and national minorities.[4] Of course, the reports were not unbiased. The police had an interest in playing up discontent so as to justify their existence; they also understood the need to provide Stalin with the kind of information he liked or else risk being purged. Yet Stalin too was a prisoner of the system. Without the control organs he would have been even worse informed about affairs. The Soviet order could not function without them.

It also needed a reinforced barrage of propaganda. The official party history textbook was published to ceaseless acclaim in 1938. So was Stalin's approved biography. *Pravda* as the central party newspaper dutifully and eagerly disseminated the changing communist line of the day.

Even so, the people of the USSR proved remarkably resistant to Marxism-Leninism. Believers of every faith had been used to the open practice of their beliefs, and the secular authorities assumed that the amputation of this tradition would bring an end to religion. This did not occur. When a census was taken in 1937, some 55 per cent of citizens said they believed in a deity. The true percentage was surely even higher; it was perilous for anyone to profess religious faith in that year of savage state terror, and millions of people must have pretended to be atheists. So beliefs went on being nurtured; and when the Third Reich invaded the USSR in the Second World War, Stalin recognised reality by calling the Metropolitan of Moscow to the Kremlin and offering a modest degree of freedom to the Russian Orthodox Church in return for its support for the military effort. Religious activity would seem to have intensified rather than diminished among some groups. This was true of various Christian sects which saw Stalin as the Antichrist. It was also the reaction of many Moslems who found consolation in the Koran after the social and economic depredations of the 1930s. The hatred for Stalin in the collectivised villages in particular was acute. If Stalin reviled religion, believers thought this a good reason for going on believing.

Atheism, however, undoubtedly picked up supporters. Youngsters at school were particularly vulnerable to indoctrination. From generation to generation the demographic arithmetic was on the side of the authorities even if secularisation was taking longer than had originally been intended. Marxist-Leninist indoctrination worked its effects; so too did the surgical removal of the public religious presence. Urbanisation itself had a secularising impact, as it did in most other countries of the world apart from the USA. The space occupied by faith in the USSR was reduced.

Yet even those Soviet citizens who came to share the official atheist notions were likely to think a lot differently in private about many matters. What George Orwell dubbed double-think was a pervasive phenomenon. Everybody but saints, daredevils and nincompoops parroted the communist verities when at the factory or office. Failure to do this could have disastrous consequences. If an old peasant woman was heard grumbling about conditions in her collective farm, forced labour in Siberia would follow. Most people were clever at keeping their dangerous private thoughts private. At most they would divulge them to their spouses or closest friends in the seclusion of their apartments. Even this was risky. The homes of high-ranking officials were often bugged. The NKVD summoned individuals and demanded that they reveal secrets of recent conversations. Maids, porters and drivers were routinely employed to file reports.[5] The USSR was a listening state with an insatiable curiosity. Anonymous denunciation was encouraged. This had a deleterious effect on ordinary social solidarity. Informing on others was a tempting way to get one's own back on overbearing foremen or awkward neighbours. It was also a method of getting rid of a rival and taking his job. No one could have complete confidence, however upright he or she was, that a false delation would not bring disaster in its train. The NKVD was not renowned for its investigative scruples, especially at times when it was under pressure to fulfil its arrest quotas.

Hypocrisy exists to a large or small extent in all societies – a dose of it is frequently a necessary lubricant for the functioning of social intercourse. But the arts of subterfuge were turned into a fundamental feature of the entire Soviet order. Double-speak became a way of life. Citizens needed to say one thing and do another if they wanted to survive the terror.

Another bolthole was supplied by Russian literary classics. Many of these were issued as exemplars of the country's greatness. It was an understandable device whereby the authorities sought to identify themselves with past cultural achievement. But it exploded in their hands. The works of Alexander Pushkin, Ivan Turgenev and Lev Tolstoi were avidly bought by readers who gained a glimpse of the world they had lost since the October Revolution. The non-Russians were allowed access to at least a few of their national literary giants. Across the USSR the light of a culture which shared nothing with Marxism-Leninism was kept aflame. Those works which were banned or heavily restricted – such as the novels of Fëdor Dostoevski and the poetry of Alexander Blok and Anna Akhmatova – became the object of furtive enthusiasm. The lesson was quickly learned. People found that it was a route towards retaining their sanity in a phantasmagorical world. At a lowly level there was the eagerness to poke fun at the authorities, including Stalin himself. His cult raised him above the rest of humankind. In popular anecdotes he was a villain and a fraud. Peasants routinely called him the Antichrist.

Meanwhile the old superstitions died hard. Party functionaries, teachers and journalists railed against ancient folk beliefs in wood demons and lake spirits. Witchcraft was derided. Gypsy astrologers were scoffed at. It was not just because the young, recently educated propagandists did not seem to have lived long enough to be convincing. Another factor was that the Soviet order had deprived most citizens of the mental comforts needed at a time of tumultuous change. Marxism-Leninism was always predicting the paradise of a distant future. Organised religion was pinioned by the commissar's jackboot. Customary ideas that might otherwise have expired instead gained second wind – and there were few priests, imams or rabbis around to expose them as irrational. The trend was abetted by the sheer rapidity of urbanisation; this was a congenial trend for communist leaderships everywhere until Pol Pot's regime in Cambodia in the mid-1970s. Peasants streamed into cities to escape the collective and obtain paid employment. Attitudes were transferred from countryside and were hard to dislodge. Having evacuated the space reserved for religion, communist officials witnessed it being filled by notions which predated the spread of Christianity to Russia.

PART THREE

DEVELOPMENT

1929–1947

14. WORLD STRATEGY

The jettisoning of the New Economic Policy in 1928 helped to buoy up the revolutionary radicalism of Soviet foreign policy. Comrades around the globe were ordered to adopt a more militant posture and 'world revolution' returned to Comintern's immediate agenda. Europe became the main arena; the prize was the spread of communism. It was a fissile situation, and no leading Bolshevik in the Soviet Union felt any comfort while so little was being done to promote revolution abroad. The policy of the 'united labour front' was thrown out. Instead the Politburo instructed its people in Comintern to treat the rest of the European labour movement – social-democrats and socialists – as the mortal enemies of communism. Communists were to refer to them as 'social-fascists'. The Sixth Congress of Comintern endorsed the 'turn to the left' in summer 1928. The October Revolution had initiated the first period, which was characterised by revolutionary upsurge. The second period, beginning with the defeat of the Red Army at the battle of Warsaw, had witnessed the 'relative stabilisation' of capitalism. Proclaiming the start of a 'Third Period', Stalin maintained that the prospects for revolution had suddenly improved. Comintern was told to instruct its member parties accordingly. The final, decisive struggle with world imperialism was heralded.

Many communist leaders in Europe were only too eager to follow Comintern's new line. They had entered their parties hoping to reproduce the achievements of Bolshevism in Russia, and their detestation of social-democrats and socialists was visceral. They relished the opportunity to prove their credentials as revolutionaries. Although the fact that they accepted orders and money from Moscow occasionally embarrassed them,[1] they took pride in the general connection with the USSR. Responding to critics in December 1929, the Czechoslovak communist leader Klement Gottwald declared: 'We go to Moscow to learn from the Russian Bolsheviks how to wring your necks!'[2]

Yet official policy continued to pull in more than a single direction.

Stalin still aspired to the construction of 'socialism in one country' and badly needed commercial ties with the advanced capitalist countries if he was going to sell Soviet grain abroad and buy foreign technology and expertise for industrialisation. Peace between the USSR and the great powers was essential and the People's Commissariat for External Trade sought out suppliers of the machinery required by the five-year plans. Stalin, however, simultaneously insisted on absolutely every communist party striving for a speedy revolution in its country. He disguised this by getting Comintern to give the appropriate orders. Perhaps Stalin calculated that world capitalism was so rotten that it was about to tumble to the ground and that the USSR would acquire its needed machinery from new revolutionary states. Politburo members were constantly gauging the revolutionary prospects in Europe. The question never absent from their minds was what measures would help in this direction without endangering the interests of the USSR. Doubtless factional considerations also prompted Stalin to be bold: if he wanted to remove the Bukharinists he needed a rationale in the shape of a new policy.

The General Secretary was the despair of his specialists in international relations. He did not go abroad after the October Revolution except when on campaign in the Polish–Soviet War in 1920; and his earlier trips before the Great War had been few and of short duration. Georgi Chicherin, who was External Affairs People's Commissar until 1930, expressed his concern: 'How good it would be if you, Stalin, were to change your appearance and travel abroad for a certain time with a genuine interpreter rather than a tendentious one. Then you'd see the reality!'[3] Chicherin, despite being a former Menshevik who depended on the Politburo's appreciation of his professional competence, did not worry about being sacked. He regarded it as dangerous nonsense to denounce the other socialists as 'social-fascists', and he made the Soviet leadership aware of his opinion.[4]

The idea got around that Stalin left foreign policy to others while he himself focused on internal party manoeuvres and on the USSR's economic transformation. He did not head Comintern, and the People's Commissariat of External Affairs appeared to create foreign policy. In fact no one dared to take an initiative without consulting Stalin – and this included Politburo members.[5] Comintern was no less tightly supervised. Osip Pyatnitski as Secretary to the Executive Committee and then, from 1935, Georgi Dimitrov as Secretary-General dutifully carried out the orders from the Kremlin. Dimitrov had made his name as a brave defendant in a trial held by the Third Reich in Leipzig in 1933. On release from prison in 1934, he was given Soviet citizenship and political asylum in Moscow. He never allowed Comintern to flout the Politburo's official line. The same was true of the People's Commissariat of External Affairs under Chicherin's successor Maxim Litvinov, who had co-operated with Stalin in the Bolshevik bank robberies before the First World War. But Stalin was no sentimentalist. If Litvinov was going to influence the shaping of foreign policy he needed to persuade Stalin and the Politburo of his case.

Not that Pyatnitski, Dimitrov or Litvinov failed to speak their minds to power. This indeed was their assigned function. With their factual knowledge and technical expertise they were expected to sound alarms and suggest initiatives. But when the Politburo had settled on a policy, they were just as firmly expected to implement it without complaint. They were treated more as senior technicians than as politicians who could determine the course of Soviet diplomacy or world communist activity.

Stalin and his cronies retained their internationalist perspective while giving their greatest attention to the political and economic tasks of the first and second five-year plans. They had been brought up this way as Marxists. They were also thinking pragmatically – and people at the time and afterwards failed to recognise this. The Soviet leadership understood very well that, until the USSR ended its isolation, it would remain vulnerable to invasion by capitalist states. All through the 1920s they had feared that the great powers would arm and let loose Poland, Finland or Romania against them. Until the USSR could compete in military and industrial strength, Soviet diplomacy would continue to be hobbled. It made sense to direct efforts at building up military and economic strength. (Not that the murderous methods of Stalinist industrialisation were necessary or justifiable.) It was also reasonable for Comintern to search out opportunities for revolutionary upsurge in Europe and elsewhere. If Germany could be destabilised and thrust towards communist revolution, the end of the USSR's political quarantine would come into sight. What is more, Comintern's activities were not very costly: Moscow could supply subsidies, party schools and advisers without excessive expenditure. Not for the first time after the October Revolution the Soviet leadership was riding two horses at once.

Years of condescension by the party's intellectuals were flaking away as Stalin's supremacy was confirmed. Even before his demotion from the Executive Committee of Comintern, Bukharin was demoralised, and in July 1928 he wrote to Stalin: 'I don't wish to and won't fight.'[6] Not all

Comintern functionaries were so craven. Trying to protect the 'rightists', Jules Humbert-Droz contended that Stalin's speeches had 'the same relation to the truth as to say that two and two make five'. Angelo Tasca, an Italian communist of independent mind, pronounced that Stalin was 'the standard bearer of counter-revolution'.[7] Both were removed from positions of any influence. It was not only Bukharin's supporters who were aghast. György Lukács in Moscow exile and Antonio Gramsci in an Italian prison protested at the neglect of slogans demanding democratic reforms in Europe.[8] Talk of revolutionary vanguards and insurrections was all very well, but thoughtful Marxists understood that the chances of early success were no greater than they had been in the mid-1920s. Stalin, however, was sure about what he wanted to do. He did not want a loyal opposition: he wanted no opposition at all. He wanted total victory and removed Bukharin from the Executive Committee of Comintern in April 1929.

Whenever foreign communists would not recognise him as the new boss, he cast them out into the wilderness. The leading supporters of Bukharin were dislodged from their parties. Only a full recantation of 'right-deviationist' ideas could save them – and even this was not always enough. Identifiable Bukharinists were removed from Comintern's posts in Moscow. No factional allegiance was tolerated except to his own side in the Kremlin's disputes. Stalin's personal supremacy was internationalised.

Three months later he had objective grounds for believing that global politics were moving in communism's favour. In October 1929, after chaotic weeks of trading in the world's stock markets, panic broke out among American brokers and bankers. Shares were frantically sold off, debts peremptorily called in. The result was the Wall Street Crash. National economies around the globe were convulsed and President Herbert Hoover, hero of famine relief in Europe after the First World War, had no practical ideas about how to ensure an American recovery. The world capitalist order was driven into a crippling depression. Stalin had already radicalised communist world strategy before the Crash. It looked as if his gamble was paying off. Communist parties everywhere expected to benefit from the global financial crisis. The calculation was a simple one: the worse the situation, the better the prospects of revolution. Germany, which had always been the focus of Bolshevik hopes, was worse hit than any other advanced economy. German unemployment and inflation rocketed. Wages failed to cover living expenses; the cities suppurated with discontent. Comintern relished the growing opportunities. Hitler and the Nazis were treated as a symptom of capitalism's rottenness, not as a force which might stave off the advance of communism on power.

Both Trotski after being deported to Turkey in 1929 and Bukharin deposited into disgrace in Moscow had disagreed with each other about Soviet foreign policy throughout the 1920s. But as veteran observers of global politics they concurred about the flaws in the thinking of Stalin and the Politburo. Mussolini, according to them, was bad enough but Hitler would be even worse. Trotski and Bukharin properly appreciated the dangers of fascist and other extreme-right politics in Europe; they foresaw that, if Hitler ever came to power, his first action would be to suppress the German Communist Party and arrest its militants. They were right that Stalin's insouciance about the Nazis was a stupendous blunder. Trotski also noted that Stalin's foreign policy in no way involved abandoning the commitment to building 'socialism in one country'. He was right: the Politburo continued to give priority to Soviet state security and to rule out foreign adventures by the Red Army in advance. What Trotski – and indeed Bukharin – failed to discern was that Stalin did not discount Germany's potential to disrupt international security and political stability in Europe. Unlike Stalin, however, they understood that communists would have a hard time under Nazism. They therefore urged that every effort should be made to thwart Hitler's accession to power.

Then the Japanese invaded Manchuria in 1931. There was consternation in the USSR as Tokyo's rulers established a puppet regime and set up their Kwantung Army on the newly conquered territory. The fear was that Japan had its eyes fixed on the natural resources of Siberia and could at any time throw its forces across the Manchurian border. Worries about the Far East remained a constant factor in the Soviet leadership's decisions through to the early weeks of the Second World War.

Right-wing organisations including fascists were on the rise in central and eastern Europe. Hitler's Nazi Party, whose popularity had been dipping, benefited from German economic depression. Yet Stalin instructed Comintern to command the communist parties to concentrate their fire on the other parties of the left. No trace of solidarity was to remain. Socialist, social-democratic and labour parties were to be denounced as promoters of 'social-fascism'. This was extremist language and dangerous politics. The policy of the 'united labour front', which enjoined communists to proselytise among the rank-and-file members of the other parties of the political left, was abandoned. Instead of arranging a combined preventive attack on Nazism, Stalin diverted the German Communist Party into vilifying potential allies. Street battles between the communists and the social-democrats were not uncommon in Berlin. Several German communist leaders were uneasy about the new policy but Stalin told them not to worry. His prediction was that, if ever the Nazis came to power, they would rip up the treaty of Versailles and cause a political crisis across Europe. This, Stalin suggested, would create a revolutionary situation for communists to exploit. Thus the Nazis would act inadvertently as facilitators of communist revolution: history was on the side of Comintern and the working class.

The German communists called loudly for a general strike. In a period when workers feared being laid off as the economy suffered depression, this was not a policy with wide appeal. In April 1929, when the party issued its first summons for such a strike, the labour force of only one factory (which made chocolates) downed tools. Things were hardly better for communists in later years even though party membership grew in number. Communism in Germany marched into a strategic impasse.

At the end of 1932 the Nazis emerged as the biggest party at the national election. Although they failed to gain an absolute majority, Hitler put pressure on President Hindenburg to make him Germany's Chancellor. This duly occurred on 30 January 1933. The USSR had had cordial relations with fascist Italy despite Mussolini's persecution of the Italian Communist Party; but the Third Reich was different. The Nazis did not seek friendship with Stalin. Hitler withdrew from the secret military collaboration with the USSR that had continued since the treaty of Rapallo in 1922. He restricted economic ties. The German Communist Party was suppressed and its leaders thrown into concentration camps. Hitler continued to inveigh against 'Judaeo-Bolshevism'. Yet Comintern went on concentrating on vilifying European socialists for their 'class collaboration' with the bourgeoisie. As the spectre of fascism had assumed bodily form at the heart of Europe, the German Communist Party merely polemicised with fellow parties on the left. Germany and its working class, according to the Marxist-Leninist prognosis, still offered the greatest chance of a successful revolutionary regime. Stalin and the Politburo were guilty of a total poverty of the political imagination, and they bore the principal responsibility for stopping parties on the political left from forming a united front.

People's Commissar Litvinov considered that something drastic had to be done to end the USSR's international isolation. The danger of a German crusade was too obvious to be ignored and Litvinov as a Jew was acutely aware of Nazi racialism. His position was shared by Secretary-General Georgi Dimitrov in Comintern. They badgered Stalin with requests to alter European policy. Individuals in the French and Czechoslovak parties had urged the same thing after Hitler outlawed the Communist Party of Germany in March 1933. They were told to keep quiet.[9] Yet they could not permanently be treated this way if international communism was to have any serious influence. France and Czechoslovakia had Comintern's biggest parties outside the USSR and China. Both had borders with Germany and their communist leaders and their militants did not want to share the fate of the German comrades.[10] Change at last started to come from below when, in February 1934, the militants of the communist and socialist parties combined in Paris to organise a general strike against the spread of fascist activity to France. Discipline was breaking down among the communists, and by then there was nothing that French Communist Party leader Maurice Thorez could do to stop the co-operation.

Unless Stalin could be persuaded, however, nobody could tamper with policy for the USSR and Comintern. The change came at last in September 1934, when he took the Soviet Union into the League of Nations. This was a complete turnabout. Previously the communist position had been that the League was merely an organisation whereby the capitalist powers victorious in the Great War secured their global dominance. Now Stalin ordered his diplomats to seek co-operation with such powers with a view to limiting the further expansion of the influence of Germany and Japan. Collective security became his slogan. Diplomatic overtures were made to all states concerned about the spread of fascism and militarism in Europe and Asia.

The implications for Comintern were profound. Instead of haranguing socialists and social-democrats as traitors to the labour movement, communists were to seek them as allies. Liberals too were to be approached. A way had to be found for all anti-fascist parties to unite their efforts. Italy and Germany were already a lost cause, but the French Communist Party – at Stalin's instigation – concluded a pact with socialists and liberals for the formation of a Popular Front in July 1935. This was not just a reheated dish of the 'united labour front' policy of the 1920s.[11] The idea was that French communists should work with their socialist partners at every level. They would enter electoral pacts with them and even governments. They were to moderate 'class struggle'. Obviously this would involve ceasing to refer to socialists as social-fascists. The Third Period was over; ultra-leftism in communist parties was disowned. Italy and Germany had gone fascist; France had to be saved from the same fate. Addressing the Seventh Congress of the Communist International in August 1935, Georgi Dimitrov defined fascism as 'the open terroristic dictatorship of the most reactionary, most chauvinistic and most imperialist elements of finance capital'.

At last the message went forth that Hitler and Mussolini represented a terrifying political order without precedent. Soviet politicians continued to treat the fascist dictators as the playthings of economic forces and to predict the imminent end of capitalism, but the new policy recognised the practical need for allies; and the USSR aligned itself with all those in Europe willing to fight fascism wherever it raised its head. Delegates to the Comintern congress found it hard to switch their ideas overnight but found a way of obfuscating this in their speeches. Several leaders were anyway relieved that the change had been made. Palmiro Togliatti, resident in Moscow exile after fleeing Italy in 1926, wrote eloquently in support of popular fronts. As a victim of Mussolini he needed no one to explain to him how pernicious a right-wing dictatorship might become to the labour movement.[12]

While focusing on matters of diplomacy and security, Stalin also had an economic dimension in mind. He talked publicly as if he was introducing industrial autarky; he never mentioned the Soviet state's purchases abroad. In reality he and the Politburo knew that technological self-reliance could only be a long-term objective. The USSR depended on being able to buy from the countries of advanced capitalism. It sold its grain and natural resources abroad so as to be able to pay its bills on time; and Western companies were more than willing to do business. The Wall Street Crash had shattered the world economy, and Stalin's eagerness to trade was a godsend to American industry. Ford Motors transferred equipment and expertise for the construction of the immense automotive works in Nizhni Novgorod by the River Volga.[13] The new city of Magnitogorsk had its main plant designed by the McKee Corporation in Cleveland, Ohio.[14] Having failed to tempt the Nobel Oil Company back to Azerbaijan during the New Economic Policy, the Politburo induced European and American companies to assist with renovating the Baku refineries and starting up production near Ufa.[15] Thus the USSR was tied into the world economy. Underlying the global political struggle between capitalism and communism was the contest between capitalists competing with each other to enable communist economic development.

And so Americans replaced Germans as Stalin's principal economic facilitators.[16] The businessmen themselves kept quiet about this. Being anti-communist in their own politics, they did not want to be seen as soft on the world's first communist state. Although they wanted to advance themselves as Stalin's little helpers, they did not want anyone noticing. Their wishes were respected by President F. D. Roosevelt. From the White House he smoothed the path towards diplomatic recognition of the USSR.

A Franco-Soviet pact had been signed in May 1935. Comintern and the French Communist Party saw these developments as the beginning of genuine collective security in Europe. Yet the international situation continued to worsen. When Italian leader Benito Mussolini conquered Abyssinia in October 1935, the League of Nations blustered a lot but remained a mere spectator. Comintern reinforced its policy of popular fronts across Europe. Communist parties were instructed to form alliances that would enable countries to stand strong against the expansionism of the Third Reich. The policy had its most notable success in France. National elections gave it a stunning victory in May 1936 and the socialist Léon Blum formed a cabinet. The French Communist Party refused to supply ministers but, with its seventy-two elected representatives, regularly supported him in the Chamber of Deputies. It also sought to put a stop to industrial conflict. When a vast strike movement erupted that summer, communists preached the need for negotiations. It was a highly volatile situation. Nearly two million workers were on strike by June and there were many occupations of factories. Yet Thorez held the line that the supreme priority was to sustain Blum in power. Revolutionary action was forbidden. 'One must', explained Thorez, 'know how to terminate a strike.'[17]

Then in July 1936 a civil war broke out in Spain when General Franco brought his rebel forces over from Africa and began his steady advance on Madrid. Blum's desire was to send arms to the Spanish government. Pressure, however, was brought to bear upon him. It was made clear in the Chamber of Deputies that such national unity as had been achieved would collapse if he took sides in Spain. The British government too warned against active involvement for fear of drawing the Germans and Italians into active assistance for Franco. London and Paris consequently declared their diplomatic neutrality and erected an arms embargo (although Blum secretly allowed military supplies across the Franco-Spanish border).[18] This self-restraint had no impact on Hitler and Mussolini, who more or less openly sent forces to Franco's aid.

Comintern, which had been urging co-operation among the parties of the left, expressed disgust at what it denounced as Blum's fecklessness. The Madrid government rallied support from the country's left-wing organisations, including the minuscule communist party, to throw back Franco's advance. Faced with the prospect of a third fascist state on France's borders and the collapse of the policy of European collective security, Stalin sent tanks, fighter aircraft, guns and military advisers;[19] and Comintern encouraged the formation of international brigades of volunteers to strengthen the cause. Madrid was saved and the Spanish Communist Party experienced a sharp growth in membership and influence.

The communist leaders agreed with the liberal Republicans and the bulk of the Socialist Party that the war effort had to take precedence over all other ambitions; they repudiated the revolutionary priorities of the anarcho-syndicalists of the CNT (National Labour Confederation) and the quasi-Trotskyists of the POUM (Workers' Party of Marxist Unification). Strict military and political discipline was imposed. And Stalin took the drive for centralisation of the war effort still further by ordering the Spanish Communist Party to conduct a violent purge of the POUM. Thus he relocated the methods, if not the scale, of the Great Terror of the USSR to Iberian soil.[20] Trotski fulminated against such barbarity. He also condemned Comintern and the French Communist Party for failing to strive for revolution in France in mid-1936. Trotski, as usual, overestimated the likelihood of success. If the communists had adopted an insurrectionary strategy, they would have isolated themselves on the French political left. Unlike Russia in 1917, France did not have an overwhelming mass of the industrial working class in favour of a seizure of power. Trotski was correct, though, in highlighting Stalin's caution. He rightly asked what kind of situation was ever going to induce Comintern to sanction a communist uprising. Comintern had long ceased to answer his criticisms. Its apparatus was the handmaiden of Soviet security interests. Anti-fascism had replaced socialist revolution as its immediate strategic objective.

Yet Stalin had grounds to conclude that neither the European democracies nor the USA had the nerve to stand up to Hitler. Franco's army seized the main cities one by one, and the result by February 1939 was the overthrow of the government and the assumption of power by Franco. Hitler shook off all restraint. In November 1936 Germany and Japan had signed a treaty aimed against international communism, and Italy joined them in the following year. This Anti-Comintern Pact, as it was known, was dedicated to extirpating communist influence around the world. Events in central Europe had yet greater immediate importance as the Third Reich expanded its power and its borders with impunity. It had started by reoccupying the demilitarised Rhineland in March 1936. Austria was annexed in March 1938. Britain and France, victors in the Great War, made concession after concession to Nazi demands. Neville Chamberlain and Edouard Daladier agreed in Munich in September 1938 to consign Czechoslovakia's Sudetenland to the Third Reich. Hitler devoured the rest of Czechoslovakia in March 1939. His anti-Soviet writings and speeches treated Moscow as the centre of a Judaeo-Bolshevik world conspiracy allied to Wall Street's financial interests.

The occupation of the Sudetenland was one act of appeasement too many for Comintern, and the French Communist Party withdrew its support for the Daladier government and organised a general strike in November.[21] The policy of popular fronts in Europe lay in pieces. The dream of collective security in Europe was defunct: the liberal democracies had been put to the test by Nazi diplomacy-by-ultimatum and found wanting.

Stalin and his subordinates were becoming desperate about the security of the USSR. At the governmental level it had no reliable allies and faced threats from east and west; and the Kremlin had to assume that the great powers might turn a blind eye if the USSR was invaded by Germany or Japan. Communism in Europe was noisy but ineffectual in its efforts to gain power. Its greatest impact – in France, Britain and the USA – was in influencing the general climate of opinion without standing a chance of forming a government. This is not to say that the more distant parties of Comintern went into oblivion. Chinese communists had undertaken their Long March to the country's north and were assembling a formidable Red Army. The Communist Party of India was prominent in the agitation against British rule. In Vietnam and the rest of Indochina the anti-colonial struggle was bolstered by communist participation. Comintern had affiliated parties throughout Latin America, and organisations were sprouting even across Africa. But this was treasure for tomorrow, not for today. The USSR was at the centre of the world communist movement. It would stand or fall because of what was done by the great powers on earth, and its vulnerability to assault had not diminished since the 1920s despite the increase in Soviet military and industrial capacity.

Politburo members including Stalin still believed in the superiority of communism over rival state orders. They went on professing that their kind of revolution was an inevitable denouement around the world. Their achievements were impressive. Much had been accomplished since 1928 to build up the USSR's industrial, educational and military might – and the Soviet leaders were not in the least troubled by the price paid in human losses. Business transactions, especially with American firms, had been numerous and successful. Even so, 'history' was proving too laggardly for Soviet interests. The USSR remained a beleaguered state. But the Politburo under Stalin could reasonably claim to be conducting foreign affairs as Lenin would have done. Stalin himself, furthermore, was forever citing the Leninist recommendation to stay out of any war among the principal capitalist states. The USSR was not going to 'pull the chestnuts' out of the fire for capitalism. Stalin also repeated – and firmly believed in – Lenin's prediction of an unending sequence of world wars until such time as capitalism was overthrown. He lived and breathed the dangers confronting the USSR.

15. STALINIST IDEOLOGY

Marxist-Leninist ideology in the Stalin years was extremely crude. But it was a house with many rooms. Stalin and his propagandists intended to appeal to the scientist and the worker, the engineer and the milkmaid, the Uzbek party functionary and the recruit to communism in France, India or the USA, so space was deliberately left at the margins for diverse interpretation and adaptation. They were successful in their own time in appealing to millions of people; and, in amended versions, basic features of the ideology were relayed to subsequent generations in the USSR and other communist states.

The constitution of 1936 categorised the Soviet Union as a 'socialist state of workers and peasants' issuing from 'the overthrow of the landlords and capitalists'. The clauses were unceasingly vaunted by the propagandists. Foreign commentators – there were of course no unofficial commentators in Moscow – failed to notice that the constitution avoided saying whether the Soviet Union remained a dictatorship. They also ignored the fact that Stalin, when introducing the document, emphasised that dictatorial methods brought benefit to the people. This inattentiveness was regrettable but unsurprising while Stalin and his spokesmen went about highlighting the claim that the exploitation of man by man had ceased in the USSR. The rights of Soviet citizens were painted in the brightest colours. The constitution upheld freedom of speech, religious conscience, the press, assembly and street demonstrations. Citizens were guaranteed rights to employment (at a time when the world's other economies were hit by the Great Depression), education, rest and leisure. There was a pledge of universal suffrage and secret ballot. Spokesmen boasted that the USSR's people enjoyed guarantees which elsewhere could only be dreamed about – a paradise on earth was being created without the need for divine intervention.

In fact the constitution did not even enshrine principles of democracy. None of its articles used the term even once. Mainly it was gullible foreigners who said Stalin stood for democratic ideas or practices. Only the article about the right to employment reflected reality. The authorities, as every worker or peasant had cause to rue, had a bottomless ingenuity in finding work for people.

Fundamental for Soviet ideology was the official history of the communist party which was published to fanfares in 1938. *Pravda* carried excerpts daily. This *Short Course* gave an account of communism from Marx and Engels to the show trials of 1936–7 and covered history, politics, economics and philosophy. Stalin himself wrote the lengthy sub-chapter on 'dialectical materialism'. The book was intended as the Bible of the regime. People were expected to read the chapters at home after work.[1] (This was rather like early Protestants studying the New Testament.) It became conventional to present a copy as a rite of passage. Students finishing school or university would be given one inscribed with comradely injunctions. No one with ambition could afford to be without the book. Stalin's idea was that the chapters would provide everyone except professional ideologists with access to a sufficient understanding of communist purposes. Tens of millions of copies were printed in smart aubergine covers and on decent paper. Instant translations into the world's main languages were prepared. Comintern proclaimed the work as the highest pinnacle of wisdom; nobody could remain in any of its parties without acknowledging the *Short Course* as the crystal-clear fount of revolutionary analysis.

Contrary to today's conventional assumptions, the book itself did not entirely lack subtlety. Stress was placed on the need for communists to weigh up policies in the light of changing situations. Marxism, it was asserted, required flexibility of theory and practice. What was suitable for one historical situation was not automatically applicable to another. The proportions in Marxism-Leninism's mixture had to be adjusted from generation to generation. Organisation, slogans, class struggle and international relations had to be adapted to circumstances which would require constant reconsideration by the communist leadership. Although the October Revolution in Russia was to be regarded as the greatest event in the liberation of humankind the supreme goal had yet to be attained: the spreading of the communist order to the entire world.[2] Evidently there had to be limits to Soviet self-congratulation in this primary text of the official doctrines of world communism. It had been written for all the parties of Comintern. Attentive readers who wanted to believe the best in pronouncements issuing from Moscow persuaded themselves to put their trust in Stalin. And they had to suspend their doubting faculties at the same time.

Stalin, like Lenin, anyhow denied that the premises of doctrine were liable to reconsideration. *Capital* was said to be infallible and, although layers of polish might be added in the light of subsequent development, the original furniture was said to be the absolute truth. The passage from Marx to Stalin via Lenin was treated as the only line of legitimate succession in Marxism.

It had become obligatory to acknowledge Stalin's wondrousness. The French writer André Gide wanted to send him a friendly telegram from the south Caucasus: 'Travelling to Gori in the course of our marvellous trip, I feel the need from the bottom of my heart to address you . . .' His Soviet translator interrupted him. Stalin could not be addressed merely as 'you'. Gide was told he should add a phrase such as 'leader of the workers' or 'teacher of the peoples'. The telegram would not be sent unless he touched it up. (When he returned home he found that Soviet journalists had meddled with his spoken and written words without permission on many occasions.)[3] Soviet citizens, of course, could not quibble like Gide. Although Stalin affected to resent all the adulation and asked for the number of references to him in the *Short Course* to be reduced, this was just a pretence. It is true that the *Short Course* quoted him less frequently than Marx and Lenin,[4] but no doubt was left that 'Stalin is the Lenin of today.' He was treated as the perfect exemplar of the human species. As builder of the Soviet state order since 1928, he had no rival. Communists were taught that 'Stalin, the party and the masses' were linked by their zeal to help communism to mount the heights of revolutionary achievement.

The rise of communism in Russia was told as a saga of continuous struggle. False prophets had arisen one after another seeking to divert true socialists from the path of truth and virtue. Russian Marxists had had to contend with those socialists – the *narodniki* – who wanted to found socialism on an idealised concept of peasant life. Then the Marxists of Russia fell into internal dispute. Lenin's Bolsheviks attacked the perfidious Mensheviks led by Martov. The Bolsheviks themselves had their own disputes stretching through to 1917 when Lenin, aided by Stalin, saw off the oppositionists who opposed the seizure of power. Through the ensuing years the pattern was repeated as a succession of groups tried to overturn correct Leninist policy. The alleged offenders were Trotski, Zinoviev, Kamenev and Bukharin. Their hostility to the dual leadership of Lenin and Stalin put them in league with anti-Soviet foreign powers, and they worked consciously for the restoration of capitalism. Stalin's courage and wisdom had saved the USSR from perdition. Everything was light against darkness. In politics there could only be one correct line at any given time. Communists were put on alert that enemies of the people, including those disguised as communists, were everywhere. Vigilance had to be constant.

Stalin contended that the 'dialectical materialism' of Marx and Engels was not simply an irrefutable mode of understanding society in the past, present and future – and this in itself was a gigantic claim – but was also the compass necessary to guide research in the natural sciences. The Soviet contention was that communist-inspired science was inherently superior to its Western rivals.[5]

The Teacher of the Peoples did not leave things at that. Despite having no training in the natural sciences, he issued rulings on genetics. He favoured the scientific charlatan Timofei Lysenko, who was trying to breed a fresh species of wheat by exposing seeds to the cold of the Russian winter. Lysenko upheld the idea that plants could adapt themselves to virtually any conditions, acquire new characteristics and pass them on to the next generation.[6] This way of thinking in the natural sciences gelled with how Stalin thought about humanity and about its potential for transformation. Outstanding genuine biologists such as Nikolai Vavilov perished in labour camps as counter-revolutionaries. Stalin later also laid down that Einstein's theory of relativity was 'bourgeois mystification'. Hitler did the same but held back from persecuting German scientists – so long as they were not Jews – who followed in Einstein's footsteps. Stalin treated any support for relativity theory as conniving at the overthrow of the Soviet order. When Beria pleaded after the Second World War that Soviet physicists needed Einstein's equations in order to make a nuclear bomb, Stalin made the magnanimous concession: 'Leave them in peace. We can always shoot them later.'[7]

The physical environment was to be conquered. Lenin had postulated that a country's economic development had to proceed by building up the capital-goods sector of industry. This meant that the demands of consumers had to be delayed and priority had to be given to the machine-tool sector. Lathes, tractors, trucks and tanks were the criterion of successful industrialisation. The output of iron, steel, nickel and gold needed to be maximised. Stalin's name derived from the Russian word for steel, Molotov's from the word for hammer. Metal was turned into an object of veneration. Ecological concerns were ignored. The USSR was not the first or last state where this happened. Yet the intensity of its commitment to industrial development regardless of the consequences was unique. The Soviet precedent was to become a template for later communist states. Forests were cut down indiscriminately. Factories belched out noxious smoke to the skies. Dams were built and rivers diverted to the detriment of the local habitat. Poisonous liquids were leached into the water courses.

Official propaganda occluded this by publishing wonderful scenes of clean rivers, virgin birchwoods and snow tigers. It also stressed that human interests were being looked after. State welfare had supposedly rendered obsolete the whole idea of charity. The giving of money to beggars was therefore prohibited. André Gide noted that the ban was ignored. People simply could not understand why they should withhold compassion from the unfortunates who approached them for help.[8] They found it less easy to avoid the demands made upon them at their place of work. *Pravda* editorials praised the unforced devotion of workers and peasants who 'chose' to toil to the point of exhaustion. Citizens were expected to sacrifice their comforts for the benefit of generations as yet unborn. Elementary safety precautions lapsed. The health of the workforce was neglected for the good of the cause. The press did not comment on this; it carried no material about how to prevent accidents – and if mention was made of them, they were routinely ascribed to acts of sabotage. Fulfilment of the quotas specified in the five-year plans was designated as the supreme goal. Animate and inanimate nature, including living human beings, had become merely a resource for exploitation.

If the USSR had not been so immense in territory and so rich in resources, the communist leadership might have faced up to the damaging effects – and then perhaps the experiment would not have been repeated in eastern Europe after 1945. Instead the ecological devastation was often distant from the main cities. Ambitious local officials knew that their promotion – and physical survival in the late 1930s – depended on their hitting the targets of the five-year plans. Lodged in the core of Marxist-Leninist ideas, it was to be transmitted to communists in later generations everywhere. The assumption was that a country should ruthlessly exploit whatever natural assets it possessed. The authorities admitted that progress would involve human hardship. Much had yet to be achieved. Many 'mistakes' and 'excesses' had been recorded but, as communists used to put it, 'You can't make an omelette without breaking an egg.' Traditional morality was to be abandoned. Communists should strive for seemingly impossible ends. 'There are no fortresses', Stalin declared in 1931, 'we Bolsheviks cannot storm.'[9]

Stalin – and Lenin before him – had stripped off many of

communism's utopian vestments. Hierarchy, discipline and punishment had become the keystones of the Soviet order. And yet even in the 1930s the authorities went on encouraging the belief that a perfect world was eventually attainable. Millenarian ideas stuck like burrs to communism. The current difficulties were ascribed to the external and internal forces ranged against the party. If perfection was not yet achieved, apparently it was not the fault of Bolshevik doctrines, analysis and practices. Christians awaiting the Second Coming of Jesus Christ in the weeks after his ascension had had to cope with the same jolt to their expectation. As their initial disappointment gave way to an acceptance that the timing of Christ's return was unpredictable, they did not abandon faith: Christ would indeed come again. Groups of Christians in subsequent centuries convinced themselves that the moment was imminent. Communists behaved similarly. They had a certainty that their analysis and policies were blessed by the omniscient contributions of the Marxist classics. They believed they were special people. The world communist movement was a gathering of the select enlightened few. The parties might make occasional mistakes in practice but the fundamental line of historical development was fixed, and the future lay with communism.

These were not the only aspects reminiscent of early Christianity. At the Council of Nicaea in AD 325 the bishops of the Church determined which books should be included in the Holy Bible. Several gospels then in circulation were ruled inauthentic or inappropriate. Thus the New Testament was assembled, and it has remained undisturbed in this shape to the present day.

A similar process occurred in Moscow in the 1930s. Certain works of Marx, Engels, Plekhanov, Lenin and Stalin were inserted into the canon. As it happens, the Institute of Marxism-Leninism was in possession of a vastly bigger cache of original texts. A call had been put out to gather every single thing written by Lenin. Even his holiday postcards were to be jealously preserved. The Bolshevik scholar David Ryazanov, who knew his Marx as well as anyone, was sent to Amsterdam to negotiate the purchase of the literary legacy of Marx and Engels. Not everything he found in Moscow and Amsterdam was acceptable to the official party line. Lenin had written much that was critical of Stalin. Marx had written newspaper pieces that repudiated the Russian role in international relations in the mid-nineteenth century whereas Stalin was increasingly showing sympathy with the statecraft of the Romanovs. Stalin's Marx-ologists also knew better than to publish the *Grundrisse* which Marx had drafted in 1857–8. The *Grundrisse* was a philosophical treatise stressing the supreme priority of creating a society wherein individuals could develop to their full human potential without external coercion. In the USSR of the Great Terror this would not have been music to the Leader's ears.

Official Marxism was emptying the minds of its adherents and then filling them with its potent tincture. (And Trotskyism, despite castigating 'the Stalinist school of historical falsification', did little to alter the essential ingredients.) Marx, Engels and Lenin had declared themselves children of the eighteenth-century Enlightenment and affirmed their commitment to science and reason; they savaged rival ideologies, including socialist ones, as being based on implausible premises. Marxists liked to brandish their scientific credentials. Yet there had always been a suspicion that the founders of Marxism themselves, while castigating metaphysical modes of thought as reactionary, were imbued with religiosity of a secular kind. Brought up in the Judaeo-Christian traditions, they never fully left them behind. They remained unconsciously influenced by religious ideas about the perfect future society and the salvation of humanity. They were fixed in their godless faith as solidly as any Jewish or Christian believer. Lenin treated Marx and, to a slightly lesser extent, Engels as infallible progenitors of an omniscient world-view; and any criticism of their works and activities were treated by Leninists as a cardinal political offence. Soviet communists quoted excerpts from books by Marx, Engels and Lenin after the fashion of religious people with their sacred texts.

The mind of Stalin himself was deeply impregnated with the religiosity he had imbibed with his mother's milk. Although he trained for the priesthood, he lived in a milieu where people blended their formal Christianity with older ideas such as belief in wood spirits, witchcraft and nocturnal maleficence. Good had to be protected, if necessary by magic spells, against attack by dark forces.

Typical of this mentality was the notion that the appearance of people and things could be deceptive. Reality could be other than it seemed, and every decent person had to be wary of being fooled. Trickery was on the loose everywhere. This outlook, handed down from generation to generation in peasant families in Russia as well as Georgia, was reproduced in Marxist language in the *Short Course*. Stalinists saw themselves as fighting in the cause of righteousness; and since many of them came from rural families it was easy for the official propaganda to take root. Stalinism was Janus-faced: in one direction it nodded towards modernity, in the other it looked fondly, albeit unknowingly, at the ancient past. Opponents were never mere opponents but were agents in the pay of foreign powers. Their only aim was to do harm to the USSR and world communism. The *Short Course* pulled no punches and delivered them well below the belt. The world had to be rid of them. No pity was to be shown. Stalin, still more than Lenin and Marx before him, condemned all softness and sentimentality. Communists had to be coolly analytical and determinedly merciless; they had to fulfil their responsibilities by carrying out repression without limit.

The 'enemies of the people', furthermore, were allegedly more dangerous after they had been politically defeated. This was one of Stalin's few original contributions to Marxist thinking. Marxists had previously believed that as enemies went down to defeat, the passage towards communism would get easier. Stalin rejected this. For him, there was a need to establish a perpetual state of alert. Conspirators were always at work. Many of them were communist party members. He offered no proof of this. The only people brave enough to contradict him in the USSR had already been executed or were being exhausted to death in the forced-labour camps.

Opponents or critics were labelled 'stooges', 'lackeys', 'toadies' or 'hirelings';[10] it was as if Stalin was stuffing official communist publications with the vocabulary of cheap historical fiction. These were words that hardly appeared in ordinary Russian speech. At the same time he used the full supply of Marxist terminology. He spoke of the 'relations of the means of production' when talking about the economy. He expatiated about the 'imperialist' powers. His descriptions of those whom he disliked drew on popular idioms: 'disgusting', 'putrid', 'foul', 'vicious'. Constantly he alleged insincerity. Everyone from internal party dissenters to hostile foreign political leaders were criminals who 'looted', 'assaulted', 'bribed', 'tricked' and 'camouflaged' their way to power and wealth. They were 'vermin' or 'swine'. They were not simply to be counteracted: they had to be 'crushed', 'exterminated', 'liquidated'.[11] Stalin and his party were not alone in using language of such violence and crudity. The Nazis matched them entirely. What was different about Marxism-Leninism-Stalinism was its greater capacity to export its discourse. The world communist movement picked up the jargon developed in Moscow and employed it with little modification for consumption in the various countries.

Yet the question arises why many millions of people in the USSR and abroad were attracted to such ideas and such discourse. What seems to have been important was the balance between unpleasant crudity and uplifting promise in the propaganda. *Pravda* and *Izvestiya* in fact carried little about the Great Terror except for detailed reports of the big show trials of 1936–8. Most issues of the central newspapers instead had a picture of a young Stakhanovite factory worker or a record-breaking milkmaid. Obviously the authorities, while expunging 'enemies of the people', wanted to concentrate on the positive future heralded for the country. This was accomplished with cleverness. Arctic explorers, long-distance aviators and leading sportsmen were celebrated even more eagerly than party officials and NKVD chiefs. Efforts were made to associate the regime with youthfulness, progress and modernity. Science and atheism were praised as antidotes to superstition, organised religion and outmoded custom.

This was strengthened by the output of novels and poems. Stalin put an end to the lingering diversity of cultural trends and insisted that writers should adhere to 'socialist realism'. This concept was very vaguely formulated. But the basic requirement was that works of art should tell stories in accessible language about noble workers, engineers or party officials. Stalinist doctrine demanded uplifting themes of revolution. Books could no longer end tragically: they had to suggest that history was moving in the direction predicted by the Soviet state. Writing would no longer be allowed to be apolitical. Socialist realism was introduced at the Congress of Writers, held in the presence of Maxim Gorki, in 1934. The intention was to extend its application to all the other arts. This was easier in representative painting than in wordless music. None the less *Lady Macbeth of Mtsensk District*, Dmitri Shostakovich's opera, offended Stalin by its display of feminine sexuality and – just as bad – its failure to supply the public with tunes they could whistle. Shostakovich was buried in an avalanche of criticism, and compelled to repudiate his own work and promise to do better in future. More compliant figures in the cultural activity of the USSR emphasised that the genuine hero in the contemporary world was the communist who strove for better conditions for the working class. The sensibilities of the bourgeoisie were no longer a fit subject for serious art.

The campaign to eradicate illiteracy and innumeracy facilitated the dissemination of such notions. Textbooks for children and adults extolled the advances being made under the 'wise leadership' of 'the Leader of the Peoples'. In some cases the entire ideology penetrated minds. In others it was the sense of successful modernisation or patriotic pride which won admirers for Stalin. The message was adjusted to particular audiences. Foreigners were assured that the internationalist purposes of Marxism-Leninism remained the fulcrum of the Politburo's activities. (Allegedly, though, Stalin confided to his entourage that Marx and Engels had been under the excessive influence of German classic philosophy, especially Kant and Hegel.)[12] But in the USSR there was a deliberate attempt to cultivate Russian national opinion. Even tsars and their generals – or at least those who were seen as having been 'progressive' – were restored to prestige. The October Revolution was depicted as predominantly the achievement of Russian workers, Russian soldiers and Russian peasants. The Russian nation was represented as the 'elder brother' of the national and ethnic groups of the USSR. Alexei Tolstoi's novel *Peter the Great* and Sergei Eisenstein's film *Alexander Nevski* reinforced the claim that the Soviet Union had built on the best elements in the traditions of old Russia.

If there was one word which was brandished more than any others it was 'modernity' (*sovremennost*). Stalin made much of his commitment to catching up with the West and then surpassing it. The USSR was going to develop more advanced forms of technology than any yet invented, and finance, training and research would be directed at making things which met popular needs and strengthened the country's power and prestige. Capitalism was excoriated as inherently wasteful and vulnerable to recurrent crisis. It was written about as 'rotten', 'decadent' and 'doomed'. Cartoons in *Pravda* settled for stereotypes of bloated American businessmen in top hats, their pockets bulging with dollar bills and armaments. Another favourite image was of the jackbooted Nazi; usually he appeared as a feckless boaster rather than the bringer of mortal danger to the USSR: Stalin told Soviet citizens or communists that the Red Army would repulse and crush any invasion. The Wall Street Crash and the Great Depression were not an accident. Communists avoided predicting whether capitalism's end would occur through a political revolution, a financial crash or a world war. Just one of these events could produce the conditions for the 'transition to socialism'. The world communist movement was put on the alert that it had to be ready to seize whatever opportunity came its way.

It was not just his vision of communist modernity which Stalin used to win over the world communist movement. Marxism-Leninism since Lenin had extolled the virtues of political leadership and ruthless methods. Suitably obfuscating the dreadful realities of terror after the October Revolution, Stalin suggested to foreign communists that firm direction by a single party could make a positive impact on every country's society. He mentioned that Russia before 1917 was economically backward and, to a large extent, was beholden to external 'imperialist powers' such as the United Kingdom and France. Soviet modernisation offered itself as a model of how to break free from both backwardness and colonial subjection. If the communists could do it in the former Russian Empire, why could not the same thing happen in China or Nigeria?

The claim was that the central planning modalities of the USSR had already rendered capitalism obsolete. Marxism-Leninism under Stalin did not promise a swift end to material and social inequalities. It might indeed be many years before this happened. The people had to toil, sweat and obey. Their comforts might be few in the factories, mines and collective farms, but, according to Stalin in 1935, 'life is becoming more joyful'. Even convicts doing forced labour had good prospects according to a book published on the digging of a canal to the White Sea and Moscow. Tens of thousands of the prisoners perished on the project. But the authors contended that convict labourers were rehabilitated by working for the common good and learning the principles of Marxism. The Gulag was compared favourably with the penal system in the USA where inmates were given next to no facilities for rehabilitation. The fact that the novelist Maxim Gorki belonged to the editorial board added lustre to the book's acclaim.[13] The Soviet order from top to bottom was proclaimed as the most progressive, most humanitarian and most sincere in the world's recorded history. Stalin applied the rule of thumb announced by Joseph Goebbels: the bigger the lie, the more influence it would have on its audience.

16. INSIDE THE PARTIES

The parties of Comintern had been organised according to the Soviet model since the early 1920s. They were centralised and disciplined. They rooted out factions and banned debate once the party line had been decreed. They propagated Marxism-Leninism, idolised Stalin and acclaimed the USSR's economic and cultural achievements. They obeyed the Comintern orders issuing from Moscow: their members had become communists because they admired the Soviet Union and their objective was to establish a dictatorship of the proletariat in their own country. Communist parties recruited a mass membership wherever political conditions allowed. While contending that the global attainment of communism was inevitable, they knew an intense effort was needed to make this happen. Their belief was that, where the Soviet comrades had gone, they would sooner or later follow.

As yet they could only dream of governmental office. Communists in most countries were outlawed, persecuted or – at the very least – subjected to police surveillance. The Third Reich and fascist Italy arrested communists on sight. When confining young German suspects, the Gestapo encouraged individuals to talk about things other than politics. The calculation was that communists would sooner or later use Marxist-Leninist jargon. Arthur Koestler recalled that if they merely used 'concrete' as an adjective – as in the concrete conditions of the moment – they would be identified as proven Marxists.[1] Usually the interrogators used more brutal methods. Nazi Germany put communist militants to hard labour in concentration camps. Mussolini locked up his communists and refused them decent care. The Italian communist theorist Antonio Gramsci died in prison of tuberculosis and medical neglect in 1937. Communist parties in Germany and Italy were pushed into the political underground. Conditions were little better in most countries of central and eastern Europe. Communists lost their mass membership and had to send representatives into Soviet exile in order to maintain party work.

People who became militants had to accept the possibility, even the probability in many countries, of eventual arrest. They who advocated a dictatorship of their own could hardly start whingeing. They believed that 'class struggle' needed to be fought with total ruthlessness, and their enemies in many countries had the same attitude. After Hitler closed down the Communist Party of Germany, only sixteen out of seventy-two parties represented in the Executive Committee of Comintern had legal status in their countries.[2]

Circumstances went on worsening for communist parties around the world. Imperial powers in Asia and Africa kept their communists under surveillance and frequently engaged in bouts of suppression. The situation was somewhat easier for Comintern in North, Central and South America. The Mexican Communist Party operated freely and noisily during the presidency of Lázaro Cárdenas from 1934 to 1940.[3] (It was Cárdenas who granted asylum to Trotski.) The country had an abundance of groups of the political far left. Less fortunate was the Communist Party of Brazil, which had to work clandestinely while its leader Luis Carlos Prestes languished in prison.[4] In the USA the communists enjoyed open conditions but, like their Mexican comrades, gained little electoral support even if their influence on public debates was on the increase.[5] Comintern worked frantically to keep abreast of events in all such countries and gave peremptory instructions to its parties whether they enjoyed legal rights or worked secretly and outside the law. Moscow's word in the many local disputes was final; but the functionaries in the USSR inevitably continued to depend on being supplied with information and suggestions from the parties themselves.

Comintern's focus remained on Europe, and it was there that communism suffered the greatest deterioration in its situation as the Third Reich expanded its borders and its political and economic influence. The only durable success for Comintern was in France, where the communists had a third of a million members by 1937. This made them the largest such organisation ouside the USSR and China. But there could be no certainty that governments would not suddenly take to suppressing communist parties. When General Franco won the Spanish civil war, he spent years arresting, maltreating and executing communists of all types. The same had been true for remnants of the Chinese Communist Party who failed to join Mao Zedong on his Long March away from harm at the hands of the Kuomintang to Yanan district in Shaanxi province in China's far north. Chiang Kai-shek dealt brutally with communists falling into his hands unless they could be dragooned into his own armed forces. In Europe – outside Scandinavia, the Low Countries, Britain and France – authoritarian right-wing regimes hounded their communist parties. Communists were more bullied than bullying outside the USSR, and they earned respect as fighters against fascism and antisemitism wherever it arose: their parties were often reckless about the risks they ordered them to take and they in turn willingly faced any danger.[6]

The average European communist militant's existence was hemmed around. If such activists stayed on working in the clandestine organisations of the party, they could be caught and maltreated by the security agencies of their country. But if they moved to the USSR, they unknowingly entered a zone of still greater danger. Hundreds of Polish communists fled Piłsudski's security agencies for exile in the USSR. There had long been concern in Moscow that this was one of the channels whereby Piłsudski infiltrated his agents through the border. In August 1938 Stalin commanded Dimitrov, Comintern's Secretary-General, to shut down the Polish Communist Party. While this was being done, the Polish communist exiles were taken into custody by Yezhov's NKVD. Most were shot. Those who avoided this end lived in fear of their lives.

The arm of Soviet security agencies stretched far beyond the frontiers of the USSR. Mongolia was formally a sovereign communist state but that did not stop Yezhov from sending his subordinates to arrest and execute political leaders in Ulan Bator. Soviet agents, working for either the NKVD or Comintern, allegedly ordered the torture and execution of POUM leader Andreu Nin as a Trotskyist and a counter-revolutionary. This is not proved beyond doubt. What is undeniable is that Nin disagreed with Trotski about revolutionary strategy and that this did not stop Stalin from trying to obliterate all communist organisations abroad which refused to recognise the Kremlin as the seat of supreme authority.[7]

The Chinese Communist Party conducted internal repression without needing to be prompted from Moscow. On the Long March from southern China in 1934 and later in the Red base in Yanan the comradely spirit was disrupted by Mao Zedong's efforts to eradicate the slightest opposition. He concocted charges against rivals. To secure himself in Stalin's eyes he cynically claimed they were Trotskyists. Stalin was not fooled and sent Wang Min – a trusted Chinese functionary of Comintern in Moscow – to act as a counterweight to Mao. But Mao accused Wang of counter-revolutionary treachery and only Moscow's support saved him.[8] Mao's reaction was to get his personal physician Dr Jin to administer poison in the course of medical treatment. After months of worsening health, Wang tossed away the pills and straightaway felt better. He had phials of his urine examined, and proved to Stalin what had been going on.[9] Yet Mao had achieved what he wanted: he remained the supreme leader of Chinese communism.

Mao was far from benign in the way he treated Red Army soldiers and party rank-and-filers. In Yanan he rounded up thousands he considered of suspect dependability and confined them in the local caves. Members of their own units guarded them; this was a way of making everyone complicit in the internal campaign of terror. Many young volunteers had trudged to Yanan expecting to find an atmosphere of free thought and egalitarianism. The young writer and communist Wang Shi-wei became their advocate by putting up wall-posters criticising the system of privileges:

> ... I do not think it necessary or justified to have multiple grades in food or clothing ... If while the sick can't even have a sip of noodle soup ... some quite healthy big shots are indulging in extremely unnecessary and unjustified perks, the lower ranks will be alienated.

Mao flew into a rage, reducing Wang Shi-wei to compliance by denouncing him as a Trotskyist. But Mao neither forgave nor forgot the incident. Years later he turned on Wang again. Wang died a grisly death in 1947, when he was chopped into pieces and pitched into a dry well.[10]

Mao had not yet founded a totalitarian state, but his was already a totalitarian army. Torture was used in interrogations of suspected dissenters. Victims might be deprived of sleep for two weeks. If this did not work, they could be whipped, hanged by the wrists or have their knees wrenched to breaking point on the 'tiger's bench'. The screams at night terrified everyone who heard them in the encampments miles from the caves. Mass rallies were held to show off the 'spies' as they publicly repeated the 'confessions' agreed with their interrogators; and those who retracted their words were dragged off for renewed torture. While waiting to resume the civil war against the Kuomintang, Red Army units underwent ideological indoctrination as well as military training. Mao scoured the minds of his soldiers before they went into battle. The Japanese army practice was adopted whereby each man was required to write out 'thought examinations' so that – as Mao put it – they would 'spill out every single thing they have ever harboured that is not so good for the party'. Informing on comrades became a party obligation. Trust between comrades was gnawed away while Mao tried to reserve confidence exclusively for himself.[11]

Mao Zedong Thought was the term already coming into use and its contents were dinned into the soldiers before they went into battle. All this was done informally since Mao lacked a formal ratification of his supreme power in party and army. Possibly he was wary of making a move until he had Stalin's support. The reliance of the Chinese communists on Soviet military supplies in the 1930s made it impolitic to annoy the Kremlin. But Mao's ambition was limitless and on 20 March 1943 he convened the Party Politburo and got himself elevated to Chairmanship of the Politburo and the Secretariat.[12] Not even Stalin, whose job title in the party remained General Secretary, regularised his grandeur like this.

At that time Stalin and Mao were unusual in battering their parties. The Soviet dictator wanted to secure communist power in the USSR and applied a policy of mass repression for that purpose. Although Mao did not yet wield state power, his Red Army was a communist state in the making and his repressive measures followed the same logic as Stalin. The Soviet and Chinese precedents were to be followed in eastern Europe, Cambodia and elsewhere after the Second World War.[13] Whether Harry Pollitt, rough of tongue but an otherwise jovial leader of the Communist Party of Great Britain, would have taken the same road can never be known. In the unlikely event of a British communist revolution there would have been fierce opposition in the country as well as attempts from abroad to foment a counter-revolution. Such a scenario would have strengthened the arguments of those in the Communist Party of Great Britain who espoused political witch-hunts and vicious methods of settling revolutionary scores. Pollitt would have had to decide whether he wanted to be a victimiser or a victim. Establishing a one-party, one-ideology state had its own harsh logic even if the leaders themselves had not been attracted to repressive measures before they held power. Few of them were monsters in human form; it was the communist system that made them behave monstrously.

Pollitt's bowing and scraping before Stalin anyhow does not induce confidence that he would have resisted an injunction from Moscow to root out 'enemies of the people'. Secret plenipotentiaries of Comintern were attached to every party outside the USSR. They lived under aliases, transmitting central directives and reporting on national communist trends. The parties had their own representatives in Moscow, but these hardly enjoyed a congenial life in the Soviet capital: by the late 1930s it was not a posting craved by anyone. Moscow's man in Paris was Eugen Fried. When he did not trust the French leadership he sought confidential conversations with lower officials and militants.[14] Maurice Thorez, Secretary-General of the French Communist Party, had to keep on the right side of him, because if Fried were to send off a negative report Thorez would be in political trouble. The French communists, moreover, remained divided by internal dissensions. Organised factions no longer existed. But, while accepting orders from Comintern, the leaders at all levels frequently engaged in conflict over how to implement strategy. Communist parties seethed with political and personal tension, and Moscow continued to be used as a means of fighting local struggles. Snitching on high-ranking comrades was the norm.

Yet communist militants, aside from their disputes with each other, continued to struggle for the cause of working people. They strongly hoped to come to power and, living in a period of tumult, saw every reason for optimism. Capitalism in the 1920s had stabilised itself, reducing the opportunities for the political far left. Fascism, though, was confined to Italy. All this changed between 1929 and 1933. First came the Wall Street Crash, then Hitler's rise to become German Chancellor. Europe's politics were shaken to their core. This only served to strengthen the determination of communist parties to prevent the further expansion of right-wing dictatorships. The USA appeared to offer important chances for communist agitation and recruitment. Elsewhere in the world the anti-colonial movements was picking up in intensity. Confidence was boosted by the existence of a USSR which yearly increased in political and military strength. History appeared to be on the side of world communism.

Young men and women continued to find satisfaction in fighting for the communist cause, and few of them had easy lives. The life of an English comrade, Ernest Darling, demonstrates the depth of dedication. Darling was born in 1905; he left formal education after elementary school in London and took a succession of jobs in various trades. He joined the labour movement and was blacklisted after a bitter strike in the booksellers' trade in 1925. Periods of unemployment followed, and Darling used his fallow periods to study communist literature. Like several on the British far left, he was not averse to living off the Labour Party and became a research assistant of the New Fabian Research Bureau as well as a Labour Party member. He joined the Communist Party of Great Britain in 1932. At last he had found his political home. As a member of the Adelaide Road communist party cell he highlighted the plight of tenants across north London. He collated statistics on poverty, poor hygiene and high rents and worked tirelessly to rectify the wrongs he saw around him. He prepared party material for parliamentary constituency elections. He joined in demonstrations against fascist meetings in Kilburn. When the Second World War broke out, he was taking an engineering course and wore himself out organising a protest against the uneatable food at his training centre: 'It was part of "wages" and seventy-five per cent of it was left on the plates.'[15]

Darling was independently minded and resented being pushed around by his own party; and he wrote in annoyance to Pollitt: 'There is only one Marxist, Party and working class answer to any one question or any one set of questions: the question is what is that answer today – in general and in particular? The answer is party policy: the question is therefore – is the Party always right?'[16] His question expressed the conundrum of the communist militant's existence. Communists were meant to be rebels; they had to stand up for themselves intellectually, politically and organisationally. But they were also expected to obey and change policies on demand. Every party member had to be like a mollusc: hard enough to repel unwanted attention from outside, yet soft enough inside to respond to pressures from Moscow. Pollitt and Darling had a lengthy exchange of letters. Darling never objected to current general strategy in a direct way and Pollitt, despite being an avid expeller, wanted to keep his awkward comrade in the party. But by September 1946 Pollitt had had enough and advised Darling to 'reconsider [his] position in the party'.[17] This brought Darling back into line: he found the thought of life outside the ranks unbearable.

The emotional existence of British communists, from Pollitt down to the latest recruit, was closely interwoven with the party's activities. By entering the party, they had given up any aspirations to making their way into the higher echelons of society. The exceptions were spies such as Kim Philby, who became a communist as a Cambridge undergraduate in the early 1930s: these individuals had to keep their party membership a secret so as to be able to enter the British establishment.[18] Most communist party members had a very different day-to-day experience. They could not imagine a life set apart from the party. Membership gave them their group of friends, their set of ideals, their whole belief system and their range of practical tasks to be discharged.

Intellectual curiosity was among the features of character that had drawn them to the party. They had sought answers about conditions in their country and the world, and they continued to discuss these questions through the 1930s and 1940s. Equipped with Marx's methods of exposing the hidden economic and political mechanisms in public life, they condemned the failure of British, French and American governments to root out fascism and militarism in Europe and Asia. Communists declared that Europe's colonies would never be liberated without the use of force. Anti-imperialism was a crusade that appealed to them. Their pamphlets denounced 'the ruling classes' for increasing the misery of the peoples they ruled. Canadian communists castigated working conditions in their mines and steel plants; communists in South Africa railed against racial discrimination in their country; Ceylon's communists attacked the global financial system which oppressed labourers in the tea plantations. Party members were eloquent – at their cell meetings, during strikes and at demonstrations – in calling for revolutionary transformation.

The Land of the Soviets remained a conveniently unobserved object of devotion since few communists visited it. No foreign loyalist published a work of intellectual substance about the Soviet Union in the inter-war years.[19] Ideological fervour and party discipline came together. The sole option for internal critics was to vote with their feet, and many did this in the 1930s. The turnover in the communist party membership in Europe and North America was high in the inter-war years. Most left their party out of boredom or disgust, others were thrown out. Suspicion of supporting Trotski or Bukharin was sufficient for a stern reprimand and, if behaviour stayed unchanged, for expulsion. Thus the communists lost some of their brightest minds. A process of inverted Darwinism was at work whereby the fittest individuals were the ones who failed to survive. Nearly all communist parties were headed by general secretaries whose chief distinction was an infinite willingness to toe the shifting line drawn for them by Stalin and explained to them by the Comintern apparatus.

The effect was to train the mental inquisitiveness out of their members. Richard Wright, the black American novelist, was to recall after leaving the communist party:

> An hour's listening disclosed the fanatical intolerance of minds sealed against new ideas, new facts, new feelings, new attitudes, new hints at ways to live. They denounced books they had never read, people they had never known, ideas they could never understand and doctrines they could not pronounce. Communism ... had frozen them at an even lower of ignorance than had been theirs before they met Communism.[20]

Liveliness of the intellect was frowned upon by the Marxist-Leninist-Stalinist adjudicators.

Most of the leavers abandoned communism for socialist parties or for political inactivity. A few turned into right-wingers who had seen communist methods from the inside and were determined to expose them to the world. Some communists, however, were attracted by the Trotskyist splinter organisations. In 1933 Trotski called for the inauguration of the Fourth International; this was duly realised five years later. Trotski designed the new organisation as the successor to the Communist (or Third) International. Until then he had hoped to win over recruits from the existing communist parties and eventually to take over the Communist International; he yearned to return to Moscow as head of the world communist movement. All Trotskyists claimed to uphold 'democratic' procedures in their internal organisation. The reality was more authoritarian. From his first place of exile on the island of Prinkipo near Istanbul he moved like a nomad to France, Norway and – at last – Mexico. He lacked the intimate knowledge to give sensible rulings to his acolytes in France, Germany and the USA. But he governed the Fourth International more firmly than Lenin had controlled the Bolshevik faction in the years of emigration.

This was to be the pattern for Trotskyist and other dissenting communist organisations. The USSR's security agencies strove to penetrate and disrupt their activity. They were very successful before 1933 in Germany, where the Sobolevicius brothers Abraham and Ruvin led the Berlin Trotskyists while working for Moscow. Trotski felt Stalin's barbarity at first hand. His younger son Sergei was arrested in the USSR in 1935; his elder son Lev died mysteriously, probably at the hands of a Soviet agent, in a Paris hospital in 1938. Trotski's followers in Russia, both the real ones and those who had charges trumped up against them, suffered torture and the Gulag. His name was paddled through deep sewers of vilification and he himself was marked down for assassination. In June 1940 an amateurish attempt to kill him led by the muralist painter David Alfaro Siqueiros nearly succeeded. (Siqueiros fancied himself as a military man and dressed up in fatigues for the assault.) Despite every precaution that he took, Trotski did not prevent the infiltration of his home and office by Soviet agents. On 22 August 1940 the inevitable happened. Ramón Mercader inveigled himself into Trotski's confidence and crashed an ice-pick into his cranium.

Trotski had supplied the intellectual rationale for the Fourth International; other leaders were to do the same in subsequent decades for the kaleidoscope of new groupings. From there it was but a short distance to establish an informal cult of the leader. Yet nothing done by the Trotskyists came near to the authority and influence exerted from Moscow. Trotski argued that the Fourth International would stand or fall depending on its capacity to recruit radical industrial workers. He had no realistic means of bringing this about. He never had more than a few thousand adherents across Europe and North America. Their financial condition was always fragile and their appeal was predominantly to young men of middle-class background. Moreover, one European state after another had moved towards right-wing dictatorship and the suppression of communism. Organisations in France, Belgium, Holland, Britain and the USA went on waving the flag of the Fourth International. But they made no general impact on the politics of the far left except in Ceylon and Bolivia. Trotski had said Stalinism could take proper root only in 'backward' Russia. He failed to note that Trotskyism was making little headway in most countries of advanced capitalism and that Stalinism was doing better.

Meanwhile no party belonging to Comintern could avoid, at the barest minimum, displaying its loyalty to Moscow. Mao Zedong succeeded in preserving a modicum of autonomy and self-esteem despite his reliance on military supplies from the USSR. Tito was to achieve the same in wartime Yugoslavia. Mao and Tito benefited from their countries' isolation from the rest of the world: Stalin lacked the means to exercise a fine-tuned control over them. Yet the Communist Party of India and the Brazilian Communist Party were also distant from the Soviet capital and had only patchy contact with the Kremlin. Nevertheless both the Indians and the Brazilians, once they had expelled their malcontents (including the most famous Indian communist Manabendra Nath Roy), were dutiful executors of the USSR's wishes.

Communist party members around the world genuinely adored Stalin; they conformed to his policies and were eager students of his works. Communism's emphasis on book learning enhanced the education of thousands of members who had missed out on their schooling. Inquisitive working-class people gained a sense of worth about themselves. Recruits of a Jewish background found that their practice in dissecting contentious passages of the Talmud fitted them well for discussion of the finer points of Marxian texts.[21] The traditions of the Protestant denominations of Christianity also assisted many newcomers to the parties. Communists who had been used to speaking out at Methodist or Congregational chapels managed the transition to far-left political activity with remarkable facility; and they were in the habit of constructing their argument with reference to the sacred texts. Thus *Capital* and the *Short Course* replaced the New Testament. Each communist party was a synod of hair-splitting political discussion. (The exceptions were the parties in the USSR and China where the internal reign of terror poisoned the wells of intellectual exchange.) The result was that communists also became more articulate than adherents of socialist, social-democratic or labour parties.

They rejected whole schools of social, political and economic thought by the act of becoming communists. Socialist openness to the general intellectual atmosphere of the time was abandoned. The choice of fundamental texts was determined in Moscow. Each party's 'theorists' in reality were mere paraphrasers. The austere Anglo-Indian Oxford graduate Rajani Palme Dutt was a notable example in the British communist party. Revered and even feared by his party comrades for his intellectual mordancy, he was like a schoolboy owning up to naughtiness whenever he found his opinions athwart Moscow's line of the day; and he delighted in rebuking comrades, including his own leader Harry Pollitt, whenever they failed to get down on their knees beside him. Europe's communists had to accept that the sun, whatever the time of day, shone always from the east.[22]

Party discipline put a blind over their natural curiosity. They became accustomed to laughing at non-communists who expressed doubts about the October Revolution or the latest five-year plan. This necessitated continuous self-deception, and some managed it better than others. Pollitt was the master of the technique. The British General Secretary had friends who disappeared in Moscow. In fact he made strenuous enquiries about his former girlfriend Rose Cohen in 1937, who had received a proposal of marriage from him fourteen times. She had run off to Moscow with a Comintern agent and, equally foolishly, given up her British citizenship. Although Stalin told him he would do his best to get her released, in fact she had already been shot.[23] Pollitt coped with the grotesque brutalities of Stalin's Soviet Union by declining to think about them. Not once did he criticise the show trials, collectivisation, the blood purges or – except for a few days in 1939 after the signature of the Nazi–Soviet pact[24] – the foreign policy of the USSR. Pollitt's case was not unusual. Selective silence was a cardinal qualification for remaining a communist. This was easier for the mass of the party than for the central leadership. Local militants were unaware that policy was peremptorily handed down to London from Moscow. Information was not fully shared even inside the leadership. Only Pollitt and a small coterie knew about the party's dependence on a regular subsidy from the USSR. The rest of the party was taught to regard talk of 'Moscow gold' as the vilest slander.

17. FRIENDS AND FOES

Stalin exerted a greater force of attraction and repulsion upon foreign minds than even Lenin had done. The whole world buzzed with interest in Soviet developments. Industrial, scientific and military success stimulated commentators to examine what was going on in the east. Few people assumed any longer that the USSR would soon implode. The Soviet Union was wielding authority on the European stage. It also constituted a model of state and society very different from those of rival powers. Efforts grew to take stock of the order which had arisen from the wreckage of the Russian Empire.

Trotski's books produced an instant éclat. As an experienced journalist he understood that if he was to attract a wide readership he had to write in suitable genres. His autobiography *My Life* and his *History of the Russian Revolution* reached out to people who would otherwise have taken little notice.[1] Sympathy for him was widespread and in 1937 the American philosopher John Dewey, no friend of communism, agreed to hold quasi-judicial proceedings in Coyoacán as if Trotski were being indicted on the very charges being laid against him in the Moscow show trials. The verdict was in Trotski's favour and against the clumsy fabrications of the Stalinists.[2] Trotski went on developing his favourite themes. The October Revolution had been betrayed by Stalin and his group. Lenin and his legacy had been rejected. Russia in 1917 had been an economically and culturally backward country. The 'class struggle' had not produced a clear winner; the working class was incapable of competent self-rule and the old middle class was much too small to dominate politics after the fall of the Imperial monarchy. A bureaucratic stratum had taken advantage of the stalemate and became the guiding force in the USSR. These ideas were the cornerstone of the Trotskyist critique of the USSR.[3]

Other writers on the political left offered their distinctive answers. The Austrian Marxist Otto Bauer and the Russian Menshevik Fëdor Dan concluded that Soviet 'socialism' was probably the best and most appropriate form of socialism available to Russia. Other commentators suggested that New Russia was merely Old Russia in red disguise. Nikolai Berdyaev, who was deported in 1922, maintained that Tsar and Orthodox Christianity had given way to Party General Secretary and Marxism-Leninism. Another variant was the notion that Russia, caught geographically between Europe and 'the East', had developed its peculiar, separate civilisation with centralist authoritarianism at its heart – and the communists were seen as having continued the tradition. Nikolai Trubetskoi and the Eurasianists, as they called themselves, published in obscure Russian émigré journals; but it can scarcely be said that the other analysts – with the notable exception of Trotski – attracted much greater notice in the West.[4]

Fabian Society luminaries Sidney and Beatrice Webb in the United Kingdom were more influential than Bauer, Dan, Berdyaev and Trubetskoi. Both were prolific writers who influenced the social and economic thinking of the Labour Party. Beatrice was a stereotypical middle-class bluestocking who wanted a fairer social system and assumed that her own 'scientific' approach was required to provide the necessary ideas. Her husband Sidney was of like mind. Trimly bearded and attired, he navigated his way through the channels of power and scholarship and helped to found the London School of Economics. They had been critics of Soviet oppression in the 1920s, thinking that the political experiment in Russia damaged the cause of socialism elsewhere. Yet they were intellectually shaken by the global effects of the Wall Street Crash. Despairing of reform in the United Kingdom, they became entranced by the case for state economic planning.[5] From elegant butterflies who reviled Lenin they turned into Stalin's admiring slugs, and in 1932 they decided to find out for themselves about the USSR by taking an Intourist trip to Moscow.

Their lack of curiosity about current Soviet propaganda was a disgrace of the intellect. Whatever they were told by their OGPU minders, they believed. When they returned from Russia they expressed nothing – absolutely nothing – but praise for the sights they had seen, and in 1935 they brought out their *Soviet Communism: A New Civilisation?*[6] Two years later they removed the question mark from the second edition – this must rank as the worst grammatical emendation of the twentieth century. The Webbs defended Stalin and his policies against Western critics; they even asserted, without the slightest expertise in the Russian language or in internal Bolshevik politics, that the show trials of 1936–8 were exemplars of due judicial process. Stalin could not have wished for more eager little helpers.

The Webbs ridiculed another visitor to the USSR who saw things differently. This was Malcolm Muggeridge, the Moscow correspondent of the *Manchester Guardian* newspaper. Muggeridge journeyed by train through the famine-stricken Ukraine, witnessing the consequences of official measures. Desperate peasants crowded railway-station platforms as he travelled south. The bloated bodies of starving children orphaned by the deaths of executed or malnourished parents horrified him. The dismissiveness of local party and government functionaries when he questioned what was going on failed to fool him. He refused to be lathered with communist soft soap. Unfortunately his editor in Manchester usually preferred a lighter treatment of the Soviet Union. Muggeridge resigned but not before he got at least some of his dispatches printed. Indeed the *Manchester Guardian* also accepted an account by Gareth Jones, the Russian-speaking former secretary of David Lloyd George. Jones was horrified by what he witnessed in Ukrainian villages, and gave vivid speeches on the subject after returning to Britain.[7] Muggeridge wrote up a searing account of his own experiences in his book *Winter in Moscow*.[8]

It happened that Muggeridge's wife Kitty was Beatrice Webb's niece. Professor and Mrs Webb treated their nephew-in-law as a silly, misguided youth. Beatrice herself – Aunt Bo as they knew her – consulted Ivan Maiski, Soviet ambassador to the Court of St James's, about conditions in the USSR. Maiski, she wrote in her diary, 'comforted us about the food shortage'. Such was their trust in the ambassador that Sidney showed him drafts of *Soviet Communism* for his comments. They saw nothing odd in the fact that they enjoyed help offered 'gratuitously from the USSR authorities'. Young Malcolm continued to write privately to them castigating the Soviet state order. Aunt Bo wondered grandly whether he might have been cured of his problems 'by psychoanalysis and early treatment in the nursery and the school'.[9]

The Webbs declined to query the outlandish charges laid in the Moscow show trials of 1936–8. Only the Nazi–Soviet pact of August 1939 gave them pause for concern, but not for long. Beatrice confided to her diary in 1943: 'we have lived the life we liked and done the work we intended to do; and we have been proved to be right about Soviet Communism: a new civilisation. What more can we want than a peaceful and painless ending of personal consciousness?'[10] To the end of their lives both she and her husband were convinced they were right. The same was true of the Revd Hewlett Johnson, Dean of Canterbury, who wrote *The Socialist Sixth of the World*. In a decade when Stalin was exterminating tens of thousands of Orthodox Church priests, this prominent English cleric declared: 'The communist puts the Christian to shame in the thoroughness of his quest for a harmonious society. Here he proves himself to be the heir of the Christian intention.'[11] Johnson's visit to the Soviet Union in 1937 left him permanently transfixed by its achievements; and as Vice-President of the Society for Cultural Relations with the USSR he spoke up for the communist spirit of the times more fervently than for the Holy Spirit.

H. G. Wells and André Gide were writers of greater renown who went out to Moscow. For Gide it was a journey to disillusionment. Even though he was shepherded away from the ghoulish sights witnessed by Muggeridge, he would not be fooled. He could not stomach the lies, the abject subordination and the official hostility to notions of charitableness.[12] Wells, now on his second visit to Russia, had a different impression which combined positive and negative aspects. He interviewed Stalin in 1934 for three hours and their exchanges were gentlemanly in manner. Wells began by telling the dictator how he had seen 'the happy faces of healthy people' in contrast with his earlier visit to Moscow in 1920. But he also bluntly criticised the lawlessness, class-based discrimination, state violence and absence of free expression.[13] Stalin enjoyed jousting with him and gave back as good as he got, and he was pleased enough with his performance to permit publication of their conversation. Wells as chairman of the London-based PEN Club, which defended the rights of authors to write without being intimidated, had gone to the USSR hoping – ever the optimist – to win Stalin over by force of argument. By the end of his short stay he appreciated that no reform was likely in the near future. No other foreigner spoke to Stalin in that way in his period of supreme rule. No Soviet citizen could do so without inviting certain execution.

The Webbs were not the only writers who rejected the anti-Soviet standpoint. The dramatist and commentator George Bernard Shaw had been out to Moscow on a brief trip in 1931, returning full of enthusiasm. With his flaming red beard and pale Irish face, Shaw had the authority of an intellectual who was used to speaking *ex cathedra*. Like the Webbs, he was a socialist. He was also a vegetarian and teetotaller: words, not food and drink, were his self-indulgence. His romantic entanglements did not satisfy him; but this failed to bother him.[14] Shaw was an intellectual peacock who preened himself on his reputation for understanding the realities of contemporary politics. It never occurred to him that he had been officially invited to visit Moscow because he was a gullible type. A flavour of his sagacity is conveyed by his comment on the purges: 'We cannot afford to give ourselves moral airs when our most enterprising neighbour [that is, the USSR] humanely and judiciously liquidates a handful of exploiters and speculators to make the world safe for honest men.' Shaw garlanded his elegant scorn round the necks of those who tried to claim otherwise.

He had no excuse. W. H. Chamberlin, Moscow correspondent for the *Christian Science Monitor*, had a Russian-Jewish émigrée wife who explained to Shaw that if they had to live on her ration book they would starve. Shaw advised her to breastfeed their infant. When she pointed out that the boy was already four years old the visitor replied that Eskimos gave mothers' milk to their children up to the age of fourteen. On hearing the story from the Chamberlins, Muggeridge recorded his verdict in his diary: 'He is a preposterous old fool.'[15]

The fools for Stalin included the American journalist Maurice Hindus. Hindus had fled the pogroms of the Russian Empire after the turn of the century, and declaimed after inspecting a Soviet prison that 'the dictatorship ... actually overflowed with kindness'.[16] *New York Times* correspondent Walter Duranty announced: 'Any report of a famine in Russia is today an exaggeration or malignant propaganda.'[17] Duranty was a fraud who benefited from privileged treatment from the Soviet authorities; he knew differently about conditions in the USSR and his distant editors suspected as much. But he was on the spot. He wrote with undiluted confidence and ridiculed Muggeridge and Jones as fabricators of falsehood.[18] Likewise the American journalist Edgar Snow journeyed out to northern China to interview Mao Zedong after the completion of the Long March. Snow produced a eulogistic account, *Red Star over China*, in which he voluntarily censored the grim conditions which had been inflicted by Mao on the local inhabitants and indeed on his own armed forces.[19] At least Snow took his studies of communism seriously. Joseph Davies, the US ambassador to Moscow in the fateful years 1937–8, was much more casual. In his reports to Washington he contended that the indictments of the defendants in the Moscow show trials had been proved 'beyond a reasonable doubt' and that 'the adjudication of the punishment' had been entirely justified.[20]

Of still greater political authority was Henry Wallace, US Secretary of Agriculture from 1932 and Roosevelt's Vice-President from 1940. Wallace visited the eastern USSR in May 1944. He would automatically have become President in April 1945 when Roosevelt died if Roosevelt had not grown suspicious of him and chosen Harry Truman as Vice-

Presidential candidate in the previous year's election. Roosevelt himself had been soft in diplomatic negotiations with Stalin. But Wallace's attitude was softer again. 'When you look at Russia,' he opined, 'you have to consider the historical background. Compared to what they had under the Czar, the Russian people are well off today ... I wouldn't want communism over here, but it makes more sense in Russia.'[21]

The authorities in the USSR handled their visitors with cunning. Wallace was given a royal welcome. To allay any lingering doubts he may have had he was invited to the Vorkuta labour camp to inspect the programme of prisoner rehabilitation. The death rate of Vorkuta's labourers was notorious. The NKVD therefore took the precaution of replacing the emaciated inmates with police operatives for the day of Wallace's arrival. They were well fed and decently clothed and spoke confidently to the American delegation. Wallace was impressed by the humanitarianism of official policy, and spoke favourably about Stalin in Washington. The whole deception had been a spectacular success.[22] Another useful device was to restrict the travel rights of correspondents. Bad as living conditions were in Moscow, they were much worse in Ukraine and Kazakhstan – and Muggeridge was unusual in snatching his chance to witness the famine while passing through Ukrainian territory on an officially sponsored trip to Dnepropetrovsk. The authorities, furthermore, got rid of uncooperative journalists by revoking their visas. Dispatches were therefore written with some caution. This was especially true if a correspondent happened to have a Russian spouse. Fear of retaliation against family members was constant – at least one Austrian writer withdrew his comments about the Gulag after threats were made.[23]

Even so, this indulgence of the Soviet order is hard to understand or condone. Walter Duranty was a scoundrel who said anything that would prolong his comfort and commercial activity in the Soviet capital; according to Muggeridge, he exported goods illegally from the USSR.[24] Edgar Snow, Joseph Davies and Hewlett Johnson were out of their intellectual depth. Yet no one could fairly say that the Webbs and Bernard Shaw were lacking in analytical capacity. What inspired them to speak for Stalin? The answer lies mainly in the purposes they entertained for their own country. They believed in central state planning for social and economic improvements. They were cultural reformers. They were also unconscious authoritarians; they thought their own policies to be the sole rational vision of the future. The weakness of their position was that they had no power but only influence. They shared a lot of the ultimate assumptions of communists and saw Stalin as the builder of a

civilisation to be admired. They suffered from a serious lack of imagination. Brought up in liberal democracies, they could not conceive that
anyone sharing their objectives in social engineering could be murderous
gangsters. They thought the USA and the United Kingdom to be the
centre of world civilisation. For their generation it was conventional to
regard Russia as an exotic country which probably needed the touch of
severe rule to achieve transformation.

From 1933 they found an additional cause for backing Stalin in Adolf
Hitler. German expansionism terrified the advocates of liberal democ-
racy, who noted the ineffectuality of their governments' reaction. No
power in Europe but the USSR was willing to stand up against the Nazis.
This did more than anything else to drum up sympathy for the Soviet
Union. Poets such as Stephen Spender quashed their doubts about
communism and went out to Spain to join the International Brigade.
Working-class young men did the same. Only when they set foot on
Spanish soil did they discover the internecine skulduggery instigated by
Stalin within the republican forces themselves. Many who lacked direct
experience simply refused to believe what was reported about his policies.
Not until August 1939, when Stalin did a deal with the Third Reich, were
supporters of Soviet policies shown beyond cavil to have erred in treating
the USSR as the adamantine bulwark against Nazism.

Sympathy for the USSR had been strengthened by the proliferation
of books and pamphlets published in the same mode by the Left Book
Club founded by Victor Gollancz in 1936. The print runs went into the
tens of thousands. Each month a new book would be recommended to
subscribers and the list included gems of analysis such as Pat Sloan's
Soviet Democracy and R. Page Arnot's *A Short History of the Russian
Revolution*. Both authors were communist party members and their
offerings took their place alongside those of authors who belonged to
other parties of the political left.[25] Communism was being lent political
respectability. Gollancz's initiative was matched by conservatives who set
up the Right Book Club in London. It never reached the public with the
same verve as its left-wing rival. One of the most striking denunciations
came from the typewriter of United Press correspondent Eugene Lyons.
Lyons had gone to Moscow as a communist sympathiser and returned
angry and disillusioned. His reports and his later book *Assignment in
Utopia*, like Muggeridge's classic, nailed the lie that Ukrainian kolkhozniks were spending their time making corn dollies and dancing at village
harvest ceremonies.[26] Lyons focused his book on Moscow politics, but

he said enough about living conditions in the capital and a few regions to get his blistering points across.

The London *Times* correspondent R. O. G. Urch published *The Rabbit King of Siberia* with the Right Book Club. The contents were more indicative than factually grounded. Urch told a tale of adventurers who allegedly tricked Stalin into believing that the problems of food supplies in the USSR could be surmounted by millions of rubles being granted to establish large collective farms where they would use the latest biogenetics to develop gigantic rabbits to be raised for consumption by urban inhabitants. 'Rabbit-wreckers' were put on trial. Another idea was to solve difficulties in livestock husbandry by feeding pigs on a tadpole diet. Neither the pigs nor the peasants were eager about the projects.[27]

Emigré memoirs also entered public discussion. Defectors from the USSR included OGPU operative Walter Krivitsky and diplomat Sergei Dmitrievski.[28] There was even a set of recollections by Boris Bazhanov, who had served in Stalin's secretarial entourage in the 1920s. Bazhanov had made a dash for Paris before he could be apprehended.[29] Such authors left no doubts about the peculiarly vicious personality of the General Secretary in a milieu populated by unpleasant politicians. They lived in constant fear of the Soviet police catching up with them. The OGPU and later the NKVD had penetrated the Russian communities across Europe and assassinations and even abductions of 'enemies of the people' were frequent. General Kutepov was kidnapped in 1930 and General Miller in 1937: both had indeed been organising anti-Soviet networks in the USSR. The Kremlin had a reach across the continents and a grip as tight as an anaconda's. But plenty of accounts were available in French and English which exposed the iniquities being perpetrated in Stalin's USSR. Their authors had turned up in Europe and, tossing aside their Soviet allegiance, had repudiated any association with left-wing politics.

At the more popular level, too, rejection of communism was widespread. The media were crucial in this. It is true that left-of-centre magazines in the USA such as the *New Republic* were impressed by Soviet policies against fascism in the second half of the 1930s. But American newspapers were less indulgent to the USSR; and although Stalin's intervention in the Spanish civil war eased the criticism of him by liberals and the moderate left, this was the exception to the pattern.

Bestselling fiction reflected and confirmed anti-Soviet opinion. The heroes of Richmal Crompton's children's books, William and the Outlaws, held a mock general election in *William – the Bad*. Ginger, a fellow Outlaw, put himself up as the communist candidate:

> 'Ladies an' Gentlemen,' he began. 'Communism means havin' a war against all the people that aren't Communists an' conquerin' 'em an' killin' 'em.'
>
> 'Killin' people's wrong,' interposed the [unnamed] hope of the Sunday School. 'People who kill people get hung. And serve them jolly well right too.'[30]

Ginger interjected that victory in the armed conflict would render the question obsolete.[31] But as a communist he stood no better a chance than Henry as socialist or Douglas a liberal candidate; and William, more by force of personality than by political persuasion, won election to the Prime Minister's office on behalf of the conservatives. The association of communism with murder and mayhem was taken for granted – and not only many children but also their parents read and took delight in the stream of books which came from Miss Crompton. Schoolboy naughtiness was condoned so long as it did not disturb the social status quo; adult communism was the infernal plague of humankind.

Another writer, Baroness Orczy, sold millions of books about the French Revolution. Her main character Sir Percy Blakeney was known to his enemies as the Scarlet Pimpernel. A master of disguise, he infiltrated himself into political circles in Paris and rescued aristocrats under threat of arrest and execution. The Baroness was Hungarian by origin and had started her series before the First World War. Although she wrote nothing directly about twentieth-century communism, her stories of terror, torture, arbitrary rule and despotism were relished by readers who made the connection between events in eighteenth-century France and more recent events in Russia and indeed her native Hungary.

Nor should Robert W. Service (no relation), one of the bestselling poets of the twentieth century, fall out of the picture. Service was born in England to Scottish parents and emigrated to Canada as a young man where he wrote verses which made his name as the poet of the Yukon. He visited the USSR in the 1930s and recorded his impressions. His *Bar-Room Ballads* contained 'The Ballad of Lenin's Tomb', which included the lines:

> I was a Cheko terrorist – Oh I served the Soviets well,
> Till they put me down on the bone-yard list, for the fear that
>   I might tell;

That I might tell the thing I saw, and that only I did see,
They held me in quod with a firing squad to make a corpse of me.
But I got away, and here today I'm telling my tale to you;
Though it may sound weird, by Lenin's beard, so help me God
    it's true.[32]

The 'Cheko' – or Cheka – operative had escaped from Moscow and ended up across the Atlantic telling his 'yarn' to a friend in 'Casey's Bar'. For Service, all was oppression, fraud and arbitrary rule in the USSR. He had seen it for himself and told the story in the doggerel style that delighted his legions of readers.

Thus the anti-communist case was not left exclusively to authors of the political right. Not only the then socialist Malcolm Muggeridge but also George Orwell of the Independent Labour Party smashed the plate glass of the USSR's international reputation. Orwell (whose real name was Eric Blair) had been a pupil of Eton College. He had gone on to work for the British Empire as a policeman in Burma. He kicked against the conventions of his upbringing. Not only did he change his name and disguise his social background but also he campaigned as a novelist of growing distinction for the radical reform of British society. The Spanish civil war drew him to volunteer to fight on the Republican side.

No sooner had he arrived in Spain than he recognised the unbridgeable chasm between the communists and other parties on the political left. On orders from Moscow, Palmiro Togliatti – alias Ercole Ercoli – instructed the Communist Party of Spain to devote itself to purging the Republican forces of anarchists and Trotskyists. This involved mass executions. The butchery and the trickery appalled Orwell, who had gone out to Barcelona with a mind not closed to co-operating with the communists. But he had miscalculated. He joined the military organisation of the Workers' Party of Marxist Unification (known by its Spanish initials POUM) founded by Andreu Nin in 1935. Nin, without being a consistent Trotskyist, was definitely a sympathiser. The POUM was therefore a particular target of Stalin's anger. Many members were shot by firing squad and Orwell himself, returning from the front, owed his escape from this fate by a timely warning from his wife. He was invalided out of the military conflict in 1937 and wrote up his experiences pungently in *Homage to Catalonia*. His disgust with official communism was total.[33]

Although he had already been published to acclaim in the Left Book Series, he could not persuade Gollancz to accept his account for publication. Orwell was saying that what he had seen in Spain was simply the transmission of Soviet political methods to foreign countries; he exposed the entire fallacy of the argument that socialists had no enemy on the left. He took his book to the Secker and Warburg publishing house and, while suffering criticism from his old comrades, did his duty as a citizen of the world. Part travelogue, part political tract, *Homage to Catalonia* remains one of the anti-Stalinist literary masterpieces.

Communism in the 1930s was the object of intense public dispute. The abrupt chasm between the left and right in the politics of the previous decade had given way to a messier landscape. Not every conservative or liberal opposed Stalin, and some of them – especially those who had business interests – positively sought warmer relations with the USSR. The White House under Roosevelt was prominent in making a gentle analysis of events in Moscow. But undoubtedly it was the socialists in Europe and North America who bowed lowest in their admiration of Stalin. If it had been otherwise, Orwell would have found it easier to get his critique of the Soviet Union into print. Above all, it was despair at the ineffectualness of liberal democracy in promoting economic and social reform and protection from fascism that addled some of the finest minds in Europe and North America. Most – but not all – of these people were to suffer a terrible shock in August 1939 when Hitler and Stalin concocted a plot to carve up the lands that lay between their two states. By then it was too late for writers who had always denounced the USSR to take pleasure in sinners who had repented.

18. COMMUNISM IN THE WORLD WAR

Hitler's Foreign Minister Joachim von Ribbentrop flew to Moscow on 23 August 1939. In the early hours of the next day, Ribbentrop and his Soviet counterpart Molotov signed a non-aggression treaty between the Third Reich and the USSR. Stalin, who looked on, was in light-hearted mood. International relations had been complex and dangerous in the preceding years and Stalin had monitored the details on a daily basis. The USSR feared being caught in the pincers of invasion by Imperial Japan and the Third Reich. The Japanese, Germans and Italians were already conjoined by the Anti-Comintern Pact. When Japan's Kwantung Army attacked Soviet forces in May 1939 at Nomonhan, Stalin sent tanks and aircraft to the Far East and appointed Georgi Zhukov to command the retaliatory action.[1]

Soviet leaders appreciated that the Japanese by themselves had the material and human resources to overrun Russia if Zhukov failed to hold them back. Yet the Soviet–Japanese conflict was happening at a time of acute tension across Europe. Germany had annexed Austria in March 1938, the Sudetenland in September 1938 and the rest of Czechoslovakia in March 1939. Hitler had never disguised his ultimate goal of attacking the USSR; his speeches had blazed with imprecations against Moscow as the centre of the 'Judaeo-Bolshevist' world conspiracy against the Aryan race. It was imperative for Stalin to seek diplomatic partners with a view to establishing 'collective security' in Europe against Nazi expansionism. Obvious candidates were the liberal democracies of the United Kingdom and France. Unfortunately for the USSR neither the British nor the French cabinet would offer reliable commitment to an alliance. There was ground for suspicion that the Western powers would not have been displeased if Hitler, instead of wreaking havoc in central Europe, turned his armed forces eastwards and demolished communism in the Soviet Union. Stalin's purge of his own officer corps in 1937–8 had anyway made him an unimpressive military partner. Who afterwards could have confidence in the Red Army as a great force against the Wehrmacht?

The depths were plumbed in summer 1939 when the British sent only a low-level functionary for talks and arranged his journey by steamship. Stalin was getting desperate. Trade talks had been taking place for months in Berlin between Soviet diplomats and the Nazi administration as each side explored whether a deal of some kind was possible. The negotiations seemed to be getting nowhere when, out of the blue, Hitler made direct overtures to Moscow and dispatched Ribbentrop to put the German proposal. Within hours, the deal was done for a non-aggression treaty. Eastern Europe would be divided into zones of influence between the Third Reich and the USSR. Publicly the pretence was made that the two powers had simply agreed to increase mutual trade and not to attack each other. But the implication of the secret protocol about the zones was unmistakable: Germany wanted to invade Poland and to ensure the USSR's compliance. Nazism and communism became allies in all but name.

It was the diplomatic sensation of the century. Maxim Litvinov, who until May had been People's Commissar of External Affairs, exclaimed to his wife: 'Do they really intend to link up with the Germans?'[2] The swastika flag was run up at the Third Reich's embassy in the Soviet capital. Anti-German films were withdrawn from circulation and *Pravda* explained that the treaty would ensure peace and security. Spokesmen for the USSR and Germany contradicted everything they had said about each other since 1933. However badly Stalin had behaved in the Spanish civil war, he had indisputably resisted the expansion of fascism. He had suddenly thrown the policy into reverse gear and enabled the Nazis to gobble up still more territory. On 1 September Hitler began a blitzkrieg against Poland and swept to victory. His great mistake was in underestimating British and French determination. But, when London and Paris delivered an ultimatum demanding his withdrawal, he ignored them and the Second World War began. Stalin held back the Red Army on the Soviet–Polish frontier for a fortnight until he could secure a peace agreement with Japan in the Far East. Then the Soviet tanks rumbled into the western lands of dismembered Poland. The USSR became Hitler's active collaborator.

Stalin called Dimitrov and ordered him to issue fresh instructions to the parties of Comintern. The conflict in western Europe was to be condemned as 'imperialist' in nature. Communists were to refuse to take sides. Like Lenin in 1914, Stalin stipulated that Marxism required avoidance of military service or any other support for national governments.

Instead, communist parties were to raise the banner of 'class struggle' and campaign against the capitalist bosses who stood to make their fortunes out of the carnage.

The world communist movement was profoundly shocked by the USSR's diplomatic and military collusion. Party members had become communists precisely because the USSR and Comintern promised unconditional struggle against fascism. In England they had fought street battles with Mosley's British Union of Fascists in London's East End. Some of them had volunteered for service in the International Brigade in the Spanish civil war. They abhorred Hitler and all he stood for. Two communist parties, the French and the British, had to make a choice between their Comintern discipline and their anti-fascist commitment. The French comrades chose instant obedience and urged their government to sue for peace with the Third Reich.[3] But, just as Lenin had failed to convince many Russian comrades in 1914, many communists in the United Kingdom could not stomach Comintern's commands. British General Secretary Harry Pollitt was among those who supported Britain's declaration of war. Comintern, however, cabled him that Moscow took the contrary position. He ignored the information, perhaps hoping that there had been some confusion in the Comintern apparatus.[4] On 2 September his Central Committee issued a manifesto calling for resistance to Nazi aggression.[5]

At the Central Committee on 2 October he argued again for support for the British war effort. By then Dave Springhall, the party's representative in Moscow, had arrived in London with Comintern's orders in his pocket. Pollitt went down fighting. The Central Committee removed him as General Secretary and a new leadership under Rajani Palme Dutt took over and announced its refusal to takes sides in the 'imperialist war'.[6] This remained the official line of British communism for nearly two years. Palme Dutt and his allies chastised any resistance to the Third Reich; instead they called, in an almost surrealistic manner, for a 'people's peace'. They recognised that neither a 'revolutionary workers' government' nor a 'dictatorship of the proletariat' was currently possible. Instead they campaigned for a 'people's government' which by implication would exclude Conservative and Labour MPs. The communist priority was to raise the political consciousness of the British people.[7] (This was the ultimate impertinence at a time when that same people was standing alone in Europe against Nazi Germany.) The understanding of Marxism had to be deepened in the party. Scotland was hailed for the success of its study groups and the London branches should emulate this.[8] Never had the country's communist organizations been so far detached from popular concerns.

Yet the British government moved cautiously. It held back from arresting communists even though it banned the party's newspapers. Pollitt jauntily toured the country espousing the party line he had previously opposed: this was good for communist discipline.[9] In Glamorganshire in October 1939 he mocked the government for its previous policy of appeasing Hitler.[10] Speaking in Cardiff in June 1940, he declared:

> We sent millions to the support of fascism in Germany when Hitler was in difficulties. Why? . . . Why has our country built up this Frankenstein – because that is what it is now beginning to be? We have done it because there are men in power who would like to see the Miners' Federation of G.B. destroyed, the Labour Party and the Communist Party destroyed, and would like to see Bolshevism destroyed . . . When someone comes to power in Germany and says that is what I intend to do, all the British gentlemen in this country were in full support . . . Somehow it has gone wrong, and we seem to have been putting money on the wrong horse.[11]

Even so, the authorities still stayed their hand. They recognized that the communist party was more a nuisance than a menace. Much more dangerous, ministers thought, were Mosley and the British Union of Fascists, 747 of whose members were interned during the war.[12]

The French Communist Party was less troubled by internal tension. Its leader Maurice Thorez deserted the French armed forces in November 1939 after being conscripted; he was needed to keep the party leadership operational. While Thorez made his escape to Moscow, the remaining leaders continued to abide by instructions. When France fell to the Wehrmacht in June 1940, however, they were cut off and on their own. Pathetically they approached the Germans for permission to go on publishing their newspapers. They hoped that, if the Nazis had signed a treaty with the USSR, Hitler would see no reason to suppress French communism. The request was given short shrift. Across central and eastern Europe the SS and the local police rounded up the remnants of support for Comintern.[13] Nevertheless the French Communist Party stuck by Moscow's demand that the military conflict should be denounced as the 'second imperialist war' and that no preference should be shown as between the British and the Germans.

On 22 June 1941 Hitler ordered his forces across the River Bug to invade the USSR in Operation Barbarossa. At first Stalin refused to recognise what had happened. For hours his army command pleaded with him to permit them to retaliate. The German advance continued to be rapid in subsequent weeks. Lithuania and Belorussia were conquered. By autumn the Germans were on the outskirts of Leningrad and Moscow and had occupied Ukraine. Communism appeared on the point of being demolished in the sole powerful state where it had established itself. Stalin reacted positively to overtures from the beleaguered United Kingdom. At the end of the year he was delighted when the Americans entered the war after the Japanese air force bombed its fleet and air force at Pearl Harbor and Hitler declared war on the USA. A Grand Alliance was formed from the United Kingdom, the USSR and the USA – and Comintern instructed its member parties to back every anti-Nazi government and join every anti-Nazi resistance movement. Workers in the USA and the United Kingdom should no longer be called out on strike. They should be told that it was their political duty either to volunteer for the armed forces or to help boost armaments production. Operation Barbarossa had changed everything. Communist parties were no longer to be neutral about the war but were to disrupt the war-making capacity of the Third Reich and its allies.

The effect on communist parties in countries sympathetic to the anti-German and anti-Japanese cause was electrifying. From being wartime subversives, communists were turned into militant advocates of the struggle against the Third Reich. The parties in the United Kingdom and the USA resumed their public prominence. In France, Greece, Italy and Yugoslavia they formed armed groups and fought as best they could against fascism. The resurgence of communism was also remarkable in Latin America. In 1939 there were only 100,000 communists across that vast area of the world; by 1947 the number had risen to half a million.[14]

And against nearly universal expectation, the Soviet Union did not collapse. The autumn mud and the snows of the winter held up the Wehrmacht, and the Red Army defended every inch of ground. Stalin ranted at his generals, demanding that they organise a counter-offensive regardless of strategic risk. He insisted on this being attempted in spring 1942. The result was yet another disaster and the Germans pushed further forward. But Stalin kept up the pressure. Order No. 270 made it illegal for soldiers to allow themselves to be taken prisoner – an extraordinary prohibition in practical and moral terms. Soviet forces were put under savage compulsion. Order No. 227 proclaimed 'not a step backwards' as the official slogan. Even temporary retreats were prohibited. Quietly, though, Stalin brought his instincts under some control and, after exhausting all alternatives, started to behave more soundly. It still took a brave commander like Zhukov to query his proposals. But Stalin, unlike Hitler, began to accept professional advice. Apparently he scolded his unambitious son Vasili: 'You should have got your diploma from the Military Academy long ago.' Vasili was ready for this. 'Well,' he snapped back, 'you haven't got a diploma either.'[15] Stalin himself worked hard at learning about war-making techniques and his commanders were glad of his growing competence.

Yet Leningrad remained under siege; Moscow was endangered. The Wehrmacht bludgeoned its way to the River Volga and planned an assault on Stalingrad. Somehow, however, the USSR found the resources to resist. Conscription at its peak placed twelve million Soviet men and women under arms. Factories were evacuated to the Urals and armaments were produced in growing abundance. The German forces were severely hampered by overstretched lines of supply. A carefully planned campaign by the Red Army encircled the Germans outside Stalingrad. Hitler prohibited a strategic withdrawal of his forces. This was a wildly foolish order and, after severe hand-to-hand fighting, Stalingrad was back in Soviet possession in January 1943. It was the first European defeat for the Third Reich in the Second World War.

The fighting on the eastern front was not yet finished. The Germans retook Kharkov in eastern Ukraine in March, proving their resilience. In July the two armies squared up for an enormous tank battle near Kursk. Although neither side achieved victory, Hitler could less afford an indecisive contest than Stalin. His factories failed to keep up with the USSR's performance in the production of tanks and aircraft – and Soviet people were determined to win through to victory. The USSR also had an advantage in the number of troops it could muster. Kharkov fell back into the Red Army's hands in August, Kiev in November. The siege of Leningrad was lifted in January 1944. On 22 June, the third anniversary of Operation Barbarossa, Stalin started Operation Bagration for the recovery of Belorussia and Lithuania. Minsk and Vilnius became Soviet cities again in July and the Red Army halted to recuperate on the east bank of the River Vistula; it stood aside as the Germans suppressed the Warsaw Uprising and razed the Polish capital to the ground. The offensive was resumed in January 1945 as Soviet forces at last crossed the Vistula. Despite a fierce defence by the Germans, the Wehrmacht could not stop the Soviet advance. The Red Army under Marshal Zhukov seized the Reichstag in Berlin on 30 April.

The spine of the Wehrmacht was shattered on the eastern front. British and American forces had taken until June 1944 to undertake their amphibious invasion of northern France across the English Channel. Stalin had frequently rebuked the Western Allies for their tardiness in opening a second front; he underestimated the logistical difficulties. Churchill bit his tongue and avoided replying that the United Kingdom had been bombed in 1940 when the USSR was an active ally of the Third Reich in all but name. The USA, moreover, needed time to counter the twin military threats of the Japanese and Germans. American factories were switched to military production. Conscripts were raised and trained. Roosevelt and his commanders were determined that, when the Americans struck back, they would hit the enemy with massively superior power. The USA's entire economy benefited and the effects of the Wall Street Crash of 1929 were finally eradicated. American business flourished and the lacerations of mass unemployment were healed. Stalin anyway appreciated that the USA, the United Kingdom and the USSR had to stick together in order to defeat Hitler, and they kept their spats to a minimum. Roosevelt in the meantime included Moscow as well as London under the Lend–Lease scheme of his government. Soviet armed forces received enormous material assistance. Jeeps, sugar, gunpowder and Spam were sent to fill the gaps in the USSR's output.

Each of the Big Three – Stalin, Roosevelt and Churchill – had an expansive ego and limitless confidence in his capacity for analysis and negotiation. Roosevelt was determined to get along with Stalin, taking this to the length of treating Churchill with some gentle ridicule in the Soviet dictator's presence at the conferences they held at Tehran in November 1943 and Yalta in February 1945.[16] US ambassador Averell Harriman was convinced that his President failed to perceive the unbridgeable gap between the Soviet order and democratic states.[17]

The Western Allies started a propaganda campaign to drum up sympathy and finance for the Soviet war effort and for the Grand Alliance. Stalin was fêted *in absentia*. Fund-raising concerts were held for the USSR and a statue of Lenin was erected near one of his former lodgings in Percy Circus off London's Pentonville Road. (This was not the most successful idea: anti-communist activists repeatedly vandalised the monument and the Metropolitan Police had to divert scarce manpower to guard it.) Soviet ambassadors were applauded whenever they stepped out in Washington and London. Pamphlets appeared, with governmental sanction, extolling the hardiness of Red Army soldiers. Stalin was made *Time* magazine's Man of the Year for the second time in January 1943 – he had first won it at the start of 1940 for no other achievement than the signature of the Nazi–Soviet pact; only Roosevelt won the accolade more times. Sir Adrian Boult conducted a BBC concert of Prokofiev pieces in honour of Stalin's birthday.[18] King George VI sent him an engraved sword to commemorate the battle of Stalingrad.[19] Churchill and Roosevelt regularly expressed their appreciation of Stalin and the Red Army in their broadcast speeches. The Allied forces went to war praising good old Uncle Joe. Gratitude for Soviet sacrifices on the eastern front was shared by everyone but a few anti-Soviet irreconcilables such as Evelyn Waugh. Polish military units in the British capital hated the USSR almost as much as Nazi Germany, but their opinion was not solicited.

British communist activists spoke at factory meetings. They even operated in the armed forces of the Western Allies. (Few rose to officer rank if ever their party allegiance was discovered: there were limits on their promotability.) Party members and sympathisers found their way into the highest echelons of the British administration. Washington and London were more eager to have warm relations with the USSR than to trouble with severe precautions against espionage – and Moscow took full advantage of this light touch. Stalin made fewer concessions. The Soviet intelligence agencies retained their 'moles' in the higher reaches of the Western establishments. American and British journalists were allowed into the country only on a restricted basis and newspapers such as *Britanski soyuznik* ('British Ally') appeared in a limited edition. Soviet citizens who were caught expressing admiration for American technology were liable to arrest, and American material assistance went largely unreported in *Pravda*.[20]

Stalin meanwhile had been contemplating a reconstruction of the world communist movement. His astonishing objective was to close down the Communist International. Dimitrov, its Secretary-General, was used to his accusations against the organisation. In 1937 Stalin had barked at him that 'all of you in Comintern are hand in glove with the enemy'.[21] Dimitrov must have wondered how long he had left to live. In April 1941 Stalin came back to the matter in more temperate tones. This time he argued that communist parties had to be seen to be independent of Moscow and protective of national interests; he probably also hoped to reassure Hitler that he was not trying to stir up trouble in the countries occupied by the Third Reich:

The International was created in Marx's time in the expectation of an approaching international revolution. Comintern was created in Lenin's time at an analogous moment. Today, *national* tasks emerge for each country as a supreme priority. Do not hold on tight to what was *yesterday*.[22]

Operation Barbarossa deflected Stalin from this purpose. The disasters on the eastern front made it imperative to concentrate through every waking hour on the defence of the USSR – and there was no longer a need to show good faith to the Nazis.

Comintern's staff – at least, those who had survived the Great Terror – were ordered to Ufa, south of the Urals. Dimitrov himself was dispatched to Kuibyshev on the Volga with several people's commissariats of the USSR. Radio stations sent inspiring messages to eastern Europe about the 'great patriotic war' being fought by the Red Army. Couriers made their way to surviving underground communist groups. The Polish Communist Party, dissolved in 1938, was rebuilt from scratch as the Polish Workers' Party from late 1941. Throughout the war there were efforts to prepare for a post-war world where the communists would be a political force. Word came back to Moscow about the achievements of communists in the resistance organisations of Europe. There was also news about the extraordinary resilience of the Yugoslav communist forces in tying down the Wehrmacht – and Comintern relayed a biographical sketch of the military leader Tito, whom Moscow had dispatched to head the communist party before the war.[23]

After the battle of Stalingrad, as he thought urgently about how to spread communism in Europe, Stalin reverted to the idea of abolishing Comintern. Dimitrov, titular leader of world communism, was told on 8 May 1943 to put himself out of a job.[24] Immediately he organized the formalities at a hastily arranged Executive Committee meeting which keenly concurred that Comintern had outlived its purposes. Needless to stress, Stalin watched carefully from behind the scenes.[25] Since 1919 the Comintern and its communist parties had caused trouble for capitalism abroad wherever they could. Perhaps Stalin wanted to reassure the Americans and the British that he was no longer aiming at world revolution. He hoped to get them to lower their political guard before the upcoming conferences of the Big Three. But of greater importance to him, probably, was the urge to maximise communist appeal in the European countries about to be overrun by the Red Army. The reality was that the central apparatus of Comintern was simply transferred to the International Department of the Central Committee Secretariat of the All-Union Communist Party (Bolsheviks). The new head of the department was none other than Georgi Dimitrov. All this was done on the quiet. The important thing for Stalin was for each communist party to appear to be acting without instructions from Moscow.

Stalin's attempt to reach out to eastern Europe in particular also involved the establishment of an All-Slavic Committee. The brotherhood of Slavic peoples was proclaimed. The fact that several peoples of the region, including the Hungarians, were not Slavs was overlooked: the idea was to appeal positively to the Poles, Czechs and others rather than to alienate the non-Slavs. This was nevertheless a chimerical plan. It was inconceivable that Hungarians would not see it as an anti-Magyar plot. A further initiative in September 1943, moreover, was surely a lightly disguised piece of Soviet-Russian imperialism. It was then that Stalin invited Russian Orthodox Church clerics to the Kremlin and offered to ease the repression on them in return for their political loyalty. This they eagerly acceded to. An additional blandishment for them was Stalin's willingness to turn over the buildings of the Ukrainian Autocephalous Church to them as the Soviet armed forces moved westwards.[26]

Something which had seemed hardly imaginable before 1941 had occurred a few years later: the USSR began to be treated as a country worthy of normal ties with the rest of the world. American businessmen were looking forward to doing deals in Moscow and helping the economic reconstruction of the USSR. Vast profits were expected. Eric Johnston, President of the US Chamber of Commerce, stated in October 1944: 'Russia will be, if not our biggest, at least our most eager customer when the war ends.' The entrepreneurial elite had greater trust in Stalin's post-war reliability than any other group in American society. The US Bureau of Foreign and Domestic Commerce fostered such optimism and reckoned that at least a third of America's exports would be directed at the Soviet Union in the post-war period.[27] President Roosevelt's respectful diplomatic exchanges with the Kremlin strengthened hopes in Washington that peaceful economics would infuse the US–Soviet relationship. Both powers wanted the demise of the European empires. The USA and the USSR were resolved that neither Germany nor Japan would ever be able to threaten them again. There seemed a reasonable prospect that Moscow and Washington might agree on how world affairs were to be organised.

Communist parties in the great Western powers – the USA, the UK and newly liberated France – were operating freely, legally and with much prestige. They had their central offices, their press and their ebullient militants. In North America and Britain they had performed a useful role as cheerleaders on the political far left for the war effort. They looked forward to a period when they could increase their popularity. Communism was not quite respectable; but it was no longer a dirty word among most people. Stalin was a hero across the entire West.

In Yugoslavia, Italy, France and Greece the communists could claim a lot more than this. Although they received much aid from the Western Allies and not a little from the USSR, Tito's partisans did a lot of the work of ridding themselves of the German occupiers. Churchill, veteran harrier of world communism, had plumped for Tito as the most effective Yugoslavian enemy of the Third Reich – and he took the controversial option of backing him rather than his Serbian nationalist foe Draža Mihailović. A bloody ethnic and civil war had been tucked into the fight against Nazism. Among other dimensions of the struggle the communist partisans had taken on and defeated the pro-German regime of the Ustashas in Croatia. The Greek Communist Party sought to match this military victory to the south. As the Germans retreated northwards in October 1944, communists rushed to seize towns and strengthen their potential to take national power. Civil war was breaking out in Greece; it was an open question whether the communists or a monarchist right-wing administration would prevail. Meanwhile the communist-led partisan groups in France and northern Italy disrupted the Wehrmacht's defences against the Western Allies. Communism in Europe was coming out of the Second World War stronger and more confident than it had been at the beginning.

19. FORCING THE PEACE

The destruction of the Third Reich crowned Stalin's career. Yet he did not give himself long to celebrate. He was already thinking about the dangerous uncertainties of world politics. When Khrushchëv congratulated him on the German surrender, Stalin froze him to the spot with invective. He was just as angry after he tried to mount a white Arab stallion in preparation for the victory parade. The frisky steed threw him to the ground, and he passed the equestrian honour to Marshal Zhukov. Stalin briefly relaxed at a banquet he held for his commanders. The tables groaned with caviar and vodka as he praised the wartime accomplishments of the Russians. 'Any other people', he declared, 'might have said to its government: "You've not lived up to our expectations, so go away and we'll install another government which will conclude a peace with Germany and secure relief for us."'[1] This was the nearest he got to apologising for his blunder at the start of Operation Barbarossa.

The last full conference of the Allies took place in July 1945 at Potsdam near Berlin. Two new members – Harry Truman and Clement Attlee – joined the Big Three after Roosevelt had died on 12 April and Churchill lost an election in the midst of the proceedings. The Potsdam decisions were quickly made. Japan was to be disarmed and Germany divided into four occupation zones. The USSR was promised the right to reparations from the defeated countries. There was agreement to eject Germans living in eastern Europe into a territorially reduced Germany. Truman, though, no longer wished to press Stalin to join the Japanese war. American scientists working on the Manhattan Project had invented a nuclear bomb. The US air force could now finish off Japan speedily and without assistance. Stalin already knew about this from his spies and insisted on making the territorial gains promised to him in the Far East at the Yalta Conference – and Truman did not demur. Other large questions of the post-war settlements were postponed. Although it was expected that Poland should have a 'provisional government of national unity', detailed planning for the political future of eastern Europe was not attempted.

As American forces fought their way to Japan by sea and air, Soviet forces overran Manchuria. Truman was eager by then to win the war with the minimum of assistance from Moscow. On 6 August US air force bombers flew over Hiroshima and exploded an atomic bomb for the first time. A second was dropped on Nagasaki two days later. The damage was on a scale unprecedented in all warfare, and Truman's obvious resolve to go on using the A-bomb terrified Emperor Hirohito and the rest of the Japanese leadership into unconditional surrender. The Second World War was over. American troops, who days earlier had been preparing for a drawn-out campaign over every inch of Japan, installed an occupying administration. The Americans had played the decisive role in the Far East; but the Red Army had done enough at the last moment to ensure the acquisition of territory on the edge of the Pacific Ocean deemed vital by Stalin for the USSR's security.

Appearances were deceptive. Although the USSR had defeated its enemies to become a world power, its internal situation was unenviable. Twenty-six million Soviet citizens had perished in the conflict with Germany. Deaths on the battlefield, in concentration camps or through malnutrition and overwork affected nearly every family. The country teemed with orphans and crippled invalids. As many as 1,710 cities lay in charred rubble. Seventy thousand villages had been razed to the ground. Stalin had not been an innocent spectator. His scorched-earth policy in 1941–2 had caused acute hardship, and the Gulag and the deportation operations of the NKVD added to the fatalities. While the economy met military requirements efficiently, this was at the expense of the other sectors. Agriculture was ruined. Factories had practically given up producing consumer goods. The strains of war had shredded the civilian administration. Officials had to confront grievous difficulties in their locality with little assistance from Moscow. At the same time the USSR had concerns about how to consolidate its authority over eastern Europe. Somehow, if Stalin was to hold on to his gains, the newly conquered half-continent needed to be fed and economically regenerated as well as administered by the USSR's overstretched ministries, police and armed forces.

Soviet leaders paraded as democrats while strengthening tyranny. Stalin was frank among his intimates, ordering them to 'land a heavy punch' on any call for a relaxation of the regime in the USSR.[2] The pre-war order was to be restored and the USSR's expanded interests abroad protected.

The government and the communist party repaired the wartime

damage to their administrative networks. The world heard that everything was in smoothly working order. If the USA were to discover the
extent of ruination in the USSR, Stalin's poker hand in negotiations
would have been a weakened one. Terror was applied to suspect groups.
Political, economic and cultural elites in Estonia, Latvia and Lithuania
were arrested and deported to Siberia – or at least individuals belonging
to them who had escaped arrest under the first Soviet annexation in
August 1940. Anyone who had studied Stalin should have expected this:
surgical removal of the canker of potential opposition had been a
constant feature of his rule. Even by his standards, though, he was
vicious in his treatment of repatriated prisoners of the Germans. Order
No. 270 had designated Soviet POWs as traitors to the Motherland.
Then the news filtered back about the severe conditions they had to
endure in the Third Reich. Stalin was implacable. Every liberated soldier
was to be interrogated by the intelligence agencies and, in half of the
cases, deposited in a forced-labour camp. Over a million people suffered
this fate. Many were sent to mines to dig for uranium; this by itself was
virtually a death sentence. Having survived the Nazi horrors, the ex-
servicemen were transferred to misery in their own land.[3]

Ordinary civilians were treated little better. Initially the state planning bodies were under instructions to increase budgetary provision for
consumer goods. The worsening of relations between the USSR and the
USA ended all that. The fourth five-year plan, inaugurated in 1946, was
jerked sharply towards the development and output of weaponry.[4] The
fiscal screws were tightened. The collective farm peasantry suffered badly
as a tax was exacted for each cow and each fruit tree. This was done
without regard to reported hardship. Famine occurred across Ukraine
and cases of cannibalism were discovered. But when Khrushchëv asked
for exemptions from the centrally assigned quotas for grain deliveries, he
was denounced by Stalin for lack of Marxist-Leninist principle.

Stalin knew the kind of USSR he wanted and the kind of rulers he
required for this. The Soviet state vaunted its military power and called
upon citizens to forgo their comforts – and their lives – to defend the
country's interests. Pride was cultivated in the Russian past. This had
been a growing trend since the early 1930s and Stalin now began to
encourage a general xenophobia. 'Bowing down before the West' was
treated as treason. Even Peter the Great, whom Stalin saw as a worthy
predecessor as a moderniser, was said to have adopted Dutch and
English models without discrimination. Soviet achievements were end-

lessly paraded. Russia had possessed a potential which allegedly the communist state alone had succeeded in fully tapping. The obstacle to the country's progress had been the Imperial system of oppression and exploitation. The October Revolution had opened an avenue for promotion of individuals on merit; at last the full potential of the people was being released and supported. The goal of Soviet modernity was an industrialised, educated and collectivist society. To Stalinists it appeared obvious that the five-year plans and the victory in war proved the superiority of the communist order. They maintained that every other nation could and should copy the model.

People mattered to Stalin only as instruments for implementing state policy. He deferred satisfying the material needs of citizens; the security police arrested any grumblers. Heavy industry was the official strategic priority through to his death. The basic assumption was anyway that the expansion of the 'means of production' was the crucial way to generate economic growth. Also axiomatic was the belief that large-scale organisation was vital for success; Stalinism involved sheer gigantomania. Ruthless leadership and state power were intrinsic to the Soviet order as it had developed. The 'masses' were to be taught to obey whatever the Leader and his acolytes commanded. These attitudes were inculcated as fundamental constants of Marxism.

The Stalin cult gained in extravagance. The Leader was the god and the chief priest, and hundreds of millions of copies of his books and images were put before his fellow citizens. He no longer considered ways of making existing institutions work better but settled down as a communist conservative. He entrusted most authority to the organs of government. The party supervised ideology and the appointment of personnel and was stopped from interfering in other business. Any idea that the armed forces, fresh from their triumph over the Wehrmacht, might assert some autonomy was dispelled. Zhukov was demoted to the Odessa Military District; other generals were made to understand that the same fate – or worse – would befall them unless they showed exuberant obedience to Stalin. The intelligence agencies were at work everywhere. Their leaders were frequently reshuffled; Stalin let no police chief feel comfortable in office: there was an unceasing demand for loyal, punctilious discharge of duties under the watchful eye of the General Secretary. Institutions operated in a peculiar condition of agitated stability. Officials were no longer thrust into high office without qualifications, as had frequently been true in the late 1930s. Professional training and proficiency as well as a course in Marxism-Leninism were a prerequisite. The newer officials were unlikely to show Stalin anything but their deepest loyalty.[5]

He himself discouraged any thought that radical economic measures might be in the offing. The kolkhozes were not going to be turned into state farms employing peasants for wages regardless of the amount of work they did. Voluntaristic changes in policy were a thing of the past.[6] Quite how the state would develop after his death was left unclear. Stalin instinctively avoided establishing formal procedures for the political succession and executed several Soviet leaders to bring the rest into line. In 1949–50 he was to liquidate the entire Leningrad political elite on suspicion of its members' lack of total obedience to his will as well as their alleged support for Russian nationalism. Among the victims was Politburo member Nikolai Voznesenski.[7] No politician was left in any doubt about Stalin's continued readiness to use the bloodiest methods.

Yet policies were not yet fixed in cement. Planners were told to project a drastic increase in the output of consumer goods. The people of the Soviet Union had won the war and now they were to reap a material benefit. (Of course, nobody was meant to dream of electing their political leadership or being consulted about anything truly important.) Stalin did not immediately revoke the minor concessions to cultural expression first granted in wartime. Nor did he go back on his informal concordat with the Russian Orthodox Church. Popular expectations of further relaxation were high. Soldiers had joined the party in wartime confident that the regime would abandon its repressive zeal: this was one of the reasons why they had fought so hard against the Nazis. Stalin was regarded by many millions of Soviet citizens as a heroic leader. The authorities had frequently talked about the need for 'party and masses' to be brought together in indissoluble and harmonious union. People now wanted words to be matched by practice. They denounced officials who abused their position. They demanded more food, better housing and improved working conditions. Many did not hesitate to put their grumbles into writing. They had fought and won the war. In victory they were in a mood to assert their rights.

Active resistance to communism continued after the Second World War. In Russia it was weak: the levers of oppression were in good repair and had been vigorously manipulated for years. Peasants complained as they always had done. There were clandestine youth groups dedicated to a restoration of 'genuine' Leninism. The toughest rebels were to be found in the labour camps where national and religious critics of the

Soviet order from the western borderlands of the USSR joined in attempts to disrupt the Gulag system. Yet generally the security police were not unduly pressed. In Estonia, Latvia, Lithuania, west Belorussia and west Ukraine it was a different matter. Anti-Soviet partisan groups challenged the annexation of their lands. Based in woods and villages, the Forest Brothers carried out a campaign of assassination and sabotage as Soviet armed forces tried to hunt them down.[8] The same happened further west. The Polish authorities treated the Home Army, which had led the Warsaw Uprising against the German occupation, as a national enemy. Patriots took to the countryside and re-formed their military units to strike at the official forces. The fighting was savage on both sides.

Meanwhile Stalin's forces in the Far East had rampaged across northern Manchuria after being transferred from European Russia as had been agreed at Yalta in February 1945. They also grabbed the territories promised to the USSR by the Western Allies when Sakhalin and the northern islands of Japan were annexed. Stalin, cognisant of the humiliation suffered by the Russian Empire in the Russo–Japanese War of 1904–5, announced that a 'blot of shame' had been removed. He would have liked to exercise some direct power over the new Japanese government, but the Americans brusquely rejected his requests. They, and not the armed might of the Soviet Union, had reduced Japan to unconditional surrender and they were unwilling to let him poke his nose into politics in Tokyo. Stalin was more successful in regard to China. He remained sceptical about the Chinese Communist Party's chances of gaining power. As its paymaster and military supplier he was able to insist that it stayed in alliance with Chiang Kai-shek's Kuomintang. Meanwhile Stalin signed a treaty with Chiang. China at the time was in no condition to resist Soviet demands. The USSR secured permission to use Port Arthur and Dairen for their naval facilities. Moscow also obtained rights over the railways in Manchuria.

The Big Three still stayed together despite rising mutual distrust. They had agreed before the end of the war to the formation of a body to succeed the League of Nations. This would be the United Nations Organisation (or UN). Inaugurated in San Francisco, it was given permanent premises in New York. Its main purpose was the prevention of war in general. The USSR took its majestic place on the UN's Security Council along with the USA, the United Kingdom, France and China. Truly Stalin led a power of global power and renown.

His steadiest attention was on eastern Europe. He had said to

Yugoslav emissary Milovan Djilas: 'This war is not as in the past; whoever occupies a territory also imposes his own social system. Everyone imposes his own system, as far as his army can reach.'[9] But as yet he was too weak to undertake comprehensive communisation in the countries of the region – and it is not impossible that he did not yet think this a feasible objective.[10] Communists were very few and inexperienced except in Yugoslavia: the Nazis and their allies had seen to that. Although the Red Army was unchallengeable, Stalin lacked a reliable administrative apparatus of political and security-police control. He lacked the resources to put the economies of the occupied countries quickly back on their feet. Furthermore, his armed forces did not possess an atomic bomb. The Americans had shown their technological superiority by obliterating two Japanese cities; they could fly over Moscow and repeat the devastation. There was a further factor in Stalin's mind. The Grand Alliance had elevated him and his country into a partnership with the USA and the United Kingdom. The USSR had received wartime material assistance from across the Atlantic, and Stalin and Molotov had not stopped hoping to obtain a loan to hasten Soviet economic recovery. Yalta, Tehran and Potsdam had left many basic matters undiscussed and Stalin resolved to act with caution.

The microfauna of Comintern in Moscow exile meanwhile returned to their native countries to lead the communist parties. There were exceptions, and one of them in Poland was Władysław Gomułka. Polish party functionaries arriving from Moscow could not tame him and complained about him to the Soviet authorities.[11] But Stalin still needed to proceed with prudence. While Gomułka appeared to him as unduly independent of mind and even somewhat nationalistic, many militants in Hungary had to be restrained from excessive impatience to communise the country.[12]

Rumours spread about Stalin's intentions. Perhaps he was going to force the countries of the region to become republics of the USSR.[13] In Romania it was being said the communist leadership was going to establish 'kolkhozes of a militarised type' and institute a twelve-hour working day.[14] Denials by communist leader Gheorghe Gheorghiu-Dej cut no ice with popular opinion. Polish peasants too dreaded the prospect of a kolkhoz system, and Poland's party boss Gomułka told Dimitrov: 'Even if anyone expresses the wish to enter a kolkhoz, we still won't be introducing them.'[15] The awful record of communism in the USSR spoke for itself: collectivisation, purges, concentration camps, one-party dictatorship. Even if some rumours were wildly inaccurate, many were very plausible. There was agreement among the Big Three that the occupied countries should become independent, democratic states. Elections had to be held and economic recovery promoted. The USSR itself had limited options. It wanted to avoid war with the USA, especially when the Soviet armed forces lacked nuclear weaponry. It sought financial assistance from the Americans. It also heard the truth from communist parties in eastern Europe, in their moments of candour, about their own deep unpopularity.[16]

A softly-softly approach to communisation was required. Communists in eastern Europe were advised by Moscow that the USSR lacked the finances to regenerate their economies; indeed some of them were compelled to accept that their first national obligation was to pay off the reparations demanded by the USSR for the damage done by their armies as allies of the Third Reich. This was true of Hungary, Romania, Bulgaria and East Germany, and the reparations paid by Budapest amounted to half the Hungarian state budget in 1947.[17] Whole factories were crated up and sent eastwards to Russia. It also suited Stalin to insist that communist leaders did not bite off more than they could chew. If they took over their economies, they would get the blame for the hardships inevitable after the war. A degree of political sobriety was called for. To this end he stipulated that communist parties should advance behind the shield of multi-party democratic coalitions. He was willing to consider a 'bloc' even between the communists and the Catholic Church.[18] Such manoeuvres would get the Western Allies off his back as well as diffuse responsibility for the difficulties of post-war rule. With a modicum of cunning the communist ministers could secure portfolios enabling them to deal ruthlessly with political enemies. Wherever possible, they were told to take posts in the security and police forces.

Moscow told the incoming communists to present themselves as patriots. National leaderships were wary of giving undue prominence to the Jews in their midst – and Stalin encouraged them in this caution.[19] This was a notable difficulty in Poland, Hungary and Romania where popular antisemitism was strong. Jews held half the leading posts in the Polish security ministry.[20] In Romania there was unease that 'the Jewess Pauker and the Hungarian Luka' held positions of power.[21] The danger was that communists would come to be seen as a party giving privileges to this disliked minority. Yet at the same time Stalin ordered Gheorghiu-Dej to hold back from comprehensive Romanisation of the party leadership; he objected to ideas about communists in Romania turning themselves into a 'racial party'.[22] Moreover, land reform proceeded without the collectivisation of farming. The old estates, including the vast holdings of the infamously right-wing Junkers in Prussia, were parcelled into smallholdings for peasants and the deserving rural poor.[23] The Soviet leadership continued to urge caution. In Romania's case Stalin maintained that the bourgeoisie had handed economic power to the communists so as to saddle them with an intractable task.[24]

Truman, Attlee and other Western leaders implicitly acknowledged that the USSR would have a preponderant influence over eastern Europe. But they did not want to leave the countries of the region entirely to Stalin's mercy. Bulgaria, Romania and Hungary had been allies of the Third Reich until late in the war. In accordance with their agreements, the Big Three set up Allied Control Commissions in their capitals. This enabled the Americans and British to witness what was going on and to hinder communist oppressiveness. They also had firm communications and eager collaborators in Poland and Czechoslovakia. The West stood for electoral democracy, an open economy and cultural and religious tolerance across the region and made this clear to Soviet ministers and diplomats.

For two whole years Stalin and the communist parties of the region probed the resolve of the other Allies; and, as he was to confide to Mao, he did not feel bound by any existing accords with the Western Allies.[25] Communists had already held most seats in the Albanian provisional government since October 1944 and had ratified their power in Yugoslavia in November through an election boycotted by the opposition parties. In Poland a coalition government was formed by communists – the Polish Workers' Party – together with the Polish Socialist Party, the Democratic Party, the Labour Party and the Peasants' Party. Communist dominance was ensured by the fact that most of the ministers had belonged to the USSR-dominated Lublin Committee which had acted previously as a provisional authority. Intimidation of Stanisław Mikołajczyk's revived Polish Peasants' Party, which was easily the country's largest political organisation, intensified. The national election in January 1947 was a travesty of due procedure. Four-fifths of the votes were allegedly cast in favour of the Democratic Bloc to which the communists belonged; and although Józef Cyrankiewicz of the Polish Socialist Party became Prime Minister, decisive power passed to the Polish Workers' Party. A similar transition took place in Hungary, but Stalin, being preoccupied with Poland, insisted that the communists took their advance at a slower pace. The Smallholders' Party won an absolute majority of votes at the election of November 1945. Yet the communists held the Ministry of the Interior and ran the security police. From this base they could do much of what they wanted without interference.

Soviet troops withdrew from Czechoslovakia in December, leaving the socialist Eduard Beneš in power. Beneš, the country's most popular politician, complied with the demands of the Soviet leadership, and the communist leader Klement Gottwald became Prime Minister. Elections were held in May 1946; the communists won 38 per cent of the votes. No communist party in the region did better in a reasonably free election. Indeed no election approached Czechoslovakia's in political freedom. This went to show that if the communists were careful and moderate it was not impossible for them to appeal successfully to their electorate; but of course this was no guarantee that the votes would stay with them in future electoral contests.

Bulgaria was a harder nut to crack even after the communist-inspired execution of political leaders on the right of the public spectrum. Persecution of the other rivals of communism followed. Georgi Dimitrov returned from his Moscow exile to increase the standing of the communists. The communist-led Fatherland Front won 86 per cent of the votes in the election of November 1945, but the Western Allies objected strenuously to the amount of fraud and violence. A further election in the following year confirmed communist supremacy and Dimitrov became Minister-President amid continuing arrests. The Romanian communists too set up joint organisations. Only one communist became minister in the first coalition government after the collapse of German military power. Soviet pressure succeeded in disbanding the cabinet of Nicolae Radescu, a general, and replacing him with Ploughman's Front leader Petru Groza, who was suitably malleable. The control of the USSR was still more direct in East Germany, but the local communists none the less needed to regularise their authority. Their preference was for fusing their organisation with the other parties of the left. Intimidation followed. In April 1946 the German Communist Party and Germany Social-Democratic Party, after months of threats from the Soviet army high command, were blended into the Socialist Unity Party. Even so, they failed to gain an absolute majority that August. The politics of eastern Europe eluded firm control.

Stalin at the same time was determined to eliminate the potential menace from Finland. This was a neighbouring state which had sided with the Third Reich in the world war. Finns were not fond of the Russians. They were also former subjects of the Russian Empire and Stalin believed they had been wrongly wrenched from Russia's grasp in the revolutionary period. Western powers judged things differently, but in the event they did not face the question of intervention. Stalin was pleased that Finnish communists won a quarter of the parliamentary seats in 1945. But the growing evidence of anti-communist sentiment was unmistakable. Instead of sending in the Soviet army, he dispatched Andrei Zhdanov to secure a political compromise. In return for staying neutral in the disputes between the USSR and the West, Finland could retain its independence. The Finns under Juho Kusti Paasikivi handled the situation cleverly: they guaranteed never to side with the enemies of the Soviet Union and to observe permanent neutrality. In return they asked for freedom to maintain a capitalist economy and a liberal democracy; they also requested, firmly but politely, not to be incorporated in the USSR as a Soviet republic. Zhdanov, on Stalin's orders, accepted the deal.[26]

Full communisation was avoided in eastern Europe, in line with Stalin's wishes, in the first years after the Second World War. Nevertheless the Poles nationalised every factory with a labour force of at least fifty workers in January 1946.[27] Mass unemployment was declared forever ended. The promise was made that a system of comprehensive state welfare would be instituted as the economy recovered after the war. There was also land reform across the region and peasants received parcels of land even from the coalition cabinets. The monarchies in Albania, Bulgaria, Romania and Yugoslavia were abolished. Leading collaborators with the Third Reich were arrested and executed; the political right, whether or not its representatives had been pro-German, was eradicated from the public scene. Reports again and again told a story of persecution of political opponents, religious leaders and critical intellectuals. The USSR fobbed off the Western Allies whenever they complained. The fact that communists had invested themselves with portfolios in the security ministries gave them the appearance of procedural regularity. Every country in eastern Europe, moreover, was chaotic after the war. The communist parties exploited the situation. Deeds were done and then denied. An atmosphere of fear was created; and no serious measures could be taken against the abusers of power while Soviet armed forces stood willing to intervene.

American policy had stiffened with the defeat of Japan and Truman's accession to power. Perhaps Roosevelt too would have gone this way. At any rate there was a growing intention in the USA to spread its military, political and economic power around the world – and Britain as well as the USSR would inevitably register the assertive pressure.

American isolationism had faded. Yet Truman did not want to risk starting the Third World War; he was genuinely appalled by the human and ecological devastation caused by the bombing of Hiroshima and Nagasaki.

PART FOUR

REPRODUCTION

1947–1957

20. THE COLD WAR AND THE
SOVIET BLOC

The temperature of relations between the USSR and the Western Allies dropped like a stone in summer 1947. This was the year when the Cold War began in earnest. Political leaders in the West no longer expected anything but bad to come out of Moscow; Stalin and his comrades reciprocated the hostility. Neither side in fact wanted military conflict with the other. Truman, while publicly reaffirming his willingness to use nuclear bombs once again if his country's vital interests were threatened, shuddered at the thought of a third world war: he well understood that nothing would be left on the planet but the insects.[1] Stalin too affected to be unruffled by the new technology of warfare; he refused to exhibit any concern about his country's security. He adhered to the Leninist precept that world wars would continue to occur among capitalist powers so long as capitalism retained its global influence. As previously, he declared that Soviet diplomacy should be geared towards keeping the USSR out of any such clash.[2] This was standard Leninism. Privately, though, he too saw that a third world war might make the world uninhabitable.[3] At the same time he pressed for the acquisition of an A-bomb of his own. A team of scientists was hastily assembled. Beria was to oversee them and no resources were spared. Stalin was not going to be intimidated into compromises by the USA's superior military technology.

Western strategy was supplied by two diplomats, George Kennan for the USA and Frank Roberts for the UK. Independently of each other they urged the need for 'containment'; their idea was to resist all attempts at expanding communist power beyond existing territorial boundaries but to avoid provoking a third world war. Force, including nuclear weaponry, was to be used only if the Kremlin failed to accept this situation. Kennan and Roberts took the long view. They contended that at some future time, as yet unpredictable, the Soviet Union would undergo internal crisis and that communism would collapse.[4]

In June 1947 American Secretary of State George Marshall announced a programme for economic recovery in Europe – including countries in the east – by means of financial grants and loans. The Americans would be assisting the continent to surmount its devastation and penury while creating a market for their own surplus of industrial goods. Governments in western Europe welcomed the initiative. Czechoslovakia too expressed interest. Stalin and Molotov had been hoping that the USSR might be eligible for financial help. But it quickly became evident that Truman and Marshall expected recipient countries to guarantee open trade and the rule of law. Stalin drew back, horrified at the idea of American businessmen behaving in the USSR as if they were at home. When he discovered that Czechoslovak ministers, including communists, planned to go to Paris and explore what kind of deal was on offer, he summoned them to Moscow and gave them a verbal blistering.[5] The European countries to the east of the Elbe were to remain strictly within the great zone of Soviet influence, and Stalin would use any means to defend that position. A turning point in post-war history was reached as the Grand Alliance of wartime, creaking since the end of the war, fell irretrievably apart.

Marshall never genuinely intended to bail out the economy of the USSR or any state under its suzerainty. Negotiations about an American loan to the Kremlin disappeared in smoke. A network of US military bases was being thrown around the globe and notice was given that friendly diplomatic relations with Washington would depend on unrestricted access being made available for the goods and services of the American economy. While offering to help Europe to recover from the war, Truman kept up the pressure on the old imperial powers – the United Kingdom, France, Holland and Portugal – to waive their commercial privileges in their colonies; his aim was that the empires should soon be dissolved.[6]

Stalin struck back by forming the Communist Information Bureau (or Cominform). This was accomplished at a founding conference in September 1947 where communist parties from several countries of eastern Europe as well as France and Italy would be represented. The purpose was to instruct communist parties to adopt a more aggressive posture. In eastern Europe this was to involve switching to a campaign of rapid communisation on the Soviet model; in western Europe it would mean a reinforced campaign against the Marshall Plan and a shift to more militant opposition to the existing governments. The possibility of reconciliation with the USA was discounted. Stalin was still not seeking war with the USA but intended to protect the gains made by the Red Army in the Second World War. European communism was to be redirected towards that objective. Stalin felt that he had nothing to lose. The USA had made its bid to become the dominant power across Europe. The Soviet economic base was weaker than the American one. Moscow had yet to develop an atomic bomb. The Soviet army, however, held the logistical advantage in eastern Europe, and communist parties in western Europe could stir up trouble.

The Conference was held in Szklarska Poręba, a secluded village for holidaymakers at the foot of the Sudety mountains in Polish Silesia. It was practically the geographical centre of Europe – and this perhaps was not an accident. The proceedings had been arranged with conspiratorial thoroughness. (As if it would have mattered a jot if the Western powers had known what was happening!) Delegates assembled like Bolsheviks attending one of their clandestine congresses. But whereas the police before 1917 regularly spied on such gatherings, the Soviet security agencies guarded the Cominform Conference from prying eyes. The Polish communist leadership was kept in the dark about the details. Secrecy was obsessive. The delegates were not told the name of the village even after they had arrived.[7] All meekly accepted this absurd way of going on.

Stalin decided who was to be invited. He refused a request from Mao Zedong, who obviously thought that the plan was to re-establish the Communist International. But Stalin had not dismantled Comintern for nothing; he wanted the world to think that communist parties operated independently of the Kremlin. More surprisingly, perhaps, he did not invite the Spanish and Portuguese. The likely reason is that they stood no chance against their fascist police and Stalin could not be bothered with them. Nor were the British given a place at the conference. Perhaps Stalin thought they were too weak a political force to merit inclusion. In any case he did not want communists in the United Kingdom to abandon the 'parliamentary road'; their presence would certainly have complicated the message he aimed to deliver to the French and the Italians.[8] Even the Greeks were kept away. This was a remarkable decision since the Greek Communist Party was fighting a civil war against a royalist army which was backed by London and Washington.[9] Their absence signalled that Stalin judged it dangerous to commit himself militarily in a country that he did not regard as essential to the security of the USSR. While responding militantly to the American challenge, Stalin wished to avoid any danger unlikely to bring him any benefit.

Conference delegates were given no prior acquaintance with the agenda and were treated like detainees on arrival. A radio transmitter was installed to keep in constant touch with Moscow, and Stalin had regular reports from his men on the spot, Malenkov and Zhdanov. Only the Soviet participants, of course, could communicate in this way with the outside world. Malenkov and Zhdanov tore into the Poles for failing to introduce radical communist measures after the Second World War. The Red Army had given them every opportunity. The USSR offered a model. Yet the communists of Poland and elsewhere in eastern Europe had wheezed and blustered rather than discharge their revolutionary duty. Zhdanov argued that two 'camps' existed in global politics: the first was the camp of progressive, peace-loving democracies and was led by the Soviet Union; it was opposed by the camp of political reaction, militarism and imperialism under the USA's leadership. The task of Malenkov and Zhdanov was made easier by the enthusiasm of the Yugoslav delegates Edvard Kardelj and Milovan Djilas, who strongly denounced the compromises of 1945–7 in the region conquered by Soviet armed forces. Western Europe's communists too came in for a pasting. The Italian and French parties were castigated for having stuck to parliamentary and peaceful methods. Zhdanov declared that this was no way for communism to advance on power. Revolutionary action was required.

Polish party leader Gomułka was unique in defending himself and his search for a specifically national road to socialism. There was no criticism of him until Malenkov and Zhdanov spoke out. The troglodytes of world communism needed to know what the Father of the Peoples wanted before they dared to say anything.[10] The Soviet leadership was behaving with transcendent hypocrisy. The communist movement in both halves of Europe had been forced to follow the Kremlin's orders throughout the previous few years. It is true that such orders had often been confined to general strategy; but not one important step had been taken without consultation with Moscow.

The Marshall Plan and Cominform were early rounds in the contest between East and West. Tito's boisterousness was no longer tolerable. The Yugoslav communists had been helpful in establishing Cominform but too often had intruded into matters of foreign policy which Stalin reserved for the Kremlin. At the Second Cominform Conference, in June 1948, Yugoslavia was expelled from the organisation without right of appeal.[11] Cominform itself was moved from Belgrade to Bucharest. It never truly imposed regular control over its member parties; its functionaries dished out propaganda and did little else. Stalin continued to use the International Department of the Central Committee Secretariat of the All-Union Communist Party in Moscow to co-ordinate and guide the activities of the rest of the world's communist parties. Information came to him both directly from those parties and from his embassies and intelligence agencies. Funds continued to be secretly disbursed to communist leaderships. The Kremlin, as previously, expected to be consulted about important changes in policy or personnel. No communist party dared to express solidarity with the Yugoslavs – and this included parties outside eastern Europe. There were glimmerings of the idea that Chinese communism's orientations towards the peasantry might offer a model for agrarian societies. The most striking example were the communists of the state of Kerala in India. But the Communist Party of India stamped on such heresy, announcing that its only figures of authority were Marx, Lenin and Stalin.[12]

After setting up Cominform, Stalin flexed his muscles in Berlin by denying the Western Allies' access to the city through East Germany. The USA and the United Kingdom reacted by airlifting supplies to the people in the districts of the city which they occupied. The flights continued until Stalin acknowledged defeat in May 1949. But he did not give up the general struggle. In January of the same year he had approved the creation of the Council of Mutual Economic Assistance (or Comecon) to bind eastern Europe together under the USSR's control. In April the Americans and their allies signed the military treaty which constituted the North Atlantic Treaty Organisation (NATO); the zones of Germany they controlled were formed into the Federal Republic of Germany while, in October, the Soviet zone was announced as a separate German Democratic Republic.

The symmetry was not total since the USSR refrained from signing an alliance to compete with NATO until 1955, when Stalin had been dead for two years: the Soviet dictator placed implicit reliance on his Soviet army and distrusted the armies under formation in eastern Europe. He was beginning to discern grounds for increased confidence. The USSR's spies and scientists worked together to produce an A-bomb and it was exploded in Beria's presence in August 1949. Global politics were becoming bipolar. The Kremlin felt more secure than at any time since the Japanese surrender. In October, quite against Stalin's prognosis, the armed forces of Mao Zedong triumphed in the Chinese civil war and took power in Beijing.[13] The map of the world was being redrawn as a quarter of the earth's surface was tugged under direct communist control.

In 1950 there was a further attempt at expansion when the Soviet and Chinese leaderships supported the military campaign of communists under Kim Il-sung's leadership in North Korea to overrun and reunite the entire country.[14] Stalin had misled himself into supposing that the Americans would lack the will to contain communist expansionism. He had also been worried that Mao might gain eminence as the world's greatest exponent of the revolutionary spirit.

Kim had badgered Stalin into giving his consent to the campaign. He had emerged among Korean communists on the coat-tails of the Soviet armed forces' campaign in the Far East in late summer 1945. Plucked from obscurity by his patrons in the USSR, he became the General Secretary of the newly amalgamated Labour Party of Korea. It was said that even his command of the Korean language was insecure after many years with the Russians in Siberia. A cult was immediately created for him. Two decades of his generalship among Korea's communist insurgents were celebrated in 1946 even though this implied that Kim had been a general since the age of fourteen. But, once ensconced in the central party apparatus, he acted as if the throne of power was his birthright.[15]

But Stalin, Mao and Kim had all badly misread the situation. The Americans, exploiting a Soviet walkout from the United Nations Security Council, obtained the UN's sanction to assemble a multinational force to defend South Korea against invasion.[16] This was an important indication of Western resolve. If the whole of Korea had fallen to communism, the policy of global containment would have been utterly discredited. The Korean War involved vast numbers of troops. The Americans and their Western allies, boosting the South Koreans, faced a confident army of North Koreans which had the open participation of the Chinese and the covert support, both in armaments and even aviators, of the USSR. The fighting stopped just short of a direct confrontation between the USA and the USSR. What is more, Truman rejected the call by General Douglas MacArthur to use nuclear bombs and sacked MacArthur for his readiness to act outside instructions. But it was a war that constantly threatened to turn into a third world war. Capitalism and liberal democracy engaged in a titanic struggle with communism. Truman was determined to prove that no further country of geostrategic importance for Washington would succumb to a communist seizure of power. The fronts of the Korean War moved backwards and forwards without either side being able to pull off victory.[17]

More discreetly, the American and British intelligence services sent agents into Albania and Ukraine in these years in an attempt to subvert communist power. The Americans were going beyond the strategy of mere containment: Truman was not averse to probing whether there were weak links in the chain of communism in eastern Europe. It was a forlorn enterprise since it was monitored by Kim Philby, then working in the British embassy in Washington and spying for the USSR – and the result was a bloody débâcle.[18]

At the same time Truman took long-term precautions against communist economic parasitism. In 1949 he had ratified an export control act to prevent strategic materials being sold to the USSR. A Coordinating Committee (CoCom) was set up to ensure that other Western countries toed the same line.[19] This was not a total economic blockade. Trade quietly continued with the USSR and eastern Europe. Ernest Bevin as British Foreign Secretary in May 1949 disliked the publicity given to commercial deals. The Canadians had been criticising the United Kingdom for buying products from communist countries – timber, metals and grain – which Canada itself could produce and sell.[20] Marshall Aid meanwhile produced its results slowly but surely. But Truman did not like to risk anything. The US State Department and the Central Intelligence Agency pumped money and political assurances into western Europe. Agents were simultaneously infiltrated into eastern Europe – this was less effective in part because the Soviet intelligence agencies had been alerted to what was going on. NATO, like its enemies, was engaged in a furious struggle short of provoking the Third World War. The USA did not expect to lose. Truman believed in national destiny and in the inherent greatness of the American political and economic model.

Stalin had ideas about historical inevitability derived from the Leninist ideological storehouse; and his regime also sought to enhance its regional security and maximise its power over eastern Europe. Communisation was reinforced. If polls of popular opinion had been held, communists would have been in the majority nowhere in the region. Communist leaders were regarded as Soviet stooges and communism itself as 'Russian slavery'.[21] Looting took place everywhere. Rape of local women by Red Army soldiers, especially when drunk, was a widespread scandal.[22] A song became popular in the Soviet occupation zone in Germany:

Welcome, liberators!
You take from us eggs, meats and butter, cattle and feed.

And also watches, rings and other things.
You liberate us from everything, from cars and machines.
You take off with you train-carriages and rail installations.
From all this rubbish – you've liberated us!
We cry for joy.
How good you are to us.
How terrible it was before – and how nice now.
You marvellous people!²³

East German communist leader Walter Ulbricht rejected complaints by his own comrades about Soviet soldiers' misbehaviour: 'People who get so worked up about such things today would have done much better to get worked up when Hitler started the war!'²⁴

Talk of national roads to socialism did not entirely cease,²⁵ but Stalin in practice now wanted eastern Europe to copy the Soviet model as closely as possible. Poland was the crucial country. Intensified persecution of Stanisław Mikołajczyk's Polish Peasants' Party (PSL) commenced. Learning that he was about to be arrested, Mikołajczyk had fled abroad in October 1947. Only the Polish Socialist Party (PPS) had any degree of independence, and pressure was applied for it to fuse itself with the communists. The PPS refused but agreed to purge itself of its right wing. The communist leadership underwent renovation in the following months. Gomułka's habit of questioning 'recommendations' from Moscow together with his advocacy of a specifically 'Polish road' to socialism had made him suspect in Stalin's eyes. Bolesław Bierut replaced Gomułka in summer and castigated him for thwarting the creation of collective farms and showing mistrust toward the USSR. Meanwhile the PPS's nerve was cracking. In December 1948 it amalgamated with the communists in a Polish United Workers' Party (PZPR). In reality the communists were gobbling up their main rivals.²⁶ Although a United Peasant Party was established in the following year, the country was already in essence a one-party dictatorship.²⁷

A similar fusion of parties on the left was engineered in Romania in autumn 1947. The atmosphere of repression thickened. The communists inside the United Workers' Party ruled as if it was already a one-party state. King Michael was forced to abdicate. The United Workers' Party pressed most of the few other surviving parties into a People's Democratic Front which, benefiting from gross electoral fraud, won an easy victory in the March 1948 election.²⁸

The Communist Party of Czechoslovakia already dominated both the army and police. From co-operation with its cabinet partners it went over to confrontation. The non-communist ministers resigned in exasperation in February 1948; but, far from unnerving the communist leadership, the exodus opened a gap the communists filled with a single-party government under Klement Gottwald. Opposition was ruthlessly suppressed and the former Foreign Minister Jan Masaryk died mysteriously (he was probably murdered) in the following month. In Hungary the transformation appeared harder to engineer. Whereas the Czechoslovak communists had won 38 per cent of the votes in the 1946 election, their Hungarian comrades remained woefully unpopular. They jumped to 22 per cent in the election of August 1947 only by fiddling the returns.[29] Their leader Rákosi, however, did not let up. He made life intolerable for leading enemies of the party and induced them to flee abroad. He forced through the amalgamation of the communists and the social-democrats into the Hungarian Workers' Party. The security police – the ÁVO, later the ÁVH – mopped up the remaining spillage of overt dissent. Hungary had been turned into a communist one-party state in all but name.[30]

Stalin reduced the new communist states to servility to the USSR. The three conferences of Cominform in September 1947, June 1948 and November 1949 were a useful weapon. Yet Cominform's offices were allocated first to Belgrade and then to Bucharest so as to sustain the fiction that the Soviet leadership allowed freedom to the communist parties. More regular channels were maintained by the International Department of the Central Committee Secretariat of the Communist Party of the Soviet Union. The Ministry of External Affairs and the Ministry of State Security (MGB) also conveyed the wishes of the Kremlin. Stalin, moreover, established a direct telephone link with the communist party leader in each of eastern Europe's capitals. Only Stalin could use it without permission. If President Bierut in Poland, for example, wanted to speak to the Kremlin, he had to arrange an appointment.[31] Stalin became the master of half a continent's chronometry: Berlin was put on to Moscow time.[32] His puppet rulers in eastern Europe had to be ready to answer his questions at any moment and usually this meant in the middle of the night because Stalin slept through most of the day and worked through the hours of darkness.[33]

Tito was not the only suspect leader in the eyes of the Soviet dictator. Every communist chief in the region had continually to prove his loyalty and obedience. Romanian communist leader Gheorghe Gheorghiu-Dej was being denounced as hankering after an economic deal with the

'Anglo-Americans'.[34] The Secretariat of the All-Union Communist Party in Moscow cooked up suitable grounds for condemning the Hungarian communists as vulnerable to 'bourgeois influence' and for indicting both the Polish and Czechoslovak communists for their 'anti-Marxist ideological positions'.[35] Soviet political leaders also had to watch their step in eastern Europe. When Politburo member Kliment Voroshilov on a visit to Budapest in October 1945 failed to consult Moscow about the orders he was giving to the Hungarian leadership, the rest of the Politburo informed on him to Stalin.[36]

A façade of inter-party formality was preserved. A typical message to the Polish Workers' Party ran: 'We express confidence that you will discuss our considerations and let us know of your decision.'[37] But sometimes the exchanges were more brusque. When the Bulgarians worked out a draft law on bank nationalisation, they were told to amend it forthwith.[38] The Soviet Military Administration conducted deep penetration of policymaking in East Germany:

> Almost all the documents which issue from the [Socialist Unity Party] are prepared by us here. If they prepare the draft, then we look at it here and introduce all our comments. There are no documents that would not be formulated by us and which would not be fully affirmed by them; such documents do not exist.[39]

So much for the Socialist Unity Party being the vanguard of revolution! The reality was that Moscow gave the orders and the communist parties obeyed them.

Behind the scenes the Soviet functionaries interviewed the national leaders, usually in one-to-one private conversations. They looked out for disagreements within a leadership. Bolesław Bierut vilified Gomułka in writing and Moscow conserved his letter for later possible use.[40] The Kremlin obtained confidences from all and sundry. The supreme leader in each country naturally hated this practice since it wrecked the possibility of an exclusive channel of communication with Moscow. Party chiefs Georghiu-Dej in Romania and Rákosi in Hungary went round asking who had snitched on them to Stalin.[41] But they were powerless to stop the practice in case they angered Stalin. The Soviet authorities surreptitiously recruited their own informers. This too caused offence but only the Yugoslavs had the nerve to remonstrate with Moscow and remove the individuals from office – and they did this even before the split between the USSR and Yugoslavia.[42] The Kremlin expected to be consulted about decisions on the composition of party leaderships and governmental cabinets in its outer empire. Georgi Dimitrov, becoming Bulgaria's Prime Minister in 1946, provided Zhdanov with a 'preliminary plan' for the composition of his cabinet.[43] If the Kremlin had objected, Dimitrov would have torn the list up. Parties in other countries behaved with similar deference. The supreme rulers of the region lived in Moscow.[44]

Thousands of advisers and instructors were sent into the countries of eastern Europe after 1945. The armed forces and state security agencies teemed with Soviet personnel empowered to reconstruct institutions on Soviet lines. This caused disquiet even among communists, but no overt complaint was made.[45] Andrei Vyshinski, Molotov's deputy in the Ministry of External Affairs, described the situation in blatant terms: 'Our friends definitely stand in need of authoritative directions for their future work in the new conditions.'[46]

Communists said they were introducing democracy to eastern Europe. But it would be democracy of a peculiar sort. Milovan Djilas in wartime had told Molotov that the Yugoslavs were aiming at a democratic republic but 'not one like the French but instead like the Mongolian'.[47] The briefest stay in the People's Republic of Mongolia might have cured Djilas of such nonsense; his visit to Moscow ought also to have performed this function. (He was to recognise his mistake about the communist order a decade later.)[48] Stalin adopted the term being used by the Yugoslavian communists: people's democracy.[49] This is how he made the case to Polish communist leaders:

> The order established in Poland is democracy, it is a new type of democracy. It has no precedent. Neither the Belgian nor English nor French democracies can be taken by you as an example or model. Your democracy is a special one. You don't have a class of big capitalists. You've carried out the nationalisation of industry in a hundred days whereas the English have been struggling for this for a hundred years. So don't copy the Western democracies, let them copy you![50]

He argued that eastern Europe, by taking advantage of Soviet military power, could be communised without the need for the proletarian dictatorship and civil war which had followed the October Revolution. According to Stalin, there was no serious danger of counter-revolution.[51] Falsifying *The State and Revolution*, Stalin contended that Lenin had never treated the dictatorship of the proletariat as a prerequisite for constructing socialism. Ideology was being conformed to the requirements of current geopolitics. Stalin was eager to prove that the communist states of the East – which were increasingly being described as the Soviet Bloc – were offering unrivalled levels of social tranquillity, progress and democracy to their peoples.

Civil rights, however, were suspended everywhere in eastern Europe; and the communists, true to their ideology, delighted in boasting that their policies discriminated in favour of the poorer citizens. The 'people' did not constitute the entire population. The gap between a manager's salary and a labourer's wages was narrowed. Universal and free schooling was introduced. Eligibility for housing, healthcare and pensions was granted to everyone in employment. The promise was made that individuals of proven talent would be enabled to rise up the ladders of public office. Communists shared a commitment to reforms with the other left-of-centre political parties. But no one implemented them with the same determination. Before the Second World War there had been practically no country in the region where the workers, peasants and other members of the lower social orders did not resent the authorities. This made it easier for communist leaderships to impose their regimes. They were realising changes that were uncontroversial among most people. But it was a class dictatorship of some kind. The truth was blurted out when Dimitrov defined people's democracy as a new form of the dictatorship of the proletariat![52]

21. THE YUGOSLAV ROAD

The split between the Soviet Union and communist Yugoslavia caused universal shock. Stalin had dominated world communism for years and could count on the obedience of most communists around the world. The searing dispute of 1948 was different from all previous quarrels in the 'world communist movement' inasmuch as it involved two sovereign states. Hardly had communism expanded beyond the frontiers of the Soviet Motherland when a deep fissure opened up. Unitary official communism was at an end.

Yugoslav communist leader Josip Broz Tito was as astonished as everyone else. He was ideologically a proven Stalinist. Son of a peasant family, he was brought up in poverty and left school early. He quickly became a communist. He was just the sort of militant being selected for training in the Moscow party schools before the Second World War. Comintern dispatched him back from Moscow in 1937 to organize the communist party in Yugoslavia, and he retained the Kremlin's confidence in wartime. By raising a serious revolt against Nazi occupation, he deflected dozens of German army divisions from the eastern front. Tito's military feats attracted the attention of the British. Emissaries from London were parachuted into Yugoslavia to assess which anti-German armed groups should be given material aid. The decision went in Tito's favour. Churchill backed the communist partisans and turned a blind eye to their savagery and ideology in the civil war they were conducting against the Chetniks of Draža Mihailović (who fought to expel the Wehrmacht from Serbian soil) and the Croat Ustashas (who held power by Nazi sanction). The communists were unusual in emphasising a commitment to ending inter-ethnic strife: they stood for a multinational federation. By October 1944 the Red Army of the USSR acting in alliance with Tito and the partisans had taken Belgrade. This was an achievement from which the German forces never recovered in Yugoslavia.

The wartime relationship between the British government and Yugoslav communism was a marriage of convenience. In summer 1945 British

Labour leader Clement Attlee, newly elected as Prime Minister, objected to the policies of Tito's regime. Likewise Tito, with Stalin's support, took no notice of the deal done between Stalin and Churchill in Moscow in 1944 whereby the USSR would share an equal interest in Yugoslavia with the Western Allies.[1] At the same time, however, Soviet officials were concerned that Yugoslav communist propaganda glorified Tito on a level with Stalin:[2] there was room for only one divinity in the world's Marxist movement.

Meanwhile Tito ripped out the pockets of Ustasha and Chetnik resistance after the communist victory in the civil war. As many as a quarter of a million people perished in mass shootings, death marches and abusive treatment in concentration camps in the first couple of years after the Second World War.[3] No political activity outside the Popular Front was allowed. Religious organisations were hounded. Communists persecuted the Catholic Church in Croatia since its priests had supported the Ustashas and the German occupation. The Moslems were harassed in Bosnia and their mosques and Koranic schools were shut down.[4] Tito despised the slowness of communisation elsewhere in eastern Europe, and the Yugoslavs criticised this at the first conference of Cominform in September 1947.[5] They also demanded the inclusion of Trieste in Yugoslavia as the price of their acquiescence in any European peace settlement. Trieste, though, was largely an Italian-inhabited city. The fact that Tito's standpoint was an electoral embarrassment to the Italian Communist Party did not inhibit him – and initially he had Stalin on his side in the diplomatic wrangle with the government in Rome. It seemed that Stalinist faith was alive and well in Belgrade and that Tito was its vicar.

Stalin was not totally content but kept the Yugoslav comrades as bloodhounds to be turned on any European communists who failed to exhibit sufficient revolutionary ardour. The breaking point came over politics in the Balkans. In January 1948 Tito thought of sending Yugoslav troops to repel a possible Greek incursion into southern Albania. Stalin rebuked him for ignoring the danger of a British intervention. The last thing wanted by the Kremlin was armed conflict among the world's great powers. If tensions increased with the West, in any case, Stalin wanted personal control of international communist policy. He ordered the preparation of a memorandum reprimanding the Yugoslavs for disregarding the USSR's position as a global power. Allegedly they aimed to dominate the Balkans. They did not adhere to Marxism-Leninism. Why, Tito had mentioned Marx only once in the past three years and had never referred to Stalin![6] The Yugoslav leadership had made trouble over Trieste and interfered in the fraternal communist politics of Bulgaria, Albania and now even Greece. Stalin had until recently supported the idea of a Balkan Federation;[7] but he came to the conclusion that Tito would exploit such a project to dominate these other countries. And while talking big about communism, Tito had underestimated the menace of the kulak in the countryside. According to the memorandum, he and his comrades were not genuine Marxists.[8]

Tito, however, stood his ground and called the USSR's bluff – and he had the support of his Central Committee. This emboldened him to tell the Soviet adviser to Belgrade:

> We consider that on a series of questions we're . . . not worse than others who've tried to criticise us – and not only to criticise us but to deliver lectures to us. I have in mind the Hungarians, Romanians and Czechs. Do we really have more capitalistic elements than they have? Do they really have fewer kulaks than we do?[9]

Stalin's démarche was a spectacular failure. Yugoslav communism was going to be a product made at home and foreign interference would be resisted.

After probing whether the Moscow–Belgrade scission was reparable, Tito went over to the attack. When his propaganda overseer Milovan Djilas drafted a newspaper article criticising Stalin, Tito at first spiked it but then changed his mind: 'Good. Let it stand. We've spared Stalin long enough.'[10] Yet Tito also went on installing a communist order remarkably similar to the USSR's. A wild campaign was initiated in 1949 to collectivise agriculture. The same peasantry which had recently received individual smallholdings was forced into 'peasant–worker co-operatives' (SRZ). When the Bosnian Moslems put up stout resistance, the police and armed forces suppressed them.[11] Many party members, including leaders such as Andrija Hebrang and Sreten Žujović, were expelled from the ranks on suspicion of pro-Soviet leanings; Hebrang was among the 16,000 put under arrest.[12] Tito and his grim security chief Aleksandar Ranković informally agreed to expand the system of prison camps for 'socially useful labour'. Conditions of detention were sometimes worse than in the USSR. Guards at the Bare Island camp in the north Adriatic got the inmates to beat up prisoners newly arrived from the mainland. The barbarity was systematic.[13]

The Yugoslav leaders soon revised their approval of Stalin's industrial and agricultural methods. Quite apart from causing millions of deaths, the ultra-centralised administrative system generated obstructiveness and a lack of initiative at lower levels of the economy right down to the workers and peasants. Politburo member and Planning Commission chairman Boris Kidrič was among the last to recognise this. He received progress reports every twenty-four hours from all the country's factories and building sites: 'Not even the Russians have managed that – they get only monthly reports. Two truckloads a day!' It was pointed out to him that his staff lacked the time and expertise to process the incoming information. Rather than improving on Soviet procedures, Kidrič was clogging the channels of production. But then he saw the light: 'You know, those daily reports from every enterprise are the purest bureaucratic idiocy – a hopeless job.'[14]

Debate began about how to introduce a looser economic system than the Soviet stereotype. Yugoslavia's communists intended 'to create Marx's free association of producers'. *De facto* decollectivisation was announced in March 1953. The compulsion for youth to carry out physical labour was revoked. Industry was reformed as the government, while retaining ownership of enterprises, set up schemes of 'workers' self-management' from June 1950. Local councils gained some freedom to set their own budgets. The rationale was to enable city councillors, factory managers and the workers themselves to acquire a firm material interest in raising productivity. Meanwhile the peasant–worker co-operatives in the countryside provided farm labourers with a share of any profits accruing from a rise in productivity. The communist leadership hoped to avoid that spirit of popular resentment which pervaded the USSR.[15] The purpose was explicit. Yugoslavia under communism was going to try to effect a revolutionary transformation without the degree of permanent coercion that was normal under Stalin. Although Tito remained eager to repress his open political enemies, he aimed at a form of communist rule that could win popular support.

Yugoslavia acquired a new constitution in 1946 and declared itself a people's republic with six federal republics: Serbia, Croatia, Slovenia, Montenegro, Bosnia-Herzegovina and Macedonia. Two autonomous provinces were created in Serbia; these were Kosovo and Vojvodina. The titular nation of each republic was assured considerable freedom of self-expression within its borders. Provision was made for schools and media in Yugoslavia's various languages. Despite official atheism, churches and mosques were left standing and in use by believers. The barbarous conflict between Serbs and Croats in the Second World War was to be dispatched to oblivion. Unfortunately the borders could not be drawn with ethno-demographic neatness. Serbs lived throughout Croatia and

Croats inhabited parts of Serbia. Bosnia-Herzegovina was a tangled skein of Croats, Serbs and others – and many of its citizens were not Christians but Moslems. Kosovo was treasured by patriotic Serbs as the site of the battle against the Turks in 1389 but was inhabited mainly by Albanians (which is why the status of autonomous province was introduced). Communism claimed to be able to solve enmities better than any other imaginable Yugoslav state system, but old mutual enmities did not die off.

Tito was half-Slovenian, half-Croat. His mixed parentage helped to allay popular concerns. His ability to stand up for the country also assisted. Yugoslavia was friendless in eastern Europe and was agitated by war scares whenever Soviet troop movements took place. When the Korean War broke out in 1950 there was serious worry in Belgrade that Stalin might exploit the moment to invade Yugoslavia. Furthermore, post-war economic regeneration was painfully slow. Yugoslavia needed industrial growth to build up its military capacity, and its people were clamouring for more food, clothing and housing. The Yugoslav leadership looked for foreign partners. Tito made overtures to socialist and social-democratic parties in western Europe. The British Labour Party was sought out, and Attlee this time responded positively.[16] The Yugoslav leadership was ceasing to bother about whether its helpers were fellow socialists. The reaction from outside the Warsaw Pact was enthusiastic. Lester Pearson, Canada's Secretary of State for External Affairs, remarked: 'I don't suppose I'll ever be a communist, but if I were, I'd be a Yugoslav communist.'[17] (Pearson was a Liberal.) The US administration was similarly encouraging since it calculated that Tito was the enemy of the West's principal enemy and should be treated as a friend regardless of his ideology and repressive practices.

Belgrade received emergency aid to the value of half a billion US dollars in 1949–52 alone.[18] This counteracted the economic siege that Stalin was conducting. Military security was enhanced when countries in western Europe sold arms to Yugoslavia.[19] This brought about the very situation which Stalin had wanted to avoid at all costs: the intrusion of Western capitalism into the communist East. Tito had also to pay a political price. He dropped active support for communist revolution in Greece and gave up his pretensions to Trieste. Greece and Italy were allies of the USA and Yugoslavia had to respect their territorial integrity or else forfeit American assistance.[20]

The communist party was redesignated so as to distance it from association with the USSR. From 1952 it was called the League of

Yugoslav Communists. Along with the change of name went a commitment to political reform. The League was meant to confine itself to
discussing and teaching and to stop handing out commands.[21] Licence
was given to intellectuals to explore the foundations of Marxism.
Critiques of Lenin and his policies began to appear. Tito sat back while
the discussions proceeded. Unlike the communist leaders who were his
contemporaries, he laid no claim to originality as a thinker. The aim was
to recapitulate what had been originally intended by Marx and Engels.
Looking at the USSR, Yugoslav writers denied that there would ever be
'a withering away of the state' in line with Lenin's predictions in *The
State and Revolution*. The Soviet political and economic system, they
contended, was not socialist at all but a regime of 'state capitalism'.[22]
The League of Yugoslav Communists claimed that its schemes of political
federalism, institutional decentralisation and workers' self-management
constituted a long-overdue return to the sources of the Marxist tradition.

Not every leading communist in Yugoslavia felt comfortable about
developments. The ruling group around Tito included Edvard Kardelj,
Aleksandar Ranković and Milovan Djilas. Steadily Djilas moved into
opposition. He detested the political cult of Tito, who he thought had
degenerated with the holding of supreme office. He also hated the Soviet
Union as an oppressive bureaucracy and an imperial bully, and he
exceeded even Tito in his willingness to say what he thought about the
Kremlin. In 1954 he handed in his party card. In November 1956 he was
arrested when Tito started to want to prove that he was committed to a
rapprochement with Moscow. Djilas refused to recant his opinion. He
went on to write *The New Class*, one of the most powerful exposures of
the separation of communist rulers from the working class in whose
name they had made the revolution. What Djilas revealed was not just
true about Yugoslavia but applicable to every country where communism
held state power.

Stalin's death had relieved Yugoslavia's situation as the Party Presidium (as the Politburo was renamed in 1952) in Moscow sought reconciliation with Belgrade. Tito welcomed the overtures of Nikita Khrushchëv,
Stalin's successor; but would not come to terms except as an equal
negotiator.[23] He absolutely refused to go to Moscow. Khrushchëv by
1955 was getting impatient and flew with Malenkov to Yugoslavia. There
he disgraced himself by telling filthy jokes at banquets and getting hope-
lessly drunk. Tito deftly pushed the Soviet leadership into accepting
Yugoslavia's right to take its own route to communism. Meanwhile he
went about the task of finding other friends in the world. Along with

Jawaharlal Nehru and Gamal Abdel Nasser, he helped to form the Non-Aligned Movement which sought to steer a neutral passage between the USSR and the USA. The idea was to protect the interests of the world's smaller powers, and Tito set himself up as a tribune for the many struggles for national liberation. This made him a rival to Khrushchëv in international diplomacy. Things might soon have deteriorated into yet another rupture between Yugoslavia and the USSR. Events, though, pushed in the opposite direction. The Hungarian Uprising against communism in 1956 scared Tito into political support for the Soviet military invasion. Preservation of the communist one-party state was axiomatic for him. Hungary's rebels, he thought, deserved to be suppressed.

Official hopes for the Yugoslav economy proved unrealistic. Although output in industry rose by 62 per cent between 1952 and 1956, most of the increase occurred in the capital-goods sector. Consumers grumbled about being neglected. There were also regional discrepancies. The north of the country had benefited from Habsburg rule and was consistently more successful than the ex-Ottoman south.[24] Slovenia, Croatia and northern Serbia made their advance while the rest of Yugoslavia moved along at a sluggish pace. Tito cultivated an overarching sense of 'Yugoslavism' (*Jugoslavenstvo*) and strove for a consensual political order and a vibrant economy.[25] It anyway made no sense to ignore the south with its abundant mineral resources and its pool of unexploited labour.[26] The strains of rulership were immense. No leader of a republic could openly profess a nationalist agenda, but each could do this on the sly by calling for an ever bigger share of the state budget for his republic. What made things worse was the rising power of Serbia. The Serbs ran the officer corps of the Yugoslav armed forces, and police chief Aleksandar Ranković quietly favoured Serbia's interests to the detriment of the rest of Yugoslavia.

In 1968 Tito sacked Ranković from the leadership. Ranković, the hard man of the Yugoslav Revolution, broke down in tears as he left the meeting but was not much missed even by his friend Kardelj. When Tito discussed his decision about Ranković, Kardelj surprised him by moaning about having had his private phone tapped for years. Tito snapped: 'Why didn't you tell me?' Kardelj replied: 'I thought *you* might have ordered it . . .'[27]

Ranković's enforced retirement was accompanied by a change of stance in national and security policy. Concessions were made to the republics. Tito demanded obedience, using his charisma and authority to stabilise the political situation. Kosovo's cultural and administrative autonomy was enhanced and the Albanians acquired their own university in Priština.[28] Croats, who had been restive, obtained concessions for their republic. Reforms continued in the direction of loosening central economic controls from the 1960s. The fiscal demands of the Yugoslav government were lowered.[29] Yet no permanent basic improvement resulted and several problems were left festering. The brightest young workers were leaving for employment in West Germany. The exodus from agriculture left behind an agrarian sector dependent on an ageing workforce.[30] Students imitated the rebellious youth of North America and western Europe. In Belgrade they blockaded academic buildings crying: 'There is no socialism without freedom, no freedom without socialism!'[31] Yugoslavia was the single country in eastern Europe which looked as if it might be convulsed by a revolt of discontented, anarchic students such as had happened in France and Italy.

Tito alone could stop things getting out of hand when the republican leaderships failed to be even-handed in dealing with their national minorities. He rebuked Croatia's leaders in 1971 in Zagreb: 'This time I'm going to speak first. You see that I am very angry. That is why I have summoned you and the meeting won't last long.' Mass resignations and sackings followed. In 1972 he turned on the leadership of Serbia and called them to order.[32] Yet the seams of the federal system were wearing thin and Tito alone held them together. Into his seventies he still seemed indestructible. The politicians of his generation were dead or no longer active in public life. He was fêted abroad as a leader who had refused to be intimidated by the USSR, and he remained an adornment of the Non-Aligned Movement.

On 4 May 1980 mortality intruded itself when the lion of Yugoslavia – founder of the post-war state and its uninterrupted leader – died. A joke had been doing the rounds:

> *Question:* What's the difference between Yugoslavia and the USA?
> *Answer:* In the USA you work for forty years and then become president for four; in Yugoslavia you fight for four years and then become president for forty.[33]

For a while the republican leaders stuck together, at least when they met in Belgrade. Agreement was reached on a collective presidency. The chair was held on a rotating basis.[34] Honour was continually paid to Tito's memory. Yet he had left an unenviable economic legacy. The foreign debt had grown to 8 per cent of gross domestic product. Willing creditors were getting fewer for eastern Europe.[35] Calls started to be voiced for the inception of a multi-party system. National resentments were expressed without the earlier inhibitions. Although the offices of preventive censorship were maintained, dissenting opinions were printed ever more frequently. Industrial stagnation deepened. Agriculture stalled. Nobody any longer believed that the 'Yugoslav model' of communism offered a credible rival to capitalist economics. The death of the patriarch aggravated an already critical situation.

The achievements of Yugoslav communism were not negligible. Tito had stood up to the USSR. Even though he would scarcely have lasted without Western economic assistance, his steadfastness was undeniable. He was also genuinely popular. As the acknowledged hero of the struggle for the country's liberation, he experienced warmth from crowds that every communist ruler in eastern Europe envied. Yugoslavia's people had the highest standard of living in the region and were the envy of the communist world. Furthermore, Tito's management of the federal constitution was masterly. Civil war could easily have broken out among the several national and religious groups, but peace and order had prevailed. Citizens of Yugoslavia could travel abroad; indeed the state recognised the benefits of remittances from West Germany and permitted workers to ply their trades there as 'guest workers'. Belgrade's television, radio and newspapers had considerable latitude to criticise abuses of power. Food and clothing were more diverse than in other communist states. Rural households got on with life with little heed for what the government decreed.

Yet this was hardly the kind of society which had been aimed at by the comrades-in-arms before 1945, and dissenters like the ex-Marxist Djilas and the questing Marxist philosopher Mihaylov saw reality more clearly than Tito's foreign groupies – from the Fourth International to the film stars Richard Burton and Elizabeth Taylor – who rendered him homage. The League of Communists ran a one-party state. Although Tito allowed wider scope for dissent than was the norm in eastern Europe, he clamped down on the slightest objection to communism. The economy was falling into a shambles long before his death: workers' self-management was code for mismanagement. Indigenous research and development was negligible. National hostilities were barely disguised and resentment of Serbian power inside the Yugoslav state was intense. People knew a lot about conditions in western Europe. Financial assistance from abroad was what kept the budget afloat. Communism as an ideology touched few hearts; there no longer existed much sense of progress obtained or obtainable in communist Yugoslavia. Travelling out to West Germany in search of work, the 'guest workers' from Yugoslavia wrote home about the attractions abroad. The gap in freedom, comfort and expectancy between Balkan communism and the West's liberal and capitalist democracies was wider than ever.[36]

22. WESTERN EUROPE

While the Soviet Bloc was being established in eastern Europe, the fraternal communist parties in most countries of the West adapted themselves to an open existence. From Greece to France there was a sustained spasm of activity in 1944–5 as liberation from Nazi occupation was achieved. The exceptions in western Europe were Spain and Portugal, where the fascist regimes of General Franco and Dr Salazar continued to ban communist parties and imprison their dwindling number of militants. Dolores Ibárruri – known as La Pasionaria – was regularly wheeled out in Moscow, where she had taken refuge after the Spanish civil war, to denounce the trampling of political and civic freedoms throughout the Iberian peninsula.

Liberal democracies had renovated their strategies for governance. Many of them in western Europe were committed to reducing social inequalities, enhancing mass education and increasing state economic ownership and regulation. Welfare provision rose on the public agenda in several countries. The British led the way with a comprehensive scheme for social security and public health. Planning was advocated by political groupings in the region. Having been general practice in all belligerent countries in time of war, it was retained as the key to industrial and agricultural recovery. Trade unions sprouted up. Multiparty democracy and cultural freedom were the norm except on the Iberian peninsula. Religion could be practised with little interference. International co-operation was hailed as a goal; there was constant talk about the need to build a just world.[1] The Truman administration was satisfied that governments in western Europe were fostering market economies, facilitating Christian worship and permitting American access to their economies. Above all, such governments were hostile towards communism. British Labour Party politicians such as Foreign Secretary Ernest Bevin matched Conservative Party leader Winston Churchill in denouncing communist abuses in the USSR and eastern Europe.

The communist parties were resilient under such pressure. Palmiro Togliatti, after years of Moscow exile, pestered Dimitrov for permission to return to Italy, where Pietro Secchia, soon to be made his party deputy, headed the Italian anti-fascist resistance.[2] French communist leader Maurice Thorez too had spent the war in the Soviet capital, while his deputy Jacques Duclos stayed behind to co-ordinate the communist activity in the Maquis – and Thorez was itching to go back to his country. The communists in France, Italy and Greece had joined the anti-Nazi resistance, carrying out sabotage, disruption and killings. Capture by the Germans had meant certain death, usually after frightful torture. They put themselves forward in 1945 as champions of their liberated peoples.

They pointed to the woeful record of the Christian clergy in their countries during the war. The Vatican had colluded with Mussolini and Hitler. French Catholic bishops had supported Marshal Pétain's puppet regime at Vichy until the moment of its collapse.[3] Communists also highlighted the unwillingness of businessmen and conservative politicians to stand up to the Third Reich or to promote fundamental social reform. Official communism in western Europe, drawing down the blind on its advocacy of the Nazi–Soviet pact, claimed to be alone in its capacity to defend the national interest and stave off 'American imperialism'. (De Gaulle, though, came to power in 1945 intending to arrest Thorez for having deserted from the French army and had to be persuaded to desist.)[4] They pointed to the corruption in government, commerce and industry since the liberation. They noted that the big companies which had flourished during the German occupation were still prominent. They ridiculed other parties of the political left for colluding with the bourgeoisie and painted a bleak picture of the future unless the countries of western Europe ceased to dally with capitalism. The struggle against fascism was not enough: there had to be a total transformation of political, economic and social conditions.

By the end of the war there were already communist ministers in the coalition governments of France, Italy, Belgium, Finland and Denmark. Thorez and Togliatti had agreed their future policy with Soviet leaders before setting off home. Stalin talked at length with Togliatti in March 1944 and with Thorez in November.[5] Information brought through from their countries was complex and fluid; and Stalin, Molotov and Dimitrov accepted, however reluctantly, that they had to rely on analysis and advice from the refugee communist leaders. At the same time both Thorez and Togliatti understood that the Kremlin was constrained by the USSR's interests and especially by the need to avoid a rupture with the western Allies; they also knew that they would require Soviet support for the foreseeable future – and as old Comintern hands they never questioned the desirability of world communist unity. The discussions produced an agreed line of action. Togliatti's instinct was to go for radical policies such as abolishing the monarchy and separating Church and state; but Togliatti and Thorez accepted Stalin's advice to avoid overestimating their own strength.[6] Stalin wished also to assure Roosevelt and Churchill that he had no desire to cause undue trouble in Europe's western half at a time when he wanted them to keep their noses out of his business in the east. He even ordered communists to avoid displaying any 'excess of zeal' in defence of the Soviet Union.[7]

Togliatti arrived in Salerno on 27 March 1944 and urged the Italian Communist Party to compromise on its previous objectives. This was a hard message to deliver. Communists in Italy were confident in their ability to advance on power. They had armed groups. They saw no political group in the country which rivalled them as potential mobilisers of popular opinion. They wanted a strategy of dynamic direct action. Instead Togliatti told them that hopes of a communist-led insurrection should be put aside. A 'national road to socialism' had to be found. A 'new party' (*partito nuovo*) had to be built through mass recruitment, and the small underground party would be no more. This would involve a focus on getting communist candidates elected to parliament and on gaining places in a coalition ministry. Alliance with Christian Democracy in government should not be excluded. Conflict with the Catholic Church should be avoided and the campaign against the monarchy suspended. Togliatti wanted the communists to gain recognition as the country's genuine patriots. In this way he hoped to win over those segments of society which had always been hostile to his party.

The French Communist Party took the same line. Thorez stated: 'Production is today the highest form of class duty, of the duty of Frenchmen.' He said this to a meeting of miners in the French north who had hoped he would lead them on strikes and demonstrations.[8] Not all communists approved of the compromises. Many militants who had fought in the anti-German resistance were itching to take up arms again. Secchia in Italy indicated, if only to leading comrades, his wish to switch policy back to insurrection.[9]

The results for Thorez and Togliatti were at first impressive. The French communists emerged from the August 1945 elections as the largest party, albeit without achieving an absolute majority. The result, however, was not a communist-led government. De Gaulle as President refused their demand for ministerial posts in foreign policy, defence and security in the ensuing coalition. Thorez was entrusted merely with the public administration portfolio.[10] Although De Gaulle resigned in January 1946, distrust of communist intentions persisted. Thorez fought on. His party was again the largest in the November 1946 elections. The socialist Paul Ramadier became Prime Minister, this time with Thorez as his deputy. It looked as though the 'parliamentary road' was a rewarding one for communists to travel. But Thorez was soon disappointed. The communist ministers were sacked from the cabinet in May 1947 and a fresh coalition was put together as the socialists sought political and financial assistance from the USA. When the First Conference of Cominform criticised the French Communist Party for its lack of revolutionary zeal, Jacques Duclos accepted the criticism without mentioning that his comrades had been toeing Moscow's line at the time. (No one worried much about his feelings: Duclos had acted as the Soviet party leadership's stooge in denouncing American communist leader Earl Browder in 1945 and setting up the situation which resulted in his expulsion from the party.)[11]

In the Italian elections of April 1948 the communists and the Christian Democrats lined up against each other as the two most popular parties. It had been a brutal campaign which Togliatti expected to win in alliance with other parties of the left; indeed his main worry was about what to do if the enemies of communism tried to overturn the result. Should the communist party organise an uprising? The strong advice from Moscow was that Togliatti should do no such thing.[12] The USSR obviously could not afford yet another complication in its relations with the West. Meanwhile the USA was active behind the scenes, showering Alcide De Gasperi and the Christian Democrats with financial support. The Americans also promised to return Trieste to Italy in the event of a non-communist government being formed, and they threatened to cut off Marshall Plan aid in the event of a communist electoral victory. US forces were secretly kept in readiness to intervene if the voting went the wrong way.[13]

The Italian communists failed to shrug off the Christian Democrats' accusation that they were Stalin's errand boys – even Umberto Terracini, a leading party veteran, upbraided Togliatti for automatically obeying orders from the Kremlin. (Terracini was cajoled into recanting his criticism.)[14] The Vatican pitched in with vitriolic attacks on atheistic communism; Pope Pius XII branded anyone voting for 'parties and powers that deny God' as 'a deserter and a traitor'. The arrival of American ships with food supplies was broadcast on cinema newsreels. The government did everything to discredit and disrupt the communists short of banning them. The election was contested fiercely but without violence. Togliatti had formed a coalition for the campaign with the Italian Socialist Party under Pietro Nenni to fight the campaign, and they banged their drum about the problems of unemployment, poverty and social inequality yet to be tackled. The outcome stayed in doubt until polling day itself. In fact the Christian Democrats won 48.5 per cent of the votes; this was not quite an absolute majority but De Gasperi could celebrate a triumph. The alliance of communists and socialists took only 31 per cent and De Gasperi formed a coalition of the parties of the centre and the centre-right; he dispensed entirely with the communists.

From that moment until the self-abolition of the Italian Communist Party in 1991 no Italian government allowed communists into coalition. Italy entered NATO at its formation in 1949, choosing an orientation towards the USA and the West. The same was true of France until the return to power of Charles de Gaulle as President in 1958. (De Gaulle withdrew his country from NATO's military structure in 1966 but continued to co-operate with the Americans behind the veil of assertive rhetoric.)

Togliatti, though, toured the great cities of north and south, affirming the party's resolve to find a way to come to power. He rejected the request of 'dear comrade Stalin' to leave Rome and head the Cominform.[15] Having escaped his cage in the USSR, he was not going to re-enter voluntarily. In July 1948 he experienced mortal danger in Italy when a student approached him and his companion Nilde Jotti and shot him in the chest. The party blamed the government and organised protest demonstrations. A general strike was called. Rumours grew that the communist leadership would organise an insurrection in reaction to the assassination attempt. Fortunately Togliatti made a quick recovery and he ordered his followers to avoid any wild action. 'Calm down,' he ordered. 'Don't lose your heads!' The communists became the largest opposition party at successive elections in the decades ahead. Despite being criticised at the First Conference of Cominform, Italian communists continued to prioritise staying within the constitution, but they were not what they seemed. Although they raised funds from members, they also begged for and received secret subsidies from Moscow.[16] They maintained a clandestine apparatus, supervised by Pietro Secchia, for any potential emergency when the government might seek to suppress the party. Togliatti planned for the worst while concentrating on progress by electoral means.

His worries that his party might be suppressed were not unusual at the time. John Gollan, Assistant General Secretary of the Communist Party of Great Britain, in a conversation with an unnamed visitor in 1948 compared the United Kingdom unfavourably with the Soviet Union. Most people in the USSR, he asserted, had 'never seen a secret policeman and never would'. The visitor retorted: 'But there is no beating here or secret executions!' Gollan was unmoved: 'No, because there is no need for executions *yet*. But one day there will be.' Asked to justify his analysis, he told the story of a man he knew in south Wales who 'was knocked down by a policeman and kicked about a bit'.[17]

Most Western governments in fact avoided violence in holding down their communists. There was recognition in Italy and France that outright suppression would provoke civil war, and the communist parties undeniably had huge support in both countries. Propaganda was intensified against Marxism, the USSR and the links between the Kremlin and European communist parties.[18] Surveillance was increased. Schemes were devised for military action in the event that communists looked likely to come to office.[19] American assistance for economic recovery was openly supplied through the Marshall Plan. But Washington also used covert techniques and poured its funds into Europe to support anti-communist parties. In the three decades from 1948 the CIA pumped in about sixty-five million dollars – and this total does not include money made available from private sources.[20] This called for a competing reaction from the USSR. The Italian Communist Party had always received funds from Moscow. These increased with Togliatti's return to open politics. Couriers moved regularly between Moscow and Rome and a special section was attached to the Italian communist apparatus to launder the American currency.[21] Italy and France were the key targets for Soviet subversion and for the USA to retain under its hegemony.

Stalin was probing ways to enhance the USSR's influence in western Europe short of provoking a world war. Contrary to widely held belief, he did not feel bound by agreements made at Tehran, Yalta and Potsdam; he frequently tested the will of the USA, Britain and France. An early example was the situation in Greece. As the German forces withdrew in October 1944, the Greek Communist Party found its armed force – ELAS – subordinated to the British army with Moscow's consent.[22] But the Greek Communist Party soon opted for insurgency.

Clashes occurred between the communists and the British together with the forces of the new British-backed Greek government. Stalin at the time, however, needed to keep good relations with the United Kingdom for strategic reasons, and he was annoyed with the Greek comrades for not having consulted him.[23] Without outside help, the Greek Communist Party did not succeed and the revolt petered out. Then Stalin changed his mind, hoping to play off the Americans and the British over Greece. To this end he was happy that party leader Nikos Zachariadis should bait the government politically. Communists accused ministers of promoting 'monarcho-fascism'; they also charged the British with wishing to dominate the whole Mediterranean.[24]

By 1946 they were eager to resume armed struggle. The headstrong Zachariadis pursued his personal line, exposing himself to lively debate among fellow party leaders.[25] He needed support from communist states for military equipment, and he gained the desired consent on his trips to Belgrade, Prague and Moscow. The plan was to conquer the villages of Greece in an unobtrusive campaign which would avoid an early intervention by the British.[26] But Stalin changed his mind yet again and advised emphasis on political measures rather than the armed struggle.[27] Tito and the Yugoslavs, however, continued to render material assistance and advice to the Greek communists. Having won their own civil war, they thought the comrades in Athens could do the same and spread communist rule to the shores of the Aegean. Stalin reverted to a militant stance after the announcement of the Marshall Plan and ceased trying to restrain the Greek Communist Party. Soviet military equipment was covertly rushed to Greece.[28] A provisional revolutionary government was proclaimed. But it became clear that the Greek communists as well as their Yugoslav sympathisers had exaggerated their strength and potential. Stalin had been misled, and called for an end to the uprising in Greece.[29]

What counted for Stalin was the fact that the enemy had vastly superior power in the Mediterranean region. He wanted to prevent the Western powers from being tempted to make incursions into Albania.[30] Eastern Europe was sacrosanct for him; he was determined to keep what had been won for the USSR by his armed forces. Pointless heroics and lost causes held no attraction for him and he expected the world communist movement to accept his judgement without demur.[31] The Kremlin would have been delighted if Greece had gone communist. But it was not to be and Stalin demanded that other communist parties should accept this denouement.

The Yugoslav communists objected to Stalin's change of policy. They were not alone. Bulgarian communist leader Traicho Kostov too urged that Soviet aid be sent to the Greek insurrectionaries.[32] This had baleful consequences for the Soviet–Yugoslav relationship; it also brought doom on Kostov, who was executed with Stalin's connivance at the end of 1948. Stalin himself wobbled on the Greek question in the following months: he was still tempted to back the insurrection or at least to cause trouble for the 'Anglo-Americans' in Greece.[33] But then he ordered the communists under Nikos Zachariadis and Markos Vafiadis to end the civil war. Zachariadis and Vafiadis were loyal Stalinists who took Stalin's side when the split between the USSR and Yugoslavia occurred. Yet, despite being deprived of supplies from Moscow, they refused to stop fighting royalist forces which had abundant assistance from the Americans. Communist measures in the mountains grew desperate. Hostages were taken. Terror-massacres were perpetrated and mass forcible conscription of adolescents was introduced. Suspect villages were razed to the ground. Torture and butchery prevailed on both sides in the war. But the communist insurgency stood no chance. By the end of 1949 the communist revolt had been crushed and the remnants of the anti-government forces fled to Albania.

The vengeance against the Greek communists was ferocious. The government had sequestered the bleak island of Makronisos as a prison colony. Supposedly it was a centre for rehabilitation. Instead the communist convicts were forced to live in tents and went hungry and thirsty most of their time. They were regularly tortured. When their spirit was broken they were forced to enlist in the armed forces and fight against their former comrades. Recalcitrant individuals were put before firing squads. Communists remained in prison long after the end of the civil war. Makronisos rivalled Franco's penal settlements after his military victory in Spain in the degree of brutality meted out to communist suspects. It was the worst instance of atrocities against communism in western Europe in the second half of the twentieth century.

Stalin's goading of the French and Italian communists ceased within months of the First Cominform Conference. Recriminations were halted against leading comrades in western Europe. At the Second and Third Conferences of Cominform, in June 1948 and November 1949, the Soviet representatives were exercised primarily by the Yugoslav question. Stalin's more sober attitude was reflected in his handling of the Communist Party of Great Britain. Its new programme, *The British Road to Socialism*, was published in 1951. This came out as a pamphlet which, according to the Executive Committee, proved that the party was not under Moscow's thumb. British communists denied wishing to reconstruct the country on the model of the USSR. They dropped 'communism' and the 'dictatorship of the proletariat' from their stated objectives. Their current aim was basic social and economic reform and they would campaign for this in parliamentary elections and by other peaceful means. They argued that only they could bring this about and that the Labour Party was merely the left wing of the Conservative Party. They presented themselves as the sole British party striving after international peace. They even claimed to have been libelled as aiming at the destruction of the British Empire; their aim, they claimed, was to reorganise relations between Britain and its colonies on a 'democratic' basis.[34]

British communist independence, however, was a fiction. Stalin vetted the draft and deftly amended its contents. At a time of war in Korea and political show trials in eastern Europe he reserved time to edit the programme of a communist party that stood no chance of achieving power. At best this would be a nuisance to the British political establishment. But co-ordination and subordination were required in the world communist movement and no exceptions could exist. Harry Pollitt, who had again become General Secretary in 1941, took his thoughts to Moscow before the document appeared. Stalin instigated revisions which stressed that the party was committed to its programme for the long term. Pollitt, who often shuttled about on foreign trips, told hardly anyone exactly where 'his' ideas had come from. He therefore had a hard job persuading the austere Stalinist Rajani Palme Dutt of the desirability of changing the party's long-term programme. But Pollitt wore down his Executive Committee. He got for Moscow what Stalin had demanded; and had Stalin not taken the initiative, the British comrades – it is now clear – would never have dreamed of issuing *The British Road to Socialism*. (The evidence of Pollitt's subservience did not come to light for another forty years.)[35]

Meanwhile Togliatti in Italy was not in the best position to refute the charge that the Kremlin lorded it over him. It was difficult to convince anyone but fellow party members that Trieste, the Italian-inhabited city on the north coast of the Adriatic, should pass to Yugoslavia. Togliatti also hated being asked by the party's enemies why Italian POWs in the USSR – usually unwilling conscripts of Mussolini – should remain in captivity. The Italian and French communist leaderships did not help themselves by repeating that Stalin was the leader of the 'democratic', 'peace-loving' camp in world politics and 'the leader of progressive humanity'.[36] They worked hard to propose a positive case for communism; but on the brink of Italy's 1948 elections the Hungarian communist leader Mátyás Rákosi told the Italian comrades he was going to lend them a hand by executing some Catholic clerics on charges of financial speculation. 'Tell him', Togliatti ordered, 'that nothing [like that] should be done!'[37] Togliatti also refused to oppose Italy's attendance at the Paris meeting in July 1947 to discuss the USA's proposals for the Marshall Plan. He and the communist party leadership had to give the impression of having 'an independent position'.[38]

Togliatti was schizophrenic about the USSR. He regarded it as the great model of contemporary communism and ceaselessly spoke up for it. This came out in ways great and small. He asked Soviet leaders to invite the Italian football team to Moscow and give them a thrashing on the field of play: 'Our gladiators strut around like peacocks too much and a lesson would be very useful for them!'[39] His argument – hardly that of an astute soccer fan – was that this would increase the USSR's popularity in Italy. The Italian Communist Party under his leadership showed unfading loyalty to Moscow even though he had lost friends and associates, including fellow Italians, in the Great Terror. He was directly acquainted with the grotesque conditions in the Soviet Union. When he flew out of Moscow with his partner Nilde Jotti, he gasped to her: 'Free at last!'[40] And he never returned until after Stalin's death.[41] Ana Pauker, a Romanian communist leader who spent the war years in the Soviet capital, put the matter in a neat aphorism: 'To Moscow whenever you please, from Moscow whenever they let go of you.'[42]

Meanwhile the American authorities appreciated – as they had done after the First World War – that communist appeal grew in direct proportion to shortages in food, shelter, employment and chances of individual and collective betterment. As economic recovery got under way, Soviet rhetoric about Europe's 'economic enslavement' cut little ice and Togliatti and Thorez were regarded by most people as Moscow's caged parrots.[43] Also important was the will of European governments and elites to press forward in the same direction. In western Europe, in contrast with countries to the east, the communist parties faced fierce competition from socialists. Communism had no monopoly in promoting the need for mass education, popular welfare and a commitment to 'progress' and an end to social privilege. It is true that material conditions were grim for several years after the war. Even in the United Kingdom, a victorious power, the government had to pursue policies of austerity. But there was also room for fun. Whereas the authorities in eastern Europe were trampling on the arts and restricting freedom, to the west there was a cultural extravaganza. Entertainment catered for high and low tastes. Who in Poland wanted to read contemporary Soviet novels? Who in the United Kingdom or Italy did not flock to the American musicals, crooners and, by the mid-1950s, rock-'n'-rollers?

People in the West valued their privacy after the wartime rigours. They were free to choose their religion, politics, hobbies and recreation and could close their door on the state. Word got about that things were not the same in eastern Europe. Communist parties continued to fight in elections and to recruit new and eager party members. They conserved the hope of gaining national power even if the immediate prospects were far from being wonderful. In France and Italy the communists maintained a serious challenge to the government. They had large followings. They were effective spokesmen for the radical sections of the labour movement. They were vocal critics of the USA, NATO and European imperialism. But they were running into the wind. Too many people knew what was happening to eastern Europe and China as they underwent communisation. Western Europe was too successful in its economic, social and political regeneration. Its communist parties did not lose their great opportunities after 1945. The reality was that their opportunities were never great.

23. WARRING PROPAGANDA

The West's political leaders, having decided that the USSR was their most menacing enemy, strove to convince their publics to abandon any lingering nostalgia about Uncle Joe and the battles of Stalingrad and Kursk. Churchill's rhetoric was at its most effective in a speech to students at Fulton, Missouri in March 1946:

> From Stettin in the Baltic to Trieste in the Adriatic, an iron curtain has descended across the Continent. Behind that line lie all the capitals of the ancient states of Central and Eastern Europe. Warsaw, Berlin, Prague, Vienna, Budapest, Belgrade, Bucharest and Sofia, all these famous cities and the populations around them lie in what I must call the Soviet sphere, and all are subject in one form or another, not only to Soviet influence but to a very high and, in many cases, increasing measure of control from Moscow.[1]

Harry Truman matched Churchill in resolve, declaring: 'We shall not realize our objectives, however, unless we are willing to help free peoples to maintain their free institutions and their national integrity against aggressive movements that seek to impose upon them totalitarian regimes.' Popular opinion was quickly transformed. The indispensable and respected military partner of 1941–5 became the object of conventional hostility.

Not all groups in western Europe and North America welcomed the strategy of containment. The most vociferous critics were the spokespersons for émigré communities in the USA from the Baltic countries and Ukraine who called on the West to deal more toughly with Stalin. Some argued that American armed forces ought to advance into the European east. Dominant opinion, however, accepted that President Truman had no realistic alternative. The certainty that the USSR would use its nuclear bombs in a world war was terrifying to most people who thought calmly about the situation.

Western politicians were a choir singing in the same anti-communist key. All wanted to reorientate popular opinion and consign the pro-Stalinist wartime propaganda to oblivion. In West Germany this was effected by careful expositions as well as by cruder means such as, in 1956, the outlawing of the German Communist Party for calling for the overthrow of the government. Countries in Europe and North America except for the Spanish and Portuguese fascist dictatorships thought that any such ban would cause more problems than it would solve. The British government needed to do little more than eavesdrop on the communist leadership chatting at its 16 King Street headquarters in London WC2 and other venues. This did not go unsuspected by the communists. John Gollan, Assistant General Secretary after the Second World War, expostulated: 'They interfere with me. That bloody telephone there – the fact that you phoned me, they know – what I said to you, they know – they open our letters – they go to our meetings . . . the spies are everywhere.'[2] The softly-softly approach of the authorities worked effectively. After communists Willie Gallacher and Phil Pirati lost their seats in the 1950 elections, the party never won a parliamentary constituency again. Surveillance of British communists, however, was maintained. Even George Orwell, hardly a great friend of official authority, secretly supplied the intelligence services with a list of persons he deemed communists or fellow travellers. His comments were not free of a racist slant. Orwell described his suspects as 'Jewess', 'Half-Caste', 'English Jew' and 'Polish Jew'.[3]

Not only in Britain but also in the USA the communists were as distant as ever from power and influence. But not every anti-communist was willing to do things on the quiet. Joe McCarthy, the rough-tongued Senator for Wisconsin, made his case inside and outside the Senate and avowed that communism was sucking the lifeblood of American public life. He dug up evidence – and sometimes invented it – that Moscow had secret collaborators everywhere. He appeared live on television brandishing his lists of communists and their supporters. Those whom he identified as subversives were required to 'name names' of communist friends or face professional ruin. McCarthy concentrated his fire on film-making and other sectors of the media. Often his accusations were ill founded but he succeeded in creating an atmosphere of suspicion which pervaded American public life. The playwright Arthur Miller refused to submit to the Senator for Wisconsin. Instead he drafted The Crucible, a play about the witch-hunt craze in seventeenth-century New England, which was an obvious allegory of hysteria and persecution. McCarthy's own activities came under scrutiny after he was accused of seeking illegal favours for his protégés. The Senate held a debate on him and by a large majority ruled that he had abused his power. McCarthy died in ignominy in 1957.

Yet his impact was enormous and permanent. No longer did the left-wing American press give gentle treatment to Marxism as had been the case before the Second World War. Words like communism and socialism – and eventually even liberalism – became widely pejorative. Mainstream political discourse in the USA underwent a drastic constriction. Sympathy for communism, where it survived outside the Communist Party of the USA, was usually confined to individual writers or students' political groups; it impinged little on popular opinion.

Academic institutes were funded in the most powerful countries of the West to establish the case against the USSR, and the study of communist politics, economics, sociology and history underwent professionalisation. The largest of them were in the USA.[4] Scholars whose published works were kind to Stalin found it difficult to get jobs. A spectacular case in the United Kingdom was the removal of Andrew Rothstein, lecturer in Russian history at London University's School of Slavonic and East European Studies. Rothstein, a founding member of the Communist Party of Great Britain who had begun work in the Soviet embassy's information department and spent years in the Comintern apparatus in Moscow, had never disguised his political allegiance. Every year he held a meeting of students to mark the anniversary of the October Revolution and deliver an emotional address.[5] The administration refused to renew his contract on the (incontrovertible) ground that he had published nothing of scholarly merit;[6] but the basic reason was his party affiliation and militancy. Further appointments were made with an eye to political reliability. The process did not need to be quite as crude in other countries of Europe and North America where communists were quietly barred from the seats of scholarship.

The Churches too joined the struggle against communism and its militant atheism. Christian-democratic parties were influential in Italy, Austria and Bavaria, and they relayed the anathema of the Pope in Rome on the behaviour and intentions of communists everywhere. Communist persecution of the Catholic Church in Poland and Hungary after the war was widely reported. Protestant denominations were equally active. One of their heroines was the English parlourmaid Gladys Aylward who with just two pounds and ninepence in her purse had gone off to China in 1930 to serve as a missionary near the Yellow river. She survived the Japanese occupation despite many misadventures and rescued a hundred

Chinese children from the invaders of her adopted country. Her problems continued after Mao Zedong came to power. Eventually she left the mainland and set up an orphanage on Taiwan. Her bravery was exactly what the editors of *Reader's Digest* were seeking.[7] Each issue of the monthly worldwide magazine highlighted instances of oppression in the communist lands. The American administration, waking up to the potential of Christianity in undermining the Marxist-Leninist 'gospel', funded the evangelical missions led by Billy Graham to the United Kingdom.[8]

Many of Stalin's victims, moreover, had been washed up like flotsam in the West in 1945. Not all of them drew attention to themselves, especially those who had committed war crimes. But a lot of them had a clean record and desired to alert their adopted countries to the horrors of rule by communists. Memoirs such as Slavomir Rawicz's *The Long Walk* became bestsellers. Rawicz was a Pole who claimed to have escaped from a Soviet labour camp in the Second World War. By his own account he trudged his way with astonishing endurance thousands of miles from Siberia across the Gobi desert and Tibet, where he splashed lemon juice on to the pupils of his eyes to make him look like a Tibetan, before stumbling down the slopes of the Himalayas into British India and personal freedom.

Confidence in Rawicz was not universal; doubts were quickly raised that anyone could endure so gruelling a journey – and eventually he was plausibly alleged to have made up his personal story.[9] But no one could reasonably reject the growing literature on the practice of communism. Accurate descriptions of Stalin's campaigns of terror appeared. No longer did they come mainly from Trotski and his supporters, who had a sectarian axe to grind and anyway were themselves communists. Many writers of Russian and east European origin piled into the debates. Grateful to have fetched up in North America or western Europe, they were frantic to avoid repatriation to communist states. Those who were Jews highlighted the iniquities of communism long before they came forward, in the 1960s, to elucidate the horrors of the Holocaust. The point they agreed on was that Marxism-Leninism in all its historical forms was characterised by dictatorship, terror, ideological intolerance and revolutionary expansionism. Most saw communism as being based on the single model already developed in the USSR. In eastern Europe and China, they asserted, the same oppressive trends were observable. Given by eyewitnesses of communisation, these accounts helped to mould popular opinion in the West.

The capture of American GIs in the Korean War heightened the alarm. Stories coming out of Korea suggested that the Chinese and Korean communists had developed techniques of indoctrination which nobody could resist. US soldiers and airmen had allegedly been turned into fervent communists. This process became known as brainwashing. Panic gripped the popular press. Perhaps such POWs, when liberated, might return home as clandestine subversives.

It was years before brainwashing was shown to be a fantasy.[10] When captives, brutalised by torture and malnutrition, professed adherence to Marxism-Leninism they were usually calculating that a pretence of ideological conversion would stop their torment. At the time, however, there was widespread belief in the effectiveness of communist indoctrination and organisation. Comic magazines led the way. Characters like Superman, Captain Marvel, Batman and Captain America did not limit their energies to combating fictitious aliens from outer space but also protected the West against the malign forces of communism. Young readers learned much about the cap badges of Red Army colonels and about the appearance and capacity of MiG jet fighters. American comics were immensely popular, in English or in translation, throughout western Europe. In the United Kingdom Captain W. E. Johns, the English writer of boys' thrillers, became a bestseller with his stories about fighter pilot Biggles and his trusty companions Algy and Ginger. Among the Biggles books was one about the hero's dramatic rescue of his ex-Nazi antagonist von Stalheim, who had unwisely opted for life in East Germany and been locked up by the Soviet political police in the Soviet Far East.[11] The adult detective fiction of Agatha Christie and her rivals also evinced an abhorrence of communism.

More refined assaults on communism were mounted in the same years. Albert Camus in *L'Homme revolté* ('Man in Revolt') looked at doctrines and practices of rebellion against authority and castigated the Soviet regime. Still more influential were George Orwell's works *Animal Farm* and *1984*. Orwell never claimed that these two novels were fired exclusively by disgust with the USSR; indeed they contain imprecations against the totalitarianism of both right and left. But *Animal Farm* is a story of pigs who lead a revolution of farm livestock against the exploitative Farmer Jones under the slogan 'Four legs good, two legs bad'. By the end the pig leaders have learned to walk on two legs and have reduced the other livestock – horses, cattle and hens – to degrading submission. The tale was unmistakably based on the author's analysis of Soviet history. Likewise Big Brother, leader of the revolutionary regime in 1984, had a distant enemy in Goldstein who was obviously based on the real Trotski; and the manipulative methods and contents of Big Brother's propaganda were reminiscent of what was already well known about Stalin. The works of Camus and Orwell became instant twentieth-century classics.

Ex-communists too joined the intellectual and political contingent denouncing communism. These renegades were typically more pugnacious than those who had always hated communists. The most famous was Eugenio Reale. As Togliatti's friend and political confidant, Reale had represented the Italian Communist Party at the first Cominform conference. His revelations about the Soviet domination of international communist relations invalidated Togliatti's claim to political independence from Moscow.[12] The British Labour politician Richard Crossman gathered statements by former communist intellectuals in *The God that Failed*.[13] This book included Arthur Koestler's vivid memoir of life as a German communist in the early 1930s. Koestler told about the rigorous techniques of securing internal party discipline. His portrait of oppositionists being humiliated into recanting perfectly reasonable opinions left a deep imprint on the minds of his readers. His novel *Darkness at Noon*, which was a fictionalised evocation of the fate of Nikolai Bukharin, was another influential account. It was Koestler's contention that Bukharin could not imagine living outside the communist milieu and that he was willing to pour filth on his own head and go to his death in the interests of the official cause.[14]

Most commentators contended that the Soviet order was an extreme form of a phenomenon not confined to state systems of the political left. This was the theory of totalitarianism. Quite apart from its analytical plausibility, it was a handy polemical concept for anti-communists. Above all, it bracketed the USSR and the Third Reich as regimes of similar structures and attitudes. Thus the present enemy of the West was conceptually associated with the West's recent Nazi foe. The global effect was electric. From being an admired partner in the Grand Alliance, the Soviet Union became the pariah power.

Several writers objected to this definition of the USSR and not all of them were communist party members. In the USA such individuals restricted themselves to quiet study and specialist monographs. (Several were volumes of pioneering analysis.)[15] In France, Italy and Germany the 'totalitarian model' prevailed. It was in the United Kingdom that debate was polarised to the greatest extent. Prominent scholars such as Leonard Schapiro and Hugh Seton-Watson described the USSR and other

communist states as totalitarian. Their standpoint was subjected to continual attack. Thus the former deputy editor of *The Times* newspaper
E. H. Carr and the freelance Trotskyist scholar Isaac Deutscher provided
a positive analysis of conditions in the USSR – and their works were also
published in substantial print runs in North America. Carr and Deutscher
believed the USSR to be capable of internal development. According to
Carr, the USSR had already provided a universal model of social and
economic development despite much nastiness. He did not explain exactly
how the situation was going to change for the better. Deutscher as a
Marxist felt no such confusion. Eventually, he predicted, the Soviet working class would stand up for itself against its masters and something like
the original Leninist vision would be realised in the country.[16]

Official communism in the USSR and China did not lack supporters
in the West in the arts, scholarship and even organised religion. Hewlett
Johnson, Dean of Canterbury, went on eulogising the achievements
of Joseph Stalin and the Soviet order. Communism around the world
earned paeans in his *What We Saw in Rumania* (1948) and *The Upsurge
of China* (which was so uncritical that the Chinese were delighted to
publish it).[17] Nothing had changed in the mind of the gaitered cleric
since his *Socialist Sixth of the World* in 1939. The British deflated his
influence by treating him as a figure of fun – and teachers and mothers
kept the boys of the King's College, Canterbury away from him.[18]

Friends of communism in literary activity included Chilean poet
Pablo Neruda, who wrote an ode to Stalin. In painting there was Pablo
Picasso, a refugee from Spain since the end of the civil war. Joining the
French Communist Party in 1944, Picasso dashed off a sketch of Stalin.
The image was not his best: Stalin appeared as a gawky young man and
– to the eyes of everyone but the artist – a trifle comic. People had been
shot for less than this in Moscow. The French party leadership in Paris
rebuked the artist for abandoning a 'realistic' style, as if Picasso usually
painted according to such a principle. Mexican painter Frida Kahlo's
last work in oils was also of Stalin; it was an unprepossessing picture
even though – or perhaps because – she used a more representational
technique than Picasso. Another supporter of world communism was
Paul Robeson. Speaking out against racial segregation in the USA,
Robeson was fêted in the USSR as a fighter for human progress. He
never joined the Communist Party of the USA. (Not that this saved him
from investigation by Joe McCarthy.) Then there was the English novelist
Graham Greene who never joined any communist party and remained a
practising Catholic. Nevertheless Greene felt a strong pull towards the

claim of Marxist-Leninists to know how to make the world better for oppressed people. He spoke up for the British defector Kim Philby, who in 1963 was exposed as a KGB agent.

American novelist John Steinbeck published his *Russian Journal* in 1949 about his Intourist trip to the USSR. Although he noted oddities in Soviet bureaucratic behaviour, he generally absolved the authorities of blame: 'Far from being watched and shadowed and followed, we could hardly get anyone to admit that we were there at all.'[19] (This was a tribute to the efficiency of the surveillance conducted on him.) Journalist Edgar Snow went on proselytising for Mao Zedong and the Chinese communists as he had done before the war. Several political and personal details in *Red Star over China* were uncongenial to the revolutionary regime in Beijing. Snow agreed to revise his work while pretending to have maintained his authorial independence.[20] Unlike Stalin, Mao was as yet in no position to organise foreign propaganda on his own behalf. But until the outbreak of the Korean War he largely escaped criticism. Snow's account led to Mao's being fêted as a hero on the Western political left.

Stalin sat in on the editorial meetings for the second edition of his official biography.[21] All human progress in recent years was attributed to him. 'Without the special care of Stalin,' it was stated in a Bulgarian newspaper, 'the present advanced techniques in meat-combines, preserve and sugar plants, fish and everything else done in the field of food industry would not exist.'[22] Stalin statues were erected, Stalin posters displayed in all communist states. Streets, factories and even whole towns were named after him. His authority was endlessly invoked. His works appeared in hundreds of millions of copies and were translated into the world's main languages. Purportedly he embodied a system of power that had proved its freedom-loving, democratic credentials in wartime and offered the only avenue towards global peace and a universal end to oppression and exploitation. The USA and its allies were portrayed as building a 'camp of international reaction'. Allegedly NATO was the successor organisation to the Third Reich and Western leaders were routinely depicted wearing swastika armbands. Konstantin Simonov wrote a play, *The Russian Question*, about an American journalist who writes a book about the peaceful intentions of the USSR and loses his job, wife, house and eventually his life in a mysterious accident.[23] Simonov's message was that people in the West could never get access to the truth about communism; the play was a favourite with Soviet audiences in the post-war years.

The Kremlin's leaders could say what they liked in eastern Europe. Open dismissal of their propaganda would have been suicidal; and although most people had their doubts about Stalin, some popularity undoubtedly accrued to him. It was not unusual for individual Czechs, Poles or Hungarians to boast that they knew somebody who knew someone else who had met him. He had the magical appeal of a leader wrapped in mystery and girded with power.

Yet the ambition of the Kremlin was wider than the countries conquered in 1944–5. Its occupants wanted to win the war of propaganda throughout the world. One of their devices was to hold anti-war meetings in Europe.[24] In August 1948 a World Congress for Peace was held in Wrocław in Poland. Intellectuals from western Europe were invited. Not every participant buckled under the pressure to praise the Kremlin. French philosopher Julien Benda accosted Soviet writer Ilya Ehrenburg: 'One of your comrades in his speech referred to Sartre and O'Neill as jackals. Is that fair or, to put it at its lowest, wise? And why do we have to clap every time Stalin's name is mentioned?'[25] Another independent spirit was the British historian A. J. P. Taylor. Speaking without notes as was his wont, he evaded being censored by the organisers and his contribution was broadcast live to the streets of the Polish city. Taylor provocatively but accurately pointed out that 'we and the French were the only peoples which went to war against Nazi Germany without waiting to be attacked'. He further infuriated the Soviet delegation by calling for 'freedom [for all peoples] from arbitrary arrest, freedom from a secret police, freedom to speak their opinion of their own government as well as of others'.[26]

In America the communist party had fallen into obscurity until Senator McCarthy had gone on the hunt for communists and their fellow travellers; and when he had finished with them the party's public influence had diminished to vanishing point. In western Europe it was a different story. Communist parties were large and vocal in France and Italy; they also operated freely in the other countries of the region except fascist Spain and Portugal. When the media turned against communism in the late 1940s, the USSR and the People's Republic of China could still count on a measure of active support.[27]

Even the wily Stalin, though, had missed some tricks. He paid little mind to the communist parties outside Europe, China and Korea. Nor did he bother himself with politics outside the world's communist parties. He scarcely thought about the colonial countries. This was odd since Stalin had made his name before the First World War as an expert on Marxism and the 'national question'; he gave speeches on the need to reach out to the national liberation movements in the European empires after the October Revolution. But by the 1930s *Realpolitik* had supervened. Not wanting to upset the other great powers, he stayed out of their spheres of influence. But there was more to it than that. Even when the Cold War started, he refrained from calling on the colonies of the United Kingdom, France and Holland to revolt against their rulers. These were the very years when the USA, Europe's creditor, called for an end to European imperialism and had the economic leverage to make things awkward for empires which failed to comply. The United Kingdom in 1947 granted independence to India – and it did this without direct American pressure. National liberation movements were springing up across Asia and Africa. They had been anticipated by Lenin and the Politburo in the early 1920s but had been weak until recently. Yet Stalin, while paying lip-service to their importance to the Marxist cause, gave them next to no practical help.

He was silent about his motives. Probably he thought the USSR had its hands full in dealing with other problems such as the Cold War, eastern Europe and industrial reconstruction. Perhaps he also felt that, unless the national liberation movements could do most of the work by themselves, any assistance would just waste Soviet resources. Even so, it is hard to deny that Stalin was failing to understand a changing world. He wrote about the iniquities of imperialism and predicted its imminent demise, but he did not earmark resources to help bring this about.

Nevertheless the leaders of the national liberation movements in the colonies, even though few of them were communists, saw communism in a sympathetic light. They were attracted to pronouncements rejecting racism and imperialism. They saw the West as transcendentally hypocritical. Blacks in the American south could not use the same schools, restaurants or buses as pale-skinned citizens; and lynching of 'uppity niggers' continued to occur without judicial retaliation. Billie Holiday's song 'Strange Fruit' drew this to public attention. In South Africa, the severities of segregation were even greater. And the Indian National Congress led by Jawaharlal Nehru was already irreconcilably offended by the combination of British oppression and condescension to its members. The USSR appeared to a significant number of Asian and African radicals as sincere and effective in dealing with its own problems of race and nationality; and the fact that hardly any of the colonial radicals had been to Moscow meant that Soviet propaganda was frequently taken at face value.

The anti-imperial leaders overlooked the subjection of eastern Europe to the USSR. Poland and neighbouring countries were the Soviet outer empire just as Ukraine was part of the inner empire. The focus of such leaders, however, was on the USA. The Americans had held hegemony in Central and South America for over a century. Panama was treated as a commercial convenience for US shipping. Guantánamo Bay in Cuba was occupied by a US military base. American armed intervention occurred in Guatemala in 1954 and in Lebanon in 1958. Americans seemed to offer no genuine solution to the colonial question around the world.

What also won admirers in the various national liberation movements was the fact that the USSR had dragged itself out of 'backwardness' through its own efforts and against the expectations of world capitalism. (The contribution of foreign technology and expertise was not yet public knowledge.) It had done this by methods of state central ownership and planning. Russia was no longer predominantly a land of uneducated peasants but a great modern power. Its society had passed from being dishevelled and disorganised to giving the appearance of superb co-ordination. Radical anti-imperialists were willing, consciously or otherwise, to ignore the abundant evidence of terrible exploitation and oppression in the USSR. This was a sign of things to come. The colonial rebels were rarely of poor backgrounds. Many had benefited from a decent education and had acquired their political ideas when studying at the metropolitan universities of empire. They expected to change their countries with popular consent, but they would – if they got the chance – do this from above. They felt they knew what was best for their societies. They suspected that if 'the people' were to be asked its opinion, the likely response would only hold things up by introducing compromises with traditionalism. The rebels had more in common with Marxist-Leninists than anyone recognised.

Yet Stalin remained indifferent to them, and Mao had had no expertise in international relations except in regard to Japan, Korea and – to his chagrin – the USSR itself. Other communist leaders appreciated the importance of the anti-imperialist movements. Stalin's successor Nikita Khrushchëv was one of them. But he could do nothing about his insight until Stalin had left the scene: the worldwide image and appeal of post-war communism until 1953 was in the hands of a man whose prejudices gave the edge to the West in the ideological contest of the Cold War. Stalin as propaganda overseer was his own worst enemy.

24. THE CHINESE REVOLUTION

Chinese communists inscribed a second great date – after 25 October 1917 – in the annals of twentieth-century communism on 1 October 1949. It was then that Mao Zedong climbed the Gate of Heavenly Peace (Tiananmen) in Beijing to announce the victory of the Revolution. The People's Liberation Army – as the Red Army was renamed in 1946 – had occupied the capital in January 1949. The Chinese civil war against the nationalist forces of Chiang Kai-shek's Kuomintang was not over; but the end was near. While he was consolidating his power in Beijing, Mao directed his armed forces southwards. The People's Liberation Army moved with remarkable speed. Crossing the Yangtze river, they took Shanghai in April. Although Tibet had yet to be overrun, Guangzhou in the south was on the point of capitulation and the outcome of the Chinese civil war was no longer in doubt. The communist leadership celebrated in pomp. Communist militants for weeks had risen early from their beds to write slogans and make paper lanterns, flowers and five-star red flags. Supporters were invited to the October ceremony; non-transferable tickets were issued to guarantee security: everything had to happen like clockwork. The neighbouring streets were cordoned off. Police and army were everywhere and Mao's arrival was greeted with deafening applause. His nerves made him keep clearing his throat, but he had the crowd in the palms of his hands when the loudspeakers relayed the words: 'The Chinese people have stood up!'[1]

Mao had not expected the Kuomintang to crumble so abruptly. Stalin, even though he had sent copious shipments of arms to the Chinese communist forces, was still more surprised; indeed he had been advising Mao to come to terms with Chiang Kai-shek until a year before the communists fought their way to Beijing.[2] Mao had drawn the obvious conclusion. If the communists were going to come to power in China, it would be through their own independent strategy. Mao had endured a lot from Stalin in the 1930s and at last had a chance at power. He had feinted diplomatically by agreeing to talks with his enemy Chiang Kai-shek about avoiding the civil war which was inevitable in the eyes of both of them. Stalin went on advising restraint. Why, he queried, did the Chinese communists have to be so ambitious? He thought they should content themselves with ruling just the northern half of a country as vast as China. Stalin did not want to place a further load on his fraught relationship with President Truman. Mao did not argue back, preferring just to ignore the advice from Moscow. He knew that, if the Chinese communists defeated Chiang, Stalin would welcome the creation of a great communist state in Asia regardless of American concerns.

The two sides in the Chinese civil war had squared up to each other again as soon as the Japanese withdrew. Pitched battles occurred, and Mao adjusted his general strategy: instead of avoiding the big cities, he decided that the time had come to conquer them. Mao entrusted Lin Biao with the military command of the Manchurian campaign. Despite several setbacks, success followed and Manchuria was overrun. Lin was ordered to the south to encircle Tianjin and Beijing. Chiang had made operational mistakes and his commanders had made still more. American equipment and money were a lot less than he needed to put up a solid fight. The People's Liberation Army outnumbered the Kuomintang's forces and had its tail up. When Beijing fell in January 1949, Chiang resigned the presidency and fled some months later with three hundred million dollars and the remnants of his army to the island of Taiwan off the Chinese mainland.

By then, far too late, he understood what had gone wrong. Corruption had spread like a plague under the Kuomintang and Chiang had hardly lifted a finger to cure it. Military commanders – warlords – had supplanted the official administration in several regions. Inflation had rocketed. Pillage of private property had been rife. Rape had been common. The Kuomintang's natural supporters felt no incentive to back it any longer. The very effective propaganda of the People's Liberation Army gave it a reputation for being uninterested in financial gain; it also won friends by making a start on agrarian reform in the regions it seized. Repression of 'local tyrants and evil landlords' pleased hundreds of millions of peasants who were short of land and money. The communists had been exacting heavy taxation in territory they occupied, but there was a growing popular belief that graft and social privilege would cease when they attained power. They had a reputation for probity and dedication. They were Marxists; they were also Chinese patriots. They were ruthless and dynamic. Their ruling group included individuals of

British communist leader Harry Pollitt seeks votes for communism before the Second World War. There is an emphasis on his continuous career as a trade-union militant and his willingness to go to prison for his principles.

БЕСПОЩАДНО РАЗГРОМИМ И УНИЧТОЖИМ ВРАГА!

ДОГОВОР о ненападении между СССР и Германией

КУКРЫНИКСЫ-41

Soviet appeal for a war to the finish against the Third Reich: 'Let us mercilessly crush and annihilate the enemy!' Hitler claws through a copy of the non-aggression treaty with the USSR only to be stabbed by a Soviet bayonet.

Australian communists call on people to join the struggle against Germany and Japan in the Second World War. This was after 1939–41 when, on Stalin's orders, they had opposed the war as imperialist on both sides.

French communist leader Maurice Thorez claims to stand for France and the Republic after the Second World War. With his necktie and ready smile he is depicted in a pose designed to appeal to a wide range of voters.

FAITES CONFIANCE
AU PARTI
DE LA FRANCE
et de
LA RÉPUBLIQUE
QUE
DANS NOTRE SECTEUR
MAURICE
THOREZ
Secrétaire Général du Parti Communiste Français
Vice-président du Conseil
Député de la Seine
CONDUIT À LA LUTTE ET À LA VICTOIRE
AU PARTI
COMMUNISTE FRANÇAIS

Глacajyħи за Народни Фронт гласамо:
за снажну Југославију
за братство и јединство Југословенских народа
за народну власт
за федеративну народну републику
за уништење трагова фашизма
за срећну будућност

Tito promises a popular revolution in Yugoslavia at the war's end. He looks rather like Thorez but the atmosphere is less compromising: his military tunic signals a determination to use force to realise the objectives of his party.

Czechoslovak communism presents itself as the party of peace throughout the world.
Simultaneously it calls for support for North Korea's cause against the
United Nations coalition in the Korean War.

East German workers are invoked to get building after the Second World War and to advance with the German Communist Party. The pointing in the brickwork does not seem to be of optimal quality.

Appeal to Bulgarian youth to get shovelling in the national interest. The spade is so shiny that the image of a curly-haired woman accordion player can be seen.

向蘇聯老大哥學習 (學習蘇聯金屬高度切削法)

Above. Chinese citizens gather attentively under the joint gaze of Stalin and Mao. Both Mao and Stalin appear in a jolly mood. A Soviet expert instructs his audience. Those were the days before the Sino-Soviet split.

Right. Chinese youths dance around the Red flag after the communist seizure of power. The diversity of their costumes is meant to celebrate the unity of all peoples in the People's Republic.

中華民族大團結

Mao's image as the object of popular devotion. He looks a lot more sombre than his young followers.

exceptional talent such as Zhou Enlai, Liu Shaoqi, Lin Biao and Deng Xiaoping. Only Mao outmatched them in forcefulness of leadership.

He was as yet little known to most Chinese. Mao was the child of well-off peasants in Hunan province – and he retained the local accent when speaking the national language.[3] Like his countrymen, he grew up resenting China's vulnerability to foreign military and economic power. He loved Chinese classical literature. As a young radical he was impressed by the October Revolution in Russia and was attracted to communism. He studied hard, largely on his own, and became a Marxist militant in Hunan. Spotted as a talented organiser, he was promoted to the Central Committee and operated in Shanghai. From 1925, under the influence of fellow communist Peng Pai, he focused his activity on the peasantry. He believed that communism in China had to concentrate its efforts on the twin problems of the village and the nation; this was to form the core of Mao Zedong Thought. In contrast with other communist leaders, he did not go to party school in the USSR. While broadly wanting to apply the Soviet model in power, he made whatever adaptations he thought necessary for the peculiarities of Chinese circumstances. He had endured adversity for decades and did not intend to surrender his independence to Moscow now that power was at last in his hands.

The communist regime set about transforming Chinese society. It was always going to be a savage process. Mass repression of 'class enemies' had been systematic in the areas occupied by the Red Army in the civil war.[4] Chinese politics had often been brutal in previous decades and had not been softened by the Japanese invasion and occupation. Recurrent famines had also coarsened attitudes. Each city, town and village was a cauldron of rivalries and resentments. The termination of military campaigning was not going to bring an end to political and social conflict.

The communists did not yet intend to calm things down. In March 1949, Mao adjured the Central Committee: 'After the enemies have been wiped out, there will still be the enemies without guns; they are bound to struggle desperately against us. We must never regard these enemies lightly. If we do not now raise and understand the problem in this way, we shall commit very grave mistakes.'[5] He urged peasants and workers to be active allies in eradicating opposition. The Soviet communists had used their security forces to carry out this task in the USSR; and from the late 1920s the Politburo in Moscow issued precise quotas for the number of victims to be arrested, deported or executed in each province.

Chinese communism proceeded differently. The 'masses' were told the general contents of Beijing's policy and then trusted to implement it. Mao felt confident that they would know whom to persecute; he also sensed that, if they participated in repression, they would go on associating themselves with the revolutionary regime – and since official policy also involved a popular redistribution of property, they would have an incentive to continue to favour the communists.

Mao defined his state not as a 'dictatorship of the proletariat' nor as a 'people's democracy' but as a 'people's democratic dictatorship'. This was a term absent from the political lexicon of the USSR: quietly he was shrugging off Soviet mental tutelage. Mao insisted that peasants could be the main revolutionary class. What is more, he insisted that, although he intended to ruin the landlords, he was picking no fight with the capitalist class in general. He claimed he was unifying the people – or most of its elements – behind him even if the methods he used were dictatorial.[6]

The party had never disguised its intention to carry 'class struggle' to a conclusion, and the propertied elites had been a main target of its hostile propaganda alongside the Japanese invaders. Stalin thought the Chinese communists were overestimating their potential. Yet they were in fact in a much more advantageous situation than the Bolsheviks in Russia after October 1917: they did not have to build a Red Army from scratch. Far from coming to power by being voted majorities in workers' councils or peasant communes, they had made their political advance by means of a military victory. The Chinese civil war preceded the accession to government. This meant that the communist order was always structurally a little different from the Soviet model. For decades to come, the army was a key agency in deliberations at the highest levels of state. Its leaders were figures of greater authority than any Soviet military figure since Trotski. There was deep interpenetration of party and army in the People's Republic of China. Party officials dressed as for a military parade. Nor was it unexpected that when the Chinese leadership drew up its budget the armed forces were constantly treated as a sector of prioritised investment.

The party worked tirelessly in the countryside while the People's Liberation Army mopped up the often large pockets of resistance. This was yet another difference from the Soviet historical experience. Dispossessions of land in China had started before the capture of the capital, and in 1950 the policy was systematically applied to the whole country. Instructions were issued from Beijing. Perhaps two or three million people were executed and millions were dispatched to labour camps.[7] Landlords were paraded with heads bowed in front of village inhabitants. They would be forced to confess to the crimes, real or imaginary, before learning their sentence. Terror was applied to the cities from spring 1951 when known or suspected enemies of the regime were given the same treatment. The camps – *laogai* – used forced labour, applied severe discipline (including capital punishment for offences that would not have attracted this sanction in the Soviet Gulag) and conducted regular indoctrination (which was hardly bothered with in the camps of the USSR). Labour was the designated route to personal reform. Really it was a gruesome process of intimidation and exploitation as the inmates mined coal, built roads and dams and farmed the fields on a near-starvation diet.[8]

The authorities dealt out labels to the other members of society. Good, 'red' categories included revolutionary veterans, their families, poor peasants and workers. The 'black' categories included landlords, rich peasants, bad elements, counter-revolutionaries and rightists; and all who were assigned to them were picked out for persecution. Everyone was attached to a work unit at the factory, farm or office. Each unit had a recognised leader who was held responsible for its loyalty and efficiency and who typically had been designated as belonging to one of the red categories. This system facilitated the supervision of the endless political and economic campaigns dreamed up in Beijing. Any dereliction of duty would initiate a hunt for the easily identifiable hostile elements.[9]

China's security from foreign threat had been jeopardised by Mao's decision to aid the communists militarily in the Korean War (although the gamble paid off inasmuch as a communist state was consolidated on the Chinese frontier as a result of the fighting).[10] But the completeness of communist control in China meant that agrarian reform could proceed without the concentrated assistance of the People's Liberation Army. By the end of 1952 only 10 per cent of rural households had been unaffected.[11] This was an astonishing achievement in the face of postwar exhaustion and continuing administrative weaknesses. The communists, handing out quotas for land to be redistributed, had done what they had promised by dispossessing the landlords.[12] The peasants were the beneficiaries. Landlords were not the only group to endure an assault. The Three Antis campaign was started up in the towns in late 1951. It was aimed against corrupt cadres; the party did this for its own sake and in order to boost its popularity: communism had to be cleansed of the taint of association with scoundrels. The Five Antis campaign quickly followed; this was aimed at known and suspected counter-revolutionaries. People strove to show their loyalty to the authorities – and executions and suicide occurred in the hundreds of thousands.[13] Two hundred thousand letters of denunciation were received in Shanghai alone.[14] Economic and political sources of organised hostility to the communist authorities were being eradicated. Soviet experts helped with the establishment of planning mechanisms to ease state regulation. Communisation was proceeding apace.

A universal literacy programme was begun. Urban sewerage and sanitation were prioritised for attention. The government energetically counteracted plagues of locusts and insects. There was a dynamism about the national effort that had not previously been seen in the twentieth century.

By 1953 the state owned up to four-fifths of heavy industry and two-fifths of light industry and handled about a half of business commerce.[15] But the greater impetus was felt by agriculture. No sooner had he handed over the land to the peasantry than Mao bristled with desire to communise agriculture. Collectivisation was announced as a priority in September 1951.[16] The communes, as the collective farms were called in China, allowed the peasants to retain small family plots.[17] Yet Mao declined simply to ape Soviet economic and social methods; he understood that Stalin's punitive campaign against the kulaks in the USSR had been a counter-productive overreaction to whatever threat they posed. In China the rich peasants were neither shot nor deported but allowed to stay in the new communes under surveillance; their skills and labour were valued. There was also a wish to avoid forcing the communes to act as the prime resource to be squeezed for the launching of industrialisation. Mao was not going to imitate Stalin by exacting a 'tribute' from the peasants to pay for foreign industrial technology. This caution helps to explain why Chinese collectivisation met much less resistance than its Soviet predecessor. It also goes some way to accounting for the reverence shown towards Mao by the hundreds of millions of rural inhabitants. At least in the early years of communist power, the authorities moved cautiously. The written decree was gaining priority over the rifle.

Mao had the instincts of a political thug and was hardly averse to using violence in pursuit of political ends – by 1955 the number of detainees of one kind and another had risen to about 9.6 million.[18] But his whole communist career had centred on the need to keep the maximum number of peasants on his side, and he did not abandon this when setting up the commune system. He was using gentleness until such time as he chose to bring thuggery to bear on a situation.

Yet collectivisation was marred by serious economic disruption. This gave rise to lively discussion in the leadership as reports flowed into Beijing about the damage done to agricultural production. Mao adamantly rejected the arguments of those who wanted a deceleration – or even a partial reversal – of the changes he had sponsored. This advice came from his deputy and presumed political heir Liu Shaoqi as well as from Zhou Enlai and Deng Xiaoping. Mao was unmoved. He had set his sights on territorial reunification, national security and economic modernisation; he regarded these targets as inextricably connected. In summer 1955 he identified himself with the side of the party which advocated greater audacity, and poured scorn on 'some of our comrades who are tottering about like a woman with bound feet' – he never failed to find a striking phrase in internal party disputes.[19] Yet he did not ditch those prominent comrades. The Politburo Standing Committee consisted of Mao Zedong, Liu Shaoqi, Peng Dehuai and Deng Xiaoping. Obviously Mao had neither ruled out a further swing to the right nor lost his confidence that he could get his subordinates to do as he bade them.[20]

Party membership grew from 2.8 million in 1949 to 5.8 million by the end of the following year.[21] By 1956 the total was to reach 10.7 million members.[22] The rapid increase was characteristic of communist seizures of power. Once everyone knew that the communists had a firm grip, recruitment to the party's ranks became an easy task. Volunteers appeared in abundance. But they remained a drop in the ocean of the general population, especially in the countryside.[23] Party members were usually ignorant of Marxism-Leninism and Mao Zedong Thought. They were inexperienced in the functions of urban political and economic management. The veteran leaders were feeling their way around the corridors of power. Huge responsibilities had accrued to them. If they were indeed convinced Marxists, they had yet to show how they would adapt their doctrines to the reality they found in a country of extraordinary cultural, ethnic and religious diversity. Many communists who had served in the armed forces felt they had nothing to learn. The mental impact of years of fighting was still with them. They had trounced their enemies. Their communism was a highly militarised variant and they were in a mood to drive the nails of their policies into Chinese society without regard to civilian niceties.

The official story of the regime's achievements was conveyed in a song taught to peasants:

Communism is heaven.
The commune is the ladder.
If we build that ladder,
We can climb the heights.[24]

Communists put themselves forward as the honest, tireless leaders who would ensure that such ladders covered the entire People's Republic of China.

Yet the communists were not untainted by corruption. As an angry popular jingle put it:

First-rank folk
Have things sent to the gate.
Second-rank folk
Rely on others.
Third-rank folk
Can only fret.[25]

Cronyism flourished. Political patrons rewarded their clients with promotion and obtained personal allegiance in return. People got what they wanted by exchanges of favours[26] – *guanxi* was the Chinese equivalent of what was known as *blat* in the USSR. Beijing could never be satisfied with their willingness to comply with its orders. Official policies were frequently modified when they reached provincial China by local leaders who disagreed with them.[27] At the bottom of the social pile were the peasants and workers; and although they could not safely criticise the regime they could withdraw their co-operation. Deliberate slowdowns in industrial production were widespread. The Chinese communists, like the party in the USSR, did not have the sanction of sacking recalcitrants.[28]

The economy went through a dire recession. Drought had afflicted the countryside in autumn 1956. Climatic conditions were dreadful in the following spring and the summer harvest was disastrous. Textile production and food-processing were severely affected. The communes tried to get their delivery quotas lowered. Morale among the peasants fell. Artisans who had been forced into communal membership abandoned their skills. Such popularity as the communists had enjoyed in late 1949 was fading. The arguments of those in the leadership who demanded a moderation of political and economic radicalism gained momentum.[29]

Mao understood the dangers and in April 1957 swung the leadership into a change of course through a 'rectification campaign'. This was better known by the slogan 'Let a Hundred Flowers Bloom! Let a Hundred Schools of Thought Contend.'[30] Mao stated: 'Our society cannot back down ... criticism of the bureaucracy is pushing the government towards the better.' He invited people to express their criticisms of state policy and make their practical proposals. Room was to be made for open debate – through the blooming of a multitude of flowers – instead of an imposed single communist line. Political, social and cultural matters came on to the agenda in a rush after Mao assured people that they would suffer no unpleasant repercussions. Often it was the trivial stuff of daily life which was exposed: too few toilets at a primary school or incompetent procedures in the local administration. But large matters also came to light. Intellectuals demanded a lifting of the ban on certain classical literary works. Former members of democratic parties objected to being banned from public activity. Many had been fobbed off with words like 'You're only a landlord's son, your ideology isn't pure, your past is complicated, you've never worked actively for us.' There was much grumbling that 'to become a boss it's necessary to join the [communist] party'.[31]

Expressions of discontent grew as fast as bamboo shoots. China in the 1920s had enjoyed a pluralism of public thought. Traditions of civil society had been growing. The Chinese elites had studied contemporary trends in the rest of the world. Foreign companies had continued to trade in the coastal cities. Intellectuals, businessmen and students retained a memory of these past times after the establishment of the Chinese communist regime.

At Beijing University they put up posters on a 'democracy wall' criticising the Chinese Communist Party for its harsh treatment of enemies, severe censorship, economic incompetence, financial corruption and slavish adherence to the Soviet model. One poster stated: 'Party members enjoy many privileges which make them a race apart.'[32] Another complained: 'The dictatorship of the proletariat is the proletariat of the few.' Yet another castigated the Mao cult. This kind of remark was not heard inside the party but internal party communist strains during the Hundred Flowers campaign broke the string of organisational unity. Some veterans – soon to be labelled as 'rightists' – sympathised with the general critique of the regime.[33] Among them was Politburo member Liu Shaoqi. It would fit a conspiratorial viewpoint that Mao had instigated the open discussions in order to get the 'poisonous weeds' to reveal themselves. This probably ascribes too much cold calculation

to one of revolutionary politics' compulsive gamblers. What is undeniable is that Mao's reaction would become severe and repressive.
Weeds had drawn sustenance from the cataclysms of political repression, administrative turmoil, social unfairness, economic mismanagement
and famine.

Mao aimed to wrench them out of the ground with the assistance of
public security minister Luo Ruiqing. People who had spoken out against
the party or its policies were targeted. Even the party was purged. About
a million of its members – some 8 or 9 per cent of the total – were
expelled for being right-wingers.[34] Many were dispatched to remote rural
areas for an indeterminate period of manual labour. The idea was that
they would learn to abandon dissent and to assimilate themselves to the
attitudes of ordinary, loyal citizens.[35] The party leadership did not halt
at the rustication of party members. It also sought out people who
belonged to other political parties, to the old administration or to the
economic and cultural elites. Denunciations of individuals were assidu-
ously collected by the security agencies. The party leadership extended
the existing forced-labour camp (laogai) network by setting up centres
for 'education through work' (laojiao); the difference between the two
types of confinement was negligible.[36] The families of the victims quaked
with fear. Wives divorced husbands. Children disowned parents. Inside
the camps there was intense pressure, confirmed by psychological and
physical torture, for convicts to make a confession of guilt; and when
convicts reached the end of their sentence, they were often constrained
to go on working in the camps as 'free labourers'.[37]

Repression was just the first step. Mao would not be deterred from
the tasks he had set himself to build an impregnable communist order
in the People's Republic of China. He aimed to complete the changes he
had started in 1949. His journey was about to be resumed as he strode
the path that was soon to lead to the Great Leap Forward and the
Cultural Revolution.

25. ORGANISING COMMUNISM

The new communist states in eastern Europe and east Asia – from Tirana to Pyongyang and from Tallinn to Shanghai – had much in common. Usually a single party governed. Sometimes other political groups, if they were left-wing and compliant, were incorporated into the communist party or allowed a semi-autonomy. Dictatorship was imposed. The courts and the press were subordinated to political command. The state expropriated large sectors of the economy and central industrial planning was introduced. Religion was persecuted. Associations of civil society were battered into submission or simply annihilated. Marxism-Leninism in its Stalinist variant was disseminated and rival ideologies were persecuted. Administration was centralised. Control of state institutions was reinforced by means of the nomenklatura system and tight interconnections were maintained among party, government, police and army. The communist leadership elaborated grand policy and scrutinised personnel appointments. Each had a dominant single figure enjoying official devotion. The rituals of public life were similar. May Day and the October Revolution anniversary were state festivals and military parades were held in the capitals. Leaders lined up in public in strict conformity to current political authority. Communist states, with the exception of expelled Yugoslavia, professed allegiance to the world communist movement headed by the USSR.

This is not to say that the Soviet model was copied in every detail or that there were no national differences among the new communist states. Specific circumstances and traditions had brought communism to power in Russia. The situation in other countries inevitably was different. What is more, big changes had occurred in Russia after 1917. Foreign communists did not always learn from Soviet mistakes; many of them suffered from historical amnesia and blundered in the same fashion. Sometimes they saw the need for avoiding precisely what had been done in the USSR and yet imposed policies which were still highly oppressive. And although a few leaders in eastern Europe saw that some moderation was required, they were restricted by fear of the Kremlin's reaction. Thus the communist order in the communist states had little elasticity. Once the parties of Marxism-Leninism had their hands on the levers of governance, the choice of structures, practices and policies was strikingly uniform.

One exception lay in the way that the 'national question' was handled. Roosevelt and Churchill had accepted the Soviet case that state boundaries had to be redrawn and that national and ethnic 'transfers' were necessary. The Big Three had moved the frontiers without waiting for peace treaties. The USSR got the consent of the Western Allies to expand its territory at the expense of pre-war Poland. An understanding was reached that Poland should be compensated by acquiring Germany's eastern territories. Behind the scenes a riot of territorial claims broke out. The Yugoslavs started a lot of trouble. Scarcely a country on their borders was safe from their greedy eyes: Albania, Bulgaria, Hungary, Austria and Italy. Even Stalin was taken aback: 'But do the Hungarians agree?'[1] He was also disconcerted by the territorial demands of the Hungarian government on Romania. Hungary had until recently been fighting as an ally of the Third Reich and it seemed inappropriate to reward the Hungarians, even though Romania too had invaded the USSR. In any case the Soviet Union could not take the decisions by itself; it had to have the agreement of the Western Allies. Whatever the Big Three decreed was obeyed. Their sharpest dispute was over Trieste. Italy and Yugoslavia competed to have the city. Eventually it was given to Italy. Inside eastern Europe, meanwhile, the new states huffed and puffed but did not seriously challenge the frontiers determined for them.

Limits anyway existed to the achievability of communist nation-states. Without rounding up the entire population of Europe east of the River Elbe and depositing them in countries according to nationality, there would always remain national and ethnic minorities. Despite the shifting of frontiers and populations, no state in eastern Europe was inhabited exclusively by a single nation. Poland came nearest to being mononational. Hitler's extermination of the Jews and the Roma left few of them alive in the country by 1945. German inhabitants had fled or been expelled. Ukrainians had been scooped into the USSR's expanded Ukrainian Soviet republic. The result was that all but 2 per cent of the population of the Polish People's Republic were 'ethnic' Poles.[2]

But Poland was exceptional. Elsewhere there were problems of managing what were still multinational states. Constitutional mechanisms had been developed in the USSR, including 'autonomous regions', for this situation. Yugoslavia led the way: the intertwined cohabitation of several nations made Tito eager to adopt something like the Soviet model.[3] The Romanians followed in 1952.[4] The Hungarian Autonomous Region was established to prove that the Romanian People's Republic guaranteed rights of national self-expression in schools, the press and culture. Romania's leader Gheorghe Gheorgiu-Dej was worried about his Hungarian minority. The autonomous region therefore did not include the long northern border area with Hungary and embraced only a third of Romania's Hungarians.[5] Gheorgiu-Dej was to be an ardent supporter of the Soviet suppression of the Hungarian Revolt in 1956: he did not want 'his' Hungarians imitating the rebelliousness of those in Budapest. A similar constitutional arrangement could have been introduced for the Hungarians in post-war Czechoslovakia, but Klement Gottwald set his face against this. He had enough on his hands trying to keep the dual federation of Czech and Slovak territories together. He also played on nationalist sensibilities. No inter-war Czech or Slovak politicians had lost followers for hammering a Hungarian minority which had kicked around the Czechs and Slovaks under the Habsburgs.

The other state where autonomous national regions were established was the People's Republic of China. Mao Zedong founded the Inner Mongolian Autonomous Region in 1947 even before taking power in Beijing. The Mongols were to be protected from 'Han chauvinism' in the newly communist China. The Han had dominated the old empire in size and influence, and communists wanted to prove their credentials as bringers of harmony among the various ethnicities. A Uigur National Region followed in 1955. Based in Xinjiang, it abutted the USSR and no doubt the rulers in Beijing thought that this concession to the Uigurs, who had co-nationals living on Soviet territory, would solidify their loyalty. Three further autonomous regions were created. The last was in Tibet. The circumstances of its foundation in 1965 demonstrated that Mao Zedong was more nationalist than he had claimed. Tibet had been independent until the Chinese Red Army's invasion in 1950. The resistance of Tibetans was brutally crushed and the conquerors sought to extirpate religious customs. They took the Panchen Lama into custody while the Dalai Lama escaped on foot across the snows of the Himalayas. Chinese spokesmen declared that Tibet had always been a province of China and that their armed forces had been welcomed as liberators. The military and judicial repression told a different story.

The Chinese and Yugoslav constitutions, unlike that of the USSR, made no provision for secession.[6] In other ways the similarity was unmistakable. Communist leaders believed in the urgent priority of industrialising their countries. Lenin had argued that heavy industry was the key to progress for pre-capitalist economies; Stalin had acted on this principle, wringing resources out of his people and pouring them into steel production for armaments, railways and tractors. Environmental considerations were flagrantly ignored and health and safety precautions were tossed aside. The universal assumption of communists was that the sooner they could 'modernise' their economies, the more quickly they would be able to distribute the goods and services on a fair basis to society.

The zeal to emulate the USSR was shared by all ruling communists. Landowners' property was expropriated and the old estates were broken up. Collectivisation was undertaken in the newly annexed Soviet republics of Estonia, Latvia and Lithuania.[7] From 1948 the process was started in the USSR's outer empire and east European leaders who disagreed were shunted to the side. (Gomułka was the best-known example.) Scarcely had peasant families received parcels of land than it was grabbed and incorporated into estate-sized collective farms. In Hungary they slaughtered their livestock as the Soviet peasantry had done in the 1930s.[8] Wartime exhaustion and fear of the Red Army's firepower and preparedness discouraged resistance. The national leaderships in eastern Europe competed to out-Stalinise each other. Bulgaria under Vulko Chervenkov won by collectivising 56 per cent of its agricultural land by 1953, narrowly beating Czechoslovakia's 54 per cent. The most sluggish was the German Democratic Republic with only 5 per cent; but this was attributable to the complexities of its international and constitutional situation; and as soon as this could be resolved the local communist leadership was keen to enter the race.[9]

The paraphernalia of Soviet-style communism were emplaced into eastern Europe's countryside. Tractors were trundled off the factory production lines for the new collective farms. Machine-tractor stations were established. Farm chairmen were appointed; usually they were local men without managerial or technical training but with a reliable political record. Preference was also given to participants in the anti-German resistance. The most talented communist veterans, however, tended to be given crucial urban postings. The lamentable outcome was predictable. The customary skills of peasants were supplanted by the ignorance of the new bosses. The tax burden on the villages rose as heavy industry was prioritised. Communist officialdom proved expert at denuding the countryside of its resources. Post-war agricultural recovery faltered and collapsed. The official data, despite being massaged by statistical functionaries to look as encouraging as possible, told a pitiful story. The fertile soil of Poland, Czechoslovakia and Hungary in 1951–2 was still registering yields much lower than the average for the years before the Second World War.[10]

The communist economic system had caused an economic disruption which was usually the consequence of defeat in wars. Robbed of its cows, horses and equipment, the peasantry resigned itself to defeat but withheld active co-operation. The dodges of Soviet kolkhozniks were learned through bitter experience in eastern Europe (and would be adopted by Chinese peasants when the drive to push them into agricultural 'communes' picked up speed in 1958). Directors of collective farms, harassed by the state's quotas for food supplies, had to turn a blind eye as the peasantry broke the rules. Household allotments tended to be bigger than was legal. More livestock was privately retained than the agrarian code of any communist state permitted. Administrative control over distant villages was weaker in mountainous Albania than in the highly industrialised and urbanised German Democratic Republic – and in the vast interior of the People's Republic of China there were thousands of settlements which rarely saw an outsider.

Most people in countryside or town in eastern Europe had been anything but prosperous before the Second World War. Communists were determined to abolish the old class system. The former aristocrats, bankers and owners of big estates vanished from eastern Europe. King Michael of Romania was forced to abdicate in 1947; he left to marry a Danish relative in Greece before settling into exile in Switzerland. Other royal dynasties too were forced out. Noble families fled. Such countries, where the Esterhazys, Zamoyskis and Radziwills had lived through centuries of upholstered splendour, were suddenly left without trace of them. This was a region which had produced a dazzling high culture. The novelists Franz Kafka and Jaroslav Hašek and the composer Antonín Dvořák had attracted the admiration of the world; and even though this efflorescence faded somewhat after the First World War, the tradition of independent thought and creativity remained in the arts and sciences. The communists were remodelling the entire social structure at breakneck speed. The owners of factories, banks and mines had been expropriated even before communist parties got rid of their government coalition partners in 1947–8.[11] The upper bourgeoisie had taken refuge abroad, hoping to return as soon as the Reds had been removed.

Policy treated society as being divided between a majority of loyal citizens and a potentially treacherous minority. Tests of allegiance came with the regular national elections. The communist triumph in each contest was a foregone conclusion, but everyone had to vote. The Polish poet Czesław Milosz recorded: 'They had to vote; for when one turned in one's ballot, one's passport was stamped. The absence of this stamp meant that the owner of the passport was an enemy of the people who had revealed his ill will by refusing to vote.'[12] The point was to get the maximum participation in collective expressions of support for communisation. It did not much matter if individuals as yet lacked personal conviction. The regimes would be stabilised and secured so long as people bought Marxist works, attended communist clubs and watched and applauded the May Day parade.[13]

With bureaucratic precision the Hungarian Party Secretariat listed the class-hostile elements they had expelled from Budapest in summer 1951:

      6 former dukes,
     52 former counts,
     41 former barons and their families,
     10 former Horthy regime ministers,
     12 former deputy ministers,
     85 former generals,
    324 former officer corps members,
     67 former police and gendarme officers,
     30 former factory owners,
     93 former large merchants,
     46 former bankers,
     53 former factory directors,
    195 former large landowners.[14]

The Secretariat noted with satisfaction that the expelled families were shunned by the local population in their new places of residence. With few exceptions the royal and aristocratic families of the region had not been characterised by opposition to right-wing political dictatorship; and the leading industrial, commercial and financial groups had typically made whatever profits were available from such regimes. Anyway, the emptying of large town-houses freed thousands of decent rooms for allocation to needy working-class families.

People were irked, however, by the campaign against urban small producers and traders. Private shops were closed. Cobblers, newsagents, bakers, grocers and pharmacists were put out of business; the best they could do was to seek state employment in their previous occupations. The landscape of the towns was radically changed. Gloomily impressive apartment blocks were thrown up. Large department stores were taken over or new ones constructed; the goods for sale were standardised: the old diversity was eliminated.

What happened in the USSR was repeated with a few modifications in every communist country. The wartime ravages in eastern Europe, China and North Korea left most people poorly clothed by pre-war standards. Communist leaders privately enjoyed better conditions while drawing up plans for the production of cheap but dour consumer goods for the 'masses'. Newspapers and magazines no longer carried pictures of the latest high fashion. Western fads were not reported. Frumpy styles for women became the norm and sexual allure was discouraged. Men's tailoring was no more imaginative. But east Europeans at least could save up to buy coloured frocks or two-piece suits. If they joined the nomenklatura, they could count on their share in the graduated scheme of perks and privileges – and Moscow encouraged the subordinate communist leaderships to ensure that loyal ordinary workers should have their turn in access to sanatoria and holiday resorts. The situation was still duller in the Far East. Mao Zedong's baggy military tunic was the standard accoutrement for the Chinese millions. Women as well as men wore it. China began to look like a gigantic ant-heap whenever newsreels of Beijing were shown abroad.

Yet communism also brought improvements to the new China. In a break with pre-revolutionary culture, nearly all urban inhabitants acquired a bicycle. Once it had been mainly the rich who got about town otherwise than on foot; they had hired taxis and rickshaws for comfort. Bikes, having been made a priority of industrial production, became a vehicle of democratisation. They were used in a spirit of strict conformity; visitors to Beijing were astounded how people rode through the streets at exactly the same speed as if obeying a central command.[15] The public cause took precedence over private privilege – at least in state policy. Parks were constructed for everyone's benefit. State healthcare and education were opened to all without charge. Shelter and food was made inexpensive (although this was not much consolation in the famine of the late 1950s). Life expectancy began to rise.[16] Most visible was the attack on outmoded and injurious custom. Women became eligible for jobs previously reserved for men. The damaging practice of binding the feet of young girls was at last prohibited.

Official policy in the new communist states in eastern Europe and

Asia was that ordinary people should be able to buy the essentials in life cheaply and easily. Prices were indeed low but availability was dire. Agriculture had still not climbed back to the pre-war level by the early 1950s. Factories, especially in heavy industry, were given huge resources and textile production rose impressively: the problem was that 70 per cent of Hungarian output was immediately grabbed by the Soviet occupation authorities as war reparations.[17] Grumbling became a way of life. The relationship between the state and its people, however, was complex in the several countries undergoing communisation. The security agencies needed co-operation with their mission to control. Many citizens were not averse to informing on their neighbours or foremen. Anonymous denunciation was encouraged by the authorities. In the German Democratic Republic the tradition of obeying governmental instructions to the letter did not die out with Hitler's removal. Enthusiastic exposures of local malfeasance and delinquency were a regular feature of the new society. Germans proved impressively compliant in helping the communist state to consolidate itself.[18]

The level of co-operation varied from country to country, and probably the Germans and Chinese showed extraordinary helpfulness to the authorities – even so, this was only by international communist standards. The East German authorities, for example, were soon reporting a drastic decline in labour productivity.[19] (The Chinese communists do not seem to have bothered about such comparisons.) People's motives were anyway conditioned by individuals having an eye for the main chance in conditions of scarcity. Informing on disliked rivals or bosses was a way of improving one's own conditions at their expense. Internal factory arrangements allowed the labour force a degree of influence over procedures – the communist authorities in eastern Europe hoped against hope to keep the workers on their side.[20]

Communist regimes bombarded their people with promises of a glorious future life. Utopia was heralded. Problems were blamed on capitalist iniquity in the past. Official spokesmen called on every well-meaning citizen to work hard and contribute to the general betterment.[21] Associations of civil society were closed down or put under severe control – and organised religion was treated with grave suspicion. The Catholic Church with its global base in the Vatican was deemed especially suspect in both China and eastern Europe. Communists sought to recruit informers among the ecclesiastical hierarchy and to influence new appointments.[22] The Orthodox Church in Romania was craven in the extreme; its Patriarch declared: 'Christ is a new man. The new man is the Soviet man. Therefore Christ is a Soviet man!'[23] Intellectuals too were suborned everywhere. Pushed to produce works of 'socialist realism' for the regime, they widely agreed to do so even when privately they detested Marxism. Their hypocrisy was salved by the thought that everybody had to earn a crust. In Poland the authorities were eager to get well-known Catholic writers to make the case for communism.[24]

The state publishing houses displayed their patriotic and cultural commitment by printing millions of copies of approved national classics. This was a high priority throughout eastern Europe. The difficulty for the Polish regime was that 'the works of the greatest Polish poets are marked by a dislike of Russia and the dose of Catholic philosophy one finds in them is alarming'.[25] But careful selection in most countries allowed communist rulers to claim that they alone were able to carry out the tasks of popular enlightenment.

Direct mass protest was anyway exceptional. The communists were feared as ruthless masters of the techniques of suppression. The labour camps developed in the USSR were introduced across the communist world. This was especially easy in eastern Europe where they inherited the punitive structures of the Third Reich. But China too was quick in developing its camp network. This became one of the defining features of communism. It is true that other types of society used forced labour as part of their penal system. Intensive manual labour in prison farms was widely found in the USA and South Africa, where the prisoners suffered terrible conditions. Such treatment, though, followed due judicial process and conviction for criminal offences even if the decisions were often arbitrary. What was different about communist rulership was the dispatch of people to the camps for no reason other than the misfortune of belonging to a suspect social class, religious group or intellectual tendency. Communist courts, if they were bothered with, frequently condemned individuals who had broken no law. Only when Stalin died and societies in eastern Europe saw a chink in the wall of communist control did workers – and indeed prisoners in some camps in Kazakhstan – risk coming out on to the streets against the regimes.

Leading offenders, if they escaped being executed, were required to engage in self-criticism. This ritual of humiliation was already entrenched in Chinese communist practice.[26] People had to be shown that nothing except endorsement of current policy was acceptable in political discourse. Opposition had to be seen as reactionary and futile. Thus the whole society would be brought to feel that communism was in the natural order of historical development.

Yet the patterns of non-acquiescence were strong. Work habits were sloppy.[27] The sole possible exception, perhaps, was East Germany; it has been surmised that the Germans were the only nation capable of making communism work: in fact the quality control in the country's factories and mines was hugely inferior to the norms across the border in West Germany. Fiddles and evasions were pervasive. Misreporting was general. Pilfering from state enterprises became a way of life. Workers caught in the act retorted that directors were guilty of gross embezzlement. Polish railwaymen defiantly shouted down trade union activists in Poland: 'We will steal!' They called on the authorities to supply families with the coal they needed for heating.[28] Cynicism about the authorities was quick to grow. An anonymous letter to Poland's Industry Minister Hilary Minc started:

> Citizen Minister! Do you think your game is not transparent to us workers, who have had enough of your democracy based on demagogy and your charlatan's road to socialism? Do you think that we, the working people, don't see your limousines, beautifully furnished apartments and in general your private rotten life?[29]

Communist regimes encouraged people to send in complaints about malpractice. Sometimes they learned things they did not greatly like.

The installation of communist regimes led to the formation of mass parties in eastern Europe. This was the easy bit. Veterans from Moscow exile or from the local political underground learned that the growth in membership introduced the virus of careerism. Party schools were established to induct promising young recruits into the ways of communism.[30] The idea was to create a cadre of reliable functionaries. The other side of the coin was to cleanse each party of undesirable newcomers. In Romania Gheorghiu-Dej was already planning a purge of 'cowardly, opportunistic and provocational elements' in early 1947.[31] The Hungarian and Polish leaders did the same with a view to ending 'corruption' in their parties and starting a fresh recruitment of workers.[32] Without a party card it was more difficult to get access to anything but the most basic goods and services. The crucial thing was to obtain a post on the nomenklatura list of jobs as the Soviet kind of order was implanted. Noteveryone succumbed to temptation. Devout Catholics in Poland, Hungary and Czechoslovakia were disgusted by the militant atheism of the Marxists. But others conquered any inhibitions they might have experienced. It was something of a risk. There was as yet no certainty that the USSR's grip on eastern Europe would last. But short of a third world war breaking out there was a diminishing prospect of the Soviet army being expelled.

Yet the bursts of centrally planned industrialisation diverted many in eastern Europe, if not yet in China, from thinking that all was bad with the communist project. Urbanisation was rapid. In Bulgaria, for instance, the percentage of the labour force employed in agriculture fell from 73 in 1950 to 57 in 1960. This was the biggest transformation in a region moving universally in the same demographic direction.[33] Workers and their families were favoured by the regimes – and in China the peasantry benefited too. Promotion in factories became easier for them. Educational and training facilities were put at their disposal. As in China, free schools and hospitals, cheap shelter and low food prices became the norm. Unemployment was eradicated. Lines of jobless men and women in search of work became a thing of the past. Wages, though, remained low by the standards of North America and most of western Europe. It also became a criminal offence to avoid being employed. 'Shirkers' were charged with parasitism. Communism certainly brought positive changes to the societies which it ruled after the Second World War; but most people did not want communist rule and objected to their conditions of oppression and exploitation.

If only one communist state had experienced the basic difficulties of Soviet society, it might be thought as a freak coincidence. In fact all those new states were troubled by problems which had afflicted the USSR from its inception. The structures, practices and ideas of communist rule were remarkably alike. The reaction to them by people, including even party officials themselves, was likewise similar. Czechoslovakia was an industrial, urbanised society integrated into the European economy before the Second World War, whereas Albania was overwhelmingly agrarian. Yet the pattern of responses to communism was a common one; national circumstances were important but only at a secondary level. There really was such a thing as communism. Until the creation of new communist states after the Second World War this was not easy to predict – and the fact that everyone at the time concentrated attention on the power of the state deflected attention from the ineffectual sides of communist authority. The consequences were going to take years to be fully appreciated. Lenin in 1917 had announced: 'There is such a party!' His supporters outside the Soviet Union could now announce: 'There is such a system!'

26. AGAINST AND FOR REFORM

The spread of communism to eastern Europe, North Korea and China was an important outcome. A third of the world's earth surface was occupied by communist states – and communists everywhere were cheered by this development. Yet this triumph disguised many deep setbacks. The onset of the Cold War brought damage to dozens of communist parties. Government after government in Latin America outlawed, suppressed or persecuted them.[1] The authorities in Australia sought the same end, and only the failure of their plebiscite stopped a complete prohibition of the communist party there.[2] In the colonies of the European powers the communists frequently joined the national-liberation movements – they were especially prominent in the struggle for independence in Vietnam and Indonesia.[3] The many anti-communist campaigns stemmed both from local pressures and from American encouragement. Soviet Politburo member Andrei Zhdanov had spoken about the growing division of the world into two rival camps led by the USSR and the USA. This description fitted global reality by the end of the 1940s.

The Soviet order in the meantime continued to petrify. This was never a spontaneous process. Nobody – alas, except for a handful of historians and political scientists in the West in a later generation[4] – doubted that Stalin continued to exert his influence. While he remained political cook of the Kremlin there was no chance of remixing the ingredients. Some in his entourage recognised that things could not last like this. Malenkov wanted a rapprochement with the USA to reduce the tensions in the Cold War. Khrushchëv placed his hopes in agrarian reform. Beria saw peril in the treatment of the non-Russians in the USSR and agreed with Malenkov and Khrushchëv that needless emergencies were arising in external and internal affairs. They could breathe no word of this in Stalin's presence. Whenever they offended him, however unintentionally, they had to beg forgiveness and to prove themselves his humble pupils and eager servants. They flattered him and his wisdom.

They could not meet except when he brought them together. No big policy could be altered without his sanction, and he held all members of the central leadership in trepidation. His whims were law for them.[5]

Official statistics in 1952 proclaimed that the USSR had completed a full agricultural recovery. This was the purest fiction. The method of counting cereal output was based on average measurements of grain standing in the field before being harvested; it made no allowance for either subsequent bad weather or poor storage and transport. By concentrating his budget on military expenditure, Stalin had starved the countryside of investment. His farming policy anyway failed to provide peasants with incentives to work harder. Although there was no outright famine after 1947, conditions in the villages remained grim. The urban diet was the worst in the industrialised world. Soviet consumers who did not belong to the administrative stratum were ill fed, ill clothed and ill housed.

If they wanted to do better than subsist in Stalin's USSR they had to glorify his name. Millions of them did this voluntarily. He had become the popular incarnation of victory over the Third Reich. Rarely appearing in public, he grew in mystery and prestige. Yet his health was deteriorating and his physician Vladimir Vinogradov advised him to retire from political activity. (Vinogradov was rewarded for his honesty by being locked up in a Lubyanka cell.) The Soviet order went on singing its own praises and lauding Stalin. The party-state bestrode the vast institutions brought into being in the inter-war years and the party itself retained crucial functions. It supervised the agencies of government and picked and scrutinised their personnel. It adjusted and propagated Marxist-Leninist-Stalinist doctrine. Tensions between party and government persisted; Stalin kept things that way to stop either of them undermining his personal power. He also wanted to prevent the party from achieving comprehensive dominance over the ministries since he aimed to promote young men and women qualified in their professions to handle the tasks of governance. Communist technocracy was on the rise.

The Ministry of State Security (MGB) mopped up all spillages of opposition to the state order. Workers and peasants could only passively obstruct the policies of the authorities. Labour discipline, like productivity, remained woeful. Directors, managers and foremen of enterprises served their personal interests at the expense of higher instructions. Localism remained the bane of central purposes. Clientelism persisted, unshaken even by the occasional arrests: the post-war purges affected particular groups and not the clientel system itself. Despite decades of indoctrination and repression, alternative ways of thinking continued to engage the minds of millions. National feelings were intensified by the punitive official campaign to eliminate them. Religious belief endured in the teeth of persecution. There was no realistic chance of a revolution from below against the ruthless power of the MGB and the Soviet army; but beneath the surface of unity there lurked stormy tendencies. It did not take a genius to work out that popular discontent would sooner or later have to be assuaged rather than suppressed. Stalin's obduracy meant that, when reformers took power in 1953, the difficulties had festered into a dangerous condition.

He was also storing up problems to the west of the USSR. Yugoslavia's disobedience was a dangerous example for other states in eastern Europe. Tito had let it be known that if Soviet agents continued to be sent to Belgrade to assassinate him, he would dispatch his own agent to Moscow – and Tito guaranteed that Stalin would not survive the visit.[6] Stalin played on the tensions in each leadership in eastern Europe. The individuals had always been eaten up with mutual jealousies; and as the pressure from Moscow increased, they eagerly ratted on each other. High politics in Romania became extremely vicious. Vasile Luca, who himself had come under suspicion in previous years, denounced Lucreţiu Pătrăşcanu for acting like the Romanian Bukharin. Luca himself was disliked by Ana Pauker, who passed on her criticisms to the Soviet authorities.[7] Various channels of communication with Moscow were kept open across eastern Europe. The Polish security chief Jakub Berman tried to discredit fellow Politburo member Gomułka in a conversation with the Soviet political adviser.[8] Rudolf Slánský, the Czechoslovak party secretary, sensing that others were ganging up against him, hung portraits of both Stalin and Gottwald in his office. Anything to prove his loyalty.[9]

If anyone took the prize as eastern Europe's biggest rat it was Hungarian party and government leader Mátyás Rákosi. This was a man who did not confine his comments to his own country's affairs. He complained to Moscow that Czechoslovak leaders had been tardy in exposing spies and provocateurs. 'It's strange', he wheedled, 'that comrade Gottwald doesn't take measures.' Rákosi also noted that an arrested American spy was carrying a letter of recommendation from Jakub Berman in Warsaw.[10] Nor was he shy about criticising the weak assistance he had experienced from the 'Soviet organs' in Hungary.[11] Whether this earned him the trust of Stalin is doubtful. Stalin knew all the tricks and automatically assumed that a display of zeal could conceal suspect purposes.

His device was to get each leadership to pick on a few of its members and parade them as accomplices of Tito as well as Western intelligence agencies.[12] Trials ensued against the broken victims. Poland's leadership held out against Soviet demands to put Gomułka in court. The Polish United Workers' Party leadership, which had a disproportionate number of Jews, may not have wished to stir up antisemitism by bringing down a native-born Pole such as Gomułka. Victims elsewhere were not so lucky. The accused were chosen in consultation with Moscow and any past softness towards Tito attracted a black mark in the record. László Rajk in Hungary and Rudolf Slánský in Czechoslovakia found themselves arrested. Koçi Xoxe fell in Albania, Traicho Kostov in Bulgaria, Pauker in Romania. After gruesome torture, the defendants confessed to crimes invented for them by their prosecutors.[13] Rajk, Slánský, Xoxe and Kostov were executed. Pauker was spared and sentenced to imprisonment. The German Democratic Republic escaped the demand for such trials. This was not for want of compliance from its leader Walter Ulbricht, who had denounced German comrades to the Soviet authorities in the 1930s.[14] Perhaps the Berlin communist leadership was thought already obedient enough to the Kremlin's wishes.

Eastern Europe's subjugation was reinforced by trade deals which privileged the USSR. Instructions were given for countries to specialise in producing goods needed by the Soviet economy; an imperial economic system was created. Those states which had been Hitler's allies, further-more, continued to have to pay reparations to Moscow. Seventy per cent of Hungarian industrial output in one fashion or another ended up in the USSR in 1953.[15] The situation in Bulgaria and Romania was little better.

Public life in the USSR underwent further degradation as Stalin exploited antisemitism. He had supported the foundation of the state of Israel in 1948 only to find that the new socialist government had a preference for the USA over the USSR; this served to aggravate his suspicion of Soviet Jews as a possible disloyal group.[16] Fears of a general pogrom grew. Jews were insulted in the street and many were beaten up. Many more were sacked from posts of influence. The rumour spread that all people of Jewish ancestry were going to be deported to Siberia. That this was really intended is unproven but prominent Jewish figures undoubtedly dreaded the possibility. He habitually applied repression against any people linked by nationality to a foreign state. In January 1953 several Kremlin doctors were accused of poisoning Soviet politicians. Almost all these medical professionals had Jewish-sounding names. The antisemitic disease was transmitted to eastern Europe. Reports were filed to Moscow claiming that the Jews in the Polish communist leadership had a 'nationalistic' tendency to give preference to fellow Jews in the appointment of personnel.[17] This was a calumny. But it was easy to get people to believe in it. And a similar trend was beginning to plant its roots elsewhere in the region. Communists abroad followed this development with horror and amazement.

Stalin remained intensely suspicious in his old age. He told Italian communist emissary Pietro Secchia: 'However good a party may be there will always be spies inside it. In our party too – the Bolshevik party – there were spies.' He affirmed that not all such spies had yet been unmasked.[18] He told the Central Committee after the Nineteenth Party Congress in 1952 that Molotov and Mikoyan were untrustworthy. Both men lived under the cloud of expected arrest. Stalin had also started the Mingrelian Affair. The Mingrelians are a people living in Georgia. Beria was a Mingrelian and had appointed many of his protégés to posts in the Georgian administration. The fact that Stalin was incarcerating hundreds of Mingrelian functionaries boded ill for Beria's future health. Molotov, Mikoyan and Beria lost influence and status in the Presidium (as the Politburo was renamed) which was formed by the Central Committee after the Congress. Panic was growing among the supreme leaders. Stalin's bodyguard-in-chief Vlasik and personal assistant Poskrëbyshev were taken into custody. The ailing Stalin seemed to be plotting to eliminate his most prominent subordinates and promote more malleable young substitutes.

But on 5 March 1953 he suddenly died. Out at his Kuntsevo dacha, alone with his guards, he had suffered a heart attack. Fear of infringing his routines had stopped anyone from entering the building for several hours, and when they plucked up courage to do this they found him collapsed on the floor. The Ministry of Internal Affairs was phoned. Its officials also were too frightened to act on their own initiative. Politburo members were rung up, and they hurried out to the dacha. Only then were the doctors summoned. It was too late: Stalin by then was breathing his last. A period in twentieth-century world history drew to a close. The chief figures in the hastily reorganised Soviet leadership were Georgi Malenkov, Lavrenti Beria and Nikita Khrushchëv. These three agreed that reform and renovation was essential. Not every leader concurred: Vyacheslav Molotov and Lazar Kaganovich were convinced believers in Stalin's policies and felt anxious about the destabilising effects of any change. But they lacked the energy and the institutional positions already held by the younger troika. Malenkov headed the governmental machine. Beria resumed control over the police and Khrushchëv increased his authority over the party apparatus. Together they edged policies away from the Stalinist legacy.

The Doctors' Plot was exposed as a sham. The announcement was made that communist principles were opposed to any 'cult of the individual'. Stalin was not expressly criticised, but his legacy was plainly under attack. Overtures were made to the USA, and Tito and the Yugoslav communists were no longer spoken about as pariahs. The forced-rate drive for industrialisation in eastern Europe was decelerated. Malenkov confided that thermonuclear war would bring disaster upon the human species.

Beria wanted to go faster and further than the others in reforming communism, and he sometimes acted without consulting Malenkov and Khrushchëv. He went round threatening to grind local police officials into 'labour camp dust'. He was also the leading advocate of reform in eastern Europe, where communist leaders were put on notice to go easier in economic policy. Compliance was not universal. Leaders across the regions had come to power by proving themselves to be reliable Stalinists. None was more dedicated to the old ways than Walter Ulbricht in the German Democratic Republic. Ignoring the changes in Soviet internal and external policies, he announced a rise in work quotas in May 1953. Mátyás Rákosi came from the same mould as Ulbricht. Summoned to the Kremlin, he was told to adopt the New Course after Beria asked him if he aimed to be the first 'Jewish king of Hungary'. Only then did Rákosi back down. The Soviet leadership punished him by insisting that he give up the post of prime minister in favour of Imre Nagy, a known supporter of reforms. Changes in personnel followed everywhere in eastern Europe. The usual procedure was to require the supreme communist ruler to drop the role of dual political leadership. Each had to choose between the party and the government. After Rákosi's humiliation they meekly complied.

Ulbricht's measures were the last straw for his exhausted populace. A strike by building workers spread like a summer forest-fire to the rest of the economy and to all cities of the German Democratic Republic. A demonstration in East Berlin against the authorities drew together a hundred thousand protesters who demanded the resignation of the government. Ulbricht called in the Soviet occupation forces and T-34 tanks trapped the crowd in a main square. When stones were thrown by demonstrators on 17 June, the Volkspolizei retaliated with gunfire and at least 125 demonstrators were killed. The massacre itself caused no palpitations in the Soviet Party Presidium: no Kremlin leader was troubled about the use of force. What worried Moscow was the fact that the German Democratic Republic had come so near to outright revolt. The Presidium had tried to restrain Ulbricht in May and get him to adopt a 'New Course'. Strikes were already taking place in Czechoslovakia and Bulgaria. The result was that the Kremlin allowed Ulbricht to stay in power and decelerate the reforms.[19]

The first political casualty was Beria. Khrushchëv talked a reluctant Malenkov into agreeing to arrest Beria at the Party Presidium on 26 June. Beria was a threat to all its members with his bloody record as a police chief and his willingness to act without consulting others. His radical policies were also dangerously destabilising. The army commanders did not need to be persuaded: they hated Beria for the way he had treated the Red Army in the Second World War. Beria was taken into military custody and executed some months later. Khrushchëv was elevated to the post of Party First Secretary in September while Malenkov remained Chairman of the Council of Ministers. Malenkov emphasised the need to avoid a third world war and to prioritise the expansion of light industry. Khrushchëv had other ideas. By calling for the ploughing up of virgin lands in Siberia and Kazakhstan, he showed he understood the difficulties faced by Soviet citizens in daily life. He cleverly put together an institutional coalition. Khrushchëv promised the armed forces and the heavy-industry ministries that he would maintain their share of the budget, and he assured the Central Committee that the party was the foundation of the Soviet order. As the doors of political discussion were prised ajar, he alone had the skill to reach out beyond the Party Presidium.

He had no shame or modesty; he spoke impromptu and sprinkled his talk with coarse condiments. (His speeches had to be cleaned up before publication.) He looked like a Russian version of the Michelin man in the tyre advertisements of the period. Yet behind his jokiness there was a pugnacity lacking in the doleful Malenkov. Khrushchëv was intuitive; he knew his inadequate schooling left him with deficiencies, but he had a boundless confidence that he knew what needed to be done in the USSR. Malenkov, pudgy and uninspiring, was continually outmanoeuvred; he looked like a victim even before he was picked on.

Khrushchëv, facing down difficulties in the Presidium, steadily increased the pressure to expose the abuses that had been systematic under Stalin.[20] He shrugged off constraints at the Twentieth Party

Congress. When his comrades advised against discussing Stalin, he retorted: 'If we don't tell the truth at the congress we'll be forced to tell the truth at some time in the future. Then it won't be us making the speeches but rather we'll be the people under investigation!'[21] Insisting on his prerogative as Party First Secretary, he delivered a speech on the 'cult of the individual' to a closed session. This was a devastating indictment of Stalin. The deceased Leader, revered by most of his audience as the greatest communist of his generation, was exposed as a mass killer with a psychological disorder. Khrushchëv pulled up short of certain hurdles. He refrained from criticising Stalin's forced-rate industrialisation and forcible mass collectivisation at the end of the 1920s. He also stressed that the Soviet order survived Stalin's abuses intact and that Leninism had been preserved. He downplayed the number and range of victims and avoided mentioning that millions of ordinary people had perished; he gave the impression that only 'several thousand' innocent functionaries in party, army and government had been killed or sent to the labour camps in the 1930s and 1940s.

Yet the speech had the effect of a political thunderbolt; and Khrushchëv insisted that its implications should be brought to bear on foreign as well as internal policy. He earnestly wanted a changed relationship with eastern Europe. The Soviet leaders had already established a military alliance for the Soviet Bloc in the form of the Warsaw Treaty Organisation – unofficially known as the Warsaw Pact – in May 1955; they also abolished Cominform in April 1956, dropping proposals to get communist parties to form new regional agencies.[22] The initiative came entirely from Moscow. No communist leadership in the USSR's outer empire would have dared to make such a proposal. Increasingly the economics of Comecon gave less advantage to Soviet interests; indeed the USSR began to supply petroleum and gas to eastern Europe at prices lower than those on the world market. The Kremlin was paying dearly for retaining its 'satellite states'. Political relations, though, remained strictly hierarchical and the USSR remained the dominant power. Khrushchëv had not become Party First Secretary in order to preside over the dissolution of the Soviet Bloc.

Abridged versions of the speech were relayed to the lower levels of the Communist Party of the Soviet Union; the contents were also passed to the leaderships of fraternal parties. Unintentionally Khrushchëv was loosening the mental fixtures of the world communist movement. Bolesław Bierut, General Secretary of the Polish United Workers' Party, had a heart attack. British communist leader Harry Pollitt was furious about the denunciation of Stalin. 'He's staying there as long as I'm alive,' he said of the portrait of Stalin that hung in his living room – and stay there it did.[23] Pollitt, however, kept his thoughts within his family. The Chinese Communist Party reacted negatively. Mao Zedong, despite his own past troubles with Stalin, refused to accept the burden of Khrushchëv's case. He adopted the formulation that Stalin was 70 per cent right and only 30 per cent wrong. This arithmetic let Stalinism off the hook: neither Mao nor the other Chinese communists leaders spoke of the horrors of agricultural collectivisation and the violent mass purges in the USSR. They wanted freedom to make their own frantic dash for economic growth. This was the beginning of a journey down the road to the split between the USSR and the People's Republic of China.[24]

Communist leaders in eastern Europe undertook a reluctant assimilation of the so-called Secret Speech. They appreciated the perils they faced better than Khrushchëv and his fellow reformers. Stalin's Red Army had conquered these countries. No communist regime had come to national power through the ballot box. All were police states. If Stalin was to be denounced as a despot, every last shred of legitimacy for communist rule in Poland and Hungary vanished. Khrushchëv had no such worry and concentrated on reforming Soviet foreign policy. The USSR had already pushed the North Koreans to sign an armistice at Panmunjom in July 1953 and agree to a partitioning of the country along the thirty-eighth parallel. In April 1955, despite all manner of objections raised by Molotov as Foreign Affairs Minister, Khrushchëv had travelled to Belgrade to effect reconciliation with Yugoslavia.[25] In May, he withdrew the Soviet occupying forces from Austria. Unlike Stalin, he was eager to journey abroad. In 1959 he met US President Dwight D. Eisenhower at Camp David and President John F. Kennedy in Vienna in 1961. A framework of 'peaceful coexistence' was being set up by the great powers. Prevention of a third world war became an acknowledged priority for Soviet and American leaders.

A rip tide of popular discontent, however, was inundating eastern Europe. There was no need for anyone to be prodded to hate Stalin, the October Revolution and Marxism-Leninism: they were a triple plague imported from Russia. The communist economies functioned poorly for consumers. Even the leaders admitted that the output of staple items was on the sub-optimal side. The East Germans had recent experience of Soviet military brutality and held themselves back. The Poles, though, had not been chastened. Industrial workers in Poland went on strike in summer 1956 and, just as in Berlin three years earlier, disputes about conditions at works spiralled up into a massive political protest. Fifty thousand people turned out in the northern city of Poznań shouting 'Free elections!' and 'Down with the Russkis!'[26] The intelligentsia and Church were ready to support any national movement against the dictatorship. Among them were communist reformers. The repression was swift and ruthless as Pole repressed Pole. There were about fifty fatalities. Yet the unpopularity of the regime was too blatant to be ignored. Władysław Gomułka, who had languished in disgrace since 1948, was invited back to supreme office on 13 October 1956. Gomułka was famous as Stalin's communist antagonist, and Poles were willing to give him a chance. Tito looked on approvingly from Belgrade. At last eastern Europe appeared capable of loosening the Soviet grip. Gomułka himself gave encouragement to communist reformers in Hungary.[27]

The Hungarian people too were indignant. The Petöfi circle of intellectuals, which met in Budapest to discuss what was wrong in the country, spread rebellious ideas. Unrest broke out in factories, mines and building sites. Rákosi lost the confidence of his fellow leaders. They no longer feared him either. In July he had to step down as party leader in favour of Ernö Gerö. This did nothing to stem the national flood of demands. Students, workers and even soldiers took to the streets in October. The security police – the ÁVH – fired upon the demonstrators but then found itself besieged in its own headquarters. The Hungarian communist leadership panicked and, backed by Soviet ambassador Yuri Andropov, got Moscow's permission for Imre Nagy to assume personal authority.[28] Nagy identified himself with the crowds in the capital. He assured the Kremlin that he could master the situation, and maintained that Hungary would remain faithful to the communist cause. At the same time his party and government released Cardinal Mindszenty and other religious and political prisoners from custody. The press shook itself free from censorship. Open demands for national independence were made throughout the country. The armed forces were plainly on the side of the demonstrators. Nagy ended up approving the country's withdrawal from the Warsaw Pact.

Budapest in autumn 1956 became the epicentre of an entire people's revolt against the USSR. Khrushchëv vacillated. On 30 October he persuaded the Soviet leadership to desist from invading Hungary. But then he reconsidered. Emboldened by the Anglo-French and Israeli attack on Egypt to resecure control of the Suez Canal, he sent tanks into Hungary on 4 November.[29] The Soviet soldiers themselves knew little or nothing about the purpose of their mission until they crossed the border.

Khrushchëv remembered Hungarians as the wartime allies of the Third Reich and saw Nagy as a traitor to the communist cause. Soviet forces in the name of communism crushed the workers' councils elected by factory labour forces. Demonstrations were broken up. The brutality was intense. When all was lost, many rebels headed for the frontier and freedom rather than stay behind and endure the military occupation. Nagy was seized and executed a couple of years later despite assurances to the contrary: Khrushchëv wanted no east European communist leader to repeat Nagy's act of defiance. The USSR approved the establishment of a puppet government under János Kádár.

Yet the entire imbroglio emboldened Khrushchëv's enemies in the Party Presidium to attack his policies. In June 1957 Molotov, Kaganovich and Malenkov plotted to demote him. Molotov and Kaganovich, Stalin's closest henchmen in the 1930s, detested the programme of reforms; Malenkov approved of it but disliked being shunted out of the central terminus of Soviet politics. They were confident of a majority in the Presidium. Khrushchëv was ready for them. Again standing up for his rights, he demanded to put his case to the larger Central Committee on which sat party, ministerial and military officials who admired him. Marshal Zhukov used the air force to ferry them from all over the USSR. They banged on the doors of the Presidium to get the Central Committee into session. The result was victory for Khrushchëv; he had turned personal disaster into the defeat of the three leaders of what he called the 'anti-party group'.

After that there was no stopping him. His policy of 'peaceful coexistence' in no way implied that he was abandoning the competition with the USA. He had confidence that the USSR had a superior order of state and society to the entire capitalist world. By 1961 he was promising that the Soviet Union would have overtaken the USA in its standard of living by the end of the decade. He asserted that the 'all-out construction' of a communist society as envisaged by Lenin in *The State and Revolution* would have begun by 1980. He called the USSR an 'all-people's state'. The gauntlet was thrown down in front of the USA. Direct military conflict was to be avoided but economic, political and ideological competition was going to be intense. Khrushchëv was eager in particular to win support from the Third World. Around the globe the empires had not yet been fully dismantled even though the British and French were already intent on this end. The Soviet leadership sought to exploit the situation. The other aim was to encourage 'non-aligned' nations to break free of American influence and cause trouble for the USA.

Khrushchëv offered financial aid and economic advisers to those states which agreed to this; he presented himself as the tireless advocate of independence for all the world's small countries.

The communist movement around the world was convulsed by the events of 1956. An exodus from the party ranks occurred with especial intensity in western Europe and North America. Admissions about Stalin's abuses undermined old loyalties; and the military suppression of the Hungarian Uprising convinced many veterans that the attitudes of the Kremlin leaders were insufficiently different from those of the deceased Soviet dictator. The Communist Party of Great Britain, for example, lost around nine thousand members – over a quarter of the total – in the two years after February 1956.[30]

Yet most communist party leaderships were willing to give the USSR the benefit of the doubt. Palmiro Togliatti in Italy had hinted that he would support an invasion even before the Soviet leadership had taken the decision.[31] The regimes in Czechoslovakia, Romania and even Yugoslavia were eager for the Hungarian experiment in self-rule to be terminated. They had Hungarian minorities of their own and did not want them to start causing similar trouble. China, despite other basic disagreements with Moscow, condoned the use of troops. Only Gomułka in Poland held out against Khrushchëv. He had been restored to power against Khrushchëv's wishes and did not want a precedent set in Budapest which might later be applied to Warsaw.[32] Nevertheless the unity of communist parties around the world was less than firm. The Chinese Communist Party had had political difficulties with Stalin before and after seizing power in 1949. But Mao endorsed most of what had been done in the USSR under Stalin; he also hesitated to lower his own claims to omniscience by recanting any cardinal features of Mao Zedong Thought. Chinese communists castigated Khrushchëv as a 'revisionist'. Yet Mao approved of the Soviet army's operation against the Hungarian Uprising. His attitude was that if the USSR had not undertaken deStalinisation, the problem in Budapest would never have arisen.

Washington's political and intelligence establishment still assumed that the USSR was the hidden hand in everything done by communist states and that Soviet domination of the world communist movement was unchecked. This was an overdrawn picture.[33] When no other communist states existed, it had been easy for Stalin and the Comintern to hand out instructions and get them obeyed. Tito had shown that it was possible to stand up to Stalin; Mao and Kim Il-sung had manipulated Stalin into making choices about war and peace according to their considerations and schedule. Even eastern Europe posed constraints on his freedom. If communist states were to endure in the region, they needed assistance from Moscow. All of them would crumble without the guarantee of Soviet military intervention. Without cheap Soviet oil and other natural resources, they would fall into difficulties. Although eastern Europe had become the Soviet Union's outer empire, the pleasures of imperialism were attenuated by the drain on the Kremlin's treasury. DeStalinisation had not put an end to the geopolitical and internal threats to the USSR.

PART FIVE

MUTATION

1957–1979

27. DÉTENTE AND EXPANSION

As soon as Nikita Khrushchëv had consolidated his position as Soviet supreme leader in 1957 he pressed forward with change in all sectors of internal and external policy in the USSR. Already the Party First Secretary, he also assumed the post of Chairman of the Council of Ministers a year later. He pulled up his younger supporters to high office, shunting his enemies in the 'anti-party group' into disgrace and retirement. He decentralised industrial organisation in the USSR by scrapping the Moscow-based ministries and establishing scores of 'councils of the people's economy'. He split the party into two sections, industrial and agricultural, at each local level: this bipartition was meant to energise economic advance. Khrushchëv encouraged a widening of public discussion, permitting the appearance of novels and poems about Stalin's Gulag.[1] He introduced a priority for investment in light industry. His purpose was to bring about a massive immediate rise in the Soviet standard of living. He brought the Twenty-Second Party Congress to its feet with his vision of the immediate fugure. Hard as nails in political struggle, the First Secretary was also a dreamer. He told the Presidium: 'Thus we'll proceed to the realisation of Lenin's tenet that every kitchen maid must know how to administer her state.'[2]

In international relations he placed emphasis on 'anti-imperialism', making overtures to countries in the Third World. This involved support for national liberation movements in the colonies of the European empire as well as assistance to those independent states in Asia, Africa and Latin America striving to break free from Western economic dominion. Furthermore, he allowed for a variety of ways, including peaceful ones, of making the 'transition to socialism'. Communist parties did not have to copy the Soviet historical experience.[3] And all this time the USSR sought a working relationship with the USA. Agreements were made to postpone atomic-bomb tests. The underlying idea was to slow down and even halt the arms race between the two superpowers.

Competition continued between the USSR and the USA as they

scrambled after global influence. Despite being the weaker superpower, Khrushchëv was willing to take a risk and see what the Americans would do. He repeatedly threatened to sign a separate peace treaty with the German Democratic Republic, proclaim all Berlin its capital and end the rights of Western powers to occupy any part of the city. The Americans reacted by building up their forces in Europe to protect West Berlin. The danger of the stand-off escalating into all-out war could not be excluded until, in summer 1962, the USSR backed down. Hardly had this happened than US reconnaissance aircraft discovered a Soviet plan to construct a nuclear-missile base on Cuba, where Fidel Castro had made his revolution in 1959.[4] President Kennedy declared a naval blockade of the island, issuing an ultimatum for the ships carrying the rockets across the Atlantic to be recalled to the USSR. Days of acute tension followed in October 1962. Khrushchëv recognised that he had over-played his hand and backed down, and the outbreak of a third world war was prevented.[5] From this episode onwards Soviet and American leaders understood how easily a diplomatic fracas could explode into a planetary holocaust.

Mao Zedong and the Chinese communist leaders berated Khrushchëv for pusillanimity. They themselves were determined to deal on more equal terms with the USSR: they wanted back the territory taken by the USSR in 1945; they aimed to renegotiate the agreements on the natural resources which they were dispatching to the Soviet Union. They sought to challenge the hegemony of the USSR over the 'world communist movement'. Like a bride regretting a shotgun wedding, Mao was suing for divorce. The decree nisi came with angry mutual consent in July 1960 after Moscow withdrew Soviet technology, finance and ten thousand advisers from China. Joint projects were abandoned at twenty-four hours' notice. Dams, factories and science laboratories were abandoned half built. Agreements were torn up and economic assistance was halted. The Soviet promise to enable the Chinese to construct nuclear weapons was nullified. Mao denounced Soviet leaders as revisionist; he personally refused to attend the world conference of communist parties in Moscow in November 1960 and ordered Chinese representatives to castigate the USSR's ideas and practices. Only Albania took China's side and eventually a compromise was reached in the proceedings.

But this only papered over the cracks of a deep schism. World communism was divided. Sino–Soviet military clashes occurred across the disputed borders. When Yugoslavia had stood up against the USSR in 1948, nobody seriously thought that Tito would take to arms. Mao was different. The possibility could not be discounted that the USSR and China might go to all-out war against each other.

Mao administered a mauling to the strategy of 'peaceful coexistence' between world capitalism and world communism. He contemplated the possibility of a third world war with a staggering insouciance:

> Let's contemplate this: how many people would die if [such a] war breaks out? There are 2.7 billion people in the world. One third could be lost; or a little more: it could be a half . . . I say that, if we take the extreme situation, half die and half live; but imperialism would be razed to the ground and the whole world would become socialist.[6]

If this had been said merely for rhetorical effect, it would not have been quite so bad. But Mao was deadly serious. He and his comrades took the outcome of the Cuban missiles crisis as a sign that the USSR and the USA were colluding in imposing a condominium over the rest of the globe. Mao regarded this as the newest and most terrifying expression of imperialism, filling the vacuum left by the European empires. China persistently made overtures to the Non-Aligned Movement, posing as the defender of the rights of small, defenceless states against political and economic depredations.

Neither Khrushchëv nor Leonid Brezhnev, who succeeded him as Soviet party chief in October 1964, had truly given up the ambition to trounce the USA in the Cold War; and while trying to build up a peaceful relationship with Washington, they sought to hold on to and legitimate all communist geopolitical gains since the Second World War. In particular, the USSR aimed at an American guarantee of military non-intervention in eastern Europe in return for the assurance that the Soviet army would never invade western Europe. Khrushchëv himself paid heavily for the failures of his leadership. There were riots in Novocherkassk and other Soviet cities when food prices were raised in July 1962. There was deep resentment among party and government officials whose job security and privileges were menaced by his frequent institutional changes. There was dissatisfaction with the humiliation he had brought on the USSR through the Cuban missiles affair. The Party Presidium, most of whose members were his promotees, removed him in a peaceful coup. Khrushchëv declared that the absence of violence in the change of leadership was among his greatest achievements, and he wept as he acknowledged his faults.[7]

Brezhnev promised to consult colleagues about policy, to maintain a 'collective leadership' and to gather expert opinion on all matters. He espoused the 'stability of cadres' as his objective: as long as officials toed the party line, they could keep their jobs for life. Brezhnev and his main colleagues Alexei Kosygin and Nikolai Podgorny scrapped Khrushchëv's bipartition of the party and restored the central ministries. They clamped down on the growing intellectual dissent and moderated any criticism of Stalin – and they were delighted that this went down well in the armed forces.[8] Kosygin in 1965 introduced a process of economic reform to give a modicum of increased authority to enterprise directors at the expense of state authorities; but Brezhnev disliked such schemes and they were dropped. The Politburo – as the inner core of the party leadership called itself again after getting rid of Krushchëv – concentrated on eliminating the eccentricities of the disgraced Khrushchëv. Politics were stabilised in the USSR by the dyes and fixative spray of Brezhnev's policies. Brezhnev's focus was on economics and international relations. Like Khrushchëv, he prioritised an expansion of supplies of food and industrial products for Soviet consumers. And he geared the state budget to the achievement of military parity with the USA while skirting any risk of a third world war.

It remained an article of faith among communists in the USSR and elsewhere that capitalism was a rotten apple which either would soon fall to earth or else would need to be pulled down from the tree. 'Class struggle' continued to be advocated from Moscow and other communist capitals. When Nicolae Ceauşescu of Romania was negotiating for his state visit to London in 1974, his heart stopped after being told of the industrial conflicts raging across the United Kingdom. Perhaps the final 'crisis of capitalism' was happening there.[9] He did not want to be seen as supporting the British Labour Party in dissuading the workers from going on strike. Moreover, leaders of communist states usually displayed greater distrust of the West's socialist, social-democratic and labour parties than of conservative and liberal parties. Khrushchëv angrily exclaimed in 1956: 'They always asked for that little bit more. Russians, therefore, would always tell them to go to Hell. They were impossible people.'[10] The doctrines of communism were maintained; and if capitalist states such as the USA, West Germany or Japan were economically resurgent, this could not be seen as a lasting phenomenon: Marxist-Leninists confidently predicted the end of private enterprise and its political systems.

Communist revolutions had been few in Khrushchëv's period of rule. The anti-colonial campaign in Indochina forced the French to leave after the victory of Ho Chi Minh and his Vietnamese communist forces at the battle of Dien Bien Phu in 1954. Civil war followed; the armistice of 1954 confined the communist regime to the area north of the seventeenth parallel. It was not long before fighting was resumed between the governments of the north and the south, and the prospect of an eventual communist triumph, adding to the success of Castro's revolution in Cuba, looked distinctly possible by the early 1960s.[11]

The world map acquired more red expanses in the 1970s. American military intervention in the Vietnamese civil war came to a humiliating end in April 1975. Within weeks the government of the communist north established its power throughout the south of the country. This event unravelled relations among several powers. Vietnam had relied on military supplies from both the USSR and China. The supreme desire of the Chinese was to get the Americans out of their backyard in Indochina. Once this had happened, Vietnam itself became an object of Chinese concern. The two countries were old enemies. When violent clashes broke out between communist Vietnam and communist Cambodia, leaders in Beijing took the Cambodian side to prevent Vietnam from asserting itself as a regional power or being turned by the USSR into an anti-Chinese vassal state.[12] The Cambodian communists – known as the Red Khmers (or Khmers Rouges) – had come to power in the mêlée caused by recent events. Prince Norodom Sihanouk had been deposed, with American connivance, by Lon Nol and the army in 1970. Sihanouk's cordial relations with Beijing had annoyed Washington. The US air force, moreover, had bombed Cambodian forests on the Vietnamese border so as to disrupt Vietnamese supply lines. All this brought recruits to the Khmers Rouges – and even Sihanouk went into alliance with them. Their leader Pol Pot became dictator in Phnom Penh in the same month as the Americans abandoned Saigon in the Vietnamese south. Laos also fell to a communist insurgency in 1975.[13]

Across the Pacific, Chile elected President Allende and his communist-inspired coalition to office in 1970; and although his administration was overturned with American support three years later, evidently the USA could no longer take its dominance in South America for granted.[14] In Africa a communist regime was established in Ethiopia in 1974 and in Angola in 1976. In both these cases the supply of financial and military assistance from the USSR was crucial for the survival of communists in power.[15] Almost to their own amazement the leaders in the Kremlin began to believe that global history had turned decisively in their favour.

American Presidents took account of the USSR's growing confidence and ambition. Richard Nixon, who entered office in January 1969, sought an accommodation with the rival superpower and together with Henry Kissinger, his National Security Adviser and later Secretary of State, designed measures to bring about a relaxation of tensions. This became known as the policy of détente. Nixon and Kissinger maintained a strategy of containment; they supported anti-communist governments where they could and were largely oblivious to considerations of democracy, the rule of law and human rights. But negotiations were also initiated for a Conference on Security and Co-Operation in Europe (CSCE). This initiative came from west European governments but Nixon's successor Gerald Ford supported it. The result was the Helsinki Final Act, signed in August 1975, which guaranteed fundamental freedom to all people throughout the continent. President Carter, entering office in January 1976, used the Act's clauses to press for a slackening of the persecution of citizens in the communist states. The main advantage to the USSR was its formal acceptance by the rival superpower as a legitimate participant in the contests of global politics. The world seemed divided for decades ahead between the two contending 'camps' led by America and the Soviet Union. A commitment to avoid a third world war appeared to have been guaranteed.

This settlement implied a weakening of the walls of Truman's containment – and certainly this was how the Kremlin understood the situation. Yet the USA's moderation was undercut by the rapprochement engineered by Nixon and Kissinger with the People's Republic of China in February 1972. The USSR was not the only possible main partner for Washington. Bets were being hedged in Washington. Equally clearly, Mao the anti-revisionist was willing to do deals with the foreign enemies of communism.

The USSR's leaders remained buoyant. The Soviet standard of living rose in the 1970s. The Politburo under Brezhnev was pleased that it avoided any serious repetition of the Novocherkassk troubles. The 'stability of cadres' policy allayed the concerns of officialdom. In 1973, moreover, the Kremlin benefited from the sharp increase in oil prices on global markets. Research and development in military technology strengthened the armed forces. A rough parity was attained with the USA, and the USSR at last became a worldwide naval power as well as the possessor of nuclear missiles with the capacity to strike at American cities from long range. Yet there was no room for complacency. The bottlenecks in economic production remained. Grain had to be imported for livestock feed and the subsidy to agricultural production was the highest in the world. Light industry was chronically under-funded. Disgruntlement with the authorities spread wide and deep in society and Marxism-Leninism was popularly discredited. Intellectuals and labour militants defied the efforts of the KGB – the new and final name for the Soviet political police – to suppress them. Party and governmental officials served their own interests at the expense of central directives. Corruption was on the increase. Non-compliance and misinformation pervaded the state order. The Politburo's grip on the rest of the country was weakening in matters of day-to-day governance.

Yet the Soviet leadership stuck to its policies: it had forgotten nothing and learned nothing. In eastern Europe it felt safe in the knowledge that the Americans would not interfere in its dispositions. When the Czechoslovak communists under Alexander Dubček embarked on a course of radical political and economic reform which came to be known as the Prague Spring, Brezhnev ordered an invasion in August 1968. The Kremlin also approved the vigorous suppression of the independent labour movement in Poland in December 1970. The USSR's reputation around the world sank ever deeper. And the cost of holding on to the 'outer empire' placed additional strain on the Soviet budget as oil and gas were transferred to eastern Europe and Cuba at artificially low prices.[16]

The Strategic Arms Limitations Talks got under way towards the end of 1969 and an agreement – known as SALT I – was signed in May 1972. Further development in military technology was not precluded and the two sides came together again and, in June 1979, agreed on SALT II. Also of importance was the initiative taken by Willy Brandt, Chancellor of West Germany, for a modus vivendi with the East Germans through his *Ostpolitik*. The two German states officially recognised each other in December 1972. The fact that American armed forces in the same period were embroiled in the war in Vietnam and proving incapable of winning it added to the feeling in the Politburo that progress for the cause of communism was steady and inevitable. The protest movement against American foreign policy mounted in the USA and western Europe. Student unrest in France in May 1968 also involved basic revulsion against the capitalist economy. Paris was convulsed by street disorders and President Charles de Gaulle and his government came close to falling. The Kremlin as well as the French Communist Party doubted that a 'revolutionary situation' was at hand. But it relished the difficulties that the West was experiencing. Anything bad for capitalist countries was considered good for the USSR.

Moscow continued to offer guidance and money to loyal and semi-loyal communist parties around the world. The People's Friendship University – later named after the murdered Congolese radical Prime Minister Patrice Lumumba – had been established in Moscow in 1960 to offer an education to young communist militants and sympathisers from the Third World. This was all done above board and in the open. Behind the scenes, though, the Soviet leadership continued to provide explosives and sabotage-training courses. The Central Committee Secretariat in 1980 approved a request from the Communist Party of Chile for such provision.[17]

Meanwhile Boris Ponomarëv, head of the International Department of the Central Committee Secretariat, went on dishing out dollars through the Assistance Fund for Communist Parties and Movements of the Left, supplemented by contributions from eastern Europe.[18] The distribution list conformed to the current objectives of Soviet foreign policy. In 1980 by far the largest grant was 2,500,000 dollars. This went into the account of the Communist Party of the USA, which stood no chance of national or even local power but was thought to perform a useful service in propaganda. Next in line were the French communists with 2,000,000 dollars; their position as a spokesman for the 'peace-loving' intentions of the USSR in western Europe was pre-eminent. The Finnish communists received 1,350,000 dollars.[19] The common border with the USSR made Finland a crucial zone for the Soviet geopolitical interest. Then, lagging behind, came Portugal (800,000 dollars), Greece (700,000 dollars) and Chile (500,000 dollars). The South African Communist Party received a paltry 100,000 dollars.[20] The Soviet leadership had no high opinion of Joe Slovo and fellow communists and instead concentrated its assistance on the African National Congress.[21]

China competed by paying out subsidies to Albania and Cambodia. Mao found that Albanian leader Enver Hoxha's reputation for wiliness was well earned when Hoxha demanded ever greater subsidies in return for his public loyalty.[22] Chinese funds were also channelled to African countries unconnected with communism. The People's Republic of China under Mao wanted to be identified as a philanthropic world power.

It was political rather than financial difficulties that limited the USSR's influence on communism around the world. Attempts by the Communist Party of the Soviet Union to impose its doctrines on other parties, at least those outside eastern Europe, met with growing opposition at the conferences of the world's communist parties held in Moscow in 1957 and 1960.[23] The Italian, French and Spanish communists since the mid-1960s had objected to the oppressive nature of the Soviet internal order. Their critique came to be known as Eurocommunism.[24] When communist parties gathered again in the Soviet capital in June 1969, the Italians robustly rejected the Kremlin's policies and angry exchanges occurred about the invasion of Czechoslovakia in the previous year. The British, who had endorsed the suppression of the Hungarian Uprising in 1956, took the Italian side. So too did the Australians, Belgians, Spanish, Swedes and Swiss. Discussions on the 'Document about the Tasks of the Anti-Imperialist Struggle' were acrimonious and several parties refused to sign it. The number would have been higher if the Chinese, Albanians, Thais and Burmese had bothered to attend; and, as Brezhnev noted in his confidential report to his Central Committee, the Koreans and Vietnamese had declined an invitation for fear of annoying Beijing.[25]

There remained many communist parties which ingested Soviet doctrine like their mothers' milk. The South African Communist Party was one of them.[26] But it was Gus Hall of the Communist Party of the USA who earned the warmest praise for saying: 'We don't regard internationalism as a burden, as a concession or as a cross to bear.'[27] Even so, Brezhnev felt obliged to acknowledge that any increase in the USSR's influence over a multitude of communist parties around the world was going to involve painstaking steady work. The Soviet leadership would have to operate 'in a differentiated fashion'. He thought that the Japanese communists with their current 'right-nationalistic' tendency could be brought to co-operate in the 'anti-imperialist' campaign. He discerned a chance for 'the normal development of relations' with the Yugoslav leadership. He affirmed that 'unremitting work' was needed to alter attitudes among Italian and British comrades. Only with Mao Zedong and China did he see no realistic chance of rapprochement.[28]

He was overestimating what he could do about the Italians. Enrico Berlinguer, leader of the Italian Communist Party, decided in 1977 to break an important remaining tie with the Soviet leadership. The Italians had secretly received four to five million dollars annually. Inside a total budget of nearly thirty million dollars this made the difference between bankruptcy and balancing the books. Boris Ponomarëv usually handed over the cheque in person.[29] Berlinguer had made up his mind to refuse Soviet largesse. The reasoning for this action was simple. Eventually the story of 'Moscow gold' was bound to reach the press in Italy; it was only surprising that this had not happened already. Berlinguer wanted to avoid a political scandal.[30] He also had positive motives. The Italian communists were beginning to believe that the 'historical compromise' was actually working. At the June 1976 elections the party had raised its proportion of the vote from 27 to 34 per cent. Gianni Cervetti delivered this message in Moscow in January 1978.[31] But Berlinguer did not stick to his decision and cheques continued to arrive in Rome from the USSR.[32]

The financial rupture between Moscow and the Italian Communist Party was finally accomplished in 1981, and the reason was not merely Berlinguer's revulsion at Soviet policy but also the Politburo's conclusion that he was no longer worth subsidising. The USSR had counted on Berlinguer's help in the Soviet propaganda campaign against American policy in Europe. Even when Italian communists were criticising their comrades in Moscow, they had been useful in attacking the USA's activities.[33] But when Berlinguer started to criticise the USSR as much as the USA, it ceased to make sense to provide him with funds. The Soviet leadership instead made payments to the pro-Soviet elements in the Italian Communist Party.[34]

The Soviet leadership kept up a barrage of abusive notes to Euro-communist leaders in Italy and Spain.[35] But it made no difference. The die was cast: a strategic decision had been taken in Rome and Madrid that any close political association with Moscow would ruin the chances of communist electoral success. By 1979 the Italian communists were telling Moscow that they intended having direct relations with the People's Republic of China.[36] Santiago Carrillo, General Secretary of the Spanish Communist Party, published fiery assaults on the reputation of the USSR. From Madrid and Rome went messages of disapproval of Soviet internal and external policy. The French Communist Party at first showed Latin solidarity. Even crusty Georges Marchais, Secretary-General from 1972, criticised Soviet abuse of human rights. He was roundly condemned by the USSR in confidential messages.[37] What is more, the party's militants and mass membership were frequently unhappy about denunciations of the Soviet order. The French Communist Party was not ready for Eurocommunism. Marchais relapsed into a display of loyalty to the USSR without entirely abandoning his objections to the Kremlin's attitudes and practices; he resisted any lingering temptation to form a west European front against Moscow.

About the desirability of détente, however, there was consensus among Berlinguer, Carrillo and Marchais. The American political estab-lishment did not speak with one voice. In 1975, the year of the Helsinki Final Act, the US Congress passed a Trade Reform Law amendment devised by Henry 'Scoop' Jackson and Charles Vanick. Its main clause denied the status of 'most favoured nation' to any state that restricted free emigration. Brezhnev was put on notice that, if he continued to prevent Soviet Jews from leaving for Israel, the USSR's access to the Western capitalist economy would be terminated. He was also made edgy by the USA's awarding of the status of 'most favoured nation' to Romania, Hungary and Poland. This was a deliberate attempt to loosen the cement of the Soviet Bloc in eastern Europe. The three countries in various ways had shown a willingness to stand up for themselves against Moscow, and the granting of this status was a reward for their endeavours.

Despite the Jackson–Vanick amendment, business had continued to be brisk with the USSR. This did not happen without objections from the US Department of Defense that exported machinery could easily be transferred to military programmes.[38] But Presidents Ford and Carter sanctioned many projects in the interests of boosting American trade and industry as well as inducing Soviet co-operation in superpower arms limitation. The USSR's computer technology was almost entirely imported from the USA and Japan.[39] Economic ties were especially close with West Germany and Italy. Germans imported most of their gas from the USSR. Italian companies increasingly traded with Soviet ministries. The city of Tolyatti – or Togliatti – was founded on the River Volga. Fiat patents were bought to produce 'Zhiguli' automobiles.[40] Yet the Kremlin was constantly playing economic catch-up. Inventions bought on licence from foreign countries – as well as those stolen by Soviet intelligence operations – were rarely implemented with speed, and the technology gap between East and West remained large in general and in certain key sectors grew decisively wider.[41] Moscow's official boasts about the USSR's programme of research and development were insubstantial.[42] The gains in nuclear missile capacity or in space rocketry disguised the simple fact that the Soviet civilian economy was woefully backward by world standards.

The end to détente came suddenly in December 1979, towards the end of Jimmy Carter's presidency, when the USSR sent its forces over the Soviet–Afghan border. Communists in Afghanistan had for months begged Moscow to help them militarily against their many religious and political enemies. The Politburo gave permission for KGB special forces and paratroops to give them secret assistance,[43] but, under Kosygin's influence, stood out against all-out intervention by the Soviet army. But the pleas from Kabul grew more insistent. Brezhnev gathered his leading confidants to a state dacha; these were Dmitri Ustinov, Andrei Gromyko and Konstantin Chernenko. Fatefully they resolved to dispatch a military contingent. For conspiratorial reasons the decision was phrased in opaque terminology and Afghanistan was referred to only as 'A'. The rest of the Politburo gave subsequent approval.[44]

This decision was motivated by the wish to prevent power being seized in Kabul by anti-communists supported by the USA, and the USSR put its troops over the border with reluctance. But a blunder is a blunder. Afghan patriots with antique weaponry had sent the British army packing in the late nineteenth century without external assistance. The situation was different in 1979. The Americans were eager to supply all the material aid requested by the insurgents. The fact that the revolt was led by Moslem fanatics – the mujehaddin – did not bother the Americans at the time. Carter, hardly a bruiser in the bargains he struck with Brezhnev, felt betrayed and pronounced the death of détente. The Americans suspended talks on arms limitation for the signature of SALT II. Civilian trade agreements were obstructed. A more vigorous strategy of anti-communist geopolitics was pursued in Africa and Latin America. Eurocommunists were furious with Moscow.[45] In order to sustain its position in the world the Kremlin had to go on squeezing the non-military sections of the USSR's state budget. Brezhnev had thought he was throwing a lasso around the neck of an adjacent country, Afghanistan. Instead he had tied a cord round the neck of the Soviet order and pulled it tight.

28. CHINA CONVULSED

The Hundred Flowers campaign of 1956–7 hurled the People's Republic of China into turmoil. People bombarded the communist party with criticism, and Mao Zedong was not exempted from their blame. Open disagreement had occurred in the communist leadership. Weary and apologetic, Mao expressed the wish to retire from daily political management and to focus his energies on strategic supervision.[1]

The Great Helmsman, as he liked to be called, was talking with monumental insincerity. In reality he was intensely anxious about opposition and determined to root it out. In summer 1957 he ordered criticism of the 'rightists' in the party as well as more widely in society. Those who had rebuked Mao or the regime were the principal targets. Although there were few arrests and executions, the psychological pressure resulted in over half a million suicides.[2] Quotas for denunciation of 'rightists' were assigned to administrative tiers right down to particular work groups.[3] Mao simultaneously readied the leadership for an intensive campaign of economic transformation. This became known as the Great Leap Forward. Aiming to eliminate the differences between town and countryside, he called for the rapid growth of rural industry. As the campaign got under way, about a tenth of the population volunteered – or, most frequently, found themselves directed – to work in makeshift iron foundries. A million of them were built. Planned output of steel was raised from six million tons in January 1958 to thirty million by the end of the following year. These were the years when Chinese communists repudiated the Soviet denunciation of Stalin and claimed that only China could supply an authentic model for communism around the world.

Mao's dominance over the Politburo was at a peak and he was as peremptory as Stalin in his ideas and methods. Among his obsessions was a campaign to exterminate the sparrow, which he thought the scourge of China's agriculture. People were told to shoot them. Mao, like Stalin in plant genetics, was balefully ignorant of zoological ecology.

Sparrows performed the useful function of feeding off insects harmful to crops; their annihilation inevitably reduced the size of harvests. Yet Mao blundered forward. All Chinese were to accept his policies as unquestionable wisdom.

The targets for transforming the economy were to be met by fair means or foul. Mothers handed over the family woks and children's brooches to be melted down for industrial use. Youths went out searching for scrap metal. Doorknobs, scissors and buckles were tossed into the furnaces. The activity was hysterical, the environment intimidating. People in the urban foundries who tried to visit their families in the villages were beaten up.[4] A vast famine afflicted the country. Drought affected some regions in 1958, but the industrialising campaign and its consequences were the main reason for the hardship. Survivor Bian Shaofeng described the result: 'When you were hungry you would eat anything. We ate all kinds of wild grass, wild roots, pumpkin leaves and peanut shells; we ate worms, baby frogs, toads. It was disgusting to eat toads as they made you sick. We ate rats if we could catch any, but often we were too weak.'[5] Her relatives died off like flies. People kept the deaths a secret so that they could go on receiving the rations of the deceased. Parents lived with the rotting corpses of their children. Cannibalism was widespread. On a trip into town, Bian Shaofeng noticed a man's head and chest by the roadside. On questioning a local woman, she was told unashamedly that he had been chopped up for his plump flesh.[6]

The exact incidence of mortality through starvation may never be known; the most plausible estimate is that at least thirty million people perished. It was the worst man-induced famine in history. Chinese state officials hid this efficiently from the world's attention and no latter-day Malcolm Muggeridge got outside the capital to investigate.[7] The disaster was a sensitive topic inside the communist leadership. Defence Minister Peng Dehuai broke the taboo at the Central Committee plenum in Lushan in June 1959 and talked about the human losses. Peng's reward for his honesty was to be branded the leader of a rightist opportunist clique and sacked. (He was to die after torture by Red Guards in the Cultural Revolution.) Lin Biao, a veteran of the civil war and an ambitious radical, replaced him at the Defence Ministry.

Supposedly this was Mao's reaction to all the suffering: 'You have only tree leaves to eat? So be it.'[8] What is undeniable is that he took no serious steps to change policy until it was too late. He continued to take satisfaction from communist successes in the decade since 1949. Land had been collectivised, industry nationalised. Rival parties had been eliminated. The non-Chinese groups in the population had been cowed. The ruling group enjoyed unchallenged supremacy; its members had the prestige and authority of men who had fought in the civil war against the Kuomintang. Yet the Great Leap Forward had not worked out as Mao had intended. The tens of millions of deaths were not the only reason why the central leaders of party and army were alarmed – and many leaders in fact were just as unconcerned about the hardship as Mao himself. What worried them to a greater extent were the consequences for state authority if the disruption was not ended. Mao had to give way: his leading position was not unconditional. After much discussion it was agreed that he should step down from the Chairmanship of the People's Republic in favour of Liu Shaoqi. Although Mao remained Chairman of the Chinese Communist Party, Liu acquired an ally in Deng Xiaoping, who held the post of its General Secretary. Mao referred to himself as a 'dead ancestor', meaning that nobody any longer had to consult him about current policy.

Yet Mao's official image remained unsullied as the media went on depicting him as a wise, altruistic supreme leader who lived the simple life. Photographs and paintings showed him in a baggy plain tunic and with a face uncreased by age. He looked more like an inflatable rubber doll than a human being. When a Danish socialist newspaper published a cartoon of him being eaten by a Chinese dragon, the Beijing authorities issued a furious protest. Disrespect to Mao was treated as an act of enmity towards the entire people of China. Implicit threats were made to Danish businessmen about to visit the country.[9] Evidently Beijing wanted a monopoly of representations of Mao: a joke was always a serious thing for communists.

Mao had no genuine leaning towards altruism and self-denial and was a serial philanderer with a penchant for ingenuous young women. In later years he infected his conquests with a sexually transmitted disease.[10] Worried about becoming impotent, he swallowed a solution of ground deer-antlers to improve his performance in bed. He believed that the Daoist love-making technique would also help – this involved physical penetration short of ejaculation, the idea being that it enhanced his virility. He kept fit by swimming every day. With characteristic one-upmanship he held poolside talks with Khrushchëv in Beijing in 1958 because the Soviet leader could not swim and had to wear a rubber ring.[11] In 1965 a doctored photo appeared in the press with Mao at the age of seventy-two swimming nine miles in sixty-five minutes in the

Yangtze river. In fact his physical prowess was already in decline. When doing a bit of digging in his campaign to get everyone to engage in manual labour, he had to give up with the sweat dripping off him. He spent most days lounging about in a bathrobe and wore the famous Mao tunic only for public appearances. He frequently relapsed into mental passivity and by the early 1970s was to suffer from a form of motor neurone disease.[12]

Since the Long March, however, Mao had outmatched every party leader in authority. His fickleness in the matter of promotions and demotions put a strain on everybody's nerves. On policy he was no less flighty. Radicalism and anti-radicalism succeeded each other with confusing rapidity. The other leaders were so buffeted that they had no time to think about trying to replace Mao. If they pondered on his career, they would have known that his instincts lay with radical politics. He wanted results and wanted them fast. Yet it was always hard to know what he was up to. Mao was master of the opaque phrase. If a policy went wrong, he distanced himself from responsibility. Whenever he changed strategy or tactics, the book could always provide an aphorism in support.

In 1961, however, Liu Shaoqi resumed the criticism of the Great Leap Forward. It was no longer possible to ignore the social and material damage. Although Mao himself was spared any rebuke, everyone in the Politburo knew who was in Liu's mind when he exposed the inanities of the campaign. Other leaders too were willing to urge a change of policy. Among them was Deng Xiaoping, who sought to restrain Mao's fanaticism. Zhou Enlai, a more sinewy figure at the court of Mao, was also reputed to have had doubts about the Great Leap Forward. Mao anyway retreated. Publicly the Great Leap Forward continued to be celebrated and the Mao cult was undiminished. And although Liu had offered a challenge behind closed doors, Mao marked him down for elimination along with all his known supporters.[13] The intention was to shake up the entire ruling group at the central and local levels. Mao had resolved upon a purge of political and cultural elites. The lesson he had learned from the Great Leap Forward was not that he needed to moderate his revolutionary zeal but that he had to rid himself and the state of those who resisted his call for greater audacity. At the same time he would reassert his personal supremacy.

Mao laid the basis in 1963 by entrusting Lin Biao with editing *Quotations from Chairman Mao Zedong* – the 'little red book' of his sayings – which was published in hundreds of millions of copies. Then, in summer 1964, Mao formed a Cultural Revolution Group under Peng Zhen to lead the campaign against those writers, lecturers and teachers who failed to accept the party's doctrines. Liu Shaoqi and Deng Xiaoping ignored the warning signs. Worse than that, they behaved brusquely towards Mao. At a Central Committee conference Liu interrupted Mao's speech with comments of his own. This was an act of *lèse-majesté*. It came after Deng had said there was no need for Mao to attend the conference unless he really wanted. Liu and Deng also advocated the re-introduction of material incentives in workplaces. This put the country's economic strategy on the agenda. Mao was cornered. 'Do I', he asked mock-plaintively, 'have any rights at all?'[14] The result was victory for Mao and the defeat of his rivals.

For the next two years he oiled the machinery of radicalism, assembling the leaders to operate it. One of them was his wife Jiang Qing. Others were Lin Biao – the Minister of Defence – and Chen Boda. Mao aimed to bring the intelligentsia to heel, reactivate mass revolutionary participation and humble the 'capitalist roaders' in the leadership. Liu and Deng were compelled to conduct self-criticism. On 31 May 1966 he instructed his follower Chen Boda to take over the *Renmin Ribao* ('People's Daily') newspaper without giving due notice to Liu. The next day's editorial was headed: 'Sweep Away All the Monsters and Ghosts'.[15] Workers could go on strike and be praised for it.[16] Students were encouraged to form groups known as Red Guards and the usual work-team tutelage over them was withdrawn. This meant that, for the first time since 1949, independent bodies were allowed to function in the Chinese public arena. The call was made in August to eradicate the so-called Four Olds. These were old ideas, old culture, old customs and old habits. The Red Guards were cheered on by Jiang Qing and Chen Boda. Mao then went further by legalising the free formation of workers' organisations. The combined élan of students and labourers, he believed, would enable him to crush any obstruction by communist party veterans, the professional elites and surviving supporters of the pre-communist order.

Mao even encouraged spontaneous activity against party and government cadres. On 1 August 1966 he wrote to the Red Guards at a Beijing school:

> Your activities show resentment to and condemnation of the landlord class, the bourgeoisie, the imperialists, the revisionists and their running dogs, who exploited and suppressed the workers,

peasants, revolutionary intellectuals and other revolutionary groups.
They also reflect justification for rebellion against the reactionaries.
I express my warmest support to you.[17]

The communist order which he had established was about to come
under attack with his full approval and at his connivance. But he himself
was to remain sacrosanct[18] – and the memory of the retaliation after the
Hundred Flowers Campaign left no one in any doubt that it would be
dangerous to offer the mildest criticism of him.

The purpose was to shake up institutions and attitudes throughout
the country. Mao and his underlings wanted a complete break with the
recent and distant past. Long experience had taught them that Chinese
popular beliefs were very tenacious. China's culture and its impregnation
with Confucian philosophy had lasted many centuries, and Maoists were
determined to dig it out of the minds of their contemporaries. Poetry,
history books and works of art from the Imperial dynasties were to be
destroyed. Just as important to Mao was his campaign to sever the
enduring allegiances of people to their extended family, their networks
of social deference and their village mentality. The informal linkages
between patron and client were also to be smashed. While expressing a
willingness for Red Guards to act on their own initiative, the ruling
group around Mao were pushing activity in this planned direction.
Students were encouraged to denounce their bosses, professors and even
parents. Like every communist leadership elsewhere, Mao and his close
supporters had discovered that their instant success in establishing a
regime was not matched by a rapid transformation in attitudes. They
had not been able to make institutions work entirely to instructions. The
party had been infiltrated with careerists, and many older communist
officials were failing to display the desired co-operation.

Mao wanted to replace – or at least to examine the activity of – post-
holders at every level. This involved action at the top as Liu Shaoqi and
Deng Xiaoping were pushed aside and Lin Biao gained preference. The
'masses' were to take hold of their own revolution. There was a menacing
comicality to events. Nien Cheng was a former employee of the Shell Oil
Company (whose offices had been closed after the communist seizure of
power). As such she had every reason to fear developments. Students
marched up and down the streets of Shanghai with drums and gongs
and shouting slogans.[19] Sofas were condemned as bourgeois. Red Guards
in the city even debated whether to change the traffic lights so that red
would be the signal for go instead of green. The city's traffic lights were

put out of action until, to general relief, the proposal was dropped. Nevertheless there was plenty of dottiness still about. Cyclists were bullied into taping pages of Mao's 'little red book' on to their handlebars. So many shops were renamed 'The East is Red' and filled with the same pictures of Mao that, together with the renaming of streets, urban inhabitants became disoriented.

Nien Cheng herself was shocked, on her way home, to see a poster denouncing her neighbour as a 'running dog of Swiss imperialism'. His crime was to have been employed as a manager at a defunct aluminium factory owned by a company based in Switzerland.[20]

When the Red Guards came for her, she was drinking coffee. A pretty student asked with obvious revulsion: 'What is this?' Nien Cheng replied that it was coffee. But this only provoked the question: 'What is coffee?' Nothing would stop the Red Guards in their campaign against every sign of middle-class and foreign influences. In the end one of them railed at her:

Why do you have to drink a foreign beverage? Why do you have to drink foreign food? Why do you have so many foreign books? Why are you so foreign altogether? In every room of this house there are imported things, but there's not a single portrait of our beloved Great Leader. We have been to many homes of the capitalist class. Your house is the worst of all, the most reactionary of all.[21]

Nien Cheng remembered smiling at this outburst. This was a perilous reaction when at that very moment the Red Guards were ransacking the house. Worse was to follow. She was put under house arrest while her daughter, an aspiring film actress, was confined to a shed at her studios while she wrote endless 'confessions' and promised to learn Mao Zedong Thought inside out. After a brief public denunciation Nien Cheng was transferred to the No.1 Detention House. Months of interrogation followed, but this was an extraordinary woman who refused to confess to imaginary crimes. Nothing broke her in six and a half years of solitary confinement. She was released only in March 1973.[22]

The apparatus of control was highly intrusive. Detainees had to study Mao Zedong Thought; other inmates were intimidated into persuading any of their fellows who might be holding out to do the same. It was not enough to work and serve out their sentence. Recalcitrance could be met with beatings, even execution. (Nien Cheng was lucky at least in this respect.) The assumption was that if you had been arrested, you must be guilty and must therefore confess to your crime and reform your thought.[23] To protest your innocence only confirmed your depravity and earned more severe punishment. Not even Kafka was tormented by such a nightmarish cycle of 'logic'.

The state reverted to capital punishment in the Cultural Revolution. Red Guards sometimes put victims on trial in the street after leading them in chains through the city. In extreme cases a defendant would be forced to confess before kneeling down and receiving a bullet in the back of the head. It was widespread practice for the families of the deceased to be sent a bill for the price of the bullet.[24] Perhaps a million people died by execution or by their own hand.[25] These gruesome rituals had a purpose. They were designed to make the maximum number of people complicit in the butchery and compliant with the policies of the authorities. Mao had no intention of doing things on the sly as Stalin had usually done. He wanted a society of active participants in the terror. According to one estimate, up to a million of the victims of the Red Guards were thrown into the prisons, the *laogai* or the reform-by-labour centres;[26] but the true number may have been much higher. Moreover, the families of victims were discriminated against. Even people who were neither killed nor arrested could suffer in various ways. Some were dispatched for re-education by means of menial labour. Others were simply demoted. Psychological trauma was a pervasive phenomenon across the country.

The five 'black' categories – landlords, rich peasants, bad elements, counter-revolutionaries and rightists – were again applied to people. Having been labelled, they were stuck with the designation. And if those doing the labelling were wondering how to discredit somebody they could also brandish the vague and menacing 'bad element'. Not that they were concerned about words. They accused people of being counter-revolutionaries and rightists who had nothing to do with either Chiang Kai-shek or Liu Shaoqi. Mao had sowed the seeds of destruction; the country reaped the whirlwind. There were plenty of volunteers to do Mao's dirty business. Some were naive youngsters who were taken in by the Mao cult and the 'little red book'. But, as the Cultural Revolution became wilder, many students who carried the burden of 'bad' personal labels had an interest in proving their radicalism. So did delinquents. Thus the Workers' Headquarters in Wuhan seemingly was staffed exclusively by individuals who had recently fallen foul of the authorities. Youths with 'good' labels and parents in official posts tended to oppose the new radicals. The result was that the Red Guards split into two factions, and cities became the ground for often physical conflict between them.[27]

At the centre, Mao totally regained control over his leading comrades. Liu Shaoqi was declared the 'First Biggest Capitalist Roader', Deng the 'Second'. Liu suffered a savage beating by Red Guards and died exhausted and demoralised in the following year.[28] Deng was sent off into provincial obscurity. Zhou Enlai escaped punishment by backing the Cultural Revolution. About 20,000 alleged supporters of Liu were purged between 1966 and 1968. Further millions of officials in party and government suffered likewise.[29] Arbitrariness pervaded the entire process. As in the Great Terror in the USSR, the purgers made decisions out of self-interest. Mao, having started the process, could not regulate how it affected most individuals.

It became clear to Mao that a continuation of the Cultural Revolution threatened to undermine the communists' grip on power in the country, and he called a halt to the hysteria before the start of 1969. Things calmed down and Mao and the leading group he had assembled were unchallenged in authority. The group itself, however, had internal tensions. The troops of the People's Liberation Army under Lin Biao had loyally backed the Red Guards in 1966–8 and just as reliably restrained the Red Guards when Mao ordered the change of policy. Mao recognised Lin Biao as his desired successor by a formal amendment to the constitution. But mutual suspicion grew. Lin wanted greater power and Mao refused to give it to him. Perhaps Lin also wanted a greater share of the budget for the armed forces. Possibly he disliked the early moves in foreign policy towards a rapprochement with the USA. By 1971 there was a growing breakdown in the relationship of the two leaders. Lin fumbled his way towards a *coup d'état*. In September he tried to strike, but Mao was too nimble for him and Lin anyway had failed to organise his military sympathisers properly. Lin fled by plane to the USSR but his plane crashed before he crossed the frontier.

Political radicalism was slackened, especially after the Sino-American rapprochement. A visible political calm was necessary. Mao turned back to Zhou Enlai and the other moderate figures in the leadership. Deng was rehabilitated in stages from April 1973. Younger newcomers, including Hua Guofeng from Hunan, were also introduced to the leadership; these had risen to prominence in the Cultural Revolution but were not devoted to its resumption.[30] Zhou, however, had advanced cancer; and while he declined in hospital, it was Deng who took the attack to Jiang Qing in the Politburo. Sessions were ill tempered. Using her last resource

– her marriage – she turned to Mao for support after Deng had stormed out of a Politburo meeting in October 1974. Deng had been unwise. Jiang had three notable allies in the leadership – Zhang Chunqiao, Yao Wenyuan and Wang Hongwen – and together they formed what became known as the Gang of Four. Wang sped to tell Mao about Deng's exodus and to denounce his policies and personal ambition.[31] Deng, though, did not let up. In September 1975 he gave a 'Report on Several Problems about Scientific and Technological Work' urging the need to prioritise a professional approach to economic construction and to confront the dogmatic leaders who had 'inherited Lin Biao's mantle'.[32]

This was a counter-attack against the Gang of Four and their allies. If popular opinion had been decisive, Deng would have had no worries. Most Chinese hated what had happened during the Great Leap Forward and the Cultural Revolution. A gauge of feelings was provided when Zhou Enlai died in January 1976 after his long illness. The leadership sought to downplay the funeral ceremony; but Zhou was widely cherished as someone who had tried to moderate the excesses of policy. He had never openly opposed the official line and had always yielded to Mao in private; but people sensed where his true preferences lay and appreciated him for doing whatever he could to improve conditions for ordinary Chinese. Troops broke up the impromptu mourning by two million people on Tiananmen Square in the weeks after the funeral. Riots took place. Jiang Qing and leading radicals told Mao that Deng's 'rightists' were responsible. Mao yet again purged Deng, who had been in trouble for some months.[33] But he refrained from appointing a Gang of Four member to replace him. Instead he selected Hua Guofeng, who was not eager for the responsibility. But Mao insisted: 'With you in charge I am at ease.' He was recognising that his time was nearly up. Hua was his chosen heir.

While moving against Deng, Mao hedged his bets by restraining the Gang of Four as well as by keeping Deng alive. He sent letters to his wife upbraiding her for speaking intemperately and acting so ambitiously. Jiang Qing was unrepentant: 'Seventy-five per cent of the old cadres inevitably follow the capitalist road!' Zhou was accused of leading this renegade tendency. Deng too was subjected to continuous criticism; Jiang obviously feared that his removal from power might prove only temporary. Her supporters outside Beijing were not afraid even to take side-swipes at Hua Guofeng.[34]

Mao himself no longer attended meetings but let his opinions be known in conversations and memoranda. He had stopped intervening in the making of policy. He ruled by controlling, right to the end, the decisions on the appointment of leading personnel. Mao had been like a great pendulum of the Chinese Revolution since the 1950s. By swinging from side to side in strategy, he showed that he knew how to hold on to power and pull up short of destroying the state order. But he had run out of ideas about how to advance the revolutionary cause in China. Maoism was a helpful way to win peasant support and make a revolutionary war. It could unify and energise a whole people by fundamental social and economic reforms. But it was a poor way to industrialise a country. It involved horrendous suffering even in its quieter periods. Its ruptures with the Soviet historical experience included both advantages and disadvantages for citizens of the People's Republic of China. But it shared many basic concepts, practices and structures with the USSR. Maoism was a variant of Marxism-Leninism. Its bankruptcy was evident to most Chinese long before Mao died.

29. REVOLUTIONARY CUBA

The revolution by Cuban guerrillas in January 1959 took communism to power in Latin America for the first time. They had started two years beforehand as a scratch force with nothing like the battlefield experience of Mao's People's Liberation Army a decade earlier. Their leader was thirty-two-year-old Fidel Castro Ruz. He was bearded and athletic and his military success took the world by surprise. Castro had been a superlative sportsman at school and a brilliant law student at the University of Havana, and had given no hint of a communist allegiance. Born to comfort and privilege, he was marked down by his Catholic teachers as a person of exceptional promise and piety. By late adolescence, however, he had lost his religious faith, and his disgust with conditions in his country turned his thoughts towards rebellion.

A military coup had brought back Fulgencio Batista, a former army sergeant, to the presidency in March 1952. Corruption was systemic and Batista its greatest beneficiary. In the Second World War he had formed a coalition which implemented some social-democratic policies; he had even brought communists into his cabinet. But power and money were his priority. By the 1950s, he was an American puppet, stashing away all the dollars he could grab while deftly suppressing the successive conspiracies against him. The Americans already had a military base at Guantánamo on the south-east coast of the island; they had established it after intervening in the Cuban war of independence against the Spanish in 1903, agreeing two thousand dollars annually for the privilege of the lease. Cuba was a source of imported sugar, rum, cigars and professional sportsmen for the USA. Rich businessmen and richer gangsters could come to Havana for casinos, whores and offshore banking facilities. The Cubans, especially the descendants of the African slaves who cultivated the sugar cane, paid a heavy price. Poverty was rife. The Catholic hierarchy had little concern for social justice. Gun crime was rampant. Educational attainment, except among the wealthy minority, was pitiful.

Batista was almost asking to be toppled. Among those plotting against him were radicals who belonged to the Orthodox Party. Castro, who was close to them, believed that a violent coup by small armed band was all that was required. In July 1953 he had led an attack on the Moncada barracks near Santiago de Cuba. It was a bungled mission of amateurs. Batista's troops shot down dozens of them, but Castro was fortunate in only being thrown into jail; in the ensuing court case he gave an exuberant speech of defiance: 'History will absolve me!'[1] Released in one of Batista's amnesties, he fled abroad seeking funds for another attempt.

In December 1956 he led his band of eighty-one insurgents on the perilous voyage back from Tuxpan in Mexico. They travelled in a dangerously over-laden cabin-cruiser, the quaintly named *Granma*, and landed at Playa de los Colorados. Batista's troops killed most of them in the first few days. Castro and leading supporters such as Che Guevara escaped to the Sierra Maestra in the south of the island while sympathisers such as Frank País fomented rebellion in the cities. Castro attracted recruits and acquired equipment and then advanced down the mountains. Support for Batista slipped away as the guerrilla forces, insisting on treating the rural inhabitants decently, gained popularity. The insurgents were a motley body of men. A few were communist sympathisers, including Castro's brother Raúl, but Fidel himself denied having any such allegiance.[2] His programme was distinctly vague: a cleansed system of justice, land reform, educational advance, democracy and an end to corruption. American officials thought they could live with this. Reformers had appeared in the past. They always came to an accommodation with existing national and foreign interest groups. Washington quietly cut the cord of assistance to Batista, who flew from the island on New Year's Day 1959.

Castro arranged a stately progress by limousine to the capital. He took obvious pleasure in the acclaim of the roadside crowds over the next few days.[3] He seemed to epitomise the carefree Latin American. He dressed casually; he washed infrequently and not very efficiently. He chased beautiful women. He turned up late to meetings, including those of his own cabinet. Whenever he was at the wheel of his Plymouth limousine, he scared the daylights out of his passengers.[4]

In fact he was calculating and inscrutable. At the beginning he seemed intent on getting rid of all communists. He said to his Finance Minister that he intended to 'do away with them with a sweep of my hat'; he told others that he was against class struggle and dictatorship.[5] His programme was disclosed gradually as he tested out his ideas against reality. He wanted to change the tax laws and root out corruption. He aimed at an agrarian reform which would give twenty-seven hectares to each peasant household while retaining the large sugar plantations. He wanted to modernise the economy. His 'maestro', he stated, was the nineteenth-century Cuban nationalist rebel José Martí; he said nothing about Marx, Engels or Lenin.[6] He avoided anti-imperialist discourse, and when he travelled to Washington in March 1959 he had expectations of economic aid.[7] He assumed that his refusal to call himself a communist would see him through. He failed to take into account the impact he made. He was calling his revolution the first in the countries of 'our America'. This was scant reassurance to President Eisenhower, who shared the conventional Yankee idea that the USA should dominate the politics of the Americas. American financial assistance was not forthcoming.

An angry Castro adopted an anti-American posture. His mood had not been lightened by the sporadic attempts at counter-revolutionary risings supported from abroad.[8] He was determined that his radical regime would not be blown away by military action conducted or sponsored by Washington. Thus it came about that a failure of mutual accommodation produced the first communist state in the history of the Americas. Washington was flabbergasted. Previously it had seen many communists where few had existed. Suddenly and without warning a real and growing communist challenge existed a few score miles from Florida. When Castro returned to the USA to address the United Nations General Assembly in 1960, he was fêted by crowds chanting: 'Fidel! Fidel! Fidel!' He declined to stay in a sumptuous Manhattan hotel and decamped to Harlem. At a time when Blacks still suffered legal discrimination this was a snub and a challenge to the White House. Castro went on the offensive at the United Nations General Assembly, calling President Kennedy 'an illiterate and ignorant millionaire'. He criticised the USA's past actions in Puerto Rico, Panama and Honduras. He castigated the Americans for holding on to their military base at Guantánamo Bay despite its having been acquired through duress. Castro compared the USSR favourably with the USA for not having colonies.[9]

Back in Havana he toughened his regime. Already the Prime Minister, he encouraged the informal title of *el Máximo Líder* while disclaiming any ambition to be a dictator.[10] He also took over the communist party and replaced its leading veterans. A Soviet delegation flew to Havana to investigate the situation. Castro, by then being avid for the USSR's support to countervail against the Americans, impressed on his visitors that he was a convinced Marxist-Leninist. He wined and dined them splendidly and some 'meetings' lasted nine hours.[11] Castro told Komsomol leader Sergei Pavlov that he was reading John Reed's *Ten Days that Shook the World* and noticing the similarity between the beleaguered Soviet republic in 1917–18 and the current condition of Cuba's revolutionary regime. Being a novice in international communism, he did not know that Reed's book was banned in the USSR for its favourable references to Trotski. Castro gushed: 'You know, the Cuban revolution didn't begin two years back: it began in 1917. If it hadn't been for your revolution, our revolution wouldn't have happened. So the Cuban revolution is forty-three years old!'[12] He pleaded for an invitation to the Soviet Union. He expressed a desire to go hunting with friends in Russian woods instead of addressing official gatherings. This last claim fooled no one who had heard his interminable speeches.

Castro hoped to sell Cuban sugar to the USSR at higher than the world market price. He wanted teachers and other experts to be sent to the island. He projected a steady advance after economic nationalisation and held the entrepreneurs in his sights for eventual expropriation: 'They're all parasites who live off others. But there are a lot of them, and for this reason we're not doing anything about them (and they're not touching anyone either) but we're thinking about it.'[13]

The Cuban authorities paid dearly for cocking a snook at the USA. On 16 April 1961 an armed contingent of anti-communist exiles left its CIA training camp in Guatemala and sailed for the Bay of Pigs on Cuba's northern coast. Kennedy had given his approval almost casually; he took it for granted that a modest deployment could easily suppress the revolution. Castro was surely just an irritating gnat to be swatted into oblivion. But the planning of the enterprise was sloppy and the prognosis of a spontaneous popular uprising against Castro proved wildly optimistic. Peasants living near the landing site had been well treated by the revolutionary government and were ill disposed to help the invaders. Castro's experience as an insurgent told him what to expect and how to organise an effective defence. The anti-communist fighters were defeated, captured and put on show on television. Castro made brilliant use of the media. Instead of delivering a long verbal tirade, he relied on the pitiful confessions of the detainees to make his case for him on radio and television. Although Kennedy made light of his government's involvement the world knew otherwise. The USA had been humiliated in Latin America for the first time in its history.

Castro concluded that invaders would keep on coming in strength

until they toppled him. Sceptical about Soviet talk of technological
superiority over the USA, he laughed in Mikoyan's face when told about
the USSR's industrial sophistication.[14] This was the common judgement
in Cuba. When the Soviet leadership sent 'economic specialists' to advise
them, Cubans welcomed them politely and left them to their own
devices. (This was no problem for the specialists, who treated a stay in
sunny, musical Cuba as a work-free privilege.) The Cubans knew better
than any Russian agronomist how to cultivate sugar cane.[15] They were
also aware of the lasting damage done to agriculture in the USSR by the
system put in place by Stalin. What is more, Castro had his own
priorities in social welfare. He went further than the Kremlin in establishing decent medical facilities. Doctors were trained in abundance.
Cuba's difficulties with its balance of foreign trade ruled out the import
of modern medicines; instead the emphasis was placed on preventive
healthcare. Cuba was renowned in Latin America for its success in
lengthening the life-span of its citizens.

But the Cuban Revolution needed a geopolitical ally of substance
and the only one available was the USSR. Raúl stiffened his brother's
resolve. Fidel came to understand that the price he would have to pay
for Moscow's military and economic support was the assimilation of his
revolution to the structures and practices of the Soviet comrades. Cuba,
if it was going to survive the hostility of the USA, would have to go right
down the line of communisation.

Castro swaggered his way into the Kremlin's embrace. Although he
claimed that he had always been a Marxist, he did this with a smile and
admitted to never having got further than page 370 of Marx's *Capital* –
and there must be a doubt that he even got that far.[16] Probably, though,
he had genuinely come to believe in the need to assimilate basic aspects
of the Soviet historical experience. Internal dissent would inevitably
proliferate and subversion was bound to be organised from abroad. A
system of political control was needed and the one-party edifice built in
the USSR offered a useful model which had stood the test of time. If the
dictatorship was to secure itself there also needed to be strict regulation
of the economy. The private sectors of industry and commerce contained
potential supporters of counter-revolution. There would simultaneously
need to be strict supervision over the media. The people of Cuba had to
be convinced that the government was doing good on their behalf. The
situation was prodding Castro into adopting structures, methods and
ideas developed by Marxism-Leninism since 1917. This was the first case

of communisation of a country by a leader who adopted communism after seizing power.

The regime for a while held back from the complete nationalisation of the economy; but in international relations Castro identified himself entirely with the USSR. He and Khrushchëv were as close as two coats of paint after their first talks. The missiles crisis in October 1962 had stemmed from this. After the Bay of Pigs invasion, Castro had begged Moscow for military assistance. Khrushchëv had surprised him by offering to install long-range nuclear missiles on Cuba to deter an American attack. Castro readily agreed. He allowed Soviet military experts to take charge of the building arrangements, and inadequate precautions were taken against everything being filmed by the U-2 spy planes which flew over the island daily. Castro later argued that the experts should have pretended to construct a vast poultry shed.[17] Alerted by his intelligence officials, President Kennedy broadcast the news on television on 22 October 1962. For him, the installation marked a dangerous and unacceptable extension of Soviet military power; he would not allow the cities of the south-east of the USA to fall within the range of the USSR's missiles. Khrushchëv countered that American missile bases existed in Turkey on the Soviet border. The globe was suddenly poised at the edge of an abyss: there was a serious possibility of the Third World War.

Castro got carried away at this point and urged Khrushchëv not to back down.[18] American bluster, he argued, should be met by launching nuclear missiles aimed at the USA. Khrushchëv, by now regretting his own impetuosity, turned to his Party Presidium for permission to make concessions. The Presidium agreed. Khrushchëv told Kennedy that a missile-carrying flotilla presently approaching Cuba would be turned around. The best he could achieve was a promise from Kennedy to close down American nuclear facilities in northern Turkey; but this was qualified by the caveat that the promise should be kept secret.[19] Kennedy also guaranteed to desist from military action against Cuba. In public, though, there was only one winner: the USA. Communism, the USSR and Khrushchëv had been humiliated. Khrushchëv concluded that the Cubans might have only a breathing space of two or three years, and he felt the lash of Castro's tongue for the imbroglio.[20]

Fidel and his brother Raúl, who was his deputy in the Cuban leadership and oversaw the army and security forces, deepened the process of communisation in subsequent years. The state expropriated and collectivised the sugar plantations. The small plots belonging to peasants were transferred into the patrimony of government. The country's mines were nationalised. Shops and cafés – including those beloved by Ernest Hemingway – were taken out of private hands. Casinos were closed down. Prostitutes were driven off the streets. The revolutionaries, whose leaders were conscious of being white men of educated and comfortable backgrounds, worked to end discrimination against Cuba's black population. The property of the American rich was seized. With a US economic blockade in place around the island the Cubans had nothing to lose. Conditions under Batista, bad as they had been, had been better than almost everywhere else in Latin America. It was therefore essential for Castro to demonstrate a capacity to bring about further improvement, especially for the poor. This was where the alliance with the USSR was vital. Although Ukraine's beet production could supply all the sugar needed by the Soviet consumers, Khrushchëv and Brezhnev bought up Cuban cane sugar at above world prices; they also shipped cheap Soviet oil to Cuba as to member countries of Comecom, which Cuba itself joined in 1972 to become eastern Europe's outpost across the Atlantic. Financial credits continued to be granted on generous terms.[21]

The regime's welfare policies and patriotic assertiveness gave it great initial popularity. Castro, keeping quiet about his geostrategic dependence on the Kremlin, seemed the first ruler of a truly independent Cuba. He frequently mocked the old elites. Businessmen and politicians from the Batista decades either retired into obscurity or fled into exile in Miami. The great landowning families joined them. Not even the Catholic Church put up an effective resistance to the regime. Catholicism was a peculiarly suspect denomination for being directed from the Vatican. Although Pope John XXIII had softened policy towards the world communist movement from 1958, his reforms had little impact in Cuba. The Cuban clergy naturally felt hostile to the policies of militant atheism. Castro for his part arrested priests who refused to hold their tongues about his regime. He was less hard on the indigenous religious traditions unassociated in their origins with Christianity. Chief among these was Santería, a set of beliefs and rituals brought over from Africa with the Negro slaves and developed in interaction with the indigenous peoples of the island. It was reliably reported that Castro's long-term lover Celia Sánchez influenced him to indulge these local sources of popular consolation. Otherwise, though, he completed a communist revolution.

Cuba's attractiveness on the global political left as a communist alternative to the Soviet order went into steep decline. He was Brezhnev's cheerleader in the Third World. Far from condemning the Warsaw Pact's invasion of Czechoslovakia in August 1968, Castro supported it. He performed this role in an idiosyncratic fashion by stressing that Dubček and the Prague Spring brought about geopolitical difficulties for world communism. He did not spell out the nature of these difficulties. Most remarkably he ignored the rights of small communist countries to decide their own path of development – and Cuba was one of those countries.[22] Castro faded from world attention until, in the 1975, he found an outlet for revolutionary commitment by aiding the efforts of the Popular Movement for the Liberation of Angola (MPLA). A quarter of a million Cuban troops under the command of Arnaldo Ochoa were sent across the Atlantic – and the USSR supplied arms and finance. Cuban propaganda was directed at Latin America. There was no serious attempt by Cuba to organise insurrection after the capture and killing of Che Guevara in Bolivia in 1967. Salvador Allende's communist-led government in Chile was welcomed in 1970 and Castro himself urged Chilean communists to adopt more radical policies than Allende thought prudent.

Little changed at home. The police arrested anyone who criticised Castro and the usual punishment was several years in custody. The Ministry of the Interior's three thousand officers penetrated society by means of informers. Treatment of prisoners was harsh; not for nothing did Castro refer to the machete as the symbol of the Revolution.[23] Yet practices usually stopped short of physical torture and Castro's personal sanction was required for the imposition of the death penalty.[24] Prisoners of conscience were few by the standards of many authoritarian states. There were 316 of them in mid-2006.[25] There would undoubtedly have been many more if thousands of people who detested the regime had not found refuge in Florida.

Revolutionary initiatives ceased as the regime consolidated the political and economic measures introduced since the early 1960s. Cuban families made the best of things. If they had a car, they kept it on the road long past the time when it would have been scrapped in most other countries. Food, though it was hardly plentiful, was adequate. Fruit, maize, rum and fish were available to all. Castro's housing programme was well intentioned. Shortage of funds and faulty planning, however, resulted in apartment blocks which lacked running water. The poor of the island benefited most from the revolution. Blacks in particular were helped by governmental efforts to improve conditions. Illiteracy was wiped out. Furthermore, Cuba had more doctors per capita than any other country in the Americas. Life expectancy for Cubans rose. Jobs in education, healthcare and administration were accessible to the newly trained youth. Cuban music retained its vigour; and Castro, far from suppressing it, enjoyed it being performed in bars and restaurants. Sports facilities were expanded. Cuba's runners, jumpers, boxers and basketball players won Olympic gold medals. (Some of them, though, defected when they had the chance.) The Revolution could not manage without its police and its prisons. But most members of its society were not itching for Castro's overthrow.

A sharp shock to revolutionary Cuba was to come in the 1980s. It was not to be the American bombs or the American economic blockade but reforms in the USSR which turned everything upside down. In 1983 Yuri Andropov, Soviet General Secretary, withdrew the military guarantee of the island's security. Cuba was told it had to defend itself. Gorbachëv later went a step further and warned the Cubans to prepare themselves for life without economic subsidy. As he and the Americans brought the Cold War to a close, he told the Cubans that intervention in civil wars in Africa no longer suited the USSR's purposes. Gorbachëv had also secured Castro's promise not to stir up a commotion in Latin America; he was insistent on the Cubans agreeing to keep out of El Salvador and Nicaragua: the last thing he needed was to have President Bush on the phone asking why the world communist movement was still kicking up dirt in the USA's 'backyard'.[26] At the same time, Soviet leaders gave oral assurances that the protection of Cuba was a 'sacred cause' for the USSR.[27] Castro continued to offer what he could to Moscow. If sugar was not enough, he was eager to provide medical supplies to the USSR and to welcome Chernobyl victims to Cuba. The fact that impoverished, unindustrialised Cuba could plug gaping holes in Soviet healthcare provision was an indictment of the general bankruptcy of communism in Russia.[28]

When the USSR collapsed at the end of 1991 and Boris Yeltsin took power in Russia, he ended the subsidy for Cuban sugar and stopped the shipments of cheap oil. Cuba was left on its own. Castro's first reaction was to expand central state control over the economy. This counter-reform, which led to the closure of the farmers' markets, at once lowered the popular standard of living. If he had known any foreign communist history, he might have anticipated such an outcome. Soon he recognised the error and opted for a very limited return to private enterprise.

Whereas Gorbachëv did this half eagerly, Castro did it in a sulk. But at least he brought back markets for farmers and allowed private handicrafts to be sold from stalls at the roadside. Ever more types of small-business activity were made legal. Private restaurants returned. Agricultural co-operatives supplanted the state farms and diversified cultivation away from sugar cane. Castro filled gaps in the state budget through deals with tourist firms from abroad. He signed a deal with a Canadian company to redevelop the nickel-mining industry at Moa Bay. Withdrawal of troops from Africa reduced a drain on revenues. Still blockaded by the Americans, the Cuban leaders made the minimum of alterations to the economics of communism in order to survive the effects of the transformation in the USSR.

What they refused to permit was any basic political reform. The one-party system with its censorship and security police was maintained in efficient fettle. Castro kept a tight grip on the situation. In 1989 his chief commander in Angola, Arnaldo Ochoa, was shot for having engaged in illicit commercial schemes. The rumour was that Ochoa desired a political overhaul like Gorbachëv's reforms and that his execution was really Castro's judicial murder of a potential rival. Castro maintained a posture of revolutionary defiance. He responded to the collapse of the Soviet Union with a dismissive joke:

> There are those who believed that when the others dissolved like a meringue, Cuba would do also. Perhaps it didn't occur to them that we are made from different egg-whites, from different eggs (Laughter and applause). And don't misinterpret my symbolism [eggs in Spanish idiom can refer to testicles] (Laughter): I'm referring to the egg-whites used in a meringue; but perhaps we [here in Cuba] are dealing with dragons' eggs.[29]

Cuba's revolution was not going to fall apart if Castro had anything to do with it. Gorbachëv was tossed into the mockery-box occupied in Castro's speeches by American presidents from John Kennedy to George H. Bush.

He did not flinch at explaining to his people why difficulties were growing. Castro explained to a young audience in November 1991:

> at the time when the Revolution triumphed we were using four million tons of petroleum, and a ton of sugar bought seven tons of petroleum, seven! . . . The point is that now, with the monopoly prices of petroleum and with the depressed prices of sugar on what

we call the world's dump market, to buy a ton of petroleum you
need almost a ton of sugar: you can buy 1.3 or 1.4 tons of petroleum
with a ton of sugar.[30]

However tough things were, Castro urged determination and pride. It
was not in Cuba that people lacked food, shelter, education and healthcare. Its example was a beacon to the rest of Latin America. Cubans
could still snub their noses at 'Yankee imperialism'.

Not all foreign leaders attracted disrespect. Castro discreetly sought
a softening of relations with the Americans after Bill Clinton won the
US presidential election of 1993. This had a slighter effect than the
attempt at conciliation with the Catholic Church. Cuba hosted a visit by
Pope John Paul II in 1998. Four years later Castro welcomed ex-President
Jimmy Carter. But simultaneously he screwed down the clamps on
incipient protest. Voluntary emigration remained illegal and captured
escapers were treated as enemies of the people. (This was the official line
even though remittances from exiles in the USA provided a lifeline to
the Cuban economy.) Castro in his seventies had grey hair and when he
greeted the ailing Pope John Paul II he looked more like a sprightly but
elderly aristocrat – he had changed his military fatigues for a smart dark
suit – than the athletic rebel of years gone by. Yet he refused to give
his enemies the pleasure of witnessing his disappointment. Repeatedly
and at length he expressed pride in his Revolution's achievements in
education, employment, sport and healthcare. The goal of an orderly
communist society and a smoothly functioning communist economy
had long since become unrealistic. But Cuba, as it re-entered the force-
field of world capitalism, had much to show for its decades of standing
up to the powers of the West.

Castro saw his Revolution as fitting the Marxist-Leninist perspective.
The USSR had laid the foundations and built the walls but its edifice
had collapsed, while Cuba, small, defenceless yet resolute Cuba, had
survived. He also regarded Cuban achievement as a model in its own
right for Latin America, for sub-Saharan Africa and for any other country
that might care to follow it.

But, much as he had done for the island, he had not succeeded in
building a vibrant economy and a settled social consensus. He could not
do without his brother's large security agencies and their prisons for
political dissenters. Communists could blame a lot on the long blockade
of their country by the USA, and their case was more robust than when
Soviet leaders had said the same about themselves in the 1920s. But, once

the Cuban Revolution had been directed towards a one-party, one-ideology state, an arbitrary police dictatorship and a state-owned economy – not to mention the *caudillo*-style despotism of *el Máximo Líder* – they were bound to come up against difficulties already experienced in other communist states. Castro could lock up the opposition but could not halt the popular grumbling, the political evasions and the economic rundown. His rhetoric soared above the speeches of his communist contemporaries. But the inherent logic of communism was irrefutable. Castro in old age knew he had long since lost the fundamental struggle even though he gave no sign of understanding why. His health suddenly deteriorated in summer 2006. Without him, public life in Cuba was thrown into confusion. Speculation about Cuban politics after Castro began in earnest.

30. COMMUNIST ORDER

Communist states isolated their peoples from alien influences. Walls, landmines, barbed wire, censorship and propaganda held the people of a third of the world's earth surface in quarantine from capitalism, representative democracy and civic freedom. Rulers in the USSR and the People's Republic of China initially assumed that seclusion was only temporary. They thought that the superiority of communism over capitalism would soon be evident to every well-intentioned person of sound mind and that the requirement for security precautions would disappear. There was never such an outcome. The immuring of citizens within prescribed territorial – and political and mental – borders became immutable policy wherever there was a communist revolution and a one-party state. The leaders themselves huddled behind the same walls. Albania's Enver Hoxha was unusual in being well read in the European literature classics – and Molotov thought his cosmopolitanism a reason for suspicion.[1] But Hoxha was a conventional communist dictator in denying his people access to disapproved alien culture.[2]

Traditions in countries such as Russia and China had an influence on this. Travellers before the twentieth century recorded most Russians as deeply xenophobic, and China's emperors, officials and people had always been inclined to regard the rest of the world with both condescension and suspicion. Yet such attitudes hardly explain by themselves why Russian and Chinese Marxists, espousing a secular ideology of Western origin, came to distrust spontaneous popular interactions with the West. Marx and Engels were proud cosmopolitans. If Lenin admired any particular people in the world, it was not the Russians but the Germans. What is more, several communist countries had a history of welcoming foreign contacts over many centuries. Czechoslovaks and Hungarians longed for admission to the community of nations after its people had been liberated from the empire of the Habsburgs in 1918–19 and subsequently from the Third Reich. Cubans were eager for better access to world trade and culture. The people of that small island flourished whenever they could make contact with friendly foreigners – it was Cuba's openness to influences from abroad that had attracted the American author Ernest Hemingway and persuaded him to take up residence almost until he died in 1961.

So why did communist rule in so many cases carry the same basic features as it emerged from its various periods of national gestation? Doubtless deliberate imitation was at work. The USSR had elaborated the model, which was widely regarded as a highly effective one. Other countries predictably copied it to a greater or lesser extent. In eastern Europe no alternative was permitted. But objective pressures of rulership were also pushing developments in this direction. Most communist states found it difficult to consolidate their rule without introducing a quarantine regime. All had citizens who resented their political, social, cultural and religious policies, and there would inevitably be some attempt to seek support from sympathetic organisations abroad. People in general would seek to know for themselves what was going on elsewhere. Whenever they found that aspects of life were better outside the communist countries they would become frustrated with an economic order that repeatedly failed to fulfil its promises.

No wonder Marxist-Leninist rulers disliked their citizens coming into unsupervised contact with foreigners from 'capitalist and developing countries'. Many rulers were agitated even about interaction with people from other communist states. The authorities in China were so suspicious of the USSR that they deported Russian emigrants who had fled the USSR in the 1920s. Leaders of Soviet republics in the west of the USSR regarded visitors from eastern Europe with suspicion in the months during and after the Hungarian Revolt of 1956 and the Prague Spring of 1968.[3] During the long emergency caused by outbreaks of popular unrest in Poland in 1970 and again from 1980 the Kremlin often lowered the quotas of Polish holidaymakers to the USSR. The worry was that the rebellious bacillus of the Gdańsk shipyards or the churches of Kraków might infect the minds of Soviet citizens. The Soviet Politburo continually gauged the level of discontent among workers of the USSR while the KGB warned of the murmurings against the authorities.[4] If the ideas of Solidarity were imported, there could be trouble on the streets of Moscow and Leningrad. Such worries were not confined to the USSR or to the 1970s and 1980s. Hostility between Hungary and Romania since the 1960s had led both governments to restrict movement across their common frontier except on official business. Nicolae Ceaușescu systematically persecuted the Hungarian minority in Transylvania. The last thing he wanted was a regular tourist exchange with communist Hungary.

Soviet citizens going abroad were issued with confidential instructions from the Central Committee Secretariat about their behaviour. There were fourteen Basic Rules. Travellers were to serve as bearers of the communist message. They were to travel in a designated group with its appointed leader. They had to show spirit in defending Soviet internal and external policies. They were to exercise unceasing vigilance since foreign intelligence agencies would pounce on any weakness. Relations with people in capitalist countries were to be restricted to official business. No personal documents were to be taken out of the USSR. On arrival in a foreign country, Soviet citizens were to present themselves at their nearest embassy or consulate. No paid private work should be undertaken abroad. No valuable gifts should be accepted. No debts should be run up. It was 'not recommended' to take an overnight train journey with a foreigner of the opposite sex. (Nothing needed to be said about homosexuals since same-sex relationships were punishable under Soviet law.) Hotel rooms were to be kept spotless. Trips around the country required the sanction of the appointed group leader. Any official taking relatives to a foreign country was to ensure that they did not pry into his or her business.[5]

Travellers had to write up their reports within a fortnight of returning home and to provide information of benefit to the Motherland. But what could they tell? By limiting the freedom of their citizens to mingle with foreigners, the average communist regime deprived itself of the full potential of economic, scientific and cultural intercourse. The truth is that the regimes were anyway averse to finding out what they did not want to know about the West. Ignorance for them was a complacent pleasure.

Only trusted citizens, of course, were allowed abroad – and trust was enjoyed by mere dozens of people in the extreme case of North Korea. Even in the Soviet Union it was a definite privilege for anyone to take a summer vacation in other countries, including those of eastern Europe. Frontiers were strictly patrolled, especially those abutting capitalist countries. Thousands of refugees fled the German Democratic Republic. After controls at the checkpoints between the eastern and western sectors in Berlin were tightened, people swam across the canals or hid themselves in car boots in order to leave East Berlin. Some sprinted through customs posts under a hail of bullets. Steadily the methods of illegal departure became more refined, as Hermann Borchert of the West Berlin fire service recalled: 'It became the custom that people who wanted to escape ... would throw little pieces of paper out of [their] windows [across the sector frontier] into Bernauer Strasse. The number of the building, the floor, the window – second or third window – was written on it, and the time, ten o'clock for example, that they wanted to jump.' It was the duty of the firemen to position themselves so as to catch the refugees on fire-fighting blankets when they leaped down.[6]

Rescues remained possible because the demarcation line between the sectors ran down the middle of Bernauer Strasse. Party leader Walter Ulbricht thought Khrushchëv was showing 'unnecessary tolerance' of the West;[7] he asked him to send him people from the USSR as a replacement for the German refugees. Khrushchëv gruffly replied: 'Imagine how a Soviet worker would feel. He won the war and now he has to clean your toilets.'[8] The constant tension led Khrushchëv to sanction Ulbricht's request to build a wall between the eastern and western sectors of Berlin in August 1961. The Soviet ambassador reported: 'We have a yes from Moscow.'[9] Since the USSR barricaded itself from foreign countries, Khrushchëv had decided that Ulbricht could not be refused his request. Despite the adverse publicity, the preliminary work was accomplished late at night on 12 August 1961. Berliners awoke next day to find a six-foot-high barbed-wire fence between East and West Berlin. Soon it was turned into a brick wall. Buildings were knocked down to clear the ground near by. Watchtowers were erected at distances suitable for marksmen to shoot down refugees who dashed across the strip towards the wall. Such measures stemmed the haemorrhage of people from East to West. The exodus of doctors, teachers and scientists was halted and East Germany became a walled garden of communist development. The political price was huge. If East Germany was paradise and West Germany was hell, why did people want to flee the heavenly conditions?

Escape attempts went on happening despite the hazards. There were youths who trained at pole-vaulting and tried to get over the wall without ladders. Ingenious tunnels were dug. Over two hundred fugitives, however, were killed before the Berlin Wall was pulled down. Equal peril faced those who sought to flee Cuba after its revolution. Sometimes whole families got into inflatable rubber dinghies and paddled across the Straits of Florida to the USA. The trip was arduous because of storms, sharks and the heat of the sun. Hundreds drowned or were taken into custody by Cuban forces.

No communist state, furthermore, lasted for long without a network of prisons and labour camps for political dissenters. Backbreaking and mind-numbing work was assigned to convicts and brutal punishments were meted out. Confidential informers were used to tell the authorities about who was criticising the state order. It is reckoned, for example, that one in 120 citizens of the German Democratic Republic in the 1970s performed this function for the state. An informer had to be thought 'an honourable, sincere and friendly person'.[10] They were seldom paid for their work; but preferential treatment was often enough to get people to agree to do it. Their victims no longer automatically ended up in jail. When he was KGB chief Yuri Andropov led the way in treating young critics as misguided delinquents. His officers visited their parents and delivered a warning that their sons or daughters would be arrested if their behaviour did not change. Adults might still escape incarceration but be placed in psychiatric wards. The People's Republic of China too adopted this technique for some prominent dissenters. Political opposition was treated as a form of madness, and victims were subjected to cocktails of dangerous anti-psychotic drugs. This was torture as bad as anything endured in the camps.[11]

Preventive censorship anyhow restricted access to undesirable ideas. Maoist Red Guards in the Cultural Revolution burned priceless old copies of the Chinese classics. The Soviet leaders retained a vestigial respect for the importance of 'world literature' as well as the Russian literary canon, and after Stalin's death they published copious translations of contemporary Western fiction – or at least those works thought to be either left-wing in orientation or apolitical and unsalacious. John Steinbeck, Graham Greene and Ernest Hemingway came into the first category while Agatha Christie and Professor C. Northcote Parkinson were placed in the second. (How did Rudyard Kipling wriggle through the sieve? Perhaps his reputation as a jingoist imperialist was thought undeserved. But Christie? Were the censors fooled or were they themselves mildly subversive?) Films were selected on the same basis. Vittorio de Sica's *Ladri di Biciclette* ('Bicycle Thieves') and the French science-fiction hero Fantomas were favourites in the 1960s. Readers in fact interpreted these writers in ways unanticipated by the censors. Hemingway, for instance, was loved less for his exposure of capitalistic corruption than for his celebration of wine, women and song.

Albania pushed the door further ajar. This was a country justifiably notorious for having the most hermetically sealed society in Europe. Yet its leader Enver Hoxha persuaded himself that the films of British comedian Norman Wisdom offered a deep critique of capitalism. Wisdom certainly spotlighted unfairness in society in his role as the sweet-natured Mr Pitkin struggling to survive in a snobbish society. Albanian audiences loved his work for its slapstick jollity – as well as for the glimpses it gave of well-dressed, well-fed people – rather than for the supposed ideology. (Wisdom's popularity outlasted communism and he was awarded the freedom of the city of Tirana in 1995.) Hoxha's predilection for British comedy was nevertheless an aberration from his norms of rulership. And all across Europe east of the River Elbe there was a cultural sanctimoniousness that bored spectators and listeners rigid. The unsmiling faces of TV presenters set the tone. The endless news programmes which claimed that communism was advancing ever upwards to a glorious future were made bearable only by the latest sports results – and of course the east Europeans adored it if any of their teams or individual athletes worsted their competition from the USSR.

It was hardly surprising that Moscow and Beijing continued to regard the Western media as a pernicious influence. Soviet radio jamming was fierce and the expertise for this facility was requested by communist leaderships in eastern Europe.[12] Voice of America, the BBC, Radio Liberty and Radio Free Europe could not be heard there for many years. Radio sets were redesigned so as to exclude the possibility of listening to undesirable short-wave frequencies.[13] Under Brezhnev, though, the jamming was suspended in the years when the USSR pursued détente with the USA. Once the Soviet television industry got under way, indeed, Estonian viewers could pick up Finnish television (which carried a lot of American and British shows in English); and, despite being chided by Erich Honecker, millions of East Germans tuned into West Germany's TV programmes. Honecker benefited economically too much from calmed relations with Bonn to disrupt the transmissions. These were breaks in the general pattern. Most citizens of communist countries were kept in ignorance about what was happening abroad except through officially approved sources.

Yet Western trends continued to seep into communist countries like a refreshing liquid. Dissenters such as Václav Havel in Czechoslovakia listened to smuggled records of the Beatles, the Rolling Stones and the Mothers of Invention. Cultural rebelliousness was alive among youngsters who wanted to taste the forbidden fruit of the West. The American and European male fashion for long hair crossed frontiers in the 1970s. Albania stood out against this. The country's few foreign tourists were inspected at the border and men were given a close trim if the length of their locks was judged improper. A close trim in Tirana was closer than anywhere in the world except for prisons. A British academic who journeyed with a tourist group that included most members of the Marxist-Leninist Party of the Faroe Islands took the precaution of having a short back-and-sides in London before departure. This failed to make him welcome at Tirana airport, where he was separated from his Faroese companions and clipped again like a straying sheep. Hoxha was determined to prevent cultural contamination.[14] Scissors were a weapon of choice against those who would defile Albanian Maoist propriety.[14]

Official distaste for rock music served only to make it more popular. Even in China the same trend was taking hold, albeit against greater obstacles. Marxist-Leninist ideology had ever fewer true believers. Mao Zedong had been able to carry through his Cultural Revolution because he could count on hundreds millions of naive peasants or poorly informed urban inhabitants to do his bidding; he had also exploited the deep feelings of social resentment. But more and more people became less gullible. The inhabitants of Chinese coastal cities knew enough about entertainment abroad to want to possess copies of its vinyl records or cassette tapes.

Unknowingly the authorities in every communist state had turned themselves into pompous, po-faced conservators of Marxist-Leninist propriety. Even in Cuba, whose popular culture was not excessively restricted, citizens had to avoid making jokes about the Castro brothers and Che Guevara. When saying something risqué about Fidel, the safe practice was to mime a beard with one's hand instead of mentioning his name. Communism could not laugh at itself – a damning indictment of its lack of basic self-confidence. The exceptions were communists who lived outside the communist states. A British communist parody of the Gilbert and Sullivan song 'I Am the Very Model of a Modern Major-General' included the memorable stanza:

> I am the very model of a modern Marxist-Leninist,
> I'm anti-war and anti-God, and very anti-feminist;
> My thinking's dialectical, my wisdom undebatable,
> When I negate negations, they're undoubtedly negatable.
> And yet I'm no ascetic – I am always full of bonhomie
> When lecturing to classes on the primitive economy;
> And comrades all agree that they have never heard a smarter cuss
> Explain the basic reasons for the slave revolt of Spartacus.
> *Chorus*: Explain the basic reasons for the slave revolt of Spartacus.[15]

Such levity, even in an amateurishly duplicated magazine, was inconceivable in Prague, Hanoi or Pyongyang.

The authorities in some communist states – most notably China and

North Korea – went on much as before. Others modified the contents
of indoctrination. (The monotonous style never changed.) Marxism-
Leninism in Brezhnev's USSR ceased to claim that the Soviet order was
catching up with the material standard of living attained in the advanced
capitalist countries.[16] Perennial shortages of agricultural and industrial
goods made this no longer believable. Khrushchëv had ineptly engaged
in an impromptu debate in July 1959 with Vice-President Richard Nixon
at the US Trade and Cultural Fair in Moscow's Sokolniki Park, where
they disputed the rival merits of the American and Soviet ways of life.
The two men stopped outside an exhibit of a kitchen built in the USA,
and Nixon praised a washing-machine as a labour-saving device; he had
earlier cooed over a colour TV set. Khrushchëv on live radio replied:
'Many things you've shown us are interesting but they are not needed in
life. They have no useful purpose. They are merely gadgets. We have a
saying: if you have bedbugs you have to catch one and pour boiling
water into its ear.' Thus he expressed his total indifference to the
drudgery of life of his Soviet female listeners. Nixon and Khrushchëv
could only agree in their dislike of jazz (although Nixon confided that
his daughters liked it – and of course they were free to enjoy it whereas
potential fans in the USSR were not).

If Soviet leaders needed a lesson about public opinion, it was given
in Novocherkassk in south Russia in June 1962 when angry crowds rioted
about meat price rises. Party and police functionaries were lynched
before the armed forces reimposed order. Presidium member Anastas
Mikoyan, sent to the city to parley with the crowds, returned a chastened
politician.[17] Moscow dealt bloodily with the inciters of trouble but also
increased the budget for consumer goods. Yet the supply was never
enough to satisfy demand. So the authorities concentrated on saying
that the collectivist principles of social order were morally superior to
the decadent West.[18] Soviet consumers lacked the meat, vegetables and
domestic equipment they wanted; but they were asked to take pride in
the spiritual benefits of their hardship. Communist collectivism was
rated higher than capitalist individualism and greed. Squalor, apparently,
was a virtue so long as it was communally suffered.

The leaders exempted themselves from any self-denial. The system
of privileges consolidated by Stalin in the USSR was replicated in other
communist countries. Central nomenklaturas enjoyed dachas, chauffeurs,
nannies, tutors and a varied diet. Not content to have their snouts in the
trough, they had their front trotters in there too. The only limits on the
self-indulgence of each leadership were those of its taste – and this had

never been a strong point among communism's luminaries. When US Secretary of State Henry Kissinger negotiated with Leonid Brezhnev, he was surprised by the tatty décor in the General Secretary's dacha. The Soviet dekulakisation campaign of the early 1930s had depleted the quality of available craftsmanship. Brezhnev, an ice-hockey fan, was a connoisseur more of American limousines than of the higher arts. He also had a passion for killing bears. His bodyguards were sickened by the sight of defenceless cubs being lined up for him to take pot-shots at.[19] No Soviet or Chinese citizen knew anything directly about this seamy side of things. The exceptions were the leadership's retainers – house-maids, bodyguards, chauffeurs, perhaps the gardeners – who knew better than to talk out of turn.

People engaged in double-think. Above all, they practised double-speak: there was no possibility of making a career for oneself unless formal obeisance was made to the pieties of Marxism-Leninism. They accepted official ideas, at least to a degree, in some parts of their lives while rejecting them in others. Work was one thing, family another. This is how Václav Havel was to describe the situation: 'All of us have become accustomed to the totalitarian system, accepted it as an unalterable fact and therefore kept it running ... None of us is merely a victim of it, because all of us helped to create it together.'[20] Popular collusion was the norm in all communist societies where people had lost hope of a realistic alternative and where the barrage of punitive sanctions was maintained by the authorities. The degree of opposition varied from country to country. Where the regimes had signed the Helsinki Final Act in 1975 the maltreatment of anti-communist militants was somewhat lightened, and Amnesty International and International PEN as well as Western governments sometimes secured liberation for leading figures. But Asian communism remained as repressive as ever; and many European com-munist states continued in the old ways regardless of their international legal commitments.

Organised dissent consequently gained few adherents in most countries. The security police were not the only problem. The technical facilities for disseminating ideas were few and far between. Printing presses, which the Bolsheviks had routinely acquired before 1917, were unavailable. While photocopiers were provided as a matter of course in offices in the West in the 1970s, they remained a rare and carefully restricted piece of equipment in communist states – and the same was true of PCs and email access in the following decade. In the USSR, China and eastern Europe the groups of dissenters made do with laboriously typed copies of pamphlets using carbon paper. They also recorded speeches on re-recordable cassette tapes. They transmitted their works abroad through trusted messengers.

Yet the majority of citizens put up with communism and only rarely engaged in strikes or demonstrations against their rulers. They resigned themselves to the boring monotony of life under communism. Styles of shoes, trousers and shirts were deliberately limited in number. No communist leadership allowed its factories to produce the bright clothing widely available in the capitalist parts of the world. Jeans were a black-market item. Indeed fashion was almost a dirty word. Soviet rulers nevertheless recognised the need at least to satisfy the popular demand for modern household equipment. Washing-machines and colour tele-visions, derided by Khrushchëv, were manufactured abundantly under Brezhnev. But poorer countries like China and Cuba stuck to the old Marxist-Leninist norms. Not even the wealthier communist states had a strong market in private cars. Belgrade in the mid-1960s was said to be the only communist capital with a parking problem.[21] Official reluctance to prioritise the manufacturing of vehicles for personal possession was influenced by ideology. Transport was meant to be a public undertaking. Castro asked an interviewer: 'What would happen if every Indian, every Eskimo had a car to drive?'[22] He clearly thought the question did not need an answer. He spoke in the long tradition of communism which put forward Spartan sufficiency and uniformity as the ideal for most people.[23]

An ecological case, it cannot be denied, could be made against gas-guzzling automobiles. But Soviet and east European leaders failed to make it; they had in fact come to assume that capitalist consumerism had to be emulated to a certain extent. The problem for them was the economic framework they had inherited. Communism was everywhere tied to central planning mechanisms as well as quantitative indices of success. Its leaders persistently criminalised entrepreneurial initiative, market freedom and personal profit. Until Deng Xiaoping's reforms in China from 1976 there was no fundamental challenge to such assump-tions. The conclusion is inescapable that the failure of communist countries to satisfy the material wants of their citizens was a derivative of their Soviet-style order.

Communist economic policy was anyway unconstrained by consider-ations of ecology or morality. The USSR, followed by the People's Republic of China, ravaged the natural environment in pursuit of industrial might. Without doubt, capitalism too has a terrible record in this respect. But, where liberal democracy, assertive newspapers and independent courts have existed, limitations on the destruction have often eventually been introduced. This was not the case in China where vast forests and lakes were devastated by the building of reservoirs and hydro-electric dams. Mining enterprises destroyed the landscape in countless regions. The Soviet Union too was afflicted. Deadly pollution was allowed to occur in Lake Baikal. The Aral Sea dried up. Large tracts of Kazakhstan were turned into a dustbowl by the virgin-lands campaign in agriculture. In Poland the air pollution in steel towns such as Katowice and Nowa Huta caused chronic bronchitis and asthma. The misuse of industrial chemicals turned the River Danube into a liquid poison flowing through Hungary, Romania and Bulgaria. The Black Sea became a poisonous waste, dangerous to swimmers and fatal to its fish. The imperatives of the central planners extinguished every inhibition as officials at the centre and in the localities struggled to hit their output targets.

Where fundamental reform was avoided, communist rulers sometimes turned to nationalism. Originally communism had been internationalist. Marx and Engels had hated nationalism. Lenin, despite his compromises with 'ideology' in the face of insurmountable problems, lived and died an internationalist. Communism had long since combined internationalist and nationalist purposes under Stalin, Mao, Gomułka and Ceaușescu. This certainly involved a betrayal of communism. But it did not mean a complete abandonment of communist purposes. From Stalin to Ceaușescu the ruling ethos appealed to the national spirit while holding close to several basic Marxist-Leninist ideas.

Ceaușescu vaunted Romania as the reincarnation of the Roman Empire's province of Dacia, and archaeologists searched for continuities with ancient culture. He endlessly goaded the Soviet Politburo and put himself forward as the nation's greatest ever protector. He aimed at economic autarky for Romania. This tin-pot dictator was treated as a hero in the struggle against the USSR. He received the Order of the Bath from Queen Elizabeth II on the recommendation of Labour Prime Minister James Callaghan. Liberal Party leader David Steel sent him a Labrador puppy. Nicolae's wife Elena strutted the world in her self-appointed role as a world-class chemist; and her penchant for clothes and shoes rivalled the record of Imelda Marcos in quantity and tastelessness. The Ceaușescus, man and wife, planned a luxurious life in the People's Palace which was being built in Bucharest's old quarter after twenty-six churches and seven thousand homes had been demolished.

The Pentagon in Washington is the only edifice with a larger cubic capacity. Yet while the Palace sparkled with 4,500 chandeliers, ordinary Romanians had to put up with regular cuts in electricity supply. It was modern communism with medieval appurtenances.

British ministers in 1978 were dreading the Ceauşescu family's visit to London; they were aware of the boorish behaviour to be expected. In Venezuela the Romanian President had thrown a tantrum when denied permission to hunt wild animals under a special conservation order. He had demanded a double bed even for short plane trips across country. (A Foreign Office official dryly noted that 'he did not specify the purpose of the double bed'.) Worries were expressed about Ceauşescu's son Nicu and his demand to be provided with a woman – 'purpose again unspecified'.[24] Nicolae Ceauşescu himself had tastes of spectacular vulgarity, astonishing diplomats in Bucharest by holding a reception seated on a large golden throne.

Communist rulers looked after themselves and if ever they worried about the people's welfare it was only after their own wants had been satisfied. There was a hierarchy of material conditions in the communist world. The Yugoslavs, with the closest commercial links with the West, did best in the range and quality of goods available. Next came the East Germans, followed by the Hungarians and the Poles. Citizens of the USSR trailed in after them; and, still more galling to Russian national pride, the Georgians and Estonians in the Soviet Union enjoyed better conditions than those available to the Russians. The stereotypical Georgian, in the Russian popular imagination, was a swarthy 'Oriental' who smuggled oranges in large suitcases from his collective farm to the large cities of the RSFSR. That fruit could be an item of internal contraband speaks volumes about communism's economic inefficiency. But plenty of nations were worse off than the Russians. Chinese, Albanian and Romanian societies contained millions of ordinary citizens who had to work hard for pitifully poor wages, food and social amenities. If it had not been for their instruments of control – one-party state, censorship, arbitrary police, labour camps and the comprehensive quarantining of their people – communist leaderships around the world would have fallen from power in an instant.

31. RETHINKING COMMUNISM

The reforms in the USSR after Stalin's death fertilised a regrowth in sympathy for the USSR in the West. But no sooner had this occurred than trouble arose. The invasions of Hungary in 1956 and Czechoslovakia in 1968 caused an immense outcry. Not a single TV or radio station in the West endorsed Moscow's cause and the only newspapers which condoned the Soviet invasions were those belonging to communist parties. Continuity was seen between the terror of the 1930s and the suppression of freedom in eastern Europe. Intellectuals lined up to condemn the USSR. Among them was the philosopher and novelist Jean-Paul Sartre. Refusing to tar all communist states with the same anti-Soviet brush, he found other shrines at which to worship in Castro's Cuba and in Mao's China.[1]

At times it seemed as if Castro had trouble in fending off Sartre and other visiting admirers. Mao rarely received visitors except foreign statesmen. As China's embassies supplied bookshops with cheap copies he became the world's bestselling – or best-donated – author. He never ventured abroad, not even to North Korea. Chinese and Cuban spokesmen composed fairy stories about their countries just as their communist forebears had done in the USSR under Lenin and Stalin. Sartre in his politics pushed aside the icy scepticism of his philosophy, swallowing the propaganda like a hungry child. Such news as emerged from Cuba and China – as had been true in the USSR in the 1930s – was heavily censored. China's propaganda was especially brazen in rejecting reports of famine, labour camps and popular discontent, and journalists who persisted with intrusive investigations were expelled. Visitors to the Soviet Union had to stay within twenty-five kilometres of their designated destinations unless special permission was granted. An innocent tourist taking a photograph of ships sailing up the River Neva in Leningrad was liable to arrest as a spy. While criticising Stalin, Khrushchëv reserved the right to set the limits for what could be said by others. Brezhnev continued the tradition.

Soviet rulers kept up the effort to disseminate a positive image of the country abroad. The Kremlin could boast of huge advances in space technology. In October 1957 the Americans were foiled in the race to be the first to put a satellite into orbit around the earth by the launch of Sputnik I. Soviet scientists went further in November by putting a stray dog named Laika into Sputnik II. (The unfortunate creature did not survive the experience and the technological achievement evoked some criticism.) In April 1961 Yuri Gagarin became the first man to circumnavigate the world in a space flight. Although the USA eventually overtook the Soviet programme, the early feats were widely remembered. Gagarin had the looks and affability of a film star and toured the world as his country's semi-official ambassador. He gave a human face to the communist order. Others did the same. Yevgeni Yevtushenko, an overrated poet but a larger-than-life personality and an advocate of deStalinisation, gave public readings in North America and Europe. Alexander Solzhenitsyn's novella *One Day in the Life of Ivan Denisovich* appeared in the world's main languages in 1963; its withering critique of the labour-camp system in the 1940s was taken as proof that the USSR was starting to look at its past with honest eyes. Soccer goalkeeper Lev Yashin was widely renowned. Soviet athletics teams had regular success at the Olympic games and brought glamour to the USSR.

Khrushchëv's record in promoting the advantages of the 'planned economy' was more mixed. Stupidly he restored the pseudobiologist Timofei Lysenko to respectability, and once again there was ludicrous boasting about wheat being growable on the Arctic ice. Khrushchëv promoted him avidly.[2] Nevertheless Soviet statistics were often taken at their face value; this was a period when only experts in Western intelligence agencies and universities discussed their doubts about them. The USSR seemingly had an economy second only to the USA in quantity and – at least in some sectors – quality of output. The continuing reliance of Soviet civilian industry on the purchase or theft of Western technology was barely ventilated; and American, European and Japanese firms doing business with the USSR as always refrained from advertising their commercial operations. This enabled Moscow to go on asserting that the Soviet order had overcome the cyclical problems of capitalist economics. Uninterrupted progress was predicted for the USSR. American presidents assumed that the rival superpower would not collapse in their lifetime. John Kennedy was impressed by the Sputniks. British Prime Minister Harold Macmillan worried that the USSR might indeed prove its superiority as a model of economic development.[3]

Both Khrushchëv and his successor Brezhnev asserted that communism around the world outdid the West's advanced capitalist countries in freedom and welfare. They ignored the point that elections were pointless when a single candidate from one party alone was allowed to stand in them; they glossed over the detention of political, intellectual and religious dissenters in the Gulag. But Soviet leaders were frequently thought to score better on other matters. There was no unemployment in the USSR. Citizens were guaranteed shelter, heating, fuel, schooling, public transport and healthcare at little or no cost. Tourists to the Soviet Union reported that muggings were rare and graffiti scrawls practically unknown; and neon-light advertisements were nowhere to be seen. What is more, Soviet spokesmen castigated racism, imperialism and nationalism. The USSR was a multinational state. Its spokesmen insisted that it had eliminated the iniquities of imperialism, nationalism and racism. Although the European empires dissolved themselves in the 1950s and 1960s, the former colonies continued to face difficulties of economic dependency and under-development. Soviet Azerbaijan was compared favourably with ex-British Nigeria, ex-French Algeria and ex-Dutch Malaysia.

Commentators – at least those who were not committed anti-communists – were often confused and under-informed in what they said about the communist order. Many experienced a mixture of fear, admiration and revulsion. Moreover, the desire to avoid policies which might spark off the Third World War prompted many people to try and think the best of the USSR. The resentments of the Ukrainians and Georgians against Moscow were overlooked. The shoddiness of Soviet clothes, shoes and furniture was rarely highlighted. Politicians and journalists in any case hardly ever visited the communist countries. Impressed by space flights, they seldom asked how efficiently the USSR's vast output of steel, diamonds, nickel, fertilisers and tractors was being integrated into the civilian economy. The shortcomings in the networks of roads, hospitals and shops were little known. Soviet spokesmen exploited this situation. Khrushchëv, brash and mouthy, sometimes made a fool of himself. He did this most notoriously when he banged a shoe on his desk in the course of a speech to the United Nations Assembly by British premier Macmillan.[4] The embarrassment was ended when Macmillan courteously asked for a translation. Brezhnev was more self-restrained, and, until his health began to fail him, he cut an imposing figure when negotiating with US politicians. These Soviet leaders and their spokesmen were masters of the arts of boastful claims and rhetorical evasion.

Khrushchëv, unlike Brezhnev, was a reformer. Many of those communists who admired him felt that his reforms had not gone far enough. Among them was Roy Medvedev, who wrote *Let History Judge* about the iniquities of Stalin and his policies but could get it published only in the West. Medvedev argued for a return to Leninist norms. He wanted electivity to be restored to internal party life. He called for multi-candidate elections to the soviets and for wider limits in public debate. He saw Stalin's despotism as marking a break with the desirable traditions of the October Revolution. Thus there was nothing essentially wrong with communism; it simply needed to be reformed for its own good.[5] Many of these ideas were shared by the East German writer Rudolf Bahro who argued in *The Alternative in Eastern Europe* that the healthier elements in the communist parties were genuinely capable of ridding the Soviet Bloc of authoritarian, bureaucratic phenomena.[6] Other dissenting analysts came to more radical conclusions. The leading nuclear physicist Andrei Sakharov developed a fundamentally liberal critique of the USSR, demanding the institution of universal civil freedoms.[7]

The glass in the official picture was also being shattered by literary writers. Two Soviet accounts in particular captivated Western opinion. The poet Boris Pasternak wrote a novel, *Doctor Zhivago*, which was banned in Moscow but appeared abroad in translations from 1957. Its panoramic viewpoint on the civil war cast a shadow over the motives and practices of the early communists. This plunged Pasternak into political hot water and he had to refuse the Nobel Prize in 1958. His role as a leading critic of the Soviet regime was picked up by Alexander Solzhenitsyn, whose later works were published in the West from the end of the 1960s. His documentary account of the labour-camp system, *The Gulag Archipelago*, was a bestseller in 1974. It pulled no punches. Solzhenitsyn had talked to survivors of the camps and assembled such documentation as was available despite the censorship. The gruesome techniques of arrest, interrogation, 'confession' and forced labour were traced from the October Revolution. When he was deported from the USSR in 1974, Solzhenitsyn continued his campaign against the iniquities of communist repression. Every year, too, novels and poems by other writers were smuggled out of eastern Europe and China with searing messages about the behaviour of communist regimes.

Meanwhile Amnesty International and the International PEN Club exposed the abuses by the Soviet, east European and Chinese authorities. Christian and Islamic organisations maintained a well-informed critique. The Campaign for Soviet Jewry raised the matter of the difficulties facing Jews who expressed a desire to emigrate. The east European diasporas in the West intensified their struggle to convince public opinion that the Iron Curtain should somehow be pulled down. Chinese communities around the world had associations dedicated to the reintroduction of freedom to their homeland.

The popular media rarely missed a chance to depict communism as a malignant force in the world. The James Bond films, like the original novels by Ian Fleming, pitched the West against the USSR. Goodness and valour fought a duel with evil. *From Russia with Love* included the character Rosa Klebb, a Soviet agent with unprepossessing looks and hatred of freedom and democracy. Some authors and filmmakers offered a more measured depiction. John le Carré, who like Fleming had once worked for British intelligence, wrote thrillers suggesting that cynicism and skulduggery were more or less the same on both sides in the Cold War. Yet he also gave a clear account of the dreary oppressiveness of the German Democratic Republic in *The Spy Who Came In from the Cold*. Likewise Stanley Kubrick's 1964 movie *Dr Strangelove* contained American characters who were even scarier than their Soviet counterparts. A bumbling US President gets into a diplomatic crisis over a nuclear alert and frantically pleads with the USSR ambassador to calm nerves in the Kremlin. Then a rogue air force commander launches a rocket at Moscow. The implication in the film's last scene is that the Third World War is about to begin. Although East and West were shown as being incompetent to the point of madness, there was no veiling of the dreadful oppressiveness of the USSR.

Marxists in the West increasingly agreed that something had gone seriously wrong with the October Revolution, and debate about the Soviet Union was rejoined after Khrushchëv's Secret Speech. While Stalin was alive, few had dared move an inch away from his analysis. The exceptions had been the Trotskyists and other grouplets on the margins of the political far left which repudiated 'Stalinism'.

Discomfort even gnawed at the mind of the Italian Communist Party's leader Palmiro Togliatti. He had been loyal to the Soviet Union since the 1920s. Unlike his contemporary Antonio Gramsci, Togliatti found nothing basically wrong with Soviet Marxism. By denouncing Stalin out of the blue, Khrushchëv put him in an awkward position. Togliatti could hardly deny the historical facts as stated, and his party remembered how closely he had collaborated with Stalin – and the Italian non-communist press never tired of pointing this out. Somehow he had to clear his own name. He did this cunningly. Instead of rehearsing his own biography, he focused on the intellectual flimsiness of Khrushchëv's case. Togliatti declared that the Secret Speech failed to offer a properly Marxist account. He denied that one malign individual – Stalin – and a few cronies such as Beria could have constituted the sole cause of the abuses in the USSR in the 1930s and 1940s. He insisted that there must have been a wide range of reasons. Like Trotski, he pointed to a 'bureaucratic degeneration' which gave power to a stratum of party officials with a political and material interest in the authoritarian kind of state which had been consolidated in the 1930s. The 'cult of the individual' was not enough to explain this.

As his health deteriorated in summer 1964, Togliatti wrote out a political testament while on holiday in Crimea. This became known as the Yalta Memorandum. Togliatti asserted that every country had to be allowed its own strategy. He called for any polemics, especially with the Chinese Communist Party, to be couched in respectful language. He asked for Soviet spokesmen to cease pretending that no serious problems existed in the USSR. Togliatti contended that unity among the various parties was possible only if the independence of each of them was protected.[8] The Italian Communist Party leadership after his death paced further in the direction he had mapped out. The Eurocommunist strategy plotted by Enrico Berlinguer went further by expressly rejecting the USSR as a model for Italian political development. The suppression of civic rights appalled him. Yet he never rejected the October Revolution[9] – he could never go that far without undermining the basic rationale for his party's existence. Some of his younger acolytes tried to resolve his intellectual contradictions for him by promoting the notion that Soviet history would have taken a more desirable path if Bukharin had won the factional struggle against Stalin in the late 1920s.

Communists in western Europe in any case introduced no new basic ideas to Marxism itself. Others saw this as a situation to be rectified. Among them were several who wished to resuscitate the old strand in Marxist thought in favour of people's self-emancipation. An ageing proponent was the Hungarian György Lukács.[10] Returning to Budapest from exile in Moscow after the Second World War, he became Minister of Culture in Imre Nagy's government in 1956. Lukács regarded himself as a Leninist while remaining true to ideas which had been denounced as anti-Leninist in the late 1920s in the USSR. Once more he argued publicly that the working class needed to assert its untrammelled authority in the revolutionary process. His point was that capitalism produced a condition of 'alienation' of people from their full human potential, and Lukács believed the workers alone to be capable of surmounting the condition and then transforming society as a whole.[11]

Another veteran communist calling for the revision of conventional contemporary Marxism was Herbert Marcuse. After emigrating from Nazi Germany in 1933, he took American citizenship and wrote prolifically about the need to graft several intellectual trends of the twentieth century – especially Freudianism and German sociology – on to the tree of the Marxist tradition. Marcuse rejected Stalin's version of communism as dogmatic, narrow and plain wrong in its interpretation of Marx.[12] He was a freer spirit than Lukács and refused to recognise Lenin as an absolute authority. He insisted that sexual drives as well as economic imperatives help to explain the mechanisms of politics and society. He scorned the Communist Party of the USA and refused to align himself with any organisation. His experiences as a young militant in Europe had eroded his faith in the revolutionary potential of the working class. Marcuse saw well-paid industrial workers as constituting one of the obstacles to humanity's liberation from oppression. Based on the San Diego campus of the University of California, he counted instead upon the unemployed, the vagabond poor and the Hispanic immigrants; he also had a soft spot for college students. He regarded these groups as living in detachment from 'bourgeois' society and ready to overcome the 'one-dimensional' aspects of contemporary capitalist existence.[13]

Marcuse's forte was as a philosopher. His preoccupation with epistemology and dialectics was typical of a growing trend among Marxist writers seeking to challenge the Marxism that had been customary since 1917. Jean-Paul Sartre, whose early philosophical work was constructed on the basis of ideas drawn from Edmund Husserl and Martin Heidegger, published his *Critique of Dialectical Reason* in 1964. This was an attempt to bring together Marxism and the existentialist school in philosophy, and – unlike any previous Marxist thinker – Sartre argued for the crucial importance of the 'autonomous' and 'self-conscious' individual in explaining and justifying social activity. Lucio Colletti in Italy went back to Marx and suggested that Immanuel Kant rather than Georg Wilhelm Friedrich Hegel had exercised the deepest influence on his thought.[14] Colletti's work was admired by the French communist writer Louis Althusser. But Althusser placed his emphasis elsewhere, acknowledging that some bits of Marx's work contradicted others. This was an extraordinary admission for a Marxist to make at that time. Althusser claimed that Marxism's claim to analytical superiority lay in the scientific method and content of Marx's later writings; he argued that the early corpus lacked the same rigour.

Marcuse, Sartre, Colletti and Althusser were style-maestros of turgidity and never tried to rise to the flights of Marx and Engels in their inspired moments. Not one of them would choose a monosyllable if a longer word could be discovered or devised. Their Marxism, if not exactly pessimistic, was cramped and cautious. What is more, they were philosophers writing mainly for other philosophers.[15] Only Marcuse became a genuine favourite of the thousands of students who rebelled in 1968 against 'bourgeois society' and university discipline, as well as the American war in Vietnam. He and his ideas were accorded a profile in *Playboy* magazine.[16] (It is hard to imagine another Marxist theorist, except perhaps Marx himself, tolerating this without complaint.) Marcuse had grown popular because of the significance he attached to the students; it also did him no harm that he was willing to discuss the erotic as well as the socio-political.[17]

French students also produced their own theorists. The charismatic Daniel Cohn-Bendit, a German citizen, led the movement in Paris. He produced *Obsolete Communism: The Left-Wing Alternative*, which was immediately translated into the other languages of the West.[18] He despised the French Communist Party for failing to put its back into helping the rebelling students. He poured scorn on the USSR, a scorn that turned into hatred when the Warsaw Pact invaded Czechoslovakia in August 1968. In France, the USA, Germany and Italy there was a confluence of Maoists, Trotskyists, anarchists and rebels of no sectarian persuasion. Cohn-Bendit's attempt at revolutionary theory was embarrassingly chaotic; it was the product of a militant on the run from meeting to meeting.[19] Making a virtue of being just an ordinary militant, he denied that the masses have to be guided by leaders in successful revolutions. Yet he defended Lenin against the charge of having acted with excessive predilection for centralism. At the same time he denounced the suppression of the Kronstadt mutiny of 1921, attributing most of the blame to Trotski. His heroes in revolutionary Russia were the anarchists, and he picked out Makhno's followers as exemplary rebels. He could only do this in ignorance of the antisemitism and wanton violence among the Makhnovites in Ukraine in the civil war.[20]

In the late 1960s, if a popularity poll had been taken among the protesters, Lev Trotski, Mao Zedong, Ho Chi Minh and Che Guevara would probably have headed the list. They were disgusted with Soviet leaders from Stalin to Brezhnev and agreed that American Presidents Lyndon B. Johnson and Richard Nixon, who had reinforced the USA's military intervention in the conflict in Vietnam, were war criminals. The esteem for Che Guevara was enhanced by his good looks. The fact that Guevara died on campaign in Bolivia even though he could have had a comfortable career in Cuba was also counted unto him for righteousness. A similar reaction was evoked by Ho Chi Minh. Like Guevara, he was taking on the might of 'American imperialism'. Data on Ho's repressive regime in Hanoi were limited and would anyway have been disbelieved by his admirers if they had learned about them. The chant went up outside American embassies and on peace marches: 'Ho! Ho! Ho Chi Minh!'

Mao Zedong's 'little red book' was the only source of information on contemporary China for many on the political far left. The Cultural Revolution was widely admired; a blind eye was turned to any newspaper reports of abuses of human rights. The generation of Westerners who liked mini-skirts, long hair and hallucinogenic drugs responded positively to Mao's portentous platitudes. They saw what they wanted to see. Mao appeared to be on the side of 'ordinary people' who were being allowed to carry out their own revolution. More tricky to explain is the posthumous rehabilitation of Lev Trotski. Why did so many leftists who professed libertarian forms of socialism fall for the blandishments of a man who had eulogised terror and dictatorship? There were several facets to the syndrome. One was the pathos of Trotski's death: the hunted last years, the ice pick in the back of the head, the trained assassin. Trotski was also a brilliant writer who presented his life in the best possible light; and he acquired a useful propagandist in his follower and biographer Isaac Deutscher, who emigrated from Poland to England in 1939.

Deutscher in fact disagreed with his hero about how change would come about in the USSR: whereas Trotski had called for political insurrection, Deutscher gave Stalin his due as an industrialiser and predicted steady internal reform as the Stalinist generation died off. But Deutscher indefatigably defended the record of Trotski in his years of power and pomp. Allegedly circumstances had simply forced Trotski to engage in repression. Deutscher proposed that if only Trotski had been Lenin's successor, the Bolshevik party leadership would have steered a passage to socialism with a human face. Another candidate was found by American academic Stephen Cohen who wrote a biography of Nikolai Bukharin. Cohen depicted his hero as a radical socialist who, building on Lenin's last writings, formulated a strategy for the introduction of socialism to Russia by peaceful means. This book played down Bukharin's continuing adherence to the axioms of the one-party dictatorship and the one-ideology society. It had the effect of dragging Trotski off the pedestal of esteem. Italian Eurocommunists in particular were attracted to Bukharin as standing for the kind of USSR that they wanted in the past and present. The memory of Bukharin also appealed to Mikhail Gorbachëv, who was to put it at the heart of his vision for a reformed Soviet Union.[21]

The young generation provided several publications that rivalled Lukács and Marcuse in arcane jargon. Among them was the *New Left Review*, founded in London in 1960. Its editors and contributors engaged in an earnest quest to find a Marxism appropriate to their times. Official Soviet ideology since the mid-1920s held no appeal to them. They venerated Lenin and Trotski while exploring whether Marcuse, Sartre, Colletti or Althusser had anything to contribute to a renewal of Marxism in general. The nature of the USSR past and present remained a bone of contention. *New Left Review* was just one among many Marxist organs in western Europe where the same questions were asked. Was the USSR a reformable workers' state? Had the Soviet bureaucratic stratum turned itself into a ruling class? Was the USSR imperialist? When did the basic 'deviations' from Leninism occur in Soviet history?

More widely read and more easily readable were the newspapers put out by various communist organisations in the same years. Perhaps the most accessible was the London publication *Black Dwarf*. Edited by Tariq Ali, a muddled Oxford student with a talent for improvising speeches, it purveyed hatred of the American and Soviet rulers in roughly equal measure. Ali, unlike Cohn-Bendit, was an admirer of Trotski. Beatles member John Lennon wrote to *Black Dwarf* criticising its sanctioning of political violence. The song 'Revolution' encapsulated his standpoint:

> You say you want a revolutio-o-on,
> We-e-ell, you know,
> We all wanna change the world.

The stanza ended:

> But when you talk about destructio-o-on,
> Don't you know that you can count me out?

Ali remonstrated in vain with Lennon; and Lennon's way of thinking was shared with many in the West whose chief wish was for an end to violent politics around the world. In the United Kingdom the Campaign for Nuclear Disarmament had been founded by Bertrand Russell, A. J. P. Taylor and others in 1958; its principal belief was that the British government should set an example by abandoning its H-bombs and that the USSR would surely follow.

This was quite a turnabout even for the mercurial Russell, who in 1945 had advocated obliterating Moscow from the air. Taylor too had been stern about the Soviet Union at the end of the war.[22] Neither the prince of mathematical logic nor the master-narrator of international history properly accounted for their confidence that British self-abnegation in weaponry would become a model for the Kremlin to give up its military-technological rivalry with the USA. Annual demonstrations took place and, from the late 1960s, were joined by groups from the Quakers to the latest Trotskyist groupuscule. 'Anti-Cold War' groups in the West were a godsend to the Soviet political and military establishment, and the Moscow-run Assistance Fund for Communist Parties and Movements of the Left did not fail to channel funds to several of them. Washington strove to reinforce any organisation working in the opposite direction. The London magazine *Encounter* robustly countered the intellectual argument for communism. Not all of its own editors were aware that its financial health depended on the Central Intelligence Agency. The poet Stephen Spender, ex-communist turned anti-communist, resigned because he thought his personal integrity had been compromised.[23]

The Cold War remained a struggle for Western minds as much as a competition in weapons development. All academic institutes and political 'think tanks' in the USA were hostile to the Soviet Union. The same was true of most such bodies in western Europe (although a few of them produced work untouched by criticism of Soviet history and politics). The great dividing line was the question what to do about the Kremlin. One wing of opinion wanted a stronger position to be adopted in any agreements with the USSR. Soviet politicians were depicted as slippery ideologues bent on internal repression and territorial expansion. If they wanted to trade with the USA, then they should be constrained to respect human rights as agreed in the Final Act of the Conference on Security and Co-Operation in Europe signed in Helsinki in August 1975. But better still would be the introduction of a cordon sanitaire around the communist states. Eventually, it was predicted, communism would implode in the USSR and elsewhere. Robert Conquest, Richard Pipes and Martin Malia were prominent in making the case. They argued that the communist order was doomed and that there was nothing to be gained by prolonging its death agony. The Soviet Union was the most pernicious existing example of totalitarianism, and the extension of its type of state to China, eastern Europe and other countries was the greatest tragedy of the second half of the twentieth century.[24]

Not only incumbents of political office but also most academic analysts distanced themselves from this standpoint. They were worried about jeopardising the benefits of 'peaceful coexistence' and 'détente'. The Cuban missiles crisis of 1962 had shown how easily the global rivalry could abruptly intensify and lead to a third world war. Prolonging peace between the superpowers and their allies was the most attractive objective.

There was an intellectual as well as a political component in the criticism of the 'totalitarian school'. Isaac Deutscher continued to contend that reform could – and probably would – come about in the USSR through a younger communist generation acceding to power. As Soviet society became more educated and complex, the impact of its demands on the regime would increase. This was also the position taken by the American sociologist Daniel Bell, who contended that existing trends in the USSR and the USA pointed towards an eventual convergence of the communist and capitalist systems. Growing state interference in the lives of individual Americans was paralleled by the gradual diminution of oppressive rulership in the Soviet Union. E. H. Carr, once the deputy editor of *The Times*, was no less insistent that the USSR's comprehensive welfare provision and state economic intervention were becoming standard features of Western governmental practice. Carr had begun as a post-Victorian liberal and ended up a quasi-Marxist.[25]

From the late 1970s the disagreement sharpened into protracted scholarly warfare. The opening attack came from what became known as the 'revisionist' trend. Its writers emphasised the popular basis of Soviet power in the decades after 1917. Some claimed that the communist dictatorship merely reflected the demands of workers and peasants and even that only a few thousand people died from repression in the 1930s. Stalin's primary responsibility for the Great Terror was denied.[26] Whereas the Webbs had done this by reliance on Soviet constitutional handouts, the newer version was based primarily on those impeccable sources, *Pravda* and the official records of party congresses. The desire to analyse the USSR and the USA in comparable terms also affected the study of contemporary communist politics. The leaderships in Moscow and Beijing, it was proposed, were decisively constrained by the frictions of bureaucratic function and by the demands of emergent interest groups. Each communist leader supposedly became a mere spokesman for the institution he headed. Revisionists had been influenced by postwar developments in the social sciences. Some of them were also alienated from the policies of their Western governments at home and abroad; a few were communists. All put the Soviet Union under a kindly gaze.

There was no consensual statement of revisionism; nobody even made an attempt at such a thing. The single unifying theme was the rejection of the totalitarian tradition of thought. Much new material was unearthed about communism in the past and present. But something was lost in the process. Writers in the 1960s – and this included Carr and Deutscher as well as Conquest and Pipes – had agreed that the Soviet state was characterised by huge central power which was frequently wielded with extreme brutality. Revisionists suffered a lapse in analytical imagination; in some cases this bordered on moral blindness.[27]

Yet the angry discussion directed light on to shadowy corners of communism. More was known than in any previous decade about conditions in Hungarian factories, North Vietnamese military units, small Chinese communes and Soviet housing estates. There was also a rising appreciation of the complexity of such states and their societies. Not only high politics but also rulership at lower levels were scrutinised. The supreme leaders were not ignored; in fact a legion of professionals were examining the minutiae of speeches by Ceauşescu, Zhivkov and Mao. Knowledge was widening and deepening. The problem was what to do with it. Throughout the 1930s there had been multi-sided and acrimonious debates about communism. The parameters of the arguments changed in the 1960s and 1970s, but people were no nearer to agreement. Political partisanship played a part in this. So too did judgements about the present and future path of developments around the world. And although a lot more came to be known about communist states than in earlier years, an immense amount of information still lay hidden by the censorship and police regulations. The consequence was that there was no such thing as 'Western opinion', only a plurality of competing and shifting standpoints. The Cold War had started with a degree of Western consensus which fell away as the years passed by.

32. EUROPE EAST AND WEST

Eastern Europe's condition as the informal outer empire of the USSR had been bloodily reconfirmed by the Soviet army's suppression of the Hungarian Uprising. Refugees flooded across the Austrian frontier. Hungary suffered savage repression and its new leader János Kádár, handpicked by the Kremlin, was left in no doubt that his job was to prevent any repetition of trouble for Moscow. Imre Nagy had reached sanctuary in the Yugoslav embassy after the fall of his government. Soviet leaders, having assured Tito that they would do no physical harm to him, took him into custody in November 1956 and held him in Romania until shooting him after a secret trial in 1958. The brutal warning to all communist regimes in the region was clear: if they failed to fulfil the USSR's requirements they would incur violent retaliation.

Moscow recognised the imperative to regularise the situation in such a fashion that the Hungarian situation would anyhow be unlikely to recur. Soviet economic subsidies to the region were increased. In particular, oil was sold to eastern Europe at prices far below the level on the world market.[1] The armed forces of the USSR garrisoned in Hungary, Poland and the German Democratic Republic were a further drain on Moscow's budget. The outer empire had not come cheap in blood: it now cost dearly in rubles. The regimes of the Soviet Bloc were still allowed to assert some national pride. They could also experiment, within limits, with economic modifications of the order in place before 1953. At the same time they were expected to communise their industry and agriculture more fully. Only Poland was permitted to exempt its countryside from collectivisation: Khrushchëv could see that too rigorous an imposition of the Soviet model might provoke yet another Polish uprising. He also sought a greater integration of eastern Europe with the USSR by increasing co-operation among the various armies of the Warsaw Pact. Co-ordinated training, equipment and planning were stepped up. All this was done subject to Soviet hegemony.[2]

The same was true of regional economic organisation. Comecon,

established in 1949, was turned into a more active agency. At Khrushchëv's insistence, countries were instructed to concentrate on the traditional strengths of their economies. Previously all had been expected
to follow the Soviet path of industrialisation. Now several of them were
confined to being the suppliers of agricultural produce or minerals for
the others, while the more industrialised ones could export factory goods
to them.[3]

This whole idea was anathema to Romanian communist leader
Gheorghiu-Dej. While maintaining a tight political order, he was
affronted by the call to abandon his ambitious plans for heavy industry
and to prioritise investment in wheat, grapes, tomatoes and petrol. By
1964 an official statement was made: 'There does not and cannot exist a
"parent" party and a "son" party, or "superior" parties and "subordinate"
parties.'[4] In 1963 he cheekily offered himself as a mediator in the Sino–
Soviet dispute. Nicolae Ceaușescu, who succeeded to the Romanian
leadership in 1965, pursued the same autonomous line. Bucharest was a
constant irritant inside Comecon and the Warsaw Pact. Romania's
ambitious industrial plans remained in place. Ceaușescu also reinforced
the collective-farm system. Like Khrushchëv earlier, he bulldozed villages
and brought peasants together in new rural townships. The rationale for
this was the zeal to bring concrete-slab, multi-storey buildings, tractors
and electric light to the countryside. National pride was asserted and the
Hungarian Autonomous Region was abolished. Opposition was vigorously suppressed by the security police. Ceaușescu was determined to
secure his regime from internal subversion as well as external interference.

What saved Romania from being invaded by its allies in the Warsaw
Pact was its retention of the one-party, one-ideology communist state.
Ceaușescu's friendliness to the powers of the West was irritating but not
a *casus belli*. Adoption of party pluralism and capitalist economics would
have been an entirely different matter. There was even less chance of
such Westernising trends in Albania. Its leader Enver Hoxha argued that
'the Khrushchëv–Tito group [had concocted] new plans against the cause
of socialism'. Hoxha sided with China in the Sino–Soviet split. He
castigated Khrushchëv and Tito as the leaders of 'modern revisionism'
who, like Eduard Bernstein and Karl Kautsky at the turn of the century,
had betrayed Marxism.[5] His was eastern Europe's only state which
refused to rehabilitate the communist leaders executed in the show
trials of Stalin's last years.[6] Most of his anger, though, was aimed at
Tito. Territorial rivalry between Albania and its more powerful Yugoslav

neighbour was the source of constant friction. Yet Albania was left alone. It maintained a communist regime, even announcing the total abolition of religion in the country in 1967. Its geostrategic importance for the USSR was small, and the fact that it criticised Tito was no problem for the Kremlin.

The authorities in the German Democratic Republic kept an even more rigid control over their people than was achieved by Hoxha in Albania, whose mountainous terrain and village traditions made things difficult for the central state authorities. Walter Ulbricht aimed to turn his state into a model of contemporary communism. It was his constant pestering that pushed the Soviet Presidium into sanctioning the building of the Berlin Wall.[7] Competition was joined with West Germany to raise the quality of material and social life, and Ulbricht constantly claimed that the German Democratic Republic was winning. In 1963 he introduced a New Economic System which provided enterprises and their managers with somewhat wider powers outside central planning control. Output rose but never as quickly as in West Germany. Although people were better off than previously, Ulbricht's unpopularity deepened. His ideological rigidity made even Brezhnev appear flexible. No one could forget that he bore responsibility for stopping people from meeting their relatives in the West. He was fired in May 1971, utterly convinced of the correctness of his policies to the very end. His successor Erich Honecker was only marginally less gloomy. Political presentation was made somewhat livelier but the basic policies remained the same. Far from being a workers' paradise, the German Democratic Republic was eastern Europe's most efficient police state.

Poland's police hardly treated opposition gently. But Gomułka did not dare to interfere blatantly with the Catholic Church, which gave quiet support to anti-communist worker–militants and intellectual dissenters. He too loosened the economic system to a certain extent immediately after returning to power in 1956, and the living conditions of Poles improved over the 1960s. Peasants were given a guarantee that the authorities would not collectivise the land. Communism by itself had not endeared itself in the country. Bidding to rally patriotic support, Gomułka started to discriminate against the Jews.[8] Few as they were in Poland after the Second World War, they remained the object of popular hostility. Grumblings about the regime grew more intense over the years. Jacek Kuroń and Karol Modzelewski wrote an open letter to the party in 1968. They could not be accused of ambiguity. Kuroń and Modzelewski were arrested and, after a brief trial, thrown into prison.[9]

János Kádár in Hungary proved more flexible than Gomułka. He too understood that improvements in the economy were badly needed, and with this in mind he cautiously began to introduce reforms rather like those mooted in Poland by communist radicals in 1956–7. Managers were granted somewhat wider powers. Enterprises were less tightly regulated by the national planning authorities. Bigger material incentives were introduced for workers. The New Economic Mechanism was formally announced in 1966 as the culmination of a series of minor reforms in previous years. Really, however, this was a very anodyne variant of an old, pre-revolutionary mechanism: the market economy. But it was bold indeed for contemporary communist economics – and Soviet reformers followed its progress with enthusiasm. The behaviour of Kádár came as a surprise to most Hungarians, who regarded him as the Quisling who had collaborated in the country's reconquest by the USSR. Nothing good had been expected of him. The martyrs of the Hungarian Revolt lived on in the public memory. Radio stations staffed by refugees continued to broadcast their anti-communist message to audiences in Budapest. (The wavelengths were quickly jammed by the authorities.) Yet Kádár's economic measures depleted any active opposition and the standard of living in Hungary steadily but slowly rose.

Kádár was clever in the way he cultivated his political appeal. He saw that Hungary would never recover from the catastrophe of 1956 if it was ruled as tightly as the other states in eastern Europe. He abandoned the goal of comprehensive indoctrination and mobilisation. 'People don't exist', he said, 'just so that we may test out Marxism on them.' His slogan became famous: 'He who is not against us is for us.'[10]

The press in Hungary, as in Poland, was no longer as severely constrained as in the USSR. The country did not have complete freedom of cultural expression, not by a long chalk. But Kádár allowed just enough space for discussion, especially about Hungary's pre-communist history, to assuage the worst frustrations in society. And Hungarians knew that, compared to most other peoples in the Soviet Bloc, they lived better. If they needed persuading, Czechs and East Germans holidaying in Hungary's campsites by Lake Balaton told them so. What the visitors liked, apart from the delights of camping and swimming, was the New Economic Mechanism's success in increasing the variety of food in the shops. Also impressive was the permission given for people to run their own little businesses as cobblers, plumbers and stall-traders. Essentially this legalised and expanded what happened in all communist economies (where tradesmen worked on the side for private gain). The idea was to shake the economy out of its bureaucratic rigidities. Kádár also stuck his neck out in international communist relations by refusing to condemn the Eurocommunists of Italy, Spain and France. He proved more irksome to Moscow than Gomułka, and the whole package became known as goulash communism.

More troublesome for the USSR was Czechoslovakia. Frustration with Antonín Novotný's obstruction of any moves towards political and economic reform was boiling up in 1967. Communist reformers allied themselves with the intelligentsia. The Central Committee was riven by barely disguised internal disputes in October 1967. The reformers gained the upper hand. Novotný was forced out of office in January 1968 and Alexander Dubček took over as communist party chief. In April the Central Committee adopted an Action Programme. Its basic goal was to develop 'a new model of socialist society, deeply democratic and adapted to Czechoslovak conditions'. Dubček abolished censorship. He permitted the formation of associations without official interference. The economic reforms of Ota Šik included allowing the closure of unprofitable factories and the growth of private economic activity.[11] Time and time again Moscow warned Dubček that he might prove unable to stop the process running out of control. Kádár, who had the Hungarian events of 1956 burned into his soul, asked him: 'Do you really not know the kind of people you're dealing with?'[12] The Czechoslovak leader was a naive reform-communist. He was confident he could persuade the Kremlin that the changes would reinforce the appeal of communism in his country and suit the USSR's geopolitical interests.

Soviet Politburo members, however, were deeply worried. They were not alone. Other communist leaders in eastern Europe, especially Gomułka and Ulbricht, saw the Prague Spring as the beginning of a counter-revolution. Negotiations were intense between Moscow and Prague. Dubček repeatedly claimed to have everything under control. Brezhnev wanted to believe him or at least to avoid drastic action, but opinion in his Politburo was moving in favour of intervention. Army manoeuvres were held near Czechoslovakia's frontiers. After much discussion it was decided in Moscow to invade with Warsaw Pact allies: Poland, the German Democratic Republic, Bulgaria and Hungary supplied forces. In the night of 20–21 August the tanks rolled across the frontiers. They moved on Prague unopposed. The day of the operation could not have been balmier. There was a slight haze in the Czech capital and a light southerly breeze was blowing. Students approached the tank crews and asked them why they had invaded. The politics of

Czechoslovakia were no longer in local hands. It was the Soviet Politburo and its agencies which ruled as Alexander Dubček, President
Ludvík Svoboda and other leading reformers were arrested, drugged and
abducted to Moscow in handcuffs.

Dubček had a nightmarish 'conversation' with Brezhnev. Either
Dubček accepted the USSR's terms or he would be killed and the
treatment of his invaded country would worsen. Forced to stay awake so
that he could not think straight, Dubček succumbed. František Kriegel,
medical doctor and veteran of the Spanish civil war, was the only one of
the five abducted Czechoslovak leaders to reject the Moscow Protocol.
Brezhnev reacted with blustering crudity: 'What's this Jew from Galicia
doing here anyway?'

The communist reformers back in Czechoslovakia had not yet been
reduced to inactivity. They could not retaliate directly against the forces
of the Warsaw Pact. Instead they held a party congress at Vysočany and
defiantly elected a new Central Committee consisting of communists
hostile to the invasion. If they were not going to go down fighting, they
were determined to make plain the illegitimacy of the Kremlin's actions.
Dubček and Svoboda were sent back to Prague and, still under Soviet
intimidation, challenged the validity of the proceedings. The USSR
stipulated that the Czechoslovak Communist Party should prioritise
the 'defence of socialist achievements'. Dubček carried out his tasks
with visible distaste. Once he had fulfilled his function of quietening
political passions and facilitating 'normalisation', he was sacked as Party
First Secretary and shunted out of sight to an obscure job in forestry
administration. His place was taken by the dour Gustáv Husák who
scurried about as the USSR's chief spaniel. All the leading reformers
were removed from office. Censorship was reintroduced and repressive
controls were strengthened. The experiments with economic decentralisation were abandoned. The Prague Spring had turned to winter without
an intervening summer and autumn.

Events in Czechoslovakia lay at the foundations of what became
known as the Brezhnev Doctrine. The USSR arrogated the right to
enforce the communist order in eastern Europe. Only the Kremlin was
empowered to judge when this order was being threatened. Brezhnev
was giving notice that the territorial and political settlement after the
Second World War would be kept firmly in place – and the West was
warned to respect the Doctrine. The countries of eastern Europe were
presented with the concept of limited sovereignty. Having been brought
under Moscow's hegemony in 1945, they were to remain loyal to the

USSR in perpetuity. Svoboda believed that he and other signatories of the Moscow Protocol had saved Czechoslovakia from a still worse fate. But he also stated: 'When our republic was occupied, it was clearly stated by the party, by the government and by myself: we invited nobody. The whole world knows that.' The idea that Ivan's tanks had arrived by fraternal invitation was one falsification too many for him. Yet the political resubjugation of Czechoslovakia was complete; and the Warsaw Pact invasion deadened all talk of reform in the whole of eastern Europe.

Yet this did not entirely root out criticism of the USSR in those countries; indeed the sheer brutality of Soviet external policy stiffened the feeling that enough was enough. Ceaușescu, who as a member of the Romanian leadership in 1956 had avidly approved of the crushing of the Hungarian Revolt, denounced Soviet military intervention in Czechoslovakia. He flatly rejected the Brezhnev Doctrine. Tito stormed around the world with his criticism of the USSR. Hoxha went further and pulled Albania out of the Warsaw Pact.

Popular protest, though, amounted to little more than rowdiness at ice hockey games against the USSR. Dissenting activity, however, did not cease and Czechoslovakia was far from becoming quiescent. The troublemakers were not communists but liberals. Among them was the playwright Václav Havel, who denounced the communist authorities at every opportunity. He was frequently arrested. A group formed around him which was eventually to call itself Charter 77. (It was created in 1977.) Persecution failed to suppress them. Havel understood how to attract attention from the West and encourage American politicians to indicate that, if Husák and his counterparts in other countries of eastern Europe were to intensify repressive measures, the USSR would pay a grievous price in diplomatic and financial relations. So Havel lived a life of arrest, release and arrest. But he was never tortured, starved or compelled to sign a false confession. The invasion of Czechoslovakia was a disaster for communism. Dubček was a communist reformer who had been lucky to escape with his life. The conclusion drawn by anti-Kremlin militants was that a communist reformation of Czechoslovakia was a futile objective. They turned to ideals of liberal democracy, national sovereignty, Christianity and market economics. They differed about which ideals they espoused. But on the need to do away with communist rule they were united.

And if armed might and military occupation did not work for the USSR in Czechoslovakia, communism was bound to encounter growing resistance elsewhere in eastern Europe. In Poland the working class was restless, the intelligentsia was resentful and the Catholic Church was troublesome. Even under tough regimes such as those of Bulgaria, Romania and the German Democratic Republic there were shoots of dissent. Albania operated the harshest repressive machinery and had the weakest organisations of opposition; Enver Hoxha proudly announced that he had extirpated the religious mentality and turned the people into eager atheists.

Gomułka's economic reforms in Poland had had a positive impact until the mid-1960s. National income in Poland grew faster than investment for the first time since the war, and wages also rose. The emphasis was put on heavy industry. As previously, the peasants bore most of the load. Compulsory delivery quotas for agricultural produce were always being revised upwards.[13] The pace of economic growth was unsustainable; without a freer system of information, management and innovation the Polish economy was bound to go on falling behind the advanced-capitalist West.[14] Gomułka's didactic speeches came to irritate most Poles; his heroic status was short lived among them. People imitated him with a joke: 'Before the war the Polish economy was on the edge of a precipice. Since liberation we have made great strides!'[15] As soon as price rises were imposed in December 1970 there were strikes. Trouble was worst in the Baltic cities. Workers in the shipyards formed unions, went on strike and took to the streets to protest against the government. Gomułka brought in the armed security forces and hundreds of demonstrators were killed. But the strikers refused to give way and Gomułka had to resign in the same month. This was a momentous event. It was the first time in eastern Europe after the Second World War that a ruler had been dislodged from office by working-class power.[16]

His place was filled by Edward Gierek, who had negotiated in a friendly fashion with the strikers. He had to make it his priority to improve living conditions, otherwise what had happened to Gomułka could happen to him too. Gierek set about contracting state loans from Western banks and attracting Soviet commercial subsidies. Poland used them to import consumer products and up-to-date industrial machinery from West Germany and elsewhere. This strategy depended on success in long-term economic regeneration. Failure would force the government to lower real wages in order to make repayments to creditors abroad. Gierek was a solid fellow with an amiable demeanour. Although he was not exactly charismatic, he gained some approval after replacing the glum Gomułka. What he lacked, though, was vision. Neither he nor his fellow leaders fully appreciated the unremitting contempt for communism among Poles. The Catholic Church stood unbowed by decades of persecution. The intelligentsia, which had once included an impressive collection of communist reformers, had turned against Marxism in all its guises. The workers in factories, mines and shipyards refused to give Gierek the benefit of the doubt.

Civil society had been battered but had not expired. Resentment of Russia was intense. The only reason why there was no revolt was the knowledge that the Warsaw Pact had the tanks. Poles feared a repetition of the bloodshed in Hungary in 1956. Older people recalled the Warsaw Uprising of 1944, when patriots rose against the German occupation and were outgunned from the start. Yet all was not lost. Many workers were eager to confront the authorities about wages, living conditions and civil rights. Linked to intellectual dissenters as well as to the patriotic clergy, the militants of the labour movement had the capacity to bring the economy to its knees if they chose to call for a general strike.

External loans bought a little time for Gierek, but the Polish economic output dipped sharply in 1977.[17] One east European ruler – Nicolae Ceaușescu – understood the dangers of the Polish strategy. Romania contracted foreign loans like every other country in eastern Europe except Czechoslovakia (where Husák had an almost compulsive aversion to contacts with the West).[18] But Ceaușescu paid his debts on the nail and did not flinch at impoverishing his people in order to keep the national accounts in the black. Oil was the country's great asset and was traded strongly on world markets. Wine too began to be exported. The Romanian government also made money from the export of people. Jews wishing to emigrate to Israel had to pay a heavy financial toll for the exit visa and the air trip. Ethnic Germans left Romania on a similar basis through an accord between Bucharest and Bonn. But there was no halt in the deterioration in economic conditions. Ceaușescu tightened his grip on party and people through his security police, the Securitate.[19] His wife Elena also acquired political influence and prominence. No shoots of political or economic reform were allowed in Romania. The cult of Ceaușescu was exaggerated beyond even the conventions of contemporary communism outside North Korea and China. Romanians who criticised the regime were locked up.

Eastern Europe caused constant alarm in the Soviet supreme leadership. The suppression of the Hungarian Uprising had been traumatic for Khrushchëv. He had thought he was relaxing communist rule for everybody's benefit but found that societies west of the Soviet Union hated their oppressors. The Prague Spring was less traumatic for Brezhnev, who had never promised reform in eastern Europe; his conscience, if he had one, was untroubled by his decision to send Warsaw Pact forces into Czechoslovakia in 1968. But military action dealt only with the symptoms. It offered no fundamental cure for the malaise of communism across the entire eastern half of the continent.

From Stalin to Brezhnev the sickly phenomena persisted. The 'colonies' in eastern Europe had turned into a multinational drain on the Soviet budget. Nuclear missile bases had to be supplied if the threat of attack by NATO was to be faced down. The Soviet army also maintained garrisons which needed equipping and financing. These disgruntled troops were locally very unpopular and Moscow took the precaution of secluding its contingents well away from regular contact with the country's civilian inhabitants. It was a most peculiar empire which resorted to such expedients. This was not all. Communised economies in eastern Europe were constructed on the Soviet model. It is true that Poland refrained from collectivising most of its peasantry; but industry, commerce, finance and transport copied the templates invented in the pre-war USSR. The result was permanent economic inadequacy. The countries of eastern Europe lacked the USSR's abundance of natural resources. If Moscow wished to salvage the situation, it had to reconcile itself to the unceasing subsidisation of gas and oil exports.

The costs were borne also in the declining impact of the USSR on politics in western Europe. Step by step, the Italian Communist Party broke free of the Soviet political and ideological embrace.[20] Its Eurocommunism involved a new and distinctive strategy. Togliatti had operated inside the constitutional framework without openly abandoning the possibility that communists might need to use other methods, especially if the political far right staged a *coup d'état*. Berlinguer wanted the party to commit itself unconditionally to a peaceful and electoral strategy. He asked for a 'historic compromise' with the Christian Democratic Party. His suggestion was that the fundamental tasks of reform in the country should be tackled by its two largest parties in tandem – and in Aldo Moro, until his murder by the Red Brigades in 1978, he found an ex-premier who was willing to take him at his word. Berlinguer dropped the traditional anti-Americanism of Italian communism. Europe, though, was at the core of his policies. He welcomed Italy's adhesion to NATO and to the European Economic Community (whereas Togliatti had treated both organisations as anti-Soviet conspiracies).[21] He also made overtures to Europe's socialist, social-democratic and labour parties. The Italian communists did well in successive elections, but in 1979 their share of the vote fell from 34 to 30 per cent.[22] Furthermore, the Christian Democrats refused Berlinguer's offer of co-operation; and the enemies of communism always succeeded in forming coalitions without the Italian Communist Party.

Santiago Carrillo, General Secretary of the Spanish Communist Party, returned to Madrid after Franco's death and the restoration of democracy in 1976. He agreed with the main practical tenets of Eurocommunism and hoped that his years of foreign exile and opposition to fascism would recommend him to the electorate.[23] It was not to be. The party did disappointingly in elections and Carrillo resigned six years later. A similar fate befell the Portuguese Communist Party. The revolution against the fascist regime had occurred in 1974, and communists had participated strongly in it. Its leadership disdained Eurocommunism, placing its trust in continuing friendly relations with Moscow. This made no difference. Next year it received only an eighth of the votes in national elections.

The French Communist Party under Waldeck Rochet, who succeeded Maurice Thorez, remained solidly pro-Soviet despite what Rochet had witnessed in the USSR in the 1920s.[24] Its candidate in the 1969 presidential elections was the gnarled old Stalinist Jacques Duclos, who gained 21 per cent of votes. Discipline in the party was strict; dissenters such as Roger Garaudy who criticised the USSR were expelled. Georges Marchais became Secretary-General in 1972 and edged towards a Eurocommunism standpoint like a man climbing out along a ledge from a skyscraper. He frequently questioned the KGB's repression of dissenters; Marchais took no notice of the instant Soviet complaint.[25] He also negotiated for an electoral coalition with François Mitterrand and the Socialist Party. But the agreement collapsed in 1974. What is more, Marchais declined to go as far as Berlinguer and Carrillo in redefining communist strategy.[26] His party remained a perennial force of protest. Even as such it had severe limitations. In 1968 all France had been ablaze with workers' strikes and students' demonstration. The French Communist Party stood aloof, refusing in particular to ally with 'bourgeois' students and denying – with justification – that there existed a truly revolutionary situation in the country. Nevertheless it did not cover itself in glory. Really the party was satisfied with the role of permanent, influential opposition. Always the bridesmaid of the Revolution, never the bride.

Communism in western Europe – with Italy, France, Spain and Greece as notable exceptions – held next to no appeal to the imagination of the industrial working class in whose name it had been invented. A case in point was the United Kingdom, where the co-founders of Marxism had written so many of their important works. The party finally turned against the USSR only in 1968, after the invasion of Czechoslovakia. The rest of the British labour movement barely noticed this transformation of consciousness. In a few trade unions the communists held a certain authority. This was especially true among the Scottish miners, who were led by party militant Mick McGahey. But young radicals in general turned not to the Communist Party of Great Britain but to communist splinter organisations or to other organisations entirely.[27] Official British communism was not yet dead, but it was dying on its feet. The only consolation for its active members – pro-Soviet or ant-Soviet, Stalinist or reformist, activist or intellectual, old or young – was that they did not yet sense that history was leaving them behind. The hurricane of global change which had favoured communism in Europe, west and east, in 1917 and 1945 had been dissipated into the ether.

33. REDUCED EXPECTATIONS

Lenin's communism had a strategic fixation with the question of how to obtain central state authority. Communist parties planned to take over whole countries and transform the framework of their politics and economy. They aimed at permanent rule; they intended that when – there was never any 'if' about it – they attained power, they would keep a tight hold on it. Like Lenin in 1917 or Mao in 1949, they believed that their policies would make them popular among most people. Communist theory never produced an alternative strategy for communist parties which lacked a 'revolutionary situation' to exploit.

Over the decades, however, most communist parties had to recognise that the chances of a successful revolution in the near future ranged from the discouraging to the non-existent. The paradox was that the greater the prospect of communists coming to power, the likelier it was for governments to adopt ruthless preventive measures. Throughout the years after the Second World War a watchful eye was kept on communist parties. The Australian labour movement had a long tradition of far-left radicalism. Between 1941 and 1945 the Communist Party of Australia under Lance Sharkey, a devotee of Stalin, had worked indefatigably to reinforce the war effort, and the consequence was a lasting influence over post-war politics.[1] The communists challenged the governing Labour cabinet by starting an industrial offensive in 1947. The army was used to break up a lengthy miners' strike two years later. In 1951 the Conservatives under Robert Menzies out-McCarthyied Senator McCarthy in the USA by trying to ban the party outright; and although the referendum on the matter went against the government, enough was said about the subversive activities of Australian communists as well as about the iniquities of Stalin's USSR for most Australians to conclude that communism was not for them. Sharkey, who had been sentenced to three years' imprisonment in 1949, was a man without influence long before Khrushchëv attacked Stalin's record.

Communists in Australia and south-east Asia kept warm ties. The

comrades in Malaya seriously threatened the British imperial administration after the Second World War. When the country gained its
independence as Malaysia in 1957, the communist party's strength and
ambition led to clashes with the government. Most party members were
ethnic Chinese and it was easy for the authorities to mobilise action
against them. The Malaysian Communist Party was no match for the
regular army and was crushed in 1960.

The Indonesian communists were also a menace to their government
after decolonisation. By the early 1960s they had acquired three million
members, making it the third largest communist party in the world.
Only the USSR and the People's Republic of China had bigger member-
ships. The Communist Party of Indonesia had played a prominent role
in fighting Dutch colonialism and had been forced into the political
underground more than once. A period of turbulence ensued when
Indonesia gained its independence. The communists supported President
Sukarno against right-wing rebels in 1958 and he brought communist
leaders Aidit and Njoto into his cabinet.[2] Fears grew that a military *coup
d'état* was being organised in 1965. The communist party sought to
frustrate this by initiating a preventive coup of its own. General Suharto
in turn forestalled the communists by mobilising his troops and starting
a process of bloody suppression. The American CIA was closely involved
as Moslem conservative groups were let loose on known communist
organisations and individuals. About a million suspected communists
were massacred. Where the mobs lacked rifles they used knives. The
heads of the dead were displayed on poles and corpses clogged the water
courses. Aidit and Njoto were murdered. Indonesian communism was
liquidated in the most comprehensive attack on communists since Stalin
had assaulted his own party in 1937–8. From sharing power and aiming
to monopolise it, the communist party had been cast into oblivion.[3]

The Communist Party of South Africa had been languishing under
persecution long before being banned outright in 1950. Strategy was
reconsidered and the leadership opted to devote itself to long-term
collaboration with the Black-led African National Congress to bring
down the apartheid regime established a couple of years earlier. The
thinking was that this would enable the communist party to increase its
impact on political events and leading communists to take a prominent
position. The African National Congress was more social-democratic
than Marxist in outlook. But it brought together many strands of opinion
and was committed to overthrowing a violently racist government; and
its resolve to conduct economic sabotage and armed resistance convinced

the Communist Party of South Africa of the benefits of such a coalition. Joe Slovo and other communists were prominent contributors to the African National Congress's operations. They had an influence out of proportion to the size of their membership and following. Essentially they had reconciled themselves to never holding supreme national power even after the desired overthrow of the Afrikaner-led apartheid regime.

Communists in several other countries came to the same conclusion and decided to concentrate on political activity below the national level. The most remarkable cases occurred in India. Led by E. M. S. Namboodiripad, the communist organisation in the state of Kerala on the south-western coast won 38 per cent of the votes in the 1957 elections. This result horrified Jawaharlal Nehru's government in Delhi. E. M. S. – as he was popularly known – quickly made a name for himself. The key to his success was his set of promises to rural voters. Agrarian reform was implemented fast. At its heart were restrictions on the rights of owners of the large estates. There was also a redistribution of land to their tenants. A minimum-wage law was passed to pull support from civil servants and urban workers – this was of particular benefit to the labour force in the coir industry. Nehru sent his daughter Indira Gandhi down to Kerala to encourage opposition to the communists even though the reforms had been introduced with constitutional and legal propriety. Her heavily publicised tour made no difference. Communists snubbed and denounced her. Exasperated, Nehru issued a peremptory decree to close down the Kerala administration in 1959. His legal grounds were largely spurious. Thus the state's communists became the victims of what elsewhere in the world they had often done to others.[4]

Rule by central fiat did not eliminate Delhi's problem with communism. Kerala quickly acquired a communist administration again and the communists have won most of the elections through to the present day. They remained popular by committing themselves to alleviating the plight of the peasantry and the rural poor. Local militants even renamed a whole town in honour of communism. They called it Moscow. The communist authorities encouraged parents to name their children after the Soviet pantheon. The result by 2005 was that India's Moscow had six residents called Mr Lenin. Stalins, Khrushchëvs and Brezhnevs have gone out of fashion in recent years. There is also a tendency for parents to pick almost any name that sounds attractively Russian. Anastasya was the daughter of Emperor Nicholas II murdered by communists in Yekaterinburg in July 1918; yet her name has been given to a present-day woman by her communist father.[5]

Kerala's communists had shown their independent streak since flirting with Maoism for a while in the late 1940s:[6] their Russophilia was a later development. In other parts of India, though, the attraction of the Chinese variant of communist exercised a permanent appeal. This was hardly surprising. Many members of the Communist Party of India were made to feel uneasy by the Kremlin's support for Nehru, who pursued a policy of 'non-alignment' with either of the world's superpowers. This reaction was natural enough. Indian communists were trying to gain in electoral strength by exposing the central government for its corruption and lack of resolve in improving the conditions of most Indians.[7] The warmth of Indo–Soviet relations at the governmental level undermined this activity. When the Sino–Soviet split forced communists to choose between China and the USSR, debate was intense on two great matters. One was the choice between the turbulent mobilisation demanded by Mao Zedong and the staid organisation preferred by Soviet leaders to be sanctioned. The second touched on the USSR's role in world politics. Those who sided with Mao's denunciation of 'Soviet hegemonism' broke away to form the Communist Party of India (Marxist-Leninist) – or the CPI(ML).[8]

The split was extremely violent in some places. In central Bihar the Maoists killed hundreds of members of the rival communist organisation.[9] At first they held the upper hand over the older party despite having fewer members.[10] Slowly the intra-communist enmities declined into peaceful political competition. And the Kerala precedent was followed by other Indian states. The West Bengal communist-led administration in particular achieved something remarkable. Coming to power in 1977, it succeeded in sustaining its electoral popularity into the twenty-first century. This has been the longest period of rule by communists who were elected to office anywhere in the world.

Thus the communists in many democracies tried to make the best of things by working hard at the local level. Communist militants contested elections in cities and provinces, putting themselves up as local champions in the struggle against the national government for social justice. They campaigned to improve living and working conditions. They listened to the grievances in their constituencies and did what they could for their voters – and they trusted that this activity, along with propaganda about the party's larger purposes, would benefit communism throughout the country. They led protests against the treatment of the poorer groups in society. They railed against capitalism and stressed that the landlords, industrialists and bankers were linked to a world system of exploitation and oppression. The old communist case was therefore not abandoned, and people were becoming communists for the traditional reasons: they wanted to fight and defeat the capitalist order at national and global levels. They coveted a reputation for resisting the temptation of corruption and castigated the privileges of political office and wealth. (This, of course, was the opposite of what happened in communist states, where communism enabled the emergence of a ruthless and self-indulgent political elite.)

The Japanese communists, disenchanted with Moscow yet reluctant to identify themselves with Beijing and its fanaticism, went their own way. They declared that the USSR and the People's Republic of China were equally guilty of 'hegemonism', which was the charge laid by Mao at the Kremlin's door; they also supported Japan's nationalist case for the restoration of the northern islands seized by Stalin's Red Army in 1945. They were turning into something like Western social-democrats as they embraced principles of elective, representative democracy.[11] By playing up the anti-American theme in their propaganda, they exploited popular resentment at Japan's post-war subjection to the geopolitical strategy required by the USA. The Japanese Communist Party never came near to obtaining national office. But in 1983 it achieved a measure of power in Osaka as part of a broadly based governing coalition. This was an impressive comeback after the brutal suppression of the communists – arrests, execution, prison maltreatment and forced exile – during the Korean War.[12] Few voters wanted to give up consumer capitalism. The country's economy depended on its continuing capacity to export cars, radios and other electronic products, and everyone knew this. But there was enough discontent among urban workers and low-level employees for the communists to maintain an influence.

The Italian Communist Party too fought hard local campaigns in successive elections after the Second World War. The need was recognised to compete with the attractions of radio, TV, the cinema and sport. Its newspaper *L'Unità* had been pretty dour in 1945. Posted on walls at the side of streets, it testified to the party's zeal to inculcate its message. Yet gradually it began to report on football matches. Similarly the Communist Party of Great Britain took to covering horse racing, a favourite pastime of the British working class – and indeed the party's London tipster had the edge over his rivals on newspapers of other political orientations. The Italian Communist Party went further and organised an annual Festa dell'Unità. These were celebrations with pasta, folksongs and carousing. Communists shrugged off their stolid image.

One party member, interviewed in the 1950s, explained the rationale: 'The [communist party] is very active in the organisation of pastimes for the members so as not to give them the opportunity to wander off and have their minds diverted from the spirit of the party even during their recreation.'[13] Political duties were simultaneously discharged. There were always bookstalls and public speeches at the Festa; and militants gave handouts about the domestic and international campaigns being waged by the party; badges and posters about foreign liberation movements were promoted. The Italian Communist Party for decades survived with bread, circuses and sermons.

While facing insurmountable obstacles in national politics, the communists of Italy did well in many local elections. Siena in Tuscany was an early success after the Second World War – indeed the party won an absolute majority of votes in the province (as distinct from the provincial capital). Their popularity faded only a little in subsequent years.[14] Communists of Siena had adjusted their policies to demography. Outside the city they obtained support from the agricultural poor by promising higher wages, more schools and better social welfare. Owners of large estates were put under direct pressure.[15]

Perhaps the greatest post-war achievement for Italian communists came when they took over the administration in Bologna. As the capital of Emilia-Romagna the city acted as a magnet attracting recruits to the party. Mayor Giuseppe Dozza held power for two decades. His rule was characterised by a reputation for honesty and dedication to popular welfare. Bolognese communists knew they needed to prove themselves as practical politicians. Buses, housing, parks, schools and litter collection had to be organised more efficiently – and, whenever possible, at a cheaper rate to the public – than under the Christian Democrats. Whereas the party at the national level under Togliatti, Longo and Berlinguer went on denouncing capitalism, Dozza did deals with the city's businessmen. The last thing that Dozza could afford was a decline in the local industrial and commercial dynamism.[16] His co-operation with capitalists became the model for how the communists came to power, often in coalition with the Italian Socialist Party, in other big Italian cities in subsequent years. Rome, Turin, Genoa and Naples at various times acquired local governments with communist representatives in leading positions. The hope – a vain one, as it turned out – was that a series of exemplary municipal records would pave the way for the party's eventual election to national government.

There was a similar attentiveness to local elections in other European countries. In France the communists had gained over fifty councils in towns with a population of over thirty thousand by the mid-1980s. Over the previous decades they had seldom lost a council once they had gained it. Le Havre and Calais were bastions of communist power. Rheims was another, at least until 1983.[17] The success in the big ferry ports was not an accident. French communists easily came to an understanding with state-owned companies in the docks, railways and shipping companies. They also frequently won power in councils in the Paris suburbs, where the party's efficient provision of social welfare and services enhanced its popularity. Communists in Spain and Portugal hoped to do the same after their liberation from fascism in the 1970s. The Spanish were more successful than the Portuguese. Córdoba, a large city in the south, fell into communist hands in 1983.[18]

The regional and urban communist administrations in India, Japan, Italy, France and Spain never succeeded in achieving national power. They accepted the existing electoral framework and expressed respect for the law. This was a trifle hypocritical in the Italian case since they had secret arrangements for bringing out armed units on to the streets in the event of a right-wing seizure of power.[19] But by and large they adhered to constitutional procedures. This meant that they continued to need to make themselves congenial to the electors. They were constantly criticised by the rival parties and remained under close scrutiny by a hostile press. They knew that if they put a foot wrong they would shatter the solid political groundwork they had laid under Togliatti and his successors. The result by the 1970s was that the Italian Communist Party in local government behaved like a social-democratic or socialist administration. It concentrated on getting the buses running and the streets swept. It offered welfare assistance to the poor. It aspired to what the Anglo-Saxons call respectability. When necessary, it shared power amicably with other parties of the left.

Usually it was parties affiliated to Moscow or Beijing which achieved most success at the local level. But once Deng had turned the People's Republic of China away from Mao's economic policies and towards capitalism, Beijing ceased to supplement the incomes of Maoist parties. This gravely weakened the Maoist cause in several countries. The Albanian communist regime, whose fondness for Mao persisted, was too poor to do more than fund a few propaganda outlets. (The little Albanian bookshop in London's Finsbury Park became the only place in the British capital where Stalin's multi-volume collected works could be bought.) The USSR was left as the only serious subsidiser of the scores of communist parties around the world.

Yet discontent in the same parties grew strongly after 1956. The result was the exodus of malcontents into little groups which claimed to be resuscitating the original Marxist-Leninist world-view. Some were Trotskyist, others Maoist; a few were Luxemburgist. Still others formed local groupuscules. Such recruits to communism had been drawn either by doctrinal study and conviction or by a general hostility to capitalism as well as by the attractions of internal-group solidarity. This was not very different from the situation on the political far left in the middle of the nineteenth century. Sectarian communism appealed to some among the disadvantaged, alienated and rootless young. Few of such groups could be bothered to scrabble for election to local councils in western Europe or anywhere else. They had been born out of despair at the behaviour of the large communist parties. They upheld revolutionary purity in doctrine and practice. Typically the groups gathered around a charismatic leader who offered his personal analysis of contemporary global capitalism and official world communism. They refused to despair. Although the immediate prospect of taking power was close to zero, they comforted themselves with the thought that the Bolsheviks had had only a handful of thousands of members before 1917.

Italy was a hotbed of Marxist sectarianism. Lotta Comunista in Genoa and Lotta Continua in Turin and other large cities argued that the defects of the Italian Communist Party had been evident for several decades. Togliatti was a figure of contempt among them because of his obedience to Stalin and Comintern. Whereas the Italian Communist Party steered away from direct confrontation with the state authorities, Lotta Comunista and Lotta Continua relished every opportunity to throw down a challenge to the political status quo. Togliatti's parliamentary strategy after the Second World War had been bad enough, but the Eurocommunism of Berlinguer was denounced as the complete betrayal of communist objectives.

The tendency was for grouplets to turn in on themselves and argue the niceties of Marxist theory without cracking the mould of European politics. Bookish disputes about the arcana of texts by Marx, Lenin, Trotsky and Mao proliferated. Pamphlets were sold at meetings and on stalls. The tiniest differences of interpretation caused organisational schism and intense polemic. Frustration with this situation led some young militants to turn to the theory and practice of terrorism. Italy had its Red Brigades, West Germany its Red Army Faction; the United Kingdom gave rise to the Angry Brigade. The Red Brigades captured and murdered the prominent Christian Democrat Aldo Moro in 1978. Moro had been Prime Minister in the 1960s and had advocated some kind of co-operation between the Italian Communist Party and Christian Democracy. There was much suspicion that the assassination had been facilitated by enemies in his own party and in the intelligence services who wanted to prevent any political deal with communism. In West Germany the Red Army Faction kidnapped and killed businessmen. Most of the terrorist groups in the United Kingdom were ineffectual. The Angry Brigade let off bombs but failed to hurt their targets.

If any terrorists succeeded in shaking the foundations of the British state it was the Provisional Irish Republican Army. Guided by Gerry Adams and Martin McGuinness, they left the old Irish Republican Army whose leaders claimed to be Marxists fighting for the liberation of Northern Ireland from London's oppressive rule. The Provisionals abandoned Marxism while the Official IRA continued to advocate it and, as a reward, was given material assistance by the Kremlin.[20] It was the bombing campaign of Adams and McGuinness, however, which brought the British government to the negotiating table.

The communist splinter parties in the United Kingdom argued with each other more eagerly than they took part in public affairs. They had 'theorists' – typically their own founders – who offered idiosyncratic analyses of Soviet history. Their ambition was to shoulder aside the Communist Party of Great Britain as the chief organisation of the political far left and to win the working class to their side. Their acronyms made up an alphabet soup of British communism:

CPB-ML	Communist Party of Britain – Marxist-Leninist
CPE-ML	Communist Party of England – Marxist-Leninist
MT	Militant Tendency
NCP	New Communist Party
RCG	Revolutionary Communist Group
RCLB	Revolutionary Communist League of Britain
RCP	Revolutionary Communist Party
RCPBM-L	Revolutionary Communist Party of Britain, Marxist-Leninist
RWP	Revolutionary Workers' Party
SF	Socialist Federation
Socialist League	Socialist League

SOA	Socialist Organiser Alliance
SPGB	Socialist Party of Great Britain
SWP	Socialist Workers' Party
Spartacist League	Spartacist League
WP	Workers' Power
WRP	Workers' Revolutionary Party

Some were Maoist (the CPE-ML and the RCLB) or, after Mao's death, pro-Albania (the CPB-ML and the RCPBM-L). The Militant Tendency's warmth for Trotski was shared by many Trotskyist organisations: the RCP, the RWP, the SF, the Socialist League, the SOA, the SWP, the Spartacist League, the WP and the WRP.

Most people found each ingredient in this mélange baffling and, if not amusing, unappealing; and the parties themselves were permanently ineffectual. The Militant Tendency was different. Recognising that it would never win political authority by straightforward means, it sought to infiltrate its members into the British Labour Party in targeted localities. This had been a Comintern tactic in the 1920s, and the Trotskyist international organisations had picked it up in the 1930s. The Militant Tendency took over Liverpool City Council by this method in the 1980s. The key to its effectiveness was clandestine parasitism. It subsisted by pretending not to exist as a separate entity and its leader Peter Taafe pretended to be a dutiful activist for the Labour Party. The Militant Tendency was a gift to Margaret Thatcher and the British Conservatives, who in the 1979 parliamentary election highlighted the Labour Party's connection with hidden organisations of the extreme left. Liverpool councillors mismanaged the city budget with stupendous incompetence. When the banks would no longer bail out the deficit, taxis were hired to deliver redundancy notices to employees of the administration and its services throughout the city. The Labour Party National Executive, fired up by a passionate speech by its leader Neil Kinnock at the Party Conference, expelled the Militant Tendency. And without its host, the parasite shrivelled into insignificance.

34. LAST OF THE COMMUNIST REVOLUTIONS

A decade and a half elapsed between the Cuban Revolution in 1959 and the next communist seizure of power. This had not been for want of trying by communists. Castro's friend and associate Che Guevara, frustrated by what he saw as the lack of independent radicalism in a Cuba under Soviet tutelage, went off to the Congo to foment and organise a revolution in the way he wanted. When this failed, he tried to do the same in the mountains of Bolivia. He raised a guerrilla contingent as he and Castro had done in Cuba, calling on workers and peasants for support. He denounced the Bolivian government as a puppet of Yankee imperialism. But his fame undid his chances of surprise. The forces of order, aided by American money and expertise, were ready for him. Guevara was cornered in Bolivia in October 1967 in the presence of a CIA agent. No one wanted to put him on open trial; there was concern about his charisma in a country where plenty of people were discontented with the government. He was shot at the site of his capture.[1]

The great powers – the USA, the USSR and the People's Republic of China – continued to exert an impact on communism around the world. Nowhere was this more obvious than in east Asia. North Korea survived as an independent state because Washington knew that Moscow and Beijing would intervene militarily if ever an American attack took place. Until the early 1970s Korean communism had an economy which performed as well as most Marxist-Leninist countries. Gross national product was roughly the same in the two halves of Korea, communist and capitalist, in the previous period. North Korea had an impressive export trade, especially in equipment for foreign armed forces. This was a highly militarised society. Conscription kept well over a million men under arms at any given time.[2] Party leader Kim Il-sung was accorded almost divine status. Mass rallies of joyful citizens praising his achievements and expressing gratitude for his wise rule were frequent. The

'Great Leader', the party and the masses were said to be in unison. Yet North Korea suffered economic atrophy as the military share of the budget got fatter. (Meanwhile South Korea experienced a boom as its imports of advanced technology and finance from Japan and the USA paid off.) Civilians went hungry throughout the north; even rice began to fail to match the state's requirements for consumption.

Kim would not be deflected. He calculated that the best way of getting co-operation from neighbouring countries was to make his armed forces feared in the region. Research and development were initiated for the acquisition of independent nuclear weapons. Labour camps were expanded in population. Millions of Koreans, in the north as in the south, had been cut off from their families since the Panmunjom agreement of July 1953. The Koreans of the north might as well have been living on a different planet, so little did they know about the situation in the south.

A more effective effort was made by the communist state in North Vietnam to reunite its country. The country had been divided after the French withdrew from Indochina after their military defeat at Dien Bien Phu and the Geneva Peace Conference in 1954. Communist leader Ho Chi Minh had been fighting for the independence of the 'Democratic Republic of Vietnam' since the Second World War and did not intend to be bound by the agreement signed in Geneva. He had travelled widely in Europe and the USA. The Soviet and Chinese leaderships were cool towards a resumption of hostilities, but Ho went his own way just as Mao had done in the late 1940s.[3] By 1958 he was ready to strike at the south. The army of North Vietnam, the Vietcong, took up the struggle in 1958. Its advances were rapid and deep, and the Eisenhower administration had to fill the gap left by the French by financing South Vietnam's defence against communism. President Kennedy dispatched troops. This failed to eliminate the Vietcong. Massive additional assistance by the USA proved necessary. Kennedy's successor President Johnson raised the number of American troops to over half a million by 1968. The American official standpoint was that, if South Vietnam were to be communised, it would be the first fallen domino in a line of countries in south-east Asia.

The Vietcong used a guerrilla strategy and avoided open pitched battle. It infiltrated villages in the south. It picked off units in the American encampments. The Pentagon sanctioned measures including the chemical defoliation of forests where the enemy was thought to be lurking. The US strategy suffered from several defects. The Americans failed to sanitise a South Vietnam government which was corrupt from top to bottom. Their own armed operations made the Vietcong appear as dedicated patriots; and although they regularly bombed Hanoi – the northern capital – and strafed the supply lines, they refrained from using the nuclear weapons which would have brought Ho to negotiations. Washington's morale was sapped by demonstrations in American cities against the waging of the war. Television news clips from South Vietnam about atrocities – as well as growing resentment of conscription – poured petrol on the flames of public protest. President Richard Nixon, despite having come to office in 1969 as a vociferous anti-communist, offered peace terms to the Vietnamese forces as they advanced relentlessly towards the southern capital Saigon. For the first time since the Second World War one of the world's two superpowers faced military defeat. Washington abruptly withdrew its forces in April 1975. American diplomats fled by helicopter at the very last moment from the roof of their embassy in Saigon.

Ho Chi Minh had not lived to witness his triumph; he died in 1969. As the northern authorities tightened their grip on Saigon, they did not forget him and the city was renamed Ho Chi Minh City in his honour. Vietnam was a single country again. Ho had organised the communist order on political and economic principles which drew on the Soviet and Chinese experiences. Agriculture was collectivised. A network of labour camps was spread across the country and hostile 'class' elements were rounded up and forced to abandon their capitalistic sympathies. A strict one-party dictatorship was imposed. A blend of patriotism and Marxism-Leninism was propagated. The party and the army were reinforced as the combined bastion of the regime. The Democratic Republic of Vietnam had been born in a colonial war and had known nothing but war since obtaining its independence. It was an even more militarised society than the People's Republic of China. Yet its industry made hardly any armaments. It had little industry at all and the Americans bombed its few factories into rubble. Financial support and military supplies from the USSR and China had been crucial for survival.

The northerners communised the south after the American withdrawal. Expropriations and arrests accompanied the expansion of the party and army presence across the newly occupied provinces. Within a year or two the southern economy had been pressed into a northern mould. Yet the wartime devastation was everywhere. Vietnam was a land of orphans, invalids, ruined houses, disrupted rice paddies and poisoned forests. Hanoi expressed the wish for a rapprochement, but the departed

Americans cut the Vietnamese off from the world economy. Peace was meant to turn the country into a desert. Although the USSR continued to proffer aid, it was never on a scale adequate for substantial reconstruction.

Hanoi was undeterred. The communist leadership under Le Duan pursued an agenda of expanding its regional influence. Vietnam refused to be managed by the USSR or the People's Republic of China. It had the forces. It had the chutzpah and experience as well as a national tradition of aggression against its neighbours. Victimised Vietnam was turning into south-east Asia's bully boy. Things in reality were more complicated. The long history of Indochina had an increasing impact. Boundaries were contentious. Every country had large national minorities. Vietnam and Cambodia were extremely ill disposed towards each other; communist internationalism was little in evidence. China was no disinterested spectator. It had helped Ho Chi Minh because he deflected the USA from any possible crusade against China. Now that Vietnam had been reunified, there was concern about a Vietnamese military assertiveness across frontiers. The Chinese withdrew assistance to Hanoi, and in February 1979, months after Vietnam had joined Comecon and allied itself firmly with the USSR, a brief war broke out between Vietnam and China. Indochina was a region of intersecting conflicts which led to the oddest of initiatives. Western leaders since the Second World War had opposed communism wherever it sprouted. But this policy was dropped in the 1970s when the USA effected a rapprochement with the People's Republic of China and even supported the communist terror-regime of Pol Pot. Geopolitics, national enmities and communist ideology were amalgamated in a witches' brew.

Or rather in an evil wizard's. The person in question was Pol Pot, leader of the Khmers Rouges, whose communist forces seized power in the Cambodian capital Phnom Penh in April 1975; he went by the soubriquet First Brother – shades of George Orwell's *1984* – and was a Maoist fanatic: he had absorbed Mao's ideas for revolutionary transformation like blotting paper.[4]

As parts of the country fell to the Khmers Rouges, they instituted instant communisation. Farming was collectivised. Even Mao had taken years to get this far; Pol Pot showed no such patience. Private property as such was abolished. Neither Stalin not Mao had attempted so extreme a measure, but Pol Pot pressed onwards. Markets and shops were prohibited. Money was abolished. The Gothic cathedral at the heart of Phnom Penh, pride of the French colonialists, was demolished.[5] The

Khmers Rouges identified two principal internal enemies. The large Vietnamese minority in Cambodia was one of them. Pol Pot ordered the razing of their villages and the butchering of the inhabitants, and there was savage ethnic cleansing. Equally miserable was the plight of urban residents of any nationality: the Khmers Rouges feared them as a fount of hostility. They wanted to work on Cambodian society with nobody around who would know more about the world than they themselves did. (Not that they knew much.) Their solution was to empty the towns of their entire population. Residents had to leave at a moment's notice for the countryside, taking only a mat, a tin bowl and the clothes they stood up in. They fended for themselves in unfriendly villages. Pol Pot was glacially indifferent: 'To have them is no gain, to lose them is no loss.'⁶

No ruler in history had engaged in such lunacy. There had been mass deportations. There had been massacres and depredations. The Chinese communists, furthermore, had engaged in brutal campaigns to push people into the countryside. But even Mao did not close down his cities. Pol Pot was unique in the Marxist tradition for treating urban life not as a prerequisite of communist progress but as an iniquity to be eliminated. It is true that he expected to revert eventually to an agenda congruent with communism elsewhere. Pol projected the total mechanisation of agriculture within ten years and the construction of an industrial base for the Cambodian economy within twenty. He aimed to double or triple the population.⁷ But all this was reserved for the future: his immediate priority was to yoke Cambodians to the party's rule.

He took power in the Cambodian capital Phnom Penh just days after the Americans scuttled from Vietnam in spring 1975. An early measure was to purge his own forces. Every follower suspected of pro-Vietnamese leanings was hauled off to an ex-secondary school redesignated as Interrogation Centre S-21. Fiendish tortures were applied to extract confessions to imaginary plots. The 'evil microbes inside the party' were liquidated. Communists were forced to attend courses of indoctrination and self-criticism. They had to go to evening 'lifestyle meetings' where they admitted to faults in their work during the day. A working cycle of nine days with the tenth off was proclaimed, but the tenth day was in fact reserved for political education.⁸ Food was used as a disciplinary instrument and the former inhabitants of the towns were given only enough rice to keep them from starvation. Everyone except the party leadership was obliged to carry out hard physical labour. Collective farming was imposed and villages had to deliver centrally determined quotas of produce to the authorities. Frugality became an official virtue. People were ordered to be satisfied with whatever food they were given. Many took to foraging for snails, mice and insects; but when Pol Pot heard about this, he made it a capital offence to pick up a fallen coconut.[9]

Few local functionaries in Cambodia had administrative or economic expertise. This was as Pol wanted it. He had no use for comrades who might relapse into ideas and practices which they had learned independently of him. Cambodian communism sealed itself off from ideological erosion. Violent, arbitrary rule was pervasive. Leaders in the country's various zones appointed their own 'strings' to jobs – strings were the equivalent of Soviet cliental 'tails'. Misreporting to higher officialdom became the norm.[10] Although repression was ordered from Phnom Penh, a lot happened in consequence of lower-level initiatives – and the scale of repression differed from area to area.[11] Ill-educated, bloodthirsty ex-guerrilla fighters became a law unto themselves. Cambodia had experienced almost continuous civil war in previous decades, and brutality had regularly been practised by all sides. The terror under Pol Pot took this to the nadir of human degradation. About a fifth of the Cambodian population died; some estimates put the losses even higher: it was demographically the most devastating of all communist revolutions in the twentieth century.[12]

The madness was brought to an end not by the resistance of the Cambodians but by Vietnamese intervention. War between Vietnam and Cambodia had broken out sporadically from the start of Pol's rule. Pol terrorised his own Vietnamese minority and idiotically made military incursions into Vietnam. The Hanoi authorities helped to establish an exile force which, with an active Vietnamese component, attacked the Khmers Rouges and overthrew Pol in January 1979. The Khmers Rouges were beaten but not eliminated, and they returned to prominence in later years; but they never again dominated the country and the nightmare of their rule had been definitively removed.

By that time the Chilean Revolution too had been suppressed. Salvador Allende won the presidential election of September 1970 against his two rival contenders, ex-President Jorge Alessandri and Radomiro Tomic, with 36 per cent of the votes cast.[13] He was sixty-two years old, tubby and bespectacled, but still a handsome figure. He radiated a reassuring avuncularity which at last won over many doubters in the electorate. It was his first successful campaign in four attempts. Allende was a Marxist heading the Socialist Party; he was the leading figure in an electoral coalition involving the Communist Party of Chile. His Popular Unity government had radical intentions. In his victory speech he declared: 'I won't be just another president; I'll be the first president of the first truly democratic, popular, national and revolutionary government in Chile's history.'[14] Allende spoke of 'the Chilean road to socialism'. He had never believed in the violent transformation. (Che had affectionately written of him 'striving after the same goal by different means'.)[15] The government planned to introduce fiscal reform to benefit the poor, end the power of the latifundia owners, establish a unicameral legislature and enable popular participation in economic management, in political decision-making and in the administration of justice. Allende boasted that he would pursue a genuinely independent foreign policy.[16]

The whole history of Latin America in the twentieth century told him that US political and economic power would be directed against him. The economic legacy of the Eduardo Frei government was grievous: there was wild inflation and wage and salary demands were strong. The price of copper, Chile's main earner of foreign currency, on the world market was falling. When Washington heard of the Chilean president's bid for independence, it withdrew financial assistance from the country and ensured that neither the International Monetary Fund nor the World Bank would help either.[17] The Popular Unity government, moreover, was a coalition of six parties including social-democrats to the right of the Communist Party of Chile and socialists to its left. Many leading figures in Allende's Socialist Party were committed to forms of revolutionary violence, and it was sometimes hard for him to restrain them from embroiling him in trouble. The opposition whipped up anti-government sentiment. The elections to the Congress and to the Chamber of Deputies in the year before Allende's presidential triumph had failed to provide Popular Unity with a majority of seats. The opportunities for destabilising the new government were ample.[18]

The huge debit in Chile's balance of payments in international trade forced Allende to seek help from friendly powers. Cuba could give little financial assistance since its own economy was reliant on subsidies from the USSR. Fidel Castro came to Santiago in 1971 to express political solidarity and to boost morale. His lengthy speeches, though, were not to Chilean popular taste – indeed they had never been wildly liked in Havana but had had to be tolerated – and his highly publicised trip, which lasted three weeks, damaged Allende's effort to allay disquiet in business, professional and military circles. Anti-communists in Chile knew that Castro had begun his own revolution by preaching moderation.

Although Allende frequently talked about his 'peaceful road' to socialism, there was no guarantee that he would stick to his word. With some difficulty the government succeeded in getting financial relief from abroad. Other countries in Central and South America were better placed than Cuba to grant the loans. The USSR and eastern Europe also supplied credits to the value of 500 million dollars.[19] The Soviet leaders felt they could not simply stand by and let Allende's Popular Unity collapse even though the communists were a minority inside it.

The Chilean government fulfilled its promise to raise the salaries of state employees. Allende nationalised many industrial companies, increasing the number of them by five times. Price controls were introduced for the benefit of the poor who had brought Popular Unity to power. Among the effects, however, was a growing disruption of the commercial process. Small business proprietors in particular felt the pinch. The economic crisis deepened. The USSR had never been confident about Allende's policies and refused to go on showing Chile the generosity it displayed to Cuba.[20] Allende suspended payments on his country's external debts.[21]

Allende and his ministers held their nerve. The copper mines were taken into state ownership in July 1971. (The feeling that national assets had been plundered by the mining companies, including foreign ones, was so widely held in Chile that the political opposition supported the government's measure.)[22] Agrarian reform was more controversial. For centuries the indigenous people had been robbed of their traditional lands as Spanish-speaking landlords seized territory for their latifundia. An agricultural oligarchy ruled the rural areas. Allende took the initiative in 1972 and announced his intention to take over 60 per cent of cultivable landed property for redistribution to the rural poor.[23] The consequence was a decreasing level of agricultural production. Many new peasant owners worked their land only for subsistence. The government also picked up the pace of industrial nationalisation. Only thirty-one enterprises were state owned in November 1970. By May 1973 the number had risen to 165 and was projected to climb higher.[24] In most cases the government took the lead. But Allende's drive for popular participation induced some workforces to seize control of their enterprises and eject their employers. If anything, there was greater commotion in the cities than in the countryside.

Discontent grew across in society. It is true that communists won 38 per cent of workers' votes in the 1972 election to the trade union movement – and socialists came second with 32 per cent. But among technical staff the Christian Democrats were out in front with 41 per cent. Across the professions there was a rising concern that Popular Unity was incapable of sound governance. Nor were even the workers solidly behind Allende. Those who remained outside the trade unions constituted a majority, and many of them were hostile to Popular Unity.[25]

The government was hit by a tidal wave of protest. Unlike Castro, Allende had no monopoly in the press and probably did not want one. His enemies relied heavily on Washington's financial and diplomatic assistance; they also made use of advice from the Central Intelligence Agency. Short of arresting the leaders of Chile's traditional elites, Allende ran a continuous risk of being overthrown in a *coup d'état*. It was not as if his handling of the economy was bringing prosperity to most people. Industry and commerce were in chaos. The government's popularity was in decline among many of its supporters. Even so, Allende retained a core of left-wing parties, trade unions, workers and peasants on his side. If he was going to be removed, the easiest option would be military action. Allende thought he had covered his back by appointing an apolitical officer, Augusto Pinochet, to head the armed forces. This was a catastrophic misjudgement. Pinochet, like many in the high command, hated communism and disorder and wanted a return to capitalist economics. US Secretary of State Henry Kissinger knew the general's inclinations better than Allende. With his sanction the CIA channelled the assistance needed for a successful attempt on power.[26]

Pinochet struck on 11 September 1973. Allende only discovered what was happening when tanks rumbled on to the lawn outside the presidential palace in Santiago. Resistance was futile. The armed forces quickly imposed their authority, but Allende refused to surrender. Recognising that his coalition government was no more, he killed himself with the rifle given him by Fidel Castro. All the parties of the left were scattered into exile or the political underground. The military junta spared no one. Communist party chief Luis Corvalán was thrown into prison. In 1976 he was included in an international prisoner-exchange. Soviet dissenter Vladimir Bukovski was allowed out to English exile while Corvalán took up residence in Moscow. Chilean communism, which had developed a strategy of radical economic and social change without violence or illegality, was crushed. Its party was outlawed. Its militants were rounded up and held in appalling conditions in the National Stadium in Santiago until they joined the ranks of the 'disappeared' after being shot.

Yet while life remained harsh for most people in Latin America there was still fertile ground for the growth of communism. Middle-class students invariably had some in their midst who resented 'Yankee imperialism' and identified their governments as repressive collaborators with the USA. Peasants and workers demanded better conditions. Castro's Cuba was widely praised for its social and economic reforms. Allende's miserable end was taken as yet another example of American selfish and ruthless interference in the politics of the hemisphere.

Communists elsewhere in the world, especially Africa, were undeterred. Angola was a focalpoint of struggle. The Cubans had encouraged the MPLA (Movimento Popular de Libertação de Angola) since the mid-1960s, and the USSR had begun to supply weapons.[27] The collapse of the Portuguese Empire in 1974–5 was followed by a civil war. Consultations between Moscow and Havana led to a division of labour: Moscow would supply money, transport and military equipment, Havana would dispatch a large expeditionary force to bolster the MPLA.[28] By spring 1976 this had resulted in victory over US-backed forces and Aghostinho Neto established a government committed to Marxism-Leninism and allied with the USSR. The fighting, however, was resumed by the anti-communist army of Jonas Savimbi; and although economic planning institutions were introduced in the Soviet style, the war against Savimbi devoured all the energies of the MPLA. South Africa and the USA supplied Savimbi with ample funds and equipment. Not until Savimbi died in 2002 did the conflict come to an end. It would be overstretching the word's meaning to say that communism was installed in Angola, despite the longevity of the regime of Neto and his successors.

Ethiopian communists were hardly more effective in setting up a stable regime. Stirrings in the armed forces against Emperor Haile Selassie led in 1974 to the formation of the Co-ordinating Committee (Derg). This body steadily stripped the Emperor of his powers. Its own members were deeply divided and its first leader Lieutenant General Aman Andom was killed in factional strife. The radical wing of the Derg, headed by Major Mengistu Haile Mariam, took dictatorial control. Mengistu declared rural land to be 'the property of the Ethiopian people' and distributed it to peasant co-operatives. He quickly moved to a communist ideological commitment. Supporters of the Imperial regime resisted him even after the murder of the Emperor in August 1975. Ethnic groups, especially the Eritreans and the Somalis, fought to secede from the Ethiopian state. Mengistu also confronted opposition in the Derg. His response was to conduct a Red Terror.[29] This finally lost him financial aid from the USA, which supported him against the Soviet-backed Eritrean rebels; but by then he could count on support from the USSR, which had ceased to favour the Eritrean rebels. In February 1977 Mengistu killed his surviving rivals and critics in the Derg. Finance, arms and military advisers in large quantities were transported to Ethiopia from Moscow. Cubans too were dispatched. Ethiopia had become a geostrategic outpost of world communism in the Horn of Africa.

Although the Derg's fighting capacity increased, the basic difficulties of communist rule got worse. Eritreans and Somalis kept up the struggle against a government which used brutal methods of suppression. Economic mismanagement was severe. Whole regions of the country experienced famine. The assault on religion and social customs caused enormous resentment. Mengistu even annoyed his Soviet advisers. They thought his propensity for political violence counter-productive; they were also disappointed by his failure to construct a communist party, mobilise the 'masses' and resolve inter-ethnic enmities. The continual executions were regarded as undesirable.[30]

Mengistu had built a confinement ward almost to rival Pol Pot's in the lunatic asylum of communist politics. Far from being controllable, he had used Soviet and Cuban assistance more or less as he liked. The same was true in Afghanistan. Two communist groups, Khalq and Parcham, had existed since the mid-1960s. These were bitter rivals but formed themselves into a united People's Democratic Party of Afghanistan and campaigned against President Mohammed Daoud and his slow pace of reform. Modernity seemed to be postponed for decades. In April 1978 the Khalq carried out a successful coup against the Daoud government and Khalq leaders Hafizullah Amin and Nur Mohammed Taraki seized power. This came as a surprise to the Kremlin, which had been supporting Daoud. Parcham warned Moscow of the dangers of Khalq extremism. Amin pressed on with executions of the regime's open enemies. Civil war broke out. Islamist rebellions of the various ethnic groups sprang up everywhere. Amin sought to win support by announcing a campaign for universal literacy and land reform. But little was achievable in an environment of unending violence and social insecurity. Amin had Taraki murdered in October 1979; he was also showing signs of wanting a rapprochement with Washington. It was in this situation of political disintegration and intensifying carnage that the Soviet leadership took its fateful decision to intervene militarily in December.[31]

The Khalq's seizure of power in Kabul was the last of the twentieth-century communist revolutions and demonstrated beyond peradventure that communism had no chance of surviving in power without resorting to massive repression. The Soviet comrades were frequently appalled by what they witnessed. They belonged to a generation which remembered the horrors of Stalin's rule, and they could hardly believe the recklessness of Pol Pot, Mengistu Haile Mariam and Hafizullah Amin. These were revolutions led by men wilder than the early Bolsheviks, wilder even than Stalin and Mao. They attempted to solve problems of economics, administration, ethnicity and religion by surgical force. Their mayhem kicked up a storm of hatred for communism. Yet the gradualist approach of Salvador Allende was hardly more successful; his regime was hurtling towards economic disaster and political disintegration even before Pinochet struck. Communist revolutionary rule proved to be a passage down a cul-de-sac.

PART SIX

ENDINGS

FROM 1980

35. ROADS FROM COMMUNISM

American presidents from Harry Truman to Jimmy Carter had acted as though the USSR was a durable fixture in world politics. It was as late as 1988 that Richard Nixon published his book *1999: Victory without War*, making the case that only a policy of renewed détente could safely wear down communism into defeat.[1] The USSR was a global power. It financed and directed dozens of communist parties and their 'front' organisations. It projected its military might and prestige across the oceans. Its missiles had the capacity to obliterate European, Japanese and American cities within minutes; its submarines docked in Vietnam. Although fewer and fewer communists thought the Soviet Union infallible or gave it automatic allegiance, its influence remained extensive. No other communist state, not even the People's Republic of China, was a close rival. Although communism had deep internal divisions around the world, communist states covered a third of the terrestrial surface of the planet. Most people assumed that things could go on like that for many years. It was widely known, of course, that communism was experiencing bottlenecks of economic development and encountering a growing tide of resentment from the societies where it had been imposed. But nobody suggested that the time was very near when most communist states would disappear.[2]

Global politics were transformed by the American presidential elections of November 1980. Carter had faced criticism for failing to secure the rescue of US diplomats held hostage in Tehran by the Iranian government under Ayatollah Khomeini. He also incurred blame for weakness in standing up to the USSR. The Soviet invasion of Afghanistan was taken as proof that the Kremlin was bent on unlimited expansion. There was a growing feeling among Americans that their country had lost its sense of purpose in the world; national pride had not yet recovered from the defeat in the Vietnam War in 1975.

Ronald Reagan easily won the election, gaining a mandate to rectify the situation on entering office in January 1981. The Soviet leadership, already discountenanced by Carter's rejection of détente, was seriously worried. *Pravda* routinely described Reagan as a war-mongering ignoramus who spurned negotiations in favour of nuclear brinkmanship. Until his election as Governor of California in 1967, he was famous as a Hollywood actor and chairman of the actors' union. His insistence on taking plenty of rest and on delegating authority to his subordinates fostered the idea that he was a figure of small substance, and he did little to counteract the image. With his dyed hair and genial demeanour, he was thought a plaything of manipulators who ratcheted up the tension in US–Soviet relations. Reagan leavened his speeches with anecdotes and avoided the complexities of affairs. He even joked, when he thought he was not being recorded, about launching missiles against Moscow. Seemingly an inmate had taken over the psychiatric ward.

His basic idea was that communism had been over-indulged. He declared the USSR an 'evil empire', asserting that totalitarian states were 'the focus of evil in the modern world'.[3] Truman, when introducing the policy of containment in 1947, had expected it to expire from its internal difficulties. Reagan was more militant: 'The West won't contain communism, it will transcend communism. It won't bother to ... denounce it, it will dismiss it as some bizarre chapter in human history whose last pages are even now being written.'[4] He refused to accept that the Cold War was a permanent condition. Reagan increased pressures on the Soviet budget by raising American military expenditure. By 1985 it had doubled in half a decade.[5]

Reagan in 1981 was as militant as Churchill in 1918 without being a warmonger. Wherever in the world a Soviet threat existed, he armed its local enemies. He licensed a gargantuan budgetary deficit. The mujehaddin resistance to the USSR's puppet regime in Afghanistan was given Stinger ground-to-air missiles.[6] Reagan funnelled cash and arms to the Contra rebels against Nicaragua's radical reformers – the Sandinistas – under Daniel Ortega, who had come to power in July 1979.[7] Washington also supported the governmental and paramilitary forces in El Salvador trying to suppress the Marxist guerrilla movement known as the Farabundo Martí National Liberation Front. In October 1983 he ordered the US Marines to suppress the Marxist-led New Jewel government on the tiny Caribbean island of Grenada. He commended Guatemala's corrupt military dictator Efrain Rios Montt as being 'totally dedicated to democracy'.[8] This was not his most convincing remark but showed his determination to inoculate world politics against the communist infection. Reagan also started tilting policy against the compromises with the

People's Republic of China negotiated by Nixon and Carter. Taiwan was no longer to be quietly abandoned. Reagan risked confrontation with Deng Xiaoping rather than drop his anti-communist commitment.

He refrained, however, from withdrawing 'most favoured nation' status from Romania, Hungary and Poland. Like Carter, he wanted to help the communist leaderships of those countries to make trouble for the USSR in Eastern Europe. Only in 1982, after Poland's armed forces had crushed the Solidarity trade union, did he withdraw the concessions being made to the Polish regime.[9] The rise in global interest rates, moreover, provided Washington with increased leverage in diplomatic relations as most states in eastern Europe fell into hopeless debt to the Western banking system.[10] The USSR, whose economy had its own problems, was constrained to bail out the Soviet Bloc or else confront increased political problems in the region.

Reagan in the same period proposed a deal to end the possibility of a third world war. He had boundless optimism. In 1981 he sent a handwritten letter to Brezhnev pleading for the 'normalisation' of relations between their two countries. (The Politburo treated this as demagogy.)[11] Tossing SALT II into the dustbin, he asked for START to be got under way. START would be the Strategic Arms Reduction Talks. Any idea of Mutually Assured Destruction (MAD), in Reagan's eyes, was madness because it remained entirely possible that a lone missile might penetrate the enemy airspace.[12] The only possible outcome would be reciprocal devastation and an uninhabitable planet. American security precautions would count for nothing. In March 1983 Reagan committed himself to financing a Strategic Defence Initiative (SDI). This instantly became known as the Star Wars Initiative – a reference to the popular sci-fi films of George Lucas. Reagan hoped that American scientists and technologists would enable his armed forces to intercept and eliminate any ballistic missile fired against the USA, and he insisted that he was willing to share such technology with the world's other powers. Soviet leaders were told that they too could receive the technology. Reagan announced his ultimate aim to be the abolition of all nuclear bombs.

The Soviet Politburo had cause to distrust him and to face him down.[13] When an international communist conference was held in Moscow in 1981, Brezhnev was in poor health; but the political line remained straight and conventional. Supposedly capitalism was decaying and communism was on the rise. Doubts existed whether the Strategic Defence Initiative was truly feasible (even though the Politburo took the precaution of ordering its scientists to work on their own rival project).[14]

Sceptics about the SDI were not uncommon in Reagan's own administration, as well as among the NATO governments. At the very least, the
American President had aroused perplexity. If he thought the USSR so
evil, why would he aim to eliminate nuclear weaponry and to share anti-
ballistic technology? Could an SDI system really be developed? Was it
sensible, if the system really could be built, to hand it over to the USSR?
Could nuclear bombs, once produced, be annihilated by politicians? And
if Reagan was going to annoy the People's Republic of China, how was
the USA going to cope with a deteriorating relationship with both of the
great communist powers at the same time?

Brezhnev died in November 1982 and the USSR acquired Yuri
Andropov as its new Party General Secretary. Andropov recognised the
need for political and economic changes if the USSR was to remain at
all competitive with the USA. He called for a renewed emphasis on
discipline and a rooting out of corruption. Dozens of central and local
party functionaries were shunted into retirement. Punctuality and conscientiousness at work was demanded. Andropov stated that the leadership had failed to understand conditions in society; by implication he
was conceding that a gap had opened between the party and most
citizens. Behind the scenes he set up a group of younger politicians
including Mikhail Gorbachëv and Nikolai Ryzhkov to explore what kind
of reforms were needed in the Soviet economy. He also put in train a
revision of the country's foreign policy. Andropov quietly proposed that
both the USA and the USSR should formally guarantee not to intervene
militarily in the countries under their control. Thus he signalled disapproval of what had happened to Hungary in 1956 and to Czechoslovakia
in 1968. Confidential indications were given to Cuba that the USSR was
withdrawing its military guarantee for the island's defence. He called not
just for limitations on the superpowers' stockpiles of nuclear weaponry
but for their drastic reduction.

Andropov, ex-Chairman of the KGB, understood that he would have
a weak bargaining hand unless the USSR could show a sustained capacity
to develop its military technology. The Politburo approved. Investment
was sanctioned for upgrading the Soviet armed forces. The military-
technological parity with the USA won by Brezhnev was to be reattained
even at the expense of the popular standard of living. Andropov wanted
to 'perfect' the communist order; he had hoped for plenty of time to do
this. But Reagan's geopolitical challenge would be met. The Cold War
was going to get hotter.

Moscow and Washington in this situation were unlikely to patch up their diplomatic relationship. Mutual distrust remained acute and events seemed to confirm the justification for it. In August 1983 a South Korean civilian plane, KAL-007, was shot down after straying into Soviet airspace in the Far East. All 269 passengers perished. Military personnel in the USSR had feared that a nuclear strike was being undertaken by subterfuge. As the innocence of the over-flight became evident, Reagan denounced the incident as a crime against humanity. Then just a few weeks later, in November, the KGB reported to Andropov that intelligences sources were indicating the possibility that the USA was planning a sudden nuclear attack on the USSR.[15] Supposedly this was going to happen under the cover of an American military exercise called Able Archer. Soviet armed forces were put on the highest state of alert. The slightest misunderstanding by one or other superpower could have triggered the Third World War and a global holocaust. In fact Andropov held his nerve, declining to take pre-emptive action. The secret emergency ended and no Soviet or American politician wanted to comment on what had been happening. This was a crisis close to the scale of the Cuban missiles crisis of October 1962; but its principal players thought it sensible to conceal it from their citizens.

Reagan recognised that his message about wishing to eliminate tensions between his country and the USSR was failing to get through:

> During my first years in Washington, I think many of us in the administration took it for granted that the Russians, like ourselves, considered it unthinkable that the United States would launch a first strike against them. But the more experience I had with Soviet leaders and other heads of state who knew them, the more I began to realize that many Soviet officials feared us not only as adversaries but as potential aggressors who might hurl nuclear weapons at them in a first strike.[16]

Re-elected in 1984, he sought to assure the Soviet leadership that he wanted peace; he also signalled that he sought a resumption of negotiations.[17] This was not going to be easy. Andropov had been in poor health at his accession to the General Secretaryship, and he died in February 1984. His successor Konstantin Chernenko had been Brezhnev's personal assistant. Mental agility beyond the routine tasks of administration had never been one of his strong features and he was already badly ill with emphysema. Reagan was trying to parley at a table at which he was the solitary sitter.

Yet fortune smiled on the American strategy when, in March 1985,

Chernenko died and was succeeded by Mikhail Gorbachëv. There was already a readiness in the West to treat the new leader differently from previous General Secretaries. British Prime Minister Margaret Thatcher had said: 'I like Mr Gorbachev. We can do business together.' Gorbachëv talked with an amiable flexibility unknown in any previous party general secretary. Thatcher's opinion of him was quickly shared by other Western leaders. Soviet internal reforms were put in motion in politics and economics,[18] and communist rulers in eastern Europe were told that they should no longer count on the armed support of the USSR to sustain their regimes.[19] President Reagan joined the crowd of Gorbachëv's admirers when, in November, they met in Geneva for the first time. They got on famously. Both men were eager to reduce the number of nuclear missiles pointed at each other's country; and they aimed, if at all possible, to eliminate such missiles from every arsenal and to end the Cold War. Only Reagan's refusal to halt support for the Strategic Defence Initiative caused the talks to founder. The two men emerged from their session knowing that a chance had been missed for a fundamental settlement of hostilities between the two countries.

The sharpening difficulties of the USSR helped to strengthen Gorbachëv's commitment to internal and external reform. Poland was a constant worry as strikes and demonstrations continued under the impetus of the Solidarity trade union. Communist-ruled eastern Europe depended on cheap oil and gas from the Soviet Union – about seventy-five billion dollars' worth of implicit commercial subsidies are thought to have passed from Moscow in the 1970s.[20] Western banks assisted in bailing out communism by continuing to lend money to communist states.[21] The strains on the Soviet budget had been increased by the invasion of Afghanistan – and they were to grow again in 1986 when the world's main countries which exported oil agreed to reduce their prices. Cuban intervention in Angola continued to cost more than the USSR could afford.

If the USSR was ever to compete with the USA in economic development, it badly needed to reduce its military expenditure. Personal computers and later the Internet were pulling things forward at break-neck speed. American firms were in the lead and there was a rapid expansion of the world market in consumer goods. The USSR had always lagged behind; now it suddenly saw its main competitors disappearing out of sight. It was no longer credible that capitalism was in its terminal global crisis. Greece and Spain joined the European Union and ceased being the backward enclaves of the continent. Ireland's commercial growth was remarkable. Elsewhere in the world there was similar progress. The People's Republic of China had learned from Taiwan and Hong Kong – territories it claimed as Chinese – that capitalism had an economic and social energy that communism lacked. South Korea was offering the same lesson (although the lesson was ignored by North Korea). So too were countries such as Indonesia and Malaysia. The 'Third World' was overtaking the USSR in industrial capacity and technological dynamism. The desirability of an improved relationship with the USA was uncontroversial among Politburo members who saw the necessity of moving their budgetary expenditure away from its preponderant emphasis on the armaments sector.

Four summit meetings followed. Gorbachëv and Reagan at Reykjavik in October 1986 nearly came to an agreement on the abolition of their nuclear weaponry but the SDI again proved an insurmountable obstacle. By December 1987, in Washington, Gorbachëv recognised that Reagan's attachment to the SDI was indissoluble and an Intermediate-Range Nuclear Forces Treaty was signed. This was a landmark on the road towards ending the Cold War. For the first time the USA and the USSR had agreed to destroy a large part of their stock of nuclear weapons. In April 1988 Gorbachëv announced his decision to withdraw Soviet forces from Afghanistan; and when visiting the United Nations Organisation in New York in December 1988, he renounced ideological principles such as 'class struggle' in international relations.[22] Afghanistan was the symbol of something bigger. Gorbachëv made clear to both his Politburo and Reagan that the Soviet Union no longer intended to make trouble for the USA in the Third World. He refused any longer to support the Nicaraguan Revolution. He forced the Cubans to get out of Africa. He questioned why the USSR should go on subsidising a regime in South Yemen of dubiously Marxist authenticity.[23] (Not that the USSR was lacking in problems on this topic.) Gorbachëv was rejecting the theory of Lenin and Stalin as well as the foreign-policy practice of Khrushchëv and Brezhnev.

While welcoming all this, Reagan sustained the diplomatic pressure. For pragmatic reasons he abandoned his anti-Beijing rhetoric and concentrated his fire on communism in the Soviet Union and eastern Europe – this change of stance was made easier for him by the perception that the Chinese under Deng Xiaoping were undertaking basic economic reform and introducing capitalism. The President did not repeat his claim that the USSR was an evil empire; he even decoupled discussions on human rights in the USSR from discussions on arms control.[24] Yet in two speeches – one at the Berlin Wall in June 1987, the other at Moscow State University in May 1988 – he said things that went far beyond what Gorbachëv currently wanted to hear. In West Berlin he demanded of the absent Soviet leader: 'Mr Gorbachëv, tear down this wall!' In Moscow in May 1988, standing incongruously beneath a huge Lenin bust, he stated: 'Freedom is the recognition that no single person, no single authority of government has a monopoly on the truth...'[25] He overruled expert diplomatic and political advice to speak like this. He understood better than his expert advisers that his words would stoke up the flames of opposition to the east European status quo without endangering his relationship with Gorbachëv.

The American intelligence agencies strengthened contact with political dissenters in eastern Europe. Agents brought messages of support and helped to publicise cases of official abuse. They also brought money. Ronald Reagan, President from 1980 to 1988, wanted to do what he could to pull down the Iron Curtain shrouding eastern Europe. He had an ally in Pope John Paul II, who as Karol Wojtyła had been Archbishop of Kraków until 1978. In the past it had been difficult for rebels against communism to subsist without gainful employment because the authorities might bring charges of 'parasitism'. The CIA and the Vatican got to work at offering discreet assistance. Informal bodies, some of them being tiny in membership and short of funds, were doing the same.[26] This was exactly what the Communist Party of the Soviet Union was doing to help the world communist movement. Thus, as dollars arrived in Rome from Moscow, dollars departed Rome and Washington for Warsaw. The finance helped, but it was not the crucial factor in weakening communism in eastern Europe. If money had been the key to political change, Italy would long ago have acquired a communist government (and the Pope would have been ejected from the Vatican). Financial subventions could only accelerate an existing motion. The same had been true in 1917: 'German gold' had been an aid to the Bolsheviks in preparing to seize power but nothing like the main resource at their disposal.

Opposition to Gorbachëv in the central party leadership was confined to home affairs. In foreign policy he had a free hand. No one in the Politburo objected to his campaign to end disputes with the USA and reduce the USSR's expenditure on nuclear weaponry. Gorbachëv was their stellar negotiator. No contemporary politician rivalled his worldwide popularity, and Reagan made things easier for him by refusing to crow about all the concessions being made from the Soviet side.

George H. Bush, before winning the presidential election of November 1988, had assured Gorbachëv that there would be no turning back on the course already pursued. Once a sceptic about the genuineness of the Soviet commitment to reform, he had become a believer – and he was not going to be browbeaten by 'the marginal intellectual thugs' to the right of Ronald Reagan.[27] Even so, he showed a coolness to Gorbachëv for some months and there was a pause in the warming of American–Soviet relations.[28] Gorbachëv's reaction to events in eastern Europe changed Bush's mind. When Henry Kissinger came to Moscow in January 1989 and proposed setting up a condominium of the USA and the USSR over Europe, Gorbachëv rejected the proposal out of hand.[29] Quite what Kissinger meant is not a topic clarified in his memoirs: was he really suggesting a mere modification of the status quo? It would seem so. Kissinger, like his former master Nixon, could not imagine a world where European countries escaped from under the umbrella of the two superpowers. At least Gorbachëv understood that the old Soviet and American understanding of geopolitics was obsolete, and he could ill afford to annoy President Bush, who had no intention of reverting to détente.

Gorbachëv seemed to be doing the work of American anti-communism better than President Bush. Conditions in China were moving towards the point of political explosion as students openly criticised the authorities. Bush set off for Beijing in February 1989 determined to ring bells for the democratic cause. At his official banquet he insisted on inviting the intellectual dissenter Fang Lizhi as his guest. The Chinese security agencies, though, made excuses to Bush and quietly detained Fang. Gorbachëv was not as easily thwarted. The Soviet leader visited Beijing in mid-May, when Tiananmen Square was being occupied by a peaceful protest by students for a month. Gorbachëv made his usual call for democracy and peaceful political methods. The Chinese media did what they could to pretend that nothing unusual was happening, but hundreds of the world's journalists had come to China to cover the visit and stayed on after his departure. The pressure of instant global media coverage was applied to the People's Republic of China for the first time. As it turned out, it made no positive difference to the line taken by the Chinese communist leadership. In the night of 3–4 June the People's Liberation Army moved tank units on to Tiananmen Square and hundreds were killed in the ensuing carnage. External intervention had ultimately failed to bend Deng Xiaoping to adopt, in Gorbachëv's repeated phrase, 'new thinking'.

Returning to Moscow, Gorbachëv had to take fundamental decisions about eastern Europe. The Polish political emergency came to a head in summer 1989. Elections were held. The communists went down to a heavy defeat and gave way to Solidarity in government. The precedent had been set. The German Democratic Republic collapsed under pressure of popular protests. Romania's Ceauşescu was overthrown. All eastern Europe was aflame with the fire of anti-communism. By the end of the year the end was in sight. Communism had already been overturned or was on the retreat in all the states of the region where it had until recently held dictatorial power. And Gorbachëv refused to lift a finger to assist his comrades in the Warsaw Pact.[30]

Bush was astounded: 'If the Soviets are going to let the communists fall in East Germany, they've got to be really serious – more serious than I thought.'[31] Country after country secured political liberation. Gorbachëv took care to obtain the Politburo's approval for military withdrawal.[32] No party, police or army leader objected to the inevitability of the strategy. Minister of Defence Dmitri Yazov was to recall: 'We had to return home some day.'[33] At the summit meeting between Bush and Gorbachëv off the coast of Malta in December 1989 Gorbachëv mooted the possibility of German reunification. By January 1990 his inner circle had made a decision along those lines.[34] Communism was dead in eastern Europe. Gorbachëv stopped bothering about communists in the old 'outer empire'. His Politburo was more eager to contact Václav Havel and former dissidents of Civic Forum in Czechoslovakia than to maintain ties with the Communist Party of Czechoslovakia.[35] Cuba was all but abandoned to its own devices, and Fidel Castro was asked to moderate his anti-American rhetoric and to avoid foreign military operations.[36] Jaime Pérez, General Secretary of the Communist Party of Uruguay, came to Moscow to plead Castro's case; but it was Gorbachëv's deputy Vladimir Ivashko, not Gorbachëv, who saw him.[37] When Bush assembled a vast force to eject Saddam Hussein's army from Kuwait in December 1990, Gorbachëv complained about the use of force to solve international problems but otherwise made no trouble for the Americans.

Yet Bush declined the $1.5 billion loan requested by Gorbachëv in spring 1991. Gorbachëv was judged incapable of undertaking comprehensive economic reform while manoeuvring to keep his more cautious comrades on his side.[38] As Soviet economic conditions became dire, Gorbachëv set out for London in June to negotiate with the leaders of the world's seven economically most powerful countries at the so-called

G7 meeting. He went cap in hand. There was nothing he could offer in return that he had not already conceded. His argument was that the world had an interest in preventing the USSR's collapse, and he played on his general popularity in the West. He ran into a brick wall and returned to Moscow empty-handed.

For many reasons, both internal and external, his leading subordinates decided that Gorbachëv was driving the USSR towards disaster. A coup was organised against him on 18 August. The putschists, as they were known, had overplayed their hand and Boris Yeltsin, the Russian President, successfully defied them. Gorbachëv returned to the Kremlin but the real power moved to Yeltsin. Bush, however, showed less than total respect to Yeltsin and continued to favour Gorbachëv. The USA did not want the USSR to fall apart. Visiting Kiev, Bush advised against secession. The downfall of communism in eastern Europe and the Soviet Union was one thing, the disintegration of a multinational power into separate and volatile units was entirely another. Yet on 8 December the decision had been taken by the presidents of Russia, Ukraine and Belarus to break up the USSR. Bush still went around speaking up for Gorbachëv. He had little historical imagination. Like Gorbachëv, he seems to have clung to the surmise that even if the 'Baltic states' – Estonia, Latvia and Lithuania – successfully seceded from the Union, no other Soviet republic would necessarily follow. Bush was backing a losing horse after the race had finished.

Gorbachëv bowed to the inevitable and accepted Yeltsin's demand for Russian independence. The USSR came to an end at the stroke of midnight on the last day of the year 1991.[39] Joy in the West was unconfined. Totalitarianism had been beaten first in eastern Europe and then in the USSR. The Cold War was over. The West had won and Soviet communism lay prostrate. Within a few years what had once seemed a distant prospect had been turned into reality. The October Revolution, Marxism-Leninism and the USSR had been tossed on to the refuse-heap of history – and this had happened with nothing like the amount of violence that might have been expected. It had taken place with fewer bangs than whimpers.

36. ANTI-COMMUNISM IN
EASTERN EUROPE

Europe to the east of the River Elbe seethed with hostility towards the USSR and communism. Every country in the region had people who could recall a different time when their nationhood, culture and religion had been respected. They resented being herded into a guarded enclave of the continent. They pointed out that countries such as Poland, Hungary and Czechoslovakia were the geographical centre of Europe. They looked on 'eastern Europe' as a degrading designation imposed on them by the way the Second World War ended.

Communist rule was at its harshest in Romania, Albania and Bulgaria, where the regimes pulled up the shoots of any opposition before they could grow. Poland was taken as a terrible example of what would happen unless repression was maintained. The rulers of Czechoslovakia and the German Democratic Republic would have liked to act with the same severity. But they were aware of their intense unpopularity, and some degree of national consent was important to them. Dissenting intellectuals were regularly thrown into prison, but they were seldom subjected to a physical battering. Václav Havel and his Charter 77 group in Czechoslovakia were a mixed group of intellectuals, Christian activists and lapsed reform-communists. Even after the end of détente they continued to operate and their confidence was growing. The German Democratic Republic had no prominent figure such as Havel; but the same sprouting of opposition was noticeable. Although the Stasi – the security police – penetrated this nascent organisation, it failed to extirpate it. It is hardly surprising that the Kremlin made little effort to exploit the opportunity offered by Tito's death in 1980. The Soviet Politburo had its hands full trying to hold on to what authority it already had. Expansion of the USSR's influence in eastern Europe was no longer a realistic possibility.

Meanwhile the protests against Polish communism grew in intensity.

Workers, intellectuals and clergy found common cause when, in July 1980, Gierek raised retail prices to correct his government's budgetary imbalance. In August the shipyard workers in Gdańsk came out on strike under Lech Wałęsa's leadership. With his ready smile and luxuriant moustache, Wałęsa immediately became the symbol of Poland's will for independence and for an end to communism. Truly he was a born orator, projecting his voice and cheekiness with or without a microphone. He was a talented negotiator. He knew what he wanted from each meeting; he never got flustered and always bargained with polite determination. Wałęsa regularly took advice from the intellectuals in the Workers' Defence Committee (KOR). He also consulted the Catholic Church. But he had a mind of his own, and it did no harm to his popularity that he was a working man of the Polish people. His project was to establish a trade union free from communist control; it was to be called Solidarity (Solidarność). A founding conference was held in Gdańsk in September 1980, and by early 1981 the union had astonishingly acquired about ten million members. Practically the entire Polish workforce, apart from communist party members (and even many of these also joined), enrolled in Solidarity.

Gierek arrested Wałęsa and other Solidarity leaders but discovered that this only stiffened the popular defiance. The failure of economic strategy and management was undeniable and the Polish United Workers' Party was in a quandary about what to do about it. The working class of Poland had organised itself into permanent confrontation with the communist state. Nothing more sharply signalled that communism oppressed the 'labouring masses'. The Soviet Politburo made no secret of its anxiety, and pressure on the USSR itself to deal firmly with Poland came from Erich Honecker in the German Democratic Republic. Honecker feared that the Polish disturbances might spill over his border; he pushed Brezhnev for sterner measures whenever they met.[1] The Kremlin's confidence in Gierek evaporated as Solidarity kept up its activity. Brezhnev and the Politburo demanded a change in personnel in the Polish United Workers' Party and the stabilisation of the communist order. They turned to a military man, General Wojciech Jaruzelski, who became Prime Minister in February 1981 and then Party First Secretary in October.

Jaruzelski introduced martial law in December 1981. He did this as much to pre-empt a Warsaw Pact invasion as to reimpose order in Poland. In fact the Soviet Politburo had decided not to intervene militarily even if Solidarity were to edge its way to power; but Jaruzelski

was not privy to this information.² Solidarity was outlawed and more of
its militants were taken into custody. Yet the strikes and demonstrations
were not abated. The network of Solidarity groups and agencies survived
the police onslaught; its presses produced pamphlets, postcards and
audiocassettes. Graffiti-artists sprayed slogans on walls such as 'The
winter is yours but the spring will be ours'.³ The Catholic priesthood
gave uncompromising sermons on the need for religious faith and
patriotism. Jaruzelski himself was reluctant to use any more force than
was absolutely necessary for the maintenance of the state order. He had
an impossible task. The communist party and the institutions it sponsored – trade unions, youth associations and cultural clubs – attracted
popular contempt. The result was chronic stalemate: although Jaruzelski
succeeded in restoring a degree of calm, he could not liquidate Solidarity
and Solidarity could not supplant his military administration. Poland
was like an insect trapped in amber. No fundamental political and
economic development was possible for the country. No end to martial
law appeared in sight.

The attempt at 'normalisation' included measures to increase the
autonomy of enterprises and expand market mechanisms. This was not
wholly ineffectual. Gross industrial output rose by 20 per cent between
1982 and 1986. Agriculture grew by 12 per cent in the same period. But
investment had drastically diminished. Shortages of factory goods and
farm produce persisted. Meat had to be rationed. Although the government managed to reschedule the servicing of its debts to western banks,
it was trapped in a budgetary cul-de-sac. Poland tumbled into dependence on the indulgence of the USSR and the rest of eastern Europe as
its trade deficit with fellow communist countries worsened.⁴ From
Brezhnev through Andropov to Chernenko, the Soviet leadership did
not know what to do. This was the only card in Jaruzelski's hand to keep
up his morale: he understood that he was the Kremlin's last chance short
of a military invasion.

Coming to power in Moscow in March 1985, Mikhail Gorbachëv
changed the principles of international relations in eastern Europe. The
world's attention was directed at his internal reforms as he reconstructed
his party, decentralised the economy and encouraged much freedom in
public debate. Quietly, though, he was setting about reforging the
Kremlin's linkage to its 'outer empire'. When the communist leaders of
eastern Europe arrived for Chernenko's funeral, Gorbachëv confidentially
indicated that the USSR would never again interfere in their political
decisions.⁵ Not everyone in the room believed his ears. Perhaps it was

Above. Italian anticommunist poster of Khrushchev as a split personality: 'Dear free people, please help a poor, starving people which I'm thinking of arming against you!!!' He is clutching a begging bucket in one hand and a nuclear missile in the other.

Right. Ordinary family in the USSR, still poor after forty-six years of the 'Soviet paradise': Italian anticommunist poster, 1963. Father, mother and son hold out a hand pleading for grain and money.

South Vietnam in 1959 struggles to hold elections in the teeth of communist aggression. The cannons blast holes in the Red Flag with its gold star.

Che Guevara, rainbow-coloured and beatified. The lines separating the colours radiate
from the star on his forehead. For once, Che is not wearing combat fatigues.

LA HUMANIDAD DEBE PERDURAR,
Y SI NOS LO PROPONEMOS
Y SOMOS CONSCIENTES,
**Y SOMOS VALIENTES,
PERDURARA.**
FIDEL CASTRO, 15 DE SEPTIEMBRE DE 1981

L'HUMANITE DOIT SURVIVRE,
ET SI NOUS NOUS LE PROPOSONS,
SI NOUS SOMMES CONSCIENTS
**ET COURAGEUX,
ELLE SURVIVRA.**
FIDEL CASTRO, 15 SEPTEMBRE 1981

MANKIND MUST LAST,
AND IF WE ARE DETERMINED,
CONSCIOUS
**AND BRAVE,
IT WILL LAST.**
FIDEL CASTRO, SEPTEMBER 15, 1981

الأنسانية لابد أن تدوم وتبقى،
وأذا ما عقدنا العزم على ذلك،
وادركناه،
وأذا ما امتلكنا الشجاعة الكافية،
فأنها ستبقى لا محالة.
فيدل كاسترو، ١٥ سبتمبر ١٩٨١

Castro presents his internationalist credentials. The mood is pensive, the light inspiring.

热烈欢呼毛泽东选集第五卷出版

Above. Chinese students make music as they implement the sayings of Mao Zedong. The artwork has become more photographic than in the early 1950s. As previously, joviality is de rigueur.

Right. Appeal for Chinese soldiers to turn their energies to economic tasks. With a mattock over his shoulder, the military veteran goes to work with his chest covered with medals.

我是戰鬥英雄, 又是勞動英雄!

DEFENDAMOS EL COBRE
por chile · unidos · produciendo más
rechacemos la agresión

Chilean communist summons for enhanced production of copper and an end to US interference. The Stars and Stripes flag mutates into the Nazi swastika.

Benign image of Allende as Chile's comrade-president. Allende has a quizzical expression. Clearly not a man to establish a dictatorship of the proletariat.

EL
COMPAÑERO **PRESIDENTE**

Portuguese communists attempt to recruit young followers. All are dressed fashionably. This would not have been allowed on posters in eastern Europe.

Questa squadra è inaffidabile

Italian communist caricature of the parties opposed to communism: 'You can have confidence in the Italian Communist Party.' The line-up of footballers includes conservative and liberal leaders.

An optimistic Brezhnev affirms that the 'unity of the Soviet nations today is as firm as never before'. Within a decade the USSR had broken apart and its republics had formed separate nation states.

just rhetoric. Surely the Soviet leadership, which had invaded Hungary in 1956 and Czechoslovakia in 1968, would not leave the region to its own devices? Only Poland was gripped by political emergency at the time. Possibly, therefore, Gorbachëv was talking about an entirely hypothetical future contingency when a member country of the Warsaw Pact might stir up unnecessary discontent with its rule. Honecker, Husák, Kádár and Zhivkov tried to persuade themselves that all would be well. Once young 'Misha' had got to grips with the realities of power east of the Elbe, they trusted he would cease his disturbing prattle. Another possibility was that he would not last long in office.

There was a patchwork of national responses to the call for fundamental reform in eastern Europe. Jaruzelski and Kádár were not in the same league as Ceauşescu in their willingness to employ force against dissent. Even Husák, Honecker and Zhivkov preferred to treat their troublemakers with a restraint which would have amazed east European communist leaders in the 1960s – and those leaders in turn were gentler with their political enemies than had been normal in Stalin's lifetime. It is true that the prominent dissenters experienced more bearable conditions than some of their more obscure supporters. But there was a tendency to avoid the harshest measures. In Hungary there was an attempt to go the other way and deepen the concessions to the dissenters. Indeed Károly Grósz, who succeeded Kádár in May 1988, emulated Gorbachëv. Most of the veteran communist leaders hated Gorbachëv, but 'ordinary' people in the region adored him. The dissenters, whether they were communist reformers or outright anti-communists, drew comfort from his policies. Emboldened by what they knew about Moscow, they increasingly adopted the Polish tactics and agitated against their regimes with whatever instruments they could obtain.

Meanwhile Misha Gorbachëv secured his political supremacy in Moscow and showed that he had meant what he said to the east European party bosses in March 1985. He wanted reforms in eastern Europe as fast and as deep as those in the USSR; and if the crusty old stagers failed to comply, he expected younger reformers to edge them out. He wanted to observe the fraternal niceties. Unlike his predecessors, he did not play the kingmaker: each country had to select its own communist leadership. He avoided the temptation to advise Kádár or even Husák to step down.[6] He rejected the request of General Militaru in Romania to back a *coup d'état* against Ceauşescu.[7] He told the communist leaders what he thought needed to be done and usually they affected to agree with him – Zhivkov was a master of this tactic.[8]

Meanwhile Gorbachëv discreetly undermined the status quo across the region. *Pravda* as well as the various Soviet weeklies disseminated the case for fundamental reform; copies of these were readily available in the newspaper kiosks of the outer empire. Gorbachëv himself eagerly toured eastern Europe. When visiting Prague in March 1988 and East Berlin in October 1989 he declared a passionate commitment to fundamental changes in the Soviet communist order. Crowds cheered him on his walkabouts. The affectionate cry went up: 'Gorby! Gorby!' They were using him as their standard bearer in the march against communism's abuses in eastern Europe since 1953.

Poland registered the impact of Gorbachëv's campaign as Jaruzelski and his ministers made conciliatory gestures to Solidarity. In September 1986 General Kiszczak released all political prisoners, and Wałęsa, without compromising his anti-communism, declared that 'dialogue must be institutionalised'.⁹ Pope John Paul II made a further visit to his native country in June 1987. The crowds who swarmed to greet him carried banners of Solidarity and the Christian faith. It was only a matter of time before the national explosion occurred. Miners and shipyard workers went on strike in 1988. The government called for talks and Jaruzelski appointed Mieczysław Rakowski, a communist reformer, as Prime Minister, but his powers of persuasion were insufficient to get non-communists to agree to join the cabinet. The Party Central Committee suffered from widening divisions. Round-table negotiations with Solidarity began in February 1989. A complicated deal was done to hold elections while reserving many seats for the communist party and its allies.¹⁰ The anti-communist forces displayed their bravado. A poster was issued depicting Gary Cooper in a scene from *High Noon* wearing a Solidarity lapel badge instead of a sheriff's star. The government was trounced in the election of 4 June 1989 as Solidarity won 160 out of the 161 available seats in the Senate. Under any other political system Jaruzelski would have resigned. But he hung on with support from none other than President George H. Bush, who visited Poland in July. Jaruzelski became President with Solidarity's consent. But it was Tadeusz Mazowiecki, a leading Catholic activist, who became Prime Minister and appointed Solidarity colleagues to a majority of cabinet posts.¹¹

A quiet revolution had taken place. It occurred on the very day that in faraway China, in Tiananmen Square, the tanks of the People's Liberation Army crushed a protest movement of unarmed students. (Honecker's regime was notable for congratulating the Chinese communist authorities on their repressive action.)¹² If Poland was a lucky country, it had worked for its luck over many years. It had undermined and brought down communism without uprising or civil war. The Mazowiecki cabinet brought in a radical free-market economist Leszek Balcerowicz to introduce capitalism. The state economy was about to be dismantled. As yet the outcome was confined to a single country. But the loosened media of eastern Europe reported on the Polish events fully enough for everyone to know what had happened. The dam had been burst. Communism had consented to its own removal in a country of huge geostrategic importance to the USSR – and the Soviet army did not interfere.

The fall of communist power in Warsaw broke the spell that held many minds in thrall. If the Poles could free themselves, other nations might be able to do the same. Communist leaders became decidedly edgy. Tensions increased and there was a growing feeling that a definitive clash was imminent in several countries. In Romania and Albania the police went on dealing brutally with opposition. Ceauşescu was no longer the darling of the Western political establishments now that Gorbachëv was doing the job of attacking the old principles of Soviet policy. Appeals to Ceauşescu to make reforms fell on stony ground. In Czechoslovakia, the German Democratic Republic and Bulgaria the tide of opposition was rising but as yet did not breach the walls of the communist order. In Hungary, Grósz aligned himself with the drive for deepened reform and had to confront the consequent public unrest. Everywhere, though, there was an atmosphere of expectation. It was difficult to see how the situation could be contained much longer. The Warsaw Pact, even if Gorbachëv had fallen from power in summer 1989, would have been difficult to mobilise against rebellious countries in eastern Europe. Popular demands were bobbing on the surface of politics where previously they had been held under water.

Hungarian politics had been tense and fluid since Kádár's departure, and it was there that the next great changes happened. On 16 June, less than a fortnight after the momentous election in Poland, the body of Imre Nagy was disinterred from its miserable grave on plot no. 301 and given a decent funeral attended by 200,000 patriots. The communist leadership tried to identify itself with Nagy, but events were running out of its control. In September it came to terms with the Opposition Round Table of oppositionist political groups. Free elections were to be called. The communists – the Hungarian Socialist Workers' Party – split into two parties. The strain of self-reform was too much. The communist government threw concessions at the people like confetti. The state was renamed, the constitution amended. The end was not long in coming. The communists fell from power in mid-October as their fingers lost their grip on institutions, policies and day-to-day decisions. The odd thing was that few of their leaders seemed to regret what was happening. The Hungarian People's Republic became simply the Hungarian Republic. The removal of the people from the name of the state was paradoxically a sign that the popular will was at last being respected. It was yet another noisy but bloodless revolution.

The troubles had meanwhile been gathering for months in the German Democratic Republic. Gorbachëv in person added to them on 7 October at the Berlin celebrations of the fortieth anniversary of the foundation of the state. 'Life itself', he declared in that ponderous style of his, 'punishes those who delay.' Honecker took no notice; immobility was really the way of life for his Germans. He just could not understand a crowd chanting: 'We are the people.' His brighter and younger comrades felt differently. They understood that only massive repression could prevent radical changes, and they knew the result would be isolation from any foreign assistance. Even the USSR was goading the anti-communist opposition into action. Honecker's comrades therefore refused to allow the police to fire on a crowd of demonstrators in Leipzig. They proceeded to sack Honecker, and Egon Krenz took up the reins of power. Citizens streamed across the border to Hungary which by then had an open frontier with Austria. The German Democratic Republic's leadership fell into confusion and despair. To general surprise they opened the checkpoints of the Berlin Wall itself on 9 November. Celebrations were immediate and joyous. Next day there was a swirl of delighted, dancing Germans of east and west travelling in both directions. Youngsters on both sides pulled out bricks from the infamous wall. Although the communist government remained in power, it no longer had the authority or will to use it.

Next it was the turn of Bulgaria's ruler Todor Zhivkov, who had dominated the country since 1954. No one in Europe, east or west, had been in power for longer. On 10 November he was abruptly removed by reformers in the Politburo led by Petar Mladenov. All were Zhivkov's appointees. They had been slow to identify themselves openly with the kind of politics approved by Gorbachëv. But the rise in anti-communist activities on the streets of Sofia disconcerted them. Mladenov took power, as Krenz had done in the German Democratic Republic, when the situation was already running out of control. Public demonstrations against the authorities had started with ecological protests and moved towards concerns with the absence of civil rights. Mladenov promised to reform the communist party and its government; he also gave a guarantee that political, social and economic reforms would follow. Thus he avoided his own instant overthrow. But the protesters could smell the sweat of reform-communists who lacked confidence. By February 1990 the party had to give up its permanent claim on power. The reformists split off from the communist party and formed a Bulgarian Socialist Party, which won the first free elections since before the Second World War. It was a popular revolution against communism carried through by ex-communist leaders. Lenin would have called it opportunistic.

What more could happen before the year 1989 came to an end? The prospects for communism in Yugoslavia were already bleak and, unusually for eastern Europe, were barely connected with events in the other countries of the region. People in Belgrade, Zagreb and Ljubljana gave hardly a thought to the latest sayings of Gorbachëv or to rumours of the recent exercises of the Soviet army. Yugoslavia's uneasy stability since the Second World War was disturbed by Tito's death in 1980 and the descent began into conflicts among its republics and its nations in subsequent years.

Trouble was acute in Bosnia-Herzegovina where Serbs and Croats lived cheek by jowl – and Moslems had their grievances against both. The Albanians in Kosovo persecuted the Serbs. The result was an intensification of conflict at the local level. The loosening of federal ties allowed republican leaderships to assert themselves in their own national cause. Serbia was to the fore in this. Although the Serbian authorities had prospered under Tito, resentments had never disappeared. Communism, what is more, was coming to count for little in Belgrade. Nationalist literature was permitted. Private economic entrepreneurship was on the rise. The Orthodox Church was strengthening its case for an increased role in Serbian affairs. The whole republic was a tinderbox. The match to set off a blaze occurred in 1987 when Serbian president Ivan Stambolić supported the candidature of his protégé Slobodan Milošević as party leader. Milošević cultivated an image as protector of Serbs everywhere. In Kosovo he declared to them: 'No one must beat you!' He ruthlessly replaced Stambolić in the presidency in 1989. He stirred up Serbs in the other republics. He bullied the non-Serbs in Kosovo and Vojvodina and abolished their status as autonomous provinces. Milošević was Yugoslavia's internal imperialist; he was gambling that Serbia's strength would intimidate the other republics into submission.

The reaction to the changes in Serbia was not long in coming in Croatia and Slovenia. As nationalist rhetoric sharpened, politics in Yugoslavia traced a vicious circle of embitterment. Outbreaks of violence between hostile national groups became common. The republican presidents found it difficult to deal with each other, and indeed Milošević showed no interest in negotiation: he wanted power for himself and for Serbia. While suppressing Croat and Albanian political organisations in Serbia, he allowed new Serbian ones – including nationalist parties – to be created; he also fostered a growing market economy and turned a blind eye to corruption, criminal gangs and paramilitary violence. Serbia was no longer a one-party republic – and in July 1990 he was to change the name of his own organisation to the Socialist Party of Serbia.[13] The communist order was dead long before Yugoslavia was cremated in the fires of its wars and ethnic cleansings in the rest of the decade.[14] This did not happen with an open denunciation of communism and the removal of its old leaders. Posters of Tito still hung in public buildings. Milošević went about the transformation with cunning, unobtrusively replacing Marxist doctrine with nationalism. The disturbances witnessed in Warsaw, Berlin and Bucharest were not repeated in Belgrade.[15]

Back in the last days of 1989 two countries alone, Albania and Romania, appeared to have rulers who might hold on to their communism. Albanian ruler Enver Hoxha had died in 1985 and was succeeded by Ramiz Alia. For a while it had been Alia's intention to make the minimum of reforms. His regime, no longer supported by the People's Republic of China, was friendless in the world. Its main asset was that its Soviet and Western critics showed little interest in active intervention. Alia made nods in the direction of changing economic policies but generally sat tight and hoped against hope that the tide of history would soon reverse itself.

Like Alia, Nicolae Ceauşescu spat on all talk of reform in Romania. He took one of his regular opportunities to strut before an adoring multitude on 21 December when he appeared on the balcony of his grandiose Central Committee premises in Bucharest. The crowd had been filtered through the usual mechanisms. The police were on guard as was customary. Ceauşescu, flanked by wife and close aides, strode forward to address the usually subservient 'masses'. Barely had he begun to speak than grumbling voices were heard. The Conducător, as he styled himself in a manner uncomfortably reminiscent of fascist dictators, was unaccustomed to this. On instinct he harangued his critics. The crowd turned surly. It was like a scene from a clichéd film 'epic' about ancient

Rome. (This was fitting since Ceauşescu had always tried to identify himself with the greatness of the Roman Empire.) People muttered, advanced, shouted and raised their fists. The security forces refrained from trying to restore order. Ceauşescu suddenly understood the danger he was in. He scuffled in panic from the scene, took a helicopter to the countryside and briefly attempted to rally support. No one came to his aid. Leading communists were among those who stepped forward to announce the collapse – the most sudden and glorious collapse in a half-year of such collapses – of communist power. There was no mercy for the Ceauşescu couple. The new authorities did not want them alive and able to tell the story of the part played by their successors in the maintenance of communism before 1989. They were shot on 25 December.

If ever the American dominoes theory was put successfully to the proof, it was in eastern Europe in the closing months of 1989. But it was validated in the opposite fashion to the predicted one. The collapsing dominoes in that half of the continent led not to an increased number of communist states but to the extirpation of communism. Violence occurred fitfully over that brief period, but rulers were wary of going over to the full available modalities of repression; they observed how their counterparts in adjacent states were getting into difficulties: none wanted the obloquy of being identified as ruling without popular consent.

The year had been a disaster for the reform-communists. Ramiz Alia went on contending that Albania could hold out against the trend; it was his opinion that a reformed communism could survive and flourish. But by March 1991, under threat from street demonstrations, even he had to concede multi-party elections.[16] His Albanian Party of Labour won most votes but the end was in sight. In 1992 the communists were defeated by the Democratic Party and removed from government: the last domino had fallen. Alia had announced himself as a reformer late in his career. Others in eastern Europe had hoped for decades to edge aside their communist-conservatives and institute the communist order of their dreams. Hungarian reformers had tried in 1956 and the Czechoslovaks in 1968 and suffered military invasion. The constant hope had been that, if such a variant of communism were tried, it would attract national support. By the time the reformers had their chance these were unrealistic ideas. Probably they had never stood much chance. The agenda of reform-communism had quickly been left behind by a Hungarian popular revolt in 1956. In western Europe, moreover, the Eurocommunists had come to appreciate that people would be satisfied only by the maintenance of a multi-party system and a pluralist society and culture. Nowhere in eastern Europe had communists come to office in the late 1940s with a majority of electoral votes.

It is true that communists were to succeed in winning elections in certain countries in the region in the 1990s;[17] but in order to do this they had to switch their policies abruptly away from communist reformism. They had to become – or to appear to become – socialists or social-democrats. Communism collapsed east of the Elbe in 1989 because Moscow released its grip and countries in one way or another stood up to their communist rulers. The situation of impatience, frustration and anger had been mounting for years. The year 1989 produced a unique conjuncture of conditions. But it is doubtful that the communist reformers would have done much better for themselves if they had enjoyed a more congenial environment.

37. CHINA'S CAPITALIST COMMUNISM

Mao Zedong died minutes after midnight on 9 September 1976. Competition for power, which had been gathering in intensity for months, became frantic. He had endeavoured to preserve his legacy by anointing Hua Guofeng as his successor. Learning from Soviet history, Mao acted nimbly to prevent de-Maoisation. Yet Hua remained vulnerable to attack from the Gang of Four. Jiang Qing and fellow Gang members were impatient to seize power and throw China back to the politics of 1966–8 when Mao had released and directed the Red Guards, cut down the intelligentsia and lunged at economic regeneration through the efforts of workers and peasants.

The Gang hurried to barge Hua aside. The headstrong Jiang Qing went about deriding him as a 'nice gentleman in the Malenkov mould'.[1] Stalin in 1953, it will be recalled, left Malenkov in the best position to succeed him and yet Malenkov was quickly supplanted by Khrushchëv. Having always fired her weapons from under her husband's parasol, Jiang was poorly equipped for unchaperoned conflict. People said she suffered from an empress syndrome and she was deeply unpopular in most layers of China's society. Few Chinese wanted to return to the era of the 'little red book', revolutionary operas and small bowls of rice; there was a longing for the authorities to guarantee a lengthy period of political stability and economic growth. Outsiders to the leadership anyway had no impact on what was decided. The problem for the Gang was that dislike of them was not confined to ordinary people. The political and military elites found them equally repugnant: officials in the army, party and government hated the prospect of resumed turbulence. Even the beneficiaries of the Cultural Revolution could not count on keeping their jobs under the rule of Mao's widow and her allies.

While Mao's corpse was being embalmed for display in its mausoleum, the Gang's members plotted a *coup d'état*. They did this without finesse. On 19 September 1976 they demanded a Politburo Standing Committee meeting to be held with Jiang in attendance despite her not being a member; they also called for the exclusion of Ye Jianying from the proceedings even though he held membership. Hua gave way on this but refused Jiang Qing's sudden request to put Mao Yuanxin, who was her shield-carrier and Mao Zedong's nephew, in charge of the late Chairman's papers. Hua had stopped dithering and was fighting back. He knew that, once in possession of such papers, the Gang would be able to concoct whatever text they liked to legitimate their measures.[2]

The Gang ordered the militia in Shanghai to remain under arms and Jiang Qing and Wang Hongwen made provocative speeches in Beijing. Hua reacted by holding an impromptu Politburo conference at the People's Liberation Army headquarters outside the capital on 5 October. The decision was made to arrest the Gang, and the task was given to Army Unit No. 8341. A servant spat on Jiang. Resistance in the rest of the country was slight and easily eliminated. Hua, though, faced a gathering economic crisis. Planning targets had not been met. Popular discontent about food and wages was on the rise. Strikes had broken out. Veterans in the leadership persuaded Hua that Deng Xiaoping's rehabilitation would help to stabilise public life and tranquillise the unrest. Deng, despite trouble with his prostate gland, returned to the fray at the Central Committee in July 1977. He had the personal contacts to create a favourable atmosphere for measures of reform. Unlike Hua, he knew every influential agency of party and government from the inside – and he understood that Hua had restored him to public life not out of mercy but because he could not handle the situation without him. By the Eleventh Party Congress in August he was third in the ranking of the Chinese communist leadership. Rejecting doctrinaire Maoism, he coined the slogan: 'Seek truth from facts.'[3]

Deng was born in 1904 to a landowning family deep in the Sichuan province. He took the path of many other young Chinese and boarded a steamer from Shanghai to France. Learning French, he made his living as a waiter, train conductor and rubber-overshoe assembler and eventually joined the Renault automobile factory as a skilled worker. He quickly became a communist agitator among the Chinese émigrés. Deng was an adaptable fellow who came to like croissants, potatoes and coffee. He watched football and played bridge – and deep into old age he was to accept appointment as honorary chairman of China's bridge-players' society: he had always liked holding political discussions during a game.[4] As a practical man he produced the local communist newsletter. In 1926 Deng was chosen to train in Moscow at the Sun Yatsen Communist University of the Toilers of the East.[5] On returning to China, he joined

Mao Zedong in forming a communist armed force after the party's disaster at the hands of Chiang Kai-shek in Shanghai. He soon rose to the highest levels of the Red Army command and stayed with it during the gruelling Long March and through to the seizure of power in 1949.

His European experience left him with some understanding of capitalist countries. This was also true of Zhou Enlai. Both were open to fresh thinking and pragmatic in the quest for national resurgence. Deng was as hard as teak. He endured as many demotions as promotions at Mao's hands from the 1950s. His son was crippled from the waist down after leaping from a window to escape physical maltreatment in the Cultural Revolution. Denounced as the 'Second Biggest Capitalist Roader', Deng might have been put on trial but instead he was sent to work as a fitter in a tractor-repair plant in Jiangxi province. The purpose was to knock the fancy ideas out of him and restore him to Maoist orthodoxy. Although it was a part-time job, this was a grim sentence: his pay barely covered his family's basic material needs.[6]

Aged seventy-three at the moment of this latest comeback in 1976, he knew he had no time to waste if he wanted to make the changes he wanted. Victims of the Gang were released from the camps.[7] Prominent leftists were dropped from the Central Committee at the Eleventh Party Congress. Such guarantees of good behaviour he had given before his political rehabilitation were no more than expedients. Hua's removal was made easier by the wide recognition that the economy had been ineptly managed. His inclination was to position himself between contending political groupings and to adopt measures that avoided risk and disturbance. He went on promising that 'whatever directives Chairman Mao issued, we shall steadfastly obey'.[8] Deng was forthright about the need for change and impressed himself on the Politburo and the People's Liberation Army as the leader in waiting. On a tour of the USA in 1978 he acted the part by wearing a cowboy hat in Texas and waving heartily at the crowds. Most Americans thought the tiny, wildly gesticulating figure faintly ridiculous; but many Chinese warmed to a politician who dispensed with the austere pomp of Mao Zedong. At the same time he refused to be pushed into undertaking comprehensive political reform, and in March 1979 he terminated the 'democracy wall' movement and jailed its leaders.

Deng pounced on Hua in September 1980 by getting the post of Prime Minister for his own protégé Zhao Ziyang. The Gang of Four were put on trial in the ensuing winter. The court proceedings against them were carried on national TV. Popular antagonism to Jiang Qing and her fellow accused was deep and wide. When the unrepentant Jiang claimed Mao's mantle as her inheritance, she met with derision. The decade before his death started to be described as the ten years of chaos. While honouring the virtues of Mao Zedong Thought, Deng asserted that the Great Helmsman had made many basic mistakes from the late 1950s.[9]

The guilty verdict against the Gang of Four was never in doubt. Its members were sentenced to life imprisonment; and in June 1981 Hua lost his post as Party Chairman to Hu Yaobang, yet another of Deng's protégés. Deng was by then the supreme leader. His only serious rival by then was Chen Yun, who had charge of economic policy; but Chen failed to make a direct bid for power. What is more, Deng knew what he wanted to do and when and how to do it; unlike Mao he did not bother with cycles of attack and retrenchment. He genuinely wanted to step down from office as soon as possible, but not until he had fixed his strategy in indestructible cement. He announced four cardinal principles: keeping to the socialist road, maintaining the dictatorship of the proletariat, upholding the party's leadership and adhering to Marxism-Leninism and Mao Zedong Thought.[10] There was much obfuscation here. 'Proletarians' were not running their own dictatorship any more than in other communist systems of power. Deng, a communist since his French sojourn, had not changed his political allegiance. Communist rule would be maintained. He regarded the one-party state as crucial for containing the pressures of what assuredly would be an explosive transition to 'modernity'. He was planning to tread down every trace of Mao Zedong Thought from economic policy; he aimed at nothing less than the restoration of an immense capitalist sector.

Deng, like Gorbachëv, had to convince the elites of the party, army and ministries that his reforms were desirable. How did Deng succeed in keeping power while Gorbachëv did not? Chinese elites, it would seem, were easier to persuade. Perhaps they were more nationalist than Soviet elites were. This is definitely possible. Possibly too China's reforms were facilitated by a sense of emergency in the communist leadership after the twin cataclysms of the Great Leap Forward and the Cultural Revolution. Deng was devising an orderly way forward and an end to chaos. Above all, he intended to leave the existing elites in post; and he offered to increase the material rewards available to them. Gorbachëv, by contrast, caused disorder in the Soviet state, undermined the elites and almost invited a coup against himself.[11]

Deng anyway got on with things. With Mao dead, he at last had a chance to choose his set of priorities. The rural communes were dismantled, with the land being handed back to individual peasant households. Fields could be reclaimed by those who had owned them early after the revolution of 1949. State procurement prices were increased. Permission was given for the setting up of private industrial companies. Capital was invited from overseas. Special economic zones were established in the cities along the Pacific coast (where foreign firms before the communist seizure of power had conducted trade through the 'treaty ports'). Businessmen from China and foreign countries were assured of finding a cheap, compliant and educated workforce and a helpful administration. Technology and organisational methods were renovated to the highest standards. The Chinese Communist Party was ordered to step back from controlling the minutiae of public life. Widened debate was allowed among communists. The People's Liberation Army was retrained and re-equipped so as to discharge its responsibility for defence and security. Veteran communist leaders began to be eased out of office without loss of respect. Deng managed the transition in such a fashion as to ensure peaceful compliance.

He was building on the minor economic reforms in process since the early 1970s. Much change was occurring at the local level. Party organisations quietly increased the scope for initiative among factory directors and managers. Red tape was cut; material incentives were increased. Rural industrial output rose in the villages of the coastal regions. Cultural relaxation was introduced, and painters who worked in a traditional style were given assignments again.[12] Even Deng was astounded by the rapidity of the Chinese economy's growth once he had raised the reforms in industry and commerce to the national level.[13]

He assumed that reforms would eventually need to be applied to internal politics. At least, this was what he said in public: 'We must create the conditions for the practice of democracy, and for this it is essential to reaffirm the principle of the "three don'ts": don't pick on others for their faults, don't put labels on people and don't use a big stick.'[14] Party Chairman Hu Yaobang said privately that China needed to move towards the rule of law, the separation of powers and even multi-party pluralism.[15] He was even willing to relax repression in Tibet.[16] Deng announced: 'Undoubtedly when the methods of dictatorship are being used it's necessary to be cautious, it's necessary to arrest the minimum number of people, it's necessary to do the very utmost to avoid bloodshed.'[17] The authorities had slackened the repression somewhat earlier in the decade. Disturbances broke out in the camps as discipline was relaxed. About 1.4 million people had succeeded in escaping in the year before September 1981; demands for rehabilitation proliferated.[18] Yet the Chinese leadership's 'liberalism' had limits: the number of detainees in the camps remained between four and six million.[19] When Deng began a campaign to 'punish criminals without mercy', he reverted to the communist technique of assigning numerical quotas to lower authorities. People were executed who would normally have been given sentences of confinement.[20]

Party Chairman Hu paid dearly for what had been only a limited enthusiasm for democratic reform. When students staged noisy protests in December 1986, the party elders successfully petitioned Deng to sack him.[21] Deng was not just yielding to pressure from old comrades. Democracy was acceptable to him only insofar as it did not get in the way of the rest of his strategy. Tensions remained in the Politburo with Zhao Ziyang advocating a degree of political liberalisaion and Li Peng urging a continued clampdown. A paralysis affected public affairs until spring 1989 when the students massed daily in Tiananmen Square, calling for the introduction of democratic and civil rights. Pamphlets were produced, wall-posters pinned up. Hundreds of thousands of party members joined in the protest movement.

Deng told US Secretary of State George Shultz that his own reforms would succeed. He scoffed at the Soviet strategy for reform.[22] China was economically on the rise whereas the USSR was entering a crisis in production and supplies. Deng, unlike Zhao Ziyang, refused to compromise with protesters. He resharpened political authoritarianism and held the unity and power of the party as sacrosanct. He felt sure that this was the only way for the Chinese to extricate themselves from the communist cul-de-sac. Deng declared martial law on 20 May and sent Premier Li Peng to negotiate with the students. Li, an implacable supporter of order and authority, told them: 'Today we will discuss one matter: how to relieve the hunger strikers of their present plight.' Student leader Wuer Kaixi, jabbing his finger at Li Peng, retorted: 'Excuse me for interrupting you, Premier Li, but time is running short. Here we are sitting in comfort while students outside are suffering from hunger. You just said that we should discuss only one matter. But the truth is, it was not you who invited us to talk but we – all of us in Tiananmen Square – who invited you to talk. So we should be the ones to name the matters to be discussed.' When Li Peng offered his hand to the students, the gesture was rejected. The Premier grunted: 'You've gone too far!'[23] The People's

Liberation Army was rushed to the central precincts with orders to clear the area of protesters.

A massacre began late on 3 June as tanks rolled across the cobbled square and crushed several students under their caterpillar tracks.[24] Leaders of the protest were sentenced to long terms in labour camps. Zhao Ziyang, the Politburo member who had shown sympathy with the students, tumbled into official disgrace and was put under virtual house arrest. Censorship was reinforced. Army and police were put out on the streets and told to nip any resistance in the bud.

Deng ignored all the international criticism. He stressed that it was for China to determine how to organise itself and that foreigners were welcome to do business with the Chinese so long as they kept their noses out of politics. The ruling group reimposed its authority. Potential trouble in the ministries and the armed forces was defused. Ministers and their families could make profits out of the expanding market sector. Commanders were promised advanced weaponry and sustained prestige and influence. Order was restored. The elderly Deng was confident that no jeopardy existed for his strategy, and he stepped down from his burdensome offices in November 1989 while retaining the unofficial power of general political oversight. His protégé Jiang Zemin became leader. The process of economic reform slowed for a while. But Deng's tour of southern provinces in 1992 revived it, and China's transformation quickened again. Private companies sprang up in all cities and many villages. The most dynamic zones lay along the Pacific coast. Investment poured in from abroad. Multinational companies long excluded from Chinese industry and commerce set up in Beijing, Shanghai and Guanzhou. Gross domestic product rose exponentially as private enterprise from home and abroad injected the most up-to-date technology into an industrial sector which offered a cheap, educated, co-operative and disciplined labour force. By 2003 China share of the world's gross production had risen to 12 per cent.

Conditions in factories were usually unhygienic and always the work was hard and the hours long. The gap between rich and poor became a chasm. Young, ambitious people had opportunities denied to the old. The urban coastland belt prospered while peasants who stayed in the villages paid with their taxes for their over-mighty state. The old patterns of communal assistance – the moral economy – broke down.[25] Welfare provision fell away. Chinese capitalism was red in tooth and claw. Not a word of objection to the abandonment of communist economics appeared in the party's central newspaper *Renmin Ribao*. Financial fraud and judicial malfeasance became deeply rooted. Criminal gangs spread their tentacles into every corner of business. Police were used to enforce the needs of the big entrepreneurs. Strikes were no longer treated gently.[26] Officials in party and government lined their pockets by taking bribes and overlooking scams. The licensing of new enterprises and the enforcement of contracts spawned corruption. Communist authorities talked about the commonweal while ignoring it in reality. The wealthy, protected by their bodyguards and living inside the walls of their new palatial cantonments, enjoyed their expensive clothes, jewellery and trips abroad. Car ownership increased exponentially and the sprawling cities no longer reserved their avenues for cyclists.

Capitalism had liberating effects. Villagers sometimes welcomed the improvements in healthcare and education even though they had to pay for them. 'Under the new system,' said veteran rural leader Wang Fucheng in Henan province, 'the people work harder and they get more.'[27] There were plenty of jobs for those who could move to the growing zones of employment; and people arriving from the countryside, however meagre their pay, improved their situation and remitted their saving to their rural relatives. Entrepreneurial initiative, furthermore, brought rewards for the businessmen who set up thriving stalls, shops and companies. But this broad process of liberation provided most people with less time and energy for private obligations and pleasures. China acquired the world's highest suicide rate.

A few glimpses of a brighter future for civil society were detectable. No capitalist society could function without the Internet, and although the parameters of usage were politically restricted there was plenty of access to news and ideas that were banned from the media. Foreign books were readily translated. Sporting links were strengthened and Manchester United and other soccer teams played exhibition matches. Rock music concerts were put on with leading bands from abroad. Even the factories and sweatshops of Shanghai had the positive feature of upgrading the skills and technical knowledge of their workforces. Advanced machinery was shipped in abundance to the People's Republic of China. The country became the workshop of the world. Yet, although people did not dare to come out on to the streets to protest against the authorities, the grumbling about official policies became louder. The regime understood that it needed to take popular opinion into account. When the SARS virus afflicted the southern provinces in summer 2004 the government at first tried to clamp down on public discussion. A combination of international and internal criticism made this unsustainable. China's rulers could no longer talk nonsense and get their subjects to parrot it automatically.

Hong Kong was reincorporated in the People's Republic in 1997 when the British ceded their colony to Beijing. The immediate effect was a restriction on liberties on the island. But the Chinese regime needed to reassure global entrepreneurs of its commitment to some degree of social freedom, and a political witch-hunt in Hong Kong would have damaged this objective. Expatriate Chinese colonies in North America and Europe also required reassurance since they acted as important intermediaries for China's entry into the world economy. Ties of commerce between the People's Republic and the USA were strengthened and the global markets teemed with Chinese exports. Chinese rulers huffed and puffed about desiring to reincorporate Taiwan but military action was avoided. Trade was preferred to conquest.

Yet China remained a one-party dictatorship and its labour camps – the infamous *laogai* – continued to hold between four and six million inmates in shocking conditions.[28] Mao's gigantic image was still displayed in Tiananmen Square. There was no true pluralism of intellectual and political discourse at the highest official levels. Interest groups of employers were not allowed to function. Trade unions were emasculated. The importance of military power went on being promoted. Tibet languished under China's despotism and its levels of literacy and material provision remained low;[29] and the construction of a railway across its territory, much vaunted in Beijing as showing its wish to share the benefits of modernisation, was seen by Tibetans as a means of reinforcing central control. Great regions such as Xinjiang in the north-west of the People's Republic were held in a suffocating grip. There the Chinese authorities feared that Islam and Uigur nationalism might breed a separatist movement. Freedom of religious expression was only patchily respected across China. Falun Gong, an indigenous faith of massive popularity, was systematically persecuted. Communist doctrines remained an obligatory ingredient in the school curriculum and a qualification for a serious public career.

Marxism-Leninism was otherwise honoured only in the breach. The discussion of Mao Zedong Thought sank to mere ritual, and the young in particular had no regrets about its reduced influence. Peasants in some districts refused to abandon their devotion to him and erected traditional religious shrines in his memory. Countless further millions of Chinese continued to think well of him as a patriot and state-builder while shuddering at the memory of his Cultural Revolution. They tended to idealise the practices of the Maoist period and contrasted them with the economic and administrative corruption after his death.

A firm line was held from 1989, and hopes for political reform were regularly dashed. From Deng Xiaoping through Jiang Zemin to Hu Jintao (who came to power in 2003) there was no vacillation. When Zhao Ziyang died in January 2005, his quiet funeral evoked memories of what might have been. He had never expressed a principled commitment to democracy and the rule of law, but he had gone further in that direction than any other leader. Young militants trying to preach the need for 'democratisation' were meanwhile regularly rounded up; they were kept strictly apart from foreign journalists and politicians. The government also patrolled the use of the Internet and secured the consent of Google and other global search-engine companies to excise politically sensitive matters from their China-based coverage. Official worries were not confined to the cities. Discontented peasants constituted by far the greatest proportion of the population, and the government became concerned that they might become infected by the propaganda of urban dissenters. Troops and local thugs were dispatched to beat up troublemakers. In 2004, according even to the Ministry of Public Security, there were 74,000 riots and other 'mass incidents' involving 3.5 million people.[30] The Ministry of Labour and Social Security suggested that instability in society had risen to the 'yellow alert' level. This was only one level below a 'red alert', the very highest level.[31]

Rural discontent was spreading. Peasants had benefited from the dissolution of the land communes under Deng Xiaoping and traded their growing harvests for profit. But they were taxed ever more heavily. Regional and local administrators illegally dispossessed them of their fields on the edges of cities. The cranes and bulldozers were kept working twenty-four hours a day in the great cities as the massive economic boom continued. Where was it going to end? There was no equivalent in the history of world communism. Ideas of 'market socialism' – for example, in the USSR in the 1920s, Czechoslovakia in 1968 and Hungary in the 1970s – had never proposed a system with the capitalist sector outgrowing the parts of the economy owned by the state. Chinese leaders from Deng Xiaoping onwards asserted that they were developing a 'communism with Chinese characteristics'. The red-dyed gauze no longer occluded reality. The communist order was retained only as a means of rigorous political and ideological control; its economic and social components were blown to the winds. Concepts of Mao Zedong Thought were abandoned except insofar as they promoted the goals of national identity, centralised administration and superpower status. An extraordinary hybrid was created. China had become the only communist state which developed a vibrant economy by giving it over to capitalism.

By the beginning of the third millennium the country was already pointed in the direction of becoming the world's largest manufacturing nation. It was its social cohesion and political durability that remained questionable. Deng was the last supreme ruler to have taken part in the Long March; his successors lacked the aureole of legitimacy as revolutionary veterans. Measures to deal with popular discontent were either crudely punitive or merely palliative. Party officials, faced with a choice between Maoist ideology and self-enrichment, invested in apartment blocks, coal mines and computer technology. No one was able to tell how long this situation could last. No one today can tell any better.

38. *PERESTROIKA*

The challenges to the communist order in eastern Europe had always annoyed the old men in the Kremlin. Most Soviet leaders had come to high office under Stalin; they had gone along with Khrushchëv's reforms because they wanted freedom from fear of arrest and recognised that greater flexibility was needed in policy. Yet they saw everything through the cobwebs of past glory and disliked the denigration of Stalin and of the industrial and military achievements that took place under his command. Khrushchëv's denunciation of their idol rankled with them for damaging the core of purpose in their lives. While stumbling towards the time of their own funerals, they felt an instinctual need to correct what they regarded as the wrong done to Stalin. Their anger spurted out at a Politburo meeting in July 1984. Minister of Defence Ustinov said Khrushchëv 'did us great harm'. Minister of Foreign Affairs Gromyko agreed, maintaining that the positive image of the USSR had been destroyed after 1953. Tikhonov, Chairman of the Council of Ministers, recalled his own humiliation in being transferred from Moscow to a provincial post in one of Khrushchëv's reorganisations. On and on they went. Inevitably they got round to their memories of glory in the Great Patriotic War. Khrushchëv had changed the name of Stalingrad to Volgograd. Ustinov proposed changing it back: 'Millions of people would receive this very well.'[1]

Some of those present must have sensed that things were getting out of hand. While millions of people from the wartime generation might have welcomed the name change, the rehabilitation of Stalin would have caused untold damage to the country's reputation. The proposal was dropped. The old men had had their rant and their anger was spent, at least until the next time one of them got worked up about the USSR's 'glorious past'.

Mikhail Gorbachëv, the youngest Politburo member, had held back from bad-mouthing Khrushchëv in the discussion. This was a small, early example of his independence of thought. Born in 1931, he had driven tractors in his village in Stavropol region, deep in the Russian south, before gaining a scholarship in jurisprudence at Moscow State University. On graduating he went back to Stavropol and climbed the high pole of local party politics. By 1970 he had been appointed party chief for the region. He caught the eye of KGB Chairman Yuri Andropov, who took his holidays down there. In 1978 Gorbachëv joined the Central Committee Secretariat. Andropov appreciated his intelligence and affability and in 1982, as Party General Secretary, recruited him to the confidential group examining the defects of the Soviet economy. Gorbachëv was being groomed by Andropov as his successor. But Andropov died too soon, in 1984, and the wheezing Konstantin Chernenko became party leader and reinstated the policies of Brezhnev. Chernenko himself expired in March 1985. At last it was Gorbachëv's turn, and he did not let the grass grow beneath his feet. From his first day as Party General Secretary he caused tremors in the Kremlin.

He had disguised the scale of his purposes until that moment. On the very eve of being appointed to the highest party office he strolled with his wife Raisa in their dacha garden. Out of range of KGB bugging devices, he confided: 'We can't go on living like this.'[2] He was referring not to themselves as a couple but to general conditions in the country. The Gorbachëvs believed that Khrushchëv had erred on the side of caution. They quietly adhered to the version of communism advocated by the dissenter Roy Medvedev. They wanted electivity as a principle of internal party organisation. They wished for broader public discussion and for a lessening of the state's reliance on force. Mikhail and Raisa Gorbachëv believed that if the ideas and practices of Lenin were reinstated, the USSR would become the most dynamic society and economy in the world. Then Soviet people would show undying enthusiasm for communist rule.

Gorbachëv's affable public manner marked him off from his predecessors. Adopting the slogan of 'acceleration', he pensioned off the gerontocrats and rapidly gathered like-minded reformers into the Politburo. Chief among these were Yegor Ligachëv, Nikolai Ryzhkov, Eduard Shevardnadze and Alexander Yakovlev. Drastic changes were made in policy. Gorbachëv brandished the Russian word *glasnost* like a sword. *Glasnost*, a difficult word to translate, basically referred to the ventilation of historical and current political 'questions' through the official media. This was to be done under close official supervision: Gorbachëv was aiming not to terminate the one-party state but to enhance its effectiveness. He also introduced a modicum of economic reform. Stressing the importance of the 'human factor', he hoped to involve the 'people' in the process. He renounced what had happened to the USSR after Stalin's attainment of dominance. Supremely optimistic, he genuinely believed that reforms in Moscow would create an order superior, in economic dynamism as well as in political and moral stature, to the best on offer from advanced capitalism. A dreamer had entered the portals of the Kremlin. But the transparent fact that he was committed to the enhancement of the Soviet order saved him from being removed from the throne.

He and the reformers had no agreed plan. Some like Ligachëv wanted to go a shorter distance and at a slower pace. But Ligachëv supported Gorbachëv's eagerness to restore friendly relations with the USA, and everyone in the Politburo accepted that Gorbachëv was their most impressive international negotiator. (Most Americans thought the same about Reagan.) If Soviet leaders could attenuate tension in the Cold War they would have an opportunity to re-aerate the USSR's crumpled budget into shape and boost the output of consumer goods.

Andropov's agenda was meanwhile being zealously extended. Discipline was insisted on. The replacement of ageing communist officials began in earnest. Ligachëv sponsored a militant temperance campaign; whole vineyards were cut down in Moldavia and Ukraine. The unifying intention was to 'perfect' the mechanisms of the Soviet order. The Politburo was divided about what to do next, and it became clear that Gorbachëv was not going to be satisfied with Andropov's limited projects. Instead he demanded comprehensive reform. With his policy of *glasnost* he encouraged the exposure of the horrors of the Stalin years; he also directed a spotlight at the 'period of stagnation' under Brezhnev. If reform was to succeed, Soviet people had to be convinced of its desirability. The changes would have to involve more than tinkering with the institutional architecture. Gorbachëv called for a process of 'restructuring' (*perestroika*). He aimed at a drastic shift in the organisation and methods of party, government and other institutions of the Soviet state. He wanted to introduce the elective principle to public posts. Even communist party secretaries were to be subject to democratic control 'from below'.[3]

Bad luck intervened. In 1986 the OPEC countries reduced their prices for oil and threw the Soviet economy into lasting imbalance. It was a grim year. In April 1986 the nuclear power-station at Chernobyl in Ukraine exploded. Local politicians and scientists, being stuck in the old ways of doing things, covered up the disaster rather than come clean and

ask for assistance. The effect on Gorbachëv was to galvanise his commitment to making changes. He met immense passive resistance. Party
officials, including those appointed under Gorbachëv, hated the thought
of losing any authority. Governmental ministers were annoyed by
demands for them to alter their ways. While holding Gorbachëv in high
esteem, citizens felt uneasy about the consequences of basic political and
economic reforms. Gorbachëv turned to the intelligentsia for help. To
demonstrate his sincerity he liberated the liberal dissenter Andrei Sakharov from administrative exile in December 1986. Such was his charisma
and confidence that he was given the benefit of the doubt. The struggle
was joined to persuade society that the old ways of the Soviet order had
to be abandoned and a fresh prototype of communism developed.
Writers and thinkers would be crucial allies.

Gorbachëv no longer defined the USSR as having attained 'developed
socialism'; instead he called it 'socialism in the process of self-develop-
ment'.[4] This terminological mouthful implicitly abandoned the conventional claims of the USSR's ideologues. His own aims remained
undefined. By 1987 he was beginning to understand the immensity of his
problems. The Soviet institutional colossus tended to preserve its habits
even after he had sacked the old incumbents of offices. Functionaries
were not used to submitting themselves to elections and conspired to
undermine him. In 1988 he encountered trouble over economic policy.
His legislation on state enterprises gave a modicum of autonomy to their
directors. They were permitted in particular to put some of their
products on sale at prices they could fix without consulting Moscow.
Directors reacted by charging more for their output rather than by
expanding it. Gorbachëv also granted much power to the regions. This
had an effect he had not foreseen as several Soviet republics followed
their own national agendas in opposition to the wishes of the 'centre'.
Likewise many members of the Russian intelligentsia, freed from fear of
retribution, advocated ideas for the future different from his own. The
genie had escaped the lamp of the Soviet order.

If he had wanted, Gorbachëv could have caught and returned it to
the lamp. The party, army and KGB were under his aegis. Gorbachëv,
though, shrank from ripping up his reform agenda; he genuinely wanted a more democratic USSR. Another possibility would have been for
him to start with small-scale changes in the direction of the market
economy while maintaining a severe regime in politics. This was what
the Chinese had been doing under Deng Xiaoping for over a decade.
Why did Gorbachëv not do the same by fostering private agriculture

and manufacturing? He might thereby have been able to attract foreign capital into the Soviet economy and boost gross domestic production as well as raise the standard of living of millions of citizens. Perhaps then he might have started a cautious process of 'democratisation'.

The General Secretary had different ideas. His political attitudes were formed in the Khrushchëv years and he truly believed that the country suffered from a deficit of democratic procedures. He detested the Stalinist legacy and felt disgust at what his country had done to Hungary in 1956 and Czechoslovakia in 1968. He was comfortable in the company of those of his generation who thought as he did, and he welcomed such politicians and intellectuals to his entourage. His conversations with Western leaders encouraged him to go on thinking that his strategy had credible chances of success. What is more, Reagan constantly nagged him about the USSR's disrespect for human rights. If Gorbachëv wanted to conserve friendly relations with President Reagan and NATO, it was certainly going to help if he started to empty the Gulag and reduce the authority of the KGB. Failure to put words into action would shatter Gorbachëv's clean image as a reformer. In fact there is no evidence that Reagan would have refused to negotiate seriously if the USSR had taken the 'Chinese road' to reform. Reagan's supreme priority was to move beyond arms limitation talks to a process of actual reduction in arma-ments. He would probably have gone easy on Gorbachëv, as he did on Deng Xiaoping, if he could have enhanced American geopolitical security.[5]

The truth is that Gorbachëv gave no thought to emulating Deng Xiaoping. Several Soviet politicians later claimed that this was a strategic blunder and that the 'Chinese road' should have been followed. But few of them said or even hinted this before the fall of the USSR. The general assumption of reformers, from Gorbachëv to Ligachëv, was that reform required some attenuation of central political authority. Whether the 'Chinese road' was a realistic alternative is a separate question. If he had started down it, Gorbachëv would doubtless have come up against perils greater than those which confronted Deng. The Soviet countryside had been denuded of its young, industrious males, who had gone off to the towns to improve their conditions. Much of the work on collective farms was carried out by old women who offered little potential for an agricultural resurgence. Gorbachëv, moreover, needed allies. Unlike China, the USSR had a party apparatus which gave lip-service to *pere-stroika* while seeking to restrict its effects. Gorbachëv had had little alternative to seeking support among intellectuals. Most of them saw the liberalisation of the media as a priority. Without their help in shifting public opinion to his side he knew he would be in difficulties.

Yet a slower pace of political and cultural reform might have been beneficial; and a faster granting of freedom for small-scale manufacturing and commerce could also have brought advantage. Such a scenario perhaps would have facilitated a more orderly and – quite possibly – more successful process. Gorbachëv went at his tasks like a bull at a gate. He was a brilliant and brave leader of his vanguard but he and his society paid dearly for his recklessness.

It needs saying in his favour that his enemies were growing in number. Moscow city party chief Boris Yeltsin, noisy and contumacious, disturbed the Politburo by advocating policies still more radical than those of Gorbachëv. He repeatedly threatened to resign. He engaged in personal criticism of Gorbachëv, accusing him of listening too much to Raisa and flagrantly exploiting his political post for his own material gain. In November 1987 Gorbachëv had had enough and pushed Yeltsin into retirement. This had the unfortunate side-effect of boosting the standing of Yeltsin's strident critic Yegor Ligachëv. Ligachëv was Gorbachëv's deputy in the party leadership and connived at reverting *perestroika* to the more restricted agenda being elaborated under Andropov; and whenever Gorbachëv left on a foreign trip, Ligachëv got up to mischief. Whereas Gorbachëv succeeded in mastering Ligachëv, he found it harder to suppress the tendency he represented. There was an increasing number of politicians at the centre and in the localities who spoke out in favour of a greater emphasis on statehood, Russian pride, reverence for Soviet historical achievements. From their vantage points in party, army, KGB and economic ministries they urged the need for reforms to be decelerated and even reversed. Gorbachëv knew he would ignore them at his peril.

Yet he pressed onward. By 1989, he was no longer seeking to adjust and revitalise the Soviet order: he wanted to transform it.[6] It is true that in his own head he was a Leninist – and he was to remain so. But the objective work of his hands told of a different goal. He was turning many basic features of the USSR into their diametrical opposites. He did this with ingenuity and audacity. If his Politburo rivals had suspected what he was up to, they could easily have removed him from power. But Gorbachëv could also trade on his enormous popularity in the country and his mastery of the central policymaking bodies. The first great step in constitutional change was to scrap the pyramid of appointed soviets in favour of elected ones. Contested hustings would underpin the entire political system. The topmost stones would be a Congress of People's Deputies whose sessions would be chaired by Gorbachëv and broadcast on television. Not all of its members would need to be communists or even declared sympathisers of Marxism-Leninism. Gorbachëv privately discussed whether to split the Communist Party of the Soviet Union into two and lead off the radical reformers into a new social-democratic party. But he refrained from this, fearing that the anti-reformers would exploit such a situation to the lasting detriment of fundamental change.

In 1990 he gave scope for the formation of rival political parties by repealing article six of the USSR Constitution which guaranteed the leading role for the communists. There had been nothing like it since the early years of the Soviet state. Cultural pluralism crossed beyond previous bounds. Gorbachëv had already reviled Stalin and ridiculed Brezhnev; he now sat back as his own hero Lenin was criticised by others. As a counterweight to his communist-conservative adversaries, he brought back Boris Yeltsin from disgrace. All the gratitude he received was Yeltsin's resumed castigation of his policies. The attacks on Gorbachëv came from several sides as political pluralism spread. And Gorbachëv's willingness to sit through the interminable proceedings of the Congress of People's Deputies did him no favours. He lost the supreme ruler's aura of mystery. The Soviet man of destiny was turning into a figure of contempt and distrust.

His unpopularity came upon him in a rush. He had collaborated with Ronald Reagan in bringing the Cold War virtually to an end. The rest of the world wished the USSR well; this had not happened since 1945. He had introduced political and cultural liberalisation even though he had not yet completed the process. But fellow citizens did not forgive him his responsibility for economic collapse. His ideas for the country's transformation included the introduction of a market sector to the economy. The trouble was that his measures were too modest and ill-formulated to bring about an expanded provision of industrial and agricultural products. The standard of living of consumers collapsed. Shops ran out of things to sell. Meat, sugar, butter and vegetables were rarely available. As the black market grew bigger, people's discontent increased. Although Gorbachëv meant well, this was not enough to turn the ship quickly in the desired direction. Disputes intensified among the reformers as they planned how to reduce the state-owned, planned share of the economy. Soviet economists lacked experience of markets; they also represented large institutional interests in the USSR. Gorbachëv tried to get the country's political leaders to agree on a compromise which became known as the 500-day programme. But this only meant that radical change was yet again postponed. The economic crisis deepened.

Moscow had always been better supplied than the Russian provinces, but in the winter of 1990–1 a visitor might have been forgiven for thinking that a horde of robbers had passed through the capital. A dairy supermarket near the prestigious metropolitan university was staffed as usual with dozens of counter-assistants in white jackets. Yet they had no milk, yoghurt or butter for sale. The only products on offer were a few small tins of sardines. It was not yet famine. But there was deep popular discontent.

Gorbachëv alluded to the deteriorating situation only in abstract terms. As opinion turned against him, he was not helped by the growing sense that the USSR was on the point of disintegration. One of his blind spots was the 'national question'. This was in some ways surprising. He came from Stavropol region on the edge of the multi-ethnic north Caucasus where tensions among nations were bitter. Both he and his wife came from a mixture of Russian and Ukrainian ancestries. Perhaps, though, this contributed to his blindness. Gorbachëv was a typical 'Soviet person' who thought that sensible citizens should assimilate to the USSR's values regardless of national background; he also unthinkingly assumed that Russian culture should lie at the core of Soviet identity. When in Kiev, he talked as if he was in Russia rather than Ukraine. Early in his time as General Secretary he had concentrated on rooting out corruption and disobedience in the various Soviet republics. He did not allow for the capacity of communist elites in Kazakhstan, Uzbekistan and elsewhere to stir up nationalist trouble. Indeed he continued to include the Soviet republics in his policy of political decentralisation. The intention was to resolve tensions by giving autonomy to the national communist leaderships: he showered them with freedoms.

It was a gamble that only a believer in the 'Leninist harmony of peoples' could have taken. For a while Gorbachëv appeared to be the winner. In March 1991 he held a referendum across the USSR. The question was: 'Do you believe it essential to preserve the USSR as a renewed federation of equal sovereign republics in which the rights and freedoms of a person of any nationality will be fully guaranteed?' The turnout was high and 76 per cent of the ballot papers had a cross in favour of Gorbachëv's objective. The federal union seemed to have been saved.

No plebiscite, however, could alter the basic trend towards break-up. As the political and economic disarray increased, the republics had to fend for themselves. The communist leaderships could no longer rule exclusively by command and intimidation. They turned to nationalism to drum up support for their continued leadership. In Estonia, Latvia and Lithuania the communists sought to identify themselves as national leaders first and communists only second. The communist leaders in the Caucasus and central Asia were more discreet but no less keen to take advantage of the rising tides of nationalism. Ukraine and Belorussia stayed firm in their allegiance to Moscow; but even their loyalist pronouncements were problematic for Gorbachëv since neither Kiev nor Minsk was led by communists who favoured his reforms. As the other Soviet republics asserted their rights to self-rule, Yeltsin claimed that the RSFSR (or just 'Russia', as he called it) was being left behind. The RSFSR was larger than all the other republics put together. Yeltsin, who had risen from his political grave, demanded that it should have its own political institutions and leadership; he obtained an overwhelming victory in the Russian presidential election of June 1991. Gorbachëv as President of the USSR had facilitated the holding of the election, and he was counting on Yeltsin as a strong ally in the campaign to save the federal union against dissolution. But Yeltsin was already signalling that a price would have to be paid for his co-operation.

What made things worse was that the men lately appointed by Gorbachëv to high office had deep misgivings about the loose constitutional structure projected in the draft Union Treaty. They were also appalled by the gathering pace of economic decline. Some now thought Gorbachëv a traitor. Meanwhile Gorbachëv had lost his magical touch with Western leaders, who began to refuse his requests for emergency financial assistance; he was no longer an asset for the USSR in international relations. His rapprochement with Yeltsin convinced several members at the core of the Soviet establishment that drastic action was called for. They plotted a *coup d'état*. They would appeal to Russian patriotism and Soviet pride, and they hoped that Gorbachëv would see the light and come over to their side, but they were determined to act regardless of his attitude. He was not to be told until they had declared a state of emergency.

The conspirators made the correct assumption that most people were fed up with Gorbachëv and his unfulfilled promises and wooden jargon. The old economic order had disintegrated as industrial output was dislocated by local administrative chaos and blunders in central policy. The legal retail trade all but vanished. Crime on the streets was growing. Pride in the USSR's history had been ridiculed; the media turned out a ceaseless stream of exposés of abuses of power from Lenin onwards. The Congress of People's Deputies frequently descended into a verbal bear-pit. Pornography was sold in kiosks. As the small steps were taken towards a market economy, already a few entrepreneurs were becoming conspicuously rich. Beggars appeared in the main cities. The maltreatment of army conscripts became a public scandal. Republican and local political elites ran their areas as fiefdoms. Strikes broke out in the mines of the Kuzbass. It was unlikely that people would come out in large numbers to defend Gorbachëv. He had lost his towering popularity; he was also dreadfully tired. The organisers of the coup made a few amateurish arrangements; they were betting on being able to deploy the traditional instruments of party, police and army without need to plan for any contingency other than total success. If the worst came to the worst, the residual fear of the punitive sanctions would surely deter resistance.

They made their move on 19 August, setting up a State Emergency Situation Committee under the nominal leadership of Vice-President Gennadi Yanaev while Gorbachëv holidayed at Foros in the south. Moscow was brought under martial law; an appeal was made to the patriotism of citizens while order and welfare were being restored to the USSR. The conspiracy was ridiculously amateurish. The State Emergency Situation Committee included experienced figures such as KGB Chairman Vladimir Kryuchkov, Interior Minister Boris Pugo and Defence Minister Dmitri Yazov. Yet they complacently omitted to arrange properly for the arrest of Yeltsin, who was just outside Moscow at his dacha. On TV they made a pathetic line-up. Their nerves jangled when Yeltsin, arriving at the RSFSR Supreme Soviet building, announced his defiance from the top of a tank put at his disposal by a friendly army officer. A delegation of the committee sent to negotiate with Gorbachëv met with the President's angry contempt. The conspiracy collapsed as Yeltsin took control of Moscow. Gorbachëv, who had been reported as having been incommoded by illness, returned to resume authority. Yet the real victor was not Gorbachëv but Yeltsin. From that time onwards Yeltsin oversaw everything done in the name of the USSR.

Estonia, Latvia and Lithuania declared their independence. The other Soviet republics raised the stakes for continued collaboration with Moscow. The exasperated Gorbachëv offered to step down in Yeltsin's favour. But Yeltsin chose a different tack. On 1 December the Ukrainians voted in favour of independence. Without Ukraine, the Union could not endure. Yeltsin cut the Gordian knot by stating that the RSFSR would also become independent. Gorbachëv implored him to avoid so drastic a course, to no effect. With deep regret he announced that the USSR would cease to exist on the stroke of midnight on the last day of 1991. Although a Commonwealth of Independent States was formally established, the reality was that Russia went its own separate way. The communist order was brusquely torn down. The communist party itself had already been outlawed. The October Revolution and Marxism-Leninism were disowned; the course of Soviet history was described as a totalitarian nightmare. Yeltsin's ministers initiated radical economic reform, starting with the liberalisation of prices for goods in the shops. A multi-party system was welcomed without the previous limitations. Citizens were promised permanent relief from state interference. The era of social mobilisation was said to be over; everyone was to have the right to a private life and to a free choice about beliefs and recreations. Communism as Russians had known it since 1917 was at an end.

Few Soviet citizens lamented Gorbachëv's going. His policies had ruined the economy and smashed the state into fragments. His critics showed him no mercy. This was ungenerous of them since without his introduction of *glasnost* and *perestroika* they could never have had the opportunity to calumniate him. Abroad, he was better respected. His disinclination to halt the decommunisation of eastern Europe by force was widely admired. His primary role in the ending of the Cold War was rightly esteemed. There had been many times when a different General Secretary would have called upon the armed forces and the KGB and reversed the reform programme. Yet the verdict on him has to take account of his inability to understand the nature of the Soviet order. He had genuinely believed that the USSR could be reformed and still remain communist. He had a passion for a democratic, humanitarian Lenin who had never existed in history.

39. THE COMRADES DEPART

Dozens of communist states vanished in the two years after mid-1989. This phenomenon was not confined to eastern Europe and the USSR: the Marxist dictatorship in Ethiopia was overturned in May 1991 and Mengistu took himself off to political sanctuary in Zimbabwe.[1] Viewed in the perspective of centuries of recorded history, it had happened in a flash of time. A state order which covered a quarter of the world's land surface underwent convulsive shrinkage, and people brought up with the pages of their atlases coloured in red could hardly recognise the new political maps of the globe. Only a handful of regimes continued to profess a commitment to the objectives of Marxism-Leninism in any of its variants.

The People's Republic of China was the sole remaining communist power of global importance, but its frenzied adoption of market economics had turned the country into a hybrid of communism and capitalism.[2] This had the effect of deflecting the criticism of the Chinese labour-camp system or the terrible working conditions of the free employees. World business was doing well out of China and, as had been true of many industrial enterprises which had contracts with the USSR in the 1930s, did not pry into the gruesome corners of the national penal system. Although Vietnam remained under communist rule, its rulers too adopted capitalism: they saw China as a model for their own development.[3] Cuba shuffled unsteadily towards a few reforms; it increased religious tolerance, welcomed foreign tourism and attracted direct investment from abroad despite the American economic blockade.[4] The communist government in Laos had little alternative. The only financial aid available to it since the seizure of power in 1975 had come from Moscow, and the authorities had built holiday hotels for Soviet tourists to earn extra revenue.[5] The USSR's collapse was a disaster for Laotian communism and change was unavoidable. By the mid-1990s the authorities even embarked on closing down its labour camps.

No longer was communism in any country interested in fomenting communist insurrections abroad. Beijing's financial aid was concentrated in countries able to supply the oil needed for Chinese economic development or territorial security. Maoist insurrectionaries in Nepal and other places received neither help nor encouragement. Communist parties of all types everywhere learned to look after themselves. They had no alternative. The world communist movement was no longer just fragmented but had been blasted to smithereens.

North Korea was an exception to the global pattern. Its rulers adhered rigidly to an unreformed communist order despite its difficulty in feeding its people. Its possession of nuclear weapons made it a danger to the regional security of the north-west Pacific. Under Kim Jong-il, son of the state's founder, it had to accept donations of food supplies for more than a fifth of its people. Two-thirds of its medicines were gifts sent from abroad. A degree of economic reform was introduced in 2002 with the purpose of shaking off the reliance on foreign aid. But Kim abandoned this policy in summer 2005. Soldiers were posted in paddy-fields to ensure that every grain of rice would be delivered to the state procurement agency. There was a ban on selling the produce from kitchen gardens to private buyers. The government in Pyongyang intimidated neighbouring countries by advertising its research and development in the field of nuclear bombs and ballistic missiles – and in October 2006 it taunted the world with a claim to have carried out an underground nuclear explosion. The claws of the political police were sharpened. Only three hundred foreigners, including diplomats, were licensed to be resident in North Korea. The insulation of popular opinion was nearer to completeness than in any long-lasting communist state. Kim Jong-il, dumpy and smiling, forwent rice and grain from the world's humanitarian agencies rather than submit to demands for visits by their inspectors.[6]

Yet the Cold War was over and the West had won it. There was no particular date when victory occurred. There was no single event such as a military surrender. The process was completed almost without being noticed. But there was no denying that communism had suffered global defeat. President George H. Bush, not a politician given to coining memorable phrases, heralded 'a new world order'.

More and more governments were being formed by popular election. Economies were being turned over to and expanded by capitalism. Political aspirations were liberated. It was widely believed that liberal democracies and market economies would become the universal way to organise societies around the globe. This thought was endorsed by Bush's successor Bill Clinton and entered common currency. The 'end of history' was proclaimed.[7] Dictatorships of the political right and left were diminishing in number. Latin America had followed a democratising trend in the 1980s and cast down several right-wing authoritarian regimes; eastern Europe and the Soviet Union had toppled communism in 1989–91. The assumption was that the successor states would co-operate to make the world safe for democracy, civic freedom, legal guarantees and material prosperity. The atmosphere of global politics exuded triumphalism. The USA became the world's unique superpower. Successive presidents promised to use American military, diplomatic and economic might in the service of universal humanitarianism and were willing to crush resistance to this progress by the use of America's unmatchable force.

The rulers of the universe forgot that all countries, collectively or individually, had enduring features which could bend the straight line of future development. Their hopes were quickly disappointed. Ethnic, cultural and inter-state conflicts arose in Yugoslavia, Chechnya and Rwanda. Religious animosities were intertwined with them. The growth in fanatical variants of Islam continued. The Al-Qaida group led by Osama bin Laden obtained a haven for its training bases in Afghanistan under the strict Moslem rule of the Taliban government. Bin Laden organised terror campaigns worldwide; and his example was followed by organisations which sprang up independently. The new world order turned out to be neither new nor worldwide nor even orderly. When American power overturned oppressive regimes the consequences were seldom what Washington had expected. The Taliban and Al-Qaida were militarily defeated in Afghanistan in 2002 but they were not eliminated, and the succeeding Afghan administration was hardly a model for the rule of law or for popular consent. Iraq was invaded in 2003 and the Baathist dictator Saddam Hussein was overthrown. The outcome was a widening insurgency and incipient civil war despite the introduction of electoral freedom. History had not finished its course.

But George H. Bush and Bill Clinton were right about one great thing in the last decade of the twentieth century: communism in most places had ended as a state order. The incoming administrations, after the comrades had departed, tried diverse ways to prevent any restoration of communist rule. The Bulgarian authorities hauled Todor Zhivkov into custody in 1990 and convicted him of embezzlement two years later. This was a bit like Al Capone being found guilty of tax evasion. Zhivkov pleaded ill-health and was let off with house arrest. The Germans pressed charges against Erich Honecker in 1993, but he was already stricken with liver cancer and the trial was suspended. He died a year later in Chile. His successor Egon Krenz enjoyed better health and was treated less leniently. In 1997 he was arrested for complicity in the shooting of individuals who had tried to clamber over the Berlin Wall. Krenz was sentenced to six years' imprisonment. (In fact he served only three of them.) Gustáv Husák and Wojciech Jaruzelski suffered little harassment. President Havel in Prague wanted no vengeance upon his tormentor Husák, who was mortally ill and died in 1991. Successive governments in Poland recognised that Jaruzelski, despite his faults, had helped his country avoid invasion by the Warsaw Pact in the 1980s.

In the Czech Republic a law was introduced prohibiting communist leaders from holding office; in reunited Germany the public was given access to the files on them gathered by the security police. Archives were opened and the horrors of communist rule were exposed. The consensus in the media was that the 'totalitarian nightmare' was over. From Siberia's Pacific coast across to Hungary, the Balkans and the former East Germany the same development took place. National pride was asserted. Religious and cultural tradition was reinstalled. Flags were redesigned and towns and streets were renamed. Statues of Marxist-Leninist heroes were pulled down. The history books were rewritten. The offices, dachas and bank accounts of the old communist parties were seized.

But then a strange thing happened: the communists began to make a political comeback. Boris Yeltsin had striven to make this impossible in Russia. Immediately after the August 1991 coup he outlawed the communist party. He sealed the party's offices, expropriated its property and locked up the coup leaders. He spoke of all the years since 1917 as a totalitarian nightmare. Whereas Gorbachëv had zigzagged his route towards market reforms, Yeltsin drove directly into capitalism. Prices were liberalised in January 1992. Preparations were made to sell off Russia's industrial assets by means of a system providing all citizens with vouchers entitling them to shares in their privatised enterprises. Consumer goods were imported to satisfy the demands of consumers. Yet the coalition which had brought Yeltsin to power peeled away from him. Vice-President Alexander Rutskoi objected to the social hardship caused by the economic transformation. Ruslan Khasbulatov, Speaker in the RSFSR Supreme Soviet, criticised Yeltsin's eagerness to rule by decree. Constitutional stalemate resulted. Yeltsin was spoiling for a fight; he and his advisers wanted to accelerate the movement towards capitalism.

Restless and imperious, he suspended the Supreme Soviet and announced the holding of a referendum on a new constitution. He sought a popular endorsement of his dismantlement of his intended programme.

Many supporters of Rutskoi and Khasbulatov were nostalgic for communism. The emergency brought even outright Stalinists to their side. Picking up Yeltsin's challenge, they formed an armed group and attacked the main TV station in Moscow. The rest holed up in the Supreme Soviet building, calling on fellow citizens to help in overthrowing the government. Yeltsin obtained the pretext he wanted for the use of force. The Russian army shelled the Supreme Soviet into surrender and, after a brief exchange of fire, Yeltsin achieved total victory.

Yet the death of communism in Russia had been much exaggerated. The December 1993 referendum endorsed Yeltsin's constitutional project but only because his officials fiddled the results. Yeltsin also suffered disappointment in the simultaneous election to the State Duma. Instead of a thumping win for his supporters there was much success for the neo-fascist party of Vladimir Zhirinovski. What is more, the Constitutional Court in November 1993 had ruled the ban on the communist party invalid. Back into the legal political arena marched the communists under Gennadi Zyuganov, and they became the most influential party of opposition by the mid-1990s. Zyuganov understood that he would win over few voters if he called for the restoration of a one-party state. He repositioned the Communist Party of the Russian Federation by asserting its sympathy with that bastion of the Russian Imperial tradition, the Orthodox Church, whereas the party of Lenin, Stalin and Khrushchëv had persecuted religion as the opium of the people. Zyuganov anyway cared little for Lenin. The communist he most admired was Stalin, who had led the USSR to victory in the Second World War. Zyuganov denounced the breaking up of the Soviet Union. He and his party hymned the welfare provision available under Brezhnev. They vilified Gorbachëv and snidely fostered antisemitism.

Zyuganov stood against Yeltsin in the presidential election of 1996. He was in the lead as the campaign opened but lacked the resources available to Yeltsin, who enlisted the wealthiest businessmen on his side. The communist campaign was anyway a jaded one and Zyuganov proved a distinctly uncharismatic candidate. Despite serious cardiac ill-health, Yeltsin pulled himself together for the electoral contest. He toured the country. He spent freely on political broadcasts. He disbursed budgetary largesse to local administrations. TV and print journalists focused attention on the past iniquities of communism. The result was a second presidential term for Yeltsin and the definitive trouncing of communism in Russia.

Yeltsin consolidated his power in the role of an anti-communist ex-communist; Algirdas Brazauskas did the same in Lithuania but in a more circumspect and less corrupt and violent fashion. Brazauskas had broken with Moscow before the collapse of the USSR. He then declared himself a social-democrat and gained such popularity that he won the presidential election in 1993 and went on to become Prime Minister in 2001. The old communist leaders in Latvia and Estonia did less well. Lacking Brazauskas's political versatility, they suffered ignominious electoral defeats. Patriotic revenge was being exacted after years of national subjugation. Latvians, Estonians and indeed Lithuanians celebrated their freedom in parades, religious services and literary and historical writings. Glad to see the back of the Soviet army, they hoped that Russian civilians would also depart. Rules on citizenship stipulated that everyone should speak the national language and know the national history. Wanting to acquire membership of the European Union, however, the three states moderated their treatment of resident Russians. Slowly but surely the democratic system and the market economy in these three Baltic states were strengthened by integration in the European Union.

The other former Soviet republics, except Georgia and Kyrgyzstan, were headed by communist party chiefs who restyled themselves as patriots and used their political patronage to secure themselves in power. Nursultan Nazarbaev in Kazakhstan was typical. He put his long-established group of clients in the main offices of state and gave outrageous benefit to his family as privatisation proceeded. He overrode constitutional and legal obstacles; his police used torture against dissenters. His policies blatantly discriminated in favour of individuals and groups of Kazakh nationality. In central Asia and the south Caucasus it was the same story. The new leaderships had familiar faces. The post-communist presidents and their regimes were more brutal than anything witnessed in the region since the death of Stalin. The cult of Saparmurat Niyazov in Turkmenistan was extravagant by any known standard. He proclaimed himself Turkmenbashi (Leader of all the Turkmens). His books were made compulsory in schools. A golden statue of him was erected, fifty feet high, on a pedestal which is rotated so as to stand constantly facing the sun. He renamed one of the months of the year after himself, another after his mother. Words in the state hymn threatened that anyone defaming him should have his arms chopped off.

Until 1991 this same Niyazov had been First Secretary of the Turkmenistan Communist Party. Only his death in December 2006 ended his savage tyranny.

Although there was peaceful abandonment of communism in most states of the former Soviet Union, some terrible exceptions occurred. Russian and Moldovan elites fought for supremacy in Moldova (which had dropped its Soviet name of Moldavia). Tribal and religious rivalries produced a vicious civil war in Tajikistan on the Afghan border. Chechnya rose in revolt against the Russian Federation. A bloody war sputtered on between Armenia and Azerbaijan about the Armenian-inhabited enclave in Karabagh.

But it could have been so much worse and most of the countries of the former USSR at least achieved independence without bloodshed. The same was true across the Kremlin's 'outer empire'. Eastern Europe's peoples coped calmly with life after communism without 'Russian' interference. There was a political emergency in Czechoslovakia when the Slovaks, after years of resenting the Czechs, demanded the right to secede. But the dispute was resolved. Not a shot was fired as the Czech Republic and Slovakia went their separate ways in January 1993. The great exception was Yugoslavia (which had anyway never submitted to Soviet Imperial control). Conflicts broke out across the borders of many republics after Milošević's rise to power in Serbia. Ethnic strife convulsed the internal affairs of Croatia, Bosnia-Herzegovina and Kosovo. Suddenly in mid-1991 Yugoslavia broke apart when Slovenia and Croatia unilaterally declared their independence. Macedonia followed in September 1991, Bosnia-Herzegovina in March 1992. Inflamed by Milošević's speeches, Serbs in Bosnia-Herzegovina demanded broad self-rule. This was reasonably interpreted by resident Moslems and Croats as the first steps towards annexation by Serbia. The Croatian government under Franjo Tudjman poured finance and arms into Bosnia-Herzegovina in support of its co-nationals. The whole federal state collapsed in concurrent processes of secessions, civil wars, inter-republican invasions and ethnic expulsions.

The barbarous violence was brought to an end in 1995 by an agreement signed in Dayton, Ohio; and Milošević was momentarily hailed around the world as a peacemaker. But he had suspended action in Croatia and Bosnia-Herzegovina only because he currently lacked the necessary military power. Kosovo, moreover, was another matter and in 1998 he carried out a campaign of ethnic cleansing which forced Albanians to flee for their lives over the border into Albania. President

Clinton convinced the UN to sanction armed intervention. In March 1999, after Milošević refused to give way, Belgrade suffered relentless NATO bombing from the air. By June he had no alternative but to pull out of Kosovo. Political demonstrations began against him in Belgrade. In the following year he went down to defeat in Serbia's elections and was ousted from office. In 2001 the Serbian authorities surrendered him for trial as a war criminal at the International Criminal Tribunal at The Hague; he died in March 2006 before any verdict was reached. Yugoslavia had long since been dismembered and its communism consigned to the dustbin of history. Nationalism, casting off the light disguise of constitutional federalism, had triumphed – and only to a partial degree did it lead to liberal democracy.

The system of political patronage and financial corruption outlived the communist order in the states carved out of Yugoslavia. Ex-communists frequently did well out of the 'transition to the market'. This was a phenomenon common to several states in the region but not in Poland, the Czech Republic or the abolished German Democratic Republic, where communists were flung out of positions of influence. Nearly everywhere the communist parties adopted fresh names, new leaders and a programme of ideas close to social-democracy rather than communism. This was usually not enough to earn them popular trust. But they were not disgraced in elections and in 1995 the ex-communist Alexander Kwasniewski won the Polish presidency and served two full terms. This had been barely imaginable in the heady years of Solidarity's supremacy. Yet capitalism had not been kind to many people in Poland and elsewhere in the 1990s. Mass unemployment, shoddy welfare facilities and a widening of the gap between rich and poor gave communists a second chance in politics. They had to adjust their appeal by wrapping themselves in the national flag, throwing Marxism to the winds and identifying themselves with the needs of downtrodden electors.

Electoral victory did not come easily or often. Kwasniewski had done better than the candidates put up by communist parties in western Europe. The leadership in Paris was demoralised. Georges Marchais, Secretary-General from 1972 to 1994, was an ageing poodle who had usually trotted obediently down the line prescribed by Moscow.[8] His successors were befuddled about how to recast the party's programme. They could no longer praise the defunct USSR. They concentrated increasingly on policies of state welfare and hostility to 'American imperialism'. The old linkage between the Kremlin and French communism was not so much regretted or disowned as overlooked. This situation was neither fish nor fowl to militant veterans, who left the party in droves.

In 2002 the post of Secretary-General was taken by Marie-Georges Buffet. This was a sign of the times. Previously the French Communist Party had seldom allowed women to get within a sniff of genuine authority. The veteran male champions of class struggle had lost their nerve. This was also what happened across the English Channel where Nina Temple became the Communist Party of Great Britain's last leader in 1990. As soon as she had risen to the top she dissolved the organisation into a new Party of the Democratic Left in November 1991, while various factions cursed her renegacy and went off to form parties of their own. Mme Buffet did not restore communist fortunes: in the parliamentary elections of 2002 the French Communist Party received less than 5 per cent of the popular vote. Its period of street demonstrations, ideological ambition and cultural influence was at an end. Ms Temple's pragmatic decision to distance her party from communism by name and ideology attracted scarcely any new followers and won not a single election even at the local level; and if the party had not inherited funds available from the USSR's earlier subventions to the Communist Party of Great Britain it would have fallen into instant oblivion.

The Italian Communist Party, redesignated as the Democratic Party of the Left, did much better. It had long ago cut its connections to Moscow. To demonstrate its rupture with old ideas it joined the Socialist International (which had been the object of hostility for all communists since the end of the First World War). The Democratic Party of the Left helped to establish a left-of-centre electoral coalition called the Olive Tree which succeeded in forming governments in 1996, 1998 and 2006. The new party retained its position as Italy's main leftist organisation. Its older members were sometimes nostalgic for Togliatti and the Italian Communist Party. But the deed had been done. Communists in Italy were the gravediggers of communism. Thousands of irreconcilables streamed out of the Democratic Party of the Left and formed new communist organisations. The Communist Refoundation party was among them; its leaders called upon all genuine communists to stand up and be counted. But this summons was largely ignored – and the leaders of Communist Refoundation were anyway scarcely sea-green incorruptibles: they fought elections from 1996 onwards as part of the Olive Tree coalition alongside both the Democratic Party of the Left and several liberal parties.

Elsewhere, in countries which had not effected reforms to assist the poorer social classes, it was a different story. Communism as ever fed off popular misery. The example of Guevara continued to exercise a strong appeal in Latin America. Nearly everywhere the indigenous peoples – the Indians who had inhabited those countries before their conquest by the Spanish and the Portuguese – suffered oppression and exploitation. Urban workers were treated abominably. Legal political parties offered little realistic hope of alleviating their conditions. The USA exercised an economic influence which benefited the commercial and landed elites in the region but prevented fundamental reform. Some countries had working parliaments, others were ruled by military dictatorships. Washington since 1945 had judged regimes by their willingness to accept American hegemony and to suppress communism. The end of the Cold War made little difference. Presidents Bush and Clinton did little to foster social fairness in Latin America even though at least Clinton backed the movement towards political democracy. The grinding poverty of Guatemalan villages or the shanty settlements on the edge of Rio de Janeiro in Brazil remained grim. In such circumstances there was a guaranteed residuum of support for clandestine communist parties which promised to liberate the downtrodden 'masses'.

Many small organisations and groupings ignored the vast changes in Moscow and Beijing. Not having been dependent on foreign assistance, they went on pursuing their own strategy with ideas. The Shining Path in Peru took up the peasantry's cause by selective assassinations of political and economic leaders, including foreigners, and indiscriminate bombings of institutions and companies. Ex-academic Abimael Guzmán and other leaders thought of themselves as Maoists even though Mao Zedong's revolutionary strategy had little to say about terrorism. (Guzmán's long and violent campaign was brought to an end after he was arrested and, in October 2006, sentenced to imprisonment.) The same story continued in Colombia where the Revolutionary Armed Forces of Colombia – the FARC – used drug-smuggling, kidnappings and assassinations as well as the operational expertise of the Provisional IRA from Northern Ireland. Maoists in Nepal constituted the only serious opposition to the ruling monarchy. Popular discontent as well as Maoist terror against those who collaborated with army and police allowed the communists to sustain their insurgency. The Beijing government disapproved. China's interests of state lay with the maintenance of orderly government in Nepal, and the Nepalese Maoists were cold-shouldered by Chinese leaders who maintained the colossal image of Mao Zedong in Tiananmen Square.

Wherever most people had a sense of economic and social despair there remained an opening for communist organisations. But, if the state was powerful, the communists had to take to the mountains and forests in order to survive. They tended to be more effective at sabotage, disruption and intimidation than at building a political movement with a realistic chance of forming a government. Not all governments attempted the systematic eradication of operations by communists. In Asia, Africa and Latin America there remained a profusion of parties. The media exposure of past abuses under Lenin, Stalin and Mao failed to stop grouplets from revering their memory. What counted for communist recruits was the lingering historical image of Marxists taking up the struggle against capitalism, imperialism and cultural backwardness. They wanted a different political, social and economic reality for their countries and were uninterested in discussions of what had gone wrong in earlier decades. If the Shining Path or the FARC were ever to hold power, their lack of curiosity about communist history – as well as their own penchant for dictatorship, terror, civil war, amoralism and societal mobilisation – would doom them to repeat the blunders of their heroes.

Much more eclectic in their handling of communism were the revolutionaries who were led to power in Nicaragua by the charismatic Daniel Ortega in 1979. They called themselves the Sandinistas after Augusto Sandino, a revolutionary from an earlier generation who had been executed by Somoza's army in 1934. The Sandinistas were communists. Their propaganda emphasised a populist set of aspirations. Their aims included agrarian reform, universal education and the involvement of all layers of society in their revolutionary project; they also intended to pull Nicaragua out of the political and economic orbit of the USA. Apart from Soviet Marxism, they drew upon Sandino, Castro, Mao, Catholic liberation theology, European social-democracy and a touch of anarcho-syndicalism.[9] They emphasised that no prior model would constrain them: 'Neither communism nor capitalism, just Nicaraguan Sandinismo!' More vaguely they proclaimed: 'The Revolution is young, fresh, creative!'[10] Defeated in the national elections of February 1990, they stood down without violence.[11] The Sadinistas revised their policies; and Ortega, having softened his economic and anti-clerical radicalism, won back the presidency at the ballot box in November 2006.

Yet the most remarkable example of communism's adaptation to changing conditions happened in Mexico. Revolutionary spurts had occurred there since the beginning of the twentieth century. Among the leaders of peasant rebellion had been the wild guerrilla Emiliano Zapata, who died in an ambush in 1919. Zapata had been committed to social justice. His memory was revived in the mid-1990s by the Zapatista Army of National Liberation (Ejército Zapatista de la Liberación Nacional or EZLN). It was led by the mysterious Sub-Comandante Marcos. His very pseudonym was a propaganda device. Instead of claiming leadership of the Zapatistas, he affected to have a subordinate position. Marcos's real name is Rafael Sebastián Guillén Vicente. He and his followers set themselves up in the mountain villages and forests of Chiapas in the Mexican south-east. Governments refused to negotiate with him and the armed forces tried to hunt him down. He was to be stopped from becoming the second Che Guevara. But Sub-Comandante Marcos proved an elusive quarry and, among the Indians of the mountains, his reputation as their protector grew. He got whole villages to adopt the habit of self-rule. He drove out the propertied elite. He also appealed to the rest of the country by organising a peaceful march – or 'caravan' – from the south on to Mexico City in 2000–1 (which was made possible by the more accommodating policy towards the EZLN introduced by President Vicente Fox from December 2000).

Marcos was resourceful in his propaganda. Like the Bolsheviks of old, he would not let his face be photographed. But his image in Zapatista uniform was on open sale in the shops of San Cristóbal de las Casas: trim figure, sparkling eyes, the irremovable pipe protruding from the woollen black balaclava which hid most of his face. Cassette tapes of Mexican revolutionary songs were offered for sale on stalls in the main square as well as little knitted dolls sporting balaclavas and AK-47s. Booklets and news sheets retailed stories of peasant heroism and police brutality. Marcos's articles avoided the dourness of earlier communist outpourings; he welcomed cartoons and even children's sketches to illustrate his journal. He and the Zapatistas were practising the idea that revolution was not just an end-goal. It was also a process designed to broaden and enliven the minds of the revolutionary militants and the peasants themselves.

Like Ortega and the Sandinistas in Nicaragua,[12] the Zapatistas attached themselves only eclectically to communist traditions. Although they treated Marxism positively, they lacked the inhibitions of most communists in previous decades. Lenin was no idol for them. Refreshingly Trotski was remembered as much for his suppression of the Kronstadt sailors as for his leadership of the Red Army. Marcos talked affectionately about Rosa Luxemburg, warming to her distaste for political authoritarianism and her strategic and tactical flexibility. (He obviously did not know of her disdain for the peasant life.) Marcos's frame of reference was contemporary as well as historical. He identified himself with the anti-globalisation protests at the Cancún summit of the World Trade Organisation in September 2003. He fulminated against President George W. Bush for invading Iraq. At the same time he quoted from rock songs. He cited the wisdom of Homer Simpson. At no point did he trouble himself with sketching a vista of the future perfect society. He had objectives rather than plans or policies. He and his Zapatistas aimed at helping the indigenous people of Mexico to help themselves – and they were willing to sacrifice their own comfort in this struggle. They educated villagers. They assisted in getting an administration in place. They promoted co-operatives. They spread ideas about agricultural development while always insisting on respect for the traditional practices of the peasantry.

Yet the Zapatistas were caught in the aspic of local preoccupations. They stood aside from conventional national politics and formed no alliance with other parties. Their internationalist agenda was little different from those of countless groups abroad. Indeed there was nothing uniquely left-wing about opposing economic globalisation and American world power. The EZNL had foreign admirers but no organisational network outside Mexico. Their routine activities were seldom reported even in the Mexican media, far less in North America and Europe. Their prospects of supplanting the government in Mexico City were negligible.

Communism in the early-twenty-first century had exhausted most of its potential to transform societies. Like the mysterious monoliths on Easter Island, the great mausoleums of Lenin, Mao, Ho and Kim continued to attract visitors. But fewer and fewer people even in supposedly communist states bothered much with their writings. Leninism in nearly all its variants was more frequently hated or ridiculed than espoused. Communist parties lost members, morale and rationale. They declined in global ambition and focused their efforts on attracting patriotic support. Wherever it was convenient, they changed leaders, names and basic ideology. Communism as it really existed became bewilderingly diverse. The world got to know Russian comrades who owned casinos and Chinese comrades who did deals with Google and Dell Computers. At the same time Cuban comrades protected what they could from their revolutionary heritage; and Korean comrades went on strengthening a regime more penetratively repressive even that Stalin's USSR. Guerrilla bands of comrades in Asia and Latin America kept up their war against national capitalism and Yankee imperialism. Most European comrades stressed that they completely dissociated themselves from the totalitarian perspective of Marxism-Leninism – and they stopped calling each other comrade.

40. ACCOUNTING FOR COMMUNISM

Communism caused astonishment around the world both when it came to power in Russia in 1917 and when it lost its political supremacy there and in many other countries towards the end of the century. Until the First World War the Marxists had everywhere talked a good revolution without doing much to achieve one. A confluence of many factors produced the Soviet order. There is little reason to believe that, if Lenin and Trotski had died while directing the October Revolution in the Smolny Institute, a permanent one-party, one-ideology dictatorship would have been established. Also crucial was the long tradition of revolutionary ideas peculiar to Russia in the second half of the nineteenth century. Terror, dictatorship, centralism and doctrinairism attracted an intense following. Deep feelings of resentment existed widely in Imperial society, and the chasm of sentiment separating workers and peasants on one side and the rich, powerful elites on the other was no figment of the revolutionaries' imagination. The waging of war against the Central Powers from 1914 caused acute strains in the Russian Empire. When the monarchy collapsed, the Provisional Government experienced a deeper emergency in society and the economy – not to mention the growing disarray on the military front – than occurred in any other belligerent country. Communists were given their best ever chance to make a revolution, and they took it.

Before establishing their dictatorship, they had few clear policies but many basic assumptions – and it was these assumptions which guided them as resistance grew to communism in Russia and Europe. Their early fumblings towards a communist order left the USSR internationally vulnerable in its economy and its defence, and there was a rising tide of discontent, alienation and potential opposition at home. Stalin's policies from the late 1920s industrialised the Soviet Union and turned it into a great power. He built on Lenin's legacy while ditching much that Lenin had held dear. But the foundation stones of the Leninist order remained intact: the one-party state, the one-ideology culture, the hyper-centralism, the state-penetrated economy and the mobilised society.

The Soviet Union succeeded in shining its lamp to the world whereas the lights of a Soviet Belgium would have been snuffed out by foreign powers. Perhaps if the first communist experiment had taken place on Christmas Island it would have been left alone; but any other country would inevitably have stirred up a crusade against it. Communism in Russia came near to being overrun by the great powers but by late 1919 the Western Allies, as a result of internal pressures as well as out of geopolitical considerations, had dropped any immediate ambition to overturn Lenin. As the power of the Red Army rose in the 1930s, democratic states were yet more reluctant to take up arms against Moscow – and their businessmen were making solid profits out of exports to the USSR. The Great Depression in the world economy could hardly have happened at a better time for the USSR. Another stroke of luck was the fact that Russia and its borderlands were rich in natural resources. Scarcely a mineral existed which could not be found there in abundance. Oil, gas, gold and nickel were plentiful, and vast forests could be felled for their timber. Without such advantages the communists would hardly have achieved what they did before the Second World War. Geography worked greatly to the advantage of the USSR.

Soviet communism's survival also resulted from the country's political and cultural insulation from the capitalist world even while trading with it. Stalin eliminated the space where alternative organisations, individuals and ideas might operate. Private entrepreneurship, national assertiveness, spiritual exploration and religious celebration were more or less eradicated. There was an internal state of siege. Khrushchëv's reforms loosened things up; and Brezhnev, despite reversing some of his reforms, refrained from reintroducing the old severe tautness. Gorbachëv went further than Khrushchëv. He lifted the siege and inadvertently brought the order tumbling down.

Yet Stalin's regime surely could not have lasted without modification even if Stalin by some freak of nature had lived out the twentieth century. (Georgians, of course, are noted for their centenarians.) He had had to reconcile himself to a state order with inefficiencies and obstructions he was powerless to eliminate. Clientelism persisted. Local 'nests' were ineradicable. Bureaucrats behaved sloppily and ignored higher instructions and popular needs. The quality of goods and services, except at the highest reaches of the hierarchy, languished far below world standards. The economy operated according to criteria of quantitative output and fulfilled the five-year plans without proportionately improving the living conditions of most people. Military objectives skewed the budget and conditioned the whole organisation and official culture of society. Stalin was an eager militarist. But he also aimed to create an affluent society, and neither he nor his successors came near to satisfying popular desires. Problems mounted as Soviet rulers came to appreciate that they were more effective in suppressing than in liquidating anti-communist tendencies. Under the surface of Stalinist totalitarianism, different kinds of order remained capable of re-germinating. The pre-revolutionary roots of society had clung to life.

This was not the only reason why the USSR was vulnerable when its rulers softened its terror-regime. Soviet people in their vast majority were more educated and better informed in the 1980s than at the beginning of the twentieth century; they knew more than was good for the communist party leadership. Acquaintance with foreign developments was growing. The communist rulers encountered tasks of increasing complexity as the economy left the first stage of industrialisation behind. Questions arose needing the expertise of scientific, academic and managerial professionals. The regime's advisers acquired a greater influence over the shaping of policy. Yet the leadership had made extravagant claims for its ability to satisfy material demands. Its repeated failure aggravated the popular resentment. The communist order, unfortunately for itself, contained components which inhibited the development of initiative outside the range of current policies. The dynamism of the armaments sector could not be reproduced throughout the entire economy. No amount of tinkering with institutions and cajoling citizens worked. Soviet-style communism spent decades engineering its institutional machinery; but although the engine made a lot of noise and moved well through the lower gears, the direction of movement was always down a cul-de-sac.

Such was the order which, with a few national adjustments, was introduced to most countries of eastern Europe after 1945. The same difficulties mounted as soon as the communists took power. There was political oppression, economic rigidification and social alienation. Apathy and disillusionment spread. Although the party in each communist state attracted a mass membership, idealism was quickly outweighed by cynicism among the recruits. Communists in government needed the assistance of technical specialists – and such specialists, including ones trained up under communism, obfuscated official policy when it conflicted with their interests. Everywhere there were the same old dodges. Functionaries huddled together as 'clients' protected by a patron. Information delivered upwards was distorted to benefit the senders and frustrate the awkward intentions of the recipients. Misleading the 'centre' became a mode of existence. Communism, even more than other types of political order, relied on administrators to transmit accurate data to the supreme leadership. It never attained this end.

Communists had abolished multi-party elections and public criticism of their policies. They had crushed independent organs in the media and turned their central party newspapers and state radio and TV stations into the sole purveyors of public information. They had eliminated due legal process. They outlawed any political parties which offered effective opposition. They thought they were being clever; their ideology told them that the separation of powers was a bourgeois sham, and they thought that unifying agencies of state would make for a more account-able order. Marx, following Rousseau, developed this way of thinking and Lenin had enthusiastically grafted it on to his own. This was disastrous in theory and practice. Communist rulers deprived themselves of crucial instruments for checking the veracity of information reaching them. Without an unofficial network of media they had no access to open-ended discussion. The absence of constitutional and judicial pro-priety forestalled the preventability of administrative abuse. Communism in eastern Europe had no choice but to follow the Soviet road. Elsewhere, in China and Cuba, the rulers were not constrained by the requirements of obedience. Doubtless they were adhering to a common ideology; but they also adopted the Soviet model because they recognised that they would otherwise collapse under the onslaught of popular discontent and resistance.

There have been communist leaders – and not just ones whose parties failed to come to power – who moderated their zeal for full communisation. They have included individuals who in their private lives would not deliberately hurt a fly. One such was Bukharin, animal lover, mountain walker and painter. But kindly Bukharin did not abjure dictatorship and terror in principle, and he condoned most of the violence perpetrated by the Bolsheviks in the early years of the Soviet state.

Multi-party elections and civil rights do not produce rule by the people. There is overwhelming evidence that they benefit the rich and powerful more than the poor and weak. Elites rule. Influential interest groups barge their way to the front of the queue of state priorities. Communists concluded that political, social and national oppression was inevitable even under liberal democracy. They also believed capital-ism to be inherently unstable and unfair; they thought its end was nigh.

Communism would prove itself superior in technological inventiveness. This analysis was a pernicious mixture of exaggeration and downright incorrectness. Countries with civil rights and political democracy have been widely more effective at eliminating abuses of power. Capitalism, moreover, has shown resilience in developing new and useful products for the mass consumer market. More and more countries have expanded their economies to the advantage of an ever larger proportion of their citizens in recent decades. The prediction of Marx and Engels about general impoverishment has not been realised. They contended that the market economy as it expanded would reduce nearly everyone to destitution. The Leninists added the prophecy that world wars were unavoidable under capitalism and they too have as yet proved unreliable soothsayers.

Sensing that communism was thwarting the achievement of their objectives, some communist leaders darted down the nationalist foxhole. This was scarcely an option for most regimes in eastern Europe where Soviet power held them in thrall. Tito and Ceauşescu were the exceptions. But they too had problems. Tito ruled not a nation-state but a federal assemblage of nations and gained only limited favour for his concept of Yugoslavism; Ceauşescu paraded as the paladin of the Romanian nation while in reality crushing the country's religion and culture – and most Romanians hated him and his henchmen. China, North Vietnam and Cuba were better positioned to burrow down into nationalism. The Chinese asserted their independence by falling out with the USSR and introducing specific policies of their own; North Vietnam and Cuba went on receiving assistance from Moscow but geographical distance gave opportunity to Ho Chi Minh and Fidel Castro to run their states more or less as they pleased. Mao, Ho and Fidel acquired a cachet as champions of the nation even among many citizens who reviled their communising purposes. This was not a new phenomenon. Lenin and Stalin had had an appeal as leaders who stood up for Russia more effectively than the last tsars.

The elements of nationalism alleviated but never solved the difficulties of rulership, and some reformers believed that the Soviet model and its many foreign variants required another kind of adaptation. This trend became known as reform communism. Ever since communists themselves started to object to the form taken by a particular communist state – to its policies, institutions, leaders or social structures – the temptation for them was to say that it was not communism itself that was in the wrong but the way the state was implementing it. This happened soon after the October Revolution. Oh, if only Lenin had not died prematurely. If only Bukharin had been a better politician and prevented Stalin's rise to power. If only Russia had not been so backward as an economy and culture and had not been confronted by so many powerful capitalist states. Such reactions missed the point. A perfect society cannot be built on the premise that its construction requires perfect conditions. Communism by its nature offers a challenge to the advanced capitalist world. Capitalists inevitably pick up the gauntlet. Indeed Marxists had always predicted that they would behave like this. It follows that no communist project anywhere can endure without surmounting internal and external difficulties. If mass repression is not used, such difficulties will eventually produce political, social and economic emergencies.

After Hungarian communism embarked on reforms in 1956, it was engulfed by a popular revolt that would have swept away the communist order but for the Soviet invasion. The Prague Spring in 1968 introduced economic decentralisation and open political discussion. Dubček was already losing his grip on the political levers when the tanks rolled into his capital. The evidence suggests that any process of reforming communism is likely to turn into a movement to transform it into something radically different. Brezhnev understood this and turned his back on reform; and his predecessor Khrushchëv, despite being a reformer, had never tampered with the load-bearing walls of the Soviet political and economic edifice. There were limits beyond which it was perilous for a communist leadership to tread if it wished to avoid being replaced by an entirely different kind of state.

The danger is easily understood. The wish to enjoy a private life, free from state interference, was never expunged. The history of communist interference with the individual and the family intensified this aspiration. What is more, the notion of making a profit on deals had never disappeared. Although the open market was drastically curtailed under communism, bartering for personal gain was not eradicated – indeed it was often more prevalent in communist countries than in the advanced capitalist economies. Nor did people stop thinking for themselves politically. Distrust of government was endemic and got deeper as communisation proceeded. Resentment of the privileges of the nomenklatura was commonplace. Religious faith was not eliminated; in some countries – the most remarkable case is Poland – organised Christianity became a formidable instrument of anti-communism. The zest for free choice in hobbies, sport and recreation remained a powerful inclination. The longing persisted for society to be treated as something other than a resource to be mobilised. Knowledge also spread about the West, and the crudities of communist propaganda were rejected by a rising number of citizens. The aspiration intensified to pull down the barriers to sharing in the material and social advantages enjoyed by societies abroad.

There was consequently a sound reason why the communist leaderships refused to put their position to the test of a fair election: they knew they would lose. It was the same in the USSR even during *perestroika*. Although Gorbachëv was immensely strong in the opinion polls, he had cause for being wary in introducing political pluralism. When in 1990 he repealed the one-party system he was taking a huge gamble – and the resultant competition did much to undermine the Soviet order. The conclusion must be that communist governments grew stronger in direct proportion to their implementation of the Soviet model developed by Lenin and Stalin. Those states which could not or would not copy its fundamental features were vulnerable to internal dissolution or external intervention. Not only Nagy and Dubček in eastern Europe but also Allende in Latin America learned this lesson the hard way.

Yet many of those communist states in eastern Europe that rejected reform – or implemented it in only a diluted fashion – were themselves briskly overturned in 1989–91. A state order crumbled which had generated awe at home and abroad. Communism had been held together by force, and an adventitious combination of factors – in geopolitics, economic failure, social assertiveness, generational change, ideological bankruptcy and political choice – pulled it down. A vista of rapid decommunisation was opened up. The strange thing is that many features of life under communism have survived its dismantlement. The situation varies from country to country but several states of the former USSR and eastern Europe continue to be characterised by political oppression, economic corruption and social privilege. Clientelism, electoral fraud and police-state methods did not disappear everywhere. Communist rulers and administrators, as they discerned that communism was doomed, cast away their formal communist commitment while retaining many institutional and operational techniques. People throughout their societies were accustomed to this situation. Those techniques had in any case not been the patent of earlier communists. Communism had picked them up, either all or some of them, from the pre-revolutionary past and then dynamically reinforced them.

It accordingly took unusually good fortune for states to make a benign transition from their Soviet-style state order. A patriotic consensus helped in Poland and other countries. So did the preservation of

traditions of civil, religious and individual freedom. A national commitment to elections, legality and constitutionality was crucial. And the new
rulers needed to fix rules of the political game which firmly bound all its
players to fair behaviour.

Fascism was much easier to eradicate than communism. The German
Federal Republic and the Italian Republic after the Second World War
quickly introduced representative democracy, the rule of law and pluralist media. The Western Allies had won the military conflict and imposed
the kind of peacetime settlement they wanted, and Germans and Italians
by and large consented to it. This success was facilitated by the limited
nature of the changes in society made by Hitler and Mussolini. Private
enterprise had flourished under them. Religion had not been subject to
a campaign of extirpation. Foreign travel had not been outlawed. Hitler
in the longer term intended to complete the Nazification of Germany
but was defeated in war before he could bring his ambitions to completion. As things stood in 1945, it was not difficult for the USA and its
allies to resuscitate the tissues of German society which were necessary
for liberal democracy. This was not widely the case in communist states.
Communism had penetrated every sector of life: politics, economy,
society and belief-systems. In the USSR it had lasted seven decades. Even
where it covered a shorter time-span it was implemented across more or
less the same range of sectors. No wonder it is taking many years and
much effort for a radically different order to be developed in several
countries.

It cannot be stressed too heavily that not every inhuman action in
the twentieth century was perpetrated by communists. Adolf Hitler
carried out the extermination of Jews, Roma, homosexuals and mental-
hospital patients in their millions in the Third Reich. No communist
was involved in the genocide in Rwanda in 1994. The napalm poisoning
of Vietnamese and Cambodian forests was carried out by the USAF.
Capitalism's social and ecological record, moreover, has scarcely been
wholly positive. Bolivian miners have suffered terrible conditions. The
Bhopal chemical disaster of 1984 was the result of an American company's gross negligence. The depletion of the rainforests of Brazil and
Indonesia was driven by private commercial greed. Nor has capitalism
always been on the side of democracy, popular welfare and education.
Most countries in Latin America, south-east Asia and Africa were run
by dictators, corrupt elites and brutal security forces for most of the
twentieth century without any of the great liberal democracies seeking to
change the situation.

What is more, the impulses which led to communism are not dormant. Political and economic oppression is still widespread. National, social and religious persecution endures. Although the old empires have passed away, the self-interested domination of the world by a handful of great powers persists. Personal security, educational opportunity and guaranteed access to food, shelter and employment have yet to be provided for billions of people. There is much scope for radical movements to arise and challenge this situation. The strongest and most dangerous phenomenon at the time of writing is Islamist terrorism. Its fanatical exponents, despite the paucity of their active following, have already succeeded in shaking the balance of political forces in the world. They owe much of their impact to a popular feeling among Moslems that advanced capitalism is wrecking the material and spiritual basis of their communities. Just as Marxist intellectuals before the First World War took up the cause of the industrial proletariat, now Islam has produced intransigent revolutionaries dedicated to realising their fundamental values. In the years ahead there may well emerge other as yet unknown movements in conflict with liberal democracy, capitalist economics and pluralist society. It cannot be discounted that such movements, like Marxism from 1917, might seize control of whole states.

Communism itself looks unlikely to return in the form it had in the USSR or in Maoist China. Indeed its restoration in any comprehensive fashion is surely inconceivable. It has been thoroughly discredited among intelligentsias and general publics even though grouplets of true believers will probably survive in liberal democracies or in many clandestine movements.

Yet ideologies and politics can mutate and spread like a virus which counteracts every medical effort to pinpoint and eradicate it. So it has been with communism. Lenin and the Bolsheviks groped their way to the creation of their new kind of state. This became the stereotype for communist systems elsewhere; and the USSR itself underwent internal variation in subsequent decades. Communism also infected other movements for the transformation of society. The totalising ideas, institutions and practices of Marxism-Leninism had a profound impact on the political far right. The one-party, one-ideology state with its disregard for law, constitution and popular consent was implanted in inter-war Italy and Germany. Neither Mussolini nor Hitler acted only in response to communism; and the forced submission of society to comprehensive control took different forms in the USSR, Italy and Germany. But the importance of precedent is scarcely deniable. The objective of an unrestrained state power penetrating all aspects of life – political, economic, social, cultural and spiritual – was a characteristic they shared. The same phenomenon emerged in the secularist Baathist regime in Iraq under Saddam Hussein and appeared in the Islamist plans of Osama bin Laden as well as in the rule of the Taliban in Afghanistan.

All such leaders from Mussolini and Hitler down to bin Laden have detested communism. They dedicated themselves to its annihilation. Yet they were influenced by communist precedents even while regarding it as a plague bacillus. Communism has proved to have metastasising features. It will have a long afterlife even when the last communist state has disappeared.

NOTES

1. Communism before Marxism

1. D. McLellan, *Karl Marx: His Life and Thought*, p. 128.
2. *Ibid.*, p. 28.
3. *Ibid.*, p. 139.
4. N. Cohn, *The Pursuit of the Millennium: Revolutionary Millenarians and Mystical Anarchists of the Middle Ages*, ch. 1.
5. Gospel according to St Matthew, chs 5–7.
6. *The Dead Sea Scrolls*.
7. T. More, *Utopia*; T. Campanella, *The City of the Sun*.
8. Cohn, *The Pursuit of the Millennium*, chs 12–13.
9. C. Hill, *The World Turned Upside Down: Radical Ideas during the English Revolution*.
10. W. Doyle, *Oxford History of the French Revolution*, pp. 324–7.
11. G. Lichtheim, *A Short History of Socialism*, pp. 54, 56 and 58–9.
12. *Ibid.*, pp. 42–3, 45–6 and 53–5.
13. *Ibid.*, pp. 53 and 55–9.
14. K. Bock, 'Theories of Progress, Development, Evolution' in T. B. Bottomore and R. Nisbet (eds), *A History of Sociological Analysis*, pp. 60–7.
15. I. Berlin, *Karl Marx: His Life and Environment*.
16. J. L. Talmon, *The Origins of Totalitarian Democracy*, pp. 41–9.
17. *Ibid.*, pp. 46–7.
18. N. Machiavelli, *The Prince*.
19. R. Porter, *The Enlightenment*.

2. Marx and Engels

1. D. McLellan, *Karl Marx: His Life and Thought*, ch. 2.
2. F. Wheen, *Karl Marx*, pp. 256–7.
3. K. Marx and F. Engels, *The Communist Manifesto*, p. 103.
4. *Ibid.*, p. 102.
5. *Theses on Feuerbach* in D. McLellan (ed.), *Karl Marx: Selected Writings*, p. 158.

6. McLellan, *Karl Marx: His Life and Thought*, pp. 155–66.
7. *Capital: A Critique of Political Economy*, vol. 1.
8. McLellan, *Karl Marx: His Life and Thought*, pp. 361 et seq.
9. *Ibid.*, pp. 391–402.
10. *Ibid.*, pp. 276–80.
11. T. Shanin, *Late Marx and the Russian Road: Marx and 'the Peripheries of Capitalism'* .
12. F. Engels, *Anti-Dühring*; *The Dialectics of Nature*; *The Origins of the Family, Private Property and the State*.
13. See note 9.
14. F. Mehring, *Karl Marx: The Story of His Life*, pp. 161–5.
15. See K. Kautsky, *The Agrarian Question*.

3. Communism in Europe

1. H. J. Steinberg, *Il socialismo tedesco da Bebel a Kautsky*, chs 1–2.
2. D. Geary, *Karl Kautsky*, ch. 3.
3. E. H. Carr, *Michael Bakunin*.
4. See R. Hilferding, *Boehm-Bawerk's Criticism of Marx*; R. Luxemburg, *The Accumulation of Capital*.
5. W. J. Mommsen, *The Age of Bureaucracy: Perspectives on the Political Sociology of Max Weber*.
6. R. Michels, *Political Parties: A Sociological Study of the Oligarchical Tendencies of Modern Democracy*, parts 1–2. See also T. B. Bottomore, *Elites and Society*, chs 2–3.
7. E. Bernstein, *Evolutionary Socialism*.
8. E. David's work had an international impact, being translated into Russian; it earned the ire of Lenin; see his *Polnoe sobranie sochinenii*, vol. 5, pp. 222–35.
9. See below, pp. 48–53.
10. K. Kautsky, *The Agrarian Question*. See also M. Salvadori, *Karl Kautsky e la rivoluzione socialista*, chs 2–3.
11. G. Haupt, *Socialism and the Great War: The Collapse of the Second International*, pp. 11–29.
12. M. S. Shatz, *Jan Waclaw Machajski: A Radical Critic of the Russian Intelligentsia*.
13. Michels, *Political Parties*, part 6.
14. J. P. Nettl, *Rosa Luxemburg*, vol. 2, ch. 13.
15. D. A. Smart (ed.), *Pannekoek and Gorter's Marxism*.
16. R. Luxemburg, *The Mass Strike*.
17. See above, p. 34.
18. *Austro-Marxism*, pp. 102–35.
19. *Ibid.*
20. Haupt, *Socialism and the Great War*, pp. 19–22.
21. See below, pp. 63–4 and 106–7.

4. Russian Variations

1. A. Walicki, *The Controversy over Capitalism: Studies in the Social Philosophy of the Russian Populists*.
2. See above, p. 30.
3. R. Service, *Lenin: A Political Life*, vol. 1, chs 4–5.
4. *Ibid.*, pp. 110–11.
5. *Ibid.*, ch. 9.
6. See above, p. 32.
7. Service, *Lenin: A Political Life*, vol. 1, pp. 33–7 and 128–33.
8. R. Service, *Lenin: A Biography*, pp. 188–9.
9. *Ibid.*, ch. 9.
10. Service, *Lenin: A Political Life*, vol. 1, pp. 165 *et seq.*
11. R. C. Williams, *The Other Bolsheviks: Lenin and his Critics, 1904–1914*, pp. 66–80.
12. R. Service, *Stalin: A Biography*, p. 65.
13. J. P. Nettl, *Rosa Luxemburg*, vol. 1, pp. 224–7.
14. Service, *Lenin: A Political Life*, vol. 2, ch. 2.
15. G. Haupt, *Socialism and the Great War: The Collapse of the Second International*; Service, *Lenin: A Biography*, p. 103.
16. Service, *Lenin: A Biography*, pp. 226–8.

5. The October Revolution

1. R. Service, *The Russian Revolution, 1900–1927*, pp. 39–40.
2. R. Service, *The Bolshevik Party in Revolution: A Study in Organisational Change*, pp. 42–62.
3. *Gosudarstvo i revolyutsiya* in V. I. Lenin, *Polnoe sobranie sochinenii*, vol. 33.
4. R. Service, *Lenin: A Political Life*, vol. 2, pp. 216–23.
5. The specific differences between Leninist communism and rival socialist and social-democratic variants are discussed below, pp. 107–8.
6. A. Rabinowitch, *The Bolsheviks Come to Power*.

6. The First Communist State

1. R. Service, *The Bolshevik Party in Revolution: A Study in Organisational Change*, pp. 82–3.
2. I. Getzler, *Kronstadt 1917–1921: The Fate of a Soviet Democracy*, pp. 233–44.
3. Service, *The Bolshevik Party in Revolution*, ch. 4.
4. *Ibid.*, pp. 101–9.
5. *Ibid.*, p. 147.
6. *Ibid.*, p. 125.

7. R. Service, *Lenin: A Biography*, pp. 268–9.
8. *Ibid.*, pp. 380–1.
9. *Ibid.*, p. 233.
10. R. Service, *Lenin: A Political Life*, vol. 3, p. 211.
11. L. Chamberlain, *The Philosophy Steamer: Lenin and the Exile of the Intelligentsia*.
12. Service, *Lenin: A Political Life*, vol. 3, pp. 244–8.
13. Service, *Lenin: A Biography*, p. 403.
14. R. Service, 'Bolshevism's Europe from Lenin to Stalin, 1914–1928', in S. Pons and A. Romano (eds), *Russia in the Age of Wars, 1914–1945*, pp. 69–78.
15. Service, *Lenin: A Political Life*, vol. 3, pp. 179–80.

7. European Revolutions

1. R. Service, *Lenin: A Political Life*, vol. 3, pp. 45–6.
2. RGASPI, f. 325, op. 1, d. 62, p. 4.
3. J. P. Nettl, *Rosa Luxemburg*, vol. 2, pp. 761–77.
4. American Legation in Belgrade to Herbert Hoover, 25 March 1919: T. T. C. Gregory Papers (HIA), box 2.
5. M. Károlyi, 'The History of my Abdication' (typescript: Vienna, 15 July 1919), pp. 3–6: T. T. C. Gregory Papers (HIA), box 2.
6. Letter of Philip Marshall Brown to Archibald Cary Coolidge, 17 April 1919: Hungarian Political Dossier, vol. 1: T. T. C. Gregory Papers (HIA), box 2. Brown met Kun on 15 April 1919.
7. American Relief Administration Bulletin, no. 19, 25 July 1919: Gibbes Lykes Papers (HIA), box 1.
8. Lt Emery Pottle and Dr E. Dana Durand, 'An Interview with Bela Kuhn [sic]', *American Relief Administration Bulletin*, no. 19, 25 July 1919, pp. 34–5.
9. A. R. Hunt, *Facts about Communist Hungary*, p. 6.
10. *Ibid.*, p. 3.
11. *Ibid.*, p. 4.
12. H. James (American representative on the Interallied Danube Commission), 'Report on trip to Germany-Austria and Czecho-Slovakia', p. 1: Henry James Papers (HIA).
13. T. T. C. Gregory (the American Relief Administration's director for central Europe), 'Stemming the Red Tide' (typescript, 1919), p. 70: T. T. C. Gregory Papers (HIA), box 1.
14. Notes on communism in central Europe (typescript, no title or date), p. 2: T. T. C. Gregory Papers (HIA), box 1.
15. Telegrams, 2 February and 19 April 1919: RGASPI, f. 17, op. 109, d. 46, pp. 1–2.
16. T. T. C. Gregory, 'Beating Back Bolshevism' (typescript, no date [possibly 1920]), p. 6: T. T. C. Gregory Papers (HIA), box 1.
17. Trotski's message to Rakovski, Podvoiski and Antonov-Ovseenko, 18 April

1919: RGASPI, f. 325, op. 1, d. 404, p. 86, and Lenin's telegram to Aralov and Vacietis, 21 April 1919, *ibid.*, p. 92; telegram of Vacietis and Aralov to Antonov, 23 April 1919, *ibid.*, op. 109, d. 46, pp. 3–5.

18. See below, pp. 95–6.

19. R. L. Tökés, *Béla Kun and the Hungarian Soviet Republic: The Origins and Role of the Communist Party of Hungary in the Revolutions of 1918–1919.*

20. Memorandum by Ferenc Julier, former Commander of the General Staff of the Red Army; it was prepared for the Hoover Library in 1933 and translated into English: Hungarian Subject Collection (HIA), p. 3.

21. Report of T. T. C. Gregory (American Relief Administration) to Herbert Hoover, 4 June 1919, pp. 1–2: T. T. C. Gregory Papers (HIA), box 1.

22. Memorandum of Ferenc Julier (see note 20), pp. 3–4 and 14.

23. Inter-Allied Military Commission (Budapest) to Supreme Council of the Peace Conference, 19 August 1919: Gibbes Lykes Papers (HIA), box 1; Logan to Paris, 13 August 1919.

24. Office diary, 13 February 1919, p. 3: Herbert Haviland Field Papers (HIA). Field was a delegate of the US peace treaty commission.

25. Office diary, 15 March 1919, p. 10: Herbert Haviland Field Papers (HIA).

26. J. Cornwell, *Hitler's Pope: The Secret History of Pius XII*, p. 75.

27. R. Leviné-Meyer, *Leviné the Spartacist*, p. 104.

28. *Ibid.*

29. *Ibid.*, p. 95.

30. R. J. Evans, *The Coming of the Third Reich*, pp. 60–76

31. Leviné-Meyer, *Leviné the Spartacist: The Life and Times of the Socialist Revolutionary Leader of the German Spartacists and Head of the Ill-Starred Munich Republic of 1919*, p. 153.

32. E. Toller, *An Appeal from the Young Workers of Germany.*

33. I. N. R. Davies, *White Eagle, Red Star*, chs 3–6.

34. Service, *Lenin: A Political Life*, vol. 3, p. 141.

35. Speech by Stalin to the Twelfth Party Congress, section on 'the national question', 25 April 1923: *ITsKKPSS*, no. 4 (1991), p. 171. See Service, *Lenin: A Political Life*, vol. 3, pp. 191–2.

36. S. White, *Britain and the Bolshevik Revolution: A Study in the Politics of Diplomacy, 1920–1924*, chs 1–2.

37. R. H. Ullman, *The Anglo-Soviet Accord*, pp. 474–8.

38. R. L. Tökés, 'Béla Kun: The Man and the Revolutionary', in I. Völgyes (ed.), *Hungary in Revolution, 1918–19*, pp. 186–9.

39. Letter of Stalin to Zinoviev, August 1923, which Zinoviev read out to the joint plenum of the Central Committee and Central Control Committee, July–August 1923: RGASPI, f. 17, op. 2, d. 317 (Viii), p. 22; Stalin's un-challenged comments to the same plenum: RGASPI, f. 17, op. 2, d. 293, pp. 99–101.

8. Communism and its Discontents

1. R. Service, *Lenin: A Political Life*, vol. 3, ch. 9.
2. R. Service, *The Bolshevik Party in Revolution: A Study on Organisational Change*, pp. 168–9.
3. I am adopting the suggestion of Brian Pearce, peerless translator of Russian historical works, that 'Change of Waymarks' best translates the name of the group.
4. Service, *The Bolshevik Party in Revolution*, p. 168.
5. D. Koenker, *Moscow Workers and the 1917 Revolution*, pp. 171–86.
6. A. Pospielovsky, 'Strikes during the NEP', *Revolutionary Russia*, no. 1 (1997).
7. C. Read, *Culture and Power in Revolutionary Russia*, chs 3–5.
8. T. Shanin, *The Awkward Class: Political Sociology of Peasantry in a Developing Society*, pp. 169–79.
9. R. Service, *Stalin: A Biography*, p. 256.
10. *Ibid.*, p. 403.
11. J. Baberowski, *Der Feind ist überall: Stalinismus im Kaukasus*, pp. 316–49.

9. The Communist International

1. RGASPI, f. 17, op. 84, d. 1: 28 September 1918.
2. See Chap. 4.
3. C. Sheridan, *Russian Portraits*, pp. 25–62.
4. H. Barbé, 'Souvenir de militant et dirigeant communiste' (typescript, HIA), p. 33.
5. RGASPI, f. 89, op. 52, d. 6.
6. I. Linder and S. Churkin, *Krasnaya pautina: tainy razvedki Kominterna, 1919–1943*, p. 31.
7. See the account by Barbé, 'Souvenir de militant et dirigeant communiste', pp. 74–5.
8. V. I. Lenin, *Polnoe sobranie sochinenii*, vol. 42, p. 112.
9. A. C. Sutton, *Western Technology and Soviet Economic Development, 1917 to 1930*, pp. 327–36.
10. P. S. Pinheiro, *Estratégias da illusão: a revolução mundial e o Brasil, 1912–1935*, p. 30.
11. A. S. Lindemann, *The 'Red Years': European Socialism versus Bolshevism, 1919–1921*.
12. P. Spriano, *Storia del Partito Comunista Italiano*, vol. 1: *Da Bordiga a Gramsci*.
13. Barbé, 'Souvenir de militant et dirigeant communiste', p. 33.
14. *Ibid.*, pp. 205–7.
15. *Ibid.*, p. 209.
16. *Ibid.*, p. 33.

17. J. Redman [B. Pearce], *The Communist Party and the Labour Left, 1925–1929*, p. 8.

18. G. S. Murphy, *Soviet Mongolia: A Study of the Oldest Political Satellite.*

19. Barbé, 'Souvenir de militant et dirigeant communiste', p. 140.

20. *Ibid.*, p. 228.

21. Memoirs of Zhen Bilan in Peng Shu-tse Papers (HIA), folder 3, pp. 11 and 29.

22. *Ibid.*, folder 21, pp. 28–9.

23. *Documents on Communism, Nationalism, and Soviet Advisers in China, 1918–1927: Papers Seized in the 1927 Peking Raid*, p. 105.

24. Linder and Churkin, *Krasnaya pautina*, pp. 195–206. See above, pp. 95–6.

10. Probing America

1. Minutes of the Central Executive Committee of the CPA, 15 November 1919: Theodore Draper Papers (HIA), box 32.

2. H. Klehr, J. E. Haynes and K. M. Anderson (eds), *The Soviet World of American Communism*, doc. 1, p. 19.

3. S. M. Lipset and G. Marks, *It Didn't Happen Here: Why Socialism Failed in the United States*, p. 35.

4. F. M. Ottanelli, *The Communist Party of the United States: From the Depression to World War II*, p. 51.

5. Communist International Instructions (HIA), folder XX695–10.V, p. 7.

6. *Ibid.*, pp. 1–10. The comment on the press (p. 7) has 'party' and 'dailies' in capital letters in the original.

7. Letter from Moscow to 'Dear Comrade' (Jay Lovestone?), 19 May 1924: Jay Lovestone Papers (HIA), box 196, folder 3.

8. Letter from 'Henry' to 'Dear Comrades', 26 February 1926: *ibid.*, folder 4. On the national composition of the party see H. Klehr, *Communist Cadre: The Social Background of the American Communist Party Elite*, p. 25.

9. Official central letters to 'Dear Comrade': Jay Lovestone Papers (HIA), box 195, folder 6.

10. M. Eastman, 'A Statement of the Problem in America and the First Step to its Solution': Theodore Draper Papers (HIA), box 31. See also Political Committee minutes, 29 June 1927, p. 5 on the 'deplorable state of affairs' in the Jewish Section: Charles Wesley Ervin Papers (HIA).

11. Klehr, *Communist Cadre: The Social Background of the American Communist Party Elite*, p. 46

12. Unsigned report, 8 October 1925: Jay Lovestone Papers (HIA), box 197, folder 1.

13. *Ibid.*

14. Official Comintern letter, 20 June 1925, p. 2: Theodore Draper Papers (HIA), box 32.

15. T. Draper, *American Communism and Soviet Russia: The Formative Period*, p. 334.

16. Secretariat minutes, 13 September 1927, p. 2: Theodore Draper Papers (HIA), box 32.

17. *Ibid.*

18. Klehr, Haynes and Anderson (eds), *The Soviet World of American Communism*, doc. 59, p. 206.

19. H. M. Wicks, speech at the American Commission of Comintern in Moscow, 21 April 1929, p. 7: Theodore Draper Papers (HIA), box 31.

20. H. Haywood, *Negro Liberation* (1948) sums up the project. See also H. Haywood, *Black Bolshevik: Autobiography of an Afro-American Communist*.

21. S. Adams, *Comrade Minister: The South African Communist Party and the Transition from Apartheid to Democracy*, pp. 27–8.

22. Letter from 'Ed.', 11 April 1920: Jay Lovestone Papers (HIA), box 195, folder 10.

23. See for example Ruthenburg cable to Lovestone, 5 December 1925: *ibid.*, box 386, folder 56.

24. *Ibid.*, box 197, folder 5.

25. James Cannon to T. Draper, 10 May 1954, p. 1: Theodore Draper Papers (HIA).

26. Telegram of 20 April 1927: Jay Lovestone Papers (HIA), box 195, folder 11.

27. Unsigned typescript copy, 25 April 1927: *ibid.*, box 197, folder 11.

28. Draper, *American Communism and Soviet Russia*, p. 200.

29. Letter to Bukharin, 9 September 1928: Jay Lovestone Papers (HIA), box 198, folder 8.

30. Unsigned typescript about Comintern to 'Dear Friends', 24 April 1929: *ibid.*, folder 12.

31. K. McDermott and J. Agnew, *The Comintern: A History of International Communism from Lenin to Stalin*, p. 88.

32. Telegram of 7 November 1924. Jay Lovestone Papers (HIA), box 368, folder 47.

33. G. Lewy, *The Cause that Failed: Communism in American Political Life*, p. 307.

34. Lipset and Marks, *It Didn't Happen Here*, p. 40.

35. See p. 174.

36. *Earl Browder Says*, p. 2.

37. *Ibid.*, pp. 4–5.

38. R. L. Benson and M. Warner (eds), *Venona: Soviet Espionage and the American Response, 1939–1957*, p. xii.

39. *Ibid.*, p. 49.

40. Ottanelli, *The Communist Party of the United States*, p. 210.

41. See the *Manual for Community Club Leaders. A Handbook for the Use of Officers and Committees of Communist Community Clubs* (prepared by the Organisational Department of the Communist National Committee).

42. Letters of Earl Browder to Elizabeth Churchill Brown, 1 January and 16

September 1954: Elizabeth Churchill Brown Papers (HIA). Browder made this call on 26 September 1943: *Chicago Herald-Examiner*, 27 September 1943; I have drawn this information from his private letter to Elizabeth Churchill Brown, 1 September 1954. Stalin was not the only communist leader annoyed. According to Browder, the British communist party criticised him for treading outside his political patch: letter to Elizabeth Churchill Brown, 16 September 1954. Both letters are in Elizabeth Churchill Brown Papers (HIA). For a more general account see Klehr, Haynes and Anderson (eds), *The Soviet World of American Communism*, pp. 98–9.

43. E. Browder, *Teheran: Our Path in War and Peace*.

44. G. Dimitrov, *Diario. Gli anni di Mosca (1934–1945)*, p. 683: 26 January 1944.

45. *Ibid.*, pp. 696–7: 8 March 1944.

46. 'À propos de la dissolution du PCA', *Cahiers du Communisme*, 6 April 1945.

47. See below, pp. 206–7.

48. See below, pp. 239–40.

49. Lewy, *The Cause that Failed*, p. 81.

50. See below, pp. 273–4.

51. Klehr, Haynes and Anderson (eds), *The Soviet World of American Communism*, p. 353.

52. See below, Chap. 27.

53. G. Hall, *The Power of Ideology: Keynote Address to the First Ideological Conference of the Communist Party USA* [sic], *July 14–16 1989, Chicago*, pp. 6, 7 and 21.

54. Klehr, Haynes and Anderson (eds), *The Soviet World of American Communism*, pp. 158–9 (including docs 44–5).

55. Hall, *The Power of Ideology*, p. 6.

56. See above, pp. 420–4.

57. G. Hall, *The Era of Crisis: Forging Unity in Struggle: Report to the Twenty Fifth National Convention, Communist Party, USA*, p. 2.

11. Making Sense of Communism

1. N. Bukharin and Ye. Preobrazhenskii, *Azbuka kommunizma*.

2. L. Kaganovich, *Kak postroena RKP(b)*.

3. R. Service, *The Bolshevik Party in Revolution: A Study in Organisational Change*, pp. 104–11.

4. R. Service, *Lenin: A Political Life*, vol. 2, ch. 7.

5. Zinoviev was unusual in being frank about the situation.

6. P. Dukes, *Red Dusk and the Morrow: Adventures and Investigations in Red Russia*, pp. 222–3; P. Dukes, *The Story of 'ST 25': Adventure and Romance in the Secret Intelligence Service in Red Russia*, pp. 276, 289 and 293.

7. Dukes, *Red Dusk and the Morrow*, pp. 11, 22, 82 and 208. His various Soviet official attestations are held in the Sir Paul Dukes Papers (HIA), box 1.

8. R. Bruce Lockhart, *Memoirs of a British Agent: Being an Account of the Author's Early Life on Many Lands and His Official Mission to Moscow in 1918*, pp. 236–348.

9. H. Radek and A. Ransome, *Radek and Ransome on Russia*, pp. 1–24.

10. H. Brogan, *The Life of Arthur Ransome*, pp. 153–4 and 281–2.

11. *Ibid.*, pp. 160–2; Y. Membery, 'Swallows, Amazons and Secret Agents', *Observer*, 21 July 2002.

12. RGASPI, f. 89, op. 52, d. 4, pp. 1–2.

13. A. Rhys Williams, *Lenin: The Man and his Work* (1919) and *Through the Russian Revolution* (1967).

14. J. Reed, *Ten Days that Shook the World* (1919).

15. RGASPI, f. 89, op. 52, d. 6.

16. G. Hicks, *John Reed: The Making of a Revolutionary*, p. 395.

17. P. Avrich, *The Russian Anarchists*, chs 6–7.

18. E. Goldman, *My Disillusionment in Russia* (1923); *My Further Disillusionment in Russia* (1924).

19. R. Luxemburg, *The Russian Revolution*.

20. K. Kautsky, *Die Diktatur des Proletariats*.

21. Yu. Martov, *Mirovoi bol'shevizm*.

22. Jonathan Davis, 'Left Out in the Cold: British Labour Witnesses the Russian Revolution', *Revolutionary Russia*, no. 1 (June 2005), pp. 71–88.

23. H. G. Wells, *Russia in the Shadows*.

24. B. Russell, *The Theory and Practice of Bolshevism*.

25. N. Glazer and D. P. Moynihan, *Beyond the Melting Pot: The Negroes, Puerto Ricans, Jews, Italians and Irish of New York City*, pp. 139–80 and 268–9.

26. M. N. Roy, *Memoirs*, p. 348.

27. See above, p. 51.

28. Testimony of Giovanni Casale in C. Bermani (ed.), *Gramsci raccontato: Testimonianze raccolte da Cesare Bermani, Gianni Bosio e Mimma Paulesu Quercioli*, p. 131.

29. Testimony of Ercole Piacentini in *ibid.*, p. 168.

30. L. Sedda, *Economia, politica e società sovietica nei quaderni del carcere*, pp. 34, 36, 48 and 82. See A. Gramsci, *Quaderni del carcere*, Q 4, p. 489, Q. 9, p. 1120, Q. 11, p. 1425, Q. 19, p. 2030.

31. Letter to Tatyana Schucht, 26 August 1929: A. Gramsci, *Lettere dal carcere*, p. 110.

12. The USSR in Torment

1. R. Service, *Stalin: A Biography*, pp. 214–17.

2. *Ibid.*, pp. 3–4 and 225–30.

3. R. Service, *The Russian Revolution, 1900–1927*, pp. 76–80; C. Merridale, *Moscow Politics and the Rise of Stalin*, p. 53.

4. J. Hessler, *A Social History of Soviet Trade: Trade Policy, Retail Practices and Consumption, 1917–1953*, pp. 142–6.

5. A. Nove, *An Economic History of the USSR*, pp. 171 and 241; S. G. Wheatcroft, 'More Light on the Scale of Repression and Excess Mortality in the Soviet Union in the 1930s', *Soviet Studies*, no. 2 (1990), p. 366.

6. S. Fitzpatrick, 'Stalin and the Making of a New Elite, 1928–1939', *Slavic Review*, no. 3 (1979).

7. *Akademicheskoe delo, 1929–1931: Delo po obvineniyu akademika S. F. Platonova*, p. xlviii.

8. *Trud*, 4 June 1992.

9. B. A. Viktorov, 'Geroi iz 37-go', *Komsomol'skaya pravda*, 21 August 1988.

10. See below, pp. 255–9.

13. The Soviet Model

1. Letter to F. Dzierżyński, n.d.: RGASPI, f. 76, op. 3, d. 345. I took this from the Volkogonov Papers, reel 9 in the Bodleian Library.

2. J. Riordan, 'The Strange Story of Nikolai Starostin, Football and Lavrentii Beria – Sports Personality and Soviet Chief of Intelligence', *Europe-Asia Studies*, July 1994.

3. P. Gregory, *The Political Economy of Stalin: Evidence from the Soviet Secret Archives*.

4. *'Sovershenno sekretno': Lubyanka – Stalinu o polozhenii v strane (1922–1934 gg.)*, vols 1 ff.

5. Yelizaveta Parshina and Leonid Parshin, 'Razvedka bez mifov' (typescript, 1994, HIA) p. 5.

14. World Strategy

1. See below, pp. 200–1.

2. K. McDermott and J. Agnew, *The Comintern: A History of International Communism from Lenin to Stalin*, p. 102.

3. *Sovetskoe rukovodstvo. Perepiska, 1928–1941*, p. 77.

4. McDermott and Agnew, *The Comintern*, p. 95.

5. In 1939, however, things reached a further stage when Stalin took the decision on the Nazi–Soviet non-aggression treaty without properly consulting even Molotov.

6. N. I. Bukharin, *Problemy teorii i praktiki sotsializma*, p. 298.

7. McDermott and Agnew, *The Comintern*, pp. 85–6.

8. G. Fiori, *Antonio Gramsci*, pp. 249–56.

9. Cilly Vassart, 'Le Front Populaire en France' (typescript, HIA), pp. 8 and 31.

10. McDermott and Agnew, *The Comintern*, pp. 121–2.

11. I am grateful to Brian Pearce for his memory and advice here.

12. G. Procacci, *Il socialismo internazionale e la Guerra d'Etiopia.*

13. A. C. Sutton, *Western Technology and Soviet Economic Development, 1917 to 1930*, pp. 246–9.

14. A. C. Sutton, *Western Technology and Soviet Economic Development, 1930 to 1945*, pp. 74–5.

15. *Ibid.*, pp. 82–90.

16. *Ibid.*, ch. 4 *et seq.*

17. D. A. L. Levy, 'The French Popular Front, 1936–1937', in H. Graham and P. Preston (eds), *The Popular Front in Europe*, pp. 67–9.

18. *Ibid.*, pp. 72–4.

19. P. Preston, *Franco: A Biography*, pp. 200–2.

20. H. Graham, *The Spanish Republic at War, 1936–1939*, pp. 285–91; P. Preston, *The Spanish Civil War: Reaction, Revolution and Revenge*, pp. 254–7 and 261–5.

21. Vassart, 'Le Front Populaire en France', p. 65.

15. Stalinist Ideology

1. R. Service, *Stalin: A Biography*, pp. 361 and 364.

2. *Ibid.*, p. 361.

3. A. Gide, *Retour de l'U.R.S.S.*, pp. 72–3.

4. F. Bettanin, *Fabbrica del mito: storia el politica nell'URSS Staliniana*, p. 174.

5. *Istoriya vsesoyuznoi kommunisticheskoi partii (bol'shevikov): kratkii kurs.*

6. Service, *Stalin: A Biography*, p. 307.

7. See D. Holloway, *Stalin and the Bomb: The Soviet Union and Atomic Energy*, p. 211.

8. Gide, *Retour de l'U.R.S.S.*, p. 65.

9. *Pravda*, no. 35, 5 February 1931.

10. G. A. Almond, *The Appeals of Communism*, pp. 74–5.

11. *Ibid.*, pp. 90–1.

12. M. Djilas, *Rise and Fall*, p. 157: this was Djilas's recollection of a post-war conversation in Stalin's dacha.

13. M. Gor'kii, L. Averbakh and S. Firin (eds), *Belomorsko–baltiiskii kanal imeni I. V. Stalina.*

16. Inside the Parties

1. A. Koestler (no title), in R. H. Crossman (ed.), *The God that Failed*, p. 54.

2. K. McDermott and J. Agnew, *The Comintern: A History of International Communism from Lenin to Stalin*, pp. 121–2.

3. I. Roxborough, 'Mexico', in L. Bethell and I. Roxborough (eds), *Latin America between the Second World War and the Cold War, 1944–1948*, p. 191.

4. L. Bethell, 'Brazil', in *ibid.*, p. 37.

5. See above, pp. 125.

6. On the German Communist Party after 1933 see A. Paucker, *German Jews in the Resistance, 1933–1945: The Facts and the Problems*, p. 45.

7. On Mongolia: RGASPI, f. 89, op. 29, d. 1, pp. 1–3: 13 September 1937; on Spain, H. Graham, *The Spanish Republic at War, 1936–1939*, pp. 287–91.

8. G. Dimitrov, *Diario. Gli anni di Mosca (1934–1945)*, p. 677.

9. J. Chang and J. Halliday, *Mao: The Unknown Story*, pp. 262–6.

10. P. Short, *Mao: A Life*, pp. 383–9; Chang and Halliday, *Mao*, pp. 251–2.

11. *Ibid.*, pp. 254–5.

12. Short, *Mao*, pp. 282.

13. See below, Chs 20 and 34.

14. H. Barbé, *Souvenir de militant et dirigeant communiste* (typescript, HIA), pp. 333–4.

15. Autobiographical notes dated 17 November 1945, pp. 1–5: E. W. Darling Papers (HIA), box 1, folder 1.

16. Darling's letter to Harry Pollitt, 6 January 1946: *ibid.*

17. Darling's letter to Harry Pollitt, 18 September 1946: *ibid.*

18. K. Philby, *My Silent War*.

19. One possible exception was communist party member and noted economist M. H. Dobb's *Russian Economic Development since the Revolution* (London, 1928).

20. Quoted from R. Wright, *American Hunger* by R. Conquest, *Reflections on a Ravaged Century*, p. 79.

21. Y. Slezkine, *The Jewish Century*, pp. 94–5.

22. See the contributions of Palme Dutt and Pollitt in *About Turn: The British Communist Party and the Second World War. The Verbatim Record of the Central Committee Meetings of 25 September and 2–3 October 1939*.

23. Ivy Litvinov Papers (HIA), box 1, Oral History, p. 3.

24. See below, p. 213.

17. Friends and Foes

1. L. Trotsky, *My Life: An Attempt at an Autobiography*; L. Trotsky, *History of the Russian Revolution*.

2. *The Case of Leon Trotsky: Report of Hearings on the Charges Made against Him in the Moscow Trials*.

3. L. Trotsky, *The Revolution Betrayed: What Is the Soviet Union and Where Is it Going?*

4. O. Bauer, *Bolschewismus oder Sozialdemokratie*; N. Berdyaev, *The Russian Idea*; T. Dan, *The Origins of Bolshevism*; N. S. Trubetskoi, *K probleme russkogo samosoznaniya: sobranie statei*.

5. J. Davis, 'Webb, (Martha) Beatrice (1858–1943)', *Oxford Dictionary of National Biography*.

6. S. and B. Webb, *Soviet Communism: A New Civilization?*
7. S. J. Taylor, *Stalin's Apologist: Walter Duranty, the New York Times's Man in Moscow*, pp. 206–9.
8. M. Muggeridge, *Winter in Moscow*.
9. *The Diaries of Beatrice Webb*, vol. 4: *The Wheel of Life, 1924–1943*, pp. 301, 308 and 414.
10. *Ibid.*, p. 495.
11. H. Johnson, *The Socialist Sixth of the World*, p. 367.
12. A. Gide, *Retour de l'U.R.S.S.*, pp. 43–55.
13. I. Stalin, *Beseda s angliiskom pisatelem G. D. Uellsom, 23 iyunya 1934 g.*, pp. 9, 13, 15–16, 18 and 20.
14. M. Holroyd, *Bernard Shaw*, vol. 2: *1898–1918: The Pursuit of Power*, pp. 301–4 and 309–14.
15. M. Muggeridge, 'Russian Journal' (HIA), 28 September 1932, p. 15.
16. See D. Caute, *The Fellow Travellers: A Postscript to the Enlightenment*, p. 100.
17. *New York Times*, 23 August 1933.
18. Taylor, *Stalin's Apologist*, pp. 208–9.
19. J. Chang and J. Halliday, *Mao: The Unknown Story*, pp. 198–200.
20. J. E. Davies, *Mission to Moscow: A Record of Confidential Dispatches to the State Department, Official and Personal Correspondence, Current Diary and Journal Entries, including Notes and Comment up to October 1941*, pp. 177–9.
21. Caute, *The Fellow Travellers*, p. 270.
22. J. S. Walker, *Henry A. Wallace and American Foreign Policy*, pp. 106–8. See also Wallace's jottings in *The Price of Vision: The Diary of Henry A. Wallace, 1942–1946*, pp. 337–9, where he recorded his impressions of the area around Magadan and Kolyma.
23. Muggeridge, 'Russian Journal, (HIA), 1 December 1932, p. 90.
24. *Ibid.*, 19 November 1932, p. 72.
25. P. Sloan, *Soviet Democracy*; R. Page Arnot, *A Short History of the Russian Revolution: From 1905 to the Present Day*.
26. E. Lyons, *Assignment in Utopia*.
27. R. O. G. Urch, *The Rabbit King of Siberia*, pp. 195–7.
28. S. Dmitrievsky, *Dans les coulisses du Kremlin*.
29. B. Bajanov, *Avec Staline dans le Kremlin*.
30. R. Crompton, *William – the Bad*, p. 68.
31. *Ibid.*, p. 69.
32. R. W. Service, *Bar-Room Ballads: A Book of Verse*, p. 90.
33. See below, p. 273.

18. Communism in the World War

1. See H. P. Bix, *Hirohito and the Making of Modern Japan*, p. 351.
2. Ivy Litvinov Papers (HIA), box 1, Oral History, p. 3.
3. D. Caute, *The Fellow Travellers: A Postscript to the Enlightenment*, p. 190.

4. A. Thorpe, *The British Communist Party and Moscow, 1920–43*, pp. 257–8.

5. Reproduced in Appendix I in J. Attfield and S. Williams (eds), *1939: The Communist Party of Great Britain and the War. Proceedings of a Conference Held on 21 April 1979, Organised by the Communist Party History Group*, pp. 147–52. See also the account by M. Johnstone, in *ibid.*, pp. 24–7.

6. *About Turn: The British Communist Party and the Second World War. The Verbatim Record of the Central Committee Meetings of 25 September and 2–3 October 1939*, p. 41 (editorial comment by M. Johnstone), pp. 197–211 (speech by Pollitt), pp. 283–91 (speech by Dutt). See also A. Thorpe, *The British Communist Party and Moscow, 1920–43*, pp. 258–60.

7. *Political Letter to the Communist Party Membership*, Political Bureau of the Communist Party of Great Britain: 15 July 1940.

8. *Marxist Study* (leaflet of the London District Committee of the CPGB): December 1940.

9. NA, KV2/1038, doc. 406a, p. 3.

10. *Ibid.*: meeting of 15 October 1939.

11. *Ibid.*, doc. 401.

12. Thorpe, *The British Communist Party and Moscow*, pp. 265–6.

13. F. W. Deakin, 'European Communism during the Second World War', in F. W. Deakin, H. Shukman and H. T. Willetts, *A History of World Communism*, p. 136.

14. F. Claudin, *The Communist Movement: From Comintern to Cominform*, p. 309.

15. S. Beria, *Beria, My Father: Life inside Stalin's Kremlin*, p. 155.

16. C. Bohlen, *Witness to History: 1929–1969*, p. 146.

17. W. A. Harriman and E. Abel, *Special Envoy to Churchill and Stalin, 1941–1946*, pp. 369–70. See A. Beichman, 'Roosevelt's Failure at Yalta', *Humanitas*, no. 1 (2003), pp. 104–5.

18. N. Lebrecht, 'Prokofiev was Stalin's Last Victim', *Evening Standard*, 4 June 2003.

19. This is now held in the Dom-muzei I. V. Stalina in Gori, Georgia.

20. J. Rossi, *Spravochnik po GULagu*, vol. 1, p. 40.

21. G. Dimitrov, *Dimitrov and Stalin: 1934–1943: Letters from the Soviet Archives*, p. 32, citing Dimitrov's diary. I have retranslated the phrase *na ruku*.

22. *Ibid.*, p. 302.

23. *Ibid.*, p. 659.

24. *Ibid.*, p. 612.

25. *Ibid.*, pp. 615–17.

26. R. Service, *Stalin: A Biography*, pp. 443–4.

27. R. Conquest, *Reflections on a Ravaged Century*, pp. 133–4.

19. Forcing the Peace

1. I. V. Stalin, *Sochineniya*, vol. 2(xv) (ed. R. MacNeal), p. 204.
2. A. S. Belyakov's recollections of A. A. Zhdanov's oral account of a meeting of central party leaders: G. Arbatov, *Zatyanuvsheesya vyzdorovlenie, 1953–1985 gg.: svidetel'stvo sovremennika*, p. 377.
3. E. Bacon, *The Gulag at War*, pp. 93–4; D. Holloway, *Stalin and the Bomb: The Soviet Union and Atomic Energy*, p. 193.
4. T. Dunmore, *The Stalinist Command Economy*, ch. 5.
5. R. Service, *Stalin: A Biography*, pp. 527–40.
6. I. V. Stalin, *Ekonomicheskie problemy v SSSR*, in *Sochineniya*, vol. 3(xvi), pp. 294–304.
7. Service, *Stalin: A Biography*, pp. 534–7.
8. M. Laar, *The War in the Woods: Estonia's Struggle for Survival, 1944–1956*.
9. M. Djilas, *Conversations with Stalin*, p. 133.
10. N. Naimark, 'Communist Regimes and Parties after the Second World War', *Journal of Modern European History*, no. 1 (2004), pp. 28–56.
11. *SSSR – Pol'sha: mekhanizmy podchineniya, 1944–1949*, p. 48.
12. M. Mevius, *Agents of Moscow*, pp. 72–5.
13. *SSSR – Pol'sha: mekhanizmy podchineniya*, p. 114.
14. *Vostochnaya Evropa v dokumentakh rossiiskikh arkhivov, 1944–1953*, vol. 1, p. 545.
15. *SSSR – Pol'sha: mekhanizmy podchineniya*, p. 113.
16. *Ibid.*, p. 111.
17. *Vostochnaya Evropa v dokumentakh rossiiskikh arkhivov*, vol. 1, p. 617.
18. Comments to Polish government delegation led by B. Bierut: *ibid.*, pp. 460–1.
19. *SSSR – Pol'sha: mekhanizmy podchineniya*, pp. 21 and 53; meeting with Polish delegation, 19 August 1946: *Vostochnaya Evropa v dokumentakh rossiiskikh arkhivov*, vol. 1, p. 511.
20. *Vostochnaya Evropa v dokumentakh rossiiskikh arkhivov*, vol. 1, p. 269.
21. *Ibid.*, p. 559.
22. *Ibid.*, p. 565.
23. N. Naimark, *The Russians in Germany: A History of the Soviet Zone of Occupation, 1945–1949*, p. 154.
24. *Vostochnaya Evropa v dokumentakh rossiiskikh arkhivov*, vol. 1, p. 580.
25. A. M. Ledovskii (ed.), 'Peregovory I. V. Stalina s Mao Tszedunom v dekabre 1949 – fevrale 1950 g.: novye arkhivnye dokumenty, *Novaya i noveishaya istoriya*, no. 1 (1997), p. 38.
26. D. G. Kirby, *Finland in the Twentieth Century*, p. 164; L. Péter, 'East of the Elbe', p. 36.
27. *SSSR – Pol'sha: mekhanizmy podchineniya*, p. 106. See also P. Kenney, *Rebuilding Poland: Workers and Communists, 1945–1950*, p. 29.

20. The Cold War and the Soviet Bloc

1. J. Gaddis, *The Cold War: A New History*, p. 43.
2. R. Service, *Stalin: A Biography*, pp. 566–7.
3. A. Fursenko and T. Naftali, *One Hell of a Gamble: Khrushchev, Castro, Kennedy, and the Cuban Missile Crisis, 1958–1964*, p. 171.
4. 'X' (George F. Kennan), 'The Sources of Soviet Conduct', *Foreign Affairs*, vol. 25 (July 1947), p. 566.
5. *Vostochnaya Evropa v dokumentakh rossiiskikh arkhivov, 1944–1953*, vol. 1, p. 675.
6. M. Leffler, *A Preponderance of Power. National Security, the Truman Administration and the Cold War*, pp. 61–76.
7. M. Djilas, *Rise and Fall*, p. 134.
8. See below, p. 269.
9. See below, pp. 266–8.
10. Djilas, *Rise and Fall*, p. 137.
11. See below, pp. 252–3.
12. 'Struggle for People's Democracy and Socialism – Some Questions of Strategy and Tactics', Central Committee of the Communist Party of India statement, 1949 (typescript): Communist Party of India Papers (HIA), pp. 85–6.
13. See Chapter 24.
14. See below, pp. 251–3.
15. L. T. Vasin, 'Kim Ir Sen. Kto on?', *Nezavisimaya gazeta*, 29 September 1993, p. 5.
16. See below, pp. 401–2.
17. A. Farrar-Hockley, *The British Part in the Korean War*, vol. 2.
18. K. Philby, *My Silent War*, pp. 117–21.
19. A. C. Sutton, *Western Technology and Soviet Economic Development, 1945 to 1965*, p. 53.
20. NA, PREM 8/1077.
21. *Vostochnaya Evropa v dokumentakh rossiiskikh arkhivov*, vol. 1, p. 558.
22. N. Naimark, *The Russians in Germany: A History of the Soviet Zone of Occupation 1945–1949*, ch. 2.
23. *Ibid.*, p. 181.
24. H. M. Harrison, *Driving the Soviets up the Wall: Soviet–East German Relations, 1953–1961*, p. 18.
25. F. Bettanin, *Stalin e l'Europa: la formazione dell'impero esterno sovietico (1941–1953)*, p. 170.
26. H. Seton-Watson, *The East European Revolution*, pp. 178–9.
27. A. Paczkowski, *The Spring Will Be Ours: Poland and the Poles from Occupation to Freedom*, pp. 205–6 and 229.
28. Seton-Watson, *The East European Revolution*, pp. 209–11.
29. C. Gati, *Hungary and the Soviet Bloc*, pp. 22–3.

30. *Ibid.*, pp. 121–2.
31. Djilas, *Rise and Fall*, p. 118.
32. Naimark, *The Russians in Germany*, p. 11.
33. A. Mgeladze, *Stalin, kakim ya ego znal. Stranitsy nedavnego proshlogo*, p. 113.
34. *Vostochnaya Evropa v dokumentakh rossiiskikh arkhivov*, vol. 1, pp. 640 and 658.
35. *Ibid.*, pp. 802–6 and 831–58; *SSSR – Pol'sha: mekhanizmy podchineniya, 1944–1949*, doc. 46.
36. *Vostochnaya Evropa v dokumentakh rossiiskikh arkhivov*, vol. 1, p. 276.
37. *Ibid.*, p. 43.
38. *Ibid.*, p. 742.
39. Naimark, *The Russians in Germany*, p. 291.
40. *Vostochnaya Evropa v dokumentakh rossiiskikh arkhivov*, vol. 1, p. 45.
41. *Ibid.*, p. 569, and vol. 2, p. 97.
42. Djilas, *Rise and Fall*, p. 85.
43. *Vostochnaya Evropa v dokumentakh rossiiskikh arkhivov*, vol. 1, pp. 539–41.
44. *Ibid.*, pp. 301, 366 and 367.
45. Djilas, *Rise and Fall*, p. 116. See also Edward Ochab's recollections in T. Toranska, *'Them': Stalin's Polish Puppets*, pp. 36 and 49.
46. *Vostochnaya Evropa v dokumentakh rossiiskikh arkhivov*, vol. 1, p. 368.
47. *Ibid.*, p. 34.
48. See below, p. 256.
49. 'People's democracy' edged out other current possible terms such as 'new democracy' and 'progressive democracy': see Bettanin, *Stalin e l'Europa*, p. 170.
50. *Vostochnaya Evropa v dokumentakh rossiiskikh arkhivov*, vol. 1, p. 457.
51. *Ibid.*, p. 458.
52. Z. Brzezinski, *The Soviet Bloc: Unity and Conflict*, p. 74.

21. The Yugoslav Road

1. C. Gati, *Hungary and the Soviet Bloc*, p. 18.
2. M. Djilas, *Rise and Fall*, p. 90.
3. B. M. Karapandzich, *The Bloodiest Yugoslav Spring, 1945 – Tito's Katyns and Gulags*, p. 20
4. N. Malcolm, *Bosnia: A Short History*, p. 195.
5. See above, p. 242.
6. Memorandum to M. A. Suslov, 18 March 1948: *Vostochnaya Evropa v dokumentakh rossiiskikh arkhivov, 1944–1953*, vol. 1, pp. 787–800.
7. G. Dimitrov, *Diario. Gli Anni di Mosca (1934–1945)*, pp. 784 and 793.
8. Memorandum to M. A. Suslov, 18 March 1948: *Vostochnaya Evropa v dokumentakh rossiiskikh arkhivov*, vol. 1, pp. 787–800.
9. *Ibid.*, p. 877.
10. Djilas, *Rise and Fall*, pp. 248–9.
11. J. R. Lampe, *Yugoslavia as History: Twice There Was a Country*, pp. 249–51.

12. *Ibid.*, p. 252.
13. Djilas, *Rise and Fall*, pp. 241 and 244–5.
14. *Ibid.*, p. 267.
15. Lampe, *Yugoslavia as History*, pp. 256–7.
16. Djilas, *Rise and Fall*, pp. 310–11.
17. *Ibid.*, p. 264.
18. Lampe, *Yugoslavia as History*, p. 273.
19. Djilas, *Rise and Fall*, p. 274.
20. Lampe, *Yugoslavia as History*, pp. 258–9.
21. Djilas, *Rise and Fall*, p. 294.
22. *Ibid.*, pp. 268 and 271.
23. See below, pp. 309 and 315.
24. D. Rusinow, *The Yugoslav Experiment, 1948–1974*, p. 99.
25. *Ibid.*, p. 106.
26. *Ibid.*, p. 132.
27. P. Lendvai, *Eagles in Cobwebs*, p. 162.
28. Rusinow, *The Yugoslav Experiment, 1948–1974*, p. 245.
29. *Ibid.*, p. 177.
30. *Ibid.*, pp. 202–3.
31. *Ibid.*, p. 234.
32. *Ibid.*, pp. 299, 310 and 324.
33. Malcolm, *Bosnia*, p. 211.
34. F. Singleton, *A Short History of the Yugoslav Peoples*, p. 271.
35. *Ibid.*, p. 276.
36. For the disintegration of Yugoslavia see below, pp. 433–4 and 456–6.

22. Western Europe

1. D. W. Ellwood, *Rebuilding Europe: Western Europe, America and Postwar Reconstruction*, p. 4.
2. Letter of 27 July 1943: *Dagli archivi di Mosca. L'URSS, il Cominform e il PCI (1943–1951)*, doc. 1, p. 223. On Secchia's career see S. Pons, *L'impossibile egemonia: L'URSS, il PCI e le origini della Guerra Fredda (1943–1948)*, p. 216.
3. Ellwood, *Rebuilding Europe*, p. 9.
4. G. Dimitrov, *Diario. Gli Anni di Mosca (1934–1945)*, p. 713.
5. E. Aga-Rossi and V. Zaslavsky, *Togliatti e Stalin*, pp. 62–3 and 66–9. The Stalin–Togliatti conversation is recorded by Dimitrov, *Diario*, p. 691; the Stalin–Thorez conversation is reproduced in *ibid.*, pp. 287–95 – see also *ibid.*, p. 769, and M. Narinskij, 'Stalin, Togliatti e Thorez, 1944–1948', in *Dagli archivi di Mosca*, pp. 79–80.
6. Ercoli [Togliatti], 'Sui compiti attuali dei compiti italiani, 1° marzo 1944': *Dagli archivi di Mosca*, doc. 9, p. 238; Dimitrov, *Diario*, p. 770.
7. Dimitrov, *Diario*, p. 694.
8. P. Ripert, *De Gaulle*, p. 95.

9. See Secchia's discussion with Stalin: Aga-Rossi and Zaslavsky, *Togliatti e Stalin*, pp. 296–300.

10. Ripert, *De Gaulle*, pp. 96–7.

11. See above, p. 127.

12. Narinskij, 'Stalin, Togliatti e Thorez, 1944–1948', pp. 82–3. See also Pons, *L'impossibile egemonia*, p. 22, and 'Una sfida mancata: l'URSS, il Cominform e il PCI (1947–1948')*, in *Dagli archivi di Mosca*, pp. 163 and 167–8.

13. Ellwood, *Rebuilding Europe*, pp. 115–16.

14. *Dagli archivi di Mosca*, pp. 301–2.

15. *Istochnik*, no. 3 (1995), p. 149.

16. Letter of D. Shevlyagin to M. A. Suslov, June 1947: *Dagli archivi di Mosca*, doc. 17, p. 275; record of conversation of A. A. Zhdanov and P. Secchia, 12 December 1947: *ibid.*, doc. 18, pp. 277, 279 and 281.

17. NA, KV2/1777, 474bc, p. 1.

18. See Chapter 23.

19. See G. C. Donno, *La Gladio Rossa del PCI (1945–1967)*; G. P. Pelizzaro, *Gladio Rossa: dossier sulla più potente banda armata esistita in Italia*.

20. Dzh. Chervetti [G. Cervetti], *Zoloto Moskvy*, p. 153: reference to the US Congress inquiry led by M. Halperin, J. J. Berman, R. L. Borosage and C. M. Marwick, *The Lawless State: The Crimes of the US Intelligence Agencies*.

21. Donno, *La Gladio Rossa del PCI (1945–1967)*, chs 2–3.

22. P. Stavrakis, *Moscow and Greek Communism, 1944–1949*, p. 33.

23. *Ibid.*, pp. 13–16.

24. *Ibid.*, p. 85.

25. *Ibid.*, pp. 92–4 and 105–7.

26. *Ibid.*, p. 109.

27. *Ibid.*, pp. 139–40.

28. Telegram of Molotov to Stalin, September 1947, about what had been sent to Zachariadis, the Greek communist leader: RGASPI, f. 89, op. 48, d. 21.

29. M. Djilas, *Conversations with Stalin*, p. 141.

30. Stavrakis, *Moscow and Greek Communism*, pp. 169–70.

31. V. Zaslavsky, *Lo Stalinismo e la sinistra italiana: dal mito dell'URSS alla fire del comunismo 1945–1991*, p. 107.

32. *Istoricheskii arkhiv*, no. 4 (1997), p. 101.

33. Message to Rákosi, 19 February 1948: *Vostochnaya Evropa v dokumentakh rossiiskikh arkhivov, 1944–1953*, vol. 1, p. 762.

34. *The British Road to Socialism*.

35. G. Matthews, member of the Executive Committee of the CPGB at that time and later to become its Assistant General Secretary, gave his account in 'Stalin's British Road?', *Changes Supplement*, 14–27 September 1991, pp. 1–3.

36. A. Nuti, *La provincia più rossa: la costruzione del Partito Nuovo a Siena (1945–1956)*, p. 218.

37. Interview with Eugenio Reale, *Sente*, 24 March 1975. It was Reale, Togliatti's close friend and confidant at the time, who was told by Rákosi about his intentions.

38. Letter of Palmiro Togliatti to Eugenio Reale (n.d.): Eugenio Reale Papers (HIA).

39. Letter of M. A. Suslov to A. A. Zhdanov, 23 May 1947: *Dagli archivi di Mosca*, doc. 16, p. 270.

40. E. Biagi, 'Usciti dall'URSS Palmiro mi disse: finalmente liberi!', *Corriere della Sera*, 21 August 2003.

41. *Dagli archivi di Mosca. L'URSS, il Cominform e il PCI (1943–1951)*, doc. 39, p. 417.

42. M. Djilas, *Rise and Fall*, p. 103.

43. See, for example, the comments of Eduardo D'Onofrio: Nuti, *La provincia più rossa*, p. 111.

23. Warring Propaganda

1. *Winston S. Churchill: His Complete Speeches 1897–1963*, vol. 7: *1943–1949*, pp. 7285–93.

2. NA, KV 2/1977, serial 474bc. On the outlawing of the German Communist Party see P. Major, *The Death of the KPD: Communism and Anti-Communism in West Germany*.

3. *The Lost Orwell: Being a Supplement to the Complete Works of George Orwell*, pp. 141–51.

4. D. C. Engerman, 'The Ironies of the Iron Curtain: The Cold War and the Rise of Russian Studies in the United States', *Cahiers du Monde Russe*, no. 45/3–4 (2004), pp. 469–73.

5. On Rothstein in general see NA, KV 2/1584. The private information on the annual meeting came from my colleague Prof. Olga Crisp at the School of Slavonic and East European Studies.

6. I. W. Roberts, *History of the School of Slavonic & East European Studies, 1915–1990*, pp. 58–9.

7. A film, *The Inn of the Sixth Happiness*, starring Ingrid Bergman, was also made of Gladys Aylward's life.

8. *Converting Britain*, BBC Radio 4, 10 August 2004.

9. S. Rawicz, *The Long Walk*. Although this book was devoid of religious content it was made available cheaply to Christian denominations. I received a copy as a nine-year-old as a Sunday school prize. A BBC Radio 4 programme, *The Long Walk* by Tim Whewell on 30 October 2006, demolished Rawicz's claim of a Siberian escape.

10. J. A. C. Brown, *Techniques of Persuasion: From Propaganda to Brainwashing*, pp. 267–93.

11. See B. Robshaw, 'Biggles Flies Again', *Independent on Sunday*, 27 July 2003.

12. E. Reale, *Avec Jacques Duclos au banc des accusés à la Réunion Constitutive du Kominform à Szklarska Poreba*. Reale published materials in the Italian press before his French-language memoir.

13. R. H. Crossman (ed.), *The God that Failed*.

14. *Ibid.*, pp. 15–75; A. Koestler, *Darkness at Noon*.

15. J. S. Berliner, *Factory and Manager in the USSR*.

16. E. H. Carr, *The Russian Revolution from Lenin to Stalin, 1917–1929*; I. Deutscher, *Russia, China, and the West: A Contemporary Chronicle, 1953–1966*; I. Deutscher, *The Unfinished Revolution: Russia, 1917–1967*.

17. H. Johnson, *What We Saw in Rumania*; H. Johnson, *The Upsurge of China*.

18. P. Shapcott, 'I Once Met the Red Dean', *Oldie*, June 2004, p. 35.

19. J. Steinbeck, *Russian Journal*, p. 20.

20. H. Klehr, J. E. Haynes and K. M. Anderson (eds), *The Soviet World of American Communism*, p. 338.

21. R. Service, *Stalin: A Biography*, pp. 543–4.

22. *Rabotnichesko delo*, 7 January 1950: see Z. Brzezinski, *The Soviet Bloc: Unity and Conflict*, p. 115.

23. K. Simonov, *Russkii vopros: p'esa v 3-kh deistviyakh, 7 kartinakh*.

24. Speech of D'Onofrio to the Third Cominform Conference, 17 November 1949: *The Cominform. Minutes of the Three Conferences, 1947/1948/1949*, p. 764.

25. D. Caute, *The Fellow Travellers: A Postscript to the Enlightenment*, p. 290.

26. K. Burk, *Troublemaker: The Life and History of A. J. P. Taylor*, pp. 193–4.

27. See above, p. 262–5.

24. The Chinese Revolution

1. Ma Feng, 'A Nation Celebrates its New Beginning', *Time Asia*, 27 September 1999; P. Short, *Mao: A Life*, pp. 419–20.

2. G. Dimitrov, *The Diary of Georgi Dimitrov, 1933–1949*, p. 443. Dimitrov's diary entry essentially concurs with Djilas's memoir, at least about the Chinese communists, in *Conversations with Stalin*, p. 141. See in particular S. Tsang, *The Cold War's Odd Couple: The Unintended Partnership between the Republic of China and the UK, 1950–58*, p. 21 and n. 121.

3. G. Benton and S. Tsang, 'Opportunism, Betrayal and Manipulation in Mao's Rise to Power', *China Journal*, no. 55 (January 2006). On Mao's domination of his leading associates see Tsang, *The Cold War's Odd Couple*, p. 23.

4. J.-L. Domenach, *Chine: l'archipel oublié*, p. 47.

5. Mao Zedong, 'Report to the Second Plenary Session of the Central Committee of the Seventh Congress of the Chinese Communist Party, 5 March 1949', *Selected Works*, vol. 4, p. 364.

6. F. C. Teiwes, 'The Establishment and Consolidation of the New Regime', in R. MacFarquhar (ed.), *The Politics of China, 1949–1989*, p. 28.

7. Domenach, *Chine: l'archipel oublié*, pp. 70–1. The total number of victims still cannot be ascertained with precision.

8. *Ibid.*, pp. 97–100.

9. L. T. White III and Kam-yee Law, 'Explanations for China's Revolution at its Peak', in Kam-yee Law (ed.), *The Chinese Cultural Revolution Reconsidered: Beyond Purge and Holocaust*, p. 8.

10. Teiwes, 'The Establishment and Consolidation of the New Regime', p. 12.

11. *Ibid.*, p. 33.

12. E. Friedman, P. G. Pickowicz and M. Selden, *Chinese Village, Socialist State*, pp. 103–4

13. Teiwes, 'The Establishment and Consolidation of the New Regime', pp. 37 and 39.

14. Domenach, *Chine: l'archipel oublié*, p. 153.

15. Teiwes, 'The Establishment and Consolidation of the New Regime', p. 42.

16. Friedman, Pickowicz and Selden, *Chinese Village, Socialist State*, p. 123.

17. *Ibid.*, p. 193.

18. Domenach, *Chine: l'archipel oublié*, p. 489.

19. Teiwes, 'The Establishment and Consolidation of the New Regime', pp. 60–3.

20. *Ibid.*, pp. 74–5.

21. *Ibid.*, p. 22.

22. *Ibid.*, p. 73.

23. J.-L. Domenach, *The Origins of the Great Leap Forward: The Case of One Chinese Province*, p. 25.

24. Friedman, Pickowicz and Selden, *Chinese Village, Socialist State*, p. 218.

25. *Ibid.*, pp. 189–90.

26. Tianjian Shi, *Political Participation in Beijing*, pp. 21, 40, 69 and 121.

27. *Ibid.*, p. 25.

28. *Ibid.*, p. 70.

29. Domenach, *The Origins of the Great Leap Forward*, pp. 53–4, 62 and 76.

30. In fact the slogan had already been in use since the previous year.

31. Domenach, *The Origins of the Great Leap Forward*, pp. 102–3.

32. J. Spence, *Mao Zedong*, pp. 540–1.

33. Domenach, *The Origins of the Great Leap Forward*, pp. 103, 105, 109.

34. Domenach, *Chine: l'archipel oublié*, p. 127.

35. *Ibid.*, p. 130.

36. *Ibid.*, pp. 128 and 145.

37. *Ibid.*, pp. 157–9 and 185.

25. Organising Communism

1. *Vostochnaya Evropa v dokumentakh rossiiskikh arkhivov, 1944–1953*, vol. 1, p. 126.

2. I. N. R. Davies, *Heart of Europe: A Short History of Poland*, pp. 326–7.

3. See above, p. 242.

4. *Vostochnaya Evropa v dokumentakh rossiiskikh arkhivov*, vol. 2, p. 532.

5. R. R. King, *Minorities under Communism: Nationalities as a Source of Tension among Balkan Communist States*, p. 150.

6. F. C. Teiwes, 'The Establishment and Consolidation of the New Regime', in R. MacFarquhar (ed.), *The Politics of China, 1949–1989*, p. 51. See also I. V. Sadchikov's report to Molotov on Yugoslavia, 17 December 1945: *Vostochnaya Evropa v dokumentakh rossiiskikh arkhivov*, vol. 1, p. 326.

7. N. P. Bugai (ed.), *L. Beriya – I. Stalinu: 'Soglasno Vashemu ukazaniyu'*, pp. 225–32.

8. Report by the American Legation to the US Department of State, 16 July 1953, p. 3: Seymour M. Finger Papers, Foreign Service Dispatches (HIA).

9. W. Brus, 'The Peak of Stalinism', in M. Kaser (ed.), *The Economic History of Eastern Europe, 1917–1975*, vol. 3: *Institutional Change within a Planned Economy*, p. 9.

10. Calculated from the tables cited by F. Fejtö, *Histoire des démocraties populaires*, vol. 1, p. 373.

11. See above, p. 246–7.

12. C. Milosz, *The Captive Mind*, p. 218.

13. *Ibid.*, pp. 189–90.

14. *Vostochnaya Evropa v dokumentakh rossiiskikh arkhivov*, vol. 2, p. 563.

15. E. Dedmon, *China Journal*, p. 19.

16. E. Friedman, P. G. Pickowicz and M. Selden, *Chinese Village, Socialist State*, p. 121.

17. Report by the American Legation to the US Department of State, 16 July 1953, p. 3: Seymour M. Finger Papers, Foreign Service Dispatches (HIA).

18. D. Childs and R. Popplewell, *The Stasi: The East German Intelligence and Security Service*, pp. 82–4.

19. N. Naimark, *The Russians in Germany: A History of the Soviet Zone of Occupation, 1945–1949*, pp. 194–5.

20. P. Kenney, *Rebuilding Poland: Workers and Communists, 1945–1950*, pp. 80–1 and 85.

21. *Ibid.*, p. 278.

22. I. Barankovics, *Catholic Church and Catholic Faith in Hungary*.

23. Milosz, *The Captive Mind*, p. 199.

24. *Ibid.*, pp. 102–4.

25. *Ibid.*, p. 21.

26. See above, pp. 192–3.

27. Kenney, *Rebuilding Poland*, p. 176.

28. *Ibid.*, p. 91.

29. *Ibid.*, p. 234.

30. *SSSR – Pol'sha: mekhanizmy podchineniya, 1944–1949*, p. 121.

31. *Vostochnaya Evropa v dokumentakh rossiiskikh arkhivov*, vol. 1, p. 558.

32. *Ibid.*, pp. 607 and 685; *SSSR – Pol'sha: mekhanizmy podchineniya, 1944–1949*, p. 123.

33. J. Triska and C. Gati (eds), *Blue Collar Workers in Eastern Europe*, p. 31.

26. Against and For Reform

1. L. Bethell and I. Roxborough, 'The Postwar Conjuncture in Latin America: Democracy, Labor and the Left', in L. Bethell and Ian Roxborough (eds), *Latin America between the Second World War and the Cold War, 1944–1948*, p. 18.

2. See below, p. 391.

3. See below, pp. 392 and 402–4.

4. See below, pp. 377–8.

5. R. Service, *Stalin: A Biography*, ch. 48.

6. Zh. and R. Medvedev, *Neizvestnyi Stalin*, pp. 82–3.

7. *Vostochnaya Evropa v dokumentakh rossiiskikh arkhivov, 1944–1953*, vol. 1, p. 766, and vol. 2, p. 82.

8. *Ibid.*, vol. 1, pp. 901–2.

9. *Ibid.*, vol. 2, p. 91.

10. *Ibid.*, pp. 317–18.

11. *Ibid.*, pp. 233 and 318.

12. *Ibid.*, p. 650.

13. *Ibid.*, pp. 150 and 258.

14. D. Childs and R. Popplewell, *The Stasi: The East German Intelligence and Security Service*, pp. 43–4.

15. Report by the American Legation to the US Department of State, 16 July 1953, p. 3: Seymour M. Finger Papers, Foreign Service Dispatches (HIA).

16. Service, *Stalin: A Biography*, p. 568.

17. *Vostochnaya Evropa v dokumentakh rossiiskikh arkhivov*, vol. 2, p. 177.

18. Record of conversation of Stalin and Secchia, 14 December 1947: *Dagli archivi di Mosca. L'URSS, il Cominform e il PCI (1943–1951)*, doc. 20, p. 289.

19. M. Kramer, 'The Early Post-Stalin Succession Struggle and Upheavals in East-Central Europe: Internal-External Linkages in Soviet Policy Making', *Journal of Cold War Studies*, part 1 (1999), pp. 12–22.

20. *Prezidium TsK KPSS, 1954–1964. Chernovye protokol'nye zapisi zasedanii: stenogrammy*, vol. 1, pp. 94–7: Presidium meetings of 30 January and 1 February 1956.

21. N. Barsukov, 'Kak sozdavalsya "zakrytyi doklad" Khrushchëva', *Literaturnaya gazeta*, 21 February 1996, p. 11.

22. *Prezidium TsK KPSS, 1954–1964*, vol. 1, pp. 106–7: Presidium meeting of 22 February 1956.

23. K. Morgan, *Harry Pollitt*, p. 176.

24. See below, p. 320–1.

25. *Prezidium TsK KPSS, 1954–1964*, vol. 1, pp. 44–5.

26. A. Paczkowski, *The Spring Will Be Ours: Poland and the Poles from Occupation to Freedom*, p. 273.

27. J. Granville, *The First Domino: International Decision Making during the Hungarian Crisis of 1956*, p. 116.

28. C. Gati, *Hungary and the Soviet Bloc*, pp. 135–8.

29. *Prezidium TsK KPSS, 1954–1964*, vol. 1, pp. 196–202: Presidium meetings of 2–4 November 1956.

30. J. Callaghan, *Cold War, Crisis and Conflict: The CPGB, 1951–1968*, pp. 76–7.

31. Letter to the Secretariat of the CPSU Central Committee, 30 October 1956: reproduced in V. Zaslavsky, *Lo Stalinismo e la sinistra italiana: dal mito dell'URSS alla fine del comunismo, 1945–1991*, pp. 190–1.

32. *Ibid.*, pp. 192–4.

33. M. P. Leffler, *A Preponderance of Power. National Security, the Truman Administration and the Cold War*, pp. 366–7.

27. Détente and Expansion

1. See below, p. 362–3.

2. *Prezidium TsK KPSS, 1954–1964. Chernovye protokol'nye zapisi zasedanii: stenogrammy*, vol. 1, p. 400: 14 December 1959.

3. *Ibid.*, p. 280: 10 November 1957.

4. See below, Chapter 29.

5. See below, p. 320.

6. J. Chang and J. Halliday, *Mao: The Unknown Story*, p. 428. I have slightly changed the run of the translated words.

7. *Prezidium TsK KPSS, 1954–1964*, vol. 1, pp. 862–72: Presidium meeting of 13 October 1964.

8. KGB report, 11 May 1965: RGASPI, f. 89, op. 65, d. 13, pp. 1–6.

9. Report from the British embassy in Bucharest, 5 February 1974: NA, FCO 28/2549, doc. 12, p. 1.

10. NA, FO 800/720, doc. 3, p. 1.

11. See below, pp. 402–3.

12. N. Chanda, *Brother Enemy: The War after the War*, p. 22.

13. See below, p. 459.

14. See below, pp. 406–10.

15. See below, pp. 410–11.

16. K. Crane, *The Soviet Economic Dilemma of Eastern Europe*, pp. 15–42.

17. RGASPI, f. 89, op. 43, d. 9.

18. *Ibid.*, op. 51, d. 28: Politburo decision of 8 January 1969.

19. *Ibid.*, op. 38, d. 47; V. Riva, *Oro da Mosca*, p. 60.

20. RGASPI, f. 89, op. 38, d. 47; Riva, *Oro da Mosca: i finanziamenti sovietici al PCI dalla Rivoluzione d'ottobre al crollo dell'URSS. Con 240 documenti inediti delgi archivi moscoviti*, p. 60.

21. O. A. Westad, *The Global Cold War: Third World Interventions and the Making of our Times*, pp. 215–16.

22. Chang and Halliday, *Mao: The Unknown Story*, pp. 607–8.

23. Z. Brzezinski, *The Soviet Bloc: Unity and Conflict*, p. 455.

24. See below, pp. 388–90.

25. RGANI, f. 2., op. 3, d. 161: Central Committee plenum, 26 June 1969, pp. 5–6 and 8–14. See S. Pons, *Berlinguer e la fine del comunismo*, p. 10.

26. S. Ellis and T. Sechaba, *Comrades against Apartheid: The African National Congress and the South African Communist Party*, p. 9.

27. RGANI, f. 2, op. 3, d. 161, p. 9.

28. *Ibid.*, pp. 14–15.

29. Dzh. Chervetti [G. Cervetti], *Zoloto Moskvy*, p. 66.

30. *Ibid.*, pp. 44, 47.

31. *Ibid.*, p. 134. This was a peculiar conversation because, as Cervetti left the room, Ponomarëv said that the Italian communists could still receive their cut of the payments made by Italy for Soviet natural gas supplies. Cervetti has declared himself mystified by this comment: *ibid.*, p. 135.

32. Memorandum by V. Zagladin, Deputy Chief of the International Department of the Central Committee of the CPSU, 4 October 1979: RGASPI, f. 89, op. 32, d. 12.

33. Andropov's report quoted in V. Bukovskii, *Moskovskii protsess*, pp. 354–5.

34. Riva, *Oro da Mosca*, p. 520.

35. Pons, *Berlinguer e la fine del comunismo*, pp. 105 and 107.

36. Chervetti, *Zoloto Moskvy*, pp. 138–9.

37. RGASPI, f. 89, op. 33, d. 15, pp. 1–2.

38. *Ibid.*, pp. 394.

39. R. W. Judy, 'The Case of Computer Technology', in S. Wasowski (ed.), *East–West Trade and the Technology Gap*, pp. 67–71.

40. *Ibid.*, p. 385.

41. P. Hanson and K. Pavitt, *The Comparative Economics of Research Development and Innovation in East and West: A Survey*, p. 79.

42. A. C. Sutton, *Western Technology and Soviet Economic Development, 1945 to 1965*, pp. 379–80.

43. R. Giles, 'The KGB in Afghanistan, 1979–1989', paper delivered at St Antony's College, Oxford: 31 May 2006.

44. RGASPI, f. 89, op. 42, d. 7, pp. 1–2.

45. Pons, *Berlinguer e la fine del comunismo*, p. 170.

28. China Convulsed

1. F. C. Teiwes, 'The Establishment and Consolidation of the New Regime', in R. MacFarquhar (ed.), *The Politics of China, 1949–1989*, p. 12.

2. *Ibid.*, p. 82; J.-L. Domenach, *Chine: l'archipel oublié*, p. 232.

3. Tianjian Shi, *Political Participation in Beijing*, p. 252.

4. Testimony of Bu Yulong: Zhang Lijia and C. Macleod (eds), *China Remembers*, p. 75.

5. Testimony of Bian Shaofeng: *ibid.*, p. 83.

6. *Ibid.*, pp. 82–3.

7. J. Becker, *Hungry Ghosts: China's Secret Famine*. See also V. Smil, 'China's Great Famine: Forty Years Later', *British Medical Journal*, 18–25 December 1999, pp. 1619–21.

8. J. Chang and J. Halliday, *Mao: The Unknown Story*, p. 400.

9. NA, FCO 9/272, docs 1 and 4.

10. Li Zhisui, *The Private Life of Chairman Mao: The Memoirs of Mao's Personal Physician*, pp. 94, 104 and 358.

11. *Ibid.*, p. 260.

12. *Ibid.*, p. 9.

13. *Ibid.*, pp. 496 and 498.

14. Shaoguang Wang, 'Between Destruction and Construction: The First Year of the Cultural Revolution', in Kam-yee Law (ed.), *The Chinese Cultural Revolution Reconsidered: Beyond Purge and Holocaust*, pp. 26–7.

15. *Ibid.*, pp. 28–30.

16. Tianjian Shi, *Political Participation in Beijing*, p. 71.

17. Xiaoxia Gong, 'The Logic of Repressive Collective Action: A Case Study of Violence in the Cultural Revolution', in Kam-yee Law (ed.), *The Chinese Cultural Revolution Reconsidered*, pp. 128.

18. Tianjian Shi, *Political Participation in Beijing*, p. 85.

19. Nien Cheng, *Life and Death in Shanghai*, p. 59.

20. *Ibid.*, pp. 63–7.

21. *Ibid.*, p. 83.

22. *Ibid.*, pp. 111, 115, 128, 309 and 351.

23. See the testimony of Fr André Bonnichon in his 'La Cellule 23', *Etudes*, September 1954, p. 189.

24. Domenach, *Chine: l'archipel oublié*, p. 269.

25. Xiaoxia Gong, 'The Logic of Repressive Collective Action', p. 129, citing an interview with Hu Yaobang in 1985.

26. Domenach, *Chine: l'archipel oublié*, p. 270.

27. L. T. White III and Kam-yee Law, 'Explanations for China's Revolution at its Peak', in Kam-yee Law (ed.), *The Chinese Cultural Revolution Reconsidered*, p. 10; Shaoguang Wang, 'The Structural Sources of the Cultural Revolution', in *ibid.*, pp. 77–9 and 81.

28. Deng Rong, *Deng Xiaoping and the Cultural Revolution*, p. 46.

29. Xiaoxia Gong, 'The Logic of Repressive Collective Action', p. 115.

30. Deng Rong, *Deng Xiaoping and the Cultural Revolution*, pp. 246 and 250.

31. *Ibid.*, pp. 275–9.

32. *Ibid.*, pp. 329–30.

33. *Ibid.*, pp. 376–81 and 389–99.

34. *Ibid.*, p. 390.

29. Revolutionary Cuba

1. The speech included the recitation of a poem, which was a sign of the ramshackle combination of repression and tolerance under Batista's rule: see F. Castro, *Historia Me Absolverá!*.
2. J. Lagas, *Memorias de un capitán rebelde*, pp. 19–20.
3. R. López-Fresquet, '14 Months with Castro' (typescript, HIA), pp. 24–5.
4. *Ibid.*, pp. 47 and 196; Mario Llerena, 'Memoir' (typescript, HIA), vol. 1, p. 24.
5. López-Fresquet, '14 Months with Castro', p. 112; Lagas, *Memorias de un capitán rebelde*, pp. 19–20.
6. See his statement of intentions in *Humanismo. Revista de insubornable orientación democrática* (Havana), January–April 1959, pp. 329–37.
7. López-Fresquet, '14 Months with Castro', pp. 106 and 108.
8. Yu. P. Gavrikov, *Fidel' Kastro: Neistovyi komandante Ostrova svobody*, p. 143.
9. F. Castro, *Speech at the United Nations: General Assembly Session, September 26, 1960*, pp. 18, 21 and 23.
10. F. Castro, *Fidel Castro Speaks on Marxism-Leninism*, p. 31: speech of 2 December 1961.
11. Meeting of Castro with Komsomol delegation, 13 January 1961: RGASPI, f. 89, op. 28, d. 5, p. 8.
12. *Ibid.*
13. *Ibid.*, p. 9.
14. López-Fresquet, '14 Months with Castro', pp. 184–5.
15. I owe this insight to my St Antony's colleague Valpy Fitzgerald.
16. Castro, *Fidel Castro Speaks on Marxism-Leninism*, p. 46: speech of 2 December 1961.
17. R. Gott, *Cuba: A New History*, p. 201.
18. *Prezidium TsK KPSS, 1954–1964. Chernovye protokol'nye zapisi zasedanii: stenogrammy*, vol. 1, p. 646: Presidium meeting of 16 November 1962; and pp. 720–1: Presidium meetings of 16 November 1962 and 7 June 1963.
19. N. S. Khrushchev, *Khrushchev Remembers: The Glasnost Tapes*, p. 179.
20. *Prezidium TsK KPSS, 1954–1964*, vol. 1, p. 621: 25 October 1962.
21. J. Haslam, *The Nixon Administration and the Death of Allende's Chile: A Case of Assisted Suicide*, p. 154.
22. F. Castro, *Comparecencia del Comandante Fidel Castro Ruz, Primer Ministro del Gobierno Revolucionario y Primer Secretario del Comité Central del Partido Comunista de Cuba, para Analizar los Acontecimientos de Checoslovaquia, Viernes 23 de Agosto de 1968*, pp. 23–9.
23. *Moncada. Órgano del Ministerio del Interior*, June 1968, p. 5.
24. J. A. Rodríguez-Menier, 'El Minint por Dentro' (typescript, HIA), ch. 7.
25. Report by C. J. Menéndez Cervera and E. Sánchez Santa Cruz, *Comisión Cubana de Derechos Humanos y Reconciliación Nacional*, 5 July 2006, p. 1.

26. Rodríguez-Menier, 'El Minint por Dentro', pp. 4–6.
27. See the remarks of Vladimir Ivashko, Gorbachëv's Deputy General Secretary, to the General Secretary of the Communist Party of Uruguay Jaime Peres, 31 May 1991: RGASPI, f. 89, op. 11, d. 188, p. 4.
28. Official diary of Yu. V. Petrov: *ibid.*, op. 8, d. 60, p. 2.
29. F. Castro, Speech to the Latin American Trade Union meeting held in Havana, 9 November 1991: *Granma International*, 24 November 1991.
30. Speech to the First Congress of Pioneers, 1 November 1991: 'Debemos preservar siempre la esperanza', p. 18.

30. Communist Order

1. J. Halliday (ed.), *The Artful Albanian: The Memoirs of Enver Hoxha*, pp. 6–7.
2. Hoxha, however, made an exception for the British comedian Norman Wisdom: see below, p. 358.
3. A. Weiner, 'The Empires Pay a Visit: Gulag Returnees, East European Rebellions and Soviet Frontier Politics', *Journal of Modern History*, June 2006, pp. 333–76; A. Weiner, 'Déjà Vu All Over Again: Prague Spring, Romanian Summer and Soviet Autumn on the Soviet Western Frontier', *Contemporary European History*, no. 2 (2006), pp. 159–91.
4. See KGB Chairman Vladimir Semichastny's report to the Politburo in 1965: RGASPI, f. 89, op. 6, d. 30.
5. Basic Rules of Behaviour for Soviet Citizens Travelling to Capitalist and Developing Countries formulated by the Central Committee Secretariat in July 1979: *ibid.*, op. 31, d. 7, pp. 1–8.
6. 'The Wall', episode 9, CNN *Cold War* series (1998).
7. H. M. Harrison, *Driving the Soviets up the Wall: Soviet–East German Relations, 1953–1961*, p. 161.
8. *Ibid.*, p. 203.
9. *Ibid.*, p. 186.
10. D. Childs and R. Popplewell, *The Stasi: The East German Intelligence and Security Service*, pp. 84–6.
11. L. Harding, 'In the Grip of the Angkang', *Guardian*, 20 December 2005.
12. *Vostochnaya Evropa v dokumentakh rossiiskikh arkhivov, 1944–1953*, vol. 2, p. 619.
13. I. Hallas, 'Radio Jamming', www.okupatsioon.ee/english/mailbox/radio/radio/html: dated 3 May 2000.
14. Personal information from my (once scalped) colleague at St Antony's, Richard Clogg.
15. *Rhyming Reasoner*, no. 2, November 1956. I am grateful to Paul Flewers for supplying this reference.
16. A. B. Evans, *Soviet Marxism-Leninism: The Decline of an Ideology*, pp. 105–6.
17. See RGASPI, f. 89, op. 6, dd. 15–25.
18. Evans, *Soviet Marxism-Leninism*, p. 142.

19. V. Medvedev, *Chelovek za spinoi*, pp. 144 and 149.

20. T. Garton Ash, *We the People: The Revolution of 89*, pp. 137–8. Havel made this comment in January 1990.

21. D. Rusinow, *The Yugoslav Experiment, 1948–1974*, p. 139.

22. A. L. Bardach, *Cuba Confidential: Love and Vengeance in Miami and Havana*, p. 230.

23. See above, p. 188.

24. NA, FCO 28/2549, doc. 3.

31. Rethinking Communism

1. J.-P. Sartre, *Sartre on Cuba*.

2. *Prezidium TsK KPSS, 1954–1964. Chernovye protokol'nye zapisi zasedanii: stenogrammy*, vol. 1, pp. 453 and 464.

3. A. Horne, *Macmillan*, vol. 2: *1957–1986*, p. 284.

4. W. Taubman, *Khrushchev: The Man and his Era*, p. 476.

5. R. Medvedev, *Let History Judge*; R. Medvedev, *On Socialist Democracy*.

6. R. Bahro, *The Alternative in Eastern Europe*, especially pp. 39, 117, 362, 368 and 453.

7. A. Sakharov, *Progress, Coexistence and Intellectual Freedom*.

8. P. Togliatti, *Il memoriale di Yalta*, pp. 28, 41 and 43–6.

9. S. Pons, *Berlinguer e la fine del comunismo*, p. 255.

10. On Lukács see above, p. 140.

11. Lukács summarised his standpoint in *The Process of Democratization*, written in the last months of his life. He died in 1971.

12. H. Marcuse, *Soviet Marxism: A Critical Analysis*.

13. H. Marcuse: *Eros and Civilization*; *One Dimensional Man*; *Essay on Liberation*; *Counterrevolution and Revolt*.

14. L. Colletti, *Il Marxismo e Hegel*.

15. P. Anderson, *Considerations on Western Marxism*, ch. 3.

16. M. G. Horowitz, 'Portrait of the Marxist as an Old Trouper', *Playboy*, September 1970, pp. 174–5.

17. Marcuse, *Eros and Civilisation*.

18. D. Cohn-Bendit and G. Cohn-Bendit, *Obsolete Communism: The Left-Wing Alternative*.

19. Daniel Cohn-Bendit's brother Gabriel was the co-author.

20. Cohn-Bendit and Cohn-Bendit, *Obsolete Communism*, pp. 204–45.

21. R. Service, *A History of Modern Russia from Nicholas II to Putin*, p. 459.

22. See above, p. 280.

23. F. Kermode, *Not Entitled: A Memoir*, pp. 234–8.

24. R. Pipes, *Vixi: Memoirs of a Non-Belonger*; R. Conquest, *The Dragons of Expectation: Reality and Delusion in the Course of History*: both books include recollections of the authors' political engagement. See the policy statement of 1979: R. Conquest, *Present Danger: Towards a Foreign Policy*.

25. J. Haslam, *The Vices of Integrity: E. H. Carr, 1892–1982*; Service, *A History of Modern Russia from Nicholas II to Putin*, p. xxv.
26. Service, *A History of Modern Russia from Nicholas II to Putin*, p. xxvii; R. Conquest, *Reflections on a Ravaged Century*, pp. 143–4.
27. Service, *A History of Modern Russia from Nicholas II to Putin*, p. xxvii.

32. Europe East and West

1. Z. Brzezinski, *The Soviet Bloc: Unity and Conflict*, p. 389.
2. *Prezidium TsK KPSS, 1954–1964. Chernovye protokol'nye zapisi zasedanii: stenogrammy*, vol. 1, p. 86: meeting of 10 January 1956.
3. M. Kaser, *Comecon: Integration Problems of the Planned Economies*, pp. 63–82; J. F. Brown, *Eastern Europe and Communist Rule*, p. 146.
4. R. Crampton, *Eastern Europe in the Twentieth Century – and After*, p. 313.
5. *The Khrushchev–Tito Revisionist Group Concoct New Plans against the Cause of Socialism*, pp. 5, 7 and 15.
6. J. Halliday (ed.), *The Artful Albanian: The Memoirs of Enver Hoxha*, p. 9.
7. See above, pp. 356–7.
8. N. Bethell, *Gomulka: His Poland and his Communism*, pp. 258–62.
9. Crampton, *Eastern Europe in the Twentieth Century – and After*, pp. 298–9.
10. C. Gati, *Hungary and the Soviet Bloc*, pp. 160–1.
11. Crampton, *Eastern Europe in the Twentieth Century – and After*, p. 321.
12. Z. Mlynář, *Night Frost in Prague: The End of Humane Socialism*, p. 157.
13. A. Paczkowski, *The Spring Will Be Ours: Poland and the Poles from Occupation to Freedom*, pp. 281 and 288–9.
14. W. Brus, 'Political System and Economic Efficiency', in S. Gomulka (ed.), *Growth, Innovation and Reform in Eastern Europe*, p. 28.
15. *Ibid.*, p. 290.
16. Crampton, *Eastern Europe in the Twentieth Century – and After*, p. 360.
17. A. H. Smith, *The Planned Economies of Eastern Europe*, pp. 230–2.
18. *Ibid.*, pp. 227–30.
19. D. Deletant, *Ceauşescu and the Securitate: Coercion and Dissent in Romania, 1965–1989*, pp. 192, 207–8 and 322–31.
20. See above, p. 371.
21. S. Pons, *Berlinguer e la fine del comunismo*, p. 48.
22. *Ibid.*, p. 140.
23. S. Carrillo, *Eurocomunismo y estado*.
24. See above, p. 113.
25. Draft letter of Secretariat of the Central Committee of the CPSU, February 1977: RGASPI, f. 89, op. 33, d. 15.
26. T. Hofnung, *Georges Marchais: l'inconnu du Parti Communiste Français*, pp. 315–17.
27. See below, pp. 399–400.

33. Reduced Expectations

1. L. L. Sharkey, *An Outline History of the Australian Communist Party*, pp. 55–68.
2. J. P. Ongkili, *Nation-Building in Malaysia, 1946–1974*; Njoto, *Strive for the Victory of the Indonesian Revolution with the Weapon of Dialectical and Historical Materialism: A Speech at the Alkiarcham Academy of Social Sciences on 3 June 1964*, pp. 3–26.
3. G. M. Kahin and A. R. Kahin, *Subversion as Foreign Policy: The Secret Eisenhower and Dulles Debacle in Indonesia.*
4. T. J. Nossiter, *Marxist State Governments in India: Politics, Economics and Society*, pp. 69–71, 73 and 80.
5. BBC News, 1 November 2005: http://news.bbc.co.uk/go/pr/fr/-/1/hi/world/south_asia/4374826.stm.
6. On Kerala communists' unorthodoxy see above, p. 243.
7. Nossiter, *Marxist State Governments in India*, p. 17.
8. *Ibid.*, pp. 21–3 and 32.
9. P. Louis, *People Power: The Naxalite Movement in Central Bihar*, pp. 58–9.
10. *Ibid.*, p. 32.
11. Z. Brzezinski, *The Grand Failure: The Birth and Death of Communism in the Twentieth Century*, p. 203.
12. R. Boyd, 'The Japanese Communist Party in Local Government', in B. Szajkowski (ed.), *Marxist Local Governments in Western Europe and Japan*, p. 192.
13. G. A. Almond, *The Appeals of Communism*, p. 151.
14. A. Nuti, *La provincia più rossa: la costruzione del Partito Nuovo a Siena (1945–1956)*, pp. 90 and 114.
15. *Ibid.*, pp. 211, 272 and 291.
16. S. Gundle, 'Models and Crises of Communist Government in Italy', in B. Szajkowski (ed.), *Marxist Local Governments in Western Europe and Japan*, pp. 74–5.
17. A. F. Knapp, 'A Receding Tide: France's Communist Municipalities', in *ibid.*, pp. 119–20, 125–7, 136–7 and 145.
18. J. Amodia, 'The Spanish Communist Party and Local Government', in *ibid.*, pp. 30 and 33.
19. G. C. Donno, *La Gladio rossa del PCI (1945–1967)*.
20. C. Andrew and V. Mitrokhin, *The Mitrokhin Archive*, vol. 1: *The KGB and the West*, p. 501.

34. Last of the Communist Revolutions

1. R. Gott, *Cuba: A New History*, p. 4.
2. N. Eberstadt, 'Pyongyang's Option: "Ordinary" Stalinism', *Far Eastern Economic Review*, no. 3 (2005), p. 31.
3. O. A. Westad, *The Global Cold War: Third World Interventions and the Making of our Times*, p. 183.
4. P. Short, *Pol Pot: History of a Nightmare*, pp. 298–300.
5. Chhang Song, 'Return to Cambodia, July–August 1989' (typescript, HIA), p. 9.
6. N. Chanda, *Brother Enemy: The War after the War*, pp. 71–2 and 80.
7. Short, *Pol Pot*, pp. 288 and 319–21.
8. *Ibid.*, p. 233.
9. *Ibid.*, p. 346.
10. *Ibid.*, pp. 347 and 353.
11. M. Vickery, *Cambodia, 1975–1982*, pp. 34–5.
12. The Cambodian Genocide Program, Yale University: www.yale.edu/cgp (p. 1).
13. A. Angell, *Chile de Alessandri a Pinochet: en busca de la Utopia*, p. 59.
14. *Ibid.*, p. 61.
15. Yu. P. Gavrikov, *Fidel' Kastro: Neistovyi komandante Ostrova svobody*, p. 138.
16. Angell, *Chile de Alessandri a Pinochet*, p. 62.
17. *Ibid.*, p. 72.
18. *Ibid.*, pp. 63–4.
19. *Ibid.*, pp. 72–3.
20. J. Haslam, *The Nixon Administration and the Death of Allende's Chile: A Case of Assisted Suicide*, pp. 74, 153–4 and 157.
21. *Ibid.*, p. 111.
22. Angell, *Chile de Alessandri a Pinochet*, p. 65.
23. *Ibid.*, p. 67.
24. *Ibid.*, p. 71.
25. *Ibid.*, pp. 76–7 and 79.
26. P. Kornbluh, *The Pinochet File: A Declassified Dossier on Atrocity and Accountability*, p. 37; Haslam, *The Nixon Administration and the Death of Allende's Chile*, ch. 7.
27. Westad, *The Global Cold War*, pp. 212–14.
28. *Ibid.*, pp. 231–5.
29. *Ibid.*, pp. 255–9.
30. *Ibid.*, pp. 277–8.
31. *Ibid.*, pp. 306–20.

35. Roads from Communism

1. R. Nixon, *1999: Victory without War*.
2. Among those who emphasised the possibility of an eventual implosion of the USSR, Richard Pipes wrote in 1984, a year before Gorbachëv came to power: 'While the Soviet government is in no danger of imminent collapse, it cannot forever "muddle through" . . .': *Survival Is Not Enough: Soviet Realities and America's Future*, p. 13.
3. R. Dallek, *Ronald Reagan: The Politics of Symbolism*, p. 192.
4. *Public Papers of the Presidents: Ronald Reagan, 1981*, p. 434.
5. J. L. Gaddis, *Strategies of Containment: A Critical Appraisal of Postwar American National Security Policy*, pp. 393–4.
6. The principle, as so often in the Cold War, was that my enemy's enemy is my friend.
7. See speech of Daniel Ortega to the United Nations Security Council on 25 March 1982: *Comunicado de Prensa: Permanent Mission to the U.N.*, no. 035. On the Sandinistas see below, p. 369.
8. Dallek, *Ronald Reagan*, pp. 181–2.
9. J. F. Brown, *Eastern Europe and Communist Rule*, pp. 104–5.
10. *Ibid.*, p. 127
11. Testimony of V. A. Alexandrov: Hoover Institution and Gorbachev Foundation Oral History Project (HIA), box 1, folder 2, p. 15.
12. Testimony of E. Meese: *ibid.*, box 2, folder 11, pp. 37 and 71.
13. Testimony of A. L. Adamishin: *ibid.*, box 1, folder 1, p. 5.
14. For rival testimonies of contemporary Soviet reactions to SDI see *ibid.*: V. A. Kryuchkov (box 2, folder 7, p. 31) and L. B. Shebarshin (box 2, folder 19, p. 18).
15. Sergei Tarasenko in W. C. Wohlforth (ed.), *Witnesses to the End of the Cold War*, p. 70.
16. R. Reagan, *An American Life*, pp. 585 and 588–9.
17. J. Matlock, *Reagan and Gorbachev: How the Cold War Ended*, pp. 97–105.
18. See below, pp. 449–53.
19. See below, pp. 428–9.
20. M. Marrese and J. Vanous, *Soviet Subsidization of Trade with Eastern Europe: A Soviet Perspective*, p. 3.
21. H. Friedmann, 'Warsaw Pact Socialism', in A. Hunter (ed.), *Rethinking the Cold War*, p. 220.
22. R. Service, *A History of Modern Russia from Nicholas II to Putin*, p. 465.
23. O. A. Westad, *The Global Cold War: Third World Interventions and the Making of our Times*, pp. 366, 382, 383 and 391.
24. Anatoli Chernyaev in Wohlforth (ed.), *Witnesses to the End of the Cold War*, p. 95.
25. P. Robinson, *How Ronald Reagan Changed my Life*, pp. 92–3.
26. J. Douglas-Home, *Once upon Another Time: Ventures behind the Iron Curtain*, pp. 17 and 25.

27. Pavel Palazchenko in Wohlforth (ed.), *Witnesses to the End of the Cold War*, p. 159.

28. D. H. Chollet and J. M. Goldgeier, 'Once Burned, Twice Shy? The Pause of 1989', in W. C. Wohlforth (ed.), *Cold War Endgame: Oral History, Analysis, Debates*, p. 149.

29. V. M. Zubok, 'Different Perspectives on the Historical Personality', in *ibid.*, p. 226, quoting A. S. Chernyaev's notes deposited with the Gorbachev Foundation in Moscow.

30. See the account in Chapter 36.

31. M. R. Beschloss and S. Talbott, *At the Highest Levels: The Inside Story of the End of the Cold War*, p. 132.

32. See, for example, Politburo meeting of 9 March 1990: RGASPI, f. 89, op. 8, d. 78, p. 1. The proposal to withdraw troops from Hungary was made by Zaikov, Shevardnadze and Yazov (Minister of Defence).

33. Dmitri Yazov in Wohlforth (ed.), *Cold War Endgame: Oral History, Analysis, Debates*, pp. 193 and 201

34. A. S. Chernyaev, *Shest' let s Gorbachëvym: po dnevnikovym zapisyam*, p. 57.

35. RGASPI, f. 89, op. 9, d. 124, p. 2.

36. Record of meeting between Castro and the Soviet ambassador, 20 June 1990: *ibid.*, op. 8, d. 60, pp. 2–3.

37. *Ibid.*, op. 11, d. 188, p. 5.

38. Beschloss and Talbott, *At the Highest Levels*, pp. 377 and 388–92.

39. See p. 457–8.

36. Anti-communism in Eastern Europe

1. Politburo meeting, 12 March 1981: RGASPI, f. 89, op. 42, d. 37, p. 3.

2. M. Kramer, 'Poland 1980–81: Soviet Policy during the Polish Crisis', *Cold War International History Papers Bulletin*, no. 5 (1995), pp. 116–23.

3. A. Paczkowski, *The Spring Will Be Ours: Poland and the Poles from Occupation to Freedom*, pp. 454–5.

4. *Ibid.*, pp. 476–7.

5. M. Gorbačov and Z. Mlynář, *Reformátoři Nebývachí Stastní*, p. 69

6. Hoover Institution and Gorbachev Foundation Oral History Project (HIA): testimonies of A. S. Chernyaev (who talked to Kádár's interpreter), box 1, folder 12, pp. 69–70, and V. A. Medvedev, box 2, folder 10, pp. 45–6 and 47–8.

7. *Ibid.*: testimony of V. A. Medvedev, box 2, folder 10, p. 35.

8. T. Zhivkov, *Memoary*, pp. 356–60. This was a Kremlin conversation of 16 October 1987.

9. Paczkowski, *The Spring Will Be Ours*, pp. 485–6.

10. *Ibid.*, pp. 492–500.

11. *Ibid.*, pp. 507–9.

12. J. L. Gaddis, *The Cold War: A New History*, p. 206.

13. I. Banac, 'Post-Communism as Post-Yugoslavism: The Yugoslav Non-Revolutions of 1989–1990', in I. Banac, *Eastern Europe in Europe*, p. 182.

14. See below, p. 465–6.

15. On the break-up of Yugoslavia see below, pp. 465–6.

16. E. Biberaj, 'Albania: The Last Domino', in I. Banac, *Eastern Europe in Europe*, pp. 189 and 195–9.

17. See below, pp. 466–7.

37. China's Capitalist Communism

1. R. MacFarquhar, 'The Succession to Mao and the End of Maoism, 1969–1982', in R. MacFarquhar (ed.), *The Politics of China, 1949–1989*, p. 300.

2. *Ibid.*, p. 309.

3. Deng Rong, *Deng Xiaoping and the Cultural Revolution*, pp. 445–9; Deng Xiaoping, *Selected Works of Deng Xiaoping (1975–1982)*, p. 154: speech of 13 December 1978.

4. Deng Maomao, *Deng Xiaoping, my Father*, pp. 50–1, 71, 95 and 102–3.

5. *Ibid.*, p. 104.

6. *Ibid.*, p. 95; Deng Rong, *Deng Xiaoping and the Cultural Revolution*, pp. 84–7 and 125–7; D. S. G. Goodman, *Deng Xiaoping and the Chinese Revolution*, p. 78.

7. J.-L. Domenach, *Chine: l'archipel oublié*, p. 331.

8. R. MacFarquhar, 'The Succession to Mao and the End of Maoism, 1969–1982', p. 312.

9. Deng Xiaoping, *Selected Works of Deng Xiaoping (1975–1982)*, p. 280.

10. *Ibid.*, p. 172: speech of 30 March 1979, 'Uphold the Four Cardinal Principles'.

11. See pp. 451–2. I am grateful to Steve Tsang for his insights into these aspects of Chinese political history.

12. L. T. White, *Unstately Power*, vol. 1: *Local Causes of China's Economic Reforms*, pp. 14–15 and 123–4; vol. 2: *Local Causes of China's Intellectual, Legal and Governmental Reforms*, p. 145.

13. White, *Unstately Power*, vol. 1: *Local Causes of China's Economic Reforms*, p. 10.

14. Deng Xiaoping, *Selected Works of Deng Xiaoping (1975–1982)*, p. 155: speech at closing session of the Central Working Conference preparing the third plenary meeting of the Central Committee, 13 December 1978.

15. This was at a dinner in 1986 for former President Carter's National Security Adviser Zbigniew Brzezinski: see Z. Brzezinski, *The Grand Failure: The Birth and Death of Communism in the Twentieth Century*, pp. 160–1.

16. Tenzin Gyatso, *Freedom in Exile: The Autobiography of the Dalai Lama*, p. 231.

17. J.-C. Tournebrise and L. MacDonald, *Le Dragon et la souris*, p. 169.

18. Domenach, *Chine: l'archipel oublié*, pp. 332–4.

19. *Ibid.*, p. 489. See also H. H. Wu, *Laogai – The Chinese Gulag*, ch. 1.

20. Tianjian Shi, *Political Participation in Beijing*, p. 252.
21. Brzezinski, *The Grand Failure*, p. 162.
22. Conversation with G. P. Shultz, Hoover Institution, 8 March 2005.
23. R. Baum, 'The Road to Tiananmen: Chinese Politics in the 1980s', in R. MacFarquhar (ed.), *The Politics of China, 1949–1989*, pp. 449–50.
24. *Tiananmen Square, 1989: The Classified History*, doc. 14.
25. Xin Liu, *In One's Shadow: An Ethnographic Account of the Condition of Post-Reform Rural Russia*, p. 182.
26. J. P. Burns, *Political Participation in Rural China*, p. 154.
27. P. J. Seybolt, *Throwing the Emperor from his Horse: Portrait of a Village Leader in China, 1923–1995*, pp. 82–3 and 85.
28. Laogai Research Foundation: report, 14 April 2004.
29. Gu Mingyan, 'Development and Reform of Education for Minority Nationalities in China' (typescript, HIA), 26 June 1989.
30. 'The Cauldron Boils', *Economist*, 29 September 2005.
31. 'Human Rights in China: Briefing Memo', submitted to President George W. Bush, 16 November 2005.

38. *Perestroika*

1. The Politburo minute is quoted by V. Bukovskii, *Moskovskii protsess*, p. 88.
2. M. S. Gorbachëv, *Zhizn' i reformy*, vol. 1, p. 265.
3. R. Service, 'Gorbachev's Reforms: The Future in the Past', *Journal of Communist Studies*, no. 3 (1987).
4. *Ibid.*
5. I am grateful to George Shultz and Martin Anderson for sharing with me their thoughts on the counterfactual possibilities in relation to the mid-1980s.
6. A. Brown, *The Gorbachev Factor*, pp. 186–7.

39. The Comrades Depart

1. O. A. Westad, *The Global Cold War: Third World Interventions and the Making of our Times*, p. 390.
2. See pp. 440–7.
3. See pp. 403–4 for the politics of Vietnam after the communist military victory.
4. See pp. 351–2.
5. Personal information from Laurence Rees, 4 October 2005.
6. J. Watts, 'North Korea Turns Away Western Aid', *Observer*, 2 October 2005.
7. F. Fukuyama, *The End of History and the Last Man*.
8. T. Hofnung, *Georges Marchais: l'inconnu du Parti Communiste Français*, chs 7 and 8.

9. P. M. La Ramée and Erica G. Polakoff, 'The Evolution of the Popular Organizations in Nicaragua', in G. Prevost and H. E. Vanden (eds), *The Undermining of the Sandinista Revolution*, pp. 42–3; C. M. Vilas, *Perfiles de la Revolución Sandinista*, pp. 359–64.

10. *El Nuevo Diario* (Managua), 22 February 1990.

11. Ortega's editorial: *La Prensa* (Managua), 26 February 1990.

12. *El Nuevo Diario* (Managua), 22 February 1990.

SELECT BIBLIOGRAPHY

This is a list of sources actively used in the Notes; it is not intended as an exhaustive list of important works on the history of communism. A typescript is noted as TS.

ARCHIVES

Bodleian Library – UK
Volkogonov Papers

Hoover Institution Archives (HIA) – USA
Henri Barbé, 'Souvenir de militant et dirigeant communiste' (TS)
Elizabeth Churchill Brown Papers
Chhang Song, 'Return to Cambodia, July–August 1989' (TS)
Communist International Instructions
Communist Party of India Papers
Communist Party of the United States Papers
E. W. Darling Papers
Theodore Draper Papers
Sir Paul Dukes Papers
Charles Wesley Ervin Papers
R. R. Fagen Papers
Herbert Haviland Field Papers
Seymour M. Finger Papers
T. T. C. Gregory Papers
Gu Mingyan, 'Development and Reform of Education for Minority Nationalities
    in China', 26 June 1989 (TS)
Hoover Institution and Gorbachev Foundation Oral History Project
Hungarian Subject Collection
Henry James Papers
Alexander Keskuela Papers
Nestor Lakoba Papers
Ivy Litvinov Papers
Mario Llerena, 'Memoir' (TS), vols 1–4

R. López-Fresquet, '14 Months with Castro' (TS)
Jay Lovestone Papers
Gibbes Lykes Papers
M. Muggeridge, 'Russian Journal' (TS)
Boris Nicolaevsky Collection
Yelizaveta Parshina and Leonid Parshin, 'Razvedka bez mifov' (TS, 1994)
Prezidium TsK KPSS
Peng Shu-tse Papers
Eugenio Reale Papers
J. A. Rodriguez-Menier, 'El Minint por Dentro' (TS)
Maurice Thorez Papers
Ernst Toller: 'An Appeal from the Young Workers of Germany'
Albert Vassart: untitled memoirs (TS)
Cilly Vassart, 'Le Front Populaire en France' (TS: Paris, 1962)
Oswald Henry Wedel, 'Recent Political Tendencies in Bavaria': MA thesis
    (Stanford, 1924)
Erich Wollenberg: untitled memoirs (TS)

The National Archives (NA) – UK

FO 800/720	KV 2/577–8	KV 2/1753–5
FCO 9/272	KV 2/1038	KV 2/1772–8
FCO 28/2549	KV 2/1977	KV 3/129–30
HW 17/37	KV 2/1584	PREM 8/1077

**Rossiiskii Gosudarstvennyi Arkhiv Noveishei Istorii (RGANI)
– Russian Federation**
    fond 2

**Rossiiskii Gosudarstvennyi Arkhiv Sotsial'no-Politicheskoi Istorii (RGASPI)
– Russian Federation**

| fond 2 | fond 17 | fond 89 | fond 325 |
| fond 3 | fond 76 | fond 109 | |

Periodicals

American Relief Administration Bulletin
Byulleten' oppozitsiya (Germany)
Corriere della Sera (Italy)
Economist (UK)
Etudes (France)
Fight (Organ of the Bolshevik-Leninist Party [Ceylon Unit]) (Ceylon)
Humanismo. Revista de insubornable orientación democrática (Cuba)
Istochnik (Russian Federation)

Izvestiya (USSR)
Kritika (USA)
Literaturnaya gazeta (USSR)
Moncada. Organo del Ministero del Interior (Cuba)
Nezavisimaya gazeta (Russian Federation)
New York Times (USA)
El Nuevo Diario (Nicaragua)
Observer (UK)
Oldie (UK)
Playboy (USA)
Pravda (USSR)
La Prensa (Nicaragua)
Principios (Santiago de Chile)
Rabotnichesko delo (Bulgaria)
Reader's Digest (USA)
Rhyming Reasoner (UK)
Sente (Italy)
Time (USA)
Time Asia (USA)
Trud (Russian Federation)

Documentary Collections

About Turn: The British Communist Party and the Second World War. The Verbatim Record of the Central Committee Meetings of 25 September and 2–3 October 1939, ed. F. King and G. Matthews (London, 1990)

Akademicheskoe delo, 1929–1931: Delo po obvineniyu akademika S. F. Platonova, ed. A. V. Kvashonkin, O. V. Khlevnyuk, L. P. Kosheleva and L. A. Rogovaya (Moscow, 1996)

C. Andrew and V. Mitrokhin, *The Mitrokhin Archive*, vol. 1: *The KGB and the West* (London, 1999); vol. 2: *The KGB and the World* (London, 2005)

Archivio Pietro Secchia, 1945–1973 (Annali Feltrinelli) (Milan, 1979)

Austro-Marxism, texts trans. and introduced by T. Bottomore (Oxford, 1978)

R. L. Benson and M. Warner (eds), *Venona: Soviet Espionage and the American Response, 1939–1957* (Washington, DC, 1996)

C. Bermani (ed.), *Gramsci raccontato. Testimonianze raccolte da Cesare Bermani, Gianni Bosio e Mimma Paulesu Quercioli* (Rome, 1987)

M. Bishop, *Maurice Bishop Speaks: The Grenada Revolution, 1979–1983* (New York, 1983)

Bol'shevistskoe rukovodstvo. Perepiska, 1912–1927, ed. A. V. Kvashonkin, O. V. Khlevnyuk, L. P. Kosheleva and L. A. Rogovaya (Moscow, 1996)

The British Road to Socialism (London, 1951)

Earl Browder Says (New York, 1991)

E. Browder, *Teheran: Our Path in War and Peace* (New York, 1944)

N. P. Bugai (ed.), *L. Beriya – I. Stalinu: 'Soglasno Vashemu ukazaniyu'* (Moscow, 1995)

N. I. Bukharin, *Problemy teorii i praktiki sotsializma* (Moscow, 1989)

The Case of Leon Trotsky: Report of Hearings on the Charges Made against Him in the Moscow Trials, ed. G. Novack (New York, 1969)

Winston S. Churchill: His Complete Speeches 1897–1963, vol. 7, ed. R. Rhodes James (London, 1974)

The Cominform. Minutes of the Three Conferences, 1947/1948/1949, ed. G. Procacci, G. Adibekov, A. Di Biagio, L. Gibianskii, F. Gori and S. Pons (Milan, 1994)

Communist Papers: Documents Selected from Those Obtained on the Arrest of the Communist Leaders on the 14th and the 21st October 1925 (London, 1926)

The Dead Sea Scrolls, trans. by M. Wise, M. Abegg Jr and E. Cook (New York, 1996)

Deng Xiaoping, *Selected Works of Deng Xiaoping (1975–1982)* (Beijing, 1984)

G. Dimitrov, *The Diary of Georgi Dimitrov, 1933–1939*, ed. I. Banac (New Haven, 2003)

G. Dimitrov, *Dimitrov and Stalin, 1934–1943: Letters from the Soviet Archives*, ed. A. Dallin and F. I. Firsov (New Haven, 2000)

Documents on Communism, Nationalism, and Soviet Advisers in China, 1918–1927: Papers Seized in the 1927 Peking Raid (New York, 1956)

A. Gramsci, *Lettere dal carcere*, ed. P. Sprinao (Turin, 1971)

A. Gramsci, *Quaderni del carcere*, ed. V. Gerratana (Turin, 1977), vols 1–4

A Guide to New China, 1953 (Peking, 1953)

J. Haynes and H. Klehr, *Venona: Soviet Espionage in America in the Stalin Era* (New Haven, 1999)

H. Klehr, *Communist Cadre: The Social Background of the American Communist Party Elite* (Stanford, 1978)

H. Klehr, J. E. Haynes and K. M. Anderson (eds), *The Soviet World of American Communism* (New Haven, 1998)

H. Klehr, J. E. Haynes and F. I. Firsov (eds), *The Secret World of American Communism* (New Haven, 1995)

The Khrushchev–Tito Revisionist Group Concoct New Plans against the Cause of Socialism (Tirana, 1963)

P. Kornbluh, *The Pinochet File: A Declassified Dossier on Atrocity and Accountability* (New York, 2003)

V. I. Lenin, *Polnoe sobranie sochinenii*, vols 1–55 (Moscow, 1958–65)

A. M. Ledovskii (ed.), 'Peregovory I. V. Stalina s Mao Tszedunom v dekabre 1949 – fevrale 1950 g.: novye arkhivnye dokumenty, *Novaya i noveishaya istoriya*, no. 1 (1997)

Yu. Martov, *Mirovoi bol'shevizm* (Berlin, 1923)

D. McLellan (ed.), *Karl Marx: Selected Writings* (Oxford, 1977)

Manual for Community Club Leaders: A Handbook for the Use of Officers and Committees of Communist Community Clubs (prepared by the Organisational Department of the Communist National Committee: New York, 1944)

G. Orwell, *The Lost Orwell: Being a Supplement to the Complete Works of George Orwell* (ed. P. Davison: London, 2006)

Prezidium TsK KPSS, 1954–1964. Chernovye protokol'nye zapisi zasedanii: stenogrammy, vol. 1, ed. A. A. Fursenko (Moscow, 2004)

The Price of Vision: The Diary of Henry A. Wallace, 1942–1946 (Boston, Mass., 1973)

Public Papers of the Presidents: Ronald Reagan, 1981 (Washington, DC, 1982)

Selected Works of Mao Tse-tung, vols 1–5 (Peking, 1961)

D. A. Smart (ed.), *Pannekoek and Gorter's Marxism* (London, 1978)

'Sovershenno sekretno': Lubyanka – Stalinu o polozhenii v strane (1922–1934 gg.), ed. G. N. Sevast'yanov, A. N. Sakharov, Ya. F. Pogonii, V. K. Vinogradov, T. Vihavainen, K. Pursiainen, T. Martin, H. Richardson and L. P. Kolodnikova, vols 1 ff. (Moscow, 2001–)

Sovetskii faktor v Vostochnoi Evrope, 1944–1953: Dokumenty, vols 1–2, ed. T. V. Volokitina, G. P. Murashko and A. F. Noskova (Moscow, 2002)

Sovetskoe rukovodstvo. Perepiska, 1928–1941 (Moscow, 1999)

SSSR – Pol'sha: mekhanizmy podchineniya, 1944–1949, ed. G. Bordyugov, G. Matveev, A. Kosewski and A. Paczkowski (Moscow, 1995)

I. Stalin, *Beseda s angliiskom pisatelem G. D. Uellsom, 23 iyunya 1934 g.* (Moscow, 1935)

I. V. Stalin, *Sochineniya*, vols 1–13 (Moscow, 1946–53)

I. V. Stalin, *Sochineniya*, vols 1(xiv)–3(xvi), ed. R. MacNeal (Stanford, 1967)

Tiananmen Square, 1989: The Classified History, ed. J. T. Richelson and M. L. Evans (National Security Archive Electronic Briefing Book, no. 16, 1 June 1999)

L. Trotskii, *Sochineniya*, vols 2–21 [incomplete] (Moscow, 1924–7)

L. Trotsky, *Leon Sedov: Son, Friend, Fighter* (London, 1967)

Vos'moi s"ezd RKP(b). Mart 1919 god: Protokoly, ed. N. I. Shatalin and M. A. Dvoinishnikov (Moscow, 1959)

Vostochnaya Evropa v dokumentakh rossiiskikh arkhivov, 1944–1953, vols 1–2, ed. N. M. Barinova, T. V. Volokitina, T. M. Islamov, G. P. Murashko, A. F. Noskova, T. A. Pokivailova, N. D. Smirnova and T. V. Tsarevskaya (Moscow, 1997–8)

Memoirs

G. Arbatov, *Zatianuvsheesia vyzdorovlenie, 1953–1985 gg.: svidetel'stvo sovremennika* (Moscow, 1991)

B. Bajanov, *Avec Staline dans le Kremlin* (Paris, 1930)

A. Balabanoff, *My Life as a Rebel* (London, 1938)

A. Barmine, *One Who Survived* (London, 1945)

S. Beria, *Beria, My Father: Life inside Stalin's Kremlin* (London, 2001)

N. Bocenina, *La segretaria di Togliatti: Memorie di Nina Bocenina* (Florence, 1993)

R. Bruce Lockhart, *Memoirs of a British Agent: Being an Account of the Author's Early Life in Many Lands and of his Official Mission to Moscow in 1918* (London, 1932)

M. Buber-Neumann, *Under Two Dictatorships* (London, 1949)

A. S. Chernyaev, *Shest' let s Gorbachëvym: po dnevnikovym zapisyam* (Moscow, 1993)

R. H. Crossman (ed.), *The God that Failed* (London, 1949)

J. E. Davies, *Mission to Moscow: A Record of Confidential Dispatches to the State Department, Official and Personal Correspondence, Current Diary and Journal Entries, Including Notes and Comment up to October 1941* (London, 1942)

V. Dedijer, *The Battle Stalin Lost: Memoirs of Yugoslavia, 1948–1953* (New York, 1972)

E. Dedmon, *China Journal* (Cambridge, 1971)

Deng Maomao, *Deng Xiaoping, my Father* (New York, 1995)

The Diaries of Beatrice Webb, vols 1–4, ed. N. Mackenzie and J. Mackenzie (London, 1982–4)

G. Dimitrov, *Diario. Gli anni di Mosca (1934–1945)*, ed. S. Pons (Turin, 2002)

M. Djilas, *Conversations with Stalin* (London, 1962)

M. Djilas, *Rise and Fall* (London, 1983)

S. Dmitrievsky, *Dans les coulisses du Kremlin* (London, 1933)

A. Dobrynin, *In Confidence: Moscow's Ambassador to America's Six Cold War Presidents, 1962–1986* (New York, 1995)

J. Douglas-Home, *Once upon Another Time: Ventures behind the Iron Curtain* (Norwich, 2000)

P. Dukes, *Red Dusk and the Morrow: Adventures and Investigations in Red Russia* (London, 1922)

P. Dukes, *The Story of 'ST 25': Adventure and Romance in the Secret Intelligence Service in Red Russia* (London, 1938)

A. Gide, *Retour de l'U.R.S.S.* (Paris, 1936)

E. Goldman, *My Disillusionment in Russia* (New York, 1923)

E. Goldman, *My Further Disillusionment in Russia* (New York, 1924)

M. Gorbachëv, *Zhizn' i reformy* (Moscow, 1995)

M. Gorbačov and Z. Mlynář, *Reformátoři Nebývachí Stastní* (Prague, 1995)

J. Halliday (ed.), *The Artful Albanian: The Memoirs of Enver Hoxha* (London, 1986)

H. Haywood, *Black Bolshevik: Autobiography of an Afro-American Communist* (Chicago, 1978)

M. Hindus, *Red Bread* (New York, 1931)

A. R. Hunt, *Facts About Communist Hungary* (London, 1919)

J.[Jenny] Humbert-Droz, *Une Pensée, Une Conscience, Un Combat: La Carrière Politique de Jules Humbert-Droz Retracée par sa Femme* (Neuchâtel, 1976)

J. Humbert-Droz, *De Lénine à Staline: Dix Ans au Service de l'Internationale Communiste, 1921–1931* (Neuchâtel, 1971)

F. Kermode, *Not Entitled: A Memoir* (London, 1996)

N. S. Khrushchëv, *Khrushchëv Remembers: The Glasnost Tapes* (New York, 1990)

A. Koestler, *Arrow in the Blue: An Autobiography* (London, 1972)

A. Koestler (no title), in R. H. Crossman (ed.), *The God that Failed* (London, 1949)

W. Krivitsky, *I Was Stalin's Agent* (London, 1940)

J. Lagas, *Memorias de un capitan rebelde* (Santiago de Chile, 1964)

W. Leonhard, *Child of the Revolution* (London, 1957)

[Dr] Li Zhisui, *The Private Life of Chairman Mao: The Memoirs of Mao's Personal Physician* (New York, 1994)

E. Lyons, *Assignment in Utopia* (New York, 1937)

'"Lyudyam svoistvenno oshibat'tsya": iz vospominanii M. Rakoshi', *Istoricheskii Arkhiv*, no. 3 (1997)

J. F. Matlock, *Autopsy on an Empire: The American Ambassador's Account of the Collapse of the Soviet Union* (New York, 1995)

Vladimir Medvedev, *Chelovek za spinoi* (Moscow, 1994)

A. Mgeladze, *Stalin, kakim ya ego znal. Stranitsy nedavnego proshlogo* (n.p., 2001)

M. Muggeridge, *Winter in Moscow* (London, 1934)

Nien Cheng, *Life and Death in Shanghai* (London, 1986)

K. Philby, *My Silent War*, introduced by G. Greene (London, 1968)

R. Pipes, *Vixi: Memoirs of a Non-Belonger* (New Haven and London, 2003)

H. Pollitt, *Serving my Time: An Apprenticeship to Politics* (London, 1940)

D. N. Pritt, *The Autobiography of D. N. Pritt*, Part One: *From Right to Left* (London, 1965)

R. Reagan, *An American Life* (London, 1990)

E. Reale, *Avec Jacques Duclos au banc des accusés à la Réunion Constitutive du Kominform à Szklarska Poreba* (Paris, 1958)

J. Reed, *Ten Days that Shook the World* (New York, 1919)

A. Rhys Williams, *Through the Russian Revolution* (New York, 1967)

P. Robinson, *How Ronald Reagan Changed my Life* (New York, 2003)

M. N. Roy, *Memoirs* (Bombay, 1964)

A. Sakharov, *Memoirs* (London, 1990)

G. Seniga, *Togliatti e Stalin* (Milan, 1978)

P. Shapcott, 'I Once Met the Red Dean', *Oldie*, June 2004

C. Sheridan, *Russian Portraits* (London, 1921)

G. P. Shultz, *Turmoil and Triumph: My Years as Secretary of State* (New York, 1993)

E. Snow, *Red Star over China* (New York, 1939)

S. Spender, *World within World: The Autobiography of Stephen Spender* (London, 1964)

J. Steinbeck, *Russian Journal* (with photographs by R. Capa: London, 1949)

Tenzin Gyatso, *Freedom in Exile: The Autobiography of the Dalai Lama* (New York, 1990)

L. Trotsky, *My Life: An Attempt at an Autobiography* (London, 1979)

R. O. G. Urch, *The Rabbit King of Siberia* (London, 1939)

H. G. Wells, *Russia in the Shadows* (London, 1920)

Zhang Lijia and C. Macleod (eds), *China Remembers* (Oxford, 1999)

T. Zhivkov, *Memoary* (private printing by author: Sofia, 1987)

Further Sources

S. Adams, *Comrade Minister: The South African Communist Party and the Transition from Apartheid to Democracy* (Huntington, NY, 2001)

E. Aga-Rossi and V. Zaslavsky, *Togliatti e Stalin: il PCI e la politica estera staliniana negli archivi di Mosca* (Bologna, 1997)

A. Agosti, *Bandiere rosse: un profilo storico dei comunisti europei* (Rome, 1999)

A. Agosti, *Palmiro Togliatti* (Torino, 1996)

G. A. Almond, *The Appeals of Communism* (Princeton, 1954)

L. Althusser, *Lire le Capital* (Paris, 1968)

L. Althusser, *Pour Marx* (Paris, 1965)

J. Amodia, 'The Spanish Communist Party and Local Government', in B. Szajkowski (ed.), *Marxist Local Governments in Western Europe and Japan* (London, 1986)

G. Amyot, *The Italian Communist Party: The Crisis of the Popular Front Strategy* (New York, 1981)

K. M. Anderson and A. O. Chubaryan (eds), *Komintern i vtoraya mirovaya voina*, vols 1–2 (Moscow, 1994–8)

P. Anderson, *Considerations on Western Marxism* (London, 1976)

C. Andrew and O. Gordievsky, *KGB: The Inside Story of its Foreign Operations from Lenin to Gorbachev* (London, 1990)

A. Angell, *Chile de Allessandri a Pinochet: en busca de la Utopia* (Santiago de Chile, 1993)

H. Arendt, *Totalitarianism* (San Diego, 1968)

R. Aron, *L'Opium des intellectuels* (Paris, 1955)

J. Attfield and S. Williams (eds), *1939: The Communist Party of Great Britain and the War. Proceedings of a Conference Held on 21 April 1979, Organised by the Communist Party History Group* (London, 1984)

P. Avrich, *The Russian Anarchists* (Princeton, 1967)

J. Baberowski, *Der Feind ist überall: Stalinismus im Kaukasus* (Munich, 2003)

E. Bacon, *The Gulag at War* (London, 1994)

R. Bahro, *The Alternative in Eastern Europe* (London, 1978)

I. Banac (ed.), *Eastern Europe in Europe* (Ithaca, 1992)

I. Banac, 'Post-Communism as Post-Yugoslavism: The Yugoslav Non-Revolutions of 1989–1990', in I. Banac, *Eastern Europe in Europe* (Ithaca, 1992)

I. Barankovics, *Catholic Church and Catholic Faith in Hungary* (New York, 1963)

A. L. Bardach, *Cuba Confidential: Love and Vengeance in Miami and Havana* (New York, 2002)

N. Barsukov, 'Kak sozdavalsya "zakrytyi doklad" Khrushchëva', *Literaturnaya gazeta*, 21 February 1996

O. Bauer, *Bolschewismus oder Sozialdemokratie* (Vienna, 1921)

R. D. Baum, *Burying Mao: Chinese Politics in the Age of Deng Xiaoping* (Princeton, 1994)

R. D. Baum, 'The Road to Tiananmen: Chinese Politics in the 1980s', in R. MacFarquhar (ed.), *The Politics of China, 1949–1989* (Cambridge, 1993)

BBC News, 1 November 2005: http://news.bbc.co.uk/go/pr/fr/-/1/hi/world/south_asia/4374826.stm

J. Becker, *Hungry Ghosts: China's Secret Famine* (London, 1996)

F. Beckett, *The Enemy Within: The Rise and Fall of the British Communist Party* (London, 1995)

A. Beichman, *Andropov* (New York, 1983)

A. Beichman, 'Roosevelt's Failure at Yalta', *Humanitas*, no. 1 (2003)

G. Benton and S. Tsang, 'Opportunism, Betrayal and Manipulation in Mao's Rise to Power', *China Journal*, no. 55 (January 2006)

N. Berdyaev, *The Russian Idea* (London, 1947)

I. Berlin, *Karl Marx: His Life and Environment* (London, 1939)

J. S. Berliner, *Factory and Manager in the USSR* (Cambridge, Mass., 1957)

E. Bernstein, *Evolutionary Socialism: A Criticism and Affirmation* (London, 1909)

M. R. Beschloss and S. Talbott, *At the Highest Levels: The Inside Story of the End of the Cold War* (Boston, 1993)

L. Bethell and Ian Roxborough (eds), *Latin America between the Second World War and the Cold War, 1944–1948* (Cambridge, 1992)

L. Bethell, 'Brazil', in L. Bethell and Ian Roxborough (eds), *Latin America between the Second World War and the Cold War, 1944–1948* (Cambridge, 1992)

L. Bethell and I. Roxborough, 'The Postwar Conjuncture in Latin America: Democracy, Labour and the Left' in L. Bethell and I. Roxborough (eds), *Latin America between the Second World War and the Cold War, 1944–1948* (Cambridge, 1992)

N. Bethell, *Gomulka: His Poland and his Communism* (London, 1969)

F. Bettanin, *Fabbrica del mito: storia e politica nell'URSS staliniana* (Naples, 1996)

F. Bettanin, *Stalin e l'Europa: la formazione dell'impero esterno sovietico (1941–1953)* (Rome, 2006)

E. Biagi, 'Usciti dall'URSS Palmiro mi disse: finalmente liberi!', *Corriere della Sera*, 21 August 2003

E. Biberaj, 'Albania: The Last Domino', in I. Banac (ed.), *Eastern Europe in Europe* (Ithaca, 1992)

G. Bischof, *Austria in the First Cold War, 1945–55* (New York, 1999)

H. P. Bix, *Hirohito and the Making of Modern Japan* (London, 2000)

D. L. M. Blackmer and S. Tarrow (eds), *Communism in Italy and France* (Princeton, 1975)

J. Bloomfield, *Passive Revolution: Communism and the Czechoslovak Working Class* (London, 1979)

G. Bocca, *Palmiro Togliatti* (Rome and Bari, 1977)

K. Bock, 'Theories of Progress, Development, Evolution', in T. B. Bottomore and R. Nisbet (eds), *History of Sociological Analysis* (London, 1979)

C. Bohlen, *Witness to History: 1929–1969* (New York, 1973)

E. Böhm-Bawerk, *Karl Marx and the Close of his System* (New York, 1949)

A. Bonnichon, 'La Cellule 23', *Etudes*, September 1954

F. Borkenau, *The Communist International* (London, 1938)

T. B. Bottomore, *Elites and Society* (London, 1966)

T. B. Bottomore and R. Nisbet (eds), *A History of Sociological Analysis* (London, 1979)

R. Boyd, 'The Japanese Communist Party in Local Government', in B. Szajkowski (ed.), *Marxist Local Governments in Western Europe and Japan* (London, 1986)

J. Braunthal, *History of the International, 1914–1943,* vols 1–3 (London, 1966–80)

B. Brecht, *The Measures Taken and Other Lehrstucke* (London, 1977)

H. Brogan, *The Life of Arthur Ransome* (London, 1984)

A. Brown, *The Gorbachev Factor* (Oxford, 1996)

J. A. C. Brown, *Techniques of Persuasion: From Propaganda to Brainwashing* (London, 1963)

J. F. Brown, *Eastern Europe and Communist Rule* (London, 1988)

R. Brubaker, *Ethnicity without Groups* (Cambridge, Mass., 2004)

W. Brus, 'The Peak of Stalinism', in M. Kaser (ed.), *The Economic History of Eastern Europe, 1917–1975,* vol. 3: *Institutional Change within a Planned Economy* (Oxford, 1986)

W. Brus, 'Political System and Economic Efficiency', in S. Gomulka (ed.), *Growth, Innovation and Reform in Eastern Europe* (Brighton, 1986)

Z. Brzezinski, *The Grand Failure: The Birth and Death of Communism in the Twentieth Century* (New York, 1989)

Z. Brzezinski, *The Soviet Bloc: Unity and Conflict* (Cambridge, Mass., 1967)

N. Bukharin and Ye. Preobrazhenskii, *Azbuka kommunizma* (Gomel, 1921)

V. Bukovskii, *Moskovskii protsess* (Paris and Moscow, 1996)

A. Bullock, *Ernest Bevin: Foreign Secretary, 1945–1951* (Oxford, 1985)

K. Burk, *Troublemaker: The Life and History of A. J. P. Taylor* (New Haven, 2000)

M. Burleigh, *Earthly Powers: Religion and Politics in Europe from the Enlightenment to the Great War* (London, 2005)

J. P. Burns, *Political Participation in Rural China* (Berkeley, 1988)

G. Bush and B. Scowcroft, *A World Transformed* (New York, 1998)

J. Callaghan, *Cold War, Crisis and Conflict: The CPGB, 1951–1968* (London, 2003)

J. Callaghan, *Rajani Palme Dutt: A Study in British Stalinism* (London, 1993)

The Cambodian Genocide Program, Yale University: www.yale.edu/cgp

T. Campanella, *The City of the Sun,* introduced by A. L. Morton (London, 1981)

E. Caretto and B. Marolo, *Made in the USA* (Milan, 1996)

B. Carr, *Marxism and Communism in Twentieth-Century Mexico* (Lincoln, Neb., 1992)

E. H. Carr, *The Bolshevik Revolution*, vols 1–3 (London, 1950–3)

E. H. Carr, *Michael Bakunin* (London, 1937)

E. H. Carr, *The Russian Revolution from Lenin to Stalin, 1917–1929* (London, 1979)

E. H. Carr, *What Is History?* (London, 1964)

S. Carrillo, *Eurocomunismo y estado* (Barcelona, 1977)

F. Castro, *Comparecencia del Comandante Fidel Castro Ruz, Primer Ministro del Gobierno Revolucionario y Primer Secretario del Comité Central del Partido Comunista de Cuba, para Analizar los Acontecimientos de Checoslovaquia, Viernes 23 de Agosto de 1968* (Havana, 1968)

F. Castro, *Fidel Castro Speaks on Marxism-Leninism* (New York, n.d.)

F. Castro, *Historia Me Absolverá!* (Havana, n.d.)

F. Castro, *The Road to Revolution in Latin America* (New York, 1963)

F. Castro, *Speech at the United Nations: General Assembly Session, September 26, 1960* (New York, 1960)

F. Castro, Speech to the First Congress of Pioneers, 1 November 1991: 'Debemos preservar siempre la esperanza', Havana

F. Castro, Speech to the Latin American Trade Union meeting held in Havana, 9 November 1991: *Granma International*, 24 November 1991

'The Cauldron Boils', *Economist*, 29 September 2005

D. Caute, *The Fellow Travellers: A Postscript to the Enlightenment* (New York, 1973)

L. Chamberlain, *The Philosophy Steamer: Lenin and the Exile of the Intelligentsia* (London, 2006)

N. Chanda, *Brother Enemy: The War after the War* (New York, 1986)

D. P. Chandler, *Brother Number One: A Political Biography of Pol Pot* (Boulder, 1992)

D. P. Chandler and B. Kiernan (eds), *Revolution and its Aftermath in Kampuchea: Eight Essays* (New Haven, 1983)

J. Chang and J. Halliday, *Mao: The Unknown Story* (London, 2005)

Dzh. Chervetti [G. Cervetti], *Zoloto Moskvy* (Moscow, 1995)

R. H. Chilcote, *The Brazilian Communist Party: Conflict and Integration, 1922–1972* (Oxford, 1974)

D. Childs and R. Popplewell, *The Stasi: The East German Intelligence and Security Service* (London, 1995)

D. H. Chollett and J. M. Goldgeier, 'Once Burned, Twice Shy? The Pause of 1989', in W. C. Wohlforth (ed.), *Cold War Endgame: Oral History, Analysis, Debates* (University Park, Penn., 1996)

A. Ciliga, *The Russian Enigma* (London, 1940)

F. Claudin, *The Communist Movement: From Comintern to Cominform* (London, 1976)

F. Claudin, *Eurocommunism and Socialism* (London, 1978)

N. Cohn, *The Pursuit of the Millennium: Revolutionary Millenarians and Mystical Anarchists of the Middle Ages* (revised edn: London, 1970)

D. Cohn-Bendit and G. Cohn-Bendit, *Obsolete Communism: The Left-Wing Alternative* (London, 1968)

L. Colletti, *Il Marxismo e Hegel* (Bari, 1969)

L. Colletti, 'A Political and Philosophical Interview', *New Left Review*, no. 86 (1974)

R. Conquest, *The Dragons of Expectation: Reality and Delusion in the Course of History* (New York, 2005)

R. Conquest, *The Great Terror* (London, 1968)

R. Conquest, *Present Danger: Towards a Foreign Policy* (Stanford, 1979)

R. Conquest, *Reflections on a Ravaged Century* (New York, 1999)

Converting Britain, BBC Radio 4, 10 August 2004

J. Cornwell, *Hitler's Pope: The Secret History of Pius XII* (London, 1999)

S. Courtois (ed.), *Une Si Longue Nuit: l'apogée des régimes totalitaires en Europe, 1935–1953* (Paris, 2003)

S. Courtois, N. Werth, J.-L. Panné, Andrzej Paczkowski, K. Bartošek and J.-L. Margolin (eds), *The Black Book of Communism: Crimes, Terror, Repression* (London, 1999)

R. Crampton, *Eastern Europe in the Twentieth Century – and After* (2nd edn: London, 1997)

K. Crane, *The Soviet Economic Dilemma of Eastern Europe* (Santa Monica, 1986)

R. Crompton, *William – the Bad* (London, 1930)

J. C. Culver, *American Dreamer: The Life and Times of Henry A. Wallace* (New York, 2000)

Dagli archivi di Mosca. L'URSS, il Cominform e il PCI (1943–1951), ed. F. Gori and S. Pons (Rome, 1998)

Dali L. Yang, *Calamity and Reform in China: State, Rural Society, and Institutional Change since the Great Leap Famine* (Stanford, 1996)

R. Dallek, *Ronald Reagan: The Politics of Symbolism* (Cambridge, 1984)

T. Dan, *The Origins of Bolshevism* (London, 1964)

I. N. R. Davies, *Heart of Europe: A Short History of Poland* (Oxford, 1984)

I. N. R. Davies, *White Eagle, Red Star* (London, 1972)

John Davis, 'Webb, (Martha) Beatrice (1858–1943)', *Oxford Dictionary of National Biography* (Oxford, 2004)

Jonathan Davis, 'Left Out in the Cold: British Labour Witnesses the Russian Revolution', *Revolutionary Russia*, no. 1 (June 2005)

R. B. Day, *Cold War Capitalism: The View from Moscow* (New York, 1995)

F. W. Deakin. H. Shukman and H. T. Willetts, *A History of World Communism* (London, 1975)

V. Dedijer, *Tito Speaks: His Self-Portrait and Struggle with Stalin* (London, 1953)

D. Deletant, *Ceauşescu and the Securitate: Coercion and Dissent in Romania, 1965–1989* (New York, 1995)

Deng Rong, *Deng Xiaoping and the Cultural Revolution* (New York, 2005)

I. Deutscher, *Russia, China, and the West: A Contemporary Chronicle, 1953–1966*, ed. F. Halliday (London, 1970)

I. Deutscher, *Trotsky: The Prophet Armed* (Oxford, 1954)

I. Deutscher, *Trotsky: The Prophet Outcast* (Oxford, 1963)

I. Deutscher, *Trotsky: The Prophet Unarmed* (Oxford, 1959)

I. Deutscher, *The Unfinished Revolution: Russia, 1917–1967* (Oxford, 1967)

A. Di Biagio, *Coesistenza e isolazionismo: Mosca, il Komintern e l'Europa di Versailles (1918–1928)* (Rome, 2004)

M. Djilas, *The New Class: An Analysis of the Communist System* (London, 1957)

J.-L. Domenach, *Chine: l'archipel oublié* (Paris, 1992)

J.-L. Domenach, *The Origins of the Great Leap Forward: The Case of One Chinese Province* (Boulder, 1995)

G. C. Donno, *La Gladio Rossa del PCI (1945–1967)* (Catanzaro, 2001)

W. Doyle, *Oxford History of the French Revolution* (2nd edn: Oxford, 2002)

T. Draper, *American Communism and Soviet Russia: The Formative Period* (New York, 1960)

J. Duclos, 'À propos de la dissolution du PCA', *Cahiers du Communisme*, 6 April 1945

J. W. F. Dulles, *Anarchists and Communists in Brazil, 1900–1935* (Austin, Texas, 1973)

T. Dunmore, *The Stalinist Command Economy* (London, 1980)

M. Dutton, *Policing and Policy in China: From Patriarchy to the 'People'* (Cambridge, 1992)

N. Eberstadt, 'Pyongyang's Option: "Ordinary" Stalinism', *Far Eastern Economic Review*, no. 3 (2005)

S. Ellis and T. Sechaba, *Comrades against Apartheid: The African National Congress and the South African Communist Party* (Bloomington, 1992)

D. W. Ellwood, *Rebuilding Europe: Western Europe, America and Postwar Reconstruction* (London, 1992)

F. Engels, *Anti-Dühring*, published as *Herr Eugen Duhring's Revolution in Science (Anti-Duhring)* (London, 1934)

F. Engels, *The Dialectics of Nature* (London, 1941)

F. Engels, *The Origins of the Family, Private Property and the State: In the Light of the Researches of Lewis H. Morgan* (London, 1946)

D. C. Engerman, 'The Ironies of the Iron Curtain: The Cold War and the Rise of Russian Studies in the United States', *Cahiers du Monde Russe*, no. 45/3–4 (2004)

D. Eudes, *The Kapetanios: Partisans and Civil War in Greece, 1943–1949* (London, 1972)

A. B. Evans, *Soviet Marxism-Leninism: The Decline of an Ideology* (Westport, Conn., 1993)

R. J. Evans, *The Coming of the Third Reich* (New York, 2004)

R. Falber, *The 1968 Czechoslovak Crisis: Inside the British Communist Party*, occasional paper, Socialist History Society (London, 1972)

A. Farrar-Hockley, *The British Part in the Korean War*, vols 1–2 (London, 1990–5)

F. Fejtö, *Histoire des démocraties populaires*, vols 1–2 (Paris, 1969)

G. Fiori, *Antonio Gramsci* (London, 1970)

First Congress of the Peoples of the East: Baku, September 1920: Stenographic Report, trans. and ed. B. Pearce (London, 1976)

R. Fischer, *Stalin and German Communism: A Study in the Origins of a State Party* (Cambridge, Mass., 1948)

S. Fitzpatrick, 'Stalin and the Making of a New Elite, 1928–1939', *Slavic Review*, no. 3 (1979)

S. Fitzpatrick, *Stalin's Peasants: Resistance and Survival in the Russian Village after Collectivisation* (Oxford, 1994)

R. Foa, M. Mafai and A. Reichlin, *Il silenzio dei comunisti* (Turin, 2002)

K. Forster, *Rebellion and Factionalism in a Chinese Province: Zhejiang, 1976* (New York, 1990)

E. Friedman, P. G. Pickowicz and M. Selden, *Chinese Village, Socialist State* (New Haven, 1991)

H. Friedmann, 'Warsaw Pact Socialism', in A. Hunter (ed.), *Rethinking the Cold War* (Philadelphia, 1998)

F. Fukuyama, *The End of History and the Last Man* (London, 1992)

M. Fulbrook, *Anatomy of a Dictatorship: Inside the GDR* (Oxford, 1995)

F. Furet, *The Passing of an Illusion: The Idea of Communism in the Twentieth Century* (Chicago, 1997)

A. Fursenko and T. Naftali, *One Hell of a Gamble: Khrushchev, Castro, Kennedy, and the Cuban Missile Crisis, 1958–1964* (London, 1997)

J. L. Gaddis, *The Cold War: A New History* (London, 2006)

J. L. Gaddis, *We Now Know: Rethinking Cold War History* (Oxford, 1997)

J. L. Gaddis, *Strategies of Containment: A Critical Appraisal of Postwar American National Security Policy* (New York, 1982)

I. V. Gaiduk, *The Soviet Union and the Vietnam War* (Chicago, 1996)

T. Garton Ash, *We the People: The Revolution of 89* (London, 1990)

C. Gati, *The Bloc that Failed: Soviet–East European Relations* (London, 1990)

C. Gati, *Hungary and the Soviet Bloc* (Durham, NC, 1986)

Yu. P. Gavrikov, *Fidel' Kastro: Neistovyi komandante Ostrova svobody* (Moscow, 2006)

D. Geary, *Karl Kautsky* (Manchester, 1987)

E. Gellner, *Plough, Sword and Book: The Structure of Human History* (London, 1988)

I. Getzler, *Kronstadt 1917–1921: The Fate of a Soviet Democracy* (Cambridge, 1983)

I. Gilbert, *El oro de Moscú* (Buenos Aires, 1994)

R. Giles, 'The KGB in Afghanistan, 1979–1989', paper delivered at St Antony's College, Oxford: 31 May 2006

P. Ginsborg, *A History of Contemporary Italy: Society and Politics, 1943–1988* (London, 1990)

N. Glazer and D. P. Moynihan, *Beyond the Melting Pot: The Negroes, Puerto*

Ricans, Jews, Italians and Irish of New York City (2nd edn: Cambridge, Mass., 1970)

Ye. P. Glazunov *et al.* (eds), *Voina vo V'etname ... kak eto bylo (1965–1973)* (Moscow, 2005)

P. Gleijeses, *Conflicting Missions: Havana, Washington and Africa, 1959–1976* (Chapel Hill, 2002)

S. Gomulka (ed.), *Growth, Innovation and Reform in Eastern Europe* (Brighton, 1986)

D. S. G. Goodman (ed.), *China's Provinces in Reform: Class, Community and Political Culture* (London, 1997)

D. S. G. Goodman, *Deng Xiaoping and the Chinese Revolution* (London, 1994)

D. S. G. Goodman and G. Segal (eds), *China Deconstructs: Politics, Trade and Regionalism* (London, 1994)

F. Gori and S. Pons (eds), *The Soviet Union and Europe in the Cold War, 1943–53* (London, 1996)

M. Gor'kii, L. Averbakh and S. Firin (eds), *Belomorsko–baltiiskii kanal imeni I. V. Stalina* (Moscow, 1934)

R. Gott, *Cuba: A New History* (London, 2004)

H. Graham, *The Spanish Republic at War, 1936–1939* (Cambridge, 2003)

H. Graham and P. Preston (eds), *The Popular Front in Europe* (London, 1987)

A. Gramsci, *Lettere dal carcere*, ed. P. Spriano (Turin, 1971)

A. Gramsci, *Quaderni del carcere*, vols 1–4, ed. V. Gerratana (Turin, 1977)

J. Granville, *The First Domino: International Decision Making during the Hungarian Crisis of 1956* (College Station, 2004)

P. Gregory, *The Political Economy of Stalin: Evidence from the Soviet Secret Archives* (Cambridge, 2004)

H. Gruber, *International Communism in the Era of Lenin and Stalin* (New York, 1972)

E. Guevara, *Guerrilla Warfare* (New York, 1961)

S. Gundle, 'Models and Crises of Communist Government in Italy', in B. Szajkowski (ed.), *Marxist Local Governments in Western Europe and Japan* (London, 1986)

G. Hall, *The Era of Crisis: Forging Unity in Struggle: Report to the Twenty Fifth National Convention, Communist Party, USA* (unedited speech: Cleveland, Ohio, 6 December 1991)

G. Hall, *The Power of Ideology: Keynote Address to the First Ideological Conference of the Communist Party USA* [sic], *July 14–16 1989, Chicago* (New York, 1989)

I. Hallas, 'Radio Jamming', www.okupatsioon.ee/english/mailbox/radio/radio/html, 3 May 2000

F. Halliday, *The Making of the Second Cold War* (London, 1986)

M. Halperin, J. J. Berman, R. L. Borosage and C. M. Marwick, *The Lawless State: The Crimes of the US Intelligence Agencies* (London, 1976)

J. Hansen, *The Theory of the Cuban Revolution* (New York, 1962)

P. Hanson, *Western Economic Statecraft in East–West Relations: Embargoes, Sanctions, Linkage, Economic Warfare and Détente* (London, 1988)

P. Hanson and K. Pavitt, *The Comparative Economics of Research Development and Innovation in East and West: A Survey* (Chur, Switzerland, and London, 1987)

L. Harding, 'In the Grip of the Angkang', *Guardian*, 20 December 2005

W. A. Harriman and E. Abel, *Special Envoy to Churchill and Stalin, 1941–1946* (New York, 1975)

H. M. Harrison, *Driving the Soviets up the Wall: Soviet–East German Relations, 1953–1961* (Princeton, 1961)

M. Harrison, *Why Secrecy? The Uses of Secrecy in Stalin's Command*, PERSA Working Paper, No. 34 (Warwick, 2003)

J. Haslam, *The Nixon Administration and the Death of Allende's Chile: A Case of Assisted Suicide* (London, 2005)

J. Haslam, *The Vices of Integrity: E. H. Carr, 1892–1982* (London, 1999)

G. Haupt, *Socialism and the Great War: The Collapse of the Second International* (Oxford, 1972)

H. Haywood, *Negro Liberation* (New York, 1948)

S. Hellman, *Italian Communism in Transition: The Rise and Fall of the Historic Compromise in Turin, 1975–1980* (Oxford, 1988)

L. W. Henderson, *A Question of Trust: The Origins of U.S.–Soviet Diplomatic Relations* (Stanford, 1987)

J. Hessler, *A Social History of Soviet Trade: Trade Policy, Retail Practices and Consumption, 1917–1953* (Princeton, 2004)

G. Hicks, *John Reed: The Making of a Revolutionary* (New York, 1936)

R. Hilferding, *Boehm-Bawerk's Criticism of Marx*, trans. E. and C. Paul (Glasgow, 1919)

R. Hilferding, *Finance Capital: A Study of the Latest Phase of Capitalist Development*, introduced by T. Bottomore (London, 1981)

C. Hill, *The World Turned Upside Down: Radical Ideas during the English Revolution* (London, 1972)

R. Hingley, *The Russian Mind* (London, 1977)

W. Hinton, *Fanshen: A Documentary History in a Chinese Village* (Berkeley, 1966)

T. Hofnung, *Georges Marchais: l'inconnu du Parti Communiste Français* (Paris, 2001)

P. Hollander, *Political Pilgrims: Western Intellectuals in Search of the Good Society* (New Brunswick, 1998)

D. Holloway, *Stalin and the Bomb: The Soviet Union and Atomic Energy* (New Haven, 1994)

M. Holroyd, *Bernard Shaw*, vol. 2: *1898–1918: The Pursuit of Power* (London, 1990)

M. Holroyd, *Bernard Shaw*, vol. 3: *1918–1950: The Lure of Fantasy* (London, 1993)

A. Horne, *Macmillan*, vol. 2: *1957–1986* (London, 1989)

M. G. Horowitz, 'Portrait of the Marxist as an Old Trouper', *Playboy*, September 1970

I. Howe and L. Coser, *The American Communist Party: A Critical History* (New York, 1962)

J. W. Hulse, *The Forming of the Communist International* (Stanford, 1964)

'Human Rights in China: Briefing Memo', submitted to President George W. Bush, 16 November 2005

A. Hunter (ed.), *Rethinking the Cold War* (Philadelphia, 1998)

J. O. Iatrides, *Revolt in Athens: The Greek Communist 'Second Round', 1944–1945* (Princeton, 1972)

J. O. Iatrides and L. Wrigley (eds), *Greece at the Crossroads: The Civil War and its Legacy* (University Park, Penn., 1998)

R. Ioanid, *The Ransom of the Jews: The Story of the Extraordinary Secret Bargain between Romania and Israel* (Chicago, 2005)

Istoriya vsesoyuznoi kommunisticheskoi partii (bol'shevikov): kratkii kurs (edited by the Commission of the Central Committee: Moscow, 1938)

P. J. Jaffe, *The Rise and Fall of Earl Browder* (London, 1972)

M. Jay, *The Dialectical Imagination* (London, 1973)

Jian Chen, *Mao's China and the Cold War* (Chapel Hill, 2001)

H. Johnson, *The Socialist Sixth of the World* (London, 1939)

H. Johnson, *The Upsurge of China* (Beijing, 1961)

H. Johnson, *What We Saw in Rumania* (London, 1948)

K. Jowitt, 'Soviet Neo-Traditionalism: The Political Corruption of a Marxist-Leninist Regime', *Soviet Studies*, no. 3 (1983)

T. Judt, *Postwar: A History of Europe since 1945* (London, 2005)

R. W. Judy, 'The Case of Computer Technology', in S. Wasowski (ed.), *East–West Trade and the Technology Gap* (New York, 1970)

L. Kaganovich, *Kak postroena RKP(b)* (Moscow, 1924)

G. M. Kahin and A. R. Kahin, *Subversion as Foreign Policy: The Secret Eisenhower and Dulles Debacle in Indonesia* (New York, 1995)

Kam-yee Law (ed.), *The Chinese Cultural Revolution Reconsidered: Beyond Purge and Holocaust* (London, 2003)

P. Kane, *Famine in China, 1959–61: Demographic and Social Implications* (London, 1988)

K. Kaplan, *The Short March: The Communist Takeover in Czechoslovakia, 1945–1948* (London, 1987)

B. M. Karapandzich, *The Bloodiest Yugoslav Spring, 1945 – Tito's Katyns and Gulags* (New York, 1980)

M. Kaser, *Comecon: Integration Problems of the Planned Economies* (Oxford, 1965)

M. Kaser (ed.), *The Economic History of Eastern Europe, 1917–1975*, vol. 3: *Institutional Change within a Planned Economy* (Oxford, 1986)

K. Kautsky, *The Agrarian Question* (London, 1988)

K. Kautsky, *Die Diktatur des Proletariats* (Vienna, 1918), published in English as *The Dictatorship of the Proletariat*, trans. H. J. Stenning (Manchester, 1919)

'X' (George F. Kennan), 'The Sources of Soviet Conduct', *Foreign Affairs*, vol. 25 (July 1947)

P. Kennedy, *The Rise and Fall of the Great Powers: Economic Change from 1500 to 2000* (New York, 1987)

P. Kenney, *Rebuilding Poland: Workers and Communists, 1945–1950* (Ithaca, 1997)

K. Kersten, *The Establishment of Communist Rule in Poland, 1943–48* (Oxford, 1991)

B. Kiernan, *The Pol Pot Regime: Race, Power and Genocide in Cambodia under the Khmer Rouge, 1975–1979* (New Haven, 1996)

R. Kindersley (ed.), *In Search of Eurocommunism* (London, 1981)

R. Kindersley, *The First Russian Revisionists: A Study of 'Legal Marxism' in Russia* (Oxford, 1962)

R. R. King, *Minorities under Communism: Nationalities as a Source of Tension among Balkan Communist States* (Cambridge, Mass., 1973)

D. G. Kirby, *Finland in the Twentieth Century* (London, 1979)

H. Klehr, *Communist Cadre: The Social Background of the American Communist Party Elite* (Stanford, 1978)

H. Klehr, J. E. Haynes and K. M. Anderson (eds), *The Soviet World of American Communism* (New Haven, 1998)

A. F. Knapp, 'A Receding Tide: France's Communist Municipalities', in B. Szajkowski (ed.), *Marxist Local Governments in Western Europe and Japan* (London, 1986)

D. Koenker, *Moscow Workers and the 1917 Revolution* (Princeton, 1981)

A. Koestler, *Darkness at Noon* (London, 1940)

L. Kolakowski, *Main Currents of Marxism: Its Rise, Growth, and Dissolution*, vols 1–3 (Oxford, 1978)

G. Konrad and I. Szelenyi, *The Intellectuals on the Road to Class Power* (New York, 1978)

M. Kramer, 'The Early Post-Stalin Succession Struggle and Upheavals in East-Central Europe: Internal–External Linkages in Soviet Policy Making', *Journal of Cold War Studies*, nos 1–3 (1999)

M. Kramer, 'Poland 1980–81: Soviet Policy during the Polish Crisis', *Cold War International History Papers Bulletin*, no. 5 (1995)

M. Laar, *The War in the Woods: Estonia's Struggle for Survival, 1944–1956* (Washington, DC, 1992)

Laogai Research Foundation: report, 14 April 2004

J. R. Lampe, *Yugoslavia as History: Twice There Was a Country* (2nd edn: Cambridge, 2000)

P. M. La Ramée and Erica G. Polakoff, 'The Evolution of the Popular Organizations in Nicaragua', in G. Prevost and H. E. Vanden (eds), *The Undermining of the Sandinista Revolution* (London, 1997)

N. Lebrecht, 'Prokofiev Was Stalin's Last Victim', *Evening Standard*, 4 June 2003

M. P. Leffler, 'The Cold War: What Do "We Now Know"?', *American Historical Review*, no. 2 (1999)

M. P. Leffler, *A Preponderance of Power. National Security, the Truman Administration and the Cold War* (Stanford, 1992)

P. Lendvai, *Eagles in Cobwebs* (London, 1969)

J. Lévesque, *The Enigma of 1989: The USSR and the Liberation of Eastern Europe* (Berkeley, 1997)

R. Leviné-Meyer, *Leviné the Spartacist: The Life and Times of the Socialist Revolutionary Leader of the German Spartacists and Head of the Ill-Starred Munich Republic of 1919* (London, 1978)

D. A. L. Levy, 'The French Popular Front, 1936–1937', in H. Graham and P. Preston (eds), *The Popular Front in Europe* (London, 1987)

G. Lewy, *The Cause that Failed: Communism in American Political Life* (Oxford, 1990)

G. Lichtheim, *Georg Lukács* (London, 1970)

G. Lichtheim, *A Short History of Socialism* (London, 1970)

A. S. Lindemann, *The 'Red Years': European Socialism versus Bolshevism, 1919–1921* (Berkeley, 1974)

I. Linder and S. Churkin, *Krasnaya pautina: tainy razvedki Kominterna, 1919–1943* (Moscow, 2005)

J. Linz, 'Authoritarian and Totalitarian Regimes', in *Handbook of Political Science*, ed. F. Greenstein and N. Polsby, vol. 3 (Reading, Mass., 1975)

V. D. Lippit, *Land Reform and Economic Development in China: A Study of Institutional Change and Development Finance* (White Plains, 1974)

A. Lipschütz, *Marx y Lenin en la América Latina y los problemas indigenistas* (Havana, 1974)

S. M. Lipset and G. Marks, *It Didn't Happen Here: Why Socialism Failed in the United States* (New York, 2000)

The Lost Orwell: Being a Supplement to the Complete Works of George Orwell, ed. P. Davison (London, 2006)

P. Louis, *People Power: The Naxalite Movement in Central Bihar* (Delhi, 2002)

V. Loupan and P. Lorraine, *L'Argent de Moscou* (Paris, 1994)

M. Löwy, *Le Marxisme en Amérique Latine de 1909 à nos jours: anthologie* (Paris, 1980)

G. Lukacs, *History and Class Consciousness: Studies in Marxist Dialectics* (London, 1971)

G. Lukács, *The Process of Democratization* (New York, 1991)

A. Luukkanen, *The Party of Unbelief: The Religious Policy of the Bolshevik Party, 1917–1929* (Helsinki, 1994)

A. Luukkanen, *The Religious Policy of the Stalinist State: A Case Study: The Central Standing Commission on Religious Questions, 1929–1938* (Helsinki, 1997)

R. Luxemburg, *The Accumulation of Capital*, trans. A. Schwarzschild (London, 1951)

R. Luxemburg, *The Mass Strike* (London, 1986)

R. Luxemburg, *The Russian Revolution* (first pub. in German, 1922; trans. B. Wolfe, New York, 1940)

J. A. McAdams, *Germany Divided: From the Wall to Reunification* (Princeton, 1993)

W. O. McCagg, *Stalin Embattled, 1943–1948* (Detroit, 1978)

The McCarran Conspiracy against the Bill of Rights: The Communist Party's Answer to the Charges of the Attorney-General under the McCarran Act (New York, 1951)

K. McDermott and J. Agnew, *The Comintern: A History of International Communism from Lenin to Stalin* (London, 1996)

R. MacFarquhar and J. K. Fairbanks (eds), *The Cambridge History of China*, vols 14 and 15, part 2 (Cambridge, 1987 and 1991)

R. MacFarquhar (ed.), *The Politics of China, 1949–1989* (Cambridge, 1993)

R. MacFarquhar, 'The Succession to Mao and the End of Maoism, 1969–1982', in R. MacFarquhar (ed.), *The Politics of China, 1949–1989*

N. Machiavelli, *The Prince* (London, 1961)

K. E. McKenzie, *Comintern and World Revolution, 1928–1943* (London, 1964)

D. McLellan, *Karl Marx: His Life and Thought* (London, 1973)

Ma Feng, 'A Nation Celebrates its New Beginning', *Time Asia*, 27 September 1999

P. Major, *The Death of the KPD: Communism and Anti-Communism in West Germany* (Oxford, 1997)

N. Malcolm, *Bosnia: A Short History* (2nd edn: London, 1996)

R. Mallick, *Development Policy of a Communist Government: West Bengal since 1977* (Cambridge, 1993)

R. Mallick, *Indian Communism: Opposition, Collaboration and Institutionalization* (Oxford, 1994)

J. Mann, *About Face: A History of America's Curious Relationship with China, from Nixon to Clinton* (New York, 1999)

H. Marcuse, *Counterrevolution and Revolt* (Boston, Mass., 1972)

H. Marcuse, *Eros and Civilization* (Boston, Mass., 1955).

H. Marcuse, *Essay on Liberation* (Boston, Mass., 1969)

H. Marcuse, *One Dimensional Man* (Boston, Mass., 1964)

H. Marcuse, *Reason and Revolution* (New York, 1941)

H. Marcuse, *Soviet Marxism: A Critical Analysis* (New York, 1958)

G. N. Marks, 'Communist Party Membership in Five Former Soviet Bloc Countries, 1945–1989', *Communist and Post-Communist Studies*, no. 37 (2004)

M. Marrese and J. Vanous, *Soviet Subsidization of Trade with Eastern Europe: A Soviet Perspective* (Berkeley, 1983)

K. Marx, *Capital*, vols 1–3 (London, 1958–60)

K. Marx and F. Engels, *The Communist Manifesto*, ed. A. J. P. Taylor (London, 1967)

Marxist Study (leaflet of the London District Committee of the CPGB: December 1940)

V. Mastny, *The Cold War and Soviet Insecurity* (Oxford, 1996)

V. Mastny, *Russia's Road to the Cold War: Diplomacy, Warfare and the Politics of Communism, 1941–1945* (New York, 1979)

J. Matlock, *Reagan and Gorbachev: How the Cold War Ended* (New York, 2004)

G. Matthews, 'Stalin's British Road?', *Changes Supplement*, 14–27 September 1991

R. von Mayenburg, *Hotel Lux* (Munich, 1978)

M. Mazower, *Dark Continent: Europe's Twentieth Century* (London, 1998)

R. Medvedev, *Let History Judge* (revised and expanded edn: Oxford, 1989)

R. Medvedev, *On Socialist Democracy* (New York, 1979)

Zh. and R. Medvedev, *Neizvestnyi Stalin* (Moscow, 2001)

V. Medvedev, *Chelovek za spinoi* (Moscow, 1994)

F. Mehring, *Karl Marx: The Story of his Life* (London, 1936)

Y. Membery, 'Swallows, Amazons and Secret Agents', *Observer*, 21 July 2002

C. J. Menéndez Cervera and E. Sánchez Santa Cruz, *Comisión Cubana de Derechos Humanos y Reconciliación Nacional*, 5 July 2006

C. Merridale, *Moscow Politics and the Rise of Stalin* (London, 1990)

M. Mevius, *Agents of Moscow: The Hungarian Communist Party and the Origins of Socialist Patriotism, 1941–1953* (Oxford, 2005)

R. Michels, *Political Parties: A Sociological Study of the Oligarchical Tendencies of Modern Democracy*, introduced by S. M. Lipset (London, 1968)

J. E. Miller, *The United States and Italy, 1940–1950* (Chapel Hill, 1986)

C. Milosz, *The Captive Mind* (New York, 1953: original edn, 1951)

A. Milward, *The Reconstruction of Western Europe, 1945–1951* (London, 1984)

R. Mitter, *A Bitter Revolution: China's Struggle with the Modern World* (Oxford, 2004)

Z. Mlynář, *Night Frost in Prague: The End of Humane Socialism* (New York, 1980)

W. J. Mommsen, *The Age of Bureaucracy: Perspectives on the Political Sociology of Max Weber* (London, 1974)

J. B. Moore, *Social Origins of Dictatorship and Democracy: Lord and Peasant in the Making of the Modern World* (London, 1967)

T. More, *Utopia*, trans. and introduced by Paul Turner (London, 2003)

K. Morgan, *Against Fascism and War: Ruptures and Continuities in British Communist Politics, 1935–41* (Manchester, 1989)

K. Morgan, *Harry Pollitt* (Manchester, 1993)

D. E. Murphy, S. A. Kondrashev and G. Bailey, *Battleground Berlin: CIA vs KGB in the Cold War* (New Haven, 1997)

G. S. Murphy, *Soviet Mongolia: A Study of the Oldest Political Satellite* (Berkeley, 1966)

N. Naimark, 'Communist Regimes and Parties after the Second World War', *Journal of Modern European History*, no. 1 (2004)

N. M. Naimark, *Fires of Hatred: Ethnic Cleansing in Twentieth Century Europe* (Cambridge, Mass., 2001)

N. M. Naimark, 'Post-Soviet Russian Historiography on the Emergence of the

Soviet Bloc', *Kritika: Explorations in Russian and Eurasian History*, no. 3 (2004)

N. Naimark, *The Russians in Germany: A History of the Soviet Zone of Occupation, 1945–1949* (Cambridge, Mass., 1995)

N. Naimark and L. Gibianskii (eds), *The Establishment of Communist Regimes in Eastern Europe, 1944–1949* (Boulder, 1997)

M. Narinskii, 'I. V. Stalin i M. Torez, 1944–1947 gg. Novye materialy', *Novaya i Noveishaya Istoriya*, no. 1 (1996)

M. Narinskij, 'Stalin, Togliatti e Thorez, 1944–1948', in *Dagli archivi di Mosca. L'URSS, il Cominform e il PCI (1943–1951)*, ed. F. Gori and S. Pons (Rome, 1998)

A. J. Nathan and P. Link, *The Tiananmen Papers* (New York, 2001)

J. P. Nettl, *Rosa Luxemburg*, vols 1–2 (Oxford, 1966)

R. Nixon, *1999: Victory without War* (New York, 1988)

Njoto, *Strive for the Victory of the Indonesian Revolution with the Weapon of Dialectical and Historical Materialism: A Speech at the Alkiarcham Academy of Social Sciences on 3 June 1964* (Peking, 1964)

G. Nollau, *International Communism and World Revolution* (London, 1961)

T. J. Nossiter, *Marxist State Governments in India: Politics, Economics and Society* (London, 1988)

A. Nove, *An Economic History of the USSR* (London, 1969)

A. Nuti, *La provincia più rossa: la costruzione del Partito Nuovo a Siena (1945–1956)* (Siena, 2003)

D. Oberdorfer, *The Turn: From the Cold War to a New Era. The United States and the Soviet Union, 1983–1990* (New York, 1991)

J. P. Ongkili, *Nation-Building in Malaysia, 1946–1974* (Oxford, 1985)

A. Orlov, *The Secret History of Stalin's Crimes* (London, 1954)

D. Ortega, Speech to the United Nations Security Council, 25 March 1982, *Comunicado de Prensa: Permanent Mission to the U.N.*, no. 035

G. Orwell, *Animal Farm* (London, 1945)

F. M. Ottanelli, *The Communist Party of the United States: From the Depression to World War II* (New Brunswick, 1991)

A. Paczkowski, *The Spring Will Be Ours: Poland and the Poles from Occupation to Freedom* (Philadelphia, 2003)

R. Page Arnot, *A Short History of the Russian Revolution: From 1905 to the Present Day* (London, 1937).

A. V. Pantsov, 'Kak Stalin pomog Mao Tsedunu stat' vozhdëm', *Voprosy Istorii*, no. 2 (2006)

J. Pasqualini, *Prisonnier de Mao* (Paris, 1977)

A. Paucker, *German Jews in the Resistance, 1933–1945: The Facts and the Problems* (n.p., 2005)

G. P. Pelizzaro, *Gladio Rossa: dossier sulla più potente banda armata esistita in Italia* (Roma, 1997)

L. Péter, '"East of the Elbe": The Communist Take-over and the Past', in R.

Pynsent (ed.), *The Phoney Peace: Power and Culture in Central Europe, 1945–1949* (London, 2000)

P. G. Pillai, *Left Movement and Agrarian Relations, 1920–1995* (New Delhi, 2003)

P. S. Pinheiro, *Estratégias da illusão: a revolução mundial e o Brasil, 1922–1935* (Sao Paulo, 1991)

R. Pipes, *Survival Is Not Enough: Soviet Realities and America's Future* (New York, 1984)

Political Letter to the Communist Party Membership, Political Bureau of the Communist Party of Great Britain: 15 July 1940.

H. Pollitt, *Britain and the Soviet Union* [leaflet], 16 September 1939 (London)

S. Pons, *Berlinguer e la fine del comunismo* (Turin, 2006)

S. Pons, *L'impossibile egemonia: L'URSS, il PCI e le origini della Guerra Fredda (1943–1948)* (Rome, 1999)

S. Pons, 'In the Aftermath of the Age of Wars: The Impact of World War II in Soviet Security Policy', in S. Pons and A. Romano (eds), *Russia in the Age of Wars, 1914–1945* (Milan, 2000)

S. Pons, 'Una sfida mancata: L'URSS, il Cominform e il PCI (1947–1948)', in *Dagli Archivi di Mosca. L'URSS, il Cominform e il PCI (1943–1951)*, ed. F. Gori and S. Pons (Rome, 1998)

S. Pons and A. Romano (eds), *Russia in the Age of Wars, 1914–1945* (Milan, 2000)

R. Porter, *The Enlightenment* (London, 2001)

A. Pospielovsky, 'Strikes during the NEP', *Revolutionary Russia*, no. 1 (1997)

Lt Emery Pottle and Dr E. Dana Durand, 'An Interview with Bela Kuhn [sic]', *American Relief Administration Bulletin*, no. 19, 25 July 1919

P. Preston, *Franco: A Biography* (London, 1993)

P. Preston, *The Spanish Civil War: Reaction, Revolution and Revenge* (London, 2006)

G. Prevost and H. E. Vanden (eds), *The Undermining of the Sandinista Revolution* (London, 1997)

G. Procacci, *Il socialismo internazionale e la Guerra d'Etiopia* (Rome, 1978)

R. Pynsent (ed.), *The Phoney Peace: Power and Culture in Central Europe, 1945–1949* (London, 2000)

A. Rabinowitch, *The Bolsheviks Come to Power in Petrograd* (London, 1976)

K. Radek and A. Ransome, *Radek and Ransome on Russia* (Brooklyn, 1918)

S. Rawicz, *The Long Walk* (London, 1956)

C. Read, *Culture and Power in Revolutionary Russia* (London, 1990)

E. Reale, *Nascita del Cominform. Documenti e testimonianze sulla conferenza costitutiva dell'Ufficio di Informazione dei Partiti Comunisti tenuta a Szklarska Poreba (Polonia) dal 22 al 27 settembre 1947* (Milan, 1958)

J. Redman [B. Pearce], *The Communist Party and the Labour Left, 1925–1929* (Hull, 1957)

A. Rhys Williams, *Lenin: The Man and his Work* (New York, 1919)

A. J. Rieber, *Stalin and the French Communist Party, 1941–1947* (New York, 1962)

J. Riordan, 'The Strange Story of Nikolai Starostin, Football and Lavrentii Beria

– Sports Personality and Soviet Chief of Intelligence', *Europe-Asia Studies*, July 1994

P. Ripert, *De Gaulle* (Paris, 2004)

V. Riva, *Oro da Mosca: i finanziamenti sovietici al PCI dalla Rivoluzione d'ottobre al crollo dell' URSS. Con 240 documenti inediti degli archivi moscoviti* (Milan, 1994)

I. W. Roberts, *History of the School of Slavonic & East European Studies, 1915–1990* (London, 1991)

P. C. Roberts, *Alienation and the Soviet Economy* (London, 1990)

B. Robshaw, 'Biggles Flies Again', *Independent on Sunday*, 27 July 2003

J. Ross, *Rebellion from the Roots: Indian Uprising in Chiapas* (Monroe, Neb., 1995)

J. Rossi, *Spravochnik po GULagu*, vols 1–2 (2nd revised edn: Moscow, 1992)

W. W. Rostow, *The Stages of Economic Growth: A Non-Communist Manifesto* (Cambridge, 1960)

J. Rothschild, *Return to Diversity: A Political History of East Central Europe since World War II* (Oxford, 1993)

I. Roxborough, 'Mexico', in L. Bethell and I. Roxborough (eds), *Latin America between the Second World War and the Cold War, 1944–1948* (Cambridge, 1992)

D. Rusinow, *The Yugoslav Experiment, 1948–1974* (Berkeley, 1977)

B. Russell, *The Theory and Practice of Bolshevism* (London, 1919)

A. Sakharov, *Progress, Coexistence and Intellectual Freedom* (London, 1968)

M. Salvadori, *Karl Kautsky e la rivoluzione socialista* (Milan, 1976)

G. Sartori, *The Theory of Democracy Revisited* (Chatham, NJ, 1987)

J.-P. Sartre, *Sartre on Cuba* (New York, 1961)

D. Sassoon, *One Hundred Years of Socialism: The West European Left in the Twentieth Century* (London, 1997)

D. Sassoon, *The Strategy of the Italian Communist Party: From the Resistance to the Historic Compromise* (New York, 1981)

L. B. Schapiro, *The Origin of the Communist Autocracy: Political Opposition in the Soviet State, First Phase, 1917–1922* (London, 1955)

L. B. Schapiro, *Totalitarianism* (London, 1972)

S. R. Schram, *Mao Zedong: A Preliminary Reassessment* (Hong Kong, 1983)

L. Sedda, *Economia, politica e società sovietica nei quaderni del carcere* (Jesi, 2000)

J. Sejna, *We Will Bury You* (London, 1982)

G. Seniga, *Un bagaglio che scotta* (Milan, 1973)

R. Service, *The Bolshevik Party in Revolution: A Study in Organisational Change* (London, 1979)

R. Service, 'Bolshevism's Europe from Lenin to Stalin, 1914–1928', in S. Pons and A. Romano (eds), *Russia in the Age of Wars, 1914–1945* (Milan, 2000)

R. Service, 'Gorbachev's Reforms: The Future in the Past', *Journal of Communist Studies*, no. 3 (1987)

R. Service, *A History of Modern Russia from Nicholas II to Putin* (2nd edn, revised and expanded: London, 2003)

R. Service, *Lenin: A Biography* (London, 2000)

R. Service, *Lenin: A Political Life*, vols 1–3 (London, 1985, 1991 and 1995)

R. Service, *The Russian Revolution, 1900–1927* (3rd edn: London, 1999)

R. Service, *Stalin: A Biography* (London, 2004)

R. W. Service, *Bar-Room Ballads: A Book of Verse* (London, 1940)

H. Seton-Watson, *The East European Revolution* (3rd edn: New York, 1956)

P. J. Seybolt, *Throwing the Emperor from his Horse: Portrait of a Village Leader in China, 1923–1995* (Boulder, 1996)

T. Shanin, *The Awkward Class: Political Sociology of Peasantry in a Developing Society* (Oxford, 1972)

T. Shanin, *Late Marx and the Russian Road: Marx and 'the Peripheries of Capitalism'* (London, 1984)

Shaoguang Wang, 'Between Destruction and Construction: The First Year of the Cultural Revolution', in Kam-yee Law (ed.), *The Chinese Cultural Revolution Reconsidered: Beyond Purge and Holocaust* (London, 2003)

Shaoguang Wang, 'The Structural Sources of the Cultural Revolution', in Kam-yee Law (ed.), *The Chinese Cultural Revolution Reconsidered: Beyond Purge and Holocaust*

L. L. Sharkey, *An Outline History of the Australian Communist Party* (Sydney, 1944)

M. S. Shatz, *Jan Waclaw Machajski: A Radical Critic of the Russian Intelligentsia* (Pittsburg, 1989)

H. Shelley, *Arthur Ransome* (London, 1968)

P. Short, *Mao: A Life* (New York, 1999)

P. Short, *Pol Pot: History of a Nightmare* (London, 2004)

K. Simonov, *Russkii vopros: p'esa v 3-kh deistviyakh, 7 kartinakh* (Moscow and Leningrad, 1947)

P. Singer, *Hegel* (London, 1983)

F. Singleton, *A Short History of the Yugoslav Peoples* (Cambridge, 1985)

G. Sirgiovanni, *An Undercurrent of Suspicion: Anticommunism in America during World War II* (New Brunswick, 1990)

Y. Slezkine, *The Jewish Century* (Princeton, 2004)

P. Sloan, *Soviet Democracy* (London, 1937)

V. Smil, 'China's Great Famine: Forty Years Later', *British Medical Journal*, 18–25 December 1999

A. H. Smith, *The Planned Economies of Eastern Europe* (London, 1983)

A. Solzhenitsyn, *The Gulag Archipelago, 1918–1956: An Experiment in Literary Investigation*, vols 1–3 (London, 1974–8)

J. Spence, *Mao Zedong* (New York, 1999)

P. Spriano, *Storia del Partito Comunista Italiano*, vols 1–7 (Turin, 1967–98)

P. Stavrakis, *Moscow and Greek Communism, 1944–1949* (Ithaca, 1989)

P. Stavrakis, 'Soviet Policy in Areas of Limited Control', in J. O. Iatrides and L. Wrigley (eds), *Greece at the Crossroads: The Civil War and its Legacy*

H. J. Steinberg, *Il socialismo tedesco da Bebel a Kautsky* (Rome, 1979)

A. C. Sutton, *Western Technology and Soviet Economic Development, 1917 to 1930* (Stanford, 1968)

A. C. Sutton, *Western Technology and Soviet Economic Development, 1930 to 1945* (Stanford, 1971)

A. C. Sutton, *Western Technology and Soviet Economic Development, 1945 to 1965* (Stanford, 1973)

N. Swain, *Collective Farms Which Work?* (Cambridge, 1985)

B. Szajkowski (ed.), *Marxist Local Governments in Western Europe and Japan* (London, 1986)

J. L. Talmon, *The Origins of Totalitarian Democracy* (London, 1955)

W. Taubman, *Khrushchev: The Man and his Era* (London, 2003)

S. J. Taylor, *Stalin's Apologist: Walter Duranty, the New York Times's Man in Moscow* (New York, 1990)

F. C. Teiwes, 'The Establishment and Consolidation of the New Regime', in R. MacFarquhar (ed.), *The Politics of China, 1949–1989* (Cambridge, 1993)

P. Ther and A. Siljak (eds), *Redrawing Nations: Ethnic Cleansing in East-Central Europe, 1944–1948* (New York, 2001)

A. Thorpe, *The British Communist Party and Moscow, 1920–43* (Manchester, 2000)

Tianjian Shi, *Political Participation in Beijing* (Cambridge, Mass., 1997)

S. Timpanaro, *Sul materialismo* (Pisa, 1970)

P. Togliatti, *Il memoriale di Yalta* (Palermo, 1988)

R. L. Tökés, *Béla Kun and the Hungarian Soviet Republic: The Origins and Role of the Communist Party of Hungary in the Revolutions of 1918–1919* (Stanford, 1967)

R. L. Tökés, 'Béla Kun: The Man and the Revolutionary', in I. Völgyes (ed.), *Hungary in Revolution, 1918–19: Nine Essays*

E. Toller, *An Appeal from the Young Workers of Germany* (Munich, 1919)

T. Toranska, *'Them': Stalin's Polish Puppets* (New York, 1987)

J.-C. Tournebrise and L. MacDonald, *Le Dragon et la souris* (Paris, 1987)

J. Triska and C. Gati (eds), *Blue Collar Workers in Eastern Europe* (London, 1981)

L. Trotsky, *History of the Russian Revolution* (London, 1934)

L. Trotsky, *The Revolution Betrayed: What Is the Soviet Union and Where Is it Going?* (London, 1937)

N. S. Trubetskoi, *K probleme russkogo samosoznaniya: sobranie statei* (Paris, 1927)

S. Tsang, *The Cold War's Odd Couple: The Unintended Partnership between the Republic of China and the UK, 1950–58* (London, 2006)

R. Tucker, *Stalin as Revolutionary, 1879–1929: A Study in History and Personality* (London 1974)

A. Tusa, *The Last Division: A History of Berlin, 1945–1989* (Reading, Mass., 1997)

A. B. Ulam, *Expansion and Coexistence: The History of Soviet Foreign Policy, 1917–1967* (New York, 1968)

R. H. Ullman, *The Anglo-Soviet Accord* (Princeton, 1972)

A. Ulunyan, *Kommunisticheskaya partiya Gretsii: aktual'nye voprosy ideologii, politiki i vnutrennei istorii* (Moscow, 1994)

J. B. Urban, *Moscow and the Italian Communist Party: From Togliatti to Berlinguer* (Ithaca, 1986)

G. Vacca, 'The Eurocommunist Perspective: The Contribution of the Italian Communist Party', in R. Kindersley (ed.), *In Search of Eurocommunism* (London, 1981)

L. T. Vasin, 'Kim Ir Sen. Kto on?', *Nezavisimaya gazeta*, 29 September 1993

M. Vickery, *Cambodia, 1975–1982* (North Sydney, NSW, 1984)

B. A. Viktorov, 'Geroi iz 37-go', *Komsomol'skaya pravda*, 21 August 1988

C. M. Vilas, *Perfiles de la Revolución Sandinista* (Havana, 1984)

M. Vinhas, *O Partidão* (Sao Paolo, 1987)

I. Völgyes (ed.), *Hungary in Revolution, 1918–1919: Nine Essays* (Lincoln, Neb., 1971)

T. V. Volokotina, *Moskva i Vostochnaya Evropa: stanovlenie politicheskikh rezhimov sovetskogo tipa, 1949–1953. Ocherki istorii*, vols 1–3 (Moscow, 2000–3)

A. Walicki, *The Controversy over Capitalism: Studies in the Social Philosophy of the Russian Populists* (Oxford, 1967)

J. S. Walker, *Henry A. Wallace and American Foreign Policy* (New York, 1976)

'The Wall', episode 9, CNN *Cold War* series (1998)

S. Wasowski (ed.), *East–West Trade and the Technology Gap* (New York, 1970)

J. Watts, 'North Korea Turns Away Western Aid', *Observer*, 2 October 2005

S. and B. Webb, *Soviet Communism: A New Civilization?* (London, 1935)

S. and B. Webb, *Soviet Communism: A New Civilization* (2nd edn: London, 1937)

A. Weiner, 'Déjà Vu All Over Again: Prague Spring, Romanian Summer and Soviet Autumn on the Soviet Western Frontier', *Contemporary European History*, no. 2 (2006)

A. Weiner, 'The Empires Pay a Visit: Gulag Returnees, East European Rebellions and Soviet Frontier Politics', *Journal of Modern History*, June 2006

K. Weller, *'Don't Be A Soldier!': The Radical Anti-War Movement in North London, 1914–1918* (London, 1985)

O. A. Westad, *The Global Cold War: Third World Interventions and the Making of our Times* (Cambridge, 2005)

S. G. Wheatcroft, 'More Light on the Scale of Repression and Excess Mortality in the Soviet Union in the 1930s', *Soviet Studies*, no. 2 (1990)

F. Wheen, *Karl Marx* (London, 1999)

L. T. White, *Unstately Power*, vol. 1: *Local Causes of China's Economic Reforms*; vol. 2: *Local Causes of China's Intellectual, Legal and Governmental Reforms* (Princeton, 1998)

L. T. White III and Kam-yee Law, 'Explanations for China's Revolution at its Peak', in Kam-yee Law (ed.), *Beyond a Purge and a Holocaust: The Cultural Revolution Reconsidered* (London, 2003)

S. White, *Britain and the Bolshevik Revolution: A Study in the Politics of Diplomacy, 1920–1924* (London, 1979)

R. C. Williams, *The Other Bolsheviks: Lenin and his Critics, 1904–1914* (Bloomington, 1986)

W. C. Wohlforth (ed.), *Cold War Endgame: Oral History, Analysis, Debates* (University Park, Penn., 1996)

W. C. Wohlforth (ed.), *Witnesses to the End of the Cold War* (Baltimore, 1996)

B. D. Wolfe, *Strange Communists I Have Known* (New York, 1982)

H. H. Wu, *Laogai: The Chinese Gulag* (Boulder, 1992)

'X', see under G. Kennan

Xiaoxia Gong, 'The Logic of Repressive Collective Action: A Case Study of Violence in the Cultural Revolution', in Kam-yee Law (ed.), *The Chinese Cultural Revolution Reconsidered: Beyond Purge and Holocaust* (London, 2003)

Xin Liu, *In One's Shadow: An Ethnographic Account of the Condition of Post-Reform Rural Russia* (Berkeley, 2000)

V. Zaslavsky, *Lo Stalinismo e la sinistra italiana: dal mito dell'URSS alla fine del comunismo, 1945–1991* (Milan, 2004)

V. Zubok and C. Pleshakov, *Inside the Kremlin's Cold War: From Stalin to Khrushchev* (Cambridge, Mass., 1996)

V. M. Zubok, 'Different Perspectives on the Historical Personality', in W. C. Wohlforth (ed.), *Cold War Endgame: Oral History, Analysis, Debates* (University Park, Penn., 1996)

INDEX

Visit **www.panmacmillan.com** to read more about all our books and to buy them. You will also find features, author interviews and news of any author events, and you can sign up for e-newsletters so that you're always first to hear about our new releases.